P9-DXG-847

GLOBAL FORCES
of the
TWENTIETH CENTURY

SECOND EDITION

E. ALYN MITCHNER & R. JOANNE TUFFS

Reidmore Books

Canadian Cataloguing in Publication Data

Mitchner, E.A.

　Global forces of the twentieth century

　Includes bibliographical references and index.

　ISBN 1-895073-53-7

　1. History, Modern—20th century. I. Tuffs, R. Joanne (Renee Joanne), 1944- II. Title.

D421.M57 1997　　909.82　　C96-910723-4

ACKNOWLEDGEMENTS

Reidmore Books wishes to thank the following professors, who reviewed drafts of the manuscript for content and fact, for their helpful suggestions:

Dr. Hugh Wilson, Professor,
Department of History, University of Alberta

Dr. Baha Abu-Laban, Professor,
Department of Sociology, University of Alberta

Dr. Brian Evans, Vice President, Academic,
University of Alberta

Dr. David Marples, Professor,
Department of History, University of Alberta

Dr. Larry Pratt, Professor,
Department of Political Science, University of Alberta

Dr. Ulrich Trumpener, Professor,
Department of History, University of Alberta

Reidmore Books wishes to thank the following people, who reviewed drafts of the manuscript for instructional design and suitability as a student textbook, for their helpful suggestions:

Bill Mills, Calgary, Alberta

Bayne McMillan, Sackville, New Brunswick

Richard B. Marien, Valleyview, Alberta

Ted Klassen, Altona, Manitoba

Doug McKenzie, Fort Nelson, British Columbia

Marilyn Shortt, Edmonton, Alberta

We also would like to thank our student editor, Carmen Thomas of Edmonton, Alberta, for helping us decide which improvements to make for the Second Edition of this textbook.

ABOUT THE AUTHORS

E. Alyn Mitchner holds a Bachelor of Education, Master of Arts, and a PhD in History. From 1980 until his retirement in 1996, Dr. Mitchner was the Director of the International Baccalaureate Program at Harry Ainlay Composite High School in Edmonton. He taught the theory of knowledge and history for grades 10 through 12.

R. Joanne Tuffs has a Bachelor of Arts, majoring in history, and a Bachelor of Education. She became the curriculum coordinator for the International Baccalaureate Program at Harry Ainlay Composite High School in 1994. She also teaches the theory of knowledge and history for grades 10 through 12.

REIDMORE BOOKS INC.
1200, 10109-106 Street
Edmonton, AB T5J 3L7
ph. (403) 424-4420
fax (403) 441-9919
http://www.reidmore.com
email: reidmore@compusmart.ab.ca

printed and bound in Canada

TABLE OF CONTENTS

INTRODUCTION

Global Forces of the Twentieth Century introduces you to four major themes. These are 1) International Confrontation and Cooperation, 2) Global Interactions during the Interwar Period and the Second World War, 3) the Rise and Interaction of the Superpowers, and 4) Contemporary Global Interactions. The authors have used a chronological order to present the information and perspectives on these four major themes.

THEME I
INTERNATIONAL CONFRONTATION AND COOPERATION

A motive is a thought or feeling that makes people or nations act in certain ways. Motives are the result of circumstance, desire, or even fear. When people or nations confront one another, they do so because of a variety of motives. As you work through *Global Forces of the Twentieth Century*, try to discern the motives behind the confrontations.

Some motives for confrontation are nationalism, ethnocentrism, a desire for independence, expansionism, or differing ideologies. Over the course of time, the forms that confrontation takes have been labeled and defined. Some of the terms are total war, limited war, guerrilla war, terrorism, brinkmanship, and economic sanctions.

What motivates cooperation? You will learn about motives such as collective security, internationalism, nationalism, balance of power, humanitarianism, and global survival. Cooperation can take different forms, including alliances, economic blocs, political groupings, international organizations, and agreements.

THEME II
GLOBAL INTERACTIONS DURING THE INTERWAR PERIOD AND THE SECOND WORLD WAR

Confrontation and cooperation will appear again and again as you examine the motives behind the two world wars and their outcomes. You will learn about the concepts of nationalism, national security, self-determination, reparations, internationalism, alliances, and global collective security. You will also learn about justice, human rights, and the ideologies influencing the interwar period.

THEME III
THE RISE AND INTERACTION OF THE SUPERPOWERS

The rivalry for global supremacy has a long history indeed. Today, balance of power remains one of the key concepts explaining the actions of superpowers. Other concepts include spheres of influence, decolonization, defense, and self-determination. You will learn that as new nations emerge, superpowers adjust their foreign policies and reassert their spheres of influence to maintain power.

THEME IV
CONTEMPORARY GLOBAL
INTERACTIONS

Increasingly, global interactions are a result of economic developments. The European Union is one example. In reading about contemporary global interaction, you will explore such concepts as regional cooperation, environmental responsibility, and multinational corporations. Through your explorations and your research, you will further develop your understanding of the problems faced by world leaders of the past and present, and you may develop your own opinions on possible solutions.

SPECIAL FEATURES
OF THE TEXTBOOK

As you read, you will be asked to evaluate the effectiveness of the methods nations have used to solve problems since the First World War. *Global Forces of the Twentieth Century* is structured in such a way as to allow you to access the information you need to help you shape informed opinions.

Each chapter opens with a TIME LINE providing a quick reference to important events and dates discussed in the chapter. Next is a quotation expressing one point of view on a major issue in the chapter. A FOCUS ON activity then highlights a generalization and key understanding of the chapter. An OVERVIEW lists the main headings of the chapter and summarizes its content.

Within each chapter, BIOGRAPHY details the life of a world leader or thinker. SIDEBARS present ancillary information of special interest. CASE STUDIES give perspectives on key issues and events.

Each chapter ends with QUESTIONS, CRITICAL ANALYSIS, RESEARCH PROJECTS, ACTIVITIES, and HISTORICAL ANALYSIS. These will ask you to present information and ideas.

The GLOSSARY at the end of the book provides the terminology you will need to speak and write effectively about the subject matter of this book. The BIBLIOGRAPHY lists references you can use in research, and the INDEX will help you quickly locate topics within the textbook.

GLOBAL FORCES
OF THE
TWENTIETH
CENTURY

FOCUS ON

POWER

A prince, therefore, must not have any other aspect nor any other thought, nor must he take anything as his profession but war, its institutions, and its discipline; and it is of such importance that not only does it maintain those who were born princes, but many times it enables men of private station to rise to that position; and, on the other hand, it is evident that when princes have given more thought to personal luxuries than to arms, they have lost their state. And the most important cause of losing it is to neglect this art; and the way to acquire it is to be well versed in this art.

Niccolo Machiavelli, *The Prince*, chapter 14, translated by Peter Bondanella and Mark Musa, Oxford University Press, New York, 1979. *The Prince* was originally published in 1532.

Even though Machiavelli wrote these words hundreds of years ago, leaders in the twentieth century have continued to heed his advice. Was Machiavelli right? Is war the ultimate, or even the most useful, expression of global relations?

OVERVIEW

In order to facilitate peaceful interaction between nation-states, to deal with conflict, systems of international relations are agreed upon and exercised.

THE NATION-STATE

The world is divided into political units which claim sovereignty and promote their own cultural identities. At the same time, these nation-states strive to further their own political power and economic well-being.

CONFLICT—*REALPOLITIK*

The desires to preserve national security, expand territory, achieve hegemony, and defend national pride are some of the reasons that nations go to war.

SYSTEMS OF INTERNATIONAL RELATIONS

In order to preserve peace nations align themselves in a balance-of-power system. NATO, the Warsaw Pact, and bodies of collective security like the League of Nations or the United Nations are examples of these systems.

THIS BOOK is an interpretation of the political and military history of the industrial powers of the twentieth century in their quest for global supremacy and national security. Wielding significantly more power than non-industrial nations, a handful of industrial states makes the important decisions affecting the human condition in the modern era. The United States, the former Soviet Union, Great Britain, Germany, France, and Japan have routinely exercised the political, military, and economic power to shape the world in their own self-interest. In the final analysis all international relationships, whether through conflict or cooperation, are governed by the existing power structure of the world's **nation-states**. The reality of power *(realpolitik)* and the knowledge that nations *always* act in their own self-interest are the concepts basic to an understanding of international relations.

In the Machiavellian world of nation-states unchecked by any supranational force, power gives shape to international events. The power of a state is usually measured in military and economic terms. In world politics, industrial capacity is inextricably linked to military preparedness in defining a nation-state's power status. The use of organized mass violence (war) to attain national goals has been a primary strategy of sovereign nation-states throughout the twentieth century. Within the world's state system, the prevailing view has been that peace is an illusory objective and unilateral disarmament yields not an easing of tensions but rather a power vacuum that rival states will seek to fill. In the world of *realpolitik* there are no power vacuums, only political alliances and **spheres of influence**. In the light of recent changes in the superpower relationship and the emergence of new centres of influence, the conventional view of international power may have to be reassessed.

The role of the state is defined by the need to defend or acquire territory, advance its cultural or religious beliefs, secure needed resources, support its allies, and improve the people's quality of life. In return, the state demands patriotism and loyalty from its citizens, who view international relations as an exercise in self-interest. Political leaders are expected to pursue foreign-policy goals that reflect this national self-interest. Within such a framework, when one nation's self-interest collides with another nation's self-interest, war results.

Through accident and war, nation-states are continually being created and destroyed. In no age has this been more apparent than in the twentieth century. The 63 nation-states of 1920 have now multiplied to over 185. Many of the new states were formed after the Second World War in a wave of **decolonization** that saw the end of the old empires. The proliferation of states has placed considerable strain on traditional patterns of international relations. Two superpowers, the United States and the former Soviet Union, emerged as industrial and military giants. They and their allies divided the world into a **bipolar** system in which each sought to promote its own culture.

At the turn of the century the industrial societies engaged in global competition for the physical resources necessary to sustain industrial growth. Their rivalry led to the establishment of overseas empires in which other less powerful nations submitted to conquest. Within a given imperial sphere, subject peoples paid allegiance to their masters' flags and laboured to increase the imperial power. As the Industrial **heartlands** in Western Europe, North America, Japan, and Russia grew in size and complexity, the gap between the world's industrial and agrarian cultures widened at an accelerating pace. Convinced that their own cultures were superior and just, the great powers partly masked global expansion as a crusade against evil. "Manifest Destiny," "White Man's Burden," "Crusade in Europe," and "**Containment**" successively became popular slogans, each in its own time not only describing a cause, but providing a motive for the creation of world-wide movements and global spheres of interest.

Supplied by expanding industrial capacity, the imperial rivals went to war in the twentieth century, unleashing destructive forces in two world wars that devastated the planet's human and physical resources. As a result of the costs of the First World War (1914-1918) and the Second World War (1939-1945), the centre of global power shifted from the great powers of Europe to the two superpowers, the United States and the Soviet Union. It was not until after the war in 1945, when the development of nuclear, biological, and chemical weapons threatened the very existence of human life, that a measure of **peaceful co-existence** and cooperation between the industrial powers emerged. This cooperation is critical for the solution of present problems like global environmental degradation, human rights violations, international **terrorism**, and a decaying standard of living for most of the world's burgeoning population.

THE NATION-STATE

During the last four centuries, the peoples of the world have arranged themselves into political units called nation-states. These states range in size, shape, and power from the few hectares of Monaco to the thousands of square kilometres of the former Soviet Union, Canada, the United States, and China. Nation-states are territorial in nature, with political boundaries that seldom bear any relationship to determinants like geography or social groupings. Their borders often cut across cultures and religions and often do not contain enough resources to sustain the desired quality of life. They are, in effect, artificial, human-made creations that demand the absolute loyalty of their people in return for a guarantee of security and an acceptable standard of living. Within each state, the interest of the nation transcends that of the individual, and **nationalism** is a virtue.

Each state claims sovereignty within its own boundaries and resists attempts at intervention in its domestic affairs. The result has been the evolution of a wealth of differing cultures and value systems determined by the aims and goals of each society. Above all, the nation-state maintains the right to determine its own destiny and preserve its own unique society. Thus, the existence of the state system divides humans into exclusive social units

Many nation-states have borders that encompass a variety of cultures and religions.

that must forge a place for themselves in the international power structure. Scarcities of resources essential to the maintenance of the desired standard of living make economic self-sufficiency (**autarky**) impossible and force nation-states to establish relationships with other nations.

Because each state must engage in trade to secure the goods and materials essential to existence, a critical interrelatedness has developed among the world's nations. Perceived need directs a given state's relations with other states; but once outside its own boundaries, the state has no supranational law to protect it. Anarchy prevails on the international stage in the absence of any sanction to enforce lawful behaviour. Therefore, agreements must be reached to facilitate trade and security. These international agreements and codes of behaviour depend solely on the good will of the signatories for conformity, however, as no machinery for enforcement is in place. As relative power, custom, convenience, or perceived advantage determines a nation's conduct, either conflict or cooperation can result.

Although a peaceful **status quo** is preferable to conflict, powerful states will resort to aggression in

The above photograph shows an Israeli Armed Forces Centurion tank withdrawing from the town of Qneitra in the Golan Heights, after Israel and Syria signed an agreement in 1974. The United Nations tries to mediate in military confrontations.

$1.1 trillion (US), more than the entire income of the poorest half of the world's population. Since then the total expenditure has decreased slightly to $821 billion (US) in 1993, and $794 billion (US) in 1994. The figure for 1994 accounts for 2.6 per cent of the worldwide gross domestic product (GDP) and represents a cost per person of $141 (US).

In the past 3500 years, there have only been 270 in which major wars did not occur. Is war then an instinctive reaction to perceived threats to one's security that crisis makes unavoidable? Is it planned aggression designed to expand a nation's territory, attain autarky, or achieve a position of **hegemony**? The immediate causes of war seem to include all of these reasons, as well as others, such as prestige, national pride, assistance to allies, or defence of religion or **ideology**. In addition, leadership can play a decisive role in instigating war or maintaining peace. In the 1860s, Bismarck, a German statesman, engineered war against a common enemy to unify the German states. In the late 1980s and early 1990s, the Reagan-Bush-Gorbachev accommodation established an atmosphere of optimism for peaceful negotiation in international problem-areas.

However, conflict in the former Yugoslavia has raised questions about the ability of the international community to effectively resolve problems stemming from ethnic dissension. Countries committed to United Nations' intervention in global trouble spots are now questioning how they should respond to the multiplicity of ethnic conflicts which have occurred since the end of the **Cold War**.

order to obtain their objectives. Military alliances, such as **NATO (North Atlantic Treaty Organization)** or the Warsaw Pact, have been the predominant form of cooperative diplomatic ventures. Self-interest and co-existence go hand in hand in the alliance structure. While these regional groupings provide less powerful nations with the prestige of being part of the group, there is an underlying perception that industrial states predominate. When peaceful alternatives fail to resolve conflict, the more powerful nations inevitably emerge victorious.

SYSTEMS OF INTERNATIONAL RELATIONS

The modern state system began at Westphalia in 1648, with the agreement of European monarchs to recognize the sovereignty of nation-states and refrain from intervention in each other's affairs. The number and location of European states have been shifting ever since. At that time, the major powers were Great Britain, Austria-Hungary, Spain, France, Prussia, and Russia, with no single power strong enough to achieve hegemony over the others. Whenever one state became too powerful, the others banded together to check its growth. Only for a brief period under Napoleon (1799-1815) was the continent dominated by a single power, France. After the decisive Battle of Waterloo,

CONFLICT—*REALPOLITIK*

The world state system is characterized by a continual preparation for war, because only national power, which is equated with prestige and security, yields freedom of action. A nation's military forces are professionally trained to destroy the enemy and maintain state security. Many nation-states commit large portions of their gross national product (GNP) to the maintenance of a defence force, contributing to an arms trade that now exceeds the trade of grain in scale. In 1985, annual world military expenditures reached a total of the major powers met in congress at Vienna to reassert their combined power.

The congress system was an attempt at **collective security**. The major powers agreed to meet periodically to maintain the status quo in the face of growing liberal unrest. Monarchs reserved the right to intervene in other states whenever it was necessary to stamp out the republicanism that threatened their hold on their peoples.

A **balance-of-power** system evolved among the major powers during the nineteenth century and lasted in one form or another through the two world wars of the twentieth century, at which time it was replaced by a **bipolar** system of superpowers. The balance-of-power system assumed that the major powers were relatively equal in strength, were rearmed to pursue hegemony, and would act in concert against any power that attempted to assert itself, thus holding it in check. Prior to the First World War (1914-1918), this system solidified into two opposing hostile camps: the Triple Alliance of Germany, Austria-Hungary, and Italy, and the Triple Entente of Great Britain, France, and Russia.

Between the two world wars, diplomats and politicians attempted to build a new international system that would terminate wars between states. President Wilson of the United States brought forward the idea of a League of Nations acting to stop aggression and make the world safe from war. The principle of collective security assumed that each state had similar objectives and would willingly act in cooperation with the others. Wilson believed that every state would agree to open diplomacy, freedom of the seas, **self-determination**, disarmament, and the other values of democratic society. He placed his faith in the power of democratic capitalism to contain the aggressive nature of the world's autocrats. In this he was mistaken. The League failed in its attempts to secure peace in a world where national self-interest prevailed over international cooperation.

The Second World War (1939-1945) completed the destruction of the balance-of-power system and replaced it with a bipolar system, with American and Soviet spheres of influence. After the war, power and threat of war once again governed the state system and once again an attempt at collective security was made. This time, the major powers were encouraged to become involved; they were offered primacy in the principal supranational institution. In creating the United Nations (UN), the major powers reserved for themselves permanent

Steps to control the stockpiling of nuclear weapons by the superpowers were taken with the SALT I (Strategic Arms Limitation Talks) treaty of 1972.

seats on the United Nations Security Council, as well as the right to veto UN action. Lacking binding authority over its members and unable to obtain consensus on any issue of importance to the superpowers, the UN has proven relatively ineffective in resolving global conflict.

The Second World War probably changed the state system more than any other event of modern times. With effective great powers reduced from five to two, world power now emanated from Washington and Moscow. Unprecedented problems of nuclear weaponry and intense ideological hostility opened up an era of conflict and competition. Virtually all the world's power was gathered

The Olympic Games, a period of friendly competition, acknowledge the rewards of international cooperation.

into two competing blocs that rivaled each other globally for supremacy. **Brinkmanship** developed as a diplomatic tool used by both the United States and the Soviet Union as they took their nations to the verge of war without actually waging it. The Cuban Missile Crisis (1962) proved to be the most frightening exercise in this nuclear diplomacy and encouraged a new era of peaceful co-existence.

Attempts to limit nuclear weaponry proved largely unsuccessful because the superpowers failed to address the impact of improved technology on advanced weapons systems. Although steps were taken to restrict the proliferation of nuclear technology and to limit some types of weapons, it was only in 1987, with the Intermediate-Range Nuclear Forces (INF) agreement, that any move was made to actually reduce nuclear armaments. It is now generally agreed by the superpowers that nuclear war must not occur and that serious measures must be taken to stop the production of nuclear arms.

In the 1960s and 1970s, the bipolar world began to change. Decolonization resulted in large numbers of new non-aligned nations that demanded their share of both the world's resources and its power. Economic growth in West Germany and Japan, as well as developments in China and the emergence of the wealthy but underdeveloped oil-producing nations of the **Organization of Petroleum Exporting Countries (OPEC)**, suggested the emergence of a new multipolar system.

Concern regarding North Korea's ability to produce atomic weaponry reinforced a commitment on the part of the major powers to extend the Nuclear Nonproliferation Treaty when it came up for renewal in 1995. In addition, in August 1995 President Clinton announced that the United States would cease all nuclear testing. Conversely, France's determination in 1995 to continue nuclear testing produced a cry of protest from the international community. A strong commitment to prevent the spread of nuclear weapons, as well as to reduce the numbers and cease the production of nuclear weapons, is of vital importance to the peace and security of the world.

SUMMARY

The year 1989 heralded revolutionary change in the world's nation-state system, with the crumbling of the Soviet sphere in Central Europe. The superpowers seemed fully aware that the survival of humans is dependent upon the avoidance of superpower war. Their determination to avoid direct conflict is reassuring in the light of the serious challenges facing the former Soviet sphere of influence. The "nationalities question" promises to dominate the next decade as peoples around the globe struggle to achieve sovereignty. However, the nation-state system has been largely unsuccessful in preserving a lasting peace. Should subject nationalities be encouraged in their quest for autonomy? Would a new political context ensure international harmony?

Two possible alternatives to the nation-state system are the development of a supranational organization that establishes a larger jurisdiction capable of making decisions on behalf of national governments, or transnational participation, where transactions occur across national boundaries, with at least one of the parties to the transaction outside of government. The burgeoning Europe of the 1990s is an example of a supranational organization, while the Red Cross, multinational corporations, or the Olympic Committee represent transnational organizations. Have we reached a stage of political maturity where we can tolerate national uniqueness and resolve differences by diplomatic negotiations? Surely this is our challenge as we approach the next century.

QUESTIONS

1. What is the nature of, and what are the objectives of, the nation-state?

2. Why are there relationships between nation-states? How is the conduct of international affairs carried out? Based on your past studies, list some of the ways disputes between nations have been resolved?

3. What twentieth century weapons of war have made warfare unthinkable? What is the danger to all of humankind from nuclear weapons? From biological or chemical warfare? Research attempts in the past to eliminate these weapons from global arsenals.

4. One of the major issues of the twentieth century has been the debate about the sovereignty of the nation-state as opposed to global government by collective security. The two systems of government are contradictory.

a. Are you prepared to give up your citizenship to become a citizen of the world? What are the advantages to you of being Canadian?

b. In the United Nations each nation has one vote. This weights any votes taken strongly in favour of non-industrialized nations, which are in the great majority. Do you think the superpowers would give up their sovereignty to join the United Nations? Will they permit domestic matters to become the property of outsiders?

c. Many claim that the problems of the twenty-first century, such as environmental degradation, the growth of world population, the threat of nuclear war, and the issues of human rights, affect everyone and thus the United Nations has a duty to interfere in the sovereignty of the nation-state. Do you think the United Nations should have the power to interfere in Canadian government?

d. Opponents of collective security claim that any world government would be weighted toward non-industrial nations and that the needs of the industrial nations would be lost. To them, national sovereignty is absolute. Neither the collective security of the League of Nations nor that of its successor, the United Nations, has shown the ability to make global decisions and to carry them out.

The superpowers work within the United Nations only when it suits their purposes and, while doing so, maintain their sovereignty. Draw up a list of advantages and disadvantages of collective security as you understand it. As you proceed through the text and study the League of Nations and the United Nations, remember this basic issue.

THE FIRST WORLD WAR:
THE INDUSTRIAL POWERS COLLIDE

FOCUS ON TOTAL WAR

You're right my boy—we'll need to pile on quite a few more if we're to see Verdun.

Kaiser Wilhelm II to his son, the crown prince Fredrik Wilhelm, standing on an enormous pile of dead soldiers while looking through binoculars toward enemy lines.
(Reproduced in *Menneskenes Historia, i kart, tekst og bilder*, Cappelens Forlag, Oslo, 1990.)

Consider motives for confrontation. In **total war**, confrontation is enacted through the marshaling of virtually all the human and industrial resources of two opposing sides.

By the time you finish this chapter, you should be able to list and describe the motives on each side of the war.

OVERVIEW

Industrialization created the great powers of Great Britain, France, Germany, the United States, Russia, and Japan. Competition for resources coupled with nationalism and an unstable balance-of-power structure created the international tension which resulted in the First World War.

THE FIRST WORLD WAR

From 1914 to 1918, the world was torn apart by a war which involved civilians as well as the military. The war introduced technological innovation to the battlefield. The Treaty of Versailles, which was imposed on Germany to end the war, proved to be an uneasy peace.

WILSON'S POINTS

US President Woodrow Wilson believed that war could be prevented through the implementation of his fourteen points.

Britain encouraged the development of Western Canada for the dual purpose of settlement and food production.

RELATIONSHIPS between the nations of the world were dramatically altered by the Industrial Revolution of the nineteenth century. Within the handful of states that had the means to industrialize, the disciplined organization of people and the mass-production of goods resulted in a spectacular increase in standard of living and military power. Economic growth, coupled with the ability to wage mechanized war and sustain long periods of fighting, gave industrialized nations an advantage over the others and established them as great powers.

Industrialization began along the iron and coal beds that stretch eastward from England through the French provinces of Alsace and Lorraine into the Ruhr Valley and Bavaria. Fortunate to have the raw materials and technology necessary to industrialize, first Great Britain, then France and Germany, rose to great-power status. They were later joined by the United States, Russia, and Japan. When their own resources were depleted, they reached outward for empires in order to secure the food supplies and mineral resources essential to continued economic expansion.

Carried across the seas in steam-powered ships, and into the interior of continents by transcontinental railroads, their armies brushed aside the defences of the non-industrial nations. Their global empires provided not only the resources vital to industrial growth, but also markets for surplus goods, places for investment, and room for their excess population. Western Canada is the classic example of a "wilderness" area developed by an imperial power for the dual purpose of food production and settlement. By 1900, almost all of the world had come under the domination of the industrial powers who made the major decisions affecting its peoples.

The transportation routes that linked the parts of the empires together were considered "lifelines," which, in every sense of the word, they were. Guarded with a vigilance befitting their importance, the sea lanes and railroads were defended by powerful battle fleets and armies to ensure that goods would always get through. Threats to these routes would almost certainly result in war. And as rival industrial empires expanded, threats would inevitably occur.

Tensions between the industrial powers grew in frequency and intensity after 1900 as each sought to expand its sphere of influence at the expense of the others. As long as strategic positions were not threatened, these tensions were resolved through diplomatic negotiations. But peaceful relations between them could not last forever, and in the summer of 1914, rivalry for global dominance turned into the First World War.

Underlying the development of rivalry into war was the change in character of the European alliances of the Triple Entente (Great Britain, Russia, and France) and the Triple Alliance (Germany, Austria-Hungary, and Italy) from one of mutual defence to one of preparedness for war. This change came about as a result of the Balkan Wars in the period of 1912 to 1913. All the major powers increased their military expenditures, both in size of forces and in the production of war *matériel*. This upset the balance of power that had existed for over half a century and threw decades of military planning into disarray. France and Russia in particular began the rapid expansion and modernization of their armies. At the same time, Great Britain began to realize plans to send an army onto the continent as well as put its battle fleets into action.

Germany, which already had a powerful army and an expanding navy, viewed the arms buildup with alarm. The increased military preparedness of its rivals posed a lethal threat to its security. Situated in the middle of Europe, it had to protect itself from France and Russia. Germany would need to win a war against both of them at the same time. The solution to the problem of a two-front war lay in the Schlieffen Plan which called for a knockout blow against France before German armies moved back across Germany to counter a Russian attack. The success of the plan, however, depended on the French and Russian armies being unprepared when war was declared. New rearmament programs thus placed Germany's security at risk.

BIOGRAPHY

ALFRED GRAF VON SCHLIEFFEN (1833–1913)

Alfred Graf von Schlieffen, German general and chief of the army general staff from 1891–1906, has been accused of basing the Schlieffen Plan on strategic principles which, long before their implementation, had hardened into rigid doctrines. The Schlieffen Plan called for a quick strike of annihilation against France before turning all of the German forces on Russia. Schlieffen's dying words are reported to have been: "It must come to a fight. Only make the right wing strong." The Schlieffen Plan was completed in 1905 and implemented in 1914; then not by Schlieffen, who had died the year previous, but by the younger Moltke. Moltke reinterpreted the plan, drastically altering its implementation.

Schlieffen was convinced of the rightness and ingenuity of his plan, in spite of the fact that it was a very daring gamble—and, in his own words, "[an] enterprise for which we are too weak." He seemed not to admit to the flaws in the plan, several being that it did not provide the formula for neutralizing the powerful garrison of Paris, and that it was too optimistic. For success in 1914 and the years following, the plan required that everything go according to predictions completed in 1905. This optimism did not take into account the numerous variables and possible permutations of events and effects and players. It also did not take into account new technologies introduced during the war.

Schlieffen's career as chief of general staff digressed significantly from the path trod by his predecessors Waldersee and the elder Moltke. Schlieffen disapproved of their defensive stance and wanted instead to secure the upper hand in the event of a war by concentrating all of his forces, including almost all of the German reserves, against France first, then Russia. Schlieffen's goals were quick, decisive victories and the complete destruction of the enemies' striking power.

Because of his fierce determination, love of thinking and planning, and possibly also because of the early death of his wife, Schlieffen pursued his duties as general staff with tireless zeal. This same commitment was exacted from his subordinates, who remembered being assigned tactical problems on Christmas Eve for completion on Boxing Day. ●

MISSIONARY ZEAL

The growth of the British Empire provided the opportunity to teach Christianity to whom were termed by a poet of the British Empire, Rudyard Kipling, the "lesser breeds without the law." The explosion of missionary activity that accompanied the economic thrust of the Imperial Age is often overlooked. Yet this activity often provided the moral impetus for military and territorial expansion.

The spark which ignited the First World War was the assassination of the heir to the Austro-Hungarian throne, Archduke Franz Ferdinand, while on a visit to Sarajevo in the recently annexed province of Bosnia in the Balkans. It was but one of numerous assassinations and political crises that characterized the turn of the century, and in itself would not have been the cause of war had the great powers not decided at this time to seek a military solution.

The importance of the Balkan states lay in their position adjacent to the straits that link the Black Sea to the Mediterranean. All the trade from Austria-Hungary that traveled down the Danube, and from Russia's southern regions, had to pass through the Turkish-controlled waterway to reach world markets. Profits from world trade were to be used to pay for industrialization. Any threat to this strategic region would therefore bring swift response from these imperial powers, as neither could afford to have the other in possession of this crucial sea lane. Yet the frequent ethnic uprisings and wars of independence against Turkey had left the Balkans unstable. The inability of Turkey to put down these nationalist movements created a situation that invited revolution and great-power intervention.

The killing of the Austro-Hungarian archduke on 28 June by the Serbian nationalist, Gavrilo Princip, gave Austria-Hungary the pretext to invade Serbia and crush the spreading Pan-Slavic movement that threatened its southern provinces. The danger was that an invasion of Serbia would bring Russia to the aid of its neighbour Slavs. This danger was offset by Germany's promise to support Austria-Hungary should Russia interfere. The Germans urged Austria-Hungary on to war in the belief that if a general European war broke out as a result, the Germans and Austrians could win in 1914. The German general staff believed there was less chance of victory in 1916, when Russia and France would be fully rearmed. When Russia mobilized its forces on 30 July in response to Austria-Hungary's demands on Serbia, the Germans reacted by giving Russia an ultimatum: to stop mobilization. Germany also gave Russia's ally France an ultimatum: to declare neutrality should war occur. As well as publicly declaring neutrality, France was to turn over the border fortresses of Toul and Verdun as hostages. Germany did not really expect France to accept either ultimatum. Germany was now intent on war. When Russia did not respond, and when France replied it would act in its own interests, Germany declared war on Russia on 1 August, and on France on 3 August.

The other powers were more than willing to settle

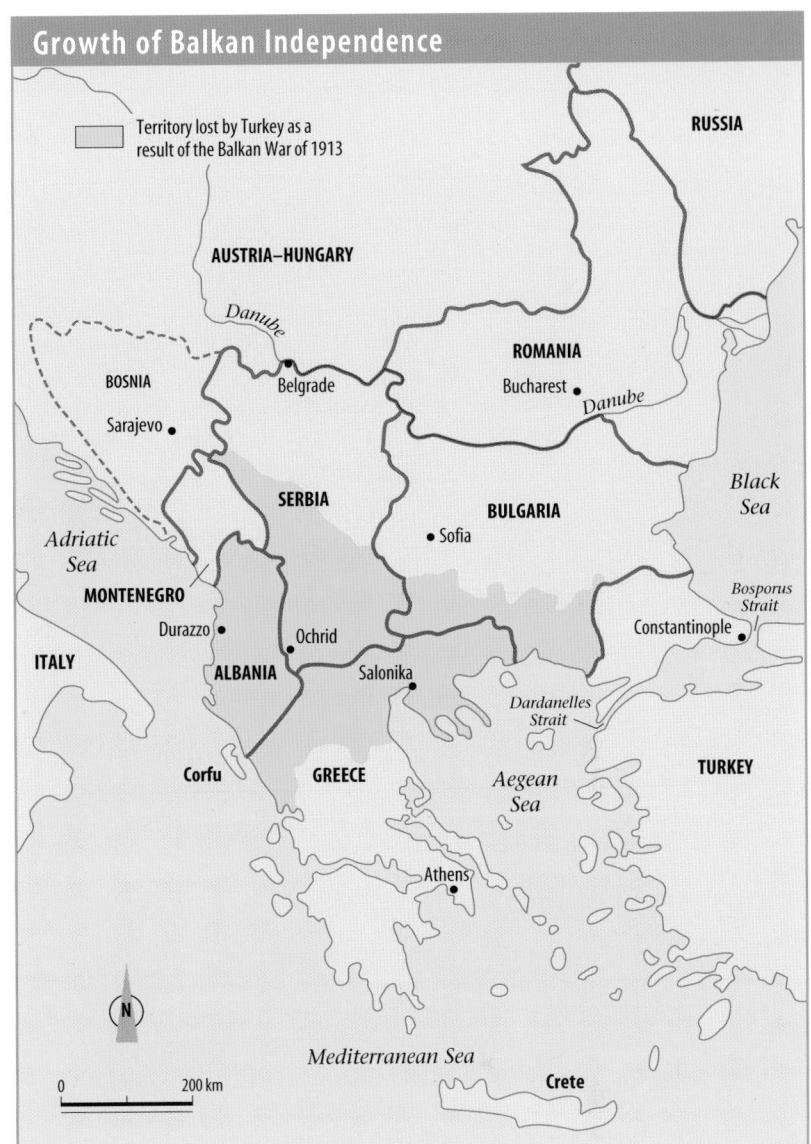

Growth of Balkan Independence

Territory lost by Turkey as a result of the Balkan War of 1913

RUSSIA

AUSTRIA–HUNGARY

Danube

ROMANIA

BOSNIA

Belgrade

Bucharest

Danube

Sarajevo

SERBIA

Black Sea

BULGARIA

Adriatic Sea

Sofia

MONTENEGRO

Bosporus Strait

Durazzo

Ochrid

Constantinople

ITALY

ALBANIA

Salonika

Corfu

GREECE

Aegean Sea

TURKEY

Dardanelles Strait

Athens

N

Mediterranean Sea

Crete

0   200 km

The Ottoman Empire (Turkey) ruled the Balkan states from the late fifteenth century until the Balkan Wars of 1913 caused the empire to lose most of its European territories.

what was then known as the German Question, by force of arms. The formation of Germany in Central Europe in 1870 had an unsettling effect on the relationships between the powers. The balance of power established by the Congress of Vienna in 1815 was upset. The unification of the German states brought together more than 60 million people with the industrial potential to form the dominant nation on the continent. This potential had been realized by 1900, when Germany had emerged as an industrial giant.

When territorial expansion became essential to sustain its economic growth, Germany ran into

Advanced weaponry, such as this Canadian siege gun, made the death and destruction of war more efficient. The result was an unprecedented loss of lives.

conflict with other countries. German economic initiatives in the direction of Turkey and the Middle East were limited by the British and French. The search for overseas markets in Latin America and the Philippines conflicted with American interests. The German concession in China, and the seizure of several Pacific island groups along with the older colonies in southern Africa, hardly amounted to what the German public saw as "a place in the sun." Unable to break out of economic encirclement, Germany faced industrial stagnation at a time when its rivals were becoming economically and militarily stronger. Fearful of being left behind and denied great-power status, the German people came to support the use of military force to secure and assert the greatness of the nation.

The German invasion of France in August 1914 began Europe's trial by fire, an agony that was not to end until 1945. Two world wars (1914–1918 and 1939–1945) would kill more people and destroy more cities and towns than ever before in world history. The human and physical resources of the European empires were squandered in a conflict that in the end destroyed both victors and vanquished. When the wars were over, most of Europe and large parts of Asia lay in ruins. The two world wars that began in Europe marked the end of one era and the beginning of another. They bridge the period of European world dominance and the present era, in which the global power structure is dominated by superpowers.

THE BALKAN WARS

In 1912 Serbia, Bulgaria, Greece, and Montenegro went to war to drive the Turks back across the Bosporus Straits and out of Europe. They readily defeated the Turkish armies and had agreed on an expansion of boundaries that they hoped to have recognized at peace talks held in London in 1913. However, Serbia's proposal for access to the Adriatic Sea by the annexation of Albania was opposed by Italy. Austria-Hungary also opposed Serbian expansion, fearing a Pan-Slavic movement would affect its southern provinces, which were populated by Slavs. Pan-Slavism would begin the breakup of the multinational empire if the Austrian Slavs united with Serbia.

Before the London talks were completed, Bulgaria attacked Serbia and set off a new round of fighting. Austria-Hungary supported Bulgaria against Serbia, while Russia came to the aid of Serbia, its only remaining Balkan ally. At subsequent peace talks in Bucharest, Turkey reaffirmed its intention of withdrawing from all but a small part of its European domain; Serbia was again denied access to the sea; Bulgaria was reduced in size; and Albania was made independent. None were happy with the solution. It failed to satisfy the nationalist aspirations that had started the fighting in the first place. Armed and highly emotional, the ethnic minorities in the Balkans continued to agitate for independence and created a political situation that only a year later would ignite the First World War.

THE FIRST WORLD WAR

The outbreak of hostilities in 1914 was greeted on all sides with wild enthusiasm. Prayers for victory were chanted as cheering mobs, eager to come to grips with the enemy, thronged the streets and avenues. It had been so long since major hostilities had taken place that many Europeans knew of war only from books and newspapers. People tended to romanticize war. Heroes and medals were what it was all about; war was seen as an adventure that would be over in a few brief months. It was a welcome diversion that broke the dull routine of the factory and office. No one thought in terms of death or defeat in battle. But this war differed fundamentally from any other that had gone before. It was the first of the industrial wars, in which machines and technology were systematically applied to the slaughter of human beings. Weapons

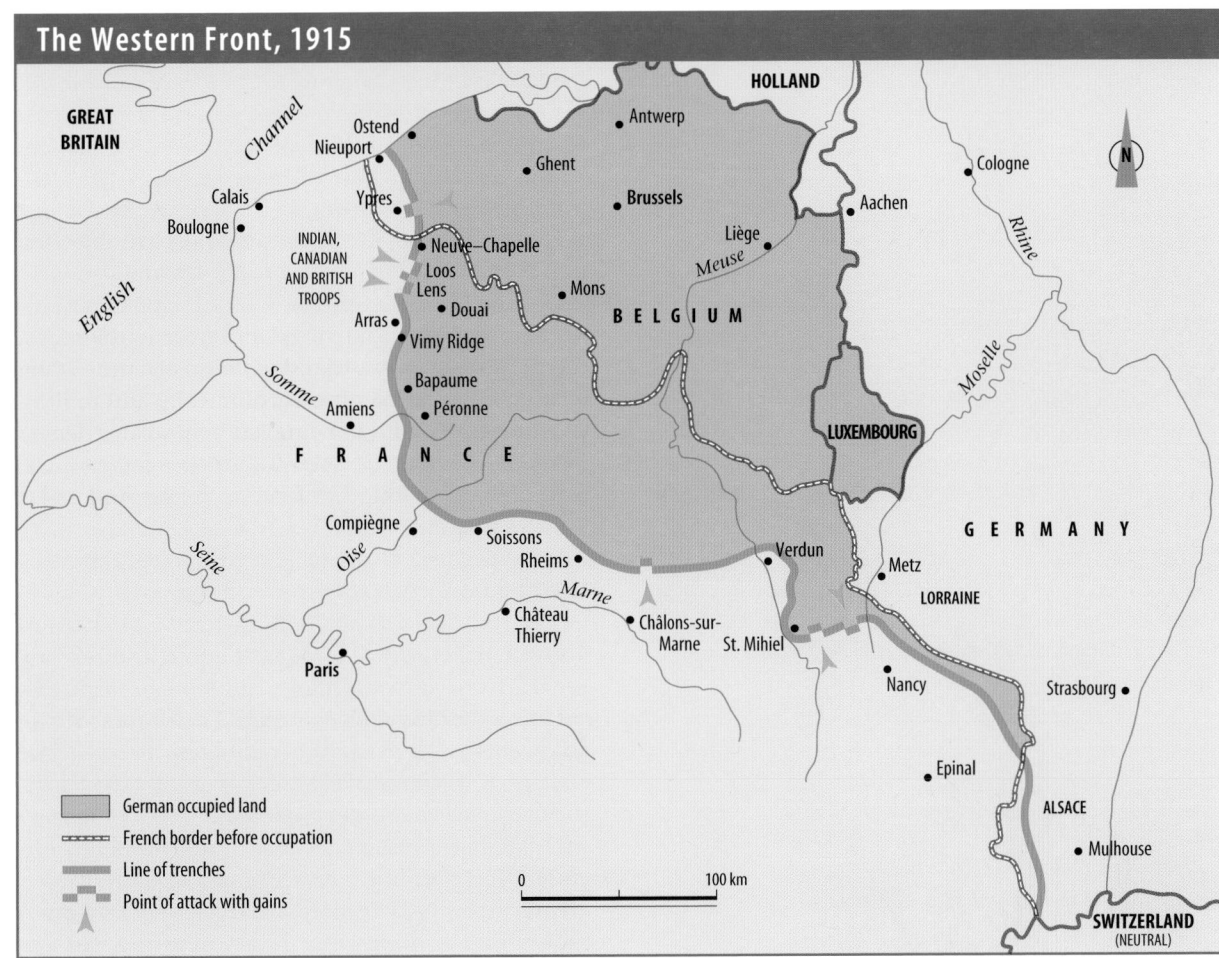

The Western Front, 1915

especially designed for efficient killing, such as machine guns and field artillery, were mass-produced for the battle fronts. The result was death and destruction on an unprecedented scale.

Within a few weeks of the declaration of war, some 6 million men stood to arms, and behind them tens of millions more were preparing to play their part. The equipping, training, and transporting of such numbers into battle could be sustained only by the industrial nations. Those nations that did not have an adequate industrial base, such as Russia, Austria-Hungary, and Italy, suffered badly. Before the war was over, their armies collapsed, unable to continue the battle. By contrast, the forces of Great Britain and Germany sustained equally terrible losses, but were able to prolong the fighting to its end four years later.

In the first weeks of the war, eight German armies pushed through Belgium and raced across its undefended border with northern France. The invasion of Belgium challenged the longtime British guarantee of Belgian neutrality and brought Britain into the war. British entry was anticipated by the

Initial attempts by the allies to push German forces out of France and Belgium were unsuccessful. Thousands of soldiers lost their lives every day until the war came to an end.

Germans and considered worth the risk; France, they thought, would be defeated before British troops could cross the English Channel. In response, the French army put into operation Plan XVII, a frontal assault on the Germans in Alsace and Lorraine. The French attack was driven back with unprecedented losses of over 600 000 men. The German armies advancing on Paris from the north were now ordered to swing away from the capital and surround the vulnerable French armies caught between Paris and Verdun. The swing north of Paris opened a 40 km gap between the German First and Second Armies. British and French forces struck into the gap, disrupting the German advance. When the Germans pulled back to regroup, a series of frontal assaults broke out along the Marne River. Between 5 and 10 September an allied counterattack stalled the German advance. Pausing only to renew stockpiles

On the home front, many women aided the war effort by taking jobs in factories that had traditionally been the domain of men. Others, like the British women illustrated above in Poland, took a more active role in the war.

CASE STUDY

THE BRITISH HOME FRONT

What dramatic social and economic change did the war introduce in the industrial nations? In Britain, increasing numbers of women entered the workplace. Assume the role of a young British woman during the 1915–1918 period. Describe your reactions to the war and the social changes it triggered in your society.

As the war progressed, seemingly without end, it made increasing demands on human and physical resources. Economies had to be centralized and managed so that fighting forces could be kept in battle. Germany was the first to adopt central planning and the rationing of goods. All combatant nations had resorted to government controls on the home front by 1915. Departments of labour were established to speed the flow of soldiers to the battlefield and replaced them in factories at home, often with women, who underwent a dramatic change in social status at this time.

During the war, the English way of life underwent major changes. While shortages reduced the standard of living, wages rose, and workers increased their bargaining power. Restrictions on every aspect of life gave a hint of the postwar regulated economies to come.

On 10 March 1915 the British army attacked at Neuve-Chapelle. It did not have enough shells for a preliminary bombardment, but went straight in, catching the Germans by surprise. The British broke through the German lines but hesitated to take advantage of the gap until reinforced. By that time, the Germans were able to close the line and a three-day stalemate resulted. General Sir John French concealed his failure by complaining about the lack of artillery shells. The British government blamed highly paid workers who, although they could not get ammunition produced, and commanded high wages, seemed to have time to spend in pubs. Legislation was at once introduced to limit the hours that drinking in public would be permitted. This was but one of the restrictions government imposed on the home front during the war.

After Neuve-Chapelle, David Lloyd George, Britain's minister of munitions and later the prime minister, believed that Britain was going to lose the war unless the government took total control of the resources of the nation. Up until 1915, the people took war as only one more concern in life. Now they were to become involved in a total reorganization of society aimed at "winning through." The government was to assume the widest powers over citizens and property. Major industries, work, unions, transportation, and leisure time all came under government supervision.

One of the major changes was the emancipation of women from the home as they took the place of men in the work force. About 1 million women were brought into shell factories and weapons-assembly plants. Others went to work in government offices. Everywhere women began working outside the home on a massive scale. This changed their lifestyle. There were policewomen, and in the later stages of the war, women were enrolled in the armed forces in an auxiliary role.

The daily round was dull, with long hours worked in the national interest. Leisure time was sharply curtailed, but the worker had more money to spend in a world in which 5000 casualties a day made most social restrictions of the past meaningless. Those at home found they could escape from societal control into the personal freedom of economic independence. Theatres and Hollywood movies had a heyday that outlasted the war.

The press blamed juvenile delinquency and the general relaxation of morals on the war. Ragtime was introduced in clubs and dance halls where couples danced the tango and fox trot. Freedom from the restraints of home and church, coupled with the especially heavy losses in 1916, seemed to indicated that life was cheap and old standards had to give way.

Real austerity did not come to Britain until 1917, when shortages in potatoes, sugar, margarine, and coal became noticeable and the queue was invented. In May, a rationing system was established to give each person three quarters of a pound of meat per week. Oatmeal puddings and bean fritters became common fare. Bread was "government bread" bulked out with starches and other oddities, and even "government tea" was tolerated. Rationing had the effect of leveling the diet of the social classes. For the first time, prime cuts of beef were made available to the poor.

During the war, all clocks were put forward one hour to give longer evening hours for recreation and to increase the efficiency of the workplace. Labour had its position strengthened as unions insisted on wages keeping up with prices if strikes were to be avoided. Families with several workers now had an abundance of extra cash to be spent on non-essentials. The piano was more often found in lower class homes, while fur coats and the gramophone became status symbols of a new found respectability. Society was becoming more homogeneous as all shared in the dislocation of war and a fairer status for women evolved. Greater wealth gave those at home greater personal freedom and independence as well as a taste for the amenities of a modern industrial society. Governments intervened in every aspect of their people's lives in order to pursue victory, and would continue to do so in the post-war era. The war had brought about an unintended social revolution.

Women of 1915 assumed a new role in society. Women attending the Women's Peace Conference at The Hague in 1915 assessed their views and took a political stance.

1. What brought the massive centralization of power to the hands of the British government?

2. Explain the government's administration of its human resources in face of total war.

3. Describe the new social roles in Britain that emerged from the war.

4. What was the purpose and effect of rationing?

5. Using the example of Britain during the First World War, argue for or against: "War is a positive force in effecting egalitarian social change."

The Canadian infantry, attacking in heavy smoke, sustained massive losses. For months, the allies continued staging offensive infantry attacks until there were temporary shortages of soldiers and *matériel*.

STAGGERING LOSSES

In the first five months of fighting, the French and Germans had lost about a million soldiers each, and the British Expeditionary Force alone lost almost half of its 160 000-soldier strength. The figures were staggering, but small by comparison to what was to come.

The objective of Britain and France was to hurl the invaders out of France and Belgium. This could be done only by infantry attacks against the machine guns, barbed wire, and mine fields that protected the German lines in places 7 km deep. These assaults would cost an average of 5000 lives every day for the next 52 months.

of *matériel*, both sides began a series of manoeuvres designed to outflank the other. Through October and November, the line of battle moved north and west until it reached the sea. Neither side could prevail as constant fighting led to mutual exhaustion. The armies began to dig in for the winter to replenish human resources and supplies in preparation for the spring; but by then the Western Front had become a long series of entrenchments stretching from the English Channel to Switzerland. This 400-km line was to remain relatively unchanged for the next three years. Repeated attempts to break through the heavily defended entrenchments by infantry assaults would cost millions of lives.

Although the knockout blow called for by the Schlieffen Plan had failed to defeat France, the German position in the west was still strong. German forces stood in occupation of the industrial regions of Belgium and France, whose coal and iron fields would now help sustain a prolonged war. Initial attempts by the French and British to throw the Germans back had failed. The Germans could not be dislodged. Confident they could not be pushed out of their trenches, the Germans decided to adopt a defensive strategy in the west while they turned their attention to the Russians on the Eastern Front in 1915.

Before the decisive battles that led to stalemate in the west were fought in the fall of 1914, Russian forces crossed the eastern borders of Germany much earlier than the Germans expected. The

Russians hoped to bring relief to their French ally by drawing German troops away from the Western Front to defend Prussia and Galicia. This tactic succeeded, but not enough German troops were drawn from the west to make a real difference. German forces already in the east were sufficient to annihilate the Russian armies before reinforcements arrived.

The Russians were more successful against the Austro-Hungarians in Galicia. Cracow was held, but fighting in the Carpathian passes threatened to break into the Hungarian Plain. The desertion of thousands of Slavic conscripts from the Austrian army brought Austria-Hungary to the verge of collapse. To forestall this disaster, German armies began a general offensive along the Eastern Front in May 1915. The Russians were driven out of Galicia and central Poland with losses so great the Germans believed Russia would be unable to mount any further attacks. The Germans now planned to regroup their armies in France to break the stalemate on the Western Front in 1916. They did not, however, count on the enormity of Russian soldier reserves or the fact they might not be able to defeat them all. During the war, Russia was able to mobilize over 12 million soldiers. Despite the early losses, Russia was far from out of the war.

None of the powers had made any plans for a protracted war, and initial supplies of soldiers and *matériel* had been used up in the first three months. In order to sustain the war governments took direct control of their domestic resources. Victory would go to the power that could provide an uninterrupted flow of goods to the battlefields. National employment agencies directed the labour force. Women entered the workplace to take the part of men gone to war. Fighting forces were kept up to strength through conscription. Legislation was passed banning strikes and lockouts. Government agencies directed the use of materials and the allocation of food and consumer goods. In the later stages, food rationing became common. All the industrial processes and domestic institutions were forged into a centralized organization directed at a total war effort.

The allies did not have the same problems of supply as the Germans. The vast resources of the British Empire and the resources of the United States after 1917 made the allies' position much easier. By contrast, the Germans were faced with a British naval blockade that cut off their overseas resources. Initially, this blockade had little effect, but in the long run, it was a major setback for the Triple Alliance. In the later months, food rationing and

178 - En Lorraine

Conditions for soldiers in the trenches were appalling, and many succumbed to illnesses contracted there.

starvation set in. German victories in Poland and Russia in 1917 came too late to permit that year's harvest of crops, and before another harvest had come, the war was over.

The Germans countered the British naval blockade with submarine warfare. German U-boats were spread out along the sea lanes that linked England with food supplies and other resources around the world. The attempt to starve England into surrender eventually provoked the United States to enter the war in 1917. The sinking of American ships sailing in the war zones around the British Isles caused a furor with the American public. The *Lusitania* was but one of many unescorted ships to fall victim to German submarines. In the worst months of 1917, some 850 000 tonnes of shipping were sunk, putting considerable pressure on Britain's ability to continue the war. The U-boat menace was overcome with the development of the convoy system, in which warships protected vital cargoes. So effective did the convoy system become that 2 million American soldiers were transported across the Atlantic to France without a single loss in 1918.

In 1916 both sides tried to achieve a breakthrough by massing soldiers and firepower against narrow fronts. In every case the attacking infantry were slaughtered by artillery barrages and machine-gun fire. Yet, despite the carnage, battles lasted as long as railways could speed reinforcements to the critical sectors. Weeks and months of attack saw

CANADA IN WORLD WAR I

As part of the British Empire, Canada was automatically at war when Britain declared war on Germany on 4 August 1914. Within a few months, the First Canadian Expeditionary Force, later to expand into a three division corps, sailed for Europe. At the time, Canada had a population of only 8 million. During the First World War, some 619 636 men and women, of whom 66 655 were lost in battle, served in Canada's armed forces.

At sea, Canada's small navy expanded to more than 100 warships to play its part in keeping the Atlantic sea lanes open. Hundreds of other Canadians served in the Royal Navy as did their compatriots in the Royal Flying Corps (RAF). Sixteen hundred Canadian pilots lost their lives. Names such as Billy Bishop, Raymond Collishaw, and W.G. Barker left a record of daring and honour as a result of their heroic conduct.

Canada's largest contribution was on land where the soldiers of the Canadian corps fought alongside the British and the French. Battle honours were earned at Arras and Amiens; in the first chlorine gas attacks before Ypres and Saint Julien where casualties climbed about 30 per cent; the capture of Vimy Ridge on Easter Monday in the midst of a driving sleet and snow storm; the capture of Passchendaele in waist-deep mud where enemy counterattacks claimed 16 000 of the 20 000 that set out the day before; and in the last months of the war when the Canadians spearheaded the final breakthrough of the German lines in 100 days of continuous action that survived the blood bath at Cambrai and the seizing of Mons on the day before the war ended.

It was Canada's outstanding war effort that gave the dominion a separate place at the peace table at Versailles. Canada was granted a separate signature on the peace document, marking international recognition that Canada was no longer only an overseas extension of Britain.

---

casualty rates climb well above the 1 million mark, until a pause in the fighting was created by temporary shortages in soldiers and *matériel*.

The first major battle in 1916 began with the German attack on Verdun. The plan was not to capture the fortress, but to threaten it in such a way that the French would rush all their reinforcements to its defence. The Germans would then proceed to destroy the French reinforcements in a battle of **attrition**. When the French ran out of soldiers, they would have to surrender. Lives lost were mere statistics. Victory went to the side with the fewest losses. During five months of battle, over 600 000 soldiers were killed, and at the end, the fortress remained in French hands. Nearly half of those killed were German.

The allies had also planned two major campaigns for 1916. The first to strike were the Russians, who mounted an unexpected and spectacular offensive in the east against the Austro-Hungarians. It threatened Berlin and Vienna before grinding to a halt at a cost of a million dead. These heavy losses were to begin the demoralization of the Russian army. But, for the moment, the victories won by General Bursilov in 1916 were the most brilliant of all allied victories in the war. So successful was this campaign that the Germans had to disengage from Verdun to move troops to the Eastern Front. This time, the Germans did not make the mistake of counting Russia out of the war. Attempts by Bursilov to repeat his earlier successes were doomed to failure, as was the final Russian offensive in the summer of 1917. From this point on, German armies put continuous pressure on the Russians, driving them back relentlessly until Russia left the war in the fall of 1917, in the midst of internal revolution.

The second allied campaign took place in the west along the Somme River, where British Imperial forces attacked along a narrow front of only 40 km. The battle began with an enormous concentration of firepower. Artillery shells smashed into the German lines for seven days and nights before the advance against what were expected to be undefended positions. The stark reality was that the Germans had survived the pounding and tenaciously defended their lines with devastating fire. The British lost 50 per cent of their soldiers on the first day of what turned into a six month battle. Fighting until winter set in, the Imperial troops gained a mere 10 km without breaking the German lines, at a cost of hundreds of thousands of casualties. As 1916 came to an end, only the British, Canadian, and German armies were capable of further effort.

The war took a decisive turn in 1917 with the elimination of Russia as a combatant and the entry of the United States of America into the war. Russia had stayed in the war despite far greater losses than any other power; but in 1917 its industrial and agricultural resources could no longer sustain the armies in the field. Russia was sick of war and its total collapse was inevitable. Successive German victories had destroyed the Russian army well before the overthrow of the tsar in the spring of 1917. Over 3.6 million Russian soldiers had been killed, a further 2.1 million had been captured, and desertion from the army had passed the 2 million mark. Many of the deserters were drawn home to their farms to take part in a rumoured land redistribution. While German forces advanced through Poland and Galicia, the Romanov dynasty came to an end. The tsarist government was replaced by two provisional governments in succession (one led by Prince Georgi Lvov, the other by Aleksandr Kerensky). Promising to hold elections in the fall, Prime Minister Kerensky proposed continuing the unpopular war, despite public unrest and an escalating casualty rate. As inflation reached 700 per cent, a series of crippling strikes broke out in June and ended any further effort to supply the fighting fronts. Severe food shortages became widespread and civil unrest grew as neither industry nor agriculture could keep pace with the demands made upon them. The inability of the provisional government to supply the people and the army led to its overthrow in the October Revolution that brought Vladimir Ilyich Lenin and the Bolsheviks to power.

Lenin's platform of peace, land, and bread won the Bolsheviks widespread public support. In October, a Bolshevik *coup d'état* ousted the provisional government, and Russia slid into revolution. The Bolsheviks acted immediately to pull Russia out of the war. Although they hoped to do this without having to cede any territory or pay any reparations, they were forced to give up all the western non-Russian parts of the empire, which contained a third of the country's population and large quantities of iron, coal, and thousands of factories, in order to stop the German advance. They were also required to pay 6 billion German marks in reparations. The signing of the Treaty of Brest-Litovsk on 3 March 1918 signaled Germany's victory in the east. All that remained was to win in the west.

Russia's surrender was balanced by the entry of the United States into the war. The American intervention was decisive because new American resources guaranteed an eventual allied victory. Although unrestricted German submarine warfare had resulted in enough public outcry to enable President Wilson to seek a declaration of war, the catalyst was a telegram from German Foreign

Canadian troops prepare unwelcome presents for Germany. Although the allies waged a massive campaign along the Somme River, shelling German lines for seven days and nights, the German troops defended their lines successfully.

A "BOLSHEVIK PLOT"?

Although it retreated into isolation and civil war, the Bolshevik government continued to affect matters in the west. The Russians seized all foreign investments and canceled all foreign debts. This had an inhibiting effect on France's post-war reconstruction. They also made public all the secret treaties agreed to by the allies during the war. For example, France was to support Russia's claim to Poland in return for Russian support in regaining Alsace and Lorraine. Italy was to get the Austrian port city of Trieste on the Adriatic as a reward for joining the allies against its former partners. Britain's foreign secretary Lord Balfour was intent on providing a homeland for the Jews, to be carved out of Palestine where in 1917 only 60 000 out of a total population of 750 000 were of the Jewish faith. All these "deals" proved embarrassing to the allied powers, who were publicly proclaiming the right of peoples to self-determination. Lenin also called for a world-wide workers' revolution that would reorganize all governments along communist lines. Although this upheaval failed to materialize, the labour unrest in Central Europe after the war gave some credence to a "Bolshevik Plot."

THE INFLUENZA EPIDEMIC

International cooperation arises from a variety of motives and results in different forms of interaction. Disease and general health concerns have often led to international cooperative efforts. Cite an appropriate instance and describe its results, emphasizing positive global outcomes.

Populations weakened by war were susceptible to the deadly influenza virus which struck in March 1918 and killed millions of people before it disappeared in 1920.

Influenza struck an American training base in Kansas in March 1918. The particularly virulent disease rapidly spread to the 30 000 soldiers in barracks. Those who recovered were sent to Europe, where they acted as carriers of the disease. Because the king of Spain was one of the first to succumb, it was known as the "Spanish flu."

Spreading outwards from Europe, mostly with troops returning home, the influenza attacked every continent during the following months. By the spring of 1919, it had killed an estimated 27 000 people. Most of them were in Africa, India, and China. In India alone more people died than had perished in the whole of the war that had just ended, and in a far shorter period of time. Over 20 million North Americans contacted the influenza in one form or another, but most of them survived. American doctors reported a 32 per cent death rate among the 70 000 cases they handled, and every soldier in the small Swiss army was infected.

Crowded barracks, towns, and cities were vulnerable, with hundreds of people dying each day. Schools and churches were closed. Public meetings were banned and people were encouraged to wear surgical masks at all times. All forms of public transport were routinely sprayed with medicinal cleansers, likely to no effect. Sporting events were abandoned, and only the very brave ventured into those movie theatres and dance halls that had not been closed by public health inspectors.

Doctors were at a loss as to what to do. All one could do was avoid contact and wait out the virus. There was no suitable vaccine and the only action taken was to quarantine affected premises. Home remedies included taking snuff to sneeze away the disease, hot towels to cure the chills, blood-letting, strong doses of whiskey, and sitting on a cane bottomed chair with a lit candle underneath.

Streets were reported to be piled high with corpses, and city squares littered with bodies. In cities on the Great Lakes, corpses were placed out on the ice to be disposed of by the spring thaw. In some instances, the dead were dragged out onto the ice near fresh-water intakes-thus compounding the difficulties in halting the spread of the disease. People were urged to stop shaving and kissing, and to refrain from shaking hands and borrowing things from neighbours.

The epidemic began to ease off in November, but in the spring of 1919 a new outbreak swept across Europe. In March, 4000 died in a single week in the London region. The mortality rate was far higher in Germany: here food and medical supplies were in short supply and the general population was already weakened by wartime malnutrition. Then, just as suddenly as it came, the virus disappeared. It was not until 1933 that scientists were able to isolate the virus that causes influenza and develop vaccines to control it.

1. Why are viruses lethal to humans? What is the best known remedy for influenza?

2. What steps do public health officials take to limit the effects of influenza?

3. Why was the mortality rate so high in Europe in the period of 1918 to 1920? Why was it high in India and Asia?

4. What stopped the virus?

5. When the flu virus strikes, what people are given vaccines? What reasons are given for their selection?

Secretary Zimmermann to the German ambassador in the United States on 19 January 1917, a telegram intercepted and decoded by the British and passed to the United States. The German ambassador was to convey to the Mexican government an offer of generous financial assistance and the understanding that after the war, Germany would support Mexico's claims to Texas, New Mexico, and Arizona if Mexico would attack the United States. This would divert the United States from Europe and permit Germany to prevail. This plan was a foolish act of desperation that incensed the American public. On 6 April 1917 the United States declared war on the Triple Alliance.

In order to resolve the debate in America over joining the war, Wilson had asked the combatants for a declaration of their war aims. This caught the European powers off guard. Their objective was simply to defeat the others' armies. After some delay, the allies replied that they hoped to drive the Germans from the occupied territories, reorganize Central Europe along the lines of self-determination for the minorities in the Austro-Hungarian Empire, and return Alsace and Lorraine to France. At this time, the Triple Alliance was winning and not inclined to reply. Germany was in occupation of the wealthy industrial regions of Belgium and northern France and could see no reason to negotiate a settlement. The overall German position was to reach a position of autarky (economic self-sufficiency) through territorial expansion in *Mittleuropa*. Food supplies essential to population growth were to come from the east, at the expense of Poland and Ukraine. The Poles and Ukrainians were to be expelled and replaced by German farmers. Poland would be reconstructed further eastward as a buffer against the Russians, and the remainder of Europe would enter into an economic union with Germany as its industrial centre.

American war aims were stated by Wilson in 14 points made public in January 1918. The US president called for Germany to withdraw from all occupied territories; the readjustment of political boundaries along the lines of nationality; self-determination for minorities; an independent Polish state with access to the sea; freedom of the seas and open world trade; and disarmament and the establishment of an association of nations for the purpose of collective security.

The American declaration of war on 6 April 1917 brought the certainty of final victory to the allies, although the United States would be unable to intervene directly for at least a year, at which time its armies would be prepared to fight. In the meantime,

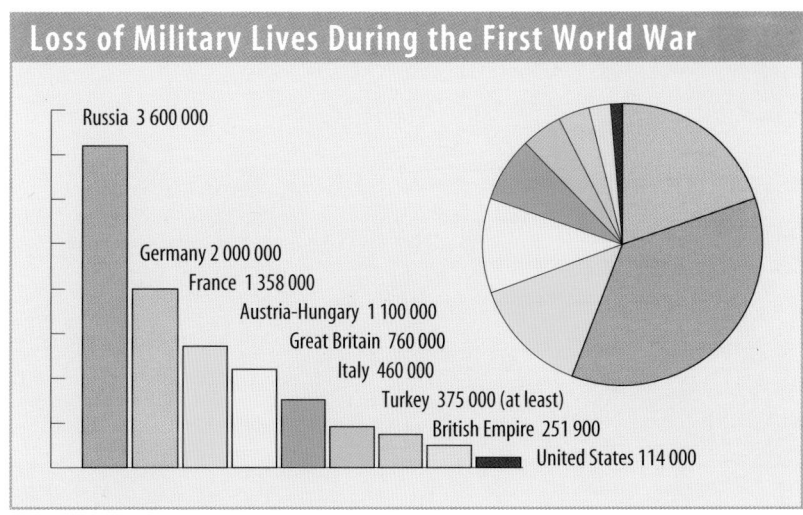

Loss of Military Lives During the First World War

Russia 3 600 000
Germany 2 000 000
France 1 358 000
Austria-Hungary 1 100 000
Great Britain 760 000
Italy 460 000
Turkey 375 000 (at least)
British Empire 251 900
United States 114 000

This chart shows the number of military lives lost during the First World War. Hundreds of thousands of civilians were also killed.

the United States would act as the arsenal for the allies. The formation of an armed force of 12 million soldiers was authorized and thousands of tanks, airplanes, and ships were to be constructed in a massive show of overwhelming industrial strength. Germany would have to win the war before this might could be brought to bear.

The final German attack along the Western Front began in the spring of 1918. With what forces they had left, the Germans drove toward Paris. They came within 40 km of the French capital before they ran out of resources. That August, the allied armies began a series of unending counterattacks that pushed the Germans back. In retreat, the German forces began to disintegrate, causing political upheaval in Germany and Austria-Hungary. Widespread anarchy and revolution resulted. Forced out of the war in August, the Austro-Hungarian Empire dissolved into a number of **successor states**. The Russian and Turkish empires also disintegrated. Germany underwent a period of chaos in which strikes and mutinies swept the homeland. The kaiser abdicated on 17 October and went into exile in Holland. On 9 November, after socialist revolutions in Munich and Berlin, and two days before the end of the war, a German republic was proclaimed under the presidency of Friedrich Ebert. Armistice terms were signed on 11 November, and the war came to an end.

The war had cost 10 million dead and 21 million wounded of the 68 million people mobilized. It was, in effect, the mass extermination of a generation of youth. The financial costs were estimated at

News of the end of First World War hostilities was joyfully received by soldiers in Moselle, France in November 1918.

$330 billion. The fighting had caused widespread destruction in northern France, and had so seriously disrupted Europe's agricultural sector that a malnourished civilian population fell prey to a terrible influenza epidemic the following winter. Some estimate that as many died in the months after the war as had fallen during the fighting. The Austro-Hungarian, Turkish, and Russian empires had disintegrated into politically unstable successor states, while the German overseas empire was placed under the League of Nations' mandate.

In January 1919 the victors gathered in Paris to repair the damage. The major decisions which led to the Treaty of Versailles were made by the Big Three—David Lloyd George for Great Britain, Georges Clémenceau for France, and Woodrow Wilson for the United States. They met privately to redraw the political map of Europe and undertake plans for political and economic reconstruction. The Treaty of Brest-Litovsk between Germany and Russia was declared null and void, even though Russia did not attend the conference. Germany was to retreat behind its 1914 boundaries both in the east and the west. Alsace-Lorraine was returned to France. Danzig was made a free city, and a corridor to it giving Poland access to the sea was established through Prussia.

WILSON'S POINTS

Wilson wanted to remove the causes of war. He saw war as a result of the tensions created by secret diplomacy, the problems of the treatment of minorities, and the autocratic manner in which a small elite managed the world's foreign affairs. He proposed to end secret treaties by introducing open diplomacy through a world association of states, self-determination and ethnic boundaries for minorities, and the democratization of government. When the hopes he raised for a better world order were not realized, and when the United States retreated into isolation, bitter disillusionment set in.

Of paramount importance was the security of France, whose 40 million people still faced a relatively undamaged German colossus of 60 million people. Germany was disarmed and allowed an army of only 100 000 men for internal security. The German armed forces were not to acquire airplanes, warships, submarines, or offensive weapons of any kind. German armies were withdrawn behind the Rhine River, and the strategic Rhineland was to be policed by an allied control commission for 15 years. The French were given bridgeheads across the Rhine River, and German fortifications within 50 km were dismantled. Britain and the United States guaranteed the neutrality of this buffer zone in compensation for refusing France's desire to annex it outright (which would have infringed upon the principle of self-determination). They also refused France's suggestion that Germany be divided into smaller, thus less powerful, states.

In order to replace the Russian counterweight it had lost in the east, France entered into a series of defensive alliances with Poland and the successor states. Politically unstable and economically immature, they could not in reality provide a strong enough deterrent to stop future German expansion. Apart from not being able to work with each other, states from the Baltic to the Balkans contained large German minorities who represented future problems.

The problem of economic reconstruction was more complex. The financial costs of the war had been staggering; neither the victors, apart from the United States, nor the vanquished had any monies left. The hardest hit were France and Russia. Russia was involved in its own horrors of civil war. As for France, the war was fought in its industrial regions, and at the end of the war, retreating German armies savaged the land. Their scorched-earth policy destroyed crops, burned houses, and flooded mines. Transportation routes were sabotaged and livestock

WILSON'S FOURTEEN POINTS

Woodrow Wilson made these recommendations for political and economic reconstruction:

1. Open covenants of peace in which there shall be no private international understandings of any kind.

2. Absolute freedom of navigation upon the seas, except by international action for the enforcement of international covenants.

3. The removal, so far as possible, of all economic barriers, and the establishment of an equality of trade conditions among all the nations.

4. The reduction of national armaments to the lowest point consistent with domestic safety. An impartial adjustment of all colonial claims, based upon the principle that the interests of the populations concerned must be considered.

5. An impartial adjustment of all colonial claims, based upon the principle that the interests of the populations concerned must be considered.

6. The evacuation of all Russian territory, and Russia to be given the opportunity for the independent determination of its own political development and national policy.

7. The evacuation and restoration of Belgium.

8. All French territory freed and the invaded portions restored, and the wrong done to France by Prussia in 1871 in the matter of Alsace-Lorraine should be righted.

9. A readjustment of the frontiers of Italy to be effected along clearly recognizable lines of nationality.

10. The assurance that the peoples of Austria-Hungary be accorded the freest opportunity for autonomous development.

Men like (from l to r) David Lloyd George (Britain), Vittorio Orlando (Italy), Georges Clémenceau (France), and Woodrow Wilson (USA) made decisions about post-war Europe at the January 1919 conference in Versailles.

11. The evacuation of Romania, Serbia, and Montenegro; the restoration of occupied territories; and the assurance of free and secure access to the sea for Serbia.

12. The assurance that the Turkish portions of the present Ottoman Empire be given an opportunity for autonomous development, and the Dardanelles be permanently opened.

13. The formation of an independent Polish state which would be assured a free and secure access to the sea.

14. The formation of a general association of nations for the purpose of affording mutual guarantees of political independence and territorial integrity to great and small states alike. All states must undertake to deal collectively with any threat to peace whenever it occurs.

BIOGRAPHY

THOMAS WOODROW WILSON
(1856–1924)

As the twenty-eighth president of the United States, Thomas Woodrow Wilson led his country through the turbulence of the First World War and was a primary architect of the League of Nations.

Wilson was a man motivated by ideas and ideals, whose moral austerity is said to have been communicated and passed on by his father, who was a Presbyterian minister. Both in his education, and in his career, Wilson was innovative in the work he did and initiatives he took. His early training was in law, but after a short and rather unsuccessful practice, he returned to his schooling and graduated from John Hopkins University in 1886 with a doctoral degree. His doctoral thesis centred on an analysis of the American political system. Some of the ideas included in that thesis he implemented during his years in the White House. Part of Wilson's success as president surely had to do with his firm academic foundation and his extensive knowledge of political and economic systems.

From 1886–1910, Wilson was a professor of Political Science at Bryn Mawr, Wesleyan, and Princeton Universities. Although Wilson is said to have excelled at teaching, in 1902 he moved into a more administrative role as president of Princeton University. In this role Wilson promoted such ideals as open communication between students and their instructors and the democratization of education, again illustrating that he was compelled by philosophical and political ideals.

Between 1910 and 1912, Wilson was the governor of New Jersey. His success at implementing, among other things, a corrupt-practices act, a direct primary law, an employers' liability act, and a law regulating the public utilities made him a prime candidate for the presidency in 1912, which office he went on to win.

Many would adulate Wilson by placing him in the sparsely populated category of great American presidents. Part of this praise is related to his role in the First World War. Wilson believed that as important as defeating Germany was the peace that would follow such a defeat. He proposed not only the ideal of an international body to ensure global justice and harmony, but also the concrete plans, political will, and energy for such a body to come into existence.

●

slaughtered. The French hoped that the United States would finance European recovery as it had financed the last months of the war. This was not to be the case. The United States put a halt to further government lending. American money could be obtained, but only from private investors at high interest rates.

The matter of reparations proved a dilemma for Britain and France. Any realistic assessment of reparations would in no way cover a fraction of the $330 billion total cost. Germany could only pay if it was admitted to world markets, but neither Britain nor France relished the thought of revived German industry. Britain saw in Germany a market for its own excess production, and France would permit reparations in coal and timber, but not in anything that would take jobs away from its own producers. In the end, Germany was required to pay an initial $5 billion in gold marks, with the final total amounting to $33 billion.

The sum was within Germany's ability to pay, but German reaction to the settlement was one of shock and disbelief. These feelings were encouraged by political and military leaders. Germany had won the war in the east and yet had been denied all its gains on the Eastern Front. The Polish corridor and the German minorities left within the buffer states went against all principles of self-determination and ethnic boundaries. Did this not make the treaty unworkable? As to the reparations, any amount would have been portrayed as barbaric. The modest amounts assessed were far lower than Germany had demanded of Russia and were easily covered by production from the Ruhr coal mines alone; yet much was to be made of the reparations question by political leaders for their own ends. In all, the people were led to believe that the treaty was repulsive and unjust. Germany had not even been allowed to participate in the negotiations. It was simply handed the finished draft and told to sign it. To the Germans, it was obvious the other powers were intent on destroying Germany's position as an industrial rival.

Germany had survived the war relatively intact; the war had been fought mainly outside its boundaries. Germany's drive for autarky and continental hegemony had been thwarted; but it was not dead, and dreams of dominating *Mittleuropa* still pervaded German society. The question of Germany's place in the ranking of the great powers had not been resolved by the war.

SUMMARY

The emergence of Germany in 1870, and its drive to become an industrial power after 1890, upset the relationships between the great powers. As each sought to secure the human and physical resources necessary for sustained industrial development, tensions developed between them. War between the powers was inevitable and broke out in August 1914. The immediate cause was the assassination of the Austro-Hungarian crown prince Franz Ferdinand and his wife, Sophie, by a Serbian nationalist in the Balkan city of Sarajevo.

The First World War was prolonged for four agonizing years as the industrial capacity of the great powers routinely replenished the battle fronts with soldiers and *matériel*. The war was different from other wars in that indiscriminate machine-killing escalated the casualties with terrifying results. Strategies used to achieve victory led to the expansion of the battle far beyond the fighting fronts to include cities and their civilian populations. The introduction of the airship, airplane, and submarine brought a third dimension to battle areas. Governments assumed absolute control of their people in order to regiment the war effort and bring their total resources to bear on the enemy. In the end, the allies won because Germany and Austria-Hungary ran out of resources first.

The Treaty of Versailles that was imposed on Germany was designed to achieve an end to war. Germany was disarmed, forced back within its boundaries, and compelled to give up its empire. Germany was also assessed $33 billion in war reparations—a sum neither draconian nor incapacitating. But the Germans viewed Versailles as an attempt by the other industrial powers to destroy Germany's future industrial growth. Not being part of the negotiations, the Germans were determined to overturn this *diktat* at the earliest opportunity.

QUESTIONS

1. How did industrialization affect the global power structure?

2. How did the Balkan Wars (1912–1913) contribute to the outbreak of the First World War?

3. What was the Schlieffen Plan?

4. Why did the assassination of Archduke Franz Ferdinand precipitate war?

5. How did the formation of Germany in 1870 affect the European balance of power? Explain where and why Germany ran into conflict with other industrial powers prior to the First World War.

6. Briefly describe the first five months of the war and explain the results. What resulted from stalemate and trench warfare?

7. Explain the significance of the battles at Verdun and the Somme.

8. Why did Russia leave the war?

9. Why did the United States enter the war?

10. What were Germany's war aims?

11. What were Wilson's war aims?

12. What was the primary contribution of the Americans upon their entry into the war on 6 April 1917?

13. List the costs of the war.

14. The Treaty of Versailles was an attempt to establish a framework for settling the war and restoring European peace. Explain the key issues under the headings:
   (a) security; (b) disarmament; (c) political; (d) territorial; (e) reparations.

CRITICAL ANALYSIS

1. How did Versailles create the grounds for future confrontation between the great powers?

2. Consider the ways in which nationalism can lead to confrontation. Is nationalism a stabilizing or a destabilizing force?

3. Contrast the principles of national security and disarmament.

4. Describe the concept and implications of total war.

5. Why did the great powers persist in mounting infantry attacks against heavily fortified positions for a period of four years?

6. Examine the conduct of twentieth century war in view of modern technologies. What effect has science had on war?

RESEARCH PROJECTS

1. New technology resulting from advances in industrialization enhanced the ability of nations to wage war. Describe new weapons, machinery, and equipment which emerged during the First World War and explain how they influenced the course of the war.

2. Research the conditions on either the Western Front or the Eastern Front. Consider supplies, fighting conditions, and morale of the fighting forces.

3. Research the role of Canadian forces in the First World War by examining their contribution to one of the following battles: (a) Ypres; (b) the Somme; (c) Vimy Ridge.

4. Research the role of women in the First World War. Examine their participation in industry, hospitals, and the military in the country of your choice.

ACTIVITIES

Role Play

Recreate the meeting at Versailles that worked out the settlement after the First World War. Assign the roles of the major powers as well as smaller participants. Students must then discuss the settlement from the point of view of the country which they represent.

HISTORICAL ANALYSIS

THE FALL OF EUROPEAN AUTOCRACIES

The First World War resulted in widespread social, economic, and political change. It spelled the end of three autocratic dynasties in central and eastern Europe: the Hapsburgs of Austria, the Hohenzollerns of Germany, and the Romanovs of Russia. The collapse of these three empires resulted in political change, which ranged from the communist experiment in Russia to the democracy of the Weimar Republic in Germany. Czechoslovakia and Yugoslavia were carved out of the old Austro-Hungarian Empire, and Poland reappeared as a sovereign state. The democratic movements of the nineteenth century had laid a foundation for change which would gain momentum in the twentieth century. The masses in the late twentieth century seemed to have lost their respect for monarchy.

The three empires had been involved in much diplomatic manoeuvring in the period prior to the First World War and were ultimately unable or unwilling to prevent the outbreak of war. Their demise is intimately connected to the events of the war, but some historians suggest that internal decay was the most significant factor contributing to their collapse.

Analyse the fall of the three autocratic dynasties. Assess the significance of the effects of the First World War and the political change it encouraged. Consider the state of these monarchies in the early twentieth century and analyse the extent to which internal decay contributed to their collapse.

A useful source to consider for this exercise is *The Fall of Eagles* by C.L. Sulszberger. You could also examine *The World in the Crucible 1914–1919* by Bernadotte E. Schmitt and Harold C. Vedeler.

The following list of questions could be used to guide your research.

1. What characteristics defined each of the three autocratic dynasties?

2. How did each emperor respond to change? Choose a specific example, such as the demand in Russia for political representation.

3. What role did the three dynasties play in the outbreak of the First World War?

4. How did each of the three dynasties lose their power? Was this inevitable or could the emperors have prevented the collapse of empires?

RECONSTRUCTION OF EUROPE 1919–1934

FOCUS ON COLLECTIVE SECURITY

The League of Nations started with good principles. But it has lost all that could give it any political meaning or historical import. In fact, the very nation that invented it took care never to join. The League has now become absurd . . .

Italian leader Benito Mussolini, in a speech to the General Assembly of the National Council of Corporations, Rome, reported in the *London Times*, 14 November 1933.

The League of Nations was the first attempt to organize an alliance of the world's nation-states, designed to promote collective security, humanitarianism, even global survival.

Assume the role of a leader of France, Germany, Japan, Great Britain, or the USA in the mid-1930s. Argue for or against the existence of the League. Use specific historical events to support your arguments.

OVERVIEW

Primary concerns after the First World War include the successor states, the League of Nations, Mussolini and Italy, and the problem of French security. In Germany, the Weimar Republic, the reparations issue, and the rise of Hitler are all important issues.

THE SUCCESSOR STATES
World War I resulted in the disintegration of the Russian, Austro-Hungarian, and the Turkish empires. The new states which were formed in Central Europe became hotbeds of nationalist unrest.

THE LEAGUE OF NATIONS
President Wilson's dream of an international system of collective security was doomed by both the structure of the League of Nations and the unwillingness of major powers to relinquish sovereignty in the interests of global cooperation.

INTERNATIONAL CRISIS
The failure of the League of Nations to successfully resolve the crisis in Manchuria in 1931 and that in Ethiopia in 1935 resulted in a fatal loss of prestige.

FRENCH SECURITY
After the First World War, France sought alliances with the United States and Britain in an effort to counterbalance German power.

GERMANY
The new Weimar Republic of Germany suffered both political and economic instability.

THE GREAT DEPRESSION
The dependence of European economies on the American economy resulted in world-wide depression when the American stock market crashed in 1929.

HITLER'S RISE TO POWER
The political and economic instability of Germany during the Weimar Republic made people susceptible to Nazi promises of a revitalized Germany.

L'EMPRUNT DE LA LIBÉRATION

This French illustration from the end of the First World War shows Kaiser Wilhelm being driven out by a united force of nations, represented by the flags. Examine the illustration for clues about how citizens and governments of the allied countries might have felt about Germany after the war ended.

THE SUCCESSOR STATES

Although the fighting had stopped, it would be another four years before any degree of normalcy returned to the continent. In defeat, the German empire shrank, and the Austro-Hungarian, Russian, and Turkish empires disintegrated into a number of successor states whose self-proclaimed boundaries made little political, social, or economic sense. Central Europe became a chaotic region in which rampant nationalist forces strove to establish their own nations in the midst of civil war and social revolution. Apart from using armed force to put down the nationalist movements, the victorious powers had no alternative but to recognize the new states as political entities.

The successor states stretched from the Baltic to the Black Sea and formed a continuous buffer between Germany and Russia. The Baltic republics tore away from Russia; Poland regained the independence lost in the eighteenth century; Serbia expanded to encompass some of its Slavic neighbours and form the state later called Yugoslavia; the Czechs and Slovaks united to form Czechoslovakia; Romania seized Transylvania from Hungary, which was separated from Austria and made independent;

Italy annexed the Austrian Tyrol and Trieste, and contended with Yugoslavia for Fiume; Austria dwindled into an insignificant state around its capital, Vienna; and Greece and Turkey went to war over Asia Minor. Although their leaders all claimed the right to self-determination, new nations held within their borders large ethnic minorities that made them politically unstable.

Czechoslovakia was the pivotal state. Its creation shattered the Austro-Hungarian Empire and encouraged other ethnic groups to pull away. Tomàŝ Masaryk and Eduard Beneš provided the spark for

THE CURZON LINE

The Curzon Line was a demarcation of territory proposed by British foreign secretary G. Curzon at the armistice of the Russo-Polish War of 1920. After the Second World War, this line became the Soviet-Polish border as a result of the treaty signed on 16 August 1945.

the Czech nationalist movement. World attention was drawn to their cause by the saga of the 100 000 soldier Czech Legion that valiantly fought its way out of Siberia along the Trans-Siberian railway. Earlier in the war these Czechs had been captured on the Russian front and sent as prisoners of war to camps in Siberia. They were freed upon Russia's surrender in 1917 and, left to their own devices, at one point considered setting up a Czech nation in Asia.

Masaryk wanted to bring the Legion out of Russia to fight in France and Italy, and before the end of the war, Czech forces were fighting alongside allied soldiers in the west. It was while Masaryk was in the United States that a constitution for the new state was drafted in Pittsburgh some six months before the war's end. With heavy financial support from Czechs and Slovaks living in the United States, the movement for independence gathered momentum. On 28 October 1918 a Czech National Council met in Prague to proclaim the new state. When formed, Czechoslovakia contained a large German minority along its western borders. Masaryk mistakenly believed that the 3 million Germans scattered about the edges of Bohemia and Moravia in the Sudetenland would eventually be absorbed into Czech culture. Instead, many of these people saw Germany as their true homeland and they provided

the excuse for the German annexation of western Czechoslovakia in 1938.

Poland was re-established as a buffer state separating Germany and Russia. The Poles were given boundaries drawn roughly along ethnic lines. The land-locked country was given access to the sea by means of a land corridor running through eastern Germany to the port of Danzig. The mixture of Poles and Germans in the corridor gave an unrealistic hope of eventual absorption of Germans into Polish culture. The port of Danzig became a free city under the administration of the League of Nations.

The allies had suggested the Curzon Line as a reasonable ethnic boundary in the east; but the Poles would not accept this line. The ensuing fighting between Polish and Soviet forces saw Soviet armies advance on Warsaw, which was held with great difficulty. The Treaty of Riga (1921) ended the fighting, but because the combatants were unable to agree on a boundary, the border became the position the rival armies held when the fighting ended. Within the new boundaries, one third of Poland's population was composed of ethnic minorities.

Italy claimed the strategically important Adriatic Coast and the cities of Trieste and Fiume as a reward for deserting the Triple Alliance (Germany, Austria-Hungary, and Italy) and joining the allied side during the war. The Americans did not support the Italian claim. They had not been party to the Treaty of London that promised Italy the new territories. Instead, Wilson gave American support to the formation of an enlarged Slavic nation, with the expansion of Serbia to engulf its neighbours. Yugoslavia quickly came into conflict with Italy over rival claims to Trieste and other key areas on the Adriatic. When Austrian troops evacuated Fiume in November 1919, the city was seized by a group of disgruntled Italian war veterans under the leadership of the poet Gabriele D'Annunzio, but this short-term government eventually collapsed. A year later, the Italian government gave the region to the League of Nations to administer as a free city. Fifteen months later, the city was retaken by the Italians. A temporary agreement was reached under the Pact of Rome in 1924, when Yugoslavia renounced its claim to the region.

Turkish nationalists would not recognize the settlement imposed upon them by the Treaty of Sèvres. Under its terms, Turkey was to give up all its European territories. Mustafa Kemal Ataturk led a rebellion that deposed the Turkish sultan, while at the same time resistance was organized to the transfer of areas of western Anatolia to the Greeks.

The League of Nations was established to prevent another war of the magnitude of the First World War. This photo shows members of the League of Nations during a visit to the United States in 1920.

Savage fighting broke out between the two nations on many of the Aegean islands and in Anatolia. Brutal massacres on both sides characterized the two years of fighting before peace was restored. In 1923, the Treaty of Lausanne arranged for an exchange of populations and Turkey's continuing control of mainland Asia Minor.

The evolution of the successor states partitioned Central Europe into a hodge-podge of small unstable political units. Created by the frenzied force of ultra-nationalism, they held minorities within their boundaries who contributed greatly to the instability of the successor states. It was only a matter of time before their very existence would be challenged.

THE LEAGUE OF NATIONS

The League of Nations was the first on the agenda at the Paris Peace Conference. President Wilson was prepared to bargain away all other goals in order to obtain support for the League, which he saw as a means to eliminate war between nations. He saw the collective action of all nations replacing the alliance system that was behind the carnage of the First World War. Only by acting together could the nations of the world stop the ultranationalism he believed responsible for the First World War. Wilson also believed in the need for international cooperation in social and humanitarian matters of a global nature. Lloyd George of Britain and Clémenceau of France were prepared to support the idea of the League as a new means of conducting international relations if it meant retaining an American commitment to the future peace and stability of Europe. They wanted the threat of American military intervention to maintain the status quo between the European powers. In reality, France and Britain preferred the traditional bilateral relationships developed over the centuries to an untried, idealistic scheme for collective security.

There had been many international organizations before the League. The Red Cross and the Permanent Court of International Justice established at The Hague in 1899 are but two examples. The League, however, was the first attempt at universal membership on a grand scale. Membership was voluntary and members were required to respect and protect each other's territories through collective action. The League was to use the combined might of all its members in collective security, to deter aggression and maintain world peace. Overwhelming power would prevent any single nation or group of nations from starting a war that could not possibly be won, and make war obsolete.

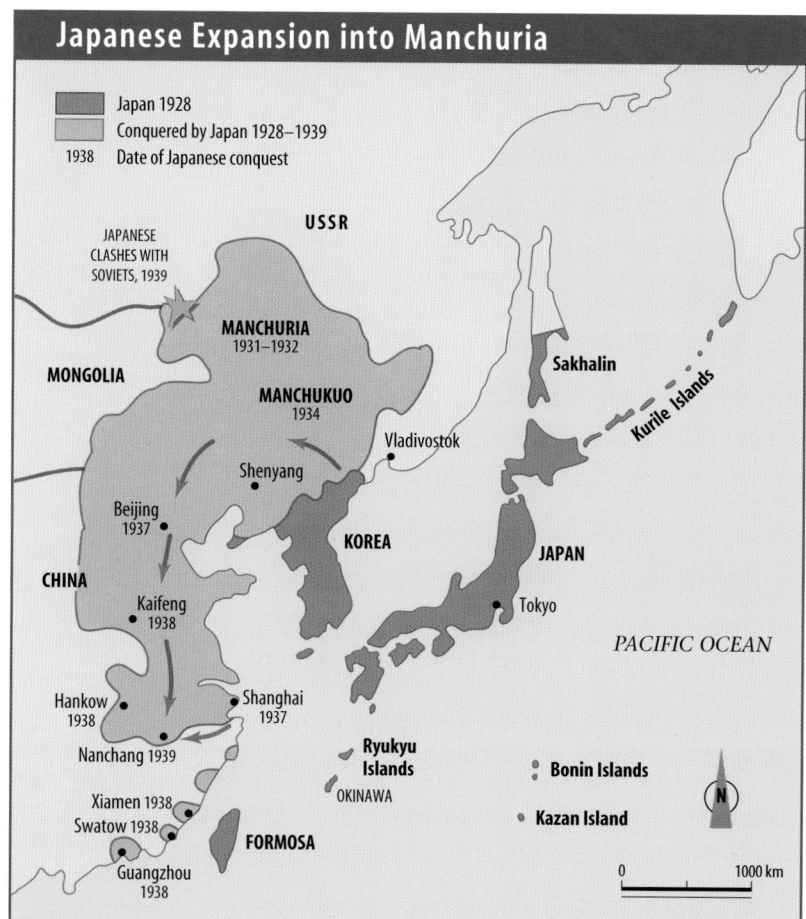

Japanese Expansion into Manchuria

Japan 1928
Conquered by Japan 1928–1939
1938 Date of Japanese conquest

JAPANESE CLASHES WITH SOVIETS, 1939

USSR

MONGOLIA

MANCHURIA 1931–1932

MANCHUKUO 1934

Sakhalin

Kurile Islands

Vladivostok

Shenyang

Beijing 1937

KOREA

CHINA

Kaifeng 1938

JAPAN

Tokyo

PACIFIC OCEAN

Hankow 1938

Shanghai 1937

Nanchang 1939

Ryukyu Islands

Bonin Islands

OKINAWA

Kazan Island

Xiamen 1938
Swatow 1938

FORMOSA

N

Guangzhou 1938

0   1000 km

The first major test of the League of Nations was the Manchurian Crisis. Members of the League were unable to agree on how to stop Japan's expansion onto the Asian mainland.

The League consisted of a council of the great powers—the USA, Britain, France, Italy, Japan, and Russia (although the USA never took its place and Russia was not admitted until 1934)—and non-permanent members elected to fixed terms; an Assembly of all members, each nation having one vote; and a Secretariat. Voluntary membership, the need for a unanimous vote (which made any action improbable), and agreement not to interfere in each other's domestic affairs left the League without the means to carry out its objectives. Some 20 satellite organizations and commissions rounded out its structure.

The power of the League resided with the major powers in the council. It was the council that determined the manner of League activity. In addition to its many responsibilities, the council was given charge of the German and Turkish colonies surrendered at the end of the war. Britain and Japan were already in possession of most of these but agreed to League supervision under a mandate system. The colonies became the responsibility of one or another of the League's members, who were given the mandate to bring them as quickly as possible to self-governing status. Those in the Middle East such as Syria and Iraq were deemed close to independence and categorized as Class A mandates. Class B mandates were in those areas of Africa that needed considerable development prior to eventual independence. The League did monitor this category of mandate to ensure some basic rights for the local populations. Class C mandates included Pacific islands so underdeveloped that they in effect became annexed to the mandated power. None of the mandates were to be armed by the supervisory power, although some of them were.

Membership in the League was almost universal. Sixty-three nations took part at one time or another. This number represented most of the world's recognized states at that time with the notable exception of the USA, which after 1919 receded into isolation. Germany became a member in 1926 and the Soviet Union in 1934. Both took permanent seats on the council. Germany and Japan left the League in 1933. In the late 1930s, there was a rash of defections as the Second World War loomed on the horizon, and the Soviet Union was expelled in 1939 for its invasion of Finland. The American failure to join left Britain and France as the only great powers involved. The League would, as a result, become eurocentric in outlook and nature. But Britain and France preferred direct negotiations between states and refused to place their affairs in the hands of an impotent organization, nor were they about to have their affairs debated in public by far less powerful states. They would make use of the League only when it suited their purposes. At all other times they would conduct their foreign affairs independently.

The League of Nations accomplished some good work in the 1920s and 1930s in the social and humanitarian fields. Its commissions and public debates helped publicize the need for cooperative action on a number of global problems. Special attention was given to: (1) the need for the just treatment of non self-governing peoples; (2) traffic in women and dangerous drugs; (3) status of women and children; (4) problems of communication and transportation; (5) the need for disarmament and arms control; (6) the need for free trade; (7) prevention of disease and other social and health problems. The work of the League in social and economic matters was valuable and laid the groundwork for the expanded activity of the future United Nations.

INTERNATIONAL CRISIS

The successes of the League in the social and economic spheres were more than offset by its failure to eliminate war. The Manchurian Crisis of 1931 brought to light the flawed nature of the League when faced by military force. The Japanese occupation of Manchuria was the first test of the League's willingness to bring collective security measures to bear against an aggressor. Japan's expansion on the Asian mainland was designed to secure minerals essential for industrial growth. To this end, the Japanese sought to acquire an empire that would sustain industrial expansion. Initially, League action was stalled by Japan's veto in the council. Only later did China appeal to the assembly to take action to throw back the invader. Great Britain and France declined to take any military action, as did all the others, especially as the war was on the far side of the globe. It is doubtful that any nation, including the USA, had the military capability to wage war in the far-off Pacific at that time: all their resources were committed to the western hemisphere, and Manchuria lay beyond their own spheres of influence.

Outside the League, the USA found itself unable to act against Japan in any effective military or economic manner and instead proclaimed the Stimson Doctrine, which stated that the USA would not recognize any boundary changes made by force of arms. The League quickly followed suit and adopted the doctrine as its own. Only belatedly was a fact-finding commission under Lord Lytton sent to Asia. Seven months after the event, the Lytton commission visited Manchuria; by this time the fighting had ended and the Japanese had established the puppet state of Manchukuo. The commission urged recognition of Japan's economic interests in the development of Manchuria and Japan's need to have military forces on the mainland to secure these interests. However, the commission did brand Japan the aggressor. The Japanese reacted by withdrawing from the League. Because Japan was no longer a member of the League, the council decided that the League had no further responsibilities in the matter and that no further action was required. The decision not to take action was greeted with relief by the members, who did not wish to incur the costs of a distant Pacific peacekeeping venture. The ineffectiveness of the League in dealing with a war between two of its own members was not lost on other expansionist regimes.

A second test of the League's peacekeeping ability arose from the Italian invasion of Ethiopia in 1935.

Again, two of the League's members were involved and this time the fighting was not in far-off Asia. Italy's invasion of the African kingdom was part of an attempt by the Mussolini regime to regain imperial prestige long since lost to his people.

Benito Mussolini and his **Fascist** party came to power in Italy after the First World War against a backdrop of social and economic unrest. Strikes and lockouts crippled the industrial centres of Milan and Turin. War-weariness and unemployment spread from the cities into the rural areas, where tenant farmers refused to pay their rents and went on a rampage against their proprietors, demanding the large estates be broken up and given to them. On the brink of economic collapse and social revolution, successive Italian governments had been unable to stabilize the volatile situation. Mussolini was only one of many leaders who gathered around him groups of unemployed war veterans in a quest for political power. Beginning in April 1919, his *fasci di combattimento* (combat units) engaged in street brawls with strikers and communists. Italian industrialists financed Mussolini's movement to restore order and to get the workers back on the job.

In 1922, Mussolini persuaded the king of Italy to appoint him prime minister after a threatened march on Rome by his supporters. Under the Italian constitution, the king first appointed the prime minister, who then tried to get a working majority in the legislature. As prime minister, Mussolini was given dictatorial powers for a year to restore order to the nation. Through the use of terror tactics, his *squadristi* had the factories working again and the trains running on time within the 12-month period.

In preparation for the 1924 elections Mussolini enacted a law that would give the winner of the election at least two thirds of the seats in the government regardless of the percentage of votes acquired. This would have the effect of eliminating many of the numerous smaller parties that fragmented the legislative process. When the socialist leader Matteotti publicized some of the beatings that took place outside polling stations, he was murdered. When the opposition parties withdrew from the legislature in protest, Mussolini declared them and their followers enemies of the state. In 1925 he appointed an all-Fascist government, making Italy a single-party state and eliminating his political opponents. The following year all government powers were invested in his person as *Il Duce* (The Leader). In 1928 only Fascist-approved candidates could run in elections.

ITALIAN FASCISM

Fascism was an extreme right-wing, militaristic European-wide phenomenon that arose out of the social chaos resulting from the First World War. It emerged in Italy but appeared later in other parts of Europe and the Americas. The Croix de Feu in France, the Mosely Fascists in England, the Belgian Rexists, the Romanian Iron Guard, General Franco in Spain, and the Heimwehr in Austria are examples of fascist movements.

In times of economic distress and social dislocation, people often look to a demagogue to restore order and bring back stability to the regime. The Italian fascist movement is a good example of how ruthless leadership, supported by the armed forces, imposed order on a chaotic situation. Benito Mussolini and his fascist cohorts came to power during a time of domestic crisis that threatened the existence of the state.

The roots of Italian fascism are the achievements of Gabriel D'Annunzio and Benito Mussolini. D'Annunzio was a poet and adventurer who appealed to Italy's younger generations. During the war he had been a pilot, lost an eye in combat, and been decorated for bravery. He called for action for action's sake. Someone had to do something to stop the worsening political and economic situation. It was an anarchist call to revolt.

It was Mussolini, a left-wing socialist turned right-wing activist, who called an organizational meeting in Milan on 23 March 1919 for the purpose of forming a new political party to stop the forces tearing Italy apart. His charisma and dynamic leadership drew in the masses. As leader of the movement, he promised to stabilize the economy, end unemployment, and restore Italy's national prestige lost at the peace tables in Versailles.

According to fascist beliefs, democracy had brought Italy to the sorry state it was in. The problems were caused by the government being turned over to the rule of the ignorant masses. The fascists would put an end to disorder with the power of a totalitarian state. Mussolini offered simple solutions to the nation's problems and, perhaps more importantly, he offered hope.

The political doctrine of the fascists evolved from taking action. Once in power a political doctrine would develop, but first the fascists would get rid of any opposition and render themselves secure in power. In *The Political and Social Doctrine of Fascism*, Mussolini wrote that what started as aspirations would later develop into a political code. It was essential to appear to be doing something.

Fascism presented itself to the people as the antidote to the liberal and democratic ideas that had brought Italy to its knees. Some of the characteristics of its right-wing radicalism were:

- a state in which the nation held absolute priority over the individual.

- an acceptance of the need for struggle and war to develop a national character. War brings nobility and energy to the people.

- a government that aspired to total control of the individual within the state.

- a belief that the state was organic and had a life of its own.

- a belief that the state was greater than its individual parts.

- a government led by the heroic élite.

- a readiness to use violence against enemies of the state.

- a contempt of upper-class values and traditional cultural mores.

- a single-party political structure.

- a dictatorship supported by the armed forces and police.

- a restructuring of government along the lines of a corporate state that controlled the economy through syndicates.

- a violent anti-labour, anti-communist, anti-liberal, and anti-democratic bias.

From 1928 to 1939, the fascists transformed Italy from a parliamentary democracy, based on geographic electoral ridings, into a corporate state that was governed by economic interests. The national legislature was composed of economic divisions: agriculture, industry, and services.

Unlike Lenin in the Soviet Union, Mussolini in Italy intended to maintain the class structure and the principles of private property but to control the economy through syndicates or economic groupings. The syndicates would also be responsible for maintaining the spirit of the nation through patriotic education of their members. All employed within an economic syndicate were members of that syndicate. The organizers of the syndicates were responsible to government for the efficient operation of their economic enterprise.

Under the electoral law of 1928, election of the 400 delegates to the Chamber of Deputies was to be confirmed by voting for an approved government list. The list was drawn from 800 names submitted by the executives of the syndicates. An additional 200 names were added by cultural and charitable organizations. From this master list of 1000 names, the Fascist Grand Council chose the 400 to stand for election. People were asked to vote yes or no to the entire list.

1. Who did the fascists see as being responsible for Italy's social and economic collapse in 1920?

2. What argument was used to discredit liberal-democratic practices? Can you propose counter-arguments?

3. What was the fascist view of the relationship between the state and the individual? What are the advantages and disadvantages of this view?

4. Give a critical analysis of the practicality of the corporate state.

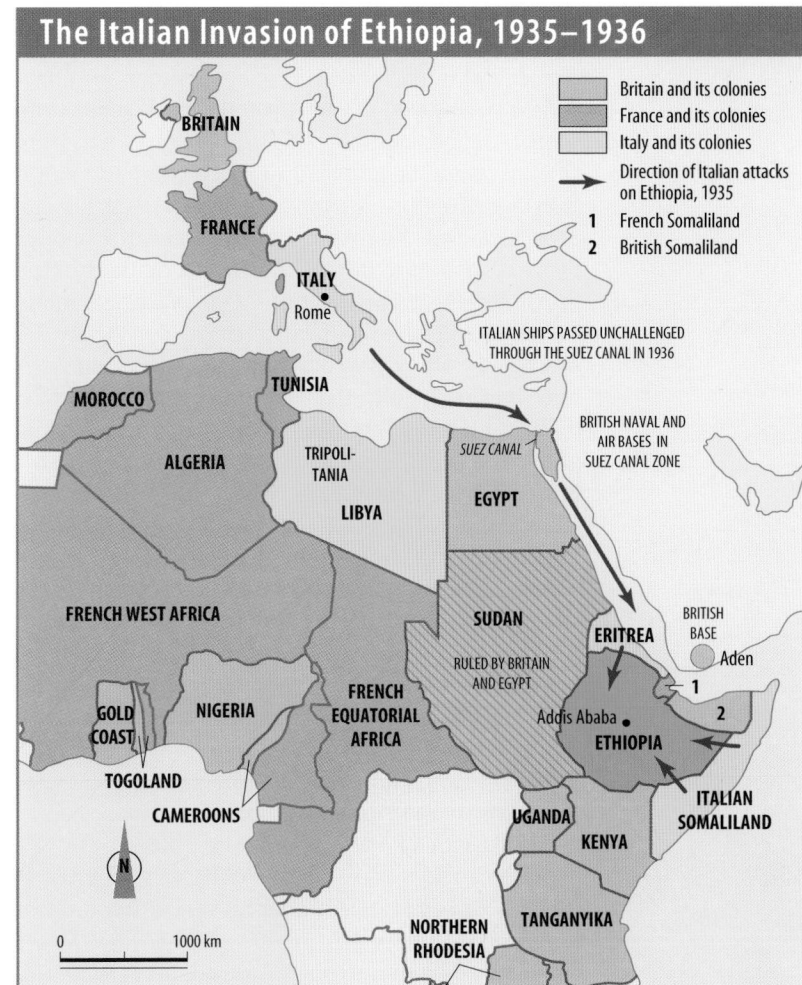

The Italian Invasion of Ethiopia, 1935–1936

Britain and its colonies
France and its colonies
Italy and its colonies
Direction of Italian attacks on Ethiopia, 1935
1 French Somaliland
2 British Somaliland

ITALIAN SHIPS PASSED UNCHALLENGED THROUGH THE SUEZ CANAL IN 1936

BRITISH NAVAL AND AIR BASES IN SUEZ CANAL ZONE

BRITAIN
FRANCE
ITALY
Rome
MOROCCO
TUNISIA
ALGERIA
TRIPOLITANIA
SUEZ CANAL
LIBYA
EGYPT
FRENCH WEST AFRICA
SUDAN
RULED BY BRITAIN AND EGYPT
ERITREA
BRITISH BASE
Aden
GOLD COAST
NIGERIA
FRENCH EQUATORIAL AFRICA
Addis Ababa
ETHIOPIA
ITALIAN SOMALILAND
TOGOLAND
CAMEROONS
UGANDA
KENYA
NORTHERN RHODESIA
TANGANYIKA

0   1000 km

N

From 1935 to 1936, Italy advanced into Ethiopia (which was called Abyssinia at the time). French and British colonies surrounded the area, but did not intervene against Italy's invasion.

Mussolini's program was one of ultranationalism, and he saw a greatly enlarged role for government in directing the nation's political and economic life. The Fascist party expanded outside the political sphere and sought to control all aspects of society, in a totalitarian regime.

The Italians launched their attack on Ethiopia, the last major independent state in Africa, in October. The League surprised everyone by taking prompt action, although both Britain and France were unwilling to take any measure that might push Mussolini into a German alliance. The balance of power in the Mediterranean was precarious. British and French interests called for caution, since a Rome-Berlin axis would threaten their lifelines through the Suez. It would also upset the balance of power on the continent. Within four days of the attack the

League condemned Italy. The sale of arms was to be cut off and trade between League members and Italy was to be stopped except for food, coal, scrap iron, rubber, copper, and oil. The United States had indicated it would be prepared to make good any world shortages in these or other products that League action caused. The American intervention would prove disastrous to British and French markets in the region. In effect, the sanctions were placed on materials that Italy had in sufficient supply. When the sanctions were removed a year later, they had been only minimally effective. The most effective action that could have been taken would have been closure of the Suez Canal to Italian military transports. This Britain refused to do. As predicted, the sanctions did change Italian foreign policy and pushed Mussolini into an alliance with Germany.

The League's inability to act effectively in either Manchuria or Ethiopia resulted in a fatal loss of prestige from which it never recovered. The League made only token resistance to foreign intervention in the Spanish Civil War, German occupation of the Rhineland in 1936, Japan's renewed war of conquest in Asia (1937), and the **Nazi** annexation of Austria and parts of Czechoslovakia in 1938.

The League of Nations was a first attempt by the nations of the world at global collective security. It was flawed because the major powers either did not join or did not support it fully. The United States did not become a member. Britain and France preferred bilateral negotiations to an untried institution. Germany, the Soviet Union, Japan, and Italy were members for only part of the League's lifetime. In theory, the process could have worked had the great powers been willing to abide by its covenant of peaceful cooperation. Because they chose military force to secure their own interests, the League was doomed to failure from the very beginning.

FRENCH SECURITY

Of the allied powers only the Soviet regime had suffered more in the war than France. The war in the west had been fought on French soil and the four long years left 1.3 million dead and 3 million wounded (one third of whom were permanently disabled). Now that peace was at hand, 40 million French people found themselves alongside 60 million Germans who had the advantage of a massive industrial complex unscarred by war. France had lost tens of thousands of buildings, over 9000 factories, and hundreds of kilometres of railways. On their evacuation of French territory, German forces had flooded the coal and iron mines in Lorraine and destroyed the land as a last injury to their foe. Still, by 1920 France was the strongest military power on the continent. The problem was how to maintain this military superiority.

In the long run France's strength and security depended on a rapid reconstruction of its war-damaged industrial base and its alliance with Britain and the USA. But it would take some time for France to recover its economic strength. Aside from war damage the French economy was precarious in part due to the loss of $3 billion in foreign loans and investments when the Bolsheviks renounced tsarist Russia's debts and seized all foreign assets. Facing a heavy burden of debt, France turned to the United States and Britain for support. The American retreat into isolation and the public outcry in Britain against further commitment on the continent left France to face the future vulnerable and alone.

The French had counted on British military strength added to its own to keep Germany submissive. However, Britain's immediate post-war objective was to regain world markets lost to the Americans and the Japanese during the war. Affairs on the continent were peripheral to Imperial needs. The British sought to rebuild the balance of power on the continent, and that meant turning a blind eye to German attempts to rearm. The British believed in any case that France and Germany should be more nearly equal in strength.

During the post-war period, British industry faced stiff competition from the USA and Japan. A decade of strikes, lockouts, and rising unemployment sabotaged attempts to regain industrial strength. The textile and shipbuilding industries were the hardest hit, primarily because of obsolete equipment and efficient foreign competition. The public mood was anything but interventionist in nature. In 1926 a nine-day general strike all but crippled the country and brought it to the verge of economic collapse. Conservative governments attempted to resolve the situation through tight-money policies and balanced budgets. Public works, which could have solved the unemployment problem, were reduced to meet the austere conditions of the time. Politicians tended to blame unrest on socialist and communist agitators, failing to see that the financial power in the world had shifted from Europe to North America. The USA had become the world's leading industrial power, in part a direct consequence of the costs of the war.

BIOGRAPHY

BENITO MUSSOLINI
(1883-1945)

Non si torna indietro. (There is no turning back.)

This fascist slogan of Benito Mussolini, head of the Italian government from 1922 to 1943, served also as the man's epitaph.

As a young man, Mussolini was unsuccessful at many of his endeavours. In his late teens and twenties, he wandered from place to place, his instinct leading him toward politics and political agitation. During these years, he wrote for various socialist or conservative papers, depending on the political climate and what he stood to gain. For a short month, he was sub-editor of the *Popolo*, a daily newspaper belonging to an Italian patriot and irredentist. Mussolini remembered, years later, having learned many of the tricks of his political trade during his month at *Popolo*, including "how to invent a news story, and how to write a whole article about some non-event without arousing disbelief."

Although the novella he wrote remained unpublished, Mussolini was attracted to, and identified with, bohemianism and the pursuits of the artistic lifestyle. Mussolini was, in essence, an actor; his stage was the national, then international, political arena. He was an opportunist to the core and could change ideologies and court opposing factions as easily as an actor could change costumes. He was eloquent and forceful in his speech and convinced many of his good will while using phrases devoid of substance. Furthermore, there was an extent to which Mussolini attempted to recreate reality after his liking—at once actor and director. Mussolini was a rising star in his Italian Empire—this "Epoch of the Third Rome"—which even adopted a new calendar to commemorate his rise to power and to affirm his tentative self-esteem.

Mussolini was influenced by the writings of German philosopher Friedrich Nietzsche (1844-1900), who wrote about exercising the "will to power" at the expense of those who did not fit the category of "Superman." It is not at all surprising that Mussolini enmeshed Italy in Hitler's politics of anti-Semitism, territorialism, and power at the cost of even his own life. In 1945, he was executed by the resistance as Italy collapsed under allied invasion.

Russian revolutionary, socialist, and intellectual, Angelica Balabanoff, who knew Mussolini well and introduced him to the classics of European socialism had this to say of him: "[Mussolini's views were] more the reflection of his early environment and his own rebellious egoism than the product of understanding and conviction; his hatred of oppression was not that impersonal hatred of a system shared by all revolutionaries; it sprang rather from his own sense of indignity and frustration, from a passion to assert his own ego and from a determination for personal revenge." ●

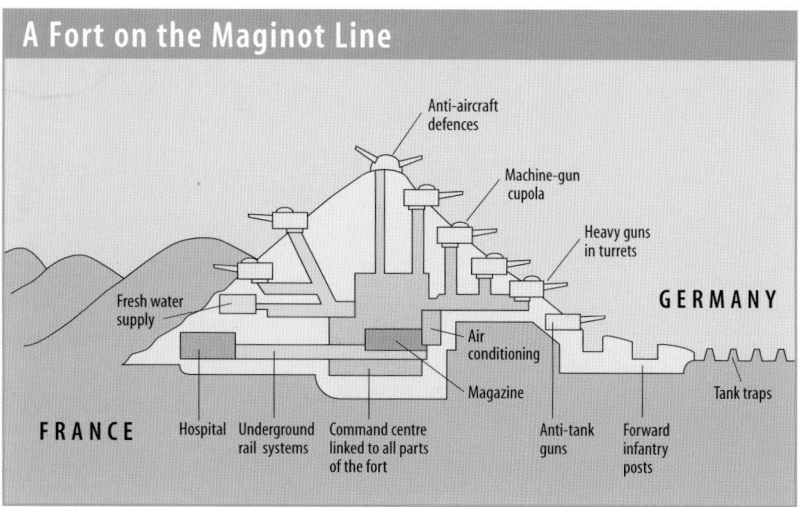

Anti-aircraft
defences

Machine-gun
cupola

Heavy guns
in turrets

GERMANY

Fresh water
supply

Air
conditioning

FRANCE

Hospital | Underground
rail systems | Command centre
linked to all parts
of the fort | Magazine | Anti-tank
guns | Forward
infantry
posts

Tank traps

This diagram shows a cutaway section of one of the forts on the Maginot Line. Examine the strengths and weaknesses of this method of defence.

FIRING ON THE HEARTLAND

The Rhineland was important because it lay a single day's march from the industrial centres of both Alsace-Lorraine and the Ruhr Valley. Occupation of the Saar region meant that French artillery could fire directly into Germany's industrial heartland.

The long-term danger to France was the prospect of a rearmed Germany, so French security meant keeping Germany weak. The French had wanted to annex the strategic region of the Rhineland. They were dissuaded by the Americans, who proposed to substitute a mutual-defence treaty for the planned occupation. When the Americans failed to ratify the treaty, France was left vulnerable along its north-eastern frontier. With the Rhineland no longer a barrier, the French decided to construct their own defence line along the border. The Maginot Line of stationary fortifications was to be the ultimate deterrent to German aggression. The fortress line was unshaken during the German attack of May 1940, but it had two vulnerable gaps. These were in Lorraine, where the Ardennes forest was considered too hilly to permit tank operations, and along the Belgian border. Both these gaps were exploited by the Germans in their invasion of France in 1940.

The French had counted on financial reparations crippling Germany's economic revival. The final amount was set at $33 billion. This amount, though seemingly large, was within the ability of Germany to pay. The treatment of Germany also was not as drastic as what Germany had handed out to the Soviet regime in 1918 or what the Germans had planned to inflict on France and Britain, had they won the war. But German political and military leaders made the reparations appear so evil that any amount would have been considered by the German public as excessive. Attempts by the German Weimar Republic to make reparation payments resulted in a considerable loss of public support.

France was prepared to accept reparations in gold or coal and timber, but not in industrial goods that would compete with those produced by its own recovering industry. Nor was Germany welcomed on the world markets where it could gain profits to pay its war debts. Denying German industry access to foreign markets made German payment of the reparations problematical. When Germany defaulted late in 1922, French troops occupied the Ruhr (January 1923). This action caused a crisis. German workers refused to work or contribute in any way to France's extraction of the mineral wealth. The French occupation came to an end a year later when American loans under the **Dawes Plan** enabled Germany to resume payments on a reduced scale.

France also sought security in a number of international agreements. It tried to revive the threat of a two-front war on Germany by allying with the successor states along Germany's eastern borders. They were to replace Russia as a counterweight to German power. Agreements with the **Little Entente** of Czechoslovakia, Romania, and Yugoslavia as well as Poland created a theoretical *cordon sanitaire* (corridor) whose potential 100 million people were considered capable of credible military action. In reality this was but an illusion, and French initiatives in Eastern Europe had the additional undesirable effect of uniting Germany and the Soviet Union against France's interference in what they considered to be their spheres of influence. In any case, the inability of the successor states to cooperate among themselves made the alliance system unworkable.

Other international agreements such as the Washington Treaties of 1921-1922, the Locarno Pact of 1925, and the Kellogg-Briand Pact of 1928 were no more effective. The Washington Treaties attempted to halt the naval race by limiting the relative tonnage of rival battle fleets. Modest success at limiting armaments was not repeated in the disarmament conferences of 1927 and 1930. The Locarno agreements of 1925 defined Germany's western borders with France and Belgium, with Britain and Italy acting as guarantors. The Germans agreed to the demilitarization of the Rhineland, and gave up any claim to Alsace-Lorraine. In return, Germany was admitted to the League of Nations in 1926. No similar agreements were signed regarding Germany's eastern frontiers with Poland and Czechoslovakia, where irreconcilable differences still existed. The good feelings of Locarno were followed by the Kellogg-Briand Pact of 1928, which gave the illusion of peace and security. The pact renounced aggressive war but offended no one nor had it any machinery for enforcement. Everyone rushed to sign it, even if it was little more than an aspiration.

From a position of being the sole effective military power in Europe in 1920, France faced the danger of German rearmament by 1929. Mutual defence treaties with the successor states in Central Europe were no substitute for the old French-Russian alliance. The fiasco over the occupation of the Ruhr and the false hopes of the Locarno and Kellogg-Briand pacts gave only the illusion of security.

GERMANY

German reaction to the Versailles settlement at the end of the First World War was one of bitter resentment. Germany had held off all the other European industrial powers for four years, had won the war in the east, and expected to keep the gains of Brest-Litovsk. The Germans expected to sit in on the peace conference as had been the tradition over the centuries. Instead, they were denied the fruits of the victory over Russia and given a *diktat* (abrupt command) to sign or face the threat of a renewed allied advance into Germany.

After all their sacrifices, the German people had come so close to victory that they could not understand what had gone wrong. In defeat, they sought a scapegoat to explain their failure to persevere. Their military leaders put about the myth that certain politicians had betrayed the army and the state, by agreeing to surrender when the army was on the point of final victory. The true reason for the defeat of the German armies on the Western Front was kept from the public by a barrage of clever propaganda. The myth of political groups stabbing the army in the back was to pervade German politics in the interwar years.

Until 1924, the German people were fighting crippling inflation. This photograph, taken in 1923, shows a German woman lighting the stove using several million marks. It was cheaper to use the almost worthless money to start a fire than it was to buy wood!

In November 1918, the kaiser left for Holland. This increased civil unrest and touched off a series of political assassinations as rival groups attempted to seize power. These uprisings were ruthlessly put down by bands of returning war veterans, as were other instances of civil disorder. It would take almost four years before any kind of political stability was established. In addition to political instability, labour unrest characterized the period.

Some German military leaders set about to save the armed forces from destruction. The idea of a German hegemony over Europe was not forgotten, nor was the role of the armed forces in achieving this goal. The officer corps was kept intact although it changed internally, and training in new methods

THE MIDDLE CLASS

Both the social mores and economic advantages of the middle class were eroded as a result of the war. Take on the role of either a teacher or a wealthy industrialist in Berlin in 1923. Describe the erosion of the middle class from the perspective you have chosen.

The standards for material wealth, consumption, and behaviour in the industrial countries were set by the British middle class. This growing group of businesspeople, bankers, entrepreneurs, and financiers lived well and had amassed the wealth that made the rapid industrial expansion of the nineteenth century possible. It was their individual initiatives, unlimited by government interference, that had resulted in spectacular economic growth. Allowed to keep all the profit they could accumulate, they reinvested their money in land and factories that returned an increasing income and made life comfortable. They were absolutely convinced that it was they who had generated the progress that benefited all of society through the creation of wealth, employment, goods, and produce.

Highly moral, at least in public, they further refined their manners in the Victorian Age. Women were adored for their beauty. Their position and status were directed to maintaining the annual rites of the family and the children. So sacrosanct was the family that even the hint of divorce (in England there were only 50 divorces in the first half of the nineteenth century) was taboo. Family and wealth were the two pillars of the British middle class.

All of this changed as a result of the war. The family unit changed as women asserted their independence. Their demands for a life of their own outside the home brought forward dramatic changes in the relationships between wife, husband, and children.

A frantic pursuit of pleasure began. A mania for dancing swept across Europe as entertainment for those who could afford it. Cocktail parties became the rage as did the cabarets, night clubs, radio, and motion pictures.

Another factor in the evolution of the middle classes was financial ruin as a result of wartime government policies. Income taxes were virtually unknown before the war; but to pay the costs of the fighting, governments began to take away part of the income essential to maintaining an acceptable middle class standard of living. Large staffs of servants dwindled or vanished, for the middle classes could not match the wages offered by business and industry. Income taxes at rates approaching 30 per cent were seen as scandalous, certain to destroy individual initiative and all that went with it. The accumulation of wealth was no longer an activity without limits.

Inflation also played its part. Most middle-class income came from long-established investments and land rents. Because prices had remained steady at the turn of the century, small increases were readily absorbed without affecting standard of living. Then the war generated inflation. Prices skyrocketed, but investment income remained steady. In Germany, for example, suitcases filled with money were required to pay for a beer. Government-imposed rent controls defeated attempts by proprietors to keep even with spiraling wages and prices. Labour could always negotiate wage increases, but the middle class could not. On the whole, prices on the continent escalated 500 per cent. The result was a rapid depression of the middle-class standard of living. During the hyper-inflation in Germany in 1923, the mark sank to 4.2 trillion to the US dollar. In efforts to stay alive, members of the German middle class bartered away their art treasures, furnishings, and real estate. Over 20 per cent of the properties in Berlin were picked up by North Americans. Incomes of 6000 marks a month, which had previously provided a good living, were now hardly enough to buy the monthly allotment of bread, milk, and butter. Potatoes, bread, and margarine became staple fare for the growing number of unemployed. Strikes and streetfighting became only too common.

Yet those who had hard currencies could live like kings in the clubs of the Kurfürstendamm or the Tiergarten. There, celebrities who had collected hard currencies of the victors, and the war profiteers, gamboled the night away in undeserved opulence. The contrast between their caviar, smoked salmon, and champagne and the starvation of the millions outside their windows was striking. During the "turnip winters" of 1916 to 1919, hundreds of thousands could not keep alive on the meagre rations they could acquire.

1. What were the expected rewards of the middle classes?

2. Describe the effect of the war on middle-class social mores.

3. Where was the wealth and power of the middle class invested?

4. Describe how middle-class wealth and power were destroyed by the after-effects of the war.

5. Draw an editorial-style cartoon (with caption) highlighting an aspect of the demise of the British middle class in the 1920s/1930s.

6. What happens to a society without a vibrant middle class of businesspeople and entrepreneurs?

7. What were the characteristics of the new wealthy classes after the war? Why was their wealth not destroyed?

of mechanized warfare took place in the Soviet Union under the terms of the Rapallo agreements of 1922. The inability of Germany to re-enter world markets and the difficulty the Soviets were having in achieving industrial growth led to an agreement between the two former enemies. In return for German skills and knowledge, the Soviet Union provided Germany with food, oil, and other natural products, and training grounds for German forces beyond the authority of the Allied Control Commission.

In 1919, political power in Germany was placed in the hands of a democratic Weimar Republic. President-elect Ebert chose Philipp Scheidemann as the first chancellor. The president was given emergency powers to rule by decree if the Reichstag failed to reach agreement. The majority of the representatives belonged to moderate parties, especially the Social Democrats, and the Catholic Centre party. Their immediate tasks were to come to terms with the Versailles settlement, achieve some semblance of civil order, and arrange for the payment of reparations. But the Reichstag was far from sympathetic to allied demands. The Reichstag was determined to overturn the Versailles agreement.

Political chaos characterized the first five years of the Weimar regime as communists and right-wing factions strove to topple the government in attempted *coups*. In January 1919, the left-wing Spartacist *putsch* took place in Berlin. Communists staged demonstrations throughout the Ruhr, and Germany sank into social revolution. A short-lived communist regime ruled in Munich until paramilitary bands restored order. In March 1920, the Kapp *putsch* created a right-wing challenge to the government, driving it temporarily from Berlin before this *putsch* too was crushed. In the midst of the chaos, government by martial law and presidential decree became the norm. Not until 1924 did any stability appear, with the surge to power of the moderate parties.

The most visible problem faced by the Weimar government was reparation payments. The initial payment of $5 billion was made good with the transfer of art treasures, jewellery, and savings of the propertied classes. The forced transfer of wealth drove public support from the Weimar government. The propertied classes never forgave the government for their losses. Subsequent reparation payments were to be made from profits made in foreign markets, but Germany was not welcomed on world

The collapse of the American stock market in 1929 was felt all over the world. This picture shows people streaming into Wall Street as they hear the news. The United States, like the rest of the world, spent the next decade trying to rebuild its economy.

markets by its industrial rivals. Unable to trade, Germany sought short-term American loans to kindle its recovery. These were secured with attractive high-interest rates that had the effect of tying German recovery to short-term American loans. Germany was now vulnerable to even the slightest fluctuation in the American economy.

The influx of large amounts of American money touched off the hyper-inflation of 1923. Hundreds of paper-mills churned out money to keep pace with skyrocketing prices. Rampant inflation erased what was left of the savings of pensioners, made life intolerable for those on fixed incomes, and lowered the real worth of the salaries of wage-earners thus further draining support from the government.

In 1922 Germany defaulted on its reparation payments and the French occupied the Ruhr in January 1923. German revulsion in the face of this French occupation touched off impassioned bursts of public censure throughout 1923. The government expressed a desire to continue to meet the payments, going against public wishes; but it dared not raise taxes or cut back public spending. Demonstrations against the government spread across the land and street-fighting resumed among rival political groups. In this many-sided civil strife the political fabric of the state broke down. In only one of hundreds of instances, Adolf Hitler and his Bavarian Nazi party attempted a coup in Munich in 1923. A massive increase in police forces took place in order to control the growing civil disorder.

In the midst of political and economic instability the United States intervened. The Americans persuaded the French to evacuate the Ruhr in return for a promise by Germany to resume reparation payments. The Dawes Plan of 1924 allocated over $30 billion in American aid to Germany to assist in reconstruction. In return for the loans, the Germans were to resume reparation payments on a modified ability-to-pay scale that would increase as German industry recovered. The Dawes Plan ushered in a five-year period of relative stability and economic growth. In 1929 further modifications to the reparation-payment arrangements were made under the Young Plan, which spread payments out over 59 years. But the collapse of the American stock market in October 1929 dashed any hopes of further payments.

The Hoover moratorium on reparation payments in 1931 was followed by attempts at the Lausanne Conference in 1932 to reduce the total due by 90 per cent. Only a year later Hitler put an end to payments of any kind.

THE GREAT DEPRESSION

As a result of the war, the world's economic structure became tied to that of the USA. The continuation of the war meant purchase of North American supplies was needed to keep the war going. Trillions of dollars worth of investments and savings from long years were directed to this need, resulting in a massive transfer of funds from Europe to North America. When these funds gave out, England and France borrowed heavily from the American government to finish the war. The result was that at war's end financial strength in the world had shifted away from Europe. With the economies of the Triple Alliance countries shattered, and with Russia in the midst of a civil war, the USA was the only solvent nation among the great powers. It was American loans that financed reconstruction and tied the world's economies to the USA.

When the American stock market collapsed in October 1929—causing the loss of $40 billion in savings and investments—it took the economies of most other nations with it. As panic set in, as bank after bank closed its doors, financial markets in the industrial nations collapsed. Industry followed suit by stopping production and laying off some 30 million workers. As unemployment rates reached astronomical proportions—as high as 30 to 40 per cent—civil unrest and public disorder emerged to challenge the existing political structure. Germany, still trying to recover from the war, was particularly hard hit as over half of its people were affected.

The peoples of the industrial nations turned against the governments that had permitted such a state of affairs to occur. An anti-parliamentary, anti-democratic mood prevailed among all economic classes. The public wanted national governments to take charge of the situation and to end the disorders. They looked for strong leadership to end the uncertainty of the times. Left-wing parties called for unemployment relief and government spending to create jobs. Right-wing parties demanded cut-backs and balanced budgets. None advocated increasing taxes. In every nation, demagogues made effective use of radio and the press to bring simplistic solutions to the visible misery people were enduring. They promised assistance in strengthening the central governments in order to force a solution on the economy. Wearied of the chaos and uncertainty, people turned to political leaders who promised a return to order and stability.

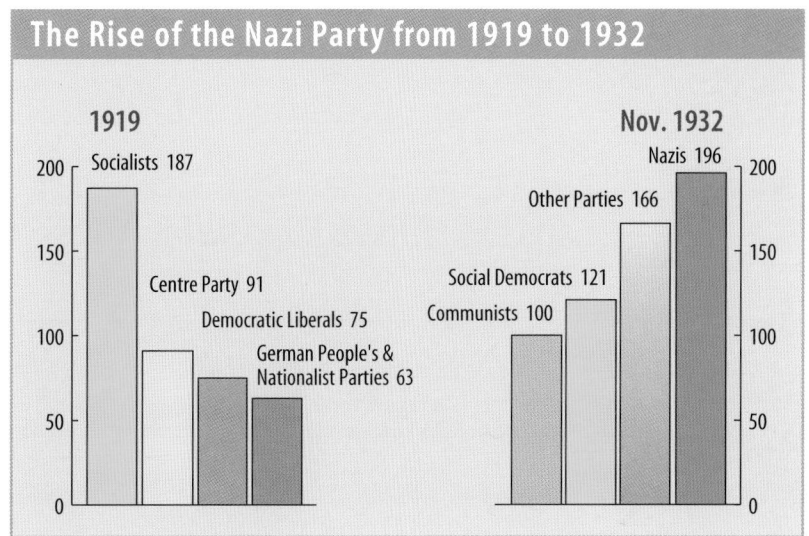

The Rise of the Nazi Party from 1919 to 1932

1919: Socialists 187; Centre Party 91; Democratic Liberals 75; German People's & Nationalist Parties 63

Nov. 1932: Nazis 196; Other Parties 166; Social Democrats 121; Communists 100

Later in 1932 the Nazis won almost another 100 seats. The Nazis continued to gain power throughout the 1930s.

HITLER'S RISE TO POWER

The civil disorders caused by the depression brought Adolf Hitler to power in Germany. In 1928 his Nazi party held only twelve seats in the Reichstag and was safely ignored. Within four years, as a result of economic turmoil, Nazis held over two hundred seats and the support of over 13 million voters. Making effective use of the radio and press and pioneering the use of the airplane in national campaigning, Hitler hammered home a simple message. The problems of the German people could be solved by overturning the Versailles Treaty, reclaiming lost territories, canceling all foreign debts, eliminating foreign elements and Jews from the country, and reaching full employment through government spending on public works and rearmament. More than anything else his message brought the hope of an end to the economic crisis and a renewal of pride and self-confidence in the German people.

The Social Democratic government of Germany was the first to fall as a result of the depression. In March 1930, a centre-right coalition under Chancellor Heinrich Brüning (1930-1932) came to power. In the elections, the Nazi party astounded everyone by gaining 107 seats and becoming the second largest political party. Brüning could not gain a majority in the Reichstag during his two years as chancellor, and as the depression deepened, he could not get his budgets approved. He reverted to government by emergency decree. In 1932, when Brüning proposed a land reform that would break

HITLER'S RISE TO POWER

One of the most important events of the twentieth century was Hitler's 12-year reign of terror. How was it possible for such a person to hold power over the German people for so long a period? Were the conditions of the time appropriate for such a leader? Could such a dictator arise again? And what lessons can be learned from studying a demagogue in power?

Alan Bullock, in his book *Hitler: A Study in Tyranny*, states that without Hitler the Nazi movement would have failed. Hitler himself was the decisive factor in the Nazi rise to power. It was Hitler's energy and oratory that attracted people to him as a political leader. Hitler was a genius at propaganda and a consummate actor who knew what his audience wanted to hear and how to generate their fanatical enthusiasm. Hitler believed that a leader must sway the masses.

There were few important centres in Germany that Hitler had not visited by 1933. His message against his opponents was simple and delivered with vehemence and passion. He appealed to hidden feelings with his talk of vast empires and racial purity. He was the forerunner of a New Order for Germany that would overcome the enemy. He appealed to the emotional, irrational side of human nature through mass rallies where his naked ambition was clothed in moral indignation. Without the man, the party would have been nothing.

A.J.P. Taylor, in *The Course of German History*, puts forward the thesis that German history was bound to produce someone like Hitler. The national German character remained militaristic in nature and it was impossible to plant democratic ideals among Germans after the First World War. The 14-year rule of the Weimar Republic was continually undermined by the military and other conservative elements within the state. The people looked more to President Hindenburg as a military leader than an agent of democracy. Brüning ended the democratic experiment in 1930 when he began continuous government by decree. At the time, there were only twelve Nazis in the Reichstag, but after the September elections, there were 107.

The government used the financial crisis of the Depression to end allied control and move to rearm. Unlike Brüning and the others, Hitler appeared as the candidate for change. What he said did not much matter because he offered decisive action to a nation seeking respect.

In the end, the army moved to take control of the legislative process through the chancellorship of General von Schleicher. In subsequent elections, the industrialists were encouraged to pay Hitler's debt and forge a national government of right-wing parties. Landowners and the army moved behind Hitler, who promised in return to protect their interests. Hitler then went on to capture the masses through a national program in a way the old governing classes of Junker and army could never do. Thus, Taylor argues, circumstances and the willingness of the German people to follow the army leadership were what brought Hitler to power.

Gerhard Ritter, in "The Fault of Mass Democracy" in Beaumont et al., *The Third Reich*, claims Hitler was a demagogue who created a grass-roots movement that brought him to power through valid democratic processes. The people, not the army, elevated Hitler to the chancellorship. Hitler had the genuine support of the masses, who chose strong leadership just as Americans elected Roosevelt. The Nazi program was seen as a salvation for those in a hopeless state of mind.

Ritter points out that only in a democracy could a minority party like the Nazis exist. In any other political system the Nazis would have been eliminated from the start. Nazism was thus a product of twentieth-century democracy. If there is a fault, states Ritter, it is in giving the masses political power. The development of a single-party state replaced the old governing classes of army and landowner with a national party of all classes; social justice became more important than liberties and individual rights. The rantings of 500 000-person rallies became the will of an entire people transferred to their leader.

These are only three explanations of why Hitler came to power. Other authors emphasize different themes, like the role of industrialists in financing the Nazi movement. Without money and the support of the army, the Nazis would not have come to power in 1933. Through Hitler, business leaders hoped to circumvent democracy and return power to their own hands. Still others argue that Hitler came to power as a result of the destabilization of the German economy during the depression of 1929. Mass unemployment and the loss of life savings created a hunger for direct action that Hitler promised. Others focus on the anti-Semitic and anti-communist appeal of the Nazi programs as bringing important support. As each historian is able to make a case, it is up to the reader to decide what it was that brought Hitler to power in 1933.

1. Discuss the validity of the leadership principle. Would the Nazis have achieved power without Hitler's charismatic manner?

2. Compare the differing viewpoints of the various authors as to what was the most important factor in Hitler's rise to power.

3. Why did the checks on the establishment of a dictatorship built into the Weimar constitution fail?

4. Could the Nazi party have survived in any political system except a democracy? How?

5. Imagine you are an honest German judge in July 1934, hearing the case of a Nazi party official accused of murder on the Night of the Long Knives. What pressures might you be working under? What are some of the implications for justice and human rights under a regime such as Hitler's?

Hitler was aware of the power of the media to shape his image. He wished the German public to see him as a kind, yet strong leader, who would look after the interests of his people.

up the aristocratic (Junker) estates, President Hindenburg, himself a landholder, forced Brüning's resignation. Brüning's successor, Franz von Papen, an aristocratic nationalist, governed solely by decree. That July, elections brought the Nazis over 270 seats and 37 per cent of the vote. They were now the largest party in the Reichstag. but Hitler still did not have a majority, despite promises that if he were named chancellor he would suppress all communist and socialist opposition.

In the midst of escalating political and labour unrest, the Nazi program of law and order appealed to the propertied classes. In many cities full-scale

A view of the demolished Reichstag after the fire of 1933. Hitler blamed the Communist party for the fire. This event marked the final ascent of nazism in Germany.

battles were fought between rival political forces. The second election in November 1932, however, saw the Nazi party short of funds and starting to lose popular support. The elections had bankrupted the party. Even the slightest loss of support meant they could no longer pose as the irresistible wave of the future going from triumph to triumph. There was even doubt that Hitler himself could hold the Nazi movement together. At this point German industrialists came to the rescue. At a meeting on 4 January 1933, German entrepreneurs promised to pay Nazi election debts in return for Hitler's promise of a hands-off policy toward German industry. Hitler also had to promise to rid the Nazi movement of its socialist elements.

Early in December 1932 a close friend of Hindenburg's son, General Kurt von Schleicher, was named chancellor. When von Schleicher began investigations into misuse of public funds by landholders during the land reform, conservative elements took alarm and demanded that President Hindenburg replace von Schleicher with Hitler. On 30 January Hindenburg asked Hitler to form a coalition government of nationalist parties, including ex-chancellor von Papen. It was thought that the other nationalist parties could keep Hitler's radicalism in check.

Within six months Hitler had acted to concentrate within the Nazi party all the political power in the state. In this he was helped by the burning of the Reichstag building in February. Blaming the fire on communist agitators, Hitler suspended civil rights and moved to destroy his left-wing political opponents. In the elections that followed, the Nazis mounted a propaganda campaign of unprecedented ferocity against dissidents and opponents. Still, they failed to win an absolute majority. In March, Hitler moved the Reichstag meetings, and after an impressive midnight military ceremony, he was able to coerce the members into passing the **Enabling Act.**

The Enabling Act of 23 March 1933 was the cornerstone of the Nazi dictatorship. It gave Hitler power to rule by decree for four years without the Reichstag's approval. Only the Social Democrats voted against the bill. He immediately abolished all other political parties and established people's courts to deal with dissidents and traitors. All regional and local police powers were centralized in Berlin under the Gestapo. The *Reichsrat,* an institution representative of the state governments, was abolished. Hitler used his power to coordinate the centralization of all power within the state, and for the first time in history Germany became a truly unitary state. Remaining centres of power, like trade unions, were in turn abolished by decree. By the end of the summer of 1933 only the churches and army remained as potential rivals. The major Christian churches remained autonomous throughout the regime, but with the death of Hindenburg in August 1934 the army began to succumb.

On 30 June 1934 Hitler carried out the promised purge of the Nazi party and eliminated his personal rivals and the party's until-now-useful socialist elements. On the **Night of the Long Knives,** Hitler struck down party dissidents. Executions were carried out by a small, élite group of storm troopers called the SS, who were from now on to play an increasingly important role within the German state.

Five weeks after the purge, the 87-year-old president Hindenburg died. In his final move to absolute power, Hitler merged the offices of chancellor and president in his own person. Now there was no competing constitutional authority to limit him. In a plebiscite held shortly thereafter, 92 per cent of the electorate voted in favour of Hitler's actions. The evidence is overwhelming that at this time a very large portion of the German people approved of the Nazi regime.

SUMMARY

As the First World War drew to a close, the Russian, Austro-Hungarian, German, and Turkish empires collapsed. Numerous successor states were created by nationalists to fill the void. These states had neither the political nor the economic stability to guarantee their existence, and each held large ethnic minorities within its borders. The only alternative to recognition was to continue the war in order to crush them. This the victorious great powers were not prepared to do.

The American proposal to establish a global organization based on collective security resulted in the establishment of the League of Nations. However, the United States did not join the organization and it became eurocentric. Although much groundwork was done by League agencies in the socioeconomic field in identifying global problems, the League was unable or unwilling to take military action against aggression. The League's failure to act decisively in the Manchurian Incident (1931), the invasion of Ethiopia (1935), or the Spanish Civil War (1936) led to its demise.

After the war, France remained the major military power on the continent. American isolationism and British indifference resulted in France seeking to re-establish the balance of power by allying with the successor states in Central Europe. These states, however, had neither the military nor the economic power to be effective. France was thrown back on its own resources. German reoccupation of the Rhineland in 1936, in violation of the Treaty of Versailles, illustrated French military weakness and the renewal of German power.

The Weimar Republic was Germany's first-ever attempt at representative democracy. It failed because of an economic crisis touched off in 1929 by the collapse of the American stock market, to which most other national economies were tied. Tired of the economic uncertainty and political chaos of the time, the German people elected an increasing number of Nazis to the Reichstag. The Nazi platform of economic stability, industrial growth, rearmament, and an end to reparations promised hope for the future. In January 1933 Hitler was appointed chancellor in an attempt by President Hindenburg to stabilize the political process. Hitler used the pretext of the Reichstag fire in February to secure dictatorial powers that resulted in the abolition of all opposition to his regime. In 1934, after the death of Hindenburg, Hitler merged the offices of president and chancellor and became the supreme authority in the Reich.

QUESTIONS

1. After the First World War, a number of successor states emerged from the fallen empires of Central Europe. Explain how these states affected the structure and stability of Central Europe.

2. Give the rationale for the establishment of the League of Nations.

3. Give three reasons for the ultimate failure of the League of Nations.

4. Explain the mandate system established by the League of Nations.

5. Identify the League's accomplishments in the 1920s and the 1930s.

6. Evaluate the effectiveness of the League in dealing with the following crises:
   (a) Manchuria, 1931; (b) Ethiopia, 1935.

7. What was the Stimson Doctrine?

8. Why did Japan invade Manchuria?

9. What did the Lytton commission decide about the Manchurian Incident?

10. Explain how Mussolini gained power in Italy.

11. What sanctions were imposed on Italy after it invaded Ethiopia?

12. Describe the effect of the First World War on France's economy.

13. Describe how the issue of German reparations affected France.

14. Why did France occupy the Ruhr in January 1923? What was the result? How was this incident resolved?

15. France attempted to counter German aggression through international agreements. Evaluate the effectiveness of each of these agreements.

16. Explain why the Weimar Republic had so many crises from 1919 to 1924.

17. How did the Americans attempt to solve Germany's reparation problems?

18. Explain the impact of the collapse of the American stock market on the international economy.

19. Explain how Adolf Hitler gained power in Germany.

20. How did the Enabling Act allow Hitler to establish a single-party dictatorship?

21. Explain the significance of the Night of the Long Knives.

22. What was the final step that gave Hitler absolute power?

CRITICAL ANALYSIS

1. Describe the instabilities of the successor states.

2. What rights should minorities have in sovereign nation-states? How can these rights be guaranteed?

3. Make a comparison of "collective security" and "balance of power" as conceptual methods for maintaining world peace.

4. Why is "self-determination" viewed as a means of reducing world tensions?

5. How does a multiplicity of parties affect the democratic process? Should marginal parties be permitted to take part in government? Why or why not?

6. How can an individual find protection in times of economic depression or inflation? Why are these periods destabilizing?

7. In a democracy, what protections are there for individual security? Should the state have ultimate authority, in the interests of the largest number? Are there inalienable rights that each individual should have?

RESEARCH PROJECTS

1. Research the following question: What responsibility did the German media have for the establishment of the Nazi regime?

2. Examine the political conditions in Germany from 1919 to 1933. Trace the development of Nazi power, explaining where support lay and how power was achieved.

3. *Mein Kampf* identifies Hitler's political program. Read 100 pages of this book and summarize his ideas. Show how he implemented these ideas after he gained power.

4. Life in Berlin in the 1920s was diverse. Some people enjoyed the cabarets while others struggled to survive. Research this era and describe how people lived in Berlin during the 1920s. Consider how they made a living, where they lived, and how they obtained food and clothing. What problems did they face as Germany struggled with post-war reconstruction and inflation?

5. Write a biographical account of one of the following individuals: (a) Hindenburg; (b) von Schleicher; (c) Brüning. Evaluate his role in the German government and assess the impact he had on Germany's political situation.

ACTIVITIES

1 Debate

Be it resolved that the Treaty of Versailles caused the Second World War.

2 League of Nations Meeting

It is 1935 and Italy has invaded Ethiopia. Assign each student the role of one of the League of Nations members, then discuss the course of action to be taken. Each student must accurately depict the point of view of the country he or she represents.

3 Panel Discussion

Establish a moderator and at least four members of a panel discussion to consider the effect of the Aryan Nations on the people of Canada. Do groups such as this threaten the minorities which they single out as "different"? Should extremist organizations of this nature be allowed to publish, promote, or even verbalize their doctrines? What similarities and differences exist between the Aryan Nations and the German Nazis?

HISTORICAL ANALYSIS

COLLECTIVE SECURITY

One of the commitments of the allied powers who emerged victorious from the First World War was the organization of a League of Nations, which would work collectively to maintain the peace and security of the world. This idea was expressed by Woodrow Wilson in his Fourteen Points and was implemented by the powers who forged the postwar peace at the Paris Conference, which convened on 18 January 1919. On 10 January 1920, the League Covenant came into effect with the ratification of the Treaty of Versailles.

Research the structure, membership, functions and peacekeeping attempts of the League of Nations. Analyse these features of the League with a view to determining why it was unable to maintain the peace.

1. What measures might have strengthened the League of Nations?

2. Was is possible at this time in history to create an international body which could act as an effective instrument of collective security?

THE THIRD REICH:

1934–1939

Today, at the close of an epoch of German history, I wish to state three clear facts:

- *The Treaty of Versailles is dead.*

- *Germany is free.*

- *The guarantor of this freedom is our own army.*

New defence forces have been built up in barely four years. Germany is not isolated, but bound in close friendship with mighty states. The natural community of interests between National Socialist Germany and Fascist Italy has continued in the last few months to prove itself an element of security between Europe and chaotic madness. It will not be possible in future anywhere to ignore this community of wills. Our agreement with Japan serves the same end, to stand together in repelling an attack on the civilized world which can take place today in Spain, tomorrow in the east, and the day after tomorrow perhaps somewhere else. We hope that other powers may understand the signs of the times and strengthen the front of reason.

Adolf Hitler, speaking to the National Socialist party congress,
Nuremberg, 7 September 1937.

TIME LINE

March	1933:	Dachau concentration camp opened
	1934:	Germany left the League of Nations
	1935:	Nuremberg Decrees
March	1935:	Remilitarization of Germany
October	1935:	Italy invaded Ethiopia
	1936:	Germany reoccupied the Rhineland
	1936:	Jewish Bureau established
June	1936:	Spanish Civil War erupted
October	1936:	Rome–Berlin axis
November	1936:	Anti-Comintern Pact between Germany and Japan
	1937:	Italy Joined Anti-Comintern Pact
5 November	1937:	Hossbach document
March	1938:	*Anschluss* (Austria merged with Germany)
September	1938:	Munich Pact
September	1938:	Germany annexes Sudetenland
November	1938:	*Kristallnacht* (Crystal Night)
March	1939:	Germany occupied remainder of Czechoslovakia
23 August	1939:	Nazi-Soviet pact
1 September	1939:	Germany invaded Poland
3 September	1939:	Britain and France declared war
17 September	1939:	Soviet Union invaded Poland

FOCUS ON EXPANSION

Expansionist foreign policy may arise from a variety of motives and circumstances. Describe German foreign policy, both as it is affecting "your" nation and the rest of Europe, either as a Czech leader in March 1939, or as a Polish or a British leader in September 1939.

OVERVIEW

The New Order describing demographic policies and German autarky is followed by rearmament and the growing power of Germany. The Western democracies of Britain and France, the Spanish Civil War, and the boundaries question of Austria, Czechoslovakia, and Poland leading to the outbreak of the Second World War are all developed.

THE NEW ORDER
As soon as he attained power, Hitler set out to achieve economic autarky and social reorganization in an expanded Germany.

HITLER'S POLICIES
From 1934-1939 Hitler implemented policies which resulted in a strengthened economy, rearmament, and diplomatic ties with Italy, Japan, and the Soviet Union.

SPANISH CIVIL WAR
In 1936, civil unrest in Spain erupted in a war which some historians suggest was a training ground for the Second World War. Right-wing Nationalist forces led by Franco were supported by Germany and Italy while Republican forces gained Soviet support. Britain, France, and the United States did not officially participate.

AUSTRIA
In 1938, Hitler engineered the union of Austria to the German state thus embarking on his policy of territorial expansion.

CZECHOSLOVAKIA
German annexation of the Sudetenland of Czechoslovakia in 1938 was accepted by the French and the British in an attempt to "appease" Hitler. Six months later, the rest of Czechoslovakia was dismembered.

POLAND
After signing a non-aggression pact with the Soviet Union in August 1939 Hitler moved his army into Poland, beginning the Second World War.

THE NEW ORDER

Adolf Hitler revived the deep-seated desire for German expansion into central and eastern Europe. His vision of a Third Reich that would last a thousand years had overwhelming support from the German people. German hegemony over the continent would concentrate all political, military, economic, social, and cultural power in Berlin. At its greatest extent the Reich was designed to encompass all the land from the Atlantic Ocean to the Ural Mountains, and from the Baltic to the Mediterranean Sea. Germany was to become the heartland of the European industrial complex. The other nations were to supply the heartland with raw materials and foodstuffs, and in return they would be guaranteed markets for their produce and manufactured goods from German suppliers. In this way, the Reich would achieve autarky and become the world's leading industrial power.

When the demand for living space—*lebensraum*—grew as a result of an increasing German population, neighbouring lands would be annexed to the Reich to accommodate them. Local populations would be removed in order to maintain the homeland or *heimat* concept, and the "purity" of the German race. Because these territories would not be given up voluntarily, Hitler assumed he would have to seize them by military force. War would have to be fought against any combination of the other industrial powers prior to 1943.

The **New Order** for Europe proposed the rationalization of agriculture and industry on a continental basis. Everything from capital goods to armaments would be concentrated in German hands. The conquered peoples would be organized to process the raw materials and food to which Germany would give absolute priority. As needed, workers would be uprooted and moved to wherever labour shortages occurred. A central planning board would direct all facets of production and establish efficient economies of scale, and redirect human resources wasted through unemployment. Although the scope of the New Order was international, the objective was to sustain the economic growth and improve the living standards only of the German people.

The creation of a German *heimat,* or homeland, implied the removal from the Reich of all non-German peoples. Racial purity was one of the pillars of the New Order. The plans for the **demographic reordering** of the continent were monstrous both in size and intent. First of all, German minorities in the border states were to be recovered and annexed to

Germany Before Nazi Control

As noted in the previous chapter, a complex set of circumstances helped set the stage for Hitler's rise to power in Germany in the 1930s. Among other factors, many Germans resented the loss of territory after the First World War. French demands for security fanned this anger.

the Reich. This in-gathering would include Austria, the Sudetenland of Czechoslovakia, and the Polish corridor (including Danzig). An additional 300 000 Germans living elsewhere would be encouraged to return to the *Grossraum,* or Greater Germany, where they would be settled in "eastern protectorates" as managers of the local people.

Racial purity would be attained by the removal of all foreigners from the homeland. People would have to be classified by race and then moved or removed to fit the plan. Heinrich Himmler, head of the SS (the Nazi headquarters guard), hoped to remove over 30 million Slavs from Poland and the western region of the USSR by the end of the twentieth century. Their place would be taken by *volksdeutsch* (ethnic Germans) garrisoning strong points along the eastern borders, where they would act as a barrier against any Soviet retaliation.

Other Nordic peoples, such as the English and the Scandinavians, would be part of the New Order, but in a way that would not interfere with German

supremacy. There was also a role for some of the non-Nordic races. These were considered inferior in nature and would have no political or civil rights and would be allowed to work for the Reich in return for the right to live. They would be controlled by limiting their education to the bare minimum so that they would read only enough to understand and obey orders. They would be totally subservient and allowed to exist so long as they were useful to the economy. A further sub-grouping was composed of "undesirables" like Jews, who could not be entrusted with even the most menial tasks. They were to be eliminated as soon as was practical.

Hitler linked the "purification" of the German race to the salvation of Europe and civilized humanity. The anti-Semitic character of his racial policies found a ready audience among those who blamed Germany's defeat in the First World War, and the plight of the German people after the depression, on world-wide Jewry. This anti-Semitism had significant support in Europe outside the Reich. The Nazis fostered an already ancient hatred of all things Jewish, and established the means to eliminate the Jewish people. After Hitler's accession to power in 1933, and the enactment of the Nuremberg Decrees of 1935, the Nazis took measures to isolate Jewish people in Germany from contact with the rest of society. In a state-organized program, German Jews and other targeted peoples were methodically identified, concentrated in ghettos, and denied all civil and social rights. They were degraded as human beings and forbidden to hold public jobs; their property was pillaged and their persons were subject to physical abuse and murder. The slightest contact between other Germans and Jews was prohibited by law. Although there were only some 370 000 Jews in Germany itself, conquest during the coming war would bring millions more under German control.

In 1936, a Jewish Bureau was established under Adolf Eichmann to systematize the state's "processing" of the Jewish population. The bureau at first attempted to remove German Jews through emigration; but no other state would take in such large numbers of "displaced persons." The exception was the British mandate of Palestine, which received 1500 people a month, provided immigrants had $1000 with them and were not a drain on local resources. No one yet believed the Nazis were planning genocide.

A foretaste of what was to come occurred on 7 November 1938 when a 17-year-old Jewish youth assassinated Ernst von Rath, a minor German diplomat in Paris. In retaliation, the Nazis brutally inflicted a night of terror on the Jewish population in Germany. Over 200 synagogues were wrecked, and 26 000 male Jews were arrested and sent to concentration camps. At least 70 were murdered and countless women and girls were raped and beaten in a public exhibition of uncontrolled rage. So much glass was broken that the event was given the name *Kristallnacht* ("Glass Night"). The Jews were then fined 25 million marks to repair the property damage that they had *not* done, and a further 1 billion marks, thereby taking away much of the wealth not already confiscated. Jews were now denied the use of all public facilities including transportation, hospitals, and retirement homes. Foreign nations did not protest the anti-Jewish pogroms—their excuse being that to do so would appear an unjustifiable interference in the domestic affairs of another nation.

Jews began to flee Germany by every means possible; but the annexation of Austria, Czechoslovakia, and Poland found many of them back under Nazi control. In 1938, Hitler and Himmler began to talk of the need to eliminate whole sections of populations that had recently come under German control. Jews, Slavs, and Gypsies were to be gathered together and transferred to places of confinement and execution. The first concentration camps, begun in Dachau in 1933 for purely political opponents, were primarily labour camps where starvation and

Hitler started persecuting the Jewish people and other minorities almost as soon as he came to power. This man is wearing the yellow, six-pointed star that all Jews were required to wear as identification.

overwork frequently led to death. The first of the outright death camps was established in Auschwitz, Poland, shortly after the German conquest in 1939. The "Final Solution," methodical genocide, was not implemented until 1942, well into the war. By that time the identification, gathering, and killing of Jews, Slavs, and Gypsies had become a separate and grimly profitable sub-economy within the Reich.

REICH SECURITY SERVICES

Totalitarian governments are maintained by force and terror. In Nazi Germany, the SA and the SS performed this "maintenance" role. Analyse this method of controlling populations.

In the turbulent months of 1919, President Ebert used returning war veterans to provide order and security in the Weimar Republic. A commission of public security was established in Berlin to control the activities of the social democrats, Jews, and communists. The old political police force of Prussia, the *Geheime Staatspolizei*, was soon to become the new central agency for repression in the Third Reich, the Gestapo.

At the same time, a rival police organization was formed in Munich. There, in January 1920, Hitler was elected head of propaganda for the German Workers party, then 64 members strong. The party accepted the 25 point program he drew up and later renamed itself the National Socialist German Workers party (NSDAP). It was to be united with the Bavarian Home Guard under the leadership of the corrupt Ernst Röhm, to create a **united front**.

Röhm had been given the task of equipping a citizen army in the wake of the deposed Red Republic. His secret arms caches held over 8 000 000 rounds of ammunition, 169 light guns, 20 000 rifles, and 300 000 hand grenades. When the Bavarian Guard was disbanded in 1920 at allied insistence, Röhm used Hitler to gain public support for his secret army. When Hitler became president of the NSDAP in 1921, Röhm's men were used as mobile squads to protect the leader. Officially known as the "gym and sporting section," they later became the SA or Storm Detachment (*Sturmabteilung*). At this time Hitler was the outsider, and Röhm gave the orders to the SA. The SA often ignored Hitler's directives. Hitler countered Röhm by recruiting the noted First World War flying ace Hermann Göring to establish an administrative headquarters staff. The headquarters guard or SS (*Schutzstaffel*) was to attain predominance. Its task was to carry out police duties within the party. In 1930, Hitler made the SS independent of the SA and placed it under Heinrich Himmler, who began expanding the force from 280 to 50 000. In 1933, around a collection of huts near an unused powder factory near Dachau, the SS began isolating communists and social democrats from the political process in the country's first concentration camp. That same year all police forces in Germany were centralized under Himmler in Berlin, when he was made deputy chief of the German state police, the Gestapo.

In December 1933, the SA ran foul of the *Wehrmacht* (Germany's army). At that time, Röhm could lay claim to a following of some 4 500 000 men. But he made the mistake of trying to usurp the army in defending the state. Hitler saw the *Wehrmacht* as a means of gaining the support of the conservative element while President Hindenburg's death loomed. If the army would follow Hitler, he would be Führer (leader) and have absolute power.

On 28 June 1934 Hitler telephoned Röhm to complain about SA troopers insulting a foreign ambassador. He demanded a meeting of all SA leaders at Röhm's holiday resort for 30 June, known in Nazi mythology as the Night of the Long Knives. At the resort, Röhm and other SA leaders were gunned down in their bedrooms. Hitler later claimed Röhm and his followers were guilty of the greatest acts of disloyalty, intending to hand Germany over to its enemies. He, Hitler, had acted to save the nation by ordering their execution. The SS began hunting down other supposed enemies of the state, including ex-chancellors von Papen and von Schleicher. When the executions ended on 2 July, 83 of Hitler's opponents had been murdered, among hundreds of others.

Within the SS, a new sub-grouping, the SD, was formed under Reinhard Heydrich as an intelligence unit that would ferret out enemies of the state before opposition to the Nazis could actually take shape. The SD's task was to cleanse the nation of all non-conformist ideas and "destructive" tendencies. The SD would become the secret power behind the new Political Police Services with the merging of SA, SS, SD, and Gestapo into the RSHA (*Reichssicherheitshauptampt*) in 1939.

One of the first activities of the expanded SD was to take into "protective custody" 2000 professionals and habitual criminals who were sent to the Sachsenhausen, Sachsenburg, Lichtenburg, and Dachau concentration camps. The camps were soon to receive whole segments of the population labeled anti-social misfits, on a prescribed seasonal quota system. The camps soon gave reality to Himmler's SS-run system of political and criminal police control over the nation. The task of the SD was to eliminate opponents within the Nazi party as well as among the general public.

On 22 August 1939 Hitler called a conference of Reich commanders to discuss war. He needed a propagandist reason for attacking Poland. In *realpolitik,* it is not right that matters, but victory. The victor would not be asked if he was telling the truth. Hitler gave Himmler the task of finding a suitable excuse for war.

Hitler had agreed with Himmler and Heydrich on staging several border incidents in Upper Silesia that would require 150 SS officers disguised in Polish uniforms. Such faked frontier incidents would make the world believe that Hitler had been provoked into action.

SD officers dressed as Polish terrorists were to attack the radio station at Gleiwitz and shout one or two anti-German slogans on the air. Dead bodies would have to be found as evidence for the attack. Prisoners from concentration camps were given lethal injections, and their bullet-riddled bodies were scattered about the entranceway.

Training of the special SS units took place throughout August. The attack took place on the night of 31 August when, shortly after 8 PM, five men entered the radio station and gathered the staff in the cellar. Then, interrupting the program on the air, they read messages in Polish over a background of shooting. After four minutes, the attack team fled, stepping over the dead body of one of the concentration-camp victims laid out at the front gate.

Similar scenes were enacted at the Hochlinden Customs House and 12 other points along the frontier. Hitler now had his excuse to invade Poland and start a war that would claim 55 000 000 victims.

During the war to come, the SS would follow hard on the heels of the army to destroy enemies of the New Order and "manage" foreign populations that came under German control. The valuable elements were to be sifted out, and the residue were to become a "substandard" labour force. Jews and Gypsies were to be completely eliminated. The SS were to form *Einsatzgruppen* and liquidate the upper classes. Five groups of SS were created for the Polish campaign—one to serve with each army. Armed with prepared lists, the SS rounded up their prey.

The Nazi invasion of the Soviet Union triggered the beginning of Jewish extermination. On 23 June 1941 Heydrich's 3000 officers set off to track down the Soviet Union's 5 million Jews. So close did Heydrich's officers follow the army that they often became involved with front-line fighting. Their method was to take control of towns, where they demanded that Jews present themselves for resettlement. Stripped of valuables and clothing, they were executed in a variety of ways. The first wave of SS was followed by a second, more thorough wave. By December 1941 some 500 000 Jews had been killed. Only later were mobile execution squads replaced by the stationary death factories in Poland.

In 1942, the SS was given the formal task of eliminating Europe's Jewry. The first death camp opened in March 1942 at Belzec. It had the facilities to kill 15 000 people per day. Sobibor, which had the facilities to kill 20 000 a day, followed in April. Then came Treblinka, with facilities for 25 000 a day. Altogether, 5 death camps and 156 labour camps were established by the SS. At Auschwitz, where Cyclon B gas replaced piped-in diesel exhaust, 4 million people were murdered.

The SS also recruited fully armed battle divisions to fight alongside the regular army. The Waffen-SS became the most ruthless of fighting forces; it took no prisoners and suffered exceptionally heavy casualties while annihilating its enemies. It was trained for merciless warfare. SS *Gruppenführer* Josef (Sepp) Dietrich chose 120 soldiers to form the headquarters guard *Leibstandarte Adolf Hitler* in 1933 as a personal bodyguard. It was this force that had carried out the executions of the Night of the Long Knives. Later it was joined by other divisions such as *Deutschland* from Munich, *Germania* from Hamburg, and *Der Führer* from Vienna. These and others were to become the German army's shock troops. When soldier requirements became strained, some 125 000 western Europeans were taken into the Waffen-SS forces. By 1944, the SS comprised close to 1 million people. Fanatical, and disdainful of losses, they were impelled by blind fury, spearheading SS attacks against enemy defence lines. So heavy were battle losses that officers often had to be drafted directly from cadet schools. *Das Reich* broke through the Moscow defences in 1941, and in the subsequent winter retreat at minus 52 degrees centigrade, *Der Führer* survived with only 35 people. The SS units provided an unparalleled example of tenacity that every German general welcomed to his command.

Near the end of the war, on 20 May 1945, Himmler attempted to escape detection by using the name Heinrich Hintzinger. He was, however, captured by British military police near Lünenburg. Under interrogation he bit into a capsule of cyanide hidden in his mouth and died within a few seconds. Only a few Nazis followed his example. The European people's courts brought charges against the others. Many were executed, including Höss, the SS commandant of Auschwitz. However, the majority of the SS were treated less severely. Most served prison sentences but were later pardoned and released.

1. How did German political officials react to the anarchy that erupted across Germany at the end of the First World War?

2. Where did the various police forces obtain their weapons and officers?

3. What was the function of the political police as compared to the criminal police?

4. What changes to the police structure were made after the Nazis came to power? Who was the leader of the federal police?

5. Why did the army oppose the power of the police forces? Why did commanders welcome SS combat divisions in their sector?

6. Explore the motives that would lead normal young people to carry out the most barbaric executions of other human beings.

HITLER'S POLICIES

Hitler did not have a well-defined program. He was an opportunist who believed the natural unfolding of events would bring him eventual success. He did not expect to establish the New Order without a war, but as to the when, where, or why, he was uncertain. France and the Soviet Union appeared to be his most dangerous enemies. In the war it would be desirable to make friends with the British to keep the resources of the British Empire out of the fray. Similarly, it was inadvisable to fight the USA, whose industrial power had been demonstrated in the First World War. Italy could distract France in the Mediterranean and Japan could distract America and the Soviet Union in Asia. Because Germany did not have sufficient stockpiles of ammunition and weapons for a prolonged war, Hitler calculated on a short struggle to gain his territorial objectives. To this end, **blitzkrieg** (lightning war) tactics were adopted to achieve victory within a three-month span.

The Hossbach Conference memorandum, written as a summation of a meeting on 5 November 1937 between Hitler and his advisors, gives a more detailed account of the Nazi strategy. The future of the German people would be secured by expansion to the east where the *volksdeutsch* would dominate. Germany would expand into Central Europe, where almost everyone, including governments of the successor states, agreed that the boundaries established after the First World War would have to be revised. The Soviet Union, Poland, Hungary, and Romania all sought changes more in line with ethnic realities. They also sought to recover nationals living as minorities in neighbouring countries. In supporting Hitler, they did not realize the result would be German hegemony. The German eastward expansion would occur by way of diplomatic manoeuvring where possible, and by armed force where necessary. Hitler did not believe the other powers would interfere because none of them would be prepared to go to war over such trifling matters. In this he was right. It was not until the invasion of Poland that the other powers overcame their reluctance to do battle.

The period 1934 to 1939 witnessed a whirlwind of Nazi activity. Hitler's first moves were to concentrate political, economic, and police powers in Berlin and make Germany a unitary state for the first time. In the economic field, the Nazis took control of the trade unions by means of a labour front that guaranteed jobs through deficit financing. Public works, modern transportation and communication, electrification, and rearmament all contributed to economic revival. A four-year plan put the concentration of industrial strength in the hands of a few large corporations. The economy was placed on a wartime footing in peacetime; full employment resulted, and became the bedrock of Nazi popularity. The construction of *autobahns* (vast highways) and the availability of consumer goods (especially radios and cars) made the regime immensely popular.

In 1936, when Germany could no longer pay for the import of industrial materials, it resorted to barter arrangements with its trading partners. Central European countries with economies in disarray were guaranteed German markets in return for weapons and technology. Imports were reduced as synthetics like plastics were developed to replace natural products like rubber and cotton. At the same time, territorial expansion to seize needed iron ore and oil supplies became a recurring theme among industrialists. They, too, saw the need for industrial expansion to sustain the momentum of growth.

On the diplomatic front, Hitler moved to overturn the Versailles and Locarno agreements by recovering the lands and people stripped from Germany in 1920. He also moved to re-establish Germany's military power. In 1933, German representatives walked out of an international disarmament conference when it was decided that Germany could not have proscribed weapons. And, for good measure, Germany withdrew from the League of Nations. In March 1935, Hitler proclaimed universal military training, and in 1936 reoccupied the Rhineland, and publicly displayed military forces far beyond those allowed under the 1919 settlement.

By 1939, the Germans had a field army of 2.75 million soldiers, a combat air force of over 4000 planes, and a growing navy of surface vessels and submarines. The rebuilding of the German military establishment paused only when industry ran out of raw materials. The economy could not provide all the service that military leaders requested. Germany was already producing more war materials than all the other powers combined. Plans for a 20 000 airplane armada would have required 85 per cent of the world's annual oil production to keep it in the air. The revival of Germany's military power in just four years made Hitler a national idol.

By all standards, it was an impressive performance. Rearmament and the overturning of the Versailles settlement rekindled national pride. At last, someone was doing something about the depressed state of German society.

Hitler used his charisma and popularity with the people to expand his powers. Rallies like this one were used to whip the populace into nationalistic frenzies.

Britain and France were the only two powers that could have done something about German resurgence, but they failed to act. They were democracies whose governments were guided by the public will; whose concerns were domestic and not given to grand strategy. Their publics were not prepared to become entangled in another war: social and financial problems of the depression had greater priority than foreign affairs. Britain was also encumbered with an empire whose views on international affairs had to be taken into account. The dominions and colonies would not support a war brought on by

Mussolini and Hitler united Italy and Germany in the Rome-Berlin axis of 1936.

Central European politics. A major issue would be required before British or, for that matter, American involvement was possible. Continental Europe was to be left alone to handle its own affairs.

Great Britain was a considerable power at the start of the 1930s, especially at sea. Its extensive global empire had the potential human and other resources to counter all threats against it. The British people were not interested in European entanglements and continually urged France to give up its alliances with the successor states. Such alliances would only drag France into another continental war. Britain also faced increased industrial competition after the war from the USA and Japan. Its energies were directed at recovery from the depression which had left millions of Britons unemployed. By 1934, as a result of reduced budgets, Britain's armed forces were not strong enough in any potential theatre of war to guarantee victory. In 1934, the advent of Germany's new *Luftwaffe* (air force) made Britain vulnerable to attack from the air. In 1935, Britain and Germany signed a naval agreement that recognized the reality of the size of Germany's naval forces. Germany agreed to limit its fleet to 35 per cent of that of Britain's, but it kept on building anyway. This agreement by one of the guarantors of the Versailles settlement dashed plans by France to react to German rearmament.

Britain did not view German rearmament as a flagrant breach of the Versailles Treaty. The British believed German rearmament was for defence purposes, and was not aimed at France any more than the reoccupation of the Rhineland was. Prime Minister Neville Chamberlain believed that once Hitler's legitimate concerns were met, the Germans would be satisfied. Even so, the British did start a modest rearmament program for its sea and air forces. At the same time, Britain and the United States were becoming more concerned about the situation in Asia that was encouraging Japanese expansion.

By 1934, France, which was the major land power in 1920, had retreated into a defensive posture behind the Maginot Line. At the beginning of the 1930s, France had the second largest army and air force among the great powers. This was to change after 1933, with the collapse of the French economy to only 83 per cent of the pre-depression scale. In addition, French national income had fallen to about 20 per cent of the 1929 income level. This retrenchment was to have significant effects on the armed forces. Although the defence budget remained at about 4 per cent of the gross national product (GNP) for most of the decade, the real budget dropped by millions of francs. It was not until 1937 that the government began pouring funds into the armed forces, and most of that went into reversing previous neglect. Even in 1938, when the defence appropriations rose to 39 per cent of the budget, it was impossible to re-equip the armed forces in a satisfactory manner. Worst off was the air force, which accepted almost 400 new aircraft in 1937, compared to the *Luftwaffe's* 5606. New fighter aircraft started to become available only in the months immediately preceding the German invasion of France in 1940.

After Locarno, the French strategy became defensive, behind what was thought to be the impregnable Maginot Line. Plans to advance into Germany in support of allies in Central Europe were blunted with Germany's occupation of the Rhineland in 1936. Then, France had to face the possibility of two hostile fascist states on its southern borders—Italy and Spain. As a result, France began to depend too heavily on Great Britain to guarantee its safety. The French assumed that in any future war, the Royal Navy would ensure food and supplies were brought across the oceans. This dependence on Britain led to increasing inertia within the French government and military staffs.

Noting the reluctance of Britain and France to act, Hitler moved to destroy the French security system. His non-aggression pact with Poland in

January 1934 breached the French alliance system and led to German economic penetration of Central Europe. Germany would guarantee markets for Polish raw materials and food, and in return would exchange technology, manufactured goods, and weapons. By 1939, all the successor states had entered into trade agreements and adopted pro-German policies as a result of Hitler's economic initiative. When the Little Entente collapsed, France attempted to resurrect the Soviet alliance. Despite ideological differences, both states had Germany as an enemy. A treaty was arranged, but without military commitment: neither of them could strike at Germany without going through other countries—in the one case Poland or Romania, and in the other, Belgium. It was unlikely either would be granted transit rights by buffer states.

The Soviets considered two alternative policies: an alliance with the Western democracies to limit German expansion, or an alliance with Germany to regain territories lost to Poland and the successor states after the First World War. At this point, the Soviets were undecided, but the expansionist regimes appeared to be unchallenged and the promise of a reorganization of Central Europe began to have a compelling attraction.

In October 1936, Hitler and Mussolini came to an understanding over previous differences and agreed to a Rome-Berlin axis. This was followed in November 1936 by Hitler's mutual non-aggression pact with Japan. The Anti-Comintern Pact did not entail any military commitments, but was a statement of intent to halt the spread of communism. Japan wanted German assurances of support for an attack on the USSR. Germany for its part wanted Japanese support in keeping Britain and the USA occupied in Asia, distracted from Europe. Italy joined the pact in 1937.

Because Spain was devastated by its civil war, Franco refused to support Germany and Italy at the outset of the Second World War. Many Spanish people, like the family above, fled to France and other countries.

SPANISH CIVIL WAR

The Spanish Civil War broke out in June 1936 and diverted world attention from the major powers at a critical time. In itself a local affair, the Spanish Civil War was never a threat to the international order; yet the major powers became involved and their intervention prolonged the war and distracted world opinion from *Mittleuropa* and Asia.

In the early part of the twentieth century, growing labour problems in the Madrid-Valencia-Barcelona triangle had led to civil unrest. Demands by the workers for better working conditions and a redistribution of the immense wealth of the church and landowners were coupled with a call for a republican form of government. At the same time, the peasants began demonstrating for the breakup of the vast estates held by the aristocracy. When General Primo de Rivera was appointed prime minister in 1923, the Spanish army crushed the disturbances and set up a military dictatorship that continued in power until 1930, when Rivera was dismissed by the king. Subsequent elections in 1931 brought a left-leaning government to power on the promise of needed reforms and the implementation of welfare legislation. The nation had divided, with the cities favouring a republic and the rural areas loyal to the monarchy. When the king left the country, a republic was proclaimed in 1931.

The pace of change brought about by Spain's republican government was not fast enough to satisfy the people. In the elections of 1933, right-wing parties won a slim majority and promptly undid most of the reforms. An even smaller majority returned the left-wing to power in February 1936. When this government moved to break up the estates of the rich, its supporters went on a rampage, plundering churches and abusing churchmen and women. The propertied classes retaliated with equal violence and turned the streets into bloody battlegrounds. In June, the army moved to restore order and overthrow the republican government. Thus began three years of civil strife characterized by massacres and atrocities on both sides. In the end, 600 000 Spaniards would be killed in battle or murdered as prisoners. And after the war, General Francisco Franco, who had led the military uprising, would have another million people arrested and sent to concentration camps.

During the civil war, the right-wing Nationalist forces under General Franco were flown into southern Spain from Africa by German and Italian aircraft. During the war, Nationalists dominated the south and rural areas while Republican forces held the cities and the isolated region of the Basque provinces in the north-west. The Basques stayed loyal to the republican government in order to protect their newly won autonomy. Franco hoped to crush the opposition quickly by advancing on Madrid. The city was besieged by four columns, but he could not prevail. Nationalist forces within the city sought to sabotage its defences and were termed the "Fifth Column"—a name used today to signal betrayal from within. The arming of the workers, and later peasants, by both sides, changed the character of the fighting. Moderation gave way to extremes of violence and atrocity.

Germany and Italy gave prompt support to Franco's forces. Both supplied airplanes and Italy contributed ground forces as well. *Luftwaffe* bombing operations against undefended Basque cities like Guernica were a prelude to larger raids on Europe's capitals—Warsaw, Rotterdam, and London—in the Second World War. The air attacks had a lasting effect on British and French strategists, who pictured their own undefended cities in ruins. The reality of the threat from the air to undefended cities was very persuasive and helped shape non-interventionist strategies.

The Republican side received a different kind of international support. The plight of the government touched the heartstrings of young idealists who came to Spain to fight in international brigades like the Mackenzie-Papineau (Canadian) or the Abraham Lincoln (American). After the stalemate of the winter of 1937, these brigades were taken over by Soviet officers and subjected to communist propaganda. By year's end, the Soviets had gained control over most of the Republican forces and transformed them into a people's army. One objective of Soviet intervention on the Republican side was to try to force mutual defence agreements with the democracies of France and Britain to oppose Germany. When the Soviet effort did not have the desired effect, the USSR dropped its support of the Republican cause in 1938. Without Soviet aid, the government forces were quickly routed by Nationalist armies in early 1939.

Hitler had hoped to receive military support in the Second World War from Franco in return for his efforts in support of the Nationalists. But Franco was a Nationalist in fact as well as name, and although Spain did supply Germany with iron ore and provide havens for German U-boats during the Second World War, it did not take the final step and join in the hostilities. Nor did Spain cut off the Straits of Gibraltar to British and American fleets. Ever the opportunist, partly by necessity, Franco pleaded Spain's exhaustion, even as he profited from dealing with both sides of the conflict.

Throughout the civil war, very little aid was given to the Republican forces by Britain and France. Instead, the two countries established a Non-Intervention Committee, hoping to gain support by localizing the fighting. Their citizens were not prepared for war and in England a "peace ballot" was signed by over 11 million people. No government could ignore the force behind such a public anti-war statement. Bound by democratic systems, neither nation could find sufficient public support for military intervention. But the message they gave other powers was not one of peace, but rather one of weakness and vacillation, when compared with Germany and Italy.

BIOGRAPHY

FRANCISCO FRANCO
(1892-1975)

The hole that Francisco Franco leaves in Spanish life and the space he goes on to fill in history is so great that any superlative would serve only to belittle him. The Chief of State has died, but above all the founder of a State and of an historical era to which his name, in all justice, has been given and which with him ends. During almost half a century his figure has stood at the top national level and his biography and the general history of Spain have been mingled to such an extent that it would be very difficult, if not impossible, to separate.

Editorial in the Spanish newspaper *Ya*
on the morning that Francisco Franco died.

It seems somewhat incongruous that Francisco Franco, the cautious and enigmatic Spanish general and dictator, would have been the lifelong ruler of a nation of people stereo-typed as passionate and volatile. Both Franco's wife and only child were named Carmen, a name that brings to mind the opera *Carmen*, with its Spanish bull fights, angry lovers, and dusty heat. Unfortunately, the Spain of the opera is only part of the story. The other part is a Spain of repression and corruption, a Spain which housed a regime that would not tolerate criticism or opposition—a regime of which no vestiges remained within only two short years of the death of its leader.

At the young age of 15, Franco joined the army. From 1907 to 1910 he attended the military academy at Toledo, where he became second lieutenant. After a short posting in El Ferrol, Franco went to Morocco (1912-1917), where Spain was involved in a colonial war. There Franco distinguished himself in the eyes of his superiors and was promoted to the rank of major for his leadership in commanding African troops against the Berbers. Franco went on to command the victorious rebel forces during the Spanish Civil War of 1936-1939.

In spite of the expectations of Germany and Italy and the aid they had lent to Franco's forces during the Spanish Civil War, and despite the fact that Franco's allegiances may have naturally fallen with Mussolini and Hitler, Franco managed to keep Spain out of World War II. His excuse was that his country needed a chance to get back on its feet after the devastation of the Spanish Civil War. Franco did, however, send troops to help the Germans against Russia. This illustrated Franco's perception that communism was the real enemy.

Although Franco broke ties with the axis powers in October 1943, in December 1946 the United Nations (UN) recommended the diplomatic isolation of Spain. The UN also refused to allow Spain to join the organization because the country was a declared fascist state. In 1947 Franco issued a constitution which declared Spain a monarchy and himself as head of state, with the power to name his successor.

The tensions created by the Cold War made other earlier tensions of less account. In 1950 the United States sponsored Spanish membership in the UN, and shortly thereafter the United States gave Spain military assistance and indirect aid in return for the establishment of Spanish bases aimed against Russia. ●

GUERNICA

The horrors of war sometimes, ironically, inspire great art. The intensive bombing of the Basque village of Guernica inspired one of the twentieth century's most powerful works of art. Research and describe a work of art (i.e., painting, book, film, symphony, etc.) inspired by an act of war. Alternatively, create your own piece of art, based on a recent example of warfare.

In the second year of the Spanish Civil War, the rebel Nationalist forces of General Francisco Franco struck northwest at the heavily defended Basque port of Bilbao. The port was protected by a series of defence lines stretching 70 km into the interior. Behind the first fortified line lay the small market town of Guernica. There was a small-arms factory on the outskirts and a bridge across a small river at the edge of town. Basque forces retreating towards Bilbao would likely use the road through Guernica to reach a second and more powerful defence position. Guernica had no significant military value and was not protected in any way, but it was symbolically important. Here, Spanish kings traditionally swore to uphold Basque local rights under the Tree of Liberties. Guernica was the centre of Basque nationalism.

With a population of only 7000, Guernica was only one of many Spanish villages that dotted the landscape. Monday, 16 April 1937, was another market day. The streets were filled with people going about their business. Farmers from the countryside had brought in their produce to trade in a generally festive atmosphere.

At 4:30 PM church bells announced an air raid. Heinkel IIIs and Junker bombers flew over the town in repeated waves, dropping incendiary bombs and strafing people running in the streets. The aircraft came every 20 minutes until 8 PM that night. Altogether 43 German aircraft were involved in the raid. Over 70 per cent of the town's buildings were destroyed, and an estimated 1000 people were killed.

The Nationalist propaganda machine swung into high gear the next day and claimed that Basque arsonists had torched the town, that there had been no air raid. A few days later, when Guernica fell to the Nationalist army, the soldiers mounted a protective guard around the Tree of Liberties. Later, they were to claim that the damage was done by artillery fire in the battle for the town the next day. Could not the explosions have come from dynamite stored in the sewers? It was not until October that senior Nationalist officers admitted that they had bombed Guernica over and over again to destroy the spirit of Basque nationalism. Much later, German war ace Alfred Galland admitted the raid had been a mistake but said the bombs had fallen on the town proper because of poor bomb-sights. Under interrogation in 1946, German air marshal Göring admitted that the bombing of the village had been a test of the effectiveness of a blanket bombing strategy.

The Nationalist forces broke through the defence lines and captured Bilbao. The Basque mines were captured intact, and soon Nationalist ships were carrying iron ore to Germany and England for their rearmament programs. Asked to do a wall mural for the Paris World's Fair, the self-exiled Spanish artist Picasso chose Guernica as his subject. The catastrophe is depicted in the burning house, animals, and the distortion of the sun. Disembodied women and children add to the confusion in this, one of his most celebrated paintings.

1. What part did Basque nationalism have in the decision by General Franco's Nationalist forces to destroy Guernica?

2. Is the Nationalist excuse that they were only following orders a valid one? This defence has been used on numerous occasions by military personnel brought to trial for alleged atrocities against civilians. What rights do civilians in battle areas have? Should they be treated differently from combatants? If so, how and why?

3. Guernica underlines the continuing difficulty of attacking military targets from the air. Unable to separate military from civilian targets, pilots have resorted on occasion to the strategy of carpet-bombing the entire area. Make a study of the effectiveness of bombing as a military tactic.

AUSTRIA

Securely in power at home, and convinced the democracies would not fight, Hitler moved quickly to expand his Reich. The first target for annexation was Austria. Even before Hitler came to power, there had been a growing movement there for union with Germany *(Anschluss)*. Hitler's coming to power in Germany added impetus to this movement. The Austrian chancellors Dollfuss and von Schuschnigg attempted, unsuccessfully, to create their own nationalist movement. In February 1934, Dollfuss banned opposition parties, including the Austrian Nazi party. Five months later, Nazis broke into his office and assassinated him. His murder touched off a political crisis. Hitler would have sent his forces into Austria at that time had it not been for Mussolini's dispatch of troops to the Brenner Pass. Italy was worried that *Anschluss* might also include the German speaking Tyrol that Italy had been granted after the First World War. Hitler backed off in the face of the Italian military threat. It would be another four years before Hitler could make his next move in Austria, only because Italy had by then assumed a pro-German stance. Once the Rome-Berlin axis had been forged, Austria was vulnerable.

Pressure on Chancellor von Schuschnigg to agree to *Anschluss* grew in intensity until the early part of 1938. After a particularly volatile propaganda campaign, von Schuschnigg called for a

Mussolini, Hitler, and Chamberlain signed the Munich Pact in 1938, allowing the German annexation of Czechoslovakia. After returning to England from Munich, Chamberlain announced that he had achieved "peace in our time." He was quickly proven wrong.

national referendum on union, scheduled for 13 March. Although the forces of union would likely have won a free vote, Hitler would not risk embarrassment and so sent his forces into Austria the day before the referendum. Not quite six months later, Czechoslovakia was to feel the brunt of forced annexation.

CZECHOSLOVAKIA

Three million Germans out of a total Czechoslovakian population of fifteen million lived in Bohemia and Moravia. They were a reasonably compact group that could easily be detached from Czechoslovakia. Hitler based his public policy of "repatriation" of the Sudetenland on the principle of self-determination. This was accepted as reasonable by most of the world's political leaders. It was not only Germany that wanted to reorder Europe's eastern boundaries. All the successor states desired an exchange of minorities and a revision of their boundaries. For example, Hungary wanted its 600 000 nationals back from Slovakia, and Poland had an eye on the Czech industrial region around Teschen.

Czechoslovakia was the cornerstone of the French security system. It was the strongest member of the Little Entente that, along with France in the west, was supposed to contain German expansion in Central Europe. Czechoslovakia's modern army was well-trained and well-equipped compared to Germany's forces, if not in fact superior. It stood behind extensive defence works that stretched back from the western mountains to Prague. However, Czechoslovakia was not to be given the chance to test its defences.

Konrad Henlein was the leader of the Nazi party in Czechoslovakia. On the directions of Berlin he mounted a noisy propaganda campaign for Sudeten independence. The complaints that Germans in Czechoslovakia were being denied government positions because of their background held enough truth to make other complaints of discrimination plausible. Henlein was ordered by Hitler to make his demands so outrageous that the Czechoslovakian president, Eduard Beneš, could not possibly accept them and would thus give Germany a pretext for intervention.

Alarmed at the possibility of a general war, France, which had treaty commitments to defend Czechoslovakia against attack, and Britain urged the Czechs to negotiate a settlement. Beneš was afraid that if autonomy were granted to the German minority, all the state's other minorities would make the same demands; soon there would be no state left. Informed that Britain and France would not stand behind him, Beneš was forced to accept German annexation of the Sudetenland.

During September 1938, British prime minister Chamberlain flew to the continent to meet with Hitler at Berchtesgaden, Godesberg, and finally Munich in efforts to solve the Czech problem and avoid a great-power war. Thinking he had reached a solution at Berchtesgaden, he returned to Godesberg to find Hitler had expanded his demands to include new demands of Poland and Hungary on the Czech state. Outraged at this duplicity, the Czechs proclaimed martial law, France put its forces on the alert, and Britain mobilized its battle fleets. Yet it seemed to some people the height of folly to begin a war over the matter.

At the last moment, Mussolini was prevailed upon to chair an emergency meeting at Munich to which the Czechs were not invited. At Munich it was agreed that German forces would move in to occupy the Sudetenland and other regions where the population was more than 50 per cent German. The Czechs would give up their western defences and withdraw their armies. The dismemberment of Czechoslovakia has been judged in hindsight as a betrayal of a smaller nation by the major powers that had agreed to defend it. At the time, however, the Munich agreement was celebrated as a diplomatic solution to avert war. Poland seized Teschen in October; and the next year, in March 1939, Slovakia proclaimed its independence as a German protectorate. The rest of what was Czechoslovakia was quickly gobbled up by its neighbours.

It was the hope of the democracies that Hitler had achieved his goals and would now give up his expansionist drive. **Appeasement** was seen as a valid instrument of negotiation, but the problem was that Hitler could not be appeased. The question raised after Munich was, Did the policy of self-determination apply to all the other minorities in Europe? Germany and Italy agreed to join France and Britain in guaranteeing the boundaries of Central Europe, but only after the Polish and Hungarian borders had been revised.

POLAND

Hitler wanted to deal with Poland prior to his attack on France. The usual complaints were orchestrated by the Germans in Danzig and in the Polish corridor; but Poland would not agree to negotiate the status of these regions. Britain and France, realizing Hitler would not be stopped by appeasement, had changed their pacifist policies and were now resolved to fight. Both democracies rushed to ready their armed forces for battle. At the end of March, Britain began to implement conscription and readied its battle fleets. Both nations then offered mutual defence treaties to all the nations of Central Europe. Although they had no way of giving direct aid, the public offer of alliance was thought to be enough to deter Hitler. The pretext no longer mattered. They had decided on war, should Germany act.

Hitler had to move before the autumn rains made mechanized warfare difficult. His principal concern in invading Poland was the reaction of Joseph Stalin. Stalin had been toying with an alliance with either Germany or the democracies. The previous months had shown Britain and France unwilling to fight. An alliance with Germany, however, meant forgiving Hitler's extermination of the German Communist party in 1934. All that aside, Germany was prepared to reorder the eastern boundaries and the democracies were not. Stalin wanted to reclaim those regions lost in 1918, and a German alliance appeared the better way of doing so. There was the danger that Hitler intended to make the Soviet Union his next victim; but when Stalin learned from Karl Sorge, his spy in Tokyo, that Hitler intended to strike west after Poland, he relaxed his guard. Threatened by Japan, Stalin did not want a two-front war. On 23 August 1939 Stalin shocked the world when he agreed to a non-aggression pact with his archenemy, Germany. Together, the Soviet Union and Germany would impose their spheres of influence on the successor states.

The Nazi-Soviet pact assured Germany of a controlled situation in the east. The Soviets would not come to the aid of Poland, but would share in its dismemberment. On the night of 31 August, bodies in Polish uniforms were scattered about the base of the radio tower at Gleiwitz. Claiming that Polish forces had attacked across the border, Hitler used the charade to justify his invasion the next day. On 3 September Britain and France declared war. Now, three of the industrial powers were involved as the Second World War began. The Polish forces did not stand a chance against Germany's mechanized armies. On 25 September, Warsaw was bombed, and on 5 October, Hitler visited the city. Poland had succumbed. Stalin took the opportunity to strike at Poland from the east on 17 September, assuring the Soviets of their agreed share of the spoils. By the end of 1939, Soviet forces had regained most of the western *irredenta*, although the Soviets' invasion of Finland resulted in their expulsion from the League of Nations.

SUMMARY

The first years of Hitler's administration were frenzied. His plans for a thousand year Reich based on the concepts of racial purity and economic autarky were greeted with enthusiasm by most of the German public. Government by decree, and the use of force to end civic unrest and bring order out of chaos, won applause from many other nations. The New Order called for the expansion of Germany's borders to secure required resources and living space for a growing population. Targeted peoples were excluded from the planning: they were to be identified, concentrated in ghettos, and then removed from the Reich. The other nations were to be given their place in the economic reorganization of the continent around the needs of a German industrial heartland. Hitler embarked on a grand strategy of public works funded through barter and deficit financing.

The Spanish Civil War (1936-1939) embroiled the great powers in debate. The people of Britain and France were reluctant to embark on another war and stayed out of what they saw as a domestic civil war. Germany and Italy gave active support to the Spanish army under General Franco, ensuring his victory. Soviet involvement on the Republican side was an effort to convince Britain and France to re-establish the Triple Entente against the growth of German power. Soviet officers commanded the international brigades and later the Republican army. When the hoped-for defence agreements with Britain and France were not forthcoming, the Soviet Union abandoned the Republican forces to their fate.

The unwillingness of the democracies to intervene in Spain resulted in Hitler's pursuit of an expansionist policy in Central Europe. The annexation of Austria, the dismemberment of Czechoslovakia, and the invasion of Poland were the immediate causes of the Second World War.

QUESTIONS

1. Explain Hitler's New Order.

2. How would implementation of the New Order affect the various peoples of Europe?

3. What were the Nuremberg Decrees? How did they affect the German people?

4. Describe the causes and results of *Kristallnacht*.

5. Explain the significance of the Hossbach document.

6. Why did Britain and France fail to act against the resurgence of German power?

7. Explain the significance of the Anti-Comintern Pact.

8. Describe the opposing sides in the Spanish Civil War.

9. Explain the international involvement in the Spanish Civil War. What was the result?

10. How did Hitler gain control of Austria?

11. Why did Britain and France allow Hitler to annex the Sudetenland of Czechoslovakia?

12. Why did Stalin sign a pact with Hitler in August 1939?

13. Give the terms and the significance of the Nazi-Soviet pact of 23 August 1939.

CRITICAL ANALYSIS

1. Nation-states claim sovereignty by mutual agreement and precedent. Are there grounds for intervention in the domestic affairs of another state? What forms can intervention take?

2. The German quest for autarky and industrialization touched off two world wars. Was Germany's desire for industrial strength valid?

3. Are ethnic boundaries the solution to the minority question?

4. Is appeasement a valid strategy? Explain.

5. How did the popular mood in Britain and France affect the power balance in Europe between 1934 and 1939? Should the people at large be fully informed of all aspects of foreign-relation negotiations?

6. How can governments ensure that the will of the people is (a) legitimate and (b) correct?

RESEARCH PROJECTS

1. Research the role of women in Nazi Germany and evaluate their position by comparison to the pre-Nazi period.

2. Trace the roots of anti-Semitism in Europe. Identify those areas of Europe that sanctioned anti-Semitism and describe how Jews were treated in one of the following countries: (a) France, (b) Poland, (c) Hungary, (d) Austria, (e) Canada, (f) United States, (g) others.

3. Trace the background of one of the following individuals: (a) Göring, (b) Himmler, (c) Heydrich, (d) Röhm. Describe the role he played in Hitler's Reich.

ACTIVITIES

1 Trial
Establish a mock trial in which you bring a Nazi war criminal to justice. Structure the charge and then assign judge, jury, prosecution lawyer, and defence lawyer. Research the issue, balancing the necessity to punish perpetrators of crimes-against-humanity with the necessity of obeying the laws and orders of superiors.

2 Map
On a large map of Europe, place concentration-camp locations and the transportation links with the prisoners' country of origin.

3 Debate
Be it resolved that the Second World War was inevitable.

HISTORICAL ANALYSIS

CAUSES OF THE SECOND WORLD WAR

In the early hours of 1 September 1939, Germany attacked Poland. Hitler's aim was not only to reclaim, but to expand the German border of 1914. In attacking Poland, Hitler understood that he was risking war with other major powers, notably Britain and France.

The following quotations provide insight into the causes of the Second World War. Compare and contrast the views presented by these world leaders on the origins of the Second World War.

1. *The aim of restoring the borders of 1914 is insufficient from a national viewpoint, unsatisfactory from a military viewpoint, and mad from the viewpoint of its consequences...*
   —Hitler-from his Second Book, 1928.

2. *There never was an easier war to stop by timely action. It could have been prevented without firing a single shot. Softness invites aggression...*
   —Churchill-from an address at Fulton, Missouri on 5 March 1946.

3. *It would be incorrect to think that the war arose accidentally or as the fault of some statesman. The war arose out of the inevitable result of the development of world economic forces on the basis of imperialist capitalism...*
   —Stalin-on Radio Moscow, 9 February 1946.

Some historians suggest that the Second World War was a natural consequence of the First World War. Evaluate this suggestion on the basis of the following information:

1. The Treaty of Versailles unjustly punished Germany and did not resolve the problem of German domination of Central Europe. As Clémenceau predicted, it provided a truce between campaigns.

2. After the First World War, political problems predominated in the newly-created states. German foreign policy was driven by the desire to reclaim power and prestige.

3. When German inflation soared out of control in 1923, the Dawes Plan stabilized German currency, provided credit, and established a payment structure which was viable for Germany. In 1929, the Young Plan arranged a further reduction in payment. In 1931, the Hoover Moratorium called for a cessation of payment for one year. The Lausanne Conference terminated the reparations issue. Sources suggest that Germany received more money in foreign loans than it paid out in reparations over this period.

4. In 1925, at Locarno, Germany agreed to the security of its western boundaries and indicated agreement on its eastern boundaries once they were revised to accommodate the 19 million people of ethnic minorities in Central Europe.

5. The Great Depression of 1929 plunged the world into economic collapse and dashed hopes of international peace. Appeasement and collaboration characterized the 1930s and prepared the way for conflict.

Consider the following questions as you make your analysis:

a. How did ethnic problems in Central Europe contribute to instability?

b. What role did international leaders play in the causes of the Second World War?

c. How did economic instability contribute to the climate for war?

THE SOVIET UNION & THE UNITED STATES
1917–1941

CHAPTER 5

SOVIET UNION TIME LINE

22 January	1905:	Bloody Sunday
27 February	1917:	Provisional government established in Russia
2 March	1917:	Nicholas II abdicated
25 October	1917:	Bolshevik revolution
3 March	1918:	Treaty of Brest-Litovsk
	1919:	Third Comintern established
1917 - 1920:		War Communism
	1921:	New Economic Policy instituted
April	1922:	Treaty of Rapallo
January	1924:	Lenin died
	1928:	First Five Year Plan
1929 - 1933:		Collectivization of agriculture
18 September	1934:	Soviet Union joined the League of Nations
2 May	1935:	Treaty of mutual assistance made between France and the Soviet Union
16 May	1935:	Soviet Union and Czechoslovakia form treaty of mutual assistance
	1936:	Great Purge began
23 August	1939:	Nazi-Soviet pact
April	1941:	Soviet-Japanese neutrality pact
22 June	1941:	Hitler invades the Soviet Union

UNITED STATES TIME LINE

	1898:	Spanish-American War
1919 - 1933:		Prohibition
	1921:	Washington Naval Conference
	1924:	Dawes Plan
	1928:	US recognition of government of Chiang Kai-shek
	1929:	Young Plan
29 October	1929:	Black Tuesday—stock market crash
	1929:	Beginning of the Great Depression
	1930:	London Naval Conference
	1931:	Hoover Moratorium
3 March	1933:	New Deal announced
9 March-16 June	1933:	Roosevelt's Hundred Days
	1935:	US Neutrality Act
November	1939:	Cash and Carry
September	1940:	Destroyers for bases
March	1941:	Lend-Lease Act
7 December	1941:	Pearl Harbor bombed by the Japanese

FOCUS ON DIPLOMACY

There never was in the whole world such a powerful and authoritarian regime as our Soviet regime, and there has never been such a powerful authoritarian party as our Bolshevik Party. If gross and unpardonable mistakes have been made ... it is wrong and very unjust to blame the peasants. The guilt is entirely ours.

Soviet leader Joseph Stalin, in a speech to the Central Committee of the USSR, Moscow, 17 January 1933.

You are a Soviet diplomat and your friend is an American diplomat. You are having dinner together in early 1942. You are discussing your respective countries' policies regarding Japan. Describe the conversation.

The test of our progress is not whether we have provided too much for those who already have abundance, but to provide enough for those who have too little.

American president Franklin Roosevelt in his inaugural address, Washington, 20 January 1937.

OVERVIEW

In the decades between the First and Second World Wars, the Soviet Union and the United States pursued similar goals of domestic development. The Soviet Union dealt with the collapse of the Romanov dynasty, the Bolshevik coup, civil war, the New Economic Policy, Stalin's agricultural and industrial policies, and Soviet foreign policy. The United States concentrated on domestic development followed by the Great Depression, the New Deal, and American foreign policy.

PRE-REVOLUTIONARY RUSSIA
The Romanov dynasty collapsed in the face of civil unrest and economic chaos after its defeat by Japan and its devastation during the First World War.

RUSSIAN REVOLUTION
The Bolsheviks seized power in October of 1917 after the summer of political instability which followed the abdication of the Romanovs in March 1917.

WAR COMMUNISM: 1917–1921
Civil war raged for the first three years of the new Bolshevik state. After defeating Royalist forces in 1920, the Red Army had to subdue nationalist unrest and the Polish army before the Soviet Union was consolidated in 1922.

THE NEW ECONOMIC POLICY
Food shortages in the new Soviet state led to the introduction of economic incentives.

LENIN'S DEATH AND THE ENSUING POWER STRUGGLE
Lenin's death in 1924 was followed by a power struggle. Joseph Stalin eventually emerged as undisputed leader.

COLLECTIVIZATION OF AGRICULTURE
In order to feed industrial labour, agriculture was collectivized by creating both state and collective farms.

INDUSTRIALIZATION
Stalin implemented a series of Five Year Plans beginning in 1928 which revolutionized industry in the Soviet Union.

SOVIET FOREIGN POLICY
Initial failure to forge an association with Western powers resulted in the Nazi-Soviet pact of 1939. The invasion of the Soviet Union in 1941, however, brought about the Grand Alliance of the Soviet Union, Great Britain, and the United States.

THE UNITED STATES
During the first half of the twentieth century, the United States evolved into a major industrial power rivaling that of European and Asian nations.

DOMESTIC GROWTH
The United States experienced phenomenal economic growth resulting in a high standard of living for its citizens until the stock market crashed in 1929.

THE GREAT DEPRESSION
Millions of Americans suffered unemployment as the economy suffered the effects of the stock market crash and disruption of global trade.

THE NEW DEAL
In order to counteract the effects of the depression Roosevelt implemented numerous government programs designed to stimulate the economy and provide employment.

FOREIGN POLICY
The United States's attempts to remain isolated were challenged by the militarism of fascist governments. Japan's attack on Pearl Harbor and Germany's declaration of war on the United States in 1941 effectively ended the United States's isolationism.

PRE-REVOLUTIONARY RUSSIA

In the half century before the Second World War, tsarist Russia had channeled its energies into Asia. The Trans-Siberian Railway, begun in 1891, would ensure Russian dominance in the Pacific. The Russians had long coveted Lüshun (Port Arthur) as a warm-water naval station that could dominate Huang Hai (Yellow Sea). The Russian presence in Manchuria could provide minerals essential to industrial development, and the timber concessions along the Yalu River promised a Russian-dominated Korea.

Russia's plans for a Pacific empire were thwarted by the Japanese, who also sought possession of the physical wealth of Korea and Manchuria for their

Tsar Nicholas II and his wife, Alexandra, were the last of the Romanov dynasty. They are shown here with four of their children some years before the revolution which cost them their lives.

own industrial needs. In 1904 and 1905, the Japanese attacked the Russian positions on the Asian mainland, determined to establish their own sphere of influence. The victorious Japanese claimed Lüshun, seized economic concessions in Manchuria, and took Korea as a protectorate (annexed in 1910).

The Russo-Japanese War was a humiliating experience for the Romanov dynasty. Never before had a non-Western nation defeated one of the great European powers. The defeat was to have a devastating effect on the tsarist regime. The regime's political authority was undermined and it could no longer ignore the growing cries for political change.

From Bloody Sunday on 22 January to 30 October 1905, Russia was wracked by labour strife and political dissension, most of which could be attributed to the war losses. On Bloody Sunday, workers led by Father Gapon marched on the Winter Palace in Saint Petersburg to make their demands known to the tsar. In the resultant melee, shots were fired and a number of workers killed. This touched off a season of unrest among the workers in the major cities. The labour unrest was only temporarily quelled when the tsar agreed to the formation of a representative *Duma.* This vehicle of self-government was hindered at every step by tsarist officials. In the next decade, strikes and work stoppages escalated until tens of thousands of labour demonstrations occurred each year. By 1914, the domestic economy was having serious economic problems.

Industrialization had made Russia the fourth major power in the world in terms of industrial output. However, only 1.75 per cent of Russia's population was employed in factories. A majority of the population was still employed in agriculture. In addition, foreign ownership, particularly of mining, oil extraction, and chemical industries, gave Russia the dubious distinction of having the largest foreign debt in the world. Textiles and food-processing were the only two areas predominantly in Russian hands. This situation, coupled with foreign ownership of mineral resources, suggested an immature economy. Technologically behind other industrial nations such as Great Britain or Germany, Russia exported agricultural products and imported manufactured goods.

These critical shortcomings in the domestic economy coupled with the outbreak of the First World War led to revolutionary change in 1917. The Romanov dynasty was overthrown and a provisional government was established on 27 February 1917 to manage the affairs of the state until elections could be held in October. Unable to find immediate solutions to the domestic crisis and at the same time manage the war, the provisional government was brushed aside when Vladimir Ilyich Lenin and his Bolshevik followers seized power in October.

RUSSIAN REVOLUTION

The problems that led to the revolution in Russia were rooted in the inability of the Romanov dynasty to deal effectively with the economic and social changes demanded by a newly industrializing state. Reforms such as progressive labour legislation and safety standards in factories were

BIOGRAPHY

TSARINA ALEXANDRA
(1872-1918)

Life is difficult to understand—tak i nado—

poterpi [so it must be, have patience] that's all one

can say.

Alexandra to Nicholas, 27 October 1914

Born Princess Alix of Hesse-Darmstadt on 6 June 1872, Alexandra Fyodorovna, wife of Nicholas Romanov, last tsar of Russia, has generated intense interest before and since the execution of her and her family in 1918. Because she came from Germany, and because her father was German Prince Louis of Hesse, Alexandra was known as the German tsarina. She was, however, more British than German in her thinking and education and could more rightly have been called the English empress.

Alexandra had a strong sense of self and of duty. Key to Alexandra's psyche were her fatalism—as illustrated by the initial quotation taken from her 27 October 1914 letter to Nicholas—her faith in God, and her emotionalism. Having grown up a devout Lutheran, Alexandra was totally distraught when, shortly after her confirmation, and due to her upcoming marriage to Nicholas, she was required to change to the Orthodox religion. Although, at the time, this seemed an unbearably hypocritical alteration, Alexandra eventually took to this oldest version of Christianity with great relish, holding onto her belief in a personal relationship with God while at the same time combining it with a veneration of Russian saints and icons, and an avid exploration of Russian mysticism.

Alexandra regarded emotions as God's tool for guiding people and therefore constantly encouraged Nicholas to listen to his heart. Grigoriy Rasputin (1871-1916), Russian mystic, peasant, and close confidant of the tsarina, exuded a compelling charismatic spirituality. In spite of Rasputin's lack of formal education and almost total illiteracy, the tsarina pressed her husband, and through him all of Russia, to listen to the "God-wisdom" of this self-styled *strannik* or holy man. Among Rasputin's beliefs was the belief that constitutional reform was a danger to Russia and undesirable on every count. This conviction suited Nicholas and Alexandra's own conservative instincts. Just before the Russian Revolution, Alexandra asserted that "All true Russians" see a constitution as "Russia's ruin."

Alexandra was disgusted by the idle decadence of high society—expressing disdain for the hedonism of some of Nicholas's own cousins and brothers—and instead chose to dedicate her own energies, and direct the energies of her four daughters and hemophiliac son, toward serving others. Because of her moralistic way of keeping to herself, Alexandra eventually came to be perceived by the Russian upper class as cold and haughty, a belief which helped to turn much of public opinion against the tsar and his family.

Besides the needlework that she is often pictured doing in photographs, Alexandra and her daughters worked with the sick, her daughters as volunteers and Alexandra as a studied and qualified war nurse. One of Alexandra's friends is recorded as having said that "suffering always made a strong appeal with the Empress." In keeping with Orthodox beliefs, Alexandra felt that suffering would bring the sufferers closer to God. Therefore, she viewed the First World War as a kind of holy war, not because of the political or economic outcomes that it would bring about, but because it would purge humanity, thereby clarifying humanity's vision. ●

ignored. The industry of agriculture still directly employed in excess of 80 per cent of the population. Most farmers worked with poor soil, little or no fertilizer, and wooden plows. Agricultural production could not keep pace with the population, which increased by 61 million people between 1890 and 1914. Clinging to an autocratic mode of government and unwilling to delegate authority to the *Duma,* the Romanovs refused to enact the changes needed to save their dynasty. Then, at a critical juncture, the economy was devastated by the heavy losses of the First World War. Inadequate rail transportation meant that when the railroads were used to move troops, food shortages resulted in the cities. Russian soldiers were ill-equipped to fight the superior German forces, and 4 million Russians died during the first year of the war alone.

In 1915, Tsar Nicholas II dismissed the *Duma* and personally took control of the armed forces, intent on leading them to victory. Now he had no one to blame for the army losses but himself. His wife, the tsarina Alexandra, was left in charge of the imperial government at home. She was strongly influenced by a mystic named Rasputin, to whom she attributed healing powers for her hemophiliac son, Alexis, heir to the throne. Rasputin virtually controlled the government through her, and scandalous dealings characterized the workings of the executive. In December 1916, a right-wing group dedicated to saving the Romanov dynasty assassinated Rasputin, hoping to prevent opposition from becoming revolution.

At this time, Germany took advantage of Russia's internal dissension by encouraging independence movements in Ukraine, Poland, and Finland. It also gave support to Russian revolutionaries (including Lenin) in the hope of causing internal collapse and forcing Russia out of the war.

The crisis came in 1917 after particularly severe battle losses and the desertion of over 2 million men. Between 23 February and 26 February 1917, shortages of bread and coal caused riots and demonstrations in the streets of Saint Petersburg (which the tsar had patriotically "Slavicized" as "Petrograd"). Although Nicholas II was still away at the front, the presence of 160 000 troops in the capital seemed to ensure its safety. However, after an initial attempt by senior officers to gain control, the battalions began fraternizing with the demonstrators. When the Cossacks, the most reliable arm of the imperial forces, went over to the people and helped give out food and raid granaries, the regime was doomed. Tsarist officials went into hiding and the people turned to the *Duma* for leadership. On 27 February 1917 the *Duma* established a provisional government. Although the Temporary Committee wanted to preserve the monarchy as a symbol of authority, the people favoured abdication. Thus, on 2 March 1917 Nicholas II abdicated both for himself and for his son Alexis, in favour of his brother, Michael. The following day, Michael refused the crown, and Russia became a republic.

In the *Duma,* liberals of the Constitutional Democrats party or "Kadets" dominated the administration. Prince Georgi Lvov became the first prime minister. The only Social Revolutionary was Aleksandr Kerensky, minister of justice. This new provisional government was supported by the Petrograd **Soviet**, a self-declared city government of workers and revolutionaries. However, dissension between the two bodies soon developed over continued Russian involvement in the war. Lvov maintained that Russia must not conclude a unilateral peace but rather must hold firm to its international obligations. The Triple Entente supported this position, and promised the Bosphorus and the Dardanelles straits to the Russians if Russia stayed in the war. The government decided to stay at war, but the Petrograd Soviet scorned this imperialist ambition and organized anti-war demonstrations that eventually brought down the Lvov government in May.

The new government, called the First Coalition, resulted from a union of all parties except the Bolsheviks. It retained Lvov as prime minister and appointed Kerensky minister of war. The coalition continued the Russian involvement in the war and launched an offensive at the end of June. The disastrous results of this campaign discredited the government and opened the door for Lenin and the Bolsheviks. Huge demonstrations on 3 and 4 July 1917 very nearly tipped the balance of power in the Bolsheviks' favour. The government, however, accused Lenin of being a German agent. Bolshevik presses were smashed, and Lenin fled to Finland while his chief aide, Leon Trotsky, was imprisoned.

The Second Coalition took office on 24 July with Kerensky as prime minister. Now, in addition to opposition from left-wing factions, the government was beset by right-wing groups that objected to its inability to control the army. The turning point in the dispute between the coalition and the local soviet was the Kornilov Affair. General Kornilov, commander-in-chief of the armies, was a conservative who disapproved of the soviet and worked out an agreement with Kerensky to dispatch troops to Petrograd

Front line at armistice, 5 December 1917

Ceded by Bolshevik government to Germany by the Treaty of Brest–Litovsk, 3 March 1918

Occupied by Germany 1918

Occupied by Austria 1918

Occupied by Romania 1918

to destroy it. Kornilov's intentions regarding the provisional government are less clear, but it is likely he wanted to purge it of radical elements. Acting as mediator between Kerensky and Kornilov, Lvov attempted to have Kornilov replace Kerensky as prime minister, with Kerensky remaining in the cabinet. Kerensky, however, feared that the government would be overthrown and appealed to the people to save the revolution from Kornilov. He garnered enough support to gain control of the army, then arrested Lvov and dismissed Kornilov. The right-wing factions felt Kornilov had been betrayed, while the left-wing factions felt the government had plotted with Kornilov to destroy them.

The Bolsheviks were prepared to take advantage of this split within the *Duma*. Bolsheviks dominated the Petrograd and Moscow soviets, and Lenin moved to seize power. On 25 October 1917 (7 November on the new calendar) strategic locations in Petrograd, including the Winter Palace, were stormed by Red Bolshevik troops. Members of the provisional government were arrested and soviet authority was established.

Lenin promised peace to the Russian people, but it proved a difficult promise to keep. Russia paid a large price for peace at the signing of the Treaty of Brest-Litovsk.

The provisional government had failed in spite of much progressive legislation. The government had given political prisoners amnesty, abolished capital punishment, granted the right to strike, and removed restrictions based on class, nationality, or religion. However, inability to solve agrarian discontent by redistribution of land, and the continuation of an unpopular and seemingly hopeless war, led to economic and social breakdown. The charismatic personality of Lenin, and his promise of bread, land, and peace, proved attractive to a population impatient for change. Lenin promised to distribute gentry land to the peasants, give control of the factories to the workers, and take Russia out of the war. These promises brought the popular support necessary for the Bolshevik seizure of power in 1917.

Soldiers and workers took part in massive demonstrations under the leadership of the Bolsheviks. This protest occurred on 18 June 1917 in Petrograd.

WAR COMMUNISM: 1917-1921

The first four years of Lenin's government were fraught with challenges, as civil war raged between the monarchy's supporters and the Bolsheviks. Lenin's leadership emanated from his charisma and his conviction that he must exercise complete control.

One of Lenin's most significant promises had been to take Russia out of the war. Peace, however, proved to be much more difficult to achieve and immensely more costly than Lenin had calculated. The Germans first offered draconian peace terms in December, and Trotsky, minister of foreign affairs, rejected them. Trotsky was determined to forge a peace treaty that would spare Russia loss of territory. When the German terms were rejected, the German army launched a new offensive in February 1918, an offensive the Russian army could not stem.

Lenin was determined to have peace at any cost, however, and in the face of the German advance was now able to persuade hold-outs in his own party to accept the German terms. The Treaty of Brest-Litovsk was signed on 3 March 1918. By its terms, the Soviet government would lose 60 million people, as Ukraine, Poland, Finland, Lithuania, Estonia, and Latvia received their independence. Some 26 per cent of the railway system, 33 per cent of the manufacturing industries, 73 per cent of the iron industries, and 75 per cent of the coal fields were confiscated in the settlement. However, the new Soviet government was not in any position to fight the German army. As disastrous as it appeared, the treaty probably saved the Bolshevik administration.

Lenin's promise of land to the peasants was fulfilled by his abolition of all private ownership, making land the property of the whole nation. Local soviets were instructed to establish collective farms. However, the peasants were more interested in keeping the fruits of their labour than in enjoying land ownership. When the government forcibly requisitioned the harvest in order to feed the cities, the peasants resisted in a number of ways. Cultivated areas dropped by 40 per cent in three years. The black market absorbed the bulk of farm produce, with 60 per cent of city bread distributed through illegal channels. By April 1920, only 29 per cent of all food was distributed through the official government system. Serious food shortages now affected industrial labour, and strikes ensued. Between 1918 and 1920, 7.5 million people perished from starvation, disease, and the ravages of civil war. Nationalization and agricultural coercion had thrown the country into chaos.

Civil war continued to rage, as royalist supporters attempted to wrest control from the Bolsheviks. Foreign intervention only added to the misery. The allies (British, Canadians, French, Japanese, Americans) landed at Vladivostok, and the British, Canadians, and the Americans seized Archangel. These landings were an attempt to retrieve large supplies of war *matériel* shipped to the Russians before the revolution. The new Soviet government had accepted no financial responsibility for the goods they had seized, although they were no longer part of the war effort against Germany. The allies also hoped to re-establish the second front against the Germans in the east, and needed the supplies sitting in Russian ports. The allied intervention was interpreted as hostile toward the Soviet government, even though military confrontation was largely avoided. By 1920, all allied troops, with the exception of the Japanese, had departed. Japan pulled out the last of its troops in 1922.

The civil war pitted the Red Bolshevik Army organized by Trotsky against the White Army, a collection of monarchists, Kadets, Social Revolutionaries, and right-wing groups whose only attitude in common was their opposition to the Red Army. The White Army could not agree on a program for Russia nor on a supreme commander. They were thus no match for Trotsky's well-disciplined forces. Perhaps the White Army's biggest problems were its inability to gain the support of the peasantry, coupled with its inability to change the common perception that it stood for tsarist autocracy and the landed gentry. In addition, its reliance on allied support branded it as treasonable. The Red Army emerged victorious in 1920. It then had to subdue nationalist uprisings and defend itself in a war against Poland, neither of which conflicts threatened the existence of the Soviet government itself. In 1922, the nation-state of Russia became the Union of Soviet Socialist Republics (USSR).

THE NEW ECONOMIC POLICY

War Communism and civil war from 1917 until 1920 devastated the economy. Food shortages, strikes, and riots characterized the cities. In March 1921, the Kronstadt naval base rebelled against Communist rule and demanded free soviets and a constituent assembly.

Even though this rebellion was soon suppressed by the Red Army, it indicated very serious dissatisfaction with Bolshevik rule. Lenin recognized that change must occur, and that consumer goods were needed immediately. He proposed to rejuvenate the economy with the **New Economic Policy (NEP)**, through a return to individual economic initiative and the profit motive. He presented the NEP as a temporary measure to introduce elements of private enterprise in small industry (plants employing less than 20 persons) and the retail trade. Peasants would be taxed, but they would be allowed to keep all produce in excess of the tax as an incentive to increase production. By 1928, the economy had recovered its pre-war strength. However, the social results of the NEP were a threat to the Communists, who disapproved of class distinctions. There was a dramatic increase in the number of "Nepmen" or small businesspeople in towns and of kulaks or prosperous peasants in villages. Official limitations on their numbers were introduced, and they would soon be dealt with harshly in the collectivization of agriculture.

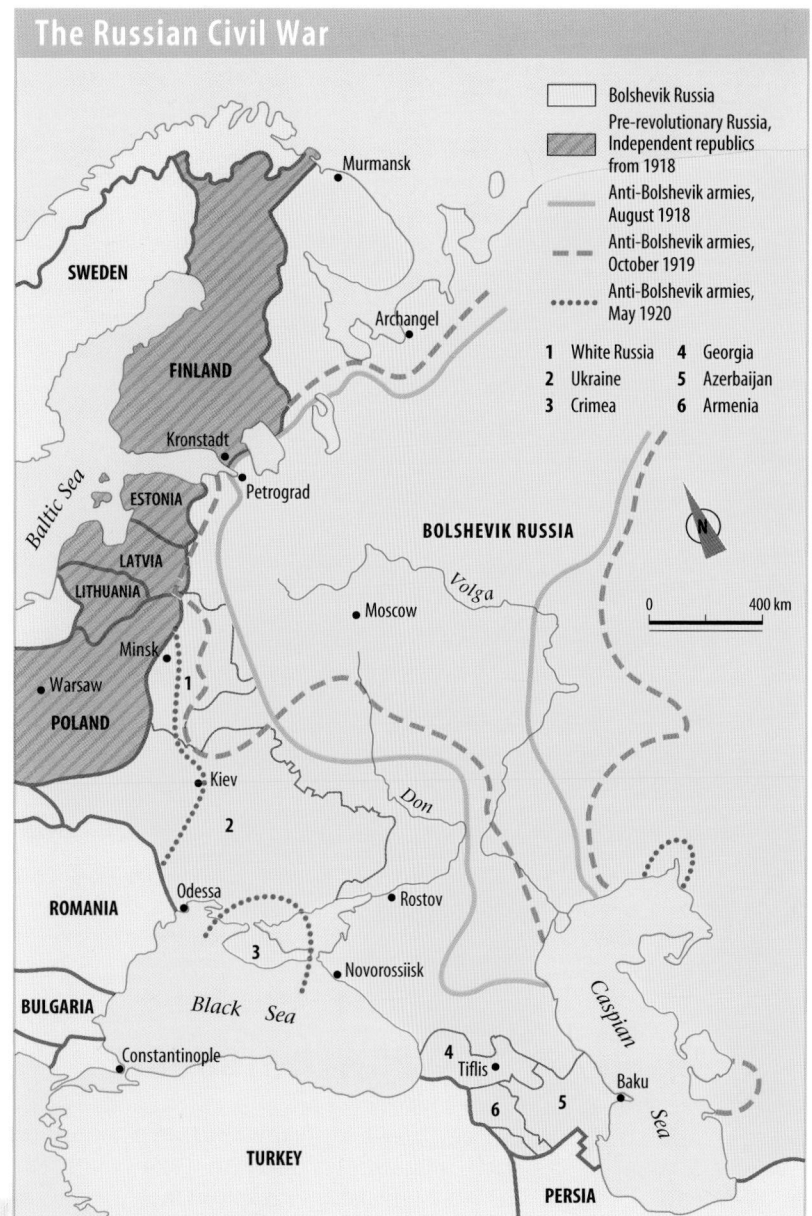

This map illustrates the erosion of the anti-Bolshevik forces during the civil war in Russia, from August 1918 to May 1920.

Vladimir Ilyich Lenin led his country into massive reforms. He is considered one of the greatest revolutionaries of all time.

LENIN'S DEATH AND THE ENSUING POWER STRUGGLE

A power struggle ensued within the Communist party after Lenin's death in 1924. Lenin had suffered a stroke after the Congress meeting in 1922, and never returned to lead the government effectively. Three basic ideological positions had emerged in the meantime.

The left-wing of the party maintained that socialism depended on world-wide revolution. The most vocal and influential supporter of this position was Trotsky. He viewed the New Economic Policy as a betrayal of communist ideology and wanted to continue a militant and socialist policy at home as well as to promote revolution abroad. Without the spread of socialism abroad, Trotsky felt that socialism in the USSR was doomed.

The right-wing of the party agreed that world revolution was ultimately essential, but it did not feel the same sense of urgency. Nikolai Bukharin, an influential Bolshevik thinker, was in favour of the New Economic Policy as a stop-gap measure to save Soviet socialism.

Between these two positions, the centre contended that whether or not world revolution occurred, socialism could be built in one country. Joseph Stalin saw the pragmatism of this approach and called for the Soviet Union to develop socialism within its borders and take a leading role in the spread of communist ideology.

Ultimately, then, it was a combination of the appeal of the centre position and Stalin's dynamic personality and his Machiavellian power politics that secured Stalin's control of the party. He promised power and prestige for the Soviet Union without the problems posed by fostering international revolution. Although Russian peasants did not favour communism, Stalin would force them to conform in order to fulfil his goal of "socialism in one country."

Trotsky, by contrast, felt that without peasant support, communism could not work. The key to communist revolution, he thought, lay in the revolt of Western industrial workers. Since the West did not contain enough seeds of revolt, Trotsky's dream of a world-wide socialist revolution was premature or perhaps ill-conceived.

The most serious challenger to Stalin for leadership, Trotsky was exiled in 1929, and murdered in Mexico on Stalin's instruction in 1940. Bukharin attempted to gain support in the Politburo (Political Bureau) for the rightist position; but Stalin successfully isolated Bukharin and his primary supporters, Tomsky and Rykov. By 1930, all three had been ejected from the Politburo. All of Stalin's rivals had been defeated.

COLLECTIVIZATION OF AGRICULTURE

The **collectivization** of agriculture was thought essential to the development of a socialist state. Economies of scale and mechanization would lead to increased yields that could feed the cities and release large numbers of workers for labour in industrial plants. Agriculture was, however, secondary to industry. It was viewed as a support for industrial activity. Farm workers suffered living standards considerably lower than their industrial colleagues. Many therefore fled to the cities where they sought industrial employment.

Two types of farms were devised during the collectivist period. The state farm can be likened to an agricultural factory operated by peasant labour, individuals who worked for a wage. Any losses in farming operations were borne by the state. The collective farm, on the other hand, rewarded labour for its input. A tax was paid to the state, overhead was also covered by earnings, and any surplus was divided on the basis of the amount of labour provided by each worker. The surplus was usually negligible, however, because market prices were strictly controlled. The collective workers were allowed to maintain small private plots (0.25-0.5 hectares) plus a limited amount of livestock. Workers on collective farms had some obvious advantages over workers on state farms.

The collectivization of farms was engineered with brutality. The class struggle which Lenin had tried in vain to sponsor in the villages in 1918 would now be forced on them. The rich peasants, or kulaks, would be destroyed and the poor peasants would emerge victorious.

A kulak was defined as a farmer who owned property valued at the equivalent of at least $800, and who hired labour for 50 days out of the year. About 5 per cent of Soviet farmers fell into this category. Kulaks were deemed to be unfit for collective farms, as their independence was unlikely to contribute to socialist production. No longer allowed to continue farming privately, they were forced out of Ukraine, long known as the USSR's breadbasket, into Siberia or Central Asia. About 5 million kulaks "disappeared."

This repression was to serve as a example to the peasants. Resistance to collectivization would not be tolerated. However, between 1929 and 1933 peasant resistance to collectivization took the form of wholesale slaughter of livestock. Roughly 50 per cent of all horses, cattle, sheep, goats, and hogs were destroyed rather than delivered to the state. Droughts during 1931 and 1932 compounded the agricultural problems, and famine swept Ukraine, claiming the lives of millions.

The government persisted in its collectivization process despite peasant resistance and its disastrous effects. By the time of the third Five Year Plan, 25 million individual farms had been collectivized. Food was more plentiful than it had been for some time, but peasants still rarely met production quotas. They tended to pay more attention to their small private plots than to the vast fields of the state farms, and the success of agricultural restructuring remained questionable.

These young women worked on a collective farm in Ukraine during the 1930s.

The social consequences of all this must not be overlooked. During collectivization, 24 million individuals left the countryside. The increase in urban population accounted for only one half of them. Some 12 million people remained uncounted for. Some may have left the country. Most of them likely perished.

INDUSTRIALIZATION

Immediately after the October revolution in 1917, the Soviet government began the nationalization of industry. In 1921, "**Gosplan**," the state planning commission, was established to draft an economic plan for the country. It was Gosplan that structured the Five Year Plans that began in 1928. While Lenin's New Economic Policy had salvaged the economy, it seemed unable to promote the rapid industrialization essential to move the Soviet Union into the ranks of modern industrial nations. In 1926, over 75 per cent of the people were still employed in agriculture. By collectivizing agriculture, Stalin had not only seized control of food production, but he had also directed a large portion of the work force into industry. By 1940, only 51 per cent of the people were employed in agriculture.

The goals of the first Five Year Plan were staggering. Total industrial output was to increase by 250 per cent. Heavy industrial production was to

THE UKRAINIAN FAMINE OF 1932–1933

In 1932 Ukraine harvested enough grain to feed its people for two years. But that year the Soviet grain requisition program caused a famine in Ukraine in which millions died of starvation. Few people outside Ukraine knew what had happened. How was it possible that millions of people could have died without the world knowing? Research and explain.

Systematic confiscation of grain by the Soviet regime led to a famine which resulted in as many as 6 million deaths. The tragedy of the Ukrainian Famine of 1932-1933 has been compared to the Armenian Massacre in 1915 and the Holocaust of the Second World War.

Industrialization had produced a shift in population from rural to urban areas. Cities were dependent on agricultural production. When food supplies became scarce, a government policy of grain procurement was implemented in order to feed urban workers. Peasant resistance to government grain procurement following the Bolshevik revolution of 1917 resulted in a shortfall of agricultural produce. In combination with a drought in southern Russia and Ukraine, this resistance led to a famine in 1921-1922. Unlike the famine of 1932, this earlier famine was acknowledged by the Soviet government, which then organized massive domestic and international relief to alleviate the hunger experienced by Ukrainian peasant farmers. Why, then, was the famine of 1932 encouraged by Soviet government policy?

Essentially, Stalin waged war on the Ukrainian peasantry in order to create the social order and economic system demanded by communist ideology. The party's attempt to reorder society resulted in a struggle with the Ukrainian peasantry and Ukrainian national aspirations. From 1928 to 1932, government policies of collectivization and dekulakization were designed to enforce conformity and eliminate characteristics of capitalism which might exist in the individual Ukrainian peasant farmer. The deaths of millions of Ukrainian peasants could be justified by Stalin as part of the cost of industrialization with the added bonus of eliminating resistance from a recalcitrant national group.

In August 1932, Communist party members were given the legal right to confiscate grain from peasant households and a law was passed making the theft of grain punishable by death. That fall, the harvest was guarded by 112 000 armed forces whose orders were to prevent the peasants from taking grain. By the beginning of 1933, it is estimated that the average peasant household of five people had only 80 kg of grain to sustain them until the next harvest. With little else to supplement the limited bread available, starvation became common. Rats, weeds, dogs, bark, leaves, and garbage kept some people alive a little longer. Reports of cannibalism surfaced. Deprivation, domination, suffering, and death characterized life in Ukraine.

Eighty per cent of the collective farms failed to pay their workers, and government policy prevented people from seeking work elsewhere. An internal passport system was implemented which prevented the peasants from selling heirlooms in the cities in order to buy bread. Over the winter, 17 people died every minute. Despite this starvation, the Soviet government exported grain and refused to accept any foreign aid. In addition, the border between the Russian Republic and Ukraine was blocked to ensure that no food supplies entered Ukraine.

Western nations refused to acknowledge the horror of the famine, choosing instead to believe the carefully staged tours of the Ukrainian collective farms which seemed to have abundant grain. Walter Duranty of *The New York Times* repeatedly denied the existence of the famine and received a Pulitzer Prize for accuracy in reporting. Privately, however, he estimated that as many as 10 million people may have died. Although Malcolm Muggeridge defied Soviet authorities and reported accurately on the famine, he was not believed by the people of the West who did not want to rupture relations with the Soviet Union. In fact, the USSR was granted a seat in the League of Nations in 1934 in spite of these atrocities.

The Soviet Union refused to acknowledge the famine of 1932-1933, referring to problems in Ukraine only as food difficulties. Open discussion of the famine was forbidden until the advent of glasnost in 1986. Only recently have Western nations been able to acknowledge that Soviet refusal of foreign aid and the export of grain did occur at a time when people were dying of starvation in Ukraine. The Ukrainian people dared to resist the tyranny of Stalin, who responded brutally with a policy designed to destroy peasant autonomy. The imposition of totalitarian control resulted in tremendous human costs and underlined Stalin's disregard for the sanctity of life and worth of the individual.

1. Explain how famine in Ukraine in 1932-1933 differed from the famine experienced in Ukraine in 1921-1922.

2. What steps did the Soviet government take to collectivize agriculture?

3. How did collectivization of agriculture in Ukraine affect the population?

4. Why did Western governments ignore the Ukrainian famine of 1932-1933?

5. Should the Canadian government intervene in the affairs of countries who are guilty of acts of terrorism against their own people?

increase by 330 per cent, pig iron by 300 per cent, coal by 200 per cent, electric power by 400 per cent, and agricultural production by 150 per cent. To attain the necessary capital at a time when foreign loans were unavailable, Stalin introduced the turnover tax. This tax was levied on the wholesale price of goods and became a major source of state revenue. The result was that while in most other industrial nations the share of GNP going to private consumption was 80 per cent, in the Soviet Union it dropped to 52 per cent. This focus on industrial consumption at the expense of domestic consumption allowed the Soviet state to deploy 25 per cent of its GNP to industry and still direct sizable funds to science, education, and the military. The Soviet state well knew it had to transform a largely illiterate population into a skilled and educated work force.

From 1928 to 1941, numerous large projects were completed. These included the Dnieper Dam, the Stalingrad tractor factory, the Magnitogorsk steel plant in the Urals, the Kuznetsk Basin mines of Siberia, and the Baltic-White Sea Canal.

Many projects were dependent on slave labour. It is estimated that 10 million political prisoners were held in concentration camps and were used in gold mining, forestry, coal mining, and the building of roads, canals, railways, and airports. About 10 per cent of these prisoners died each year. The camps were continually replenished with non-party workers and other political opponents of the Soviet regime.

This brutal program of industrialization produced results unprecedented in industrial history. In only 12 years, the USSR's industrial output surpassed that of France, Japan, and Italy. It rivaled and possibly even exceeded that of Great Britain.

While the results were impressive, an objective evaluation reveals many deficiencies. Agriculture was fraught with problems and the Soviet state was less able to feed its people in the late 1930s than it had been before the First World War. Industrial systems were still relatively primitive, and the system of planning imposed by the state made innovation and adjustments in design difficult. By 1937, awareness of the Nazi buildup of power in Germany necessitated a redirection of resources toward a massive rearmament program. Tractor factories began to produce tanks and aircraft in greater numbers. However, even though tremendous numbers of military goods rolled off the production lines, the quality of these goods lagged far behind that of the output of the industrial giants, particularly Germany and Japan.

STALIN'S ARMY PURGE

From 1936-1938, on Stalin's orders, both the government and the military were "purged" of dissenters. Two years later, German armies crushed Soviet opposition as they invaded the USSR. Explain how Stalin's army purges may have been an important cause of this shocking military defeat.

Between 1936 and 1938, a wave of terror engulfed Soviet government and military leaders as Stalin carried out a "purge" of those in the USSR who could oppose him. He moved in particular against the old Bolsheviks still powerful within the Communist party, the intelligentsia, and the Red Army. The resulting arrests and show trials were known as the Great Purge. Just five months after Hitler had reoccupied the Rhineland, State Prosecutor Vyshinski demanded the death sentence for 16 leading politicians for the crime of plotting to kill Stalin.

Purges were not new in the Soviet Union. What distinguished the Great Purge from others was its extremity. It grew out of deep philosophical divisions within the party. Trotsky led the left-wing opposition and Rykov the right-wing opposition. They both opposed Stalin's draconian, forced industrialization and collectivization policies. Already showing signs of megalomania, Stalin would not tolerate dissent and insisted on a party united behind him. Between 1933 and 1934, a million suspects were expelled from the party. Then, in December 1934, the fourth most important man in the party, Sergei Kirov, was gunned down in Leningrad, probably with Stalin's approval. This event gave the dictator the excuse he needed to act against all his opponents—especially the followers of Trotsky. The assassins of Kirov were hunted down in a far-ranging witch hunt that saw thousands executed. All party members found their memberships suddenly subject to review. The purge continued throughout 1936 in efforts to rid the party of all Trotskyites.

In 1937, Stalin turned his paranoia on the army command, with the popular military hero Marshal Tukhachevsky his next target. Documentary proof of the general's duplicity had to be manufactured, and this "proof" was obligingly provided by German security forces.

Late in 1936, Reinhard Heydrich, a senior SS official, received information that a group was forming in the Soviet Union to overthrow Stalin. The alleged leader of the coup was Tukhachevsky. Heydrich plotted to feed information about the intended coup to Stalin, hoping to destroy the Soviet officer corps in the process.

After the First World War, the relationship between German and Soviet armed forces had been close. The Soviets had assisted German rearmament and training in return for technical assistance in rebuilding their industrial base. Now, altering letters and documents written by Soviet generals to their German counterparts, German forgers made it appear that the Red Army was about to move against Stalin. Incriminating documents were created bearing the signatures of Tukhachevsky, General von Seekt, and Trotsky.

Only *SS-Hauptsturmführer* Janke raised any objections to sending the false documents. Heydrich arrested Janke and got Hitler's permission to proceed with his ruse. Some of the doctored letters were passed to Soviet intelligence through Prime Minister Beneš of Czechoslovakia. Moscow reacted swiftly by buying the remaining forgeries for 3 million rubles—appropriately enough, in forged notes.

On 11 June, Tass, the Soviet news agency, reported the arrest of Tukhachevsky and seven other senior generals, and their subsequent execution. This touched off one of the bloodiest of purges among the Soviet officer corps. Squads of NKVD agents (the Soviet secret police) descended on military bases and carted off entire staffs. Within two years, 35 000 officers were dead, including 90 per cent of the army's generals, 80 per cent of its colonels, 3 out of 5 marshals, 13 out of 15 army commanders, 57 out of 885 corps commanders, 167 out of 280 division commanders, 11 vice-commissars for war, and 75 of the 80 members of the Supreme Military Soviet. Much the same happened in the air force, and only 1 senior naval commander survived.

Many of the accused confessed to save family and friends. After days of interrogation, others confessed "to save the state." Sentences were prepared in advance of trial and approved by Stalin.

Not just the armed forces, but half the Politburo and two thirds of the Central Committee met a similar fate. In 1940, a NKVD agent assassinated Trotsky in Mexico City, where Trotsky had fled from Stalin's fury. The last to be purged were the executioners themselves. In 1939, Lavrenti Beria became head of the NKVD with the task of wiping clean the slate, eliminating those involved in the killings.

Heydrich reported to Hitler that his ploy had worked, that the SS was responsible for the Soviet army purges. But most of the arrests and executions had been carried out before the faked or doctored documents reached Moscow. The Soviet secret police had merely used the SS to provide them with false evidence. Even without evidence, Stalin would have proceeded with the executions.

1. What is the fate of opposition in a single-party state?

2. Why did so many of those accused confess to their alleged crimes?

3. What was the crime of the army?

It is estimated, then, that in spite of the spectacular gains in industry, the Soviet Union was actually weaker in relation to other powers at the end of the 1930s than it had been 10 years earlier.

SOVIET FOREIGN POLICY

Marxist philosophy predicted a world-wide revolution of the working class and eventually a utopian society that would operate without the administrative function of the state system (the "withering away of the state"). When the Bolsheviks seized power in Russia in 1917, they had to deal with the issue of communism's introduction into only one country. As a result the USSR had to recognize the international state system and make an effort to take its place within this system. Soviet foreign policy was based on two tenets. One of these was the belief that the communist revolution would spread to the rest of the world as fellow proletarians renounced their nation in favour of the class with which they shared the struggle against the bourgeoisie. The second tenet underpinning Soviet foreign policy was that capitalist nations were determined to destroy the new socialist state and thus its borders and internal security must be defended vigorously.

The realization that world-wide revolution was not imminent led Lenin to take a practical approach in foreign affairs after 1917. Peace had to be secured to consolidate the gains of the revolution. Powerful German troops still faced a Soviet army that was ill-equipped, ill-fed, and unwilling to fight any longer. Hence on 3 March 1918, Lenin accepted the Treaty of Brest-Litovsk, a humiliating and economically devastating agreement. The decision to sign the treaty was rationalized as securing the political survival of the new state, so that it would eventually be able to promote revolution abroad. This treaty would be overturned by the Treaty of Versailles, even though Russia was not present at the negotiations.

After the war, the new Soviet government was preoccupied with eliminating the resistance of royalist forces and foreign intervention in order to consolidate its power. But, in March of 1919, Lenin established the **Communist International (Comintern)** to further the Soviet goal of world revolution. Through a network of foreign communist parties, Lenin hoped to counteract allied intervention in the USSR's civil war and strengthen the

Soviet state. Revolutionary propaganda, labour strife, protest movements, and subversion would be the tactics used against the capitalist world. By 1920, the Comintern structure identified Moscow as the leader in a world-wide system of communist parties. A characteristic feature of Soviet foreign policy would be its acceptance of communist doctrine, and its attempts to conform to Marxist-Leninist ideology.

George Chicherin became commissar of foreign affairs in 1918 and held that position until 1930. His responsibility was to establish diplomatic relations between the USSR and other major powers—at the same time stabilizing its position in the world power structure. The first step in securing the Soviet state on the international level came in April 1922, when the Soviet and German foreign ministers, Chicherin and Rathenau, signed the Treaty of Rapallo. The treaty provided for diplomatic relations and economic cooperation between the two states. Germany was thus the first major country to officially recognize the new Soviet state. The Treaty of Rapallo provided for the mutual repudiation of war costs and damages, expansion of trade between the two countries, and above all, a German promise of economic assistance to the Soviet Union. In return, the USSR would allow Germany to conduct military manoeuvres on Soviet soil. This involved the testing of military equipment and the training of troops, and was in violation of the Treaty of Versailles.

The significance of the relationship between Germany and the Soviet Union at the international level must not be ignored. It ended the isolation endured by both states and undermined the French attempt to ensure Germany's complete adherence to the terms of the Treaty of Versailles.

Great Britain accorded the Soviet Union full diplomatic recognition in January 1924; but a "Red scare" in the fall of the same year, and the subsequent election of a Conservative British government, ended relations until 1930. China recognized the USSR in May 1924 and made far-reaching concessions in Manchuria and Outer Mongolia. However, the death of Sun Yat-sen and the succession of Chiang Kai-shek shifted China's foreign overtures to the Western powers, and Stalin finally broke off relations in 1927. A Sino-Soviet tie became possible after the Japanese expansion in Manchuria in 1931, as both China and the Soviet Union braced themselves against the threat of Japan.

Despite Trotsky's warnings of the dangers of fascism, Stalin continued his relationship with Germany. The Treaty of Rapallo was renewed in 1931. Stalin identified German social democrats as enemies of communism, and he actually supported Hitler's rise to power in 1933 by encouraging the German Communist party to side with Hitler. At the end of 1933, however, Hitler ended military cooperation with the Soviet Union. He also acted to create a single-party state. The German Communist party fell in the process, which gave Stalin some forewarning of the future.

Concerned about this change in the relationship, Stalin began to look to the West for potential allies, particularly France. He especially wanted to prevent any collusion between France and Germany that would allow Germany to expand its eastern territories. On 18 September 1934 the Soviet Union joined the League of Nations, after France pressed for its inclusion. On 2 May 1935 France and the USSR signed a treaty of mutual assistance.

A similar treaty was signed between the Soviet Union and Czechoslovakia two weeks later. Stalin was attempting to secure his position. The treaty pledged him to assist Czechoslovakia only if France first took action in fulfilment of its obligations to Czechoslovakia.

Throughout the 1930s, suspicion of Stalin's motives prevented the Western powers from cooperating fully with the Soviet Union. Although they were concerned about Hitler's rise to power, they continued to fear communism. The United States recognized the Soviet Union after Franklin Roosevelt came to power in 1933; but the Western powers' general attitude toward the Soviet Union remained one of suspicion and mistrust. This vacillation finally drove Stalin to reopen ties with Germany. After Britain's guarantee to Poland in March 1939, and aware of Poland's anti-Soviet attitude, Stalin began talks with Germany.

On 23 August 1939 the talks were formalized in the Nazi-Soviet pact. This agreement pledged that each nation would remain neutral in the event of war. A secret protocol provided for the partition of Poland between Germany and the Soviet Union. This would allow the Soviet Union a buffer zone if Hitler attacked Poland. It would also allow the Soviet Union to reclaim the neighbouring Baltic states of Estonia, Latvia, and Lithuania. Both Hitler and Stalin were acting out of expediency. For Stalin, this agreement offered some assurance of security on the Soviet Union's western border and allowed him to strengthen his beleaguered armed forces and prepare for war.

In April 1941, the Soviet-Japanese neutrality pact was signed. Japan had begun its war in Asia by occupying China. It had, however, been deterred from expanding into the Soviet Union as the Red Army was able to maintain the Manchurian and Mongolian borders. Stalin encouraged the Japanese to look southward rather than to the Soviet Union for the fulfilment of their imperialist ambitions.

The Nazi-Soviet alliance gave Stalin a false sense of security. He ignored warnings of a German attack from the west, from Churchill as well as his own intelligence sources. It was not until Germans had been on Soviet soil for eight hours that Stalin finally acknowledged the gravity of his situation. Some 3.2 million German troops poured into the Soviet Union along a 1600 km front. Although the Soviets had seven times as many tanks and four times as many aircraft as the Germans, they had lost most of their skilled officers in the purges. Only 7 per cent of Red Army officers had advanced military education. The Germans relied on the superior training of their forces, plus the shock effect of blitzkrieg. "Operation Barbarossa"—launched by the Germans against the USSR on 22 June 1941—at last forced Stalin to look to the West. The "Grand Alliance" between the Soviet Union, Great Britain, and the United States would soon be forged in an attempt to defeat Hitler.

Henry Ford sits behind the wheel of a 1903 Model A. His company produced 1708 Model As in its first 15 months in business. Ford went on to revolutionize American industry with the assembly line technology used to build his automobiles.

THE UNITED STATES

For the first century of its existence, the United States followed a foreign policy dominated by themes of international neutrality and expansionism within North America. However, this detachment from international affairs came to an end in 1898, with the Spanish-American War. When the Americans defeated the Spanish, they found themselves in possession of the Philippines. Unwilling to relinquish control to the local population which they, like the Spanish before them, felt would be unable govern itself, the Americans also felt compelled to step in to prevent the Germans or Japanese from expanding into this area. Thus at the turn of the century the Americans had begun a new era in their foreign policy as heirs to a "sphere of influence."

For the first half of the twentieth century, the United States underwent tremendous change as it rode a rollercoaster of economic boom and bust to eventually become a superpower after the Second World War. Throughout this period, the USA resisted formal political ties to Europe, even though it needed economic ties to fuel its domestic economy. A change in the balance of power had been evident at the turn of the century, as rising Germany and Japan had challenged the old order. The United States would soon join Great Britain in deterring these new powers from upsetting the balance.

DOMESTIC GROWTH

By 1900, the United States had become the greatest industrial nation in the world. Rich agricultural land, vast mineral resources, modern technology, and an abundance of both foreign and domestic capital had transformed the American economy between 1865 and 1900. In 1901, Andrew Carnegie's single company was producing more steel than all the steel-makers of England. Some 400 000 km of railway coursed across the land by 1914—compared to Russia's 73 600 km. Efficiency and mechanization in both production and transportation made American agricultural products less expensive than any in Europe. Coal production soared to 455 million tonnes per year, ahead of Great Britain at 292 million tonnes and Germany at 277 million.

83

The United States became the largest producer of both oil and pig iron, and the largest consumer of copper in the world. As a leading manufacturer of both consumer and industrial goods, the United States consumed more energy than most of the nations of Europe put together. In 1914, the national income of the United States was $37 billion, compared to Great Britain at $11 billion, Germany at $12 billion, and Russia at $7 billion. These advantages were only enhanced by the First World War. American industry expanded even more to produce military supplies. European powers faced economic dislocation after the war, and the United States, as their chief creditor, was left in the dominant economic position.

Following the war, New York was a financial centre comparable to London. Though anxious to return to an isolationist position in their foreign policy, Americans recognized the necessity of maintaining trade associations to fuel their industrial economy. While they refused to join the League of Nations, they wished to see the European nations rebuild their domestic economies and become viable trading partners once more.

At the end of the war, the United States, strengthened economically, wished to focus on domestic development. It seemed to live in a world of its own. In 1919, the Eighteenth Amendment to the US constitution outlawed the sale of alcohol and set the tone for the "roaring twenties" characterized by illicit consumption of alcohol in "speakeasies," the Charleston danced in flapper dresses, and the age of jazz. Sale of alcohol was controlled by gangsters, like Chicago's Al Capone, who earned huge profits from their underworld empires. It was the age of the automobile and the radio. More Americans owned automobiles than citizens of all the rest of the world combined. Commercial radio and development of the motion picture industry contributed to a new era of communications and entertainment.

The isolationist tendencies promoted after the First World War were expressed both in tariffs on foreign goods and in quotas in immigration. In 1922, the Fordney-McCumber tariff, and in 1930, the Hawley-Smoot tariff, raised import duties on foreign goods and effectively closed the American market to European countries attempting to rebuild their economies and repay wartime debts. An influx of immigrants from southern and eastern Europe, as well as from Asia, had occurred after 1900. In 1924, the American government established an annual quota limit of 2 per cent of the nationals of a given country that had been resident in the United States in 1890. This restriction sharply limited the flow of Catholics, Jews, and Asians, most of whom had come *after* 1890, even as it encouraged greater numbers of British, Germans, and Scandinavians, whose numbers had been greatest *before* 1890.

From 1923 to 1929, the American stock market boomed. The rise in its people's standard of living made the United States the first mass consumer society. By 1928, there were 26 million cars, many produced by Henry Ford, in use. This mode of transportation made possible frequent visits to the supermarkets that were appearing in major cities, a trend which would change American eating habits as a greater variety of food became available. Refrigerators were becoming an essential. Entertainment was provided by the 13 million radios in American homes, and hundreds of silent movies. In 1927, "talkies" took over the movie theatres and a new age of entertainment was born. Everyone was living on borrowed money: as new goods came on the market, it was easy to buy on credit. Why not enjoy a new car today and repay the loan tomorrow?

The same mentality applied to stock-market transactions. Large numbers of speculators made "leveraged" purchases of stocks—with borrowed money. The American economy was still largely unregulated. There were few controls in place to prevent the speculation that eventually led to the stock market crash of October 1929.

Shrewd investors, sensing the impending disaster, began selling on 24 October. By 29 October 1929 panic had set in. Some 16 million shares of stock were sold on Black Tuesday. Stocks purchased on margin with borrowed money now plunged in value. Investors unable to meet their obligations faced bankruptcy. The crash climaxed on 13 November 1929, when the Dow Jones average dropped to 1987. Even blue-chip stocks plummeted in value. Stock of American Telephone and Telegraph, for example, fell from $304 to $97.25, while General Motors shares dropped from $72.75 to $36. By 1933, the market had hit bottom. As many as 9 million savings accounts vanished as banks went out of business. More than 85 000 businesses went bankrupt and thousands of homes and farms were lost to mortgagers, who themselves found resale very difficult, if not impossible. The GNP of the United States was cut in half by 1933, and 16 million people, one-third of the labour force, were unemployed.

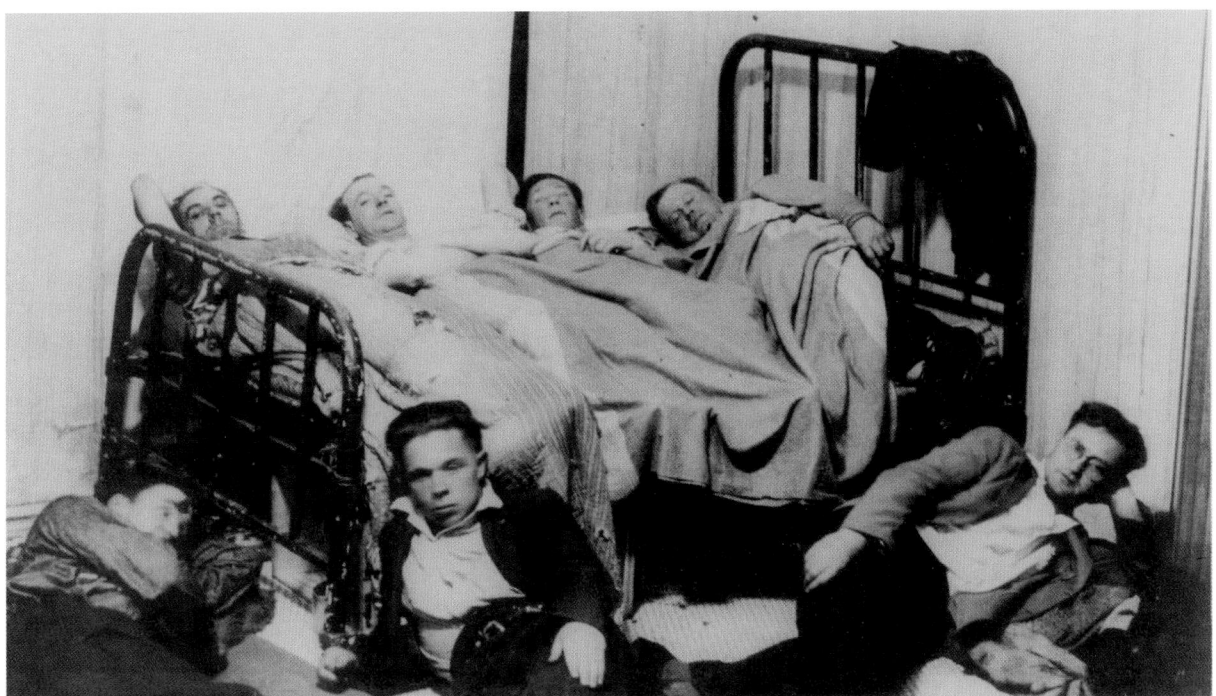

THE GREAT DEPRESSION

The average worker suffered incredibly during the Great Depression. Millions were jobless and homeless.

The stock market crash of 1929 ushered in the Great Depression. Although the depression was international in scope, it was perhaps most devastating in the United States, for it followed a period of rapid growth and rising expectations. Crash and depression brought to a head problems that had been building in the booming unregulated post-war economy of the United States. American capitalism was wildly innovative, and the lack of control by any regulatory bodies led to a financial instability that was unprecedented in the modern world.

The internal weakness of the American economy was only one reason for the depression. A second reason was the interrelatedness of global trade, which encouraged nations like Germany and Austria to borrow much more money than the scale and health of their economies justified, in order to provide the consumer goods their populations craved after the First World War. Unable to repay foreign loans—many from the United States— nations moved to tariff protection and deflationary budgets to salvage their economies. Such disruption of the world economy played havoc with an exporting nation like the United States. World-wide protectionism had a more severe impact on the United States than it did on most European nations.

Agriculture had enjoyed high prices in 1918, but during the 1920s foreign markets collapsed, the home market shrank, and prices fell. New farmlands were opened in Canada and Australia, and European nations were attempting to become self-sufficient in foodstuffs. From 1922 to 1932 American wheat exports plummeted from $200 million in annual revenue to $5 million. A slowdown in American population growth and a simplification of eating habits reduced agricultural sales. In addition, synthetic fibres reduced the demand for cotton, and improved machinery allowed large-scale farmers to produce more and displace sharecroppers. Farmers burdened by debt suffered foreclosure and joined the ranks of the unemployed.

The uneven distribution of wealth in the USA has been pointed out as another reason for the depression. Some 8.2 per cent of the country's families enjoyed 42 per cent of the nation's total income, while 59.5 per cent of America's families received only 2.7 per cent of total national income. Hence, a large proportion of Americans did not earn enough money to buy the very consumer goods they produced on the job. Wage earners had received small increases in salary throughout the 1920s, but they were tempted by the vast quantities of consumer goods, and improved their standard of living by the use of credit. Social welfare benefits, such as unemployment insurance or health insurance, were nonexistent. When the depression

Franklin Delano Roosevelt led the United States through four presidential terms, from 1933 until his death in 1945.

occurred 13 million unemployed Americans had to stand in bread lines and some were forced to sleep outdoors as they lost their homes to mortgage companies. By 1932, one out of every four families was on relief. The Emergency Relief Act was passed in July by the Hoover administration to assist cities in funding relief projects.

THE NEW DEAL

It was not until the inauguration of Franklin Delano Roosevelt as president on 3 March 1933 that any significant action was taken to turn the tide. In his inaugural address, Roosevelt told the American people, "the only thing we have to fear is fear itself," and instilled a renewed sense of confidence in the American way of life. Roosevelt's first measure was to declare a four-day bank holiday. During the first years of the depression, 4000 banks had failed, with untold losses to depositors. By March 1933, all major banks had closed their doors, leaving the nation without banking services.

The bank holiday proclaimed by Roosevelt helped stabilize the situation, and Roosevelt's administration took the opportunity to pass the Emergency Banking Act, which forbade the export of gold and the redemption of currency in gold, and thus effectively took the United States off the gold standard. The new law also allowed for government regulation of banking activities and left it to the Treasury Department to determine which banks were solvent enough to reopen their doors for business. By 15 March 1933 approximately one-half of the country's banks, representing 90 per cent of US banking resources, were declared fit to reopen. With a renewed sense of confidence, people began to trust their deposits to the banks once more.

The **New Deal** was truly revolutionary in its reorganization of the American economy, for it brought about massive government intervention in the marketplace. It was, however, conservative in philosophy: its primary purpose was to feed people and revive industry. It was not designed to overturn the capitalist system, but rather to remedy some of the abuses now apparent in the system. Despite the economic collapse, there was a sense of faith in capitalism and a lack of any real leadership or drive toward any radical departure from it. The New Deal would preserve capitalism by providing interim relief immediately and by restructuring the economic system for the future.

The blueprint for recovery and reform was outlined during the Hundred Days from 9 March to 16 June 1933. The numerous pieces of major legislation included: the Federal Deposit Insurance Corporation, which insured individual bank accounts; the Civilian Conservation Corps, which employed 3 million young people on conservation projects; the Federal Emergency Relief Administration, which provided emergency relief for the needy; and perhaps the most revolutionary of all, the Tennessee Valley Authority (TVA), which established a system of dams for electricity and irrigation in the southeastern United States. Two other pieces of legislation had a direct effect on the average citizen. The Home Owners' Loans program saved about 1 million homes, and the National Recovery Administration regulated wages and prices in industry.

In summary, these programs safeguarded bank deposits, relieved unemployment, provided emergency relief, extended credit, regulated competition, and ensured labour's right to organize and bargain collectively. In December 1933, the Twenty-First Amendment repealed-prohibition. Thus, in a year when government involved itself to a large extent in American business, it disengaged itself from at least one area of private life.

The New Deal permanently altered the structure of American capitalism, while preserving the ideological commitment to free enterprise. The Social Security Act of 1935 introduced unemployment insurance and old-age pensions. Redistribution of wealth was extended by revision of the income-tax act introduced in 1913. It was not until the outbreak of the Second World War, however, that the ravages of the depression would be fully overcome. From then on, the stimulation of science and technology would provide an impetus to the American economy unmatched in history.

FOREIGN POLICY

The United States emerged from the First World War with greatly increased economic power. It had suffered 115 000 dead and 206 000 wounded during the war, but had gained tremendous material advantage as its heavy industry expanded to meet the demands of the allied war effort. Despite Woodrow Wilson's role in fashioning the peace settlement, the United States retreated into an isolationist position, determined to focus on its own internal development. The Treaty of Versailles was rejected by the American Senate on 19 March 1920. The United States was thus not a part of the new international peacekeeping body, the League of Nations, and it remained technically at war with Germany until a separate peace was signed in July 1921. Since the United States refused to ratify the Treaty of Versailles, it was not represented on the reparations committee that established Germany's war indebtedness at $33 billion.

The United States did become involved in German affairs, however, when the German economy foundered in 1923. German businesspeople were converting their money into foreign currency and refusing to pay taxes toward reparations payments. Inflation raged as the government repaid war loans with paper money not backed by gold. The inflationary spiral was fueled by increased prices and demands for higher wages. By December 1923, the German mark had slipped to 7000 per American dollar. Germany defaulted on its reparations payments. As noted earlier, in January 1923, the French occupied the Ruhr Valley, seizing mines and factories in order to collect their own reparations. German workers in the Ruhr resorted to passive resistance, refusing to do any work. The German government continued to pay the striking workers, thus contributing to the inflation that was already rampant in the country. The German economy was in chaos.

The Dawes Plan of 1924 established loans from American bankers to stabilize the German currency, scale down reparations payments, and encourage removal of French troops from the Ruhr. In 1929, US businessman Owen D. Young was sent back to Europe to reschedule reparations payments once more. The total bill was reduced substantially, and lower rates of payments were set. However, by this time, the international economy was in disarray and Germany was suffering from both social and economic problems. In 1931, President Hoover declared a one-year moratorium on reparations payments. Finally, at Lausanne in 1932, the European powers agreed to reduce Germany's reparation payments by 90 per cent if the United States would do the same for their war debts. These discussions proved to be futile. Hitler soon came to power and removed any possibility of further reparations payments.

Despite its isolationist stance, the United States became involved in disarmament talks with the other major powers. The USA hosted the Washington Naval Conference of 1921, for example. The resulting treaty froze the number of capital ships for a period of 10 years at the ratio of 5 each for the United States and Great Britain, 3 for Japan, and 1.75 for Italy and France. The conference was viewed as an unqualified success for the United States since it allowed them to avoid political entanglements while both achieving their goal of maintaining naval superiority over Japan, and terminating the 1902 alliance between Japan and Great Britain. This alliance was replaced by the Four Power Treaty between the United States, Great Britain, Japan, and France that bound the signatories to consult one another in the event of a dispute over territorial possessions. A subsequent Nine Power Treaty called for the respect of China's territorial integrity, and the Open Door policy assured trade access to China—both of which the United States had sought in order to check Japanese hegemony in Asia.

In 1928, the United States gave formal recognition to the government of Chiang Kai-shek and

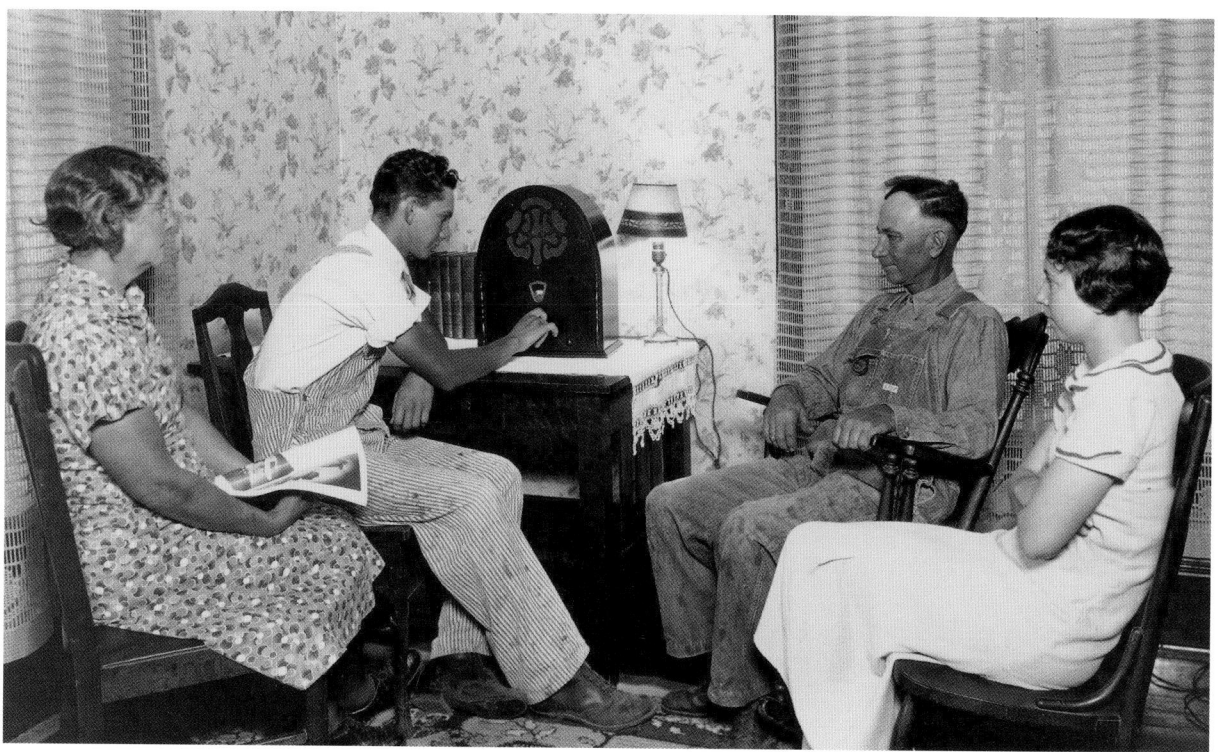

The United States kept a neutral stance in foreign policies for most of the 1930s. Average Americans, like this Kansas family, might have heard about the crisis in Europe, but most did not feel it affected their lives.

reiterated its commitment to the territorial integrity of China. The Washington Conference seemed to promote peace and stability in the world, but both Japan and France resisted attempts to subvert their power. Discontent characterized naval disarmament throughout the 1920s, and there was a growing awareness of the threat of Japanese expansion in Asia. The London Naval Conference of 1930 was an attempt to meet Japan's demands in the area of naval armaments without upsetting the balance of power in Asia. The British and the Americans agreed to allocate the higher ratio of 5 to Japanese auxiliary ships while maintaining the ratio of 3 on capital ships. There was a desire on the part of the Western nations to maintain dominance in Asia, but the Japanese move into Manchuria in 1931 confirmed Japan's intention to expand into China.

In 1935, isolationist American members of Congress successfully blocked efforts to have the United States join the World Court. During this same year, Roosevelt once again introduced a Neutrality Act to prevent activity he believed had been instrumental in involving the United States in the First World War. The issue of arms embargoes

had stalled an attempt to pass a Neutrality Act in 1933. The Neutrality Act of 1935 included an impartial arms embargo, with a six-month limit on the bill. Internationalists in Congress argued that the president must be able to limit arms embargoes. By supplying arms to the victim of an aggressor, but denying them to the aggressor, the United States could influence the war. Isolationists, by contrast, insisted that all belligerent nations should be treated equally.

The invasion of Ethiopia by Mussolini in 1935 allowed Roosevelt to invoke the Neutrality Act almost as soon as it was passed. An immediate arms embargo went into effect, and American citizens were warned not to sail on belligerent ships or to trade with the nations at war. When the League of Nations imposed a long list of goods to be denied Italy, the Americans did not formally concur. They felt that the exclusion of oil would make the embargo ineffective. The British and the French were afraid that if they imposed an embargo that included oil, Mussolini would go directly to Hitler for help. Western action against Italy was a dismal failure. Italians continued to dominate Ethiopia, and American businesspeople increased their trade with Italy.

The Neutrality Act was extended in 1937, but once again presidential discretion was denied. However, this time trade in domestic goods was allowed. This was the first of the "cash and carry" bills that allowed trade with belligerent nations, but required them to transport American goods on their own ships. Over the next two years, Roosevelt worked to remove the arms embargo as he watched Hitler reoccupy the Rhineland, then move into Austria and Czechoslovakia. The American foreign-policy position in 1938 was to support the status quo. Although the United States did not want German domination of Europe or Japanese domination of Asia, it was still unwilling to take an active role in preventing either from happening.

The outbreak of war in September 1939 challenged the American isolationist position. Hitler had now upset the balance of power and Britain and France were scrambling to prepare for war. Finally, in November 1939, Congress agreed to repeal the arms embargo and allow the sale of war *matériel* to Britain and France. Cash and Carry, as this bill was called, provided for the sale of arms to Britain on the condition that the British come to the United States and carry the goods away. Although the USA was still unwilling to be officially involved in the war effort, its cash and carry policy aligned it with the democracies, against Hitler.

By the summer of 1940, the British, stunned by the capitulation and subsequent German occupation of France in June, appealed to the United States for destroyers to protect the Atlantic supply line. On 2 September 1940 the "destroyers for bases" deal was formalized. It provided for the exchange of 50 American destroyers for a 99 year lease on British bases in the Caribbean. On 16 September 1940 American involvement in the war became more likely with passage of the Selective Training and Service Act. This act provided for the first peacetime draft in American history. Talks between British and American military personnel emphasized the importance of the European theatre of war over an Asian one in the event of a war with both Germany and Japan.

When Germany began air attacks on Britain, it became evident that Britain would not be able to carry on with the limited supplies allowed for in the cash and carry plan. Churchill appealed to Roosevelt for direct aid. In March 1941, Congress passed a bill appropriating $7 billion in war *matériel* to Britain. This was the first transfer of American goods under the Lend-Lease Act. Lend-lease marked the end of American neutrality and was, in effect, a declaration of economic war against Germany and Italy. It provided for the lending or leasing of any war *matériel* deemed necessary by the president to any nation whose defence was vital to that of the United States. In April 1941, American naval and air bases were established on Greenland, and in July 1941, Iceland was occupied by the United States. Roosevelt declared a neutrality zone in the Atlantic extending to Iceland, and American ships began to patrol the Atlantic to protect vessels carrying goods to Britain. By September, undeclared warfare was being waged by the United States against German submarines.

While the European war raged on, the Japanese continued to expand in Asia. As they moved southward in search of raw materials, and eventually occupied French Indo-China, the United States moved to protect its interests in the Philippines and prevent Japanese domination of the entire area. The Japanese had become dependent on a large trading volume with the United States. In September 1940, the United States banned exports of iron and steel to Japan, and the following July, froze all Japanese assets in the United States. Demands that Japan withdraw from China were ignored. On 7 December 1941 the Japanese air force attacked Pearl Harbor in Hawaii, headquarters of the American Pacific Fleet. The following day the United States responded with a declaration of war on Japan. On 11 December 1941 Germany and Italy, as allies of Japan, declared war on the United States and brought its policy of isolationism to an end.

SUMMARY

The collapse of the Romanov dynasty in Russia in 1917 gave way to political chaos ending in civil war. Attempting to continue a war they had already lost brought an end to the provisional *Duma* and saw the rise to power of the radical Bolshevik faction led by Lenin. In the midst of collapse, Lenin's proposals for land redistribution, an end to the war, and food for everyone held hope for the Russian people. Lenin was able to engineer the *coup d'état* that toppled the provisional government and seize power in October 1917. Three years of brutal civil war followed the revolution, leading to the establishment of the Union of Soviet Socialist Republics in 1922. Following Lenin's death in 1924, Stalin embarked on a program of forced industrialization based on a series of Five Year Plans designed to allow the USSR to forge ahead economically. As the United States did at this time, the USSR gave considerable priority to internal domestic development, remaining relatively uninvolved in international relations.

In the early part of the twentieth century the United States, Russia, and Japan emerged as industrial powers to challenge the existing world order. Since its inception in 1783, the United States had followed a policy of continental expansion that was largely divorced from international affairs. Only in specific instances, such as the Spanish-American War of 1898, did the Americans become entangled in foreign conflict. It was only after long and bitter debate that the USA broke with its isolationism in 1917 to take part in the First World War. Despite President Wilson's determination to have the United States pursue an interventionist role after the war, Congress voted down American membership in the League of Nations. A booming post-war economy encouraged a return to domestic matters. Only in foreign investment aimed at European reconstruction did the Americans seek to play an international role.

In the decades between the First and Second World Wars, the United States and the Soviet Union pursued similar goals of domestic development. What foreign policy they had was designed to protect their borders and enhance their industrial development. Not until 1941, when Hitler drew them into the Second World War, would the two major powers reluctantly become fully involved on the international scene.

QUESTIONS: THE SOVIET UNION

1. What caused the Russo-Japanese War of 1904-1905?

2. Explain the effects of the Russo-Japanese War on both Japan and Russia.

3. Describe what occurred on Bloody Sunday.

4. Describe Russia's domestic economy, both industrial and agricultural sectors, before 1914.

5. Give four major reasons for the Russian Revolution.

6. In point form, list the events from 23 February 1917 to 25 October 1917 that led to the Bolshevik takeover of the Russian government.

7. List four achievements of the provisional government.

8. Why did the provisional government fail to hold power?

9. Give three promises made by Lenin prior to the Russian Revolution. Why did these promises bring him public support?

10. What were the terms of the Treaty of Brest-Litovsk?

11. Give the reasons for, and the results of, Lenin's nationalization of agriculture.

12. Describe the civil war between 1917 and 1920. Why did the Bolsheviks win?

13. Describe Lenin's New Economic Policy. Why was it necessary?

14. Describe the power struggle that occurred at Lenin's death in 1924. What was the result?

15. Define: (a) collective farm; (b) state farm; (c) kulak; (d) Nepmen.

16. Why was collectivization of agriculture considered essential?

17. Evaluate the collectivization of agriculture.

18. How was industrialization carried out by Stalin? Evaluate the results of this program.

19. What was the basis of the new Soviet government's foreign policy?

20. What was the purpose of the Comintern?

21. What were the terms and the significance of the Treaty of Rapallo in 1922?

22. Explain the foreign-policy negotiations of the 1930s that culminated in the Nazi-Soviet pact of 23 August 1939.

23. What were the advantages to Germany and to the Soviet Union of the Nazi-Soviet pact?

24. Why was the Soviet-Japanese neutrality pact signed in 1941? Explain what each country hoped to gain.

QUESTIONS: THE UNITED STATES

1. How did the Spanish-American War of 1898 influence American foreign policy?

2. Describe the domestic economy of the United States before the First World War.

3. Describe life during the roaring twenties.

4. What was the Eighteenth Amendment?

5. Describe US policy in the area of trade and immigration after the First World War.

6. Detail the causes and effects of the stock market crash of 1929.

7. Name and explain three causes of the Great Depression.

8. Why did Roosevelt declare a bank holiday in March 1933? What was the result?

9. Describe Roosevelt's Emergency Banking Act.

10. Explain the philosophy of the New Deal and evaluate its effectiveness.

11. What were the Hundred Days of 9 March to 16 June 1933?

12. Name and explain four pieces of legislation passed under the New Deal. Evaluate their effectiveness.

13. What was the American foreign-policy position after the First World War?

14. Explain the American involvement in Germany's reparations problems from 1924 to 1931.

15. Explain the terms of the Washington Naval Conference of 1921. What was the intent and the result of limiting naval forces?

16. Summarize, briefly, American foreign policy in the interwar period.

17. What was the American response to the League of Nations' sanctions against Italy in 1935?

18. Define each of the following policies and explain their significance in American foreign policy: (a) cash and carry; (b) destroyers for bases; (c) lend-lease.

CRITICAL ANALYSIS

1. Is isolationism a valid policy in today's world? Explain.

2. Explain why the United States and the Soviet Union directed their energies to domestic issues in the interwar years.

3. Evaluate Stalin's plan for the modernization of the USSR.

4. What is the role of government in an economy? Explain.

5. Why is government intervention in an economy never temporary? Make specific reference to measures adopted by the USA during the 1930s.

6. Compare the ways in which the United States and the Soviet Union attempted to reach economic security in the interwar period.

7. Explain why neutrality legislation passed by the United States did not keep it out of the Second World War.

RESEARCH PROJECTS

1. Research the work of either Lenin or Stalin and evaluate the impact of their leadership on the Soviet Union. Include both positive and negative features of their leadership and assess whether their overall contribution to the Soviet Union was positive or negative. Be sure to provide justification for your assessment.

2. Research the Ukrainian Famine, or Stalin's war on the kulaks, and evaluate the impact of this event on Soviet society and on the economy.

3. Research Stalin's Great Purge and evaluate its impact on Soviet society.

4. Compare and contrast life in the United States in the 1920s with life in the Soviet Union in the 1920s. Consider the composition of society, availability of consumer goods, employment opportunities, and recreational opportunities.

5. Research the causes and effects of the Great Depression. Focus on the impact of the depression on the United States, but identify how the depression affected international economic conditions.

6. Research the improvements in technology in the United States from 1917 to 1940. Identify specific inventions and improvements in technology, and explain how advances affected either the lifestyle of the average American or the security of the nation.

ACTIVITIES

1 Panel Discussion

It is November 1930. The American stock market has crashed (October 1929), and by this time it is evident the global economy is headed for disaster. Structure a panel to deal with the impact of the economic dislocation of the United States both within the United States and in the international economy. Deal specifically with the issue of German reparation payments. Choose heads of state, foreign ministers, finance ministers, or economists for your panel. The chairperson must monitor the discussion and make provision for questions or comments from the audience.

2 Map

(a) On a large map of the Soviet Union place the following: (i) major industrial centres; (ii) primary resources; (iii) labour camps.

(b) On a large map of the United States place the following: (i) major industrial centres; (ii) 60 primary resources; (iii) New Deal projects.

3 Interview

Establish a television news program in which one student will play the role of Peter Mansbridge interviewing Stalin and Roosevelt on their solutions to domestic economic problems during the 1930s.

HISTORICAL ANALYSIS

THE NEW DEAL

In 1929, the American stock market crashed and the United States entered an era of depression characterized by widespread unemployment and social dislocation. In order to revitalize the economy, President Roosevelt introduced a number of government programs. The following lists a number of problems experienced by the United States in the early 1930s with solutions proposed by Roosevelt's government:

	PROBLEM	PROPOSED SOLUTION
1.	Overproduction in agriculture and industry	Impose tariffs and limit production
2.	Inflationary prices	Enact anti-monopoly legislation
3.	Low wages and under-utilization of labour	Permit unionization and enact minimum wage laws
4.	Heavy debt burden in industry and agriculture	Debt reduction programs
5.	Slow growth of power utilities industry	Creation of the Tennessee Valley Authority (TVA)
6.	Unemployment	Social security, insurance, make-work programs
7.	Inadequate low income housing	Government housing subsidies
8.	Contraction of bank loans	Government guaranteed loans

Analyse Roosevelt's measures in conjunction with the following quotations in order to determine whether or not the American government's assumption of responsibility for health, welfare, and employment was a social and political revolution.

1. *Roosevelt began a revolution in the government's massive intervention in the market. The New Deal was a new beginning...*
   −Louis M. Hacker

2. *Critical breaks with past forces do not occur in history even if the New Deal appears to be a drastic departure in what was a free enterprise system...*
   −Richard Hofstadter

3. *Whether or not the New Deal was revolutionary misses the point that it restored confidence to the American people in a time of crisis. The speed with which Roosevelt put his programs in place made them revolutionary in nature...*
   −Arthur M. Schlesinger, Jr.

JAPAN'S ASCENDENCY IN ASIA

We, by the grace of heaven, Emperor of Japan, seated on the throne of a line unbroken for ages eternal, enjoin upon you, our loyal and brave subjects: we hereby declare war on the United States of America and the British Empire.

Eager for the realization of their inordinate ambition to dominate the Orient, both America and Britain, in giving support to the Chungking regime, have aggravated the disturbances in East Asia. Moreover, these two powers, inducing other countries to follow suit, increased military preparations on all sides of our Empire to challenge us. They obstructed by every means our peaceful commerce, and finally resorted to direct severance of economic relations, menacing gravely the existence of our Empire.

Hallowed spirits of our imperial ancestors guarding us from above, we rely upon the loyalty and courage of our subjects in our confident expectation that the task bequeathed by our forefathers will be carried forward.

Emperor Hirohito, declaring war on the United States and Great Britain, 7 December 1941.

FOCUS ON SPHERES OF INFLUENCE

As a Japanese diplomat in the 1930s, explain your country's policies in Manchuria and the rest of Asia in light of Japan's economic priorities and its desire to establish political and economic spheres of influence.

OVERVIEW

With the pressures of European imperialism, Japan industrialized and westernized. Japan adapted the ways of its conquerors, and tried to claim Korea and Manchuria as its own. Following the Manchurian Incident, Japan invaded China in 1937 and bombed Pearl Harbor in 1941.

JAPAN'S QUEST FOR IMPERIAL STATUS

Japan was determined to rid Asia of Western imperialism and establish hegemony in the region itself.

RESURGENT CHINA

Nationalist and Communist forces struggled for control of China during the first half of the twentieth century.

THE MANCHURIAN INCIDENT

Manchuria's rich resources were coveted by the Japanese who occupied the area in 1931. Failure of the League of Nations to resolve the issue in China's favour was followed in 1937 by the Japanese invasion of northern China.

JAPAN'S QUEST FOR IMPERIAL STATUS

In the middle of the nineteenth century the ancient lands of China and Japan fell prey to European and American traders seeking new markets in East Asia. Unable to defend themselves against the modern battle fleets of the industrial nations, the Asian peoples were forced to come to terms with these nations.

After the first invasion by the British (1837-1842), the Chinese gave up the island of Hong Kong and agreed to grant the British exclusive trading concessions in five of their port cities. Within these concessions, the British were given **extraterritorial** rights, which made them immune to every aspect of Chinese civil authority. Inside the enclaves (known as "Treaty Ports"), protected by military forces, the British lived under their own laws and customs. The British success set off a scramble for similar privileges by the other imperial powers.

The pursuit of wealth and profit was not the only incentive for imperial expansion. Britain and the United States were in an industrial stage that brought rising prosperity to their peoples. They came to believe they should impose their political and economic systems on the "less fortunate nations." This conviction grew into world-wide evangelical and humanitarian movements at the end of the nineteenth century. The British and the Americans believed it was their duty to bring Christianity, law, and order to the rest of the world. The resultant frenzy of missionary activity was aimed at converting other peoples to Christianity—and to give them all the other advantages of Western industrialized society. Christianity as well as commerce would have a major impact on Asia, though generally less in Japan than elsewhere.

Hundreds of missionaries, from the USA, Britain, Canada, and elsewhere, were active in China, and through them, links were formed between the Chinese and American peoples. The movement was spontaneous, inspired not by government policy, but by an outpouring of Western social and religious fervour. However, so widespread was the overseas-mission movement that it had a profound influence on Western political decision-makers.

When the Chinese government attempted to stop further encroachments on its territory and authority, British and French forces occupied Canton and later captured Beijing (Peking), burning down the Summer Palace in the process. At each subsequent Chinese defeat, foreign powers seized additional privileges. An attempt to overthrow the throne was never made, however, since this would only have hurried China into the chaos of a prolonged civil war. War would bring to an end the exorbitant profits made from the export of teas, silks, and porcelains sped to waiting Western markets by tall clipper ships.

The feudal society of Japan had remained largely cut off from ties with the rest of the world for over 200 years of self-imposed isolation. Foreigners had been unwelcome in Japan since 1642, with few exceptions, when the dominant Tokugawa family had discouraged most contacts with the outside. All of this was to change when Commodore Matthew Perry sailed an American squadron into Edo (Tokyo) Bay in 1853 bearing guns, whiskey, farm implements, and clocks to trade. Perry's orders were to establish an American concession and "bring this isolated people into the family of the world's nations." Later, American senator William Seward was to publicly proclaim the American policy of "reforming their laws, customs and constitution in order to civilize the island people whose land greets the rising sun." Before the United States could consolidate its position in Japan, it was engulfed in its own civil war. While the Americans were preoccupied, the British and French forced their own concessions from the Japanese.

Foreign intrusions helped trigger revolution, and in 1867 the last Tokugawa shogun was replaced by the boy emperor, Meiji Mutsuhito. The young ruler was supported by a council of samurai, intent on transforming their feudal nation into a modern industrial giant. The first objective was to acquire the military strength to resist further intrusion. Warships and technology were purchased from the British, while Russian, French, and German officers modernized the army. Other reforms also aimed at bringing the Japanese people into the modern world. Feudal privileges were abolished. Small farm plots were consolidated into larger units, to free human resources needed by growing industries. At the same time, thousands of Japanese students were sent abroad to attain the knowledge and skills of an industrial society. As they returned, their zeal further fueled the rate of change.

As its industrial and military strength grew, Japan began to look to the Asian mainland as a source of vital raw materials and expanded territory. The first of Japan's major wars on the Chinese mainland began in 1894. The Japanese were victorious, capturing the offshore islands of Formosa and the Pescadores, and gaining an economic interest in Korea.

Meanwhile, the European powers continued to push for agreements granting new trade concessions in China. Chinese resentment erupted in the Boxer Rebellion in 1900. The Boxers, an anti-foreign movement, laid siege to the foreign legations in Beijing. This siege was raised only when a multinational force fought its way to their relief. During the uprising, missionaries and traders caught outside the concessions were murdered by frenzied mobs. In the aftermath of the rebellion, the Europeans sought to extract indemnities from China. Meanwhile, the USA advocated a new trading system that would allow virtually free access of every nation to the Chinese market. No nation would have its own sphere of influence in China. Dubbed the "Open Door policy," this idea was not well received by the foreign powers already well-established in China.

The Japanese sought to improve their status and power by forming an alliance with the British, whose Asian interests were to coincide with their

During the Boxer Rebellion, Chinese who resented the power wielded by foreign interests in China attacked foreigners and Chinese Christians in Beijing. An international force including British, French, Russian, American, German, and Japanese troops swiftly ended the fighting. The net effect of the rebellion was to strengthen rather than weaken foreign influences in China.

own. After lengthy negotiations, Japan and Britain signed a treaty in 1902, in which the two powers agreed to recognize and protect each other's spheres of influence. As a result of this treaty, Britain was able to re-position much of its Asian fleet to European waters. This in turn facilitated Japan's ability to expand its position on the Asian mainland.

The immediate threat to Japanese expansion, however, was Russia. The Russians had carried the Trans-Siberian Railway across Manchuria to Vladivostok, and had driven a spur southward from Harbin to Lüshun (Port Arthur) on the Huang Hai (Yellow Sea). At the same time, Russian interests in timber concessions along the Yalu River were thought by the Japanese to be the beginning of an attempt to annex the peninsula. While in the midst of negotiations with the Russians, the Japanese attacked Lüshen in 1904, and sank the Russian Far East Squadron as it lay at anchor. This brilliant *coup* was followed by direct invasion: the Japanese army, once landed, overran the Russian positions.

Japan's isolation from the rest of the world ended when the American, Commodore Perry, sailed into Tokyo Bay. This image shows Perry being received by the Japanese Imperial Commissioners.

The following year the Japanese moved up the peninsula and captured Shenyang (Mukden). At the same time, Admiral Tojo sank the hapless Russian Baltic fleet (which for months had laboured to reach East Asia) in the Straits of Tsushima. But 18 months of war had left Japan exhausted. An American offer of mediation was accepted by both sides. In Russia, Nicholas II hoped to avoid a revolution inflamed by the crushing defeats his forces had suffered at the hands of an Asian nation.

Under the Treaty of Portsmouth (New Hampshire) in 1905, the Japanese acquired Lüshen, the southern half of Sakhalin Island, and special economic interests in the southern Manchurian railway system. From this base they intended to dominate the mainland.

One other aspect of the Russo-Japanese War that should not go unnoticed was the change in attitude of Asians towards foreigners. The awe in which Europeans and Americans had once been held vanished. The realization that Asians, properly armed and competently led, could defeat Western imperial powers was to pervade Asia.

During the First World War Japan, as an ally of Britain, occupied Germany's Asian colonies, and most of them remained in Japanese hands after the war as part of the League of Nations mandate system. Possession of the Marianna, Marshall, and Carolina island chains gave Japan control over the sea lanes linking North America to Australia and the Philippines. When Russia left the war in 1917 and collapsed into civil war, the Japanese took the opportunity to send 60 000 soldiers into Siberia, along the Trans-Siberian Railway as far as Lake Baykal, supposedly in support of the tsarist regime. They were joined in this venture by 13 other nations, in one of the most obscure episodes of the First World War. It was not until 1922 that Japan withdrew its forces from Siberia.

The world's major powers met in Washington in 1921 to discuss disarmament and stabilize the situation in the Pacific. The Americans and the British wanted to bring a halt to an escalating naval race by limiting the size and tonnage of all the world's battle fleets. This would be accomplished by reducing the number of battleships each major power had. The battleship was still the wonder weapon of the age, but its continued costly construction could bankrupt them all. The Japanese anticipated being allowed a fleet size equal to that of Britain and the United States, but they were forced to accept one of only 60 per cent the size of its rivals. Despite this loss of face, the Japanese accepted their inferior position—providing the Americans and the British agreed not to fortify their possessions in the Pacific, save for British-held Singapore and American-held Hawaii. The relative fleet ratio of 5:3 still left the Japanese navy unrivaled in the Pacific: the other major powers had to spread their ships over two or three oceans. Agreement was also reached banning the construction of any new battleship for 10 years. The terms of the treaty were renewed in London in 1930, but further attempts at naval arms control failed when the Japanese walked out of the 1934 talks.

In other negotiations aimed at stabilizing the situation in Asia, the American position was to strengthen China in the belief that its population and resources would eventually make it a world power. The Nine Power Treaty brought to an end the humiliating treaty ports, implemented a modified Open Door policy, and guaranteed China's borders. In effect, this restrained Japanese expansion on the mainland. But the question of whether or not Manchuria—the homeland of the last imperial dynasty—was part of China was left unanswered. Any Chinese claim to Manchuria would imperil Japanese interests in the region. Despite the Nine Power Treaty, both Britain and the United States maintained their gunboats on China's rivers, and Japan reinforced its Kwantung army in Manchuria.

At this time, the Anglo-Japanese alliance of 1902 was permitted to lapse because of pressure from Canada and the United States. Americans and Canadians were concerned over the large numbers of Asian immigrants arriving on their west coasts, worried they might trigger disturbances in the local labour markets. The Exclusion Act implemented in the USA was designed to cut down drastically on Asian immigration. Similar legislation was adopted by Canada in 1923. Halting immigration in North America was an affront to Japan, and could lead to war. If war did come, there was no doubt Britain would choose the American side. Because the British wished to strengthen their ties with the Americans, the Anglo-Japanese alliance was replaced by the Four Power Pact. In this pact Britain, the USA, France, and Japan agreed to respect each other's spheres of influence in the Pacific.

These **Washington Treaties** were a final rebuff to the Japanese, who had sought recognition as a great power for over a quarter of a century. Continuously denied equal status in world politics, Japan now changed its foreign policy. Because its relations with

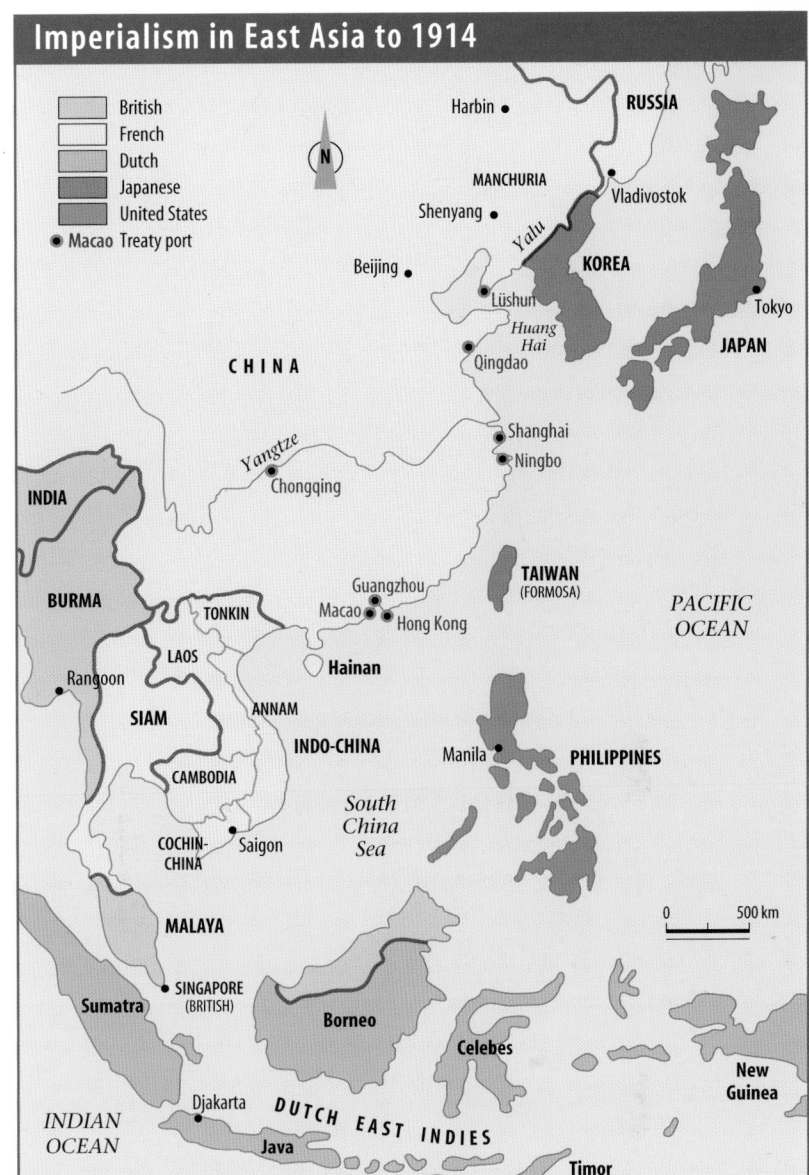

Asia represented the biggest potential market on the planet, therefore, there were many foreign interests in East Asia.

the Americans and the Europeans had been unfruitful, and would likely remain so, Japan chose to seek its future in Asia. In the eyes of Japan's leaders, the world was dividing along racial lines in which Asians would never be accepted as equals.

Japan began to prepare for the conflict that was certain to come. Japan would champion the Asian cause and force the imperialists out of the Pacific. In so doing, it would assure its own hegemony in the region. The only possible rival for dominance in the Pacific was the rising nationalist movement in China.

Russian troops marched through Manchouli, China, in 1914.

RESURGENT CHINA

When the Manchu dynasty that had ruled China since 1644 collapsed, the Middle Kingdom plunged into civil war in 1911. The 250-year-old ruling class, along with all its institutions and bureaucracy, simply vanished overnight. In its place, military leaders fought to carve out their own kingdoms. Of those seeking power, the Chinese Nationalist party, or the Kuomintang, was to become predominant.

The Kuomintang (founded in 1912) grew out of a movement started in 1905 by Dr. Sun Yat-sen, based on the principles of nationalism, democracy, and socialism. By 1927, the Kuomintang (or Nationalist party) had attracted enough support in the south to enable it to proclaim itself the Republic of China.

A small communist party, founded in 1921, was admitted to a share of power. Good feelings toward the USSR had come when the new Soviet Union had renounced all claims and concessions tsarist Russia had on Chinese soil prior to the Bolshevik revolution. Chinese leaders had gone abroad to study in Moscow, and Soviet advisors had been sent to Guangzhou (Canton) to help with the organization of what they thought was to be a new communist state.

A resurgent Nationalist China gave hope for the future unification of all Chinese territories under a modern central government. It also presented a potentially lethal threat to Japanese interests in Manchuria.

After the death of Sun Yat-sen in 1925, the movement was taken over by Generalissimo Chiang Kai-shek, who expanded the Nationalists' control over the military leaders in the central and northern parts of the country. As victory followed victory, the Kuomintang became a party of generals and landowners. Although Chiang continued to espouse democracy in order to curry favour with the United States, he had in fact established a military dictatorship.

When Nationalist forces captured Shanghai in 1927, some historians believe Chiang received large sums of money from businesspeople and bankers, with the stipulation that he remove all communists from the Kuomintang. Whatever the actual causes, the ensuing massacre was particularly savage. The few who learned of the purge in advance fled the cities to take refuge among landless peasants in the countryside. The Communist party was to be reshaped by Mao Zedong. It was the landless and disaffected who turned to the Communists and their policies of land reform, equal social rights, and a better life for all.

To Chiang, communists were a dangerous enemy from within that had to be eradicated. He knew only too well the strength of the millions of landless people who, once organized, could topple him from power. Mao's appeal to the peasantry was a major threat to the Kuomintang, and Chiang made certain throughout this period that his armies pressed remaining communists at every opportunity. In opposing Mao, the Nationalist leader misread the popular mood in China.

THE MANCHURIAN INCIDENT

As the strength of the Nationalist movement grew, the Japanese plotted to secure recognition of their claim to Manchuria before the Kuomintang became even stronger. To this end, Japan went to war in 1931.

After the revolution of 1911, the three provinces of Manchuria that lay north of the Great Wall came under the control of the military leader Chang Tso-lin. His position was secure as long as he governed in the interests of the Japanese businesspeople who had come to regard Manchuria as their own. He also had lands south of the Great Wall which he agreed to turn over to the Kuomintang in 1927, who in turn made no secret of their desire to oust the Japanese from the mainland.

The following year, Chang Tso-lin was killed when his train was blown up. He was succeeded by his son Chang Hsueh-liang, an ardent Nationalist who agreed to surrender all of Manchuria to the Kuomintang. This was not acceptable to the Japanese who used the pretext of a bomb blast on the railway lines near Shenyang to carry out a long planned military occupation of all of Manchuria.

Manchuria was crucial to Japan's economic prosperity. Japan's trade was deeply undercut by tariff barriers erected by the world's leading nations as a result of the Great Depression of 1929. It could not lose its remaining source of raw materials and markets without risking total economic collapse. The silk trade with Britain and the United States was particularly vulnerable, and the collapse of these markets had left Japanese industry in a state of disarray. The plunging economy proved the army's case that military expansion was essential to survival. Conquest could put an end to the desperate plight of their stricken Japanese economy, and war would provide an additional dividend—heightened national prestige.

The occupation of Manchuria went smoothly. By 1932, Manchuria was firmly under Japanese control as the puppet state of Manchukuo. Chiang refused to send his armies north of the Great Wall because he was just then drawing the noose tightly around

In 1937, Japan sent increasing numbers of troops into northern China. Japanese soldiers sometimes wore nose masks to guard against infections.

Mao's Communist forces in the interior. Instead, he appealed to the League of Nations to take collective action against the aggressor.

Over the previous decade the League had had some minor successes in mediating disputes between less powerful nations. It had never before been asked to take action against a major power. Manchuria would be a test case of the effectiveness of the League in preventing war. Somewhat embarrassed by the confidence placed in it, the League reluctantly agreed to take action, though protecting China was the furthest thing from the minds of the great powers. Despite the lack of support from its more powerful members, the League sent out a commission under Lord Lytton to investigate the situation in the summer of 1932.

The commission report was for the most part sympathetic to the Japanese position. It recognized Japan's long-standing economic interests in Manchuria as well as its heavy financial investments there. These special interests were to be safeguarded in the future by international treaty. Lytton also recommended that Japan be permitted to maintain military forces in Manchuria to guard against attack from either China or the USSR. However, Lytton did not hesitate to name Japan as the aggressor. This was too much for the Japanese, who believed they had been provoked by the Kuomintang's attempts to annex Manchuria. They interpreted Lytton's report as a serious loss of face, and promptly withdrew from the League. This

THE LONG MARCH

As the struggle for control intensified, the Chinese Communists were forced by the Nationalists to seek refuge in the hills of Yan'an (Yenan). Evaluate the role played by Mao in the failure of the Nationalists to destroy Communist forces.

Trapped by Chiang Kai-shek's Nationalist armies, the Chinese Communists embarked on an epic march rather than face extermination. Forced out of its stronghold in south China, the Communist party retreated across the country to the hills of Yan'an, in the northern province of Shensi. Today the march is seen as the greatest triumph of the party's early struggles. In the safety of the north, the Communists built up their strength to defeat the Nationalists in the civil war that broke out after the Second World War.

On 12 April 1927, Nationalist forces carried out a purge of communists in Shanghai. The communists were expelled from the Nationalist government in Nanjing (Nanking) and faced obliteration at the hands of agents of the Kuomintang. In August, the Communist party began recruiting an armed force named the People's Liberation Army. Abandoning the idea of occupying the cities, the Red Army moved off into the interior and became a wandering force harried by Nationalist troops. In 1928, the Red Army under Chu Teh joined forces with Mao Zedong. In the relative security of Chingkangshan on the border between Hunan and Kiangsi, the Chinese Communist party was remodeled. The older party members were steeped in the Soviet model that ignored the peasantry and sought revolution among the urban proletariat. With Soviet advisors, they tended to ignore Mao and his rural-oriented dogmas. Mao believed the revolution could and should be carried out by the peasantry, who were oppressed by absentee landlords, harried by bandits, plundered by military leaders, and reduced to near starvation. They were in a revolutionary mood. Mao would give them leadership.

Mao depended on the peasants for support in return for freeing them from their oppressors, including Nationalist forces. By 1930, the Red Army had more than 10 000 men and women, and Mao began to extend his control over adjacent areas. Toward the end of 1930 this prompted Chiang to undertake his Communist bandit extermination campaigns. The Red Army refused to come to battle; it melted away among the peasants to avoid open battles it could not win. The peasants helped the Communists cut the Nationalist supply lines, forcing the latter to withdraw.

A second Nationalist campaign was undertaken the following year—only to meet the same fate at the hands of the Red Army, now swollen to 300 000 men and women. This posed a serious threat to Chiang's control. Only with the establishment of the Japanese puppet-state of Manchukuo and the probability of war with Japan did the Nationalists call off their campaign, in 1931.

Then the Communists established a rival government in Kiangsi and developed closer ties with the USSR. The Kiangsi Soviet acted as a sovereign state and declared war on Japan. It was an empty gesture, but it garnered support among the Chinese, who were disgruntled at the Nationalist appeasement of Japanese occupation forces.

It was at this time, in 1934, that Chiang acted on the advice of his German advisors, Generals von Seekt and Wetzell, to give up frontal attacks (which had proved costly and unsuccessful) in favour of a blockade of Kiangsi province. Blockhouses were erected to interdict all the supply routes into the region. More than 700 000 soldiers were deployed against the Communists in an ever-shrinking circle.

The fifth extermination campaign was launched in October 1933. Communist plans to meet the Nationalists in open battle proved to be a disastrous mistake. By the summer of 1934 the Communists had only two alternatives: break out or perish.

The breakout occurred in October 1934. Some 90 000 soldiers determined to fight their way across China to safety in the north in Shensi, a remote and barren province. Only 30 000 survived the physically demanding trip, called the Long March. Shensi was chosen in part because the nearby Japanese presence would make it difficult for Chiang to fight the Communists if the Communists were fighting the Japanese. The Long March took the Red Army into territories ruled by poorly armed military leaders. They could offer no resistance and Chiang followed the trail at a leisurely pace, mopping up military governments as he went. The Communists did not attempt to take defended cities, and were left alone to pass through the countryside as quickly as possible. They paid for their food and supplies and acted with unusual restraint.

The Red Army set a hurried pace across the southern parts of the nation, never marching less than 50 km a day. In one stretch of 24 hours they made 110 km over mountains and passes. Those who could not keep up were left behind with friendly peasants. Keeping well ahead of the Nationalist forces, the Communists passed into Xinjiang (Sinkiang) in eastern Tibet before crossing the great snow mountains and descending into Szechuan, where they encountered the Communist Fourth Route army under Chiang Kuo-t'ao. He would stay to establish a soviet while Mao pushed on to the hills of Yan'an—which he reached on 2 October 1935.

This was the end of the Long March for the First Front Army. Chiang Kuo-t'ao re-crossed the Mongolian marshlands in an effort to reach Xinjiang, bordering on the USSR. In 1937, he was forced to find sanctuary with Mao in Shensi. He later deserted to the Nationalists and lived out his final days in Hong Kong.

Meanwhile, the Second Front Army arrived in Yan'an in 1936 to boost Communist strength to 80 000. With its arrival, the Red Army was re-established in a fixed base protected by ranges of barren mountains and high wilderness plateaus. Chiang had failed to exterminate the Communists, and now both he and the Japanese had to contend with the Red Army in Yan'an.

1. What part did ideology play in the differences between the Kuomintang and the Chinese Communist party?

2. What characteristics of communist ideology make it intolerable to other political parties and businesspeople?

3. Describe how Mao won the peasants over to his side. Why was this important?

4. Why were the Nationalist forces unable to eliminate the Communists?

brought to an end any necessity of the organization to take collective action. The decision of the League not to act was applauded by those who now did not have to contribute to costly military ventures in the Pacific.

The American reaction to the establishment of Manchukuo was tempered by its inability to mount any kind of a military response. President Roosevelt proposed a principle of non-recognition of any territorial changes made by aggression. This non-recognition doctrine, called the **Stimson Doctrine**, made the United States a potential enemy of Japan. For the moment, the absence of American military strength in the Pacific, and the inability of Roosevelt to increase the USA's armed strength because of Congressional opposition, meant that the Americans could safely be ignored by the Japanese.

During this time, Chiang kept a million troops ranged against the Communists, hoping to draw them into a final battle. Then in 1934 Mao broke out of the encirclement with 90 000 of his followers and fled westward toward the Himalayas in search

THE XIAN INCIDENT

When the Communists, led by Mao, arrived in north-west China at the end of the Long March, Chiang was poised for the kill. The troops he intended to employ against Mao were the soldiers who had been forced out of Manchuria by the Japanese.

Understandably, these forces were sympathetic to the Communists' argument that they should be fighting the Japanese, not fellow Chinese.

Their commander, the son of a former Manchurian military leader, refused to attack Mao's army. Chiang flew to Xian to gain his commander's obedience, but was instead kidnapped by the Manchurian forces.

In the negotiations that followed, Chiang agreed to cooperate with the Communists, forming a united front against the Japanese. He was released on 25 December 1936, 13 days after his capture.

of sanctuary. The Long March was an extraordinary feat of endurance. Ever harried by Nationalist forces, the Communists fought their way across China to the bitterly cold plateaus of Tibet before turning northward and, after many months, gaining the safety of the hills of Yan'an. There Mao paused to regroup his scattered forces. It was in Yan'an that he refined his strategy of liberating the landless peasants from their dreadful life through a protracted guerrilla war in the rural areas. It was also from Yan'an that the call went out to drive the Japanese from China's soil. This exhortation struck a responsive chord among the people. Unlike Chiang, Mao was prepared to fight foreigners first and wage war against Chinese military leaders later.

Chiang's strategy of avoiding war with Japan came to an end in 1937, when the Japanese army invaded northern China and began the Pacific War. On the night of 1 July, a nervous Japanese patrol guarding the Marco Polo Bridge at Beijing fired upon Nationalist soldiers a few yards away. The soldiers believed that one of their men, who had in fact slipped away to relieve himself, had been kidnapped by the Chinese. The incident quickly escalated to an exchange of shots. This event was the pretext for a full-scale invasion. War was begun by the army in the field which not only ignored orders from the Japanese government to halt the fighting, but went on to victory.

One by one, China's coastal cities fell to the Japanese Kwantung army. Beijing was taken and Shanghai besieged. By December the capital, Nanjing, was threatened, but Chiang would not surrender. He moved his capital up the Yangtze River to the mountains surrounding Chongqing (Chungking). There he hoped to hold out until fortune turned in his favour. Calls went out to the **China Lobby** to urge greater amounts of American and British aid for his beleaguered government.

Desperate to get Chiang to the peace table and exact an agreement on the recognition of Manchukuo as part of Japan, General Matsui led his army into Nanjing for a four week orgy of pillaging and destruction. Matsui did not believe that Chiang would stand by and watch his capital be torn apart day by day. The Rape of Nanjing was to take upwards of a quarter of a million lives. Unrestrained, Japanese troops took part in the systematic butchery of the civilian population. Far from convincing Chiang to surrender, this savagery transformed Chinese resolve into implacable hatred.

One final act of destruction took place in the opening months of the Pacific War. Intent on

slowing the Japanese advance, Chiang ordered the dykes along the Yangtze cut, to flood the low-lying plains. The rampaging waters slowed the invaders for only a few days, but, in the interval, one million peasants lost their lives. The Japanese invasion finally came to a halt in front of the Yangtze gorges, where the river tumbles out of the mountains in a series of narrow canyons. This passageway was too heavily defended to be carried by the forces available, and was at the outer limits of the range of Japanese aircraft. Stalemated, the war began to wind down into a six-year undeclared truce. Major fighting on the mainland was not to resume until 1944.

For his part, Chiang felt secure in the mountain retreat where he continued to receive aid from his allies. Soviet supplies came down the northern road from Turkestan, while American and British goods were driven in over the tortuous road from Burma. Chiang calculated that if the war with Japan were to continue, one of the allies would eventually come in on his side. He could then let his more powerful allies deal with Japan. Chinese Nationalist strength would be saved for the civil war with the Communists that would follow Japan's inevitable defeat.

By 1939, Japan was in control of most of eastern China. A vast quantity of foodstuffs and resources lay at hand. Properly exploited, they would have made Japan so powerful that it would never have seen defeat. But although the Japanese armies won many battles, they had not brought the Kuomintang to its knees. There was no indication Nationalist forces would agree to a peace.

In order to put an end to the China incident, the Japanese planned to cut off the final supply links to Chongqing. The caravan routes in the north through Xinjiang and the Burma Road were to be captured. It would mean risking an expansion of the war, but if successful, it would see Chiang acknowledge Japanese sovereignty in Manchuria.

The question was in which direction the Japanese should move. The army wanted to pursue a land strategy by striking northward against the USSR. Taking matters into its own hands, it attacked the Soviet armies guarding Vladivostok. The Japanese counted on German support promised them in the 1936 Anti-Comintern Pact. They also counted on the Soviet forces being weak and unprepared. Unlike the incident in 1904, however, the Soviet counterattack was swift and certain. Badly mauled, the Japanese withdrew.

A few months later the Japanese army struck again, this time at Nomonhan in Mongolia. After a

BIOGRAPHY

JIANG QING (1914-1991)

I must find out which is right—the world or I.
Jiang Qing as Nora in Ibsen's play *A Doll's House*

If there are two basic types of Chinese women—the amah—who are in the vast majority, ever meek and submissive, absorbing within themselves the sins of their family and the world outside—and the empress—a rare spirit at once yearning and domineering, seeking to avenge the fate of every amah since the beginning of time; Jiang Qing is definitely an empress. Jiang Qing, a revolutionary and politician in her own right, but also the third wife of Chairman Mao (1893-1976), was an empress with a twist. For although she would take up the cause of women's rights—or the socialist cause, as in actuality was the case—with great ferocity and flair, the important thing for her was not so much the cause itself as the drama it inspired. A cause provided Jiang with the opportunity to bridge the gap between the way things were and the way they should have been, according to her own, at times, fantastic perceptions. Biographer Ross Terrill says that Jiang would "[blow] up her own individual will into a universe of its own, finally in a surge of political action relevant only to the imperious demands of her personality." Terrill goes on to say that "for Yunhe (an earlier name Jiang went by) the point of it seemed to be her self-expression as a person trying to command a response from the world."

In her early twenties, and after already exhausting two marriages, Jiang went to university and studied literature and drama. In Ibsen's play, *A Doll's House*, Jiang played the role of Nora, who, after being accused of talking like a child and not understanding the world she lives in, replies, "No I don't [understand the world]. But now I mean to go into that . . . I must find out which is right—the world or I." Being out of sorts with the world was also Jiang's experience, whose early life was fraught with harsh realities. Jiang, first known as Li Yunhe "Crane in the Clouds," grew up in the homes of her concubine mother's rich lovers. She was an only child who was never doted upon and whose instincts were never curbed. At 24, Jiang, then known by yet another name—Lan Ping "Blue Apple"—left her life on the stage behind and went to the Chinese Communist headquarters in Yan'an to study Marxist-Leninist theory. There she

Jiang Qing (Madame Mao) is shown on the far right of this photo. To the left of her is Chu Teh, reporter Earl Leaf, and Mao Zedong (far left).

met and became the third wife of Mao Zedong (1939), who had just returned from the Long March.

Madame Mao was involved with the Ministry of Culture in the 1950s and a leader in the 1965-69 Cultural Revolution. During these years, Madame and Chairman Mao were often seen quarreling in public. The impression these scenes would leave on observers was that Mao was only half-intellectual—his other half was still peasant—and that Jiang had gone far beyond the role of amah—supporting and comforting wife—to the point where she was, in large part, responsible for many of the failures of Chinese government.

In 1969, Madame Mao was elected to the Politburo, but after Mao died in 1976, she and three others were arrested for attempting to seize power by setting up militia coups in Shanghai and Beijing. When Madame Mao was tried in 1980 for crimes against innocent people and subverting the government, it was as if her trial was a theatrical encore. There was a command that she exacted from her audience. She appeared in the courtroom looking ten years younger than her age, her hair glossy, her skin silky, supposedly from daily drinking the water from eight boiled chickens. Although when Mao was still alive, he asserted that Jiang's views were not his own, during the trial Jiang claimed that Mao controlled her: "Everything I did, Mao told me to do. I was his dog; what he said to bite, I bit."

In the drama of the courtroom, and afterwards when her death sentence was changed to life imprisonment, Madame Mao seemed still to be asking the question: Who was right, the world or she? ●

PEARL HARBOR

On 7 December 1941, American battleships stationed in Pearl Harbor were attacked by Japanese bombers bringing the Americans into the Second World War. Evaluate the decision of the Americans to direct their attention to the war in Europe before turning their full attention to war against Japan.

Unsuccessful in their attacks on Soviet forces in Asia, the Japanese decided to strike south-west by sea in order to capture essential fuel and mineral resources. They calculated on a short, victorious conquest of Southeast Asia that would result in the expulsion of the other imperial powers, bring an end to their support of Chiang Kai-shek, and force the Chinese to negotiate a settlement of the Manchurian question. The only military force that stood in their way was the American Pacific Fleet stationed in Hawaii.

The Japanese surprise attack on Pearl Harbor devastated the American battleship forces in the Pacific, giving Hitler the occasion to declare war on the United States. Instead of surrendering, however, the Americans entered the war bent on revenge. Their immense industrial capacity would be directed to the destruction of both enemies, and the occupation of the enemies' homelands.

During the interwar years the British and Americans had gradually withdrawn their military forces from the western Pacific. Only Singapore and Honolulu had any significant military strength. The Japanese were intent upon stepping into the area. Without a credible military presence in the western Pacific, the Americans resorted to economic sanctions against Japan in attempts to control its aggressive behaviour. The Americans had demanded Japan evacuate non-Japanese territories on the Asian mainland. This the Japanese military refused to consider.

Toward the end of November 1941, American authorities sent a war warning notice to their Pacific commanders. At the same time, the large aircraft carriers *Lexington* and *Enterprise* were away from Pearl Harbor, ferrying fighters to Wake and Midway Islands.

Japanese training for the attack on Pearl Harbor had begun in earnest in August. A strike force of 6 aircraft carriers supported by 2 battleships, and a host of other warships, including 20 submarine scouts, rehearsed the battle plans. The attack force left Japan at the end of November and approached Hawaii from the north. On the morning of 7 December, it had arrived undetected within 600 km of Pearl Harbor. The planes were launched at 6 AM. The first wave of 200 planes was followed by a second wave of 180. Pearl Harbor was hardly in a condition of readiness. Main batteries were not ready for action, and ammunition for them was still under lock and key. Even as the first bombs began dropping at 7:55 AM, the Americans could not believe they were under attack.

The Japanese planes swept in unopposed. Kate torpedo bombers streaked low over the quiet harbor and launched their torpedoes at American battleships moored side by side on Battleship Row, while Val dive-bombers and Zero fighter aircraft hit nearby American air bases. By 9:45 AM, the raid was over.

The American battleship *Arizona* was hardest hit; it capsized and carried a thousand of its crew to a watery grave. Of the other battleships, *West Virginia* was repeatedly hit, as were the *Nevada, Oklahoma, Tennessee, Maryland,* and *California.* Many other ships were hit in the attack, including the battleship *Pennsylvania*, which was in dry dock at the time. Yet American air power suffered greater relative damage than the naval forces. The Japanese practically eliminated American air power by strafing fighters and bombers that had been bunched together as a precaution against sabotage.

By the end of the day the Americans had suffered 2403 deaths. Three battleships had been sunk, and two thirds of the air force had been destroyed. Only 16 serviceable air force bombers were left standing. By comparison, the Japanese lost 5 midget submarines and 29 airplanes out of 360 in the attack. Nearby Honolulu suffered minor damage from fires caused by misdirected anti-aircraft fire from the dockyard basin.

Within a few hours, American military strength in the Pacific had been blunted, yet this raid would eventually bring tragedy home to the Japanese. The surprise attack rallied even American isolationists in support of war. Without this or a similar incident, the American public would not likely have favoured entering the fighting. Instead, they would have remained content to supply their allies with goods and *matériel*. The First World War had not endeared them to foreign entanglements.

The attack was also unnecessary. The American fleet had not been able to halt previous Japanese expansion in Asia and was in fact assigned a defence role. It would not have dared move within range of Japanese land-based aircraft. As well, the American aircraft carriers were not then in harbor. And even those ships that had been hit were quickly put back in action. It would have been more productive for the Japanese to have destroyed the American oil-storage facilities, the loss of which would have delayed the American war effort in the Pacific longer than the destruction of ships and aircraft.

Perhaps the final blunder was Hitler's decision to declare war on the United States. Had he not done so, the American public might well have insisted on fighting only the visible enemy, and the grand alliance of Atlantic partners might never have come about in the manner in which it did.

1. How did Japan's military leaders view Southeast Asia in the interwar years?

2. Was the attack on the American fleet at Pearl Harbor necessary to Japan's expansionist plans?

3. How did the economic crisis attributable to the American oil embargo affect Japanese strategy?

4. How can industrial powers secure needed resources if not by conquest?

5. Why were American forces not prepared for an attack?

ferocious week long battle, it was pushed back with a loss of 20 000 dead. North was not the direction to go.

The Japanese navy supported an alternative plan in which it would strike south across the Pacific Islands to capture the mineral wealth of Southeast Asia. Calling for a Co-Prosperity Sphere from which the Western imperialists would be driven, the admirals hoped to mask their drive for hegemony in an anti-imperialist crusade. The slogan "Asia for the Asians" had widespread appeal and, with the colonial powers occupied with the European war, the time to strike would never be more favourable.

In the spring of 1941 Matsuoko Yosuke, Japan's foreign minister, visited both Germany and the Soviet Union. Hitler expressed a desire to see Japanese armies attack the USSR in Siberia at the same time as German forces attacked it from the west. Together they would share the wealth of the northern colossus. The prize of Siberia was tempting, but Matsuoko was unconvinced of the USSR's vulnerability and declined to make any firm commitments. Later, while visiting Stalin, he became convinced that in a prolonged war with Germany the Soviets would win. On his own initiative, Matsuoko agreed to a non-aggression pact with the Soviet Union. Stalin considered this pact one of his master strokes, since he could now withdraw his Siberian armies from Asia and throw them against the *Wermacht* in the west.

The British and Americans were alarmed at Japan's warlike intentions. Preoccupied with the war in Europe, they gambled that with very little effort they could dissuade Japan from aggression. A British task force was to be moved from the Atlantic to Singapore in a show of naval strength. The Americans at the same time accelerated the rate of delivery of their new B-17 bombers to Manila. The combination of token air power and token sea power was thought to be a sufficient deterrent. Neither country could afford to risk the opening of a second battlefront in Asia.

Unable to concentrate any credible military deterrence against Japan, the British and especially the Americans turned to economic sanctions, restricting delivery of strategic *matériel* and fuel oil to Japan. In July 1940, the Americans embargoed shipments of aviation fuel, scrap metal, and crude oil to Japan. The embargoing of the latter was particularly dangerous since Japan was gobbling up oil reserves at the rate of 15 000

Advance of Japanese Forces from 1941–1942

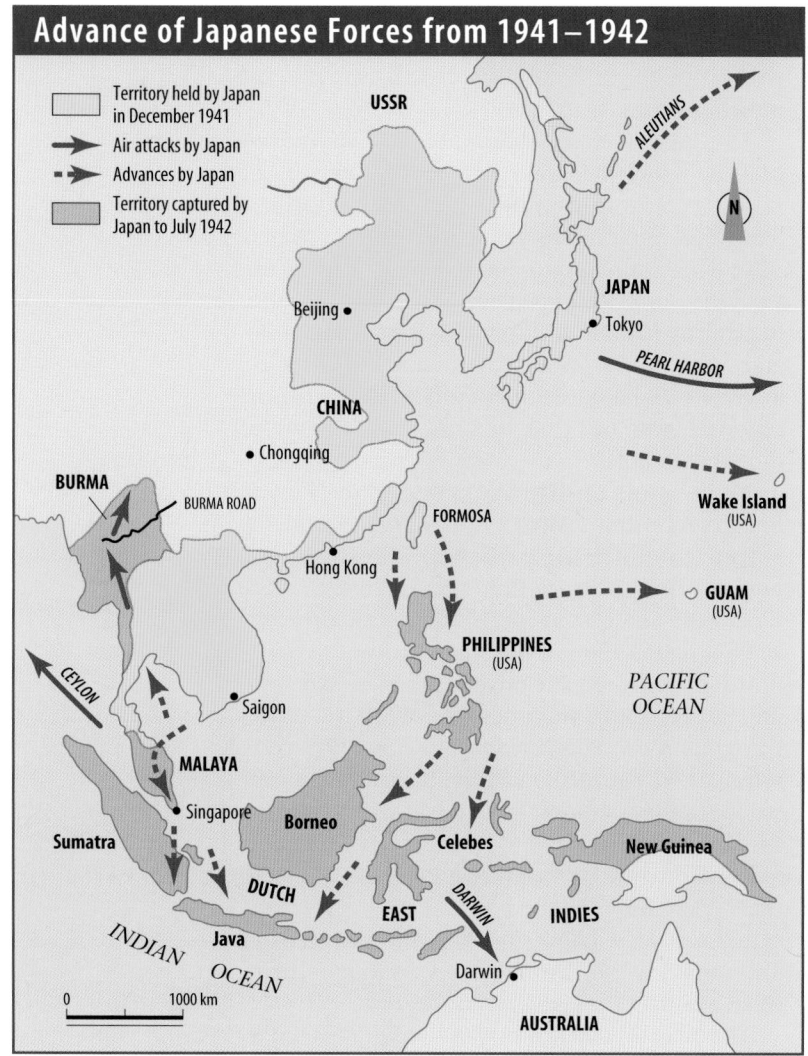

Territory held by Japan in December 1941

Air attacks by Japan

Advances by Japan

Territory captured by Japan to July 1942

USSR

ALEUTIANS

N

Beijing

JAPAN

Tokyo

PEARL HARBOR

CHINA

Chongqing

BURMA

BURMA ROAD

Wake Island (USA)

FORMOSA

Hong Kong

GUAM (USA)

PHILIPPINES (USA)

PACIFIC OCEAN

CEYLON

Saigon

MALAYA

Singapore

Borneo

Celebes

New Guinea

Sumatra

DUTCH

EAST

DARWIN

INDIES

INDIAN OCEAN

Java

Darwin

0   1000 km

AUSTRALIA

This map shows Japan's early successes in the Second World War. Japan abruptly entered the war on 7 December 1941, when Japanese forces attacked American ships anchored in Pearl Harbor, Hawaii.

tonnes a day. As their fuel supply dwindled, the Japanese were forced into negotiations with the Americans. So critical had the shortage become that in the summer of 1941 it was decided that if a solution to the fuel problem could not be found by the end of November, war would result. Japan would have to attack to seize oil resources in Southeast Asia.

The Japanese wanted to force the pace of negotiations, and were at first prepared to give up some of their mainland possessions if need be. After the fall of France in 1940, they had taken over most of the French air bases in Indo-China, from which they could strike at Malaya, Burma, and the Philippines. But with the ascent to power of General Tojo in October, plans to use these bases as pawns were scrapped. The war on the mainland had lasted four years and had cost Japan 1 million soldiers. The army would not retreat from any of its conquests.

The American tactic was to draw the talks out as long possible, to enable the maximum military forces to gather in Manila and Singapore before hostilities broke out. Each week a new flight of bombers was ferried to Clark Field in the Philippines. The Americans demanded that the Japanese respect the territorial integrity of China and withdraw from their occupation zones. The USA refused to recognize Japan's right to large parts of China.

Delay, if not postponement, of any aggression in the Pacific was crucial to American planning. Yet on 25 November 1941 President Roosevelt sent a final ultimatum to the Japanese demanding their withdrawal from the Asian mainland. He knew the result would likely be war, but he had learned from intelligence sources that even as negotiations went forward, the Japanese invasion fleets had been put to sea.

There was now little anyone could do to avert a general Pacific war. The question was where to expect the Japanese attack. American fighter planes were sent to Guam and Midway, and secret war warnings went out to US military commanders throughout the Pacific. Singapore and Manila, the most likely targets, went on full alert. Little did anyone suspect the Japanese were going to attack all the major cities in the Pacific, including Pearl Harbor itself.

SUMMARY

Europe and the USA began the economic exploitation of Asia in the middle of the nineteenth century when traders, backed by powerful battle fleets, won concessions throughout the western Pacific. These vast empires remained in place until 1942, when Japan drove the foreigners out, shattering the myth of their military invincibility.

Only the Japanese met the intrusion by adapting to the ways of the conquerors. Through industrialization they acquired a large military force that was then directed at expansion in Korea and Manchuria. On the mainland they ran into competition from Russia and later from China. Failure to gain recognition of their conquests on the mainland was the underlying cause of the Pacific War of 1930 to 1945.

Rebuffed as an equal partner, Japan plotted to attain a position of hegemony in Asia by driving other imperial forces out. In this quest the Japanese put forward the concept of a "**Greater East Asia Co-Prosperity Sphere**" based on self-development and the expulsion of foreigners (other than Japanese, of course). The Japanese gained support from other nationalist groups as far away as India, by stirring the fires of independence amongst the colonial peoples.

The most dangerous threat to Japanese hegemony over Asia lay in the Chinese Nationalist movement or Kuomintang. Led by Chiang Kai-shek, the Kuomintang was intent on unifying China under its central authority. Chiang claimed the provinces of Manchuria under Japanese control as part of China.

Chiang had powerful allies in the United States and, to a lesser extent, in the Soviet Union. In 1937, when Japan mounted a full-scale invasion of China, Chiang moved his government into the interior at Chongqing. There he was safe from attack. He was convinced that sooner or later one of the other powers would defeat Japan and restore him to full power in China. In the meantime, Chiang's soldiers would continue their war against Mao's Communist forces. It was in an effort to end the impasse that Japan attempted to cut off all outside aid by expanding the war first against the Soviet Union and then against the United States and the other imperial powers.

QUESTIONS

1. Describe nineteenth-century British involvement in Asia.

2. Explain the American Open Door policy. Why did Americans support this policy?

3. Explain the nineteenth-century reforms that propelled Japan into the industrial world.

4. What was the purpose of the mutual defence treaty of 1902 signed by Britain and Japan?

5. Give three results for Japan of the Russo-Japanese War of 1904-1905. What was its long-term significance for Japan's foreign policy?

6. What was the result for Japan of the Washington Naval Conference? Why did Japan accept its final terms?

7. Why was the 1902 Anglo-Japanese alliance permitted to lapse?

8. Explain the Four Power Pact that replaced the Anglo-Japanese alliance.

9. Explain the program put forward by the Kuomintang in China.

10. What was the basis for Mao Zedong's revival of China's Communist party?

11. Explain the conflict over Manchuria. What was the result?

12. What were Lytton's recommendations following the Manchurian incident?

13. What was Japan's response to the Lytton report? What was the significance of this response for global affairs?

14. What was the Long March?

15. Describe the incident at the Marco Polo Bridge on 1 July 1937. Explain its significance.

16. Explain how the Japanese and the Americans ultimately went to war.

CRITICAL ANALYSIS

1. Compare Japan and Britain in their bids to become industrial powers.

2. Describe how the United States hoped to limit Japan's aggressiveness in the Pacific.

3. Evaluate the effectiveness of economic sanctions. By what right can they be imposed?

RESEARCH PROJECTS

1. Write a biographical account of either Chiang Kai-shek or Mao Zedong. Evaluate the role either played in China's emergence as an independent power.

2. Evaluate the impact of the Russo-Japanese War on the development of Japanese power. Consider both political and economic power and comment on Japan's place in the international community as a result of the war.

3. Research the Japanese occupation of China from 1937 to 1945. Identify the impact on the British and the Chinese. Describe Japan's treatment of prisoners.

4. Research the American and Japanese relationship before Pearl Harbor. Describe Japanese investment in the United States and American interests in Asia.

ACTIVITIES

1 Map
On a large map of Asia identify resources, major military bases, and industrial centres before 1941. If resources are owned or controlled by foreigners, indicate their country of origin.

2 Cartoon
Create a cartoon illustrating one of the following:
 (a) Russo-Japanese War;
 (b) Japan's occupation of Manchuria;
 (c) Lord Lytton's report on the Japanese invasion of Manchuria;
 (d) Founding of the Chinese Communist party.

3 Radio Broadcast
Propaganda is one of the tools of war. Create a radio broadcast aimed at the enemy. "Tokyo Rose" was famous for such broadcasts. Re-create a broadcast which might have been given by Tokyo Rose or devise your own propagandist from the country of your choice.

HISTORICAL ANALYSIS

THE POWER OF JAPAN
Early in the twentieth century Japan emerged as a significant power in Asia, a power which was determined to drive Europeans out of the region and maintain "Asia for the Asians" with Japan dominant. The first indication that Japan was a power to be reckoned with was its defeat of Russia in 1904-1905. Subsequently, the Japanese moved into Korea in 1910 and in 1937 invaded mainland China. At this time, Japan was a very small island nation with limited resources and a small population. China on the other hand was a very large country with 20 per cent of the world's population.

Research the political and economic history of Japan in the 1930s to determine why it became such a strong military power. Analyse the strengths which Japan developed and contrast these to the political and economic condition of China during this period. Why would Japan emerge the dominant power rather than China?

THE SECOND WORLD WAR:
WAR IN EUROPE 1939–1945

CHAPTER 7

TIME LINE

1 September	1939:	German invasion of Poland
3 September	1939:	Britain and France declared war on Germany
17 September	1939:	Soviet Union invaded Poland
10 May	1940:	German invasion of France
10 June	1940:	Battle of Britain began
14 June	1940:	Paris fell
22 June	1940:	France surrendered
22 June	1941:	Germans invaded the USSR
7 December	1941:	Japanese bombed Pearl Harbor
1941 - 1943:		Battle of the Atlantic
August	1941:	Atlantic Charter
June	1942:	Battle of Midway
September	1942:	Battle of Stalingrad began
October	1942:	Battle of El Alamein
January	1943:	Casablanca Conference
28 November	1943:	Teheran Conference
6 June	1944:	D-day
9 October	1944:	Moscow Conference
February	1945:	Yalta Conference
30 April	1945:	Hitler committed suicide
8 May	1945:	V-E Day—European war won by Allies
July	1945:	Potsdam Conference

FOCUS ON

THE NATURE OF WARFARE

My very good friends, this is the second time in our history that there has come back from Germany to Downing Street 'peace with honour.' I believe it is peace for our time. We thank you from the bottom of our hearts. And now I recommend you to go home and sleep quietly in your beds.

Britain's prime minister Neville Chamberlain, speaking to a crowd of well-wishers upon his return from negotiations with Adolf Hitler, 31 September 1938.

The Second World War altered both the nature of warfare and the international balance of power. Assume that you are: a Canadian soldier during the raid at Dieppe; a young mother during the siege at Stalingrad; a Polish gypsy interned at the Dachau concentration camp. Describe the Second World War from your perspective. Place your personal observations into the context of the shifting global balance of power which occurred during the war.

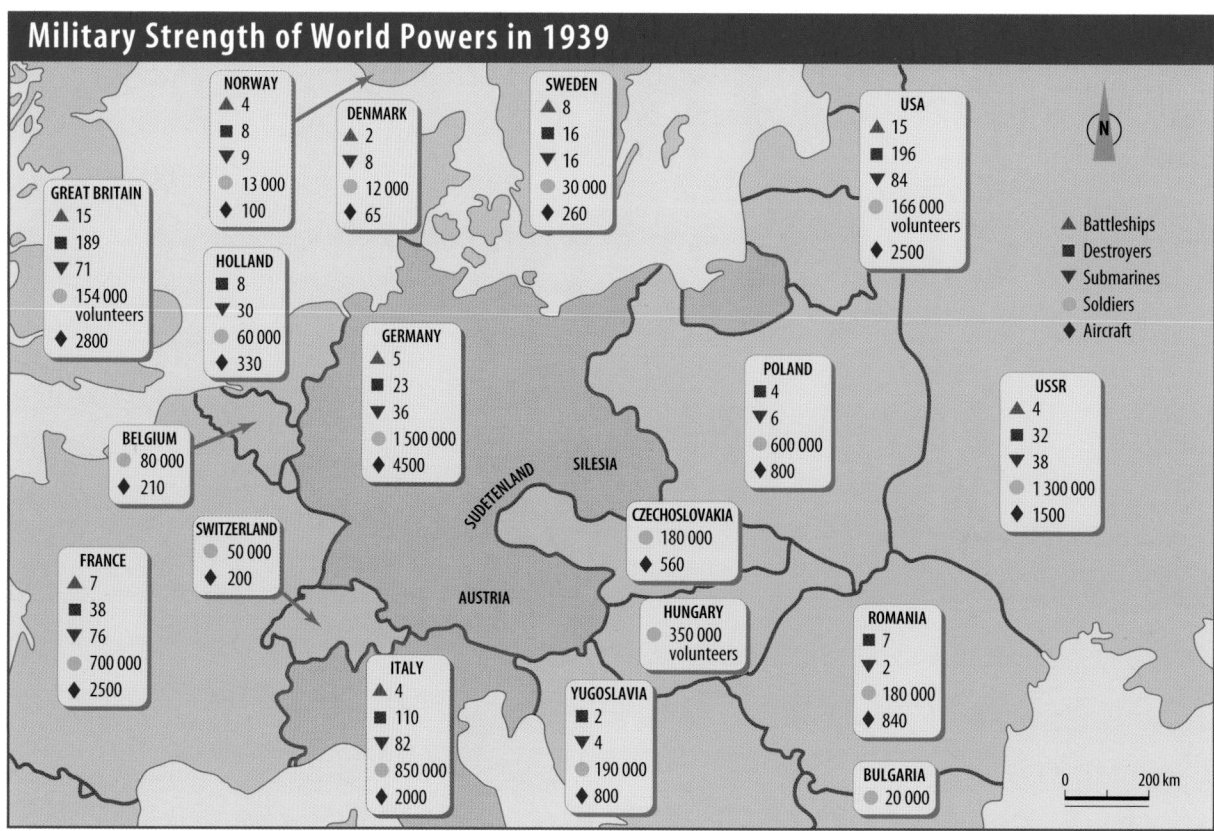

Military Strength of World Powers in 1939

NORWAY
▲ 4
■ 8
▼ 9
● 13 000
◆ 100

DENMARK
▲ 2
▼ 8
● 12 000
◆ 65

SWEDEN
▲ 8
■ 16
▼ 16
● 30 000
◆ 260

USA
▲ 15
■ 196
▼ 84
● 166 000 volunteers
◆ 2500

GREAT BRITAIN
▲ 15
■ 189
▼ 71
● 154 000 volunteers
◆ 2800

HOLLAND
■ 8
▼ 30
● 60 000
◆ 330

GERMANY
▲ 5
■ 23
▼ 36
● 1 500 000
◆ 4500

POLAND
■ 4
▼ 6
● 600 000
◆ 800

USSR
▲ 4
■ 32
▼ 38
● 1 300 000
◆ 1500

BELGIUM
● 80 000
◆ 210

SWITZERLAND
● 50 000
◆ 200

SUDETENLAND   SILESIA

CZECHOSLOVAKIA
● 180 000
◆ 560

FRANCE
▲ 7
■ 38
▼ 76
● 700 000
◆ 2500

AUSTRIA

HUNGARY
● 350 000 volunteers

ROMANIA
■ 7
▼ 2
● 180 000
◆ 840

ITALY
▲ 4
■ 110
▼ 82
● 850 000
◆ 2000

YUGOSLAVIA
■ 2
▼ 4
● 190 000
◆ 800

BULGARIA
● 20 000

▲ Battleships
■ Destroyers
▼ Submarines
● Soldiers
◆ Aircraft

0   200 km

This map shows the relative military strength of various countries just before the start of the Second World War. Compare the size of the armies of Germany, Italy, and the Soviet Union to those of the other countries.

OVERVIEW

This chapter explores the conduct and strategy of the Second World War followed by the strategy in major conferences, the Grand Alliance, the **Holocaust**, the **Resistance**, and results of the war.

THE GREATER REICH
Germany was successful in subduing western Poland, Denmark, and Norway while Soviet forces occupied eastern Poland, the Baltic states, and Finland.

THE BATTLE FOR FRANCE AND BRITAIN
Although France succumbed to the Nazi forces in a matter of weeks, the British survived relentless bombing by the Germans for three months.

BARBAROSSA AND PEARL HARBOR: 1941
In 1941 , the Soviet Union and the United States entered the war after attacks by fascist forces.

BATTLE OF THE ATLANTIC: 1941-1943
German submarine warfare on the Atlantic forced the development of Allied convoy systems to effectively

ward off the attacks on supply ships headed for Great Britain.

THE NEW ORDER
Territories occupied by German forces were subject to totalitarian control by Nazi officials. Both labour and resources were directed to the German state. Deportation and genocide were implemented for the "undesirables."

THE HOLOCAUST
As many as 12 million people, of whom 6 million were Jews, were exterminated in Hitler's attempt to achieve racial purity.

RESISTANCE
Resistance movements developed all over Europe and in many instances played important roles in the reconstruction of national governments after the war.

TURNING THE TIDE: 1942–1943
German reversals in North Africa and the Soviet Union followed by Allied bombing of Germany paved the way for the eventual Allied victory in Europe.

THE GREATER REICH

The Second World War began with Germany's invasion of Poland on 1 September 1939. German forces unleashed a blitzkrieg across the Polish plains in the first phase of Hitler's drive on the east. With the *Luftwaffe* commanding the air, German armoured columns burst through what defences there were and headed for Warsaw, which was bombed on 25 September. Within a few days, western Poland became a Reich protectorate.

On 17 September, the Soviet Union invaded Poland from the east to claim its share of the prey. By the end of the month, Poland had been partitioned between Germany and the USSR. Poland had disappeared from the map of Europe. The Soviets did not stop with Poland, but continued to expand their sphere of influence by reclaiming the Baltic republics and then, at the end of November, attacking Finland. They were determined to regain territory lost in the aftermath of the First World War. Surprisingly, a stout Finnish resistance held the Red Army at bay until the following March. Soviet expansion caused considerable debate as to which of the aggressors was the greater threat to international stability.

Anglo-French guarantees of mutual defence given to Poland and the successor states were meant as a warning to Hitler, not as an offer of concrete assistance. Both Britain and France declared war on Germany on 3 September, made their battle fleets ready for war, and began to bolster their armies and air forces. Hitler considered all of this a diplomatic show that would end in negotiation over the winter. In this he was mistaken. Despite several months of posturing—the "phony war"—an agreement that would restore peace between the three powers could not be reached.

After betrayal over Czechoslovakia, the French and British would not be tricked again into giving way, and were now determined to go to war.

The new year, 1940, found Britain and France formally at war with Germany, although no actual battles were being fought. British fleets had been active in mounting a naval blockade and in tracking down German shipping on the high seas. They had scored a stunning success with the destruction of the German battleship *GrafSpee* in Montevideo (Uruguay) harbour in December, but apart from this, the three powers had not engaged in much actual fighting. There was considerable doubt that they ever would because of the strong peace lobbies in England and France, where opposition to entering yet another European war was significant.

Although war was declared by the end of 1939, no actual battles were fought until later in 1940. England and its allies needed time to build up and train their armies. The soldiers in this picture are training in Canada.

In April 1940, German forces overran Denmark and invaded Norway. Attempts by Anglo-French forces to counter the invasion of Norway were futile, and most of both nations' soldiers were withdrawn in May. The German victory was not without cost. Coastal guns and British warships destroyed a large part of the German surface fleet. Although Germany still had the two most powerful ships afloat, the *Bismarck* and *Tirpitz,* the German navy's effectiveness had been seriously reduced.

THE BATTLE FOR FRANCE AND BRITAIN

Fighting began in earnest on 10 May 1940 with the German invasion of France. During the intervening months, Britain and France had rushed to coordinate their defences. Britain had sent its small army and some air force units onto the continent while the French continued to strengthen the Maginot Line. Plans called for a dash forward into Belgium to meet the Germans along the Meuse River and Albert Canal. In the end this gambit was to no avail. German forces smashed through Belgium and Holland in a matter of days. The day before Holland surrendered, Rotterdam became the second major city after Warsaw to experience German bombing. In Rotterdam, 1000 civilians died.

The major German thrust, however, came through the Ardennes at Sedan. Thought to be too difficult a terrain for tank operations, the French had neglected the area in planning. It was here that German Panzer divisions broke through the French lines, and in three days drove 500 km into France, splitting the Allied forces (French and British). In the north the Anglo-French armies fell back on the coastal port of Dunkirk, France. In one of the stranger twists of the war, the Germans—apparently at Hitler's instruction—paused for a period before resuming their attack on the bridgehead. In that time between 27 May and 4 June, 338 226 British and French soldiers escaped to Britain by sea. The Germans had let a significant number of their enemy escape because they had not even considered the possibility of evacuating troops by sea. A further evacuation of 190 000 Anglo-French soldiers from southern French ports occurred later in the month.

German mechanized forces entered Paris on 14 June, and the French government fled to Bordeaux. On 22 June, an armistice was signed at Compiègne. Under the terms of surrender, the Germans were to occupy the north of France and Atlantic coastal regions but leave about a third of France unoccupied. The French would be permitted to govern the interior. Marshal Pétain was selected to head the new government at Vichy, where he ruled unoccupied France by decree. All civil liberties were abolished under a regime dedicated to trying to get the best deal it could for France within Germany's New Order.

As long as the French cooperated, there was a chance the Germans would repatriate the 2 million French prisoners of war (POWs) held in camps in Germany. The Vichy government complied with German orders to take French hostages, of whom some 30 000 were eventually shot; to confine a further 80 000 anti-fascists and most of French Jewry to concentration camps; and to transport French Jews and 640 000 skilled labourers to the Reich. In the belief that the defeat of France had been final and irrevocable, some French youths enlisted in SS divisions and fought on the eastern front against the Soviet Union. Those who openly collaborated with the Germans were brought to trial after the liberation of France in 1944. Of the 126 000 tried, more than 7000 were given the death penalty, although only 767 were actually executed.

France's reparations payments were set at 300 million francs a day to cover the cost of the German forces of occupation. This figure was increased to 700 million francs a day after Allied landings in French North Africa in November 1942. German forces then occupied the remainder of France. The total French reparations paid amounted to 200 billion francs—about nine times the reparations assessed on Germany under the Dawes Plan of 1924. The French African colonies were left untouched under Vichy administration, and the colonial armies were left where they were. It was further agreed that Japan would move into France's Asian colonies—in particular into Indo-China. Those French citizens who could not bring themselves to surrender fled to England (some joining the Free French forces based there under General Charles de Gaulle) or secretly joined the resistance in France itself.

Two final actions ended the battle for France. Italian forces struck across the Alps on 10 June and gained Nice and Savoy. Immediately after the French surrender, the British destroyed the major part of the French battle fleet so it would not fall into German hands. French crews were given the choice of removing bunker fuel and disarming their ships, sailing to internment in a neutral port, or being destroyed by gunfire. For the most part, those ships outside of French ports voluntarily disarmed, but some chose to fight and were sunk. This policy caused a severe strain on Anglo-French relations for some time to come.

The fall of France left Britain and Germany as the only real adversaries left in Europe. Hitler hoped that with its ally gone, Britain would now make peace. Britain posed a considerable danger to the Germans, since the global resources of the British Empire and Commonwealth were formidable. Britain was the wrong kind of enemy for German forces whose greatest strength lay on land. Unconquered, the British Isles could become a base for subsequent North American intervention.

The German problem was how to get Great Britain out of the war. If negotiations failed, the island would have to be invaded and London captured. But any attack on England would present special difficulties for Germany's armed forces, such as getting the German army across the English Channel onto British soil and, once there, supplying it. The reverse problem occupied Allied planners until the Normandy landings in June 1944.

Plans for the invasion of Britain—Operation Sea Lion—were hastily drafted after the precipitate fall of France. The first priority was gaining command of

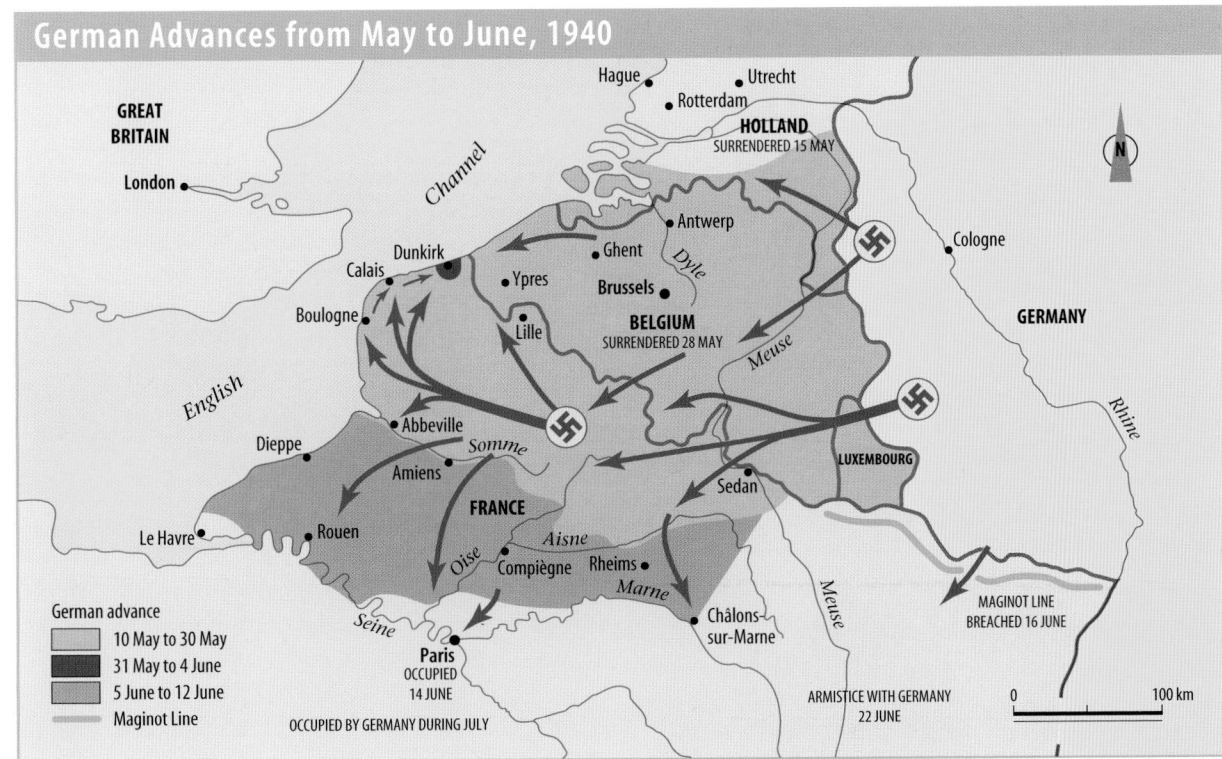

German Advances from May to June, 1940

GREAT BRITAIN

London

Channel

English

Dieppe

Le Havre

Rouen

Seine

Oise

Amiens

Abbeville

Somme

Compiègne

FRANCE

Paris
OCCUPIED
14 JUNE

OCCUPIED BY GERMANY DURING JULY

Aisne

Rheims

Marne

Châlons-
sur-Marne

Sedan

LUXEMBOURG

Meuse

MAGINOT LINE
BREACHED 16 JUNE

ARMISTICE WITH GERMANY
22 JUNE

Hague

Rotterdam

Utrecht

HOLLAND
SURRENDERED 15 MAY

Antwerp

Ghent

Dyle

Brussels

BELGIUM
SURRENDERED 28 MAY

Meuse

Dunkirk

Calais

Boulogne

Ypres

Lille

Cologne

GERMANY

Rhine

N

German advance
- 10 May to 30 May
- 31 May to 4 June
- 5 June to 12 June
- Maginot Line

0   100 km

the air over the English Channel. Once command of the air was achieved, German submarines and surface ships were to block the ends of the English Channel to English fleets and permit an armada of barges to carry 190 000 soldiers onto the southern beaches. The target was London, the loss of which the Germans calculated would result in British surrender. The possibility that England would not surrender with the capture of London or that the sprawling capital would be resolutely defended by its citizens was not considered. Another priority was timing. The invasion had to take place before the autumn storms that make channel crossings hazardous.

Neither the German army nor the navy was keen about plans they both knew had little chance of success. The German navy simply did not have the capacity to transport and supply such large numbers of soldiers, not to mention doing battle with Royal Navy fleets. Only the *Luftwaffe* showed any signs of enthusiasm. Having played largely a supporting role in the previous battles, German air force commanders were eager to assume a leadership position. It was their turn to play the major role.

The Battle of Britain began in the air on 10 June with attacks on coastal ports and shipping. The strategy was to bring the Royal Air Force to battle over the channel. When this did not work, *Luftwaffe* attacks moved inland to eliminate British fighter bases protecting the coast. Here, over the next

Germany had taken Belgium, France, and Luxembourg by the early summer of 1940. It would take nearly four years for the Allies to recapture these countries.

weeks, the eight-gun Hurricane and Spitfire fighters proved too much for the Messerschmidts and Stukas. Operating at maximum range German bombers were often left without fighter escort over targets, and were vulnerable to British fighters. The British also had the advantage of a chain of radar stations along the coast, which gave reasonable warning of enemy raids and allowed pilots to get additional rest and reduced the time it took to intercept German planes. Even so, it was a close battle, with both air fleets losing approximately the same number of machines. The actual figures were far lower than pilots claimed; in the confusion of dogfights both sides routinely reported downing more enemy planes than were in the battle. However, replacing airplanes was not the problem. There were always enough airplanes; they came off the assembly lines at the rate of 500 a month. The real problem was loss of trained pilots.

In a macabre twist of fate, a misdirected German bombing raid on London resulted in a retaliatory raid on Berlin. The latter embarrassed Hitler, and he gave the *Luftwaffe* orders to shift their raids from British fighter bases to London and other major

BIOGRAPHY

CHARLES DE GAULLE
(1890-1970)

All my life I have thought of France in a certain way. This is inspired by sentiment as much as by reason. The emotional side of me tends to imagine France, like the princess in the fairy stories or the Madonna in the frescoes, as dedicated to an exalted and exceptional destiny. Instinctively I have the feeling that providence has created her either

for complete successes or for exemplary misfortunes. If, in spite of this, mediocrity shows in her acts and deeds, it strikes me as an absurd anomaly, to be imputed to the faults of Frenchmen, not to the genius of the land. But the positive side of my mind also assures me that France is not really herself unless in the front rank; that only vast enterprises are capable of counterbalancing the ferments of dispersal which are inherent in her people; that our country, as it is, surrounded by the others, as they are, must aim high and hold itself straight, on pain of mortal danger. In short, to my mind, France cannot be France without greatness.

Charles de Gaulle

Charles de Gaulle, French general and statesman, was a man who imposed himself on events, affecting major change in France after the Second World War. When all of his Second World War contemporaries were long out of their respective political pictures, de Gaulle was once again called to leadership in France from 1958-1969.

From his early childhood days, de Gaulle agonized over French history:

Nothing affected me more than the evidence of our national successes . . . Nothing saddened me more profoundly than our weaknesses and our mistakes, as revealed to my childhood gaze by the way people looked and the things they said: the surrender at Fashoda, the Dreyfus case, social conflicts, religious strife. As an adolescent, the fate of France, whether as a subject of history or the stake in public life, interested me above everything.

De Gaulle's father, Henri, a veteran of the Franco-Prussian War of 1870, vowed he would live to avenge France's loss of Alsace and Lorraine. Henri's passionate love of his country and concern for its pride and national destiny had a profound effect on Charles and his brothers. When for his 10th birthday Charles received a popular history of Paris written by his grandfather, he read it again and again. Charles's namesake and uncle, who was another major influence in his life, had also written a book (calling for the union of Bretons, Scots, Irish, and Welsh peoples), from which the young Charles transcribed the following sentence into his own pages:

In a camp, surprised by enemy attack under cover of night, where each man is fighting alone, in dark confusion, no one asks for the grade or rank of the man who lifts up the standard and makes the first call to rally resistance.

Shortly after Germany defeated France in 1940, de Gaulle—then only an obscure brigadier general—insisted over the air on BBC radio in London that the French had lost a battle but not a war. He urged patriotic French to resist the Germans. From London he organized the Free French forces with the intent of rallying troops in French colonies to liberate France from German occupation.

In 1945, de Gaulle was elected president of the provisional government in France. His relationship with his war-time allies—Stalin, Churchill, and Roosevelt—was marked by intransigence and uncooperativeness. De Gaulle would not budge from considerations he had arrived at as to the best course for France, even though these considerations had been made in solitude, without counsel, and often stood in opposition to his allies' interpretation of events. De Gaulle's politics were marked by certain themes, among them protectionism for France. He believed that if France were to serve itself, it would be serving the whole world.

De Gaulle resigned as president in 1946 when it became clear that the new French constitution would not provide him with as many powers as he felt were necessary. In 1958, however, de Gaulle became premier with the power to rule by decree when the Algerian civil war caused a political crisis in France. He was elected president again the next year and amended the constitution to give his office more power. In 1962, de Gaulle granted Algeria its independence from France, after seven years of bitter fighting between Algerians and French. He resigned in 1969 after his proposals for senate and regional reforms were rejected.

In response to criticisms that he was a better general than prime minister, de Gaulle responded with an inversion of Clémenceau's famous epigram: "I have come to the conclusion that politics is far too serious a business to leave to the politicians." ●

cities. The plan was not simply revenge but to cause panic among British civilians who would then demand an end to the fighting. *Luftwaffe* raids on British cities did not have the desired effect. Instead of demoralizing the British, they hardened British resolve to fight until the end.

By mid-September it was apparent the *Luftwaffe* was not going to gain command of the skies. The German invasion plans were postponed indefinitely, although the air war continued. During the rest of 1940, the *Luftwaffe* continued its blitz on Britain's cities until the air fleet was withdrawn the following year for an assault on the USSR. During the aerial conflicts, which came to be known as the Battle of Britain, 51 509 British civilians were killed and another 80 000 were wounded.

BARBAROSSA AND PEARL HARBOR: 1941

In 1941, the German invasion of the Soviet Union —code named Barbarossa—and the Japanese attack on Pearl Harbor in December brought the war to a truly global scale. These were turning points as the entry of the USA and the USSR into the fighting brought an overwhelming amount of human and physical resources to the Allied side.

During the second winter and spring of the war, fighting shifted to the Mediterranean. Mussolini's vain attempts to emulate Hitler's successes resulted in a military fiasco. The Italian army in North Africa attacked British forces in Egypt and was soundly beaten, as were its armies in Ethiopia and Greece. Late in the spring of 1941, Hitler sent German forces to assist his Italian ally. General Rommel took command of the North African army, renamed the Afrika Corps, and turned the tide of battle. Other German forces crushed Yugoslavia and Greece in "Operation Punishment." In Yugoslavia, resistance began almost immediately in the mountains under the leadership of Josip Broz, known as Tito. Tito was a federalist who stood for a unified Yugoslavia. He was opposed by other guerrilla forces under the Serbian nationalist Dragoljub Mikhailovich, who fought for an enlarged Serbia. Tito's and Mikhailovich's guerrilla forces spent much of the war fighting one another. At times, the Yugoslavian situation paralleled the one in Greece, where royalist and communist guerrilla factions spent as much time fighting each

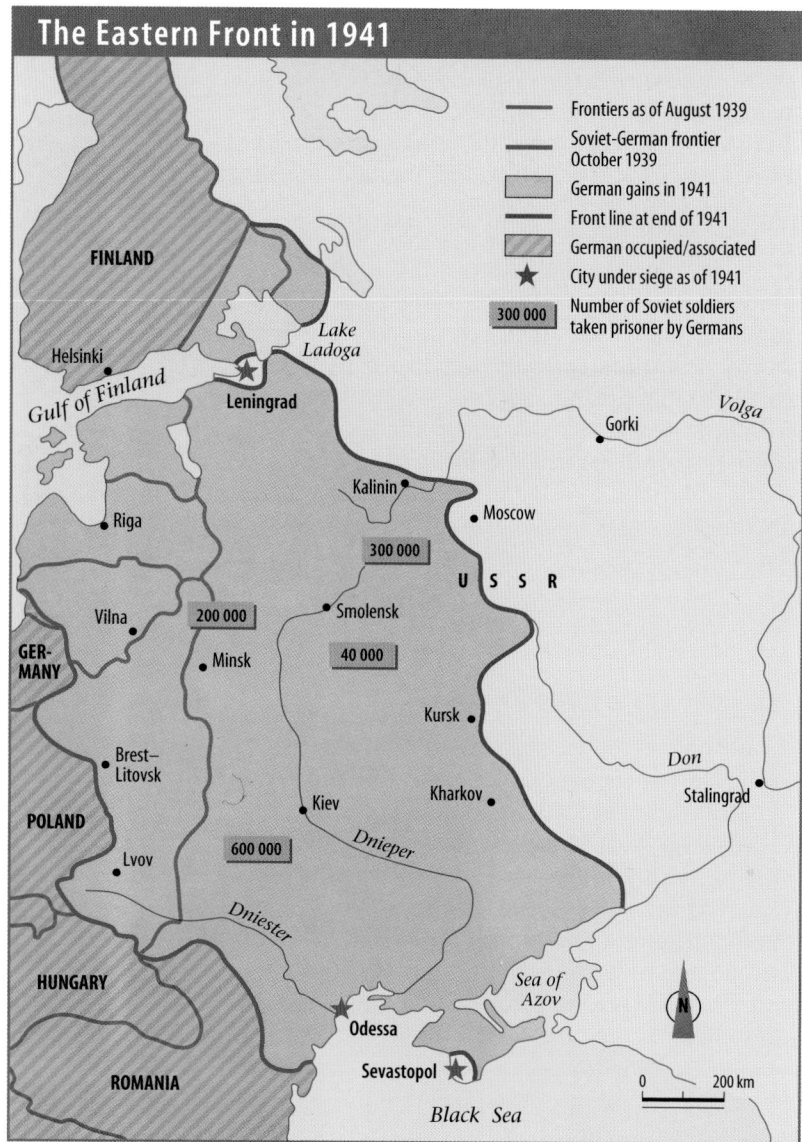

The Eastern Front in 1941

Legend:
- Frontiers as of August 1939
- Soviet-German frontier October 1939
- German gains in 1941
- Front line at end of 1941
- German occupied/associated
- ★ City under siege as of 1941
- 300 000 Number of Soviet soldiers taken prisoner by Germans

FINLAND

Helsinki

Lake Ladoga

Gulf of Finland

Leningrad ★

Gorki

Volga

Kalinin

Moscow

Riga

300 000

U S S R

Vilna

200 000

Smolensk

GER-MANY

Minsk

40 000

Kursk

Brest–Litovsk

Don

Kharkov

Stalingrad

POLAND

Kiev

Dnieper

600 000

Lvov

Dniester

HUNGARY

Sea of Azov

Odessa ★

ROMANIA

Sevastopol ★

Black Sea

N

0   200 km

The Soviet Union suffered great losses in the early stages of the German invasion. Later Germany would suffer devastating losses due to weather and the inability to supply the front lines.

other as fighting the Germans. In both cases, warring factions were to continue their struggle for power after Germany's defeat in 1945.

Intended as a swift operation, Germany's Balkan campaign bogged down. Large numbers of German soldiers were tied up in the struggle against highly effective guerrilla forces. Although the Germans held the cities, the partisans held the countryside.

British forces acted to stop the formation of pro-German governments in the Middle East, partitioning Iran with Soviet forces. General de Gaulle released Lebanon and Syria from French mandate,

thereby giving them their independence. When the French attempted to renege on this agreement after the war, and bombed Damascus, the Americans intervened to stop French aggression.

On 22 June 1941 German armies poured into the Soviet Union and crushed Soviet army and air forces in their path. In the first 24 hours, the Panzers slashed their way behind Soviet lines and took all designated targets. As Stuka dive bombers obliterated Soviet defences, three separate army groups drove eastward in the largest land battle staged so far. Millions of people took part in the initial stages. Within weeks the Germans had destroyed 5000 aircraft, 15 000 tanks, and entire Soviet armies. More than 3 million Soviets were killed or taken prisoner. So complete were the victories that the Germans for a time believed the USSR was defeated. Yet despite staggering losses in lives and *matériel*, the Soviets still had 4.7 million people under arms and could call up millions more.

The German northern army group reached Leningrad, the USSR's second most important city after Moscow, and laid siege to it. There was little fresh water or food in the beleaguered metropolis, and in the winter months thousands died of starvation each day. Supply columns struggled over the ice of Lake Ladoga to bring pitifully inadequate relief. Yet the Germans were never strong enough to take the city, and after 30 months, in January 1944, the siege was lifted.

Germany's central army group fought its way across Ukraine, engaging in major battles of annihilation. Much of the damage done to the Red Army occurred in this sector. Entire armies were destroyed by sweeping pincer movements. By 1 August, the Germans were within 320 km of Moscow, but a three-week halt was called in operations. In the meantime, Germany's southern army group made its way victoriously toward the Crimea. The August strategy meetings of the German generals wasted some of the best campaigning weather. Their gains had been so great that they did not have the human resources to supply all three battle groups at the same time. One worrisome problem was the 500 000 Soviet soldiers who had been bypassed by rapidly advancing German armies, now dangerously in their rear. A quarter of a million German troops were required simply for garrison duties. Sabotage against German forces led to retaliatory burning of entire Soviet villages and orgies of civilian killings.

Germany's fall campaign of 1941 called for a southerly advance toward the industrial heartland of the Dnieper River and Donets' basin. The offensive resumed at the end of August. Within a month, the Germans had captured Kiev and laid siege to Sevastopol in the Crimea. Heady with victory, they now gambled on Soviet weakness, not German strength. The Germans decided to capture Moscow and force surrender before the winter set in.

The final battle of the initial German campaign began in the last week of October as the central German army group launched its much-awaited attack on Moscow. The first two weeks went reasonably well, but then the weather turned bad. Heavy autumn rains turned the fields into quagmires, impassable to motorized vehicles. On some days, an advance of 2 or 3 km was considered outstanding. Then, in November, when the ground froze, driving snow and sub-zero temperatures devastated the invaders. The German army suffered horribly from the intense cold. There were 100 000 cases of frostbite; soldiers stuffed paper into their uniforms to give them protection from the cold. Guns and machines would not operate in the extreme conditions. So confident had the Germans been of a quick victory that only occupation troops had been supplied with winter clothing. At first, front-line troops had none.

Still the advance continued, and by December German troops were in the suburbs of Moscow, trying to encircle the city. On 5 December they almost succeeded in closing the gap behind Moscow, but at that critical juncture they ran out of troops and supplies. The last 5 km might as well have been a million. The Germans had reached the limit of their endurance. On 8 December the German army shifted to winter-operations status and gave up the attack. Space, snow, and time had saved the city. It is unlikely the capture of Moscow would have ended in Soviet surrender. Most of the government had already been removed from the capital and some 2 million citizens evacuated.

The Germans' failure to defeat the USSR in the first three months of their invasion placed them in a precarious position. All their battle victories aside, Germany did not have the resources to fight a prolonged war. Despite the loss of 40 per cent of its industrial and food-production areas, half of its armed forces with almost all of their equipment, the entire Ukraine, and a third of its population, the USSR would not surrender. The Germans would have to make a final supreme effort to knock the Soviet Union out of the war. This effort was made in 1942.

At the height of the battle for Moscow, Germans had noted a disturbing presence in the Soviet lines:

The German army quickly lost its advantage as winter fell. Soviet soldiers are shown here engaged in combat near Moscow during the winter of 1941.

Asian troops. On the very day he was captured in Tokyo, the Soviet master spy Richard Sorge had sent Stalin information that confirmed Japan would not renew its attacks on the USSR but would instead strike southward by sea into Southeast Asia. Confident that his Siberian borders were for the time being secure, Stalin had begun moving troops and airplanes westward from the Pacific for the defence of Moscow.

As the battle for Moscow drew to a close, events on the other side of the world were to bring the Americans into the conflict. This was a catastrophe for the Germans, since they could not match the Americans' industrial strength. On 7 December 1941, the Japanese attacked the American fleet at anchor in Pearl Harbor, Hawaii. Like the Germans, the Japanese had calculated on a short three-to-four-month war to give them the resources and living space needed to complete their industrialization. Both were unable to fight a prolonged war and counted on swift victory followed by favourable negotiations.

The attack on Pearl Harbor ignited war fever in the United States. Safe behind ocean barriers, the USA had let its military forces atrophy since the First World War. Although technically speaking neutral, the USA had done everything short of declare war to help Britain and later the Soviet Union overcome Nazi aggression. The destroyers-for-bases deal, the cash and carry, and lend-lease programs, the rearming of Anglo-French forces after Dunkirk, and the

CASE STUDY

BARBAROSSA

Although Germany and the Soviet Union had signed a non-aggression pact, Nazi forces attacked the Soviet Union on 22 June 1941. Analyse the rationale on the part of both the Germans and the Soviets for the signing of the Nazi-Soviet pact. Evaluate the impact of this agreement on the area of Central Europe which was first occupied by Soviet forces in 1939 and then German forces in 1941.

On the morning of 22 June 1941 the longest battle front in history came alive as 6000 German guns lit up the sky to pound Soviet defences. From the Baltic coast to the Black Sea, a distance of 1600 km, 3 million troops lay awake awaiting the order to rush Soviet frontier posts. Each German soldier had been given 30 cigarettes, and every four shared a bottle of brandy as the tents were taken down and the tanks made ready to roll. At 3:15 AM, after the last Soviet freight train of the day had crossed into Germany, the order was given to attack. Since 1940, Stalin had delivered a million tonnes of mineral oil, 2700 kg of platinum, and quantities of magnesium, chrome, and cotton to the value of 239 000 000 marks as part of a negotiated trade agreement with the Nazis.

As the last Soviet train advanced onto German soil, the German offensive began. The night blazed with green flares signaling that all bridges had been taken, and armoured vehicles now sped across them. German planes had crossed the border just in advance of the ground attack and were now beginning their dives on Soviet air bases. Parked row upon row, Soviet planes were easy targets for the *Luftwaffe*. In the first 24 hours, some 2000 Soviet airplanes, including 500 bombers, were destroyed. Germany had control of the air.

The Germans deployed 3 million soldiers, 600 000 vehicles, 750 000 horses, 1830 aircraft, and 7184 guns. The USSR had 4.5 million soldiers deployed evenly along the front, divided into ten army groups.

Unknown to the Soviets, their positions had been photographed by a special unit of the German air corps. Flying in pressurized cabins at altitudes as high as 11 887 m, the Germans had methodically photographed the entire Soviet front to a depth of 400 km. The extreme height of the reconnaissance planes had made them undetectable to the Soviets.

The Germans achieved complete tactical surprise. Every objective and every bridge along the 850 km Bug River was taken intact. General Pavlov's frontier armies melted away before the onslaught. After the war, General Yeremko claimed that Stalin knew of the impending attack but would not alert his generals: Stalin had dismissed warnings from his own intelligence officers, unable to believe Germany would ever attack his country. Stalin was warned by the Rote Kapelle—the Red Chapel, his spy ring in the West—of the precise date of the coming attack. Leopold Trepper, who moved freely about Hitler's entourage, Victor Sokolov in Brussels, Rudolf Rossler ("Lucy") in Switzerland, and Richard Sorge in Tokyo all forwarded mountains of information about Hitler's plans. So effective was the Rote Kapelle that German battle orders at the highest level were in Moscow within two days of being drawn up. Yet Stalin was convinced it was all a bluff to mask a German invasion of Great Britain. He wanted the Western powers to destroy themselves so that he could pick up the pieces.

Stalin even punished those who spread rumours of a German attack. He halted all reconnaissance along the front so as not to provoke an incident that might lead to war. Long-range guns were left uselessly far behind the front line. Commanders were forbidden to fire their weapons in either attack or defence without orders from Stalin's general staff, and the 7000 tanks on the front were evenly spread in support of infantry regiments, not massed at strategic points. As German armies rolled forward, Soviet soldiers held their ground, waiting for orders to open fire. When orders never came, the Soviet soldiers disappeared into the marshes and forests where they organized a clandestine resistance.

Concentrating their armour, the Germans smashed through enemy lines and headed into the open countryside beyond them. By late afternoon the mechanized columns were motoring along quiet country roads at 60 km per hour, well clear of the fighting zones. In the north General von Manstein's forces were 85 km behind the front lines on the first day and moving forward. All targeted sectors fell into German hands on the first day.

How unready Soviet forces were is evident from the fact that the German northern group under Manstein was able to capture intact the rail and road bridges at Dvinsk, 600 km behind Soviet lines. After four days fighting across open country, the armour halted, while Germans dressed as Soviet soldiers escorted what appeared to be German prisoners through Dvinsk and onto the bridges. On a signal, the Germans revealed their identities and raced to cut the demolition charges. These small units held the bridges until the tanks, now careening through the narrow streets, could reach them. The capture of the bridges opened up the road to Leningrad, which would come under siege that fall.

The central army group stormed across the Bug River, tearing apart frontier defences and penetrating deep behind the opposing lines in wide encirclements designed to destroy the bulk of Soviet armies. The Soviets could not handle the massive firepower and rapid movement of the Panzer groups. Surrounded, the Soviets linked arms and marched into the German guns, hoping somehow to break out. Soviet cavalry regiments charged into mortar and machine-gun fire shouting "Urra, urra!" in a futile effort to escape. As divisions were destroyed, fresh reserves stepped in and were also destroyed by German artillery fire.

In the first days of the assault the Germans identified over 200 Soviet divisions that had been annihilated. They reasoned that the reckless expenditure of Soviet lives could not go on forever. But endless counterattacks began to worry some German commanders, who were uneasy about the lack of prisoners and the stubborn resistance on their flanks. The Soviets were taking a ferocious beating, but they were not out of the war.

After eight weeks, the bulk of the Soviet frontier armies had been eliminated, and a bold advance on Moscow was considered. Should cities be the new targets? What of the seemingly inexhaustible Soviet reserves? What of the industrial heartlands near Stalingrad and east of the Ural mountains? The Germans had accomplished their initial objectives so quickly they had not formulated plans of what to do next. Out of an August conference came the fatal decision to strike at the USSR's political capital before the snow came.

Although Operation Barbarossa was outstandingly successful, the USSR had not surrendered. There were millions more Soviet troops yet to appear. Some German generals began to realize that the German armed forces had attempted too much and questioned whether Germany could support

The Germans dominated the eastern front throughout the early campaigns, and they were confident of a quick victory. This picture shows German armour at the beginning of the invasion.

three separate army groups operating in the USSR at the same time.

1. Consider the resources needed to arm, feed, transport, clothe, and shelter armed forces numbering more than 8 million people. What problems do you think the Germans might have encountered in supporting three separate army groups in the USSR?

2. What changes were made to war as a result of the increased killing power of modern weapons, the longer range of modern combat weapons, the addition of aircraft and submarines as a "third dimension" to the battlefield, and the size of the armies involved?

3. Why did the Germans begin to feel they had won the war on the eastern front by August 1941? Why were they wrong?

4. What are the military advantages of the size of the USSR? Would the Soviets have surrendered had Moscow been captured?

5. Evaluate the early successes of the German armed forces in their attack on the USSR.

The success of an army hinges on the dependable supply of equipment and food supplies. As in the First World War, women stepped into jobs traditionally held by men. These British workers are refurbishing a bomber plane.

AMERICAN LEND-LEASE EXPENDITURES FROM 1941–1945

Early in the Second World War, the United States supported the Allied effort without directly joining the fighting. Faced with a powerful neutrality lobby in Congress, the Roosevelt administration arranged huge transfers of money and equipment to the Allies. These transactions continued after the United States entered the fighting.

Amount in Millions of Dollars	
31 385 m$	Great Britain
10 982 m$	Soviet Union & Empire
3 224 m$	France & Empire
1 627 m$	China
501 m$	Central & South America
159 m$	Belgium & Empire
82 m$	Greece
47 m$	Norway
43 m$	Turkey
32 m$	Yugoslavia
19 m$	Saudi Arabia
12 m$	Liberia
8 m$	Iceland
5 m$	Abyssinia (Ethiopia)
5 m$	Iran
2 m$	Egypt
1 m$	Iraq

mounting of active war patrols at sea left no doubt whose side the USA was on. It would take the Americans time to rearm, but in less than two years there were 12 million soldiers under arms. Their enormous industrial plant was quickly on its way to providing a 1200-ship battle fleet, a 20 000 plane armada, and the equipment for several army groups. The decision as to whom and where to fight was made easier by Hitler's unilateral declaration of war on the United States on 11 December. The Americans would strike at Germany first, to defeat the potentially most dangerous enemy, and then deal with Japan. The decision to strike Europe first was politically courageous for President Roosevelt, in the face of the demand for revenge raised against Japan in all parts of the American press and public.

The new year, 1942, would see the war expand to global proportions. Circumstance had brought all the industrial powers into play, with Allies (Britain, the Soviet Union, the United States, Australia/New Zealand, and Canada) arrayed against the Axis (Germany, Italy, and Japan). For the next three years the Allies were bound together by a common enemy, but there were deep differences between them. Apart from their opposing political and economic ideologies, there were major disagreements on the conduct of the war. Whereas Stalin wanted to extend the Soviet sphere of influence as far west as possible, Franklin Roosevelt and Winston Churchill talked of self-determination and freely elected governments in Central Europe. Whereas Churchill and Stalin sought to retain if not expand their global positions, Roosevelt supported the ideal of independence for all peoples and would not support his colleagues in regaining their lost colonies. Whereas the American strategy was to strike directly at Germany through France, the British, aware of the difficulties of a sea-borne invasion against a fortified coast, sought to begin with strikes at North Africa, Italy, and the Balkans. Meanwhile, Stalin wondered when his allies were going to open a second front of any kind to relieve German pressure on him. He began to believe that his Anglo-American allies were purposely delaying their attack, in the hope that the Germans and Soviets could destroy each other. An absolute dictator in his own country, Stalin did not appreciate the problems involved in getting American armies across the Atlantic, or the time it would take to build landing craft to carry hundreds of thousands of men across the English Channel.

BATTLE OF THE ATLANTIC: 1941–1943

The critical factor in a prolonged war is the mass-production of equipment and *matériel*. Men and women can almost always be found and trained to use equipment. Britain's surprising ability to stay in the war depended on getting food, fuel, and raw materials from North America. It was this principal weakness that Germany sought to exploit through submarine warfare. With only two months' supplies on hand, Britain might be forced to surrender after even a brief stoppage of imports. On more than one occasion in the period 1941-1943, German U-boats came close to forcing Britain out of the war.

Under wartime conditions, British imports fell from an annual 50 million tonnes to 22 million tonnes. In 1941, the Axis powers sank 1299 merchant ships. In 1942, when the ocean-going submarines roamed off the east coast of North America and up the Saint Lawrence River, 1664 ships were lost—273 in March alone.

An added drain on shipping was the institution of Arctic convoys to send aid to the beleaguered USSR. Almost all the 3000-km trip through ice-choked waters to Murmansk and Archangel was within reach of German aircraft and surface ships. These planes and ships took their toll: 100 ships and 2800 crew members were lost from only 40 convoys. So great was the danger that during the Arctic daylight months of 1943, no convoys at all were sent out. Anglo-American aid, including an American $6 billion line of credit, amounted to about 4 per cent of the Soviet Union's war needs. Though small, this aid came at a crucial time, and was more than the Allies could comfortably spare. Among tonnes of uniforms, medical supplies, and food were 22 000 aircraft and 13 000 tanks, although much of the heavier equipment was sent to the Soviet Union by land through Iran.

It took time to organize an effective convoy system. The range of ocean escorts and air patrols had to be increased to cover every part of the 15-day Atlantic crossing. By the end of 1943, the Allies had several escort groups at sea, each with an aircraft carrier and the latest in anti-submarine warfare devices, to hound the U-boats out of the Atlantic. Of the 1162 German submarines built, 1069 were sunk or surrendered. With the sea lanes more or less secured, the Allies could focus soldiers and *matériel* on the battle fronts.

By 1943, the Allies had begun to establish control of the seas. They started planning to launch an invasion of France from the sea.

Most of the U-boats Germany lost were in the Atlantic. The Allies lost 2789 merchant vessels. The German submarine command lost 28 000 of 40 000 submariners, while the Allies lost 30 000 merchant sailors and an equivalent number of naval officers.

THE NEW ORDER

For four years Germany dominated the European continent more completely than any nation had ever done before. Although the Germans had a grand design for a New Order in Europe, their vision yielded to the realistic requirements of battle. Initially, the Germans saw their conquests as assets to be exploited for winning the war. Taken as a whole, the human and physical resources under German control were considerable, and had they been coordinated, would have been formidable.

In the west, the Germans administered the conquered peoples through their own existing institutions. The local authority of governments, mayors, and city councillors was more or less left in place. Outwardly, after the shock of defeat had passed, life reverted to routine, though diets were reduced and ration cards came into effect to control the distribution of food and consumer goods. Outside of strategic areas under direct military rule, control by German

GERMAN U-BOATS (SUBMARINES)

Britain's dependence on imported goods made it vulnerable to German submarine attacks on supply ships. There have been many books written and films made on the subject of submarine warfare. Review a book on the subject or view a video ("Run Silent, Run Deep," "Das Boot," etc.). Write a report taking the point of view of either a surface vessel crewperson, or a submariner.

German naval strategy during the Second World War included a blockade of England by Admiral Dönitz's submarine force. Needing over 50 million tonnes of imported goods each year, Britain was vulnerable to economic strangulation.

During the first two years of the war, more than 3 million tonnes of Allied shipping were destroyed in the western approaches to Britain. For the next two years, Britain's ability to stay at war hung on a battle fought the length and breadth of the Atlantic Ocean by German submarine wolf packs and merchant convoys protected by a growing number of naval escorts and anti-submarine aircraft.

During the war, 14.5 million tonnes of merchant vessels were destroyed, with British shipyards able to replace only 6 per cent. In the worst months of 1942, tonnage afloat had shrunk to 22.9 million tonnes—just over half of peacetime requirements. But American shipyards more than made good the losses by launching 10 million tonnes of new shipping that same year. Almost 20 million tonnes of shipping was launched, mostly from American yards, in 1943.

In the interwar years, the British population had grown by 4 million people, increasing the nation's need for offshore supplies. But the danger posed by submarines had been largely ignored. In the First World War, the U-boat had proven vulnerable to convoys and aircraft. To attain any speed, submarines had to travel on the surface and the underwater firing of torpedoes often caused leaks in the hulls. Submarines were considered barbaric. Whereas surface ships were expected to stop their targets and make certain crews were safely away before sinking enemy vessels, submarines struck from the depths without warning. In the First World War, the U-boats were defeated by escorted convoys: only 250 surface ships out of 84 000 sailings had been sunk by submarines.

When the Second World War broke out, the British were woefully short of escorts for the 2500 ships which were at sea on any given day.

All was not well on the German side either. Dönitz had not been able to convince his superiors to build a large submarine fleet. German naval strategy had planned for the creation of a war-ready high-seas surface fleet by 1946 with an ancillary 129 submarines ready by 1944. Dönitz argued for a U-boat fleet of 300. When war broke out, he had only 56 effective sea-going boats, some tied up in the training and refit cycle. As a result, Dönitz could rarely send out more than 6 or 7 U-boats to sea during the first year of the war. Yet this handful sank 102 ships in the first four months.

The U-boats were immune to detection except in the immediate vicinity of other shipping; they roamed the oceans at will until 1943, when long-range escorts and aircraft could patrol and protect shipping lanes from one end to the other. The submerged speed of the U-boats averaged only from 4 to 7 knots per hour, and most convoys could outrun a single U-boat on its attack course. This disadvantage led to German development of wolf-pack strategies, in which a number of submarines deployed across a convoy's path. Attacking at night, often within the convoy perimeter, and on the surface, U-boats were able to make their kills and escape.

The heyday for German U-boats was the period from July 1940 to December 1941. After the fall of France, German boats were able to use French harbours, thus cutting down travel distance to sea lanes dramatically and avoiding the British-patrolled North Sea and the English Channel. German boats took control of the western approaches and forced convoys to divert north around Ireland to reach new harbourages on Britain's west coast. During that autumn, a total blockade of Britain became a possibility as 2.5 million tonnes of shipping sank to the bottom. Larger, longer-range German boats began to move across the Atlantic to war zones in the Caribbean and up the Saint Lawrence estuary as far as Quebec City. Beginning in January 1942, German U-boats now controlled the sea lanes from Quebec City to Bermuda.

With the addition of 105 Italian submarines to the Axis fleet, the battle for the Atlantic reached critical proportions. The Americans agreed to provide Britain and Canada with 50 older destroyer escorts in return for air bases in Newfoundland and the British Caribbean. The subsequent British-American occupation of Iceland provided for increased Allied air surveillance of the sea lanes.

The critical stages of the battle came between August 1942 and May 1943, when German submarines were deployed across the sea lanes in 10 wolf packs. The packs needed to sink an average of 700 000 tonnes a month to achieve victory; in some months they came close to that figure. But sweeping back and forth across the ocean they now came upon more and larger convoy escorts and maritime patrol craft equipped with sonar detection gear and acoustic homing torpedoes. The battle waged primarily by British and Canadian surface ships began to turn against the German U-boat packs.

The last German U-boat victory was in March 1943, when gales and driving snow gave them the advantage. Fifty boats were sent out and in the first three weeks accounted for eighty-five ships sunk, with the loss of only one submarine. This was followed by disasters for the Germans in May when Canadian and British escort groups sank forty-one submarines—a quarter of the Axis's operational strength. As a result, Germany withdrew its U-boats and conceded the sea lanes to the Allies.

1. What factors make a naval blockade effective? Did German U-boat strategy incorporate these factors?

2. How did submarine warfare change the nature of the sea war?

3. Describe how technology played a critical role in defeating the submarines.

4. Make a study of submarine warfare in other theatres of war, such as the Mediterranean or the Pacific.

5. Research the role of submarines today.

officials was evident in only three areas of life: police, education, and labour. All police forces were centralized under Berlin. Sentences meted out in the courts were reviewed and, if found too lenient, German authorities spirited the accused away to Germany for resentencing. In some cases, hundreds of hostages were taken at random and later shot to "encourage" cooperation with the authorities. German officials sat on school boards to ensure proper direction. Germans also sat on the labour boards that provided work permits, identification, and travel papers. Work was the only means to obtain ration cards, and through control of work permits and ration cards the Germans kept subject societies subservient.

Control over the labour boards gave the Germans control over society. Without papers one became a non-person. Germans established quotas of production in factories and in the fields. Only if farms and businesses met their quotas were they allocated workers and materials. If they did not, they were not permitted to operate, and their workers were liable to be shipped to the Reich to work there. Almost all factory managers had to collaborate to protect their employees from deportation. Three quarters of all production went to Germany, billed as "occupation costs."

Initially, the Germans were successful in recruiting hundreds of thousands of volunteer workers with promises of better jobs, higher wages, and entertainment. However, it was soon discovered that foreign workers were not welcome in the Reich. They were housed in quarters resembling concentration camps, paid low wages if they were paid at all, liable to be hit by bombs, and not permitted to return home. As a result, the voluntary labour pool dried up except in the SS, where entire divisions composed of foreign nationals were sent off to fight on the eastern front. As the war progressed, the Germans used more forceful methods to recruit labour from the occupied nations. Recruits often were taken from the streets in random round-ups. In one instance in Marseilles, 1000 police on manoeuvres were dragged off without notice to fulfil labour quotas. Of those taken, a large portion escaped en route and joined the resistance. Still, 5 million foreign workers were in the Reich by 1944, accounting for one fifth of the work force and making a considerable contribution to the German war effort. Workers were also conscripted from prisoner-of-war and concentration camps on the payment of a portion of their produce to the SS.

The situation in the east was far different. There Nazis imposed direct rule by Reich Protectors on what they considered "sub-humans." These were the regions designated for future German settlement after the "disposal" of local populations. The prime function of the Protectorates—the Government General of Poland, the Protectorate of Bohemia and Moravia, and the Baltic Ostland—was to provide materials for the war machine. Special detachments followed hard on the heels of the front-line troops to seize or requisition food, *matériel,* artwork, and everything else they could lay their hands on. All goods not essential for a bare subsistence for local populations were to be transferred to the Reich. Captured industrial plants were initially left idle since the master plan called for turning these areas to agricultural production. But in 1942, as the war progressed, some of the factories were brought back into production. A Reich Food Office set quotas, but transportation bottlenecks prevented much of this output from reaching Germany. An entire year's harvest from Ukraine—25 million tonnes of grain—rotted on sidings for lack of transportation to flour mills. Erich Koch, the Nazi Commissioner in Ukraine, grew so desperate that he began sending grain packages with soldiers going back to Germany on leave. Germany received less grain from Ukraine in war than in peace.

THE HOLOCAUST

Nazi racial policies were carried forward, with depopulation programs of mass extermination killing more people than fell in battle. This grand-scale massacre affected every nation under German hegemony. The objective was genocide for all the Jews, Gypsies, and most Slavs in Europe. No person designated a sub-human or an opponent of the New Order was safe. An additional 500 000 people who were believed to oppose the New Order were among the victims. In the west, the state seized Jewish property and identified individuals for transportation to death camps. About a quarter of French Jewry, half of Belgium's, and three quarters of Netherlands' Jewry were deported. Of the 7500 Danish Jews, almost all escaped across the Baltic to neutral Sweden, with the courageous assistance of fellow Danes. Germany itself was declared Jew-free in 1943, but at the end of the war there were still some 33 000 German Jews who had somehow survived. In Central Europe and the eastern protectorates, anti-Semitic movements needed little

German encouragement. A million Jews were taken from Romania, while Croatian and Serbian Jews were often killed on the spot. Hungary's Jewish community was reduced from 800 000 to 100 000 in a single year. But the worst horrors were in Poland, where Europe's largest Jewish community was concentrated.

Four special squads of between 300 and 800 German commandos—*Einsatzgruppen*—were sent into the occupied territories to clear them of unwanted populations. These included prisoners of war. Of the 3 million Soviet prisoners of war taken by this time, over 2 million vanished without a trace. Death squads operated by a standard procedure. Leading Jews were identified and asked to gather their co-religionists with their valuables. Victims were then stripped of their goods and clothing and marched away to be shot, their bodies tumbled into hastily dug ditches.

In one two-day period in Kiev, 33 000 people were murdered in this manner. When the execution ground had filled up with 100 000 corpses, the Germans pushed a layer of dirt over the decomposing bodies. When decomposition caused gas explosions and minor earth tremors, authorities uncovered the bodies and strewed chemicals on them before replacing the soil. In other cases, bodies were pulverized to control decay. The whole process was meticulously photographed and observed by hundreds of the curious who felt no danger to themselves. In another instance, at Pinsk, 1000 victims were axed to death after dogs had been turned on them.

Burning alive, drowning, grenades, and cavalry charges were also used in mass-killings. In this fashion an estimated 2 million people were killed in the first days after the German armies had passed through. The survivors were gathered in ghettos in preparation for deportation to death camps, where a further 5 to 7 million were killed.

There were five death camps. Hundreds of thousands of Jews, Slavs, prisoners of war, political opponents, and Gypsies died in other concentration camps, where malnutrition, disease, beatings, and murder were common. But the complexes in Poland at Auschwitz, Chelmno, Treblinka, Sobibor, and Belzec were especially designed for mass murder. Auschwitz was a showcase for the poison gas Cyclon B, which replaced the lengthier and less efficient practice of using automotive exhausts. Auschwitz could kill as many as 12 000 people a day, and was a model for the other camps. The victims were incinerated and their ashes were sold by the bushel to cover icy streets and roads in winter.

Throughout Europe, those Jews who could be held hostage for hard cash from abroad, or those who had done noteworthy service to the state (such as iron-cross winners from the First World War) or other work of a prominent nature, were initially spared. Many were later sent to Theresienstadt in Czechoslovakia where a model camp was established to deflect world attention from the others. Visits by Red Cross officials and diplomats from neutral nations were commonplace. Because of relatively more humane treatment here, about a third of the inmates survived to the end of the war.

Resistance within the camps was feeble and infrequent. Soviet prisoners rioted and attacked their guards in Sobibor, killing 10 of them before being shot down. Himmler was so outraged by this incident that he ordered the camp razed to the ground and all evidence of it destroyed. In 1941, an uprising of 455 prisoners at Auschwitz resulted in the deaths of 4 guards. But for the most part, the victims were too physically weak to make even a gesture of defiance. At the end of the war, as Soviet forces moved into Poland, the Germans poisoned their remaining prisoners and made hurried attempts to destroy all evidence of the camps. Had Germany won the war, or had the war lasted much longer, there is no doubt Himmler's plan to rid Europe of 30 million subject people would have been carried out to the bitter end.

RESISTANCE

The earliest forms of resistance were intelligence-gathering and the establishment of escape routes. Economic resistance developed in occupied areas throughout Europe. Work slowdowns and stoppages, the production of inferior goods, the mislabeling and misdirection of parcels, and outright sabotage hampered German attempts to harness the economic power of their subject nations. Later, organized and abetted by 12 000 British and American agents who parachuted onto the continent, resistance movements were able to carry out full-scale raids on fuel dumps and transportation facilities. The Germans were forced to divert more and more soldiers to hunt them down. For example, 108 000 German troops were needed to police Norway's relatively small population of 3 million.

Sabotage invited retaliation. In one instance in Ukraine, the Germans burned 158 villages and shot

The death camps established by Germany to exterminate targeted peoples still stand today as grim reminders of the atrocities human beings have committed against other humans. This picture shows a crematorium in Dachau.

all their inhabitants in retaliation for just one bombing incident. In the most famous case, the Czechoslovakian village of Lidice was razed to the ground. Its male population was shot over a 10-hour period, and its women and children sent to Ravensbrück concentration camp in retribution for the assassination of Reinhard Heydrich, who was then protector of Bohemia. In the week Heydrich took to die, 1500 Czechs were picked at random for execution, 3000 Jews were sent to death camps, and Lezaky (a smaller village) was dealt the same fate as Lidice.

As resistance movements grew in size and organization, they began to rival national governments in exile in London and Alexandria. Removal of national governments to safety abroad seemed the right thing to do at the time. But as the war continued, their absence came to be felt. The gap was filled by the resistances, who over the months gained the loyalty and support of some of the people. After liberation, resistance leaders would claim the right to form new governments. These well-armed groups would play important political and military roles in both Europe and Asia after the war.

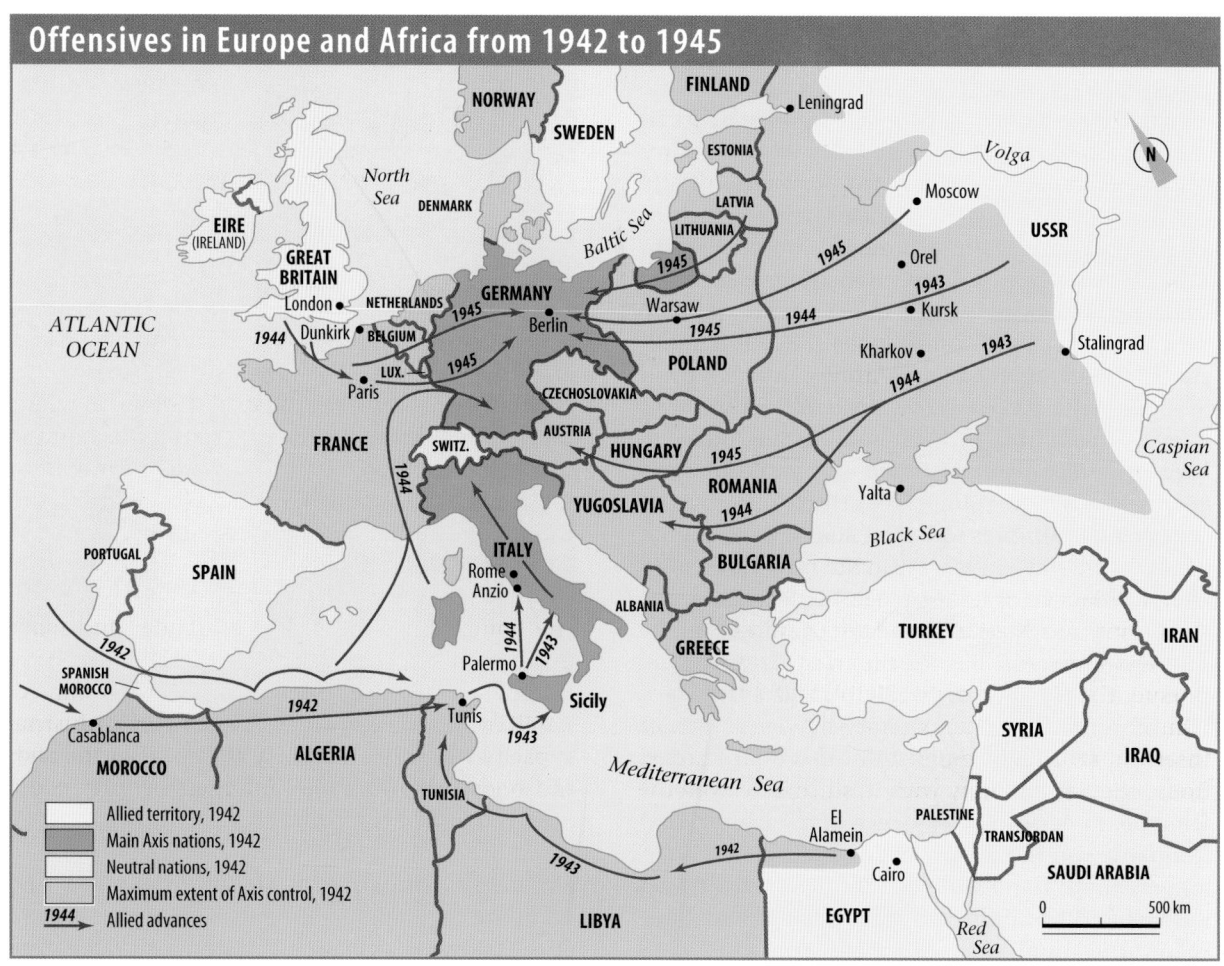

Offensives in Europe and Africa from 1942 to 1945

Allied territory, 1942
Main Axis nations, 1942
Neutral nations, 1942
Maximum extent of Axis control, 1942
1944 ─── Allied advances

After 1942 the Axis began to crumble under the force of Allied attacks.

TURNING THE TIDE: 1942–1943

The year 1942 saw the turning of the tide, with the battles of Midway in the Pacific, El Alamein in Egypt, and Stalingrad in the southern USSR. In the spring, the Germans renewed their offensive toward the industrial complex of Stalingrad on the Volga River. Stalingrad was a strategic transportation and communication hub, and the largest city near the Caspian Sea. Its capture would cut off the land route carrying British and American supplies to the Soviets and provide the Germans with a base for attacks on the USSR's second industrial centre, east of the Ural Mountains. It was this area that produced most of the Soviet Union's war equipment, including 40 000 aircraft, 30 000 tanks, 150 000 pieces of artillery, and 500 000 machine guns. This second industrial centre would not come into full production until 1944.

The battle for Stalingrad began with the bombing of the city in September. The German Sixth Army under Field Marshal von Paulus then set about leveling the southern part of the city over the next four months. In fierce house-to-house fighting, buildings were taken and retaken until they were totally destroyed by tank fire. What territory the Soviets lost during the day, their snipers and commandos regained by night. By November, the Germans had penetrated to the Volga River at several points, but were never able to silence the Soviet artillery on the north bank. As the battle for the city was brutally waged, the Soviets built up their forces to the north and south, and in November attacked along the German flanks. Striking deep behind the German lines, they completed a pincer movement in December and cut off Stalingrad from the outside.

German reaction was surprising. Instead of breaking out, the Germans decided to stay in the pocket for the winter and rely on air supply. However, the *Luftwaffe* was unable to bring in the 500 tonnes of daily supplies required. The largest *Luftwaffe* delivery was 65 tonnes, far short of what was required. Unable to hold out, the Germans surrendered on 22 February 1943, and the 90 000 survivors marched across the barren snow-swept plains into captivity. The Soviet victory at Stalingrad was the prelude to the USSR's counter-offensive in 1943.

While the battle for Stalingrad was at its height, the Germans suffered a serious reversal in North Africa. The 10-day battle at El Alamein near the Suez Canal was the beginning of the liberation of North Africa. Advancing westward along the Mediterranean coast, the British Eighth Army under General Montgomery pushed General Rommel's Afrika Corps steadily back. That November, an Anglo-American landing on both sides of the Straits of Gibraltar brought a second Allied army onto the continent. Together these armies squeezed Rommel's forces out of Africa. The Allied landings in Morocco and Algeria were to have far-reaching repercussions, one being the German occupation of the rest of France.

The second Allied decision was to continue to pursue the enemy onto Sicily and into Italy. Churchill proposed this strategy as a means of inserting an Allied presence into Central Europe. Roosevelt was unhappy with it, since it delayed the invasion of France another year. The Americans did not believe Allied armies could bring the enemy to a decisive battle in Italy.

In the summer of 1943, however, British, American, and Canadian armies landed in Sicily. In an emergency meeting, the Grand Fascist Council deposed Mussolini by a vote of 19 to 9. Mussolini was arrested and placed under guard. Later he was rescued by the Germans in a daring alpine escapade and put in charge of German-occupied northern Italy. At the end of the war, he was captured by resistance forces in Milan and executed.

After the change in Italian leadership, Marshal Badoglio agreed to a cease-fire. On 8 September Italy left the war and turned its military bases over to the Allies. The 500 000 Italian soldiers in the Balkans, the 217 000 in the USSR, and the 200 000 in southern France were to surrender themselves and their weapons.

To complicate matters further, Italy declared war on its former ally Germany on 13 October. In response, battle hardened German forces raced southward through Italy to recover as much of the situation as possible. They were able to establish several defence lines that were grudgingly given up in the next year and a half of bitter fighting.

Instead of establishing a second front in France, Roosevelt and Churchill agreed to bomb strategic targets in what the Germans called Fortress Europe.

The difficulty of hitting specifically military targets from the air led to a shift in strategy to the area bombing of larger targets like communications and transportation centres, industrial and power-generation plants, and selected cities like Regensburg and Schweinfort, to delay aircraft fighter production. As the size of the air fleets grew, other cities came in for attack. Berlin, Hamburg, Cologne, and Dresden were added to the list of targets. Strategists believed that bombing would directly affect civilian morale and destroy their will to resist. The first 1000-bomber raid went out against Cologne, where incendiary bombs were used to start a fire storm in the centre of the city. The heat was so intense it melted steel. Fed on fresh air sucked in from surrounding areas, an updraft was created, causing a storm that lasted for hours. City after city was to experience the horror of strategic bombing. Ideally, the bombing would lead to surrender and make unnecessary the sending of ground troops into Europe. In practice, though, results were mixed. Civilian morale did not collapse and industrial capacity was only marginally affected. But the raids did boost Allied morale, for their peoples could rejoice that they were now striking back.

FRANCE: THE SECOND FRONT

In January 1943, Churchill and Roosevelt met at Casablanca to coordinate future Anglo-American strategy. The second front in France would have to be postponed because there was not enough equipment ready to transport the large forces needed for the seaborne assault. In the meantime, British, American, and Canadian armies would pursue the more immediate targets of Sicily and Italy. But something had to be done to convince Stalin they were sincere about relieving the pressure on the Red Army by opening a major battle front in France. For some time, the Red Army had born the brunt of the land war, suffering millions of casualties. Stalin's demands for an invasion of France grew more strident.

Conferences between Churchill, Roosevelt, and Stalin were filled with tension. This photograph was taken at their meeting in Yalta, in February 1945.

As the Allies pursued the air war over Europe and began to land troops in Sicily, the largest tank battle of the war took place at Kursk between 5 and 12 July 1943. The Germans were attempting to cut off a Soviet salient and struck at the "bulge" from Orel and Kharkov. A million soldiers and 2700 tanks were involved in fierce fighting. Soviet air superiority and their use of anti-tank rockets and weapons brought decisive defeat to the German Panzer corps (500 000 casualties). After Kursk, the Soviets were able to advance along a broad front of 1200 km, with forces numbering 6 million soldiers. By 1944, the Soviets had superiority in weapons on a 5 to 1 ratio, except in the air, where the ratio was 17 to 1.

The first of two meetings between Stalin, Churchill, and Roosevelt took place at Teheran, between 28 November and 5 December 1943. An agreement was reached on the creation of a second front in France, to be launched in June 1944. Allied efforts in the eastern Mediterranean and Churchill's proposal to strike for Vienna and the Balkans were set aside. They would in any event come under the

Soviet sphere. Churchill could not convince Roosevelt of the political danger of permitting the Red Army to liberate Central Europe. Roosevelt was adamant that all political matters be left to a post-war conference. The Americans needed Stalin's help in Asia against Japan, and Roosevelt believed the Soviet dictator could be brought to a reasonable position on the future of a liberated Europe. To this end he accepted Stalin's vague promises of self-determination and free elections for Europeans after fighting had come to an end. In reality, Stalin had no intention of giving up any of the territorial gains the Soviets might win. At Teheran, the spheres of influence that would dominate the post-war world were beginning to take shape, with the Anglo-American Allies giving up their interests in Central Europe.

At Teheran, the Polish question bedeviled the comrades in arms. The USSR demanded the re-establishment of its 1939 boundary with Poland. Thus, it was decided to restructure Poland by setting its eastern boundary at the Curzon line, and compensating the Poles with German territory. Although agreement was reached on Poland's borders, no agreement was made on Poland's government. England and France had gone to war over Polish independence. They had supported both the

Polish government in exile in London, and the Polish resistance. They had an obligation to the Poles and to themselves.

The USSR acknowledged the Polish government in London, until that government asked the Red Cross to investigate the massacre of 1700 Polish officers in the forests at Katyn. Had they been killed by Germans or Soviets? At this, Stalin refused an investigation and used this affront as a pretext to break off relations with the government in exile. He then recognized a pro-Soviet group in Lublin as the provisional government.

On 6 June 1944, D-day, the long-awaited second front in Europe came with the Allied invasion of Normandy. Eight American, British, and Canadian divisions landed by sea or parachuted down along a 100 km arc of French coastline. By the end of the month, 640 000 soldiers were ashore, and by the end of July they had broken out into open territory and were racing for Paris. The French capital was liberated on 25 August by General Leclerc, just two days after the Soviets entered Vienna. There was a second invasion of France in the south, on 15 August. By December, Allied armies had pushed the Germans back within their own borders, and were preparing the final advance into Germany itself.

On 9 October 1944 a concerned Churchill flew to Moscow to meet with Stalin about the fate of Central Europe, now effectively under Soviet control. Roosevelt was in the middle of an election campaign and did not attend the meeting, but he went along with Churchill's and Stalin's agreement on post-war spheres of influence. Churchill proposed establishing spheres of influence in the Balkans and Central Europe that mirrored the reality of the situation: the Soviet army was in control of Central Europe and could not be dislodged without force. The Soviets would have a 90 per cent interest in Romania, a 70 per cent interest in Bulgaria and Hungary, a 50 per cent interest in Yugoslavia, and a 10 per cent interest in Greece. Stalin lived up to this agreement and did not support the communist guerrillas in Greece. Nor did he give support to communist parties in France and Italy, which he considered to be in the Western sphere. He expected his hands-off policy in the Western zone would be reciprocated by the Americans and the British in the Soviet zone.

As the war drew to a close, the Big Three met for a second time at Yalta, in February 1945. Germany was to be partitioned along the Elbe River, where it was expected the Allied armies would meet. The capital, Berlin, was to be divided into three zones

On 6 June 1944, D-day, British, Canadian, and American troops began landing at Normandy. This was the beginning of the end for Germany.

DEFINING WAR CRIMES

In 1950, the International Law Commission formulated seven principles relating to the conduct of war. Among these principles were the following assertions: an individual who commits an international criminal act can be punished for it; heads of state are liable for punishment, and "following orders" is no defence in law; there are crimes against peace, including the planning and waging of war; **war crimes** and crimes against humanity such as genocide, deportation, slave labour, plunder, killing of hostages, and the devastation of cities are not to be tolerated. The basic principle was that war is a planned human activity and is a crime that is punishable.

After the Second World War much of Europe was in ruins. It would take decades and billions of dollars for these countries to rebuild themselves. This 1945 photograph of a street in Calcar, Germany is representative of the scope of the damage.

a liberated Poland. Under the terms of secret clauses, Stalin also agreed to enter the war against Japan within three months of victory in Europe. Stalin thought the Anglo-American insistence on elections and self-determination for liberated peoples was mere window-dressing, designed to placate their own electorates. He was firmly committed to the concept of spheres of influence and the defence of the Soviet homeland.

Roosevelt left the conference a sick man, and was shortly to die. He was succeeded as president by Harry Truman, in whom Stalin found a formidable opponent and, like himself, a believer in spheres of influence. Under Truman, the Americans would embark on a program of global economic and military expansion.

The end of the war in Europe came in May 1945. On 30 April, Hitler committed suicide. Surrender of German forces took place shortly thereafter, between 7 and 9 May. The final meeting of Allied war leaders took place at Potsdam at the end of July. There the harmony that had marked Allied cooperation came to an end. Quarrels quickly broke out between Truman and Stalin on virtually every issue. Differing views on the treatment of Germany and Poland had begun to spawn a cold war between the two superpowers.

Unable to reach agreement, the military commanders, General Eisenhower and Marshal Zhukov, took over the administration of their respective occupation zones. The peoples within each zone adopted the system of government preferred by their liberators.

Despite differing views on the future of Europe, the Allies carried out a denazification program, interviewing 6 million former members of the party. Twenty-four major Nazi leaders were brought to trial for crimes against humanity. Fifty thousand others were brought to trial locally. Of the major leaders, Martin Bormann was sentenced to death inabsentia, Göring committed suicide, twelve were given death sentences, three were given life imprisonment, four were given prison terms from 10 to 20 years, and three were acquitted. The crimes they were guilty of were the planning and waging of war. The tribunal did not rule on genocide because it was a domestic matter, nor did it rule on mass-bombing because it was not asked to. It found that there was nothing in the laws of war that prohibited taking hostages.

The cost of the Second World War was a staggering 50 to 60 million dead. The figures are large beyond comprehension. Exact statistics were never

and put under military occupation. Later, France was accorded a zone constructed from portions of the British and American sectors. German industries were to be dismantled and reparations levied. Stalin suggested the sum of $20 billion as a starting point. The Americans and British were more concerned with reconstruction in their zones than they were with stripping captured zones of resources. The Soviets, however, wanted to seize German resources to help rebuild the war-ravaged USSR. The Allies could not reach agreement on whether to levy reparations before or after reconstruction. Stalin insisted on recognition of the Lublin Poles as the Polish government, although he agreed to allow some of the London Poles to participate in the administration of kept, but estimates of the dead are probably in the range of 20 million Soviets, 10 million Chinese, 5 million Germans, 2 million Japanese, 2 million for British, French, and Italians combined, and perhaps as many as 14 million Central Europeans, including victims of the genocide programs. About 259 000 Americans were killed. Add to these figures a far larger number left homeless, and the material and environmental cost of industrial devastation. Mere figures fail to convey the horrifying breadth of the human cost of this war.

The war altered the balance of power between the industrial nations. At its conclusion, the United States and the Soviet Union emerged as superpowers and the world's power structure became bipolar in nature. Despite its losses in battle, the Soviet Union maintained a formidable fighting force of 12 million and stood in occupation of Central Europe.

At the end of the war, the United States emerged as the supreme world power. It escaped relatively unscathed from the war, and had reached industrial maturity. The USA held $20 billion of the world's bullion supplies, accounted for over half of the world's industrial output, and also had 12 million soldiers under arms. Its factories were producing over half of the world's manufactured products, and it could project its military might anywhere in the world. What is more, the USA had a temporary monopoly on the atomic bomb.

Britain and France were exhausted by the war and could in no way match the new-found strength of the two superpowers. Devastated financially, they would have roles as middle powers and as allies of the United States. The development of the bipolar world in part shifted global power from Europe to North America and Asia.

SUMMARY

The Second World War saw the industrial powers at war in Europe and Asia. Hitler's Germany sought to establish hegemony over Europe. Hitler's ultimate aim was to make Germany an autarky, the most powerful nation in Europe, if not the world.

The German plan was to establish a New Order by expansion to the east for living space and resources. The Nazi concept of a master race required that "sub-humans" be eliminated. German genocide programs massacred some 10 to 12 million people, including most of Europe's Jewish community.

Expansion by force of arms won Germany an ally in Italy, and enemies in Britain, France, the USA, and the USSR. The latter two industrial giants, once mobilized, were able to crush Germany's armed forces. The war in Europe ended in 1945 with the occupation of Germany. Unable to reach agreement on post-war Europe, the USA and the USSR developed competing spheres of influence that led to the Cold War.

QUESTIONS

1. What Soviet action caused concern among Western nations in the period 1939-40?

2. Why was the initial phase of the Second World War called the phony war?

3. Describe the fall of France in 1940.

4. Explain the partition of France after June 1940. How was each section administered?

5. How did the Battle of Britain affect the conduct of the war?

6. How did the entry of the United States and the Soviet Union change the outlook of the war?

7. What factors contributed to the inability of the Germans to defeat the Soviet Union in their initial invasion?

8. Why was control of the Atlantic critical for Great Britain and its allies?

9. Compare and contrast the German occupation of western Europe with its occupation of eastern Europe and the Soviet Union.

10. Define the term holocaust. Explain how Nazi policy affected Jews during the war.

11. Identify forms of resistance against the Germans during the Second World War. How did the Germans respond?

12. Explain the significance of the following battles:
    (a) Stalingrad;
    (b) El Alamein.

13. Outline the agreements made at the following wartime conferences:
    (a) Casablanca;
    (b) Teheran;
    (c) Moscow;
    (d) Yalta.

14. Describe how the Second World War changed the international power structure.

CRITICAL ANALYSIS

1. Consider the practice of genocide in relation to the concept of sovereignty.

2. Evaluate the policy of air attacks on cities.

3. Discuss the moral implications of the establishment of resistance movements during the Second World War.

4. What effective methods should an occupation force use against civilian sabotage and terror?

5. Why did those sent to the death camps usually not fight their captors?

RESEARCH PROJECTS

1. Research the attack, course of events, and results of any of the following battles:
   (a) Battle of Britain;
   (b) Stalingrad;
   (c) El Alamein;
   (d) D-day.

2. Research the Manhattan Project. Comment on the morality of developing atomic weaponry.

3. Choose a resistance movement in any of the Nazi occupied countries during the Second World War. Describe the individuals who resisted, the means of resistance, and evaluate their success.

4. Describe the role of women in Canada during the Second World War, and compare and contrast their role with that of women in the Soviet Union.

ACTIVITIES

1 Chart
Find pictures or develop drawings to show the types of weaponry used in the Second World War.

2 Debate
Be it resolved that Stalin and the Red Army won the European war against the Nazis.

3 Role Play
Play the part of Churchill, Stalin, Hitler, Roosevelt, or any Second World War leader and prepare a speech designed to bolster confidence and support in your nation's ability to win the war. Choose words and actions which bring your personality to life.

HISTORICAL ANALYSIS

FACTORIES OF DEATH

Genocide is the systematic extermination of a particular culture or group of people. Armenians, Cambodians, and hosts of other peoples have suffered genocide in the course of history. The fate of the Jewish people during the Third Reich exemplifies genocide within the context of a modern industrial society.

In 1935, the Nuremberg Laws effectively removed Jewish people from German society by denying them political, social, and economic rights. Ghettos were established to isolate the Jews, and, by the time the Second World War broke out, Jews were routinely persecuted and imprisoned. In 1942, the Final Solution was implemented to methodically eliminate all Jews from Europe. Five death camps were established in Poland to gas and cremate Jews who were transported from all over Europe. The task of deporting and disposing of such large numbers of people required enormous resources. More than six million Jews were exterminated in the camps. They were "factories of death" staffed by thousands of ordinary people.

Analyse the rationale for the Holocaust's destruction of Jewish life with the help of the following questions:

1. How could the Nazi government enlist the cooperation of enough people to carry out its program of death?

2. Why would ordinary people allow their neighbours to be carted away? Why would someone work at a death camp?

3. Was anti-Semitism so well established in Europe that the Nazis could use it to their advantage?

4. Why did the Allied powers not make any attempt to free Jewish prisoners from the concentration camps before the end of the war?

There are many excellent resources on this subject. The following are suggested as useful for this particular project.

Buckley, William F. *In Search of Anti-Semitism*. New York: The Continuum Publishing Company, 1992.

Goldhagen, Daniel Jonah. *Hitler's Willing Executioners*. New York: Alfred A. Knopf, 1996.

Yahil, Leni. *The Holocaust: The Fate of European Jewry*. New York: Oxford University Press, 1990.

THE PACIFIC WAR

FOCUS ON GENOCIDE

A large part of Hiroshima simply dissolved into a vast cloud of dust when the bomb exploded. What had been a city going about its business on a sunny morning went up in a mountain of dust-filled black smoke, black at the base and towering into a plume of white to 40 000 feet.

The official US communiqué announcing to the world the dropping of an atomic bomb on the Japanese city of Hiroshima, 6 August 1945.

New words and expressions, many describing horrible new phenomena, came into being during the Second World War. Genocide is one of them. Take the point of view of a survivor of the Hiroshima atom bomb attack of 1945. Describe your experience and feelings. Could the fate of your friends, family, and neighbours be described as genocide?

OVERVIEW

Worlds conflict came to the Pacific with the attack on Pearl Harbor in 1941, and ended with the surrender of Japan in 1945.

VICTORIOUS JAPAN

Japan's occupation of China and control of the Pacific theatre of war until 1945 gave the Japanese a commanding presence in Asia.

THE GREATER EAST ASIA CO-PROSPERITY SPHERE

Asian nations wishing to rid themselves of colonial rule welcomed Japanese leadership in establishing a commonwealth of Asian nations. However, Japanese interest in establishing hegemony in the area subverted goals of independence.

ALLIED STRATEGY

By 1943, with the European war appearing to turn in their favour, the Allies were ready to go on the offensive in Asia.

ASSAULT BY AIR

The bombing of Japanese cities began in November 1944 and culminated with the dropping of atomic bombs on Hiroshima and Nagasaki in August 1945.

At dawn of 7 December 1941, most of the American Pacific Fleet was anchored at Pearl Harbor, Hawaii, completely unprepared for what was about to happen. Within an hour, this would be the scene.

VICTORIOUS JAPAN

The Pacific War had its origins in the struggle between Japan, China, and Russia/USSR over the mineral-rich regions of Korea and Manchuria. Beginning in 1876, this long and often bitter contest drew in other nations until, in 1941, all of Asia was drawn into a war of global dimensions. After that date the decisive battles were fought between the Americans, British, and Japanese—the war ending only with the dropping of atomic bombs on Hiroshima and Nagasaki in the summer of 1945.

When the Japanese invaded China in 1937, Chiang Kai-shek withdrew his Nationalist forces up the Yangtze River to Chongqing (Chungking). Within this mountain vastness he was safe from Japanese attack. Here he continued to receive aid from his British, American, and Soviet allies. It was in an effort to cut off this aid that Japan made the decision to expand the war. When land and air attacks against the USSR were driven back, the Japanese adopted a naval strategy that would give them control of Southeast Asia. The main battle plan called for a simultaneous strike against all foreign colonial possessions in Asia. The main thrust was to be directed at the mineral wealth of Malaya, the Philippines, and the Dutch East Indies.

Once the imperial powers had been driven out of Asia, the Japanese planned to fortify an arc of islands stretching out into the Pacific toward North America as an outer defence perimeter. Attempts to break through the island chain would result in such heavy losses, the enemy would be forced to negotiate an end to the war. The major objective was always to gain recognition of the Japanese right to Manchuria. In making the decision to expand the war, the Japanese were under no illusions about their ability to remain indefinitely in the occupied territories. They simply did not have sufficient forces. Nor did they possess the resources to fight a protracted war against their greatest potential foe, the United States. The whole plan depended upon forcing negotiations after the first six months of war. Prime Minister Tojo likened the exercise to a blind man jumping from the heights of a temple into a dark ravine below: "sometimes," he said, "it has to be done."

On the morning of 7 December 1941, the Japanese struck across a 10 000 km arc from Hawaii to Singapore and Manila, in one of the single most successful military operations in history. At one and the same time they attacked Pearl Harbor, Hong Kong, Rangoon, Manila, and Midway, even as the larger part of their armed forces remained in occupation of China. This was the beginning of six months of continuous victories that threw the colonial powers out of Asia.

Pearl Harbor was, as noted, only one of the targets on the first day. While Japanese planes were racing toward Oahu, General Yamashita's forces were landing in Malaya. They were to cut off the Burma Road that wound over the Himalayas to Chongqing. Hong Kong suffered two air raids on the first day of the war. A contingent of Canadian, Indian, and Scottish troops held out in the face of land and air attacks for two weeks before the invaders cut off the island's water supplies and forced surrender. In frustration over the delay, General Saki unleashed an orgy of pillage and murder in Hong Kong that was to be the pattern for captured cities all over Asia. Supporters of Chiang Kai-shek faced instant execution.

In other parts of the Pacific, the Japanese rounded up British and American gunboats on China's rivers while their air force bombed Guam, which fell on 10 December, Wake Island, which fell on 23 December, and Midway. In the Philippines, at Clark Field air base, General Brereton watched helplessly as Japanese airplanes destroyed the fleet of B-17 bombers ferried there at great cost over the previous months. General Douglas MacArthur's refusal to put the B-17s in the air until he was certain war had been declared ruined a planned American air raid on Formosa. The destruction of Clark Field left the Philippines without air defences.

Midway Island was the last target of the day, coming under bombing attacks just before midnight, Hawaii time. Before the Pacific War came to an end, the Japanese would have landed troops in Alaska, tried to set fire to Canada's northern forests, occupied all of Southeast Asia except Thailand, and threatened India and Australia with invasion.

The day after the attack on Pearl Harbor, President Roosevelt announced a massive armaments program. More than 45 000 airplanes were to be built, along with 45 000 tanks, 20 000 anti-aircraft guns, and 8 million tonnes of shipping. Roosevelt called for a 1000-ship navy of fast aircraft carriers and powerful battleships. The USA would out build its enemies, which would soon include Germany and Italy, and it would prevail. It would take time, but once awakened, the productive power of American industry would mount a war effort second to none.

Faced with war in both Europe and Asia, the United States established a "Europe First" strategy. Believing that Germany was the most dangerous enemy because of its industrial capacity, the USA gave priority to the European theatre. This meant maintaining a defensive posture against Japan until enough *matériel* and personnel could be readied to fight major campaigns on both sides of the globe.

For the Japanese it was a heady time. At home, people celebrated each victory of arms with toasts of *sake*, Japanese wine. Children were given bags of candy and ceremonies were held to praise the exploits of heroic soldiers. In January 1942, the Japanese took the Dutch East Indies. Singapore and Manila were soon to be occupied. Only when the monsoons came was there a temporary respite. By the summer of 1942, the Japanese were in a state of euphoria. Never in their wildest dreams had they imagined their victories would come so easily. Buoyed by their successes, plans were made for attacks against India and Australia. In preparation for the invasion of Australia, they began to construct air bases on Florida Island and Guadalcanal in the Solomons.

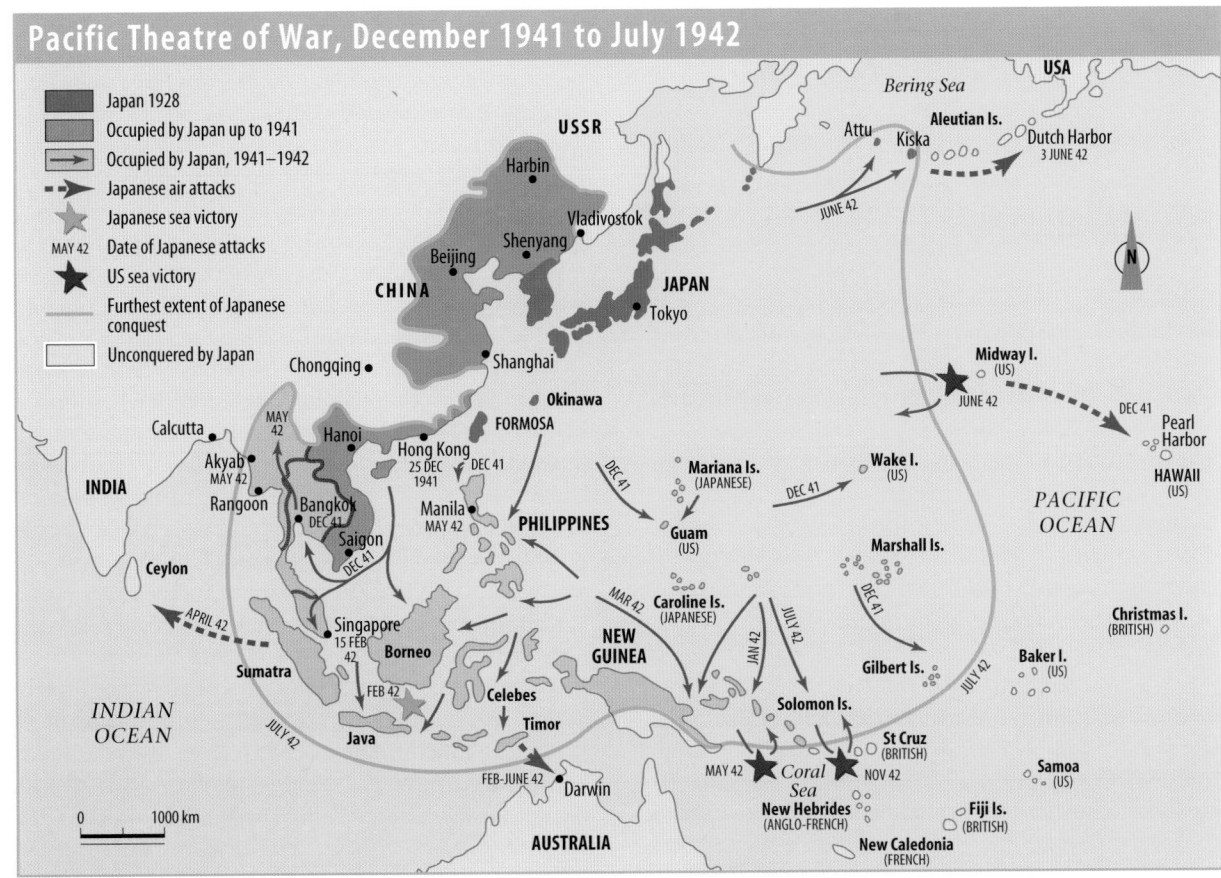

Pacific Theatre of War, December 1941 to July 1942

Legend:
- Japan 1928
- Occupied by Japan up to 1941
- Occupied by Japan, 1941–1942
- Japanese air attacks
- Japanese sea victory
- MAY 42 Date of Japanese attacks
- US sea victory
- Furthest extent of Japanese conquest
- Unconquered by Japan

The decision to expand the war was hotly debated. The army would not release its soldiers from mainland China or from along the long frontier with the USSR. Although the Soviet and Chinese fronts were quiet, there was no guarantee they would remain so. The generals argued that further expansion was foolish, unnecessary, and impractical. It was the navy that wanted to maintain the momentum of conquest. The admirals were convinced that only by continuing the pressure could the Americans and British be forced to negotiate.

At this point the war took a decisive turn. The change came as a result of American General Doolittle's scheme to fly a handful of bombers off an aircraft carrier and attack Tokyo. His fifteen B-25 bombers raced over the Japanese capital one noon hour, its streets choked with lunch-hour traffic. As sirens wailed, the falling American bombs caused shock and panic. The bombers overshot Japan and made for Chinese air bases on the mainland. One plane landed in Vladivostok, where its crew was interned for the rest of the war.

Not much damage was done as only a few buildings were destroyed and fewer than 50 people killed. But Doolittle's raid set off a chain reaction. Pursuit of the American bombers by fighter planes, and the

The Japanese were unrelenting after Pearl Harbor. They carried out a massive number of offensives, hoping to neutralize the American Pacific Fleet.

sailing of the Japanese home fleet to find the American aircraft carriers, saturated the airwaves with radio signals. From these signals, the Americans were able to break the major Japanese codes. For the rest of the war, Allied commanders in Asia would be well informed about their enemy's plans.

On the mainland, the Japanese Kwantung army reacted to the bombing by going on a rampage to revenge the insult to the emperor. Hundreds of thousands of Chinese peasants were killed in a bloodletting that outdid the savagery at Nanjing (Nanking) in 1937. The fanatical response to the raid by army and civilian leaders, many of whom contemplated *sepukku* (suicide), amazed even the most hardened observers. But the most critical result of the Doolittle raid was the Japanese decision to capture Midway Island, to serve as a forward outpost in the Pacific defence perimeter. Reconnaissance planes patrolling far out from Midway toward the west coast of North America would bring ample warning of any new threats to the home islands.

THE KAMIKAZE

Suicide missions flown by Japanese kamikaze pilots illustrated the determination of Japan to win the war at any cost. Analyse the differences between Japanese society and American society which would encourage Japanese pilots to make this sacrifice for their country.

According to the Japanese warrior code, those who fall in battle are heroes who are held in honour by their ancestors. Those who fail in battle are considered less than human. Imbued with the willingness to die for their emperor, Japanese forces proved formidable opponents and exacted a heavy toll of casualties on their enemies. Nowhere was the Japanese willingness to die more visibly demonstrated than in the kamikaze attacks that began in 1944. The word kamikaze, "divine wind," refers to the storms that drove Mongol invaders from the shores of Japan centuries earlier.

Faced with invasion of their home islands, Japanese pilots volunteered to crash their bomb-laden planes into enemy warships and other military targets. They had been told by Admiral Onishi that the salvation of the nation depended on their sacrifice. On their last mission they would be with the gods, and without earthly desires. They would perform a duel or *tokko* in which one of the combatants must die. They would gain time for the preparation of insurmountable defences to be built in the Philippines and at home. They were to inflict huge losses on the enemy, losses that would result in a negotiated end to the war, not the occupation of Japan.

The pilots were joined by the ships of the home fleet, which sailed with only enough fuel oil to reach the Philippines for a last decisive naval battle in support of the 250 000 troops defending Manila. In that battle, more than 100 000 civilians were killed before the Americans liberated the city.

The Japanese plan was to have 10 000 aircraft ready to strike at the enemy. Because of the inferiority of their planes, the Japanese pilots would have great difficulty in approaching their targets, and they had no way of returning to base. This was to be a war of attrition, in which 4160 Japanese pilots lost their lives. That greater numbers were not killed was due more to a lack of aircraft than of volunteers.

These pilots flew in groups of two or three, intent on crashing their planes into enemy warships and supply vessels. In the four months from October 1944 to January 1945, they had significant success, hitting 121 ships and sinking 19. At Okinawa—in mass attacks over a number of days, in which 1900 sorties were flown—they sank 34 ships and heavily damaged another 368, including an aircraft carrier and 10 destroyers. Many of the 4900 American sailors who were killed had been burned by the gasoline fires that usually accompanied a kamikaze attack. Ten battleships were among those that suffered damage. With these results, plans were drawn up to launch three times as many kamikazes against enemy ships when the invasion of the home islands began. So dangerous were the kamikazes that one of the first acts of the occupation forces was to render all Japanese aircraft inoperable, by smashing their propellers and landing gear.

The kamikazes failed to stop the Allied advance. The Americans had adopted a bombing strategy that would negate the need to land troops on the home islands. From June 1944 onward, American B-29 raids from bases in China began Japan's ordeal. Initially the raids were high-altitude sorties aimed at industrial targets. Later, they were to be low-altitude incendiary raids during the night. The bombers approached their targets unhindered since the Japanese had few anti-aircraft guns and no warning radar.

1. Why did the Japanese sacrifice their pilots in suicide missions instead of considering surrender?

2. Assess the effectiveness of the kamikazes. In what circumstances would a country consider using suicide bombers? In what circumstances would you follow such orders?

Japanese naval units were recalled from the Indian Ocean in a carefully timed manoeuvre, so that they could escort invasion forces against Australia prior to the Midway operation. The invasion was turned back after a fierce naval battle in the Coral Sea.

The first phase of the Midway operation was the landing of Japanese troops on Alaskan islands as a feint to draw North Americans away from the main battle. The trick did not work, for the Americans did not divert their forces. It was not until 1943 that the Japanese were driven off the islands by a joint Canadian-American sortie. In the meantime, the Americans were able to ambush Japanese fleets converging on Midway. By a stroke of luck, American torpedo planes and dive-bombers caught the Japanese aircraft carriers as they were refueling and rearming their own planes. Hurling bombs amongst the crowded fighters on the Japanese flight decks, the American planes started raging infernos that destroyed the core of Japan's naval air arm. In just over five minutes, the war in the Pacific had been turned around. No longer would the Japanese navy dominate the Pacific. So severe was the loss that survivors brought back to Tokyo were kept isolated for the rest of the war, so that news of the defeat would not be made public.

Following the Battle of Midway, the Allies went on the offensive in Asia. The first assaults were against the Japanese air bases on Florida and Guadalcanal islands. It took American marines six months to dislodge the Japanese from Guadalcanal—which came to be known as the "island of death." Hand-to-hand combat was so routine that (it was said) uncommon valour became a common thing. Before the war was through, there would be many Guadalcanals. In 1945, on Iwo Jima, Japanese defenders had to be dug out of their defensive positions one by one. At the end of that battle, some Japanese injected themselves with poison while others, including women and children, leaped from cliffs into the sea rather than be captured. Only 216 of the 50 000 defenders were taken alive, at a cost of 6000 American dead.

Okinawa was worse. There the Americans came under attack by kamikazes. Thousands of Japanese pilots volunteered to fly their bomb-laden planes in suicide missions against the invasion fleet. In every battle, the lesson learned and relearned was the high cost in lives exacted by the stubborn Japanese defence. The question constantly asked was, if the Japanese were so fanatical about defending the outer islands, how would they behave when defending their homeland? Many doubted the Americans would stand for the heavy casualties an invasion of Honshu would require.

While Allied naval forces were assaulting the island defences, Australian and American land forces set about clearing New Guinea and then, in 1944, drove on to the Philippines. The initial battles were fought by Australian forces in New Guinea's Owen Stanley Mountains, along the Kokoda Trail. Bitter fighting lasted over a year before General MacArthur could focus on the liberation of the Philippines. From the Philippines, he planned to invade Japan on Christmas 1945.

THE GREATER EAST ASIA CO-PROSPERITY SPHERE

Wherever Japanese forces advanced, they were greeted by a significant portion of the local population who viewed them as liberators from European colonial rule. Had the Japanese harnessed this support, they would have found themselves a military and economic match for any combination of powers ranged against them. By 1942, they had captured more resources than they could ever use, and had a population several times larger than that of the United States. There was considerable support for the idea of "Co-Prosperity Sphere" of independent nations in the Pacific. Nationalist movements throughout the region were encouraged to embrace self-government. Burma and the Philippines were granted a form of independence, but the other colonies were told they would have to wait until after the war.

Although the Japanese gave lip-service to the idea of a commonwealth of independent Asian nations, they had no desire to turn the fruits of military victory over to nationalist leaders. Japanese hegemony could not admit a rival power which might emerge from the nationalism that quickly spread with the expulsion of the colonial powers. This would only weaken Japan's predominance. The Japanese tried to direct independence movements along lines beneficial to Japan, and in so doing, lost the support of millions of potential allies.

Nationalist leaders were incensed at Japanese treatment of their peoples and the ruthless exploitation of their resources. Japanese agents scoured the Pacific for food and supplies to be shipped back to Japan's hungry war machine.

These Japanese soldiers are shown celebrating another victory. The Japanese forces were often welcomed by local populations as they advanced along the mainland. However, as Japanese losses piled up, Japanese rule in these countries became increasingly brutal.

shown to both captives and their allies inflamed hatred towards the Japanese occupation forces. With too few soldiers to go around, the Japanese believed exemplary violence was the way to maintain public order. Troops often bayoneted civilians in the streets for no apparent reason. In Singapore, hospitals were sacked: the wounded were murdered in their beds, and nurses and babies were killed. Thousands of Chinese were used for bayonet practice on the shores of the fortress city, and prisoners of war were brutalized. The latter were considered to have disgraced themselves by surrendering. They were herded on long marches to concentration camps, only to find their numbers far exceeded the stores of water and food set aside for them. Those who left the straggling lines were clubbed to death by the wayside. The most savage treatment was meted out during the Bataan death march in which some 7000 Filipinos died on the way to camps, along with many American victims.

In order to consolidate Japan's rule, Prime Minister Tojo brought nationalist leaders to Tokyo in the fall of 1943. Agreement was reached on the creation of a common market that would take advantage of the economies of scale in the region. Burma and the Philippines were given immediate republic status, more or less free from Japanese control. Independence for the others was promised for the near future. The army did not approve of these measures, and continued to treat all nationalists as inferior. Closer to the realities of occupation, the army chose force as the best means of control over the Asian allies. Their brutality made a mockery of the "Co-Prosperity Sphere."

ALLIED STRATEGY

Anglo-American strategy in the Pacific took shape in the fall of 1943. British and Commonwealth forces would strike back from India into Burma. American forces would mount their attacks on the Philippines and Japanese-held islands. They would settle for nothing less than **unconditional surrender**, as well as a return of China to its traditional boundaries, including Manchuria, and the elimination of all trade concessions on the mainland. At the same time, every effort was made to enlist active Chinese support in the war. Chiang Kai-shek was brought to Cairo, where he met with Roosevelt and Churchill in 1943. Roosevelt still believed that China had the population and

In addition, hundreds of thousands of people were sent to work in the mines of Korea, or to build railways and air bases far from their homes. Disillusionment quickly led to resentment and organized sabotage. As a result, Japan received less from these regions than it had in peacetime through normal trade.

The Japanese resorted to terror to govern the large populations under their control. The cruelty

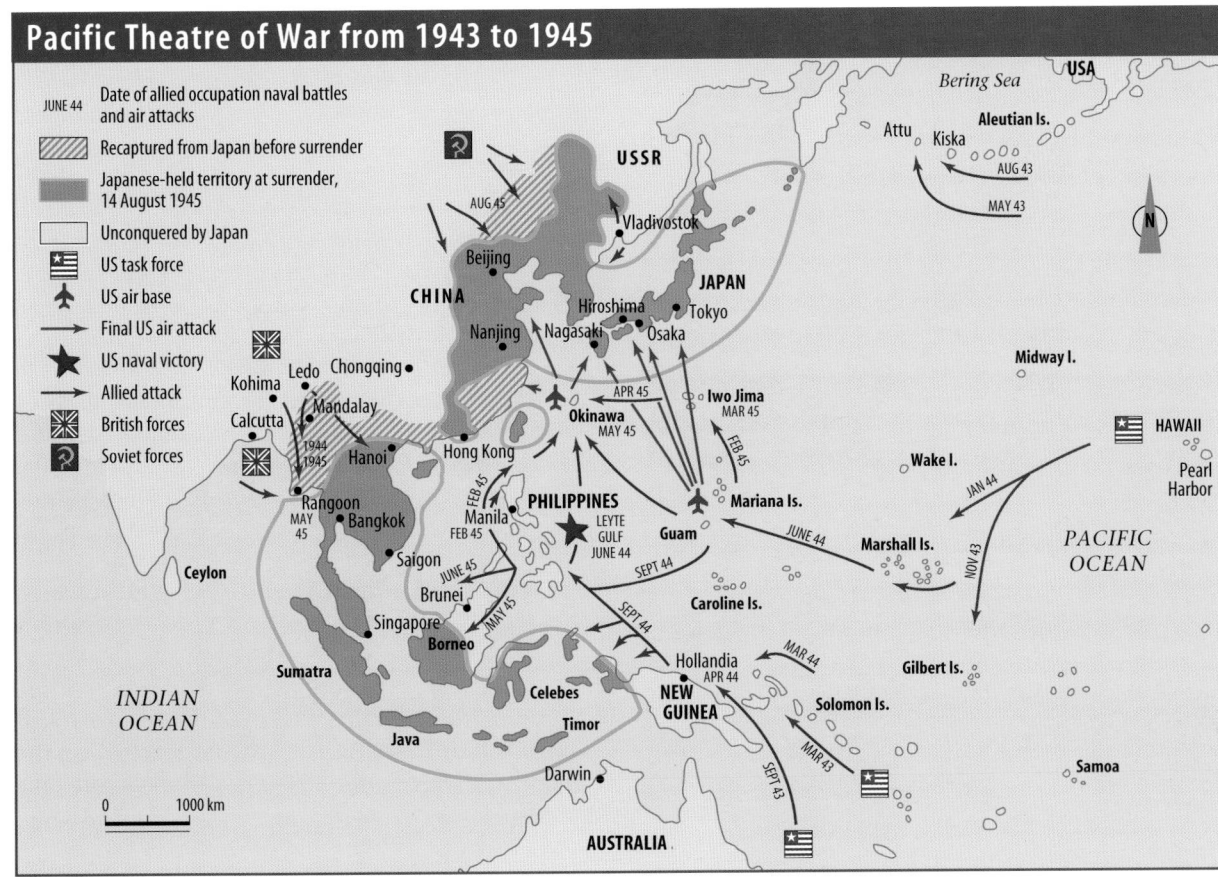

Legend:

- JUNE 44 — Date of allied occupation naval battles and air attacks
- Recaptured from Japan before surrender
- Japanese-held territory at surrender, 14 August 1945
- Unconquered by Japan
- US task force
- US air base
- Final US air attack
- US naval victory
- Allied attack
- British forces
- Soviet forces

resources to stabilize Asia after the war. The British were not as enamoured of Chiang, and would rather have strengthened ties with Mao Zedong, who appeared to have the support of the Chinese people. However, as the Pacific was chiefly an American theatre, the British relented. The British were more interested in regaining their position in Burma and Malaya, even though the Americans insisted they were not fighting the war merely to reinstate the old colonial empires. The USA was adamant that no American lives be lost in restoring Asia to colonial status. Differing views on the future of colonialism in Asia drove a wedge between the Allies that was temporarily overcome by personal orders from Roosevelt and Churchill.

At Cairo, Chiang agreed to the construction of a number of air bases for American B-29 bombers in return for more loans, although constant demands for money and supplies and avoidance of confrontation with the Japanese were wearing American patience thin. The B-29s could reach Japan from Chiang's bases. A half-million workers started construction on the 9000 m runways needed for the "flying fortresses." These bases near Chongqing would rekindle the war on the Chinese

As the war wound down in Europe, the tide turned against Japan in the Pacific. Japanese defeats at the hands of the Allies mounted, and plans for the attack on the home islands of Japan were finalized.

mainland that had been largely dormant since 1937. Alert to the dangers of long-range bombers, the Japanese army overran the air bases and drove their foes even deeper inland.

After the Cairo meetings, Roosevelt and Churchill met with Stalin in Teheran. They accepted Stalin's offer to declare war on Japan after the defeat of Germany. Soviet armies would sweep across Manchuria, reconquering areas lost in the Russo-Japanese War of 1904. Soviet support meant the Americans could do without Chiang Kai-shek. In return, the Soviets would regain their Eastern empire. Lüshen (Port Arthur) would be returned; control over the Manchurian railway system would be regained; and the southern half of Sakhalin Island, which had changed hands several times in the century, would revert to Soviet control.

In order to bring the war to a quick and decisive end, the Americans dropped atomic bombs on Hiroshima and Nagasaki. The full effects of an atomic explosion had not yet been tested, and the results were horrific. After the war, tests like the one above continued.

ASSAULT BY AIR

The air assault on Japan began in November 1944, and continued with few interruptions, until August 1945. Initially, the raids were carried out at high altitudes on specific military or industrial targets. These high-altitude raids were ineffective: the bombs usually missed their targets. The strategy was then modified to one of "saturation" or carpet bombing of whole areas suspected of having military value. Entire regions were laid waste by waves of bombers, in the hope a specific target would be hit. This tactic was also ineffective. The Japanese simply dispersed and scattered their military and industrial assets. A more effective strategy had to be found.

General LeMay proposed turning the American air strategy into one of terrorism against civilian populations. Low-level incendiary raids against densely populated cities would weaken the public's will to continue the war, and the collapse of civilian morale would lead to surrender of the armed forces. The raids on Japan were more persistent than raids against Germany. Japan was to be set afire.

The first of the raids was aimed at the industrial suburbs of Tokyo. Hundreds of bombers dropped their sticks of phosphorus on the city and created a fire storm far hotter than those at Hamburg and Dresden. Red-hot cinders spread down the streets and ignited the closely packed wooden buildings. As the temperatures rose, spontaneous combustion ignited both people and buildings. At the centre, the intense heat reached 1000°C and boiled rivers dry. The great fire raced down and across the cramped streets feeding on fresh air sucked in from the countryside. Towering pillars of hot, rolling, charcoal-black clouds bounced some of the bombers out of the sky. That night, a 26 square kilometre section of Tokyo ceased to exist.

BIOGRAPHY

EMPEROR HIROHITO
(1901–1989)

Hirohito, Japan's 124th emperor in a lineage said to descend from the sun-goddess, was emperor of Japan for 63 years. Because of the constitution instituted by his grandfather, Emperor Meiji, Hirohito was a monarch with no political powers beyond that of a mere figurehead. Only a few times throughout his years as emperor did Hirohito take significant political action, and then only because the normal governmental procedures had broken down.

There are many indications that Hirohito was uneasy with the way events were going at the start of the Second World War, and that he opposed Japan's union with Nazi Germany and Fascist Italy. He did not, however, attempt to sway Japan's course, but accepted the position of his advisers and military leaders. With the Potsdam Declaration at the end of the Second World War, Hirohito spoke of "endur[ing] the unendurable" when he admitted Japan's defeat and surrendered to the Allies. Hirohito had taken the lead in Japan's surrender in the wake of a deadlocked government and military.

Although Hirohito would not intervene in the decision-making process, he willingly accepted responsibility for the decisions made in his name during the war. After Japan's surrender, US General MacArthur (1880-1964) quoted Hirohito as having said the following:

> *I bear sole responsibility for whatever happened, for whatever incidents occurred in conjunction with Japan's prosecution of the war. Furthermore, I bear direct and sole responsibility for every action taken in Japan's name by every commander, every soldier, and every politician. As for my own life, whatever judgment you choose to make, it does not matter to me. I bear sole responsibility.*

Hirohito's acceptance of blame is reminiscent of the loyalty and selflessness of General Nogi, principal of the Peers School which Hirohito attended as a young boy. When Emperor Meiji died on 30 July 1912, General Nogi and his wife began to prepare for their own suicide one day later. This action was taken to honour their emperor, and in keeping with the spirit of Junshi, the ancient Japanese custom of following one's lord into death. Likewise, at the war's end, Hirohito counted his own life as nothing in light of the tragedies the Japanese people had suffered. In keeping with the spirit of Junshi, he would willingly take whatever measures necessary to restore some semblance of justice and harmony inside Japan, and between Japan and the outside world. He would take these measures even if they led to extreme personal hardship. The Allies decided, however, that retaining Hirohito as emperor of Japan would allow for the rapid restoration of order and the democratization of Japan. General MacArthur is quoted as saying that "having the emperor around is as good as twenty divisions of US troops."

Hirohito was the first Japanese emperor to travel outside of Japan. When as a young man he visited the Somme, he was aghast by the evidence of the horrors of war still etched on the faces of the people and on the land. The observation he made then—"war is a truly cruel thing; anyone who admires war should come see this place"—was also made in response to the atomic bombing of Hiroshima and Nagasaki 24 years later. ●

With the signing of the surrender on the *USS Missouri,* over five years of global warfare ended. The world now turned to the serious task of building a lasting peace.

Tokyo was only the first to suffer. Sixty-one major Japanese cities would soon be ravaged. Despite all this destruction, there was no indication of weakening resolve on the part of the people. LeMay estimated it could take his 1000-bomber armada another 12 months to finish the task. The air assault had not brought about surrender; it only hardened the Japanese resolve to persevere.

In Manila, General MacArthur began assembling the invasion forces to go ashore on Honshu in December. No one looked forward to the million American deaths expected during the assault on the Japanese home islands. A variety of plans were discussed on how to avoid the invasion. One plan was to stand offshore and let the winds carry mustard and other gases to Japan. Another was to burn the rice crops and force surrender through winter starvation. None of the plans were thought to be acceptable to the American people, who might not even support a prolonged air attack. There was always the chance that a war-weary United States might unilaterally end the fighting.

At this time, President Roosevelt died and was followed in office by Harry Truman. Truman had just been informed about a new "wonder weapon" called the atomic bomb, which would solve the problem of how to end the Pacific War. This was the weapon that would eliminate the need to invade the home islands and thereby save countless American battle casualties. The decision to use the bomb was never in doubt. The atomic bomb also meant that the Americans no longer needed the Soviets as allies in the Pacific. The war could now be won without them.

The age of atomic warfare was ushered in on 6 August 1945, when the first atomic bomb fell on Hiroshima. There was a glaring white pinpoint of light that flashed into a mushroom-shaped cloud that towered over the centre of the city. Everything within the fireball ceased to exist in milliseconds. Victims never knew what happened. The mind cannot react fast enough to record such an event. Outside the fireball, shock waves swept forth, flattening buildings, while the intense heat—10 times hotter than the surface of the sun—vaporized human beings and objects alike. When the Japanese did not immediately surrender, the USA dropped a second bomb, on Nagasaki, three days later. In the interval, Soviet armies marched into Manchuria.

The Japanese cabinet could not believe Hiroshima had vanished. Was it not the result of just another fire-bombing raid? Even the second bomb did little to weaken their resolve. But the Soviet invasion of Manchuria was another matter. As long as the Soviets stayed out, there was the chance of inflicting huge casualties on the Americans by bringing the armies in China and Manchuria back to Japan to defend the homeland. But now that the Soviets were engaging Japanese armies on the mainland, nothing could save them. The cabinet leaders took the unprecedented step of asking the emperor for his advice. Hirohito visited them in a sweltering bunker, and advised them to end the war.

On 28 August, the American battleship *Missouri* entered Tokyo harbour. Five days later formal surrender ceremonies were conducted on its quarterdeck. Speaking for the assembled representatives, General MacArthur voiced the view that a "better world shall emerge out of the carnage of the past ... a world dedicated to the dignity of Man and the fulfilment of his most cherished wish for freedom, tolerance, and justice." The flag flown by Commodore Perry on his visit to the same harbour in 1853 was brought from the United States especially for the occasion. The guns were now silent but the tragedy would be acutely experienced for decades to come.

As the surrender documents were signed, the first of 19 aircraft began to descend onto Japanese runways, bringing the hundreds of thousands of men and women making up the American occupation forces.

SUMMARY

The Japanese expanded the Pacific War in order to force recognition by China of their claims to Manchuria. Striking southward and deep into the Pacific, they sought to cut off supplies being sent to Chiang Kai-shek in Chongqing and seize the mineral wealth of Southeast Asia. While the armies fought through the jungles of Burma and Malaya, other forces were constructing island fortresses far out in the Pacific. When the fortresses were completed, their capture would be so costly that the British and Americans would have to negotiate with the Japanese. The Japanese did not, however, realize how deeply the American people resented the attack on Pearl Harbor, as well as the Japanese treatment of prisoners of war in the Philippines. It would take some time to bring the industrial might of the United States to bear, but once this happened, the final result of the war in the Pacific was never in doubt.

Wherever the Japanese forces went, they were usually first greeted as liberators by the local people. The Japanese had ousted the colonial powers from Asia. Had they harnessed this support, the war might have turned out differently. Support for the Greater East Asia Co-Prosperity Sphere, however, began to wane almost immediately, as a result of the treatment of occupied nations by the Japanese army. People soon realized that one colonial power had merely replaced another. Japanese hegemony was the immediate goal, not national liberation.

Because of the "Europe First" strategy, the Allied campaign in the Pacific gained momentum slowly. Only the British campaign in Burma continued throughout the war. It was not until the end of 1942 that the Allies took the offensive and struck north from Australia—one arm by sea, the other via the Philippines. The success of these campaigns in 1944 permitted the use of Okinawa and Iwo Jima as bomber bases for the Allied air assault on the home islands. The dropping of the atomic bombs on Hiroshima and Nagasaki in August 1945 removed the need to invade Japan, and saved millions of Allied lives. Stunned by the power of the new weapons, and by the news of Soviet troops flooding into Manchuria, the emperor advised the surrender of Japan, and with it an end to the Pacific War.

QUESTIONS

1. What was the primary cause of the Pacific War? How did the war begin?

2. Explain the significance of the Battle of Midway.

3. Explain the Allied strategy in the Pacific theatre of war. What part did the Soviet Union play?

4. What was the strategy for using air weapons and making incendiary raids on Japan? What was the result of these attacks?

5. Explain the twofold significance of the American possession of the atomic bomb by July 1945.

6. How and when did the Pacific War end?

CRITICAL ANALYSIS

1. Study and write about the factors that led soldiers to volunteer for suicide missions.

2. What unusual thing about the atomic bombs led to public condemnation of their use?

3. Is the use of atomic weapons a form of genocide?

4. Why do you think Japanese war crimes did not receive the same publicity that similar practices committed by the Nazis did?

5. Why should prisoners of war be given special rights?

RESEARCH PROJECTS

1. Research the role played by Japanese women in the Second World War.

2. Research the bombing of Pearl Harbor. Comment on the speculation that the British knew of the impending attack. If they knew, why did they not act to prevent it?

ACTIVITIES

1 Debate

Be it resolved that the Americans should not have used the atomic bomb in the Second World War.

2 Chart

Use pictures or drawings to show the power of atomic weaponry in 1945 in relation to weaponry in the 1990s.

3 Panel Discussion

Select one student to act as moderator and a number of students to sit on a panel which discusses the role played by individuals during wartime. The rest of the students should be prepared to ask questions. Some suggestions for the panel participants are:

    a) Japanese kamikaze pilot
    b) American anti-war protester
    c) French resistance fighter
    d) British naval officer
    e) German doctor
    f) Chinese Nationalist
    g) Canadian army private.

In each case, identify role, reasons for action, and feelings for the speaker's own country and for the war in which the country is involved.

HISTORICAL ANALYSIS

THE ATOMIC BOMB

The Second World War ended with the atomic bombing of Japan. Prior to dropping the bombs on Hiroshima and Nagasaki, the Americans had considered the possibility of defeating Japan by invading the islands. Analyse the immediate and long term consequences of dropping the bombs on Japan. Consider the following questions as you make your analysis:

1. What might the Americans have suffered if they had launched a ground attack? How would a ground attack have affected Japan?

2. What were the effects of the atomic explosion on Japan at the time, and how have the survivors fared over time?

3. How were the Americans affected by the atomic bombing?

Consider the following insightful novel as supplementary reading for this project:

Hersey, John. *Hiroshima*. New York: Alfred A. Knopf, 1946.

THE UNITED NATIONS

TIME LINE

	1942:	Washington Pact
	1944:	Bretton Woods conference
September	1944:	Dumbarton Oaks
April	1945:	San Francisco agreement on United Nations
26 June	1945:	Charter of United Nations signed
24 October	1945:	UN Charter became effective
	1947:	General Agreement on Tariffs and Trade (GATT) established
	1950:	Uniting for Peace resolution
1950 - 1953:		Korean War
	1956:	Suez Crisis
1960 - 1964:		Congo Crisis
12 November	1974:	South Africa expelled from United Nations
	1977:	UN arms embargo on South Africa
	1991:	UN forces eject Iraq from Kuwait, take steps to protect Kurdish population in northern Iraq
January	1991:	UN aid teams to Somalia
February	1992:	UN peacekeeping force to Bosnia
December	1992:	American troops to Somalia to protect UN aid workers
April	1994:	Americans withdraw from Somalia
June	1994:	UN peacekeeping force to Rwanda
June	1994:	South Africa allowed back into the United Nations
	1995:	World Trade Organization supersedes GATT

Above all, we must not permit differences in economic and social systems to stand in the way of peace. To permit the United Nations to be broken into irreconcilable parts by different political philosophies would be disaster to the world.

It is essential to the future of the United Nations that the members should use the Council as a means for promoting the settlement of disputes as well as for airing them. The exercise of neither veto rights nor majority rights can make peace secure. There is no substitute for agreements that are universally acceptable because they are just to all concerned. The Security Council is intended to promote that kind of agreement and is fully qualified for that purpose.

US president Harry Truman, speaking on the occasion of the opening of the United Nations General Assembly, 23 October 1946.

FOCUS ON GLOBAL COOPERATION

International cooperation arises from a variety of motives, and results in different forms of global interaction. Select a significant international crisis or event which has led to a collective, cooperative response. Take the position of one of the major players, and describe cause and effect.

The flag of the United Nations flies all over the world as a symbol of international lawmaking and peacekeeping.

THE GENERAL ASSEMBLY

All member nations sit in the General Assembly and have one vote. Discussion and recommendation can occur, but the General Assembly has no power to enforce its decisions.

THE SECRETARIAT

Administration is handled by the Secretariat which is under the control of the secretary general.

THE ECONOMIC AND SOCIAL COUNCIL

The 27 member nations work toward improving the standard of living of the world's people.

THE INTERNATIONAL COURT OF JUSTICE

Advice on international law and the UN Charter is given by the International Court of Justice which is located in The Hague.

THE TRUSTEESHIP COUNCIL

The administration of territories unable to govern themselves after the Second World War was given to the Trusteeship Council.

PEACEKEEPING OPERATIONS

A primary role of the United Nations has been to place itself between nations in dispute.

KOREA: 1950–1953

UN support for the South Koreans in 1950 was the first example of its attempt to maintain world peace by collective action.

SUEZ: 1956–1967

A United Nations Emergency Force was sent to the Suez region to maintain the peace between Israel and Egypt.

THE CONGO: 1960–1964

Peacekeeping operations in the Congo did ultimately achieve stability in the region but proved to be both difficult and costly.

INTERNATIONAL ECONOMIC COOPERATION

Global interdependence has resulted in the evolution of a number of organizations which regulate trade and currency exchange.

THE UNITED NATIONS IN THE 1990s

In the 1990s, the majority of UN actions were to support human rights within nations embroiled in civil wars.

OVERVIEW

Chapter 9 explores the structure and function of the United Nations, including examples of major peacekeeping operations. International cooperation also comes in the form of economic cooperation provided by the World Bank, IMF, EEC, and WTO.

THE UNITED NATIONS

Determination by the major powers to establish an effective international body of collective security following the Second World War resulted in the formation of the United Nations in 1945.

THE SECURITY COUNCIL

The 15 nations which make up the Security Council have the power to pass resolutions and settle international disputes.

THE UNITED NATIONS

The United Nations (UN) evolved out of the wartime conferences between Roosevelt, Churchill, and Stalin. These leaders wanted to create an international organization that would help in the rehabilitation of the world's war-torn regions, and in the preservation of peace and security in the future. In 1942, the 26 nations at war with the Axis powers signed the Washington Pact, which became the nucleus of future discussions for a global security organization. The basic plan for this international body was then proposed by the Americans at Dumbarton Oaks in Washington, D.C., in September 1944. Building on the **"Four Policemen" concept**—in which Roosevelt had envisaged the United States, Great Britain, the Soviet Union, and China managing global affairs—the Big Four would dominate a security council in this new international organization. All other nations would be invited to participate in a general assembly. Originally the Soviet Union demanded 15 seats in such an assembly, to represent the 15 constituent republics of the Soviet Union. However, at Yalta in February 1945, Stalin agreed to take only 3 seats, and to admit France as a permanent member of the Security Council.

Thus, before the proposal was presented to the other nations for adoption at San Francisco in April 1945, the major powers had agreed on the basic structure and could present a united front against attempts by other nations to change the framework. Positions of primacy were guaranteed the major powers by virtue of veto power in the proposed Security Council. Without this primacy it is unlikely that the United Nations would have come to fruition, for both the Soviet Union and the United States demanded protection of their sovereign interests. The Charter of the United Nations was signed by 50 nations on 26 June 1945, with Poland becoming the fifty-first signatory before the Charter became effective on 24 October 1945. The following year, the final meeting of the old League of Nations was held for purpose of dissolution.

The United Nations concern with economic and social problems gave it a broader mandate than that of the League of Nations. The most significant difference between the United Nations and the League, however, was the preparedness of the United States and the Soviet Union to play a prominent role in the new institution. In the past, the United States had refused to join the League of Nations, and the Soviet Union was expelled in

The Universal Declaration of Human Rights was one of the first accomplishments of the United Nations. The photo above shows some of the original authors and their advisors in New York in 1949. They are (from left to right): Dr. Charles Malik (Lebanon), Professor Rene Cassin (France), Marjorie Whiteman (advisor), Eleanor Roosevelt (USA), and James Simsarian (advisor).

1939. The participation of these superpowers effectively gave the United Nations a global stance that the League of Nations had lacked. Although in some instances, superpower involvement provided for a greater possibility of action in United Nations resolutions, the United Nations was sometimes hampered by the rival ideologies of the USA and the USSR. Only when the superpowers agreed could the United Nations function effectively. The desire of the major powers to pursue their own national, political, economic, and ideological interests became a major stumbling block to effective UN action.

The first sessions of the United Nations were held in London, Paris, and New York, before permanent headquarters were established on land donated along the East River in New York City. The first years were frustrating, as the infant organization attempted to find a role in global affairs. Items on the first agendas were problems of disarmament, control of atomic power, persons displaced by the war, denial of membership to Spain on the grounds of its fascist history (Spain was admitted in 1955), and recognition of Israel as a nation-state in 1948.

The most persistent problem was the refusal of the Union of South Africa to place its League of

Nations mandate in South West Africa under the new Trusteeship Council. As well, South Africa's violation of human rights through apartheid policies, which denied education, health, and government facilities to 80 per cent of its population on the ground of their race and colour, was offensive to other nations. The UN believed this situation required interference in what South Africa declared was a domestic issue. After the Sharpesville Massacre in 1960, the Security Council adopted a resolution stating that international peace and security might be endangered by South Africa's racial policies. In 1962 the General Assembly called upon member states to impose sanctions on South Africa. Finally, on 12 November 1974 South Africa was expelled from the United Nations. In 1977, a mandatory arms embargo was applied to the recalcitrant nation. However, South Africa's strategic position and relationship to major powers, particularly Britain, prevented stringent punishment. The arms embargo was lifted in May 1994 when South Africa held its first all-race multiparty election and established a democratic, non-racial government under the leadership of Nelson Mandela. South Africa rejoined the UN the next month.

The sovereign members of the United Nations agreed to safeguard the peace by non-violent means. As well, the Charter expressly forbids interference in the domestic affairs of any nation. No action of the United Nations binds any of its members against their will, and therefore many of its objectives remain beyond reach. The division of Europe into two spheres of influence at the end of the war underscored the preference of the major powers for settling differences between themselves, rather than through an international forum. In addition, the principle of non-interference in domestic affairs effectively restricts the enforcement of the Universal Declaration of Human Rights in authoritarian and totalitarian states.

In spite of these impediments, the United Nations remains a valuable forum for international discussion and mediation, as well as a means of promoting the improvement of living standards throughout the world.

THE SECURITY COUNCIL

The work of the United Nations is divided among six principal organs and a host of specialized agencies and commissions. The most powerful organ is the Security Council, which has five permanent members: the United States, Russia (occupying the seat which the Soviet Union held until its dissolution), Great Britain, France, and China. Initially six but now ten non-permanent members are elected by the General Assembly for two-year terms on the Council. These non-permanent members represent the world's geographic regions: five seats are allocated to African and Asian nations, two to Latin America, one for Eastern Europe, and two for Western Europe and other states. The presidency of the Council rotates monthly by English-language alphabetical order of its members.

It is the responsibility of the Security Council to maintain peace and security, and the Security Council therefore has the power to determine the course of action to be taken in the resolution of international disputes. Any measure brought before the Council may be vetoed by any one or more of the five permanent members. The major powers see this veto as their safeguard against the combined vote of smaller and less powerful states. The veto cannot be used in a procedural matter, nor by a power that is party to a dispute. Absence from the Council does not constitute a veto, nor does an abstention from voting. From 1946 to 1964, the Soviet Union exercised its veto power 103 times, Great Britain 4 times, France 3 times, and Nationalist China once. In 1970, the United States vetoed the resolution demanding that communications be cut off with Rhodesia, and throughout the 1970s, exercised the veto an average of twice per year.

All recommendations made by the Council are binding on the member states. The existence of the veto, however, has in the past prevented the United Nations from acting in any conflict which involved the vital interests of the superpowers. As a result, the USA and USSR had to engage in bilateral negotiations to work out whatever arrangements were deemed necessary.

In an effort to avoid public confrontation, the superpowers tempered their use of the veto during the 1980s. In the era of cooperation between Russia and the USA, since the end of the Cold War, resolutions that in the past would have resulted in a veto are now agreed to beforehand. This does not mean that the major powers will not use their veto to protect their sovereign interests, but rather that the instances in need of a veto have been significantly reduced.

THE GENERAL ASSEMBLY

All 185 member nations are represented in the General Assembly. Each nation may send five delegates, as well as five alternate delegates, to the Assembly, but each nation has only one vote. The General Assembly has now almost reached universal membership. The exceptions are Switzerland, Taiwan, and 17 former colonies which now have some measure of independence and have been given limited recognition by the international community. The Western Sahara is an example of a disputed territory which is still considered a colony but has some international status.

The influx of new members has shifted the direction of the United Nations, from its initial efforts in post-war reconstruction, to efforts to aid impoverished nations of the developing world. On the basis of national equality and the concept of "one state, one vote," the Assembly more often than not represents the views of the non-industrialized nations. The initial focus of the General Assembly was also altered by the **"Uniting for Peace"** resolution in 1950, which gave the General Assembly the power to act with a two thirds majority in matters of **peacekeeping** when the Security Council failed to act, perhaps because of the use of the veto.

The General Assembly has the power to debate any matter and initiate any action. However, it can only recommend, not mandate. Unlike those of the Security Council, General Assembly recommendations can be ignored by individual states without punishment. The weakness of the United Nations as a federation of nation-states, then, lies in its inability to enforce its demands in any way except through cooperation and good will. However, the effective use of the Assembly as a world forum to debate matters of global concern has been a positive one, as has been the practice since the 1960s of calling international conferences on a wide range of subjects of universal importance.

The Assembly session opens on the third Tuesday of September each year, and has as working languages English, French, Russian, Chinese, and Spanish. In times of emergency, nine members of the Council or a simple majority of the members of the Assembly can call for a special session within 24 hours.

The General Assembly also supervises and monitors the activities of the agencies and commissions of the United Nations. Its expanding programs are costly and have on occasion brought the UN to the verge of bankruptcy. Initially, nations were to be assessed a percentage of their GNP, depending on

This photograph shows a regular opening meeting of the General Assembly. Almost every country in the world now participates in the Assembly.

their ability to pay. The United States agreed to pay 39.89 per cent of the organization's initial budget, until the remainder of the states had recovered from the costs of the Second World War. This amount was to be reduced to 25 per cent once other nations were able to pay their share. Today, the 10 largest nations contribute most of the money but have only 7 per cent of the votes, while over 70 nations who contribute less than 0.01 per cent of their GNP hold majority voting power. The USA pays 25 per cent of the UN budget, followed by Japan which contributes 12 per cent.

This disproportionate fee schedule has resulted in a two-fold problem. The UN membership fears American domination of the organization, yet the United States government resents paying such a sizable portion of the budget without being granted corresponding influence. It has been suggested that the assessment formula be changed to one which is based on the GNP per head with a maximum of 4 per cent of the UN budget per state. This formula would require no country to contribute more that $US 40 million per year and would transfer some of the financial burden to small, wealthy states which are sometimes in need of UN protection. Kuwait and South Korea are examples of these smaller states.

Appeals for donations through agencies like UNICEF and attempts to garner additional financing from the sale of bonds to the private sector have been modestly successful.

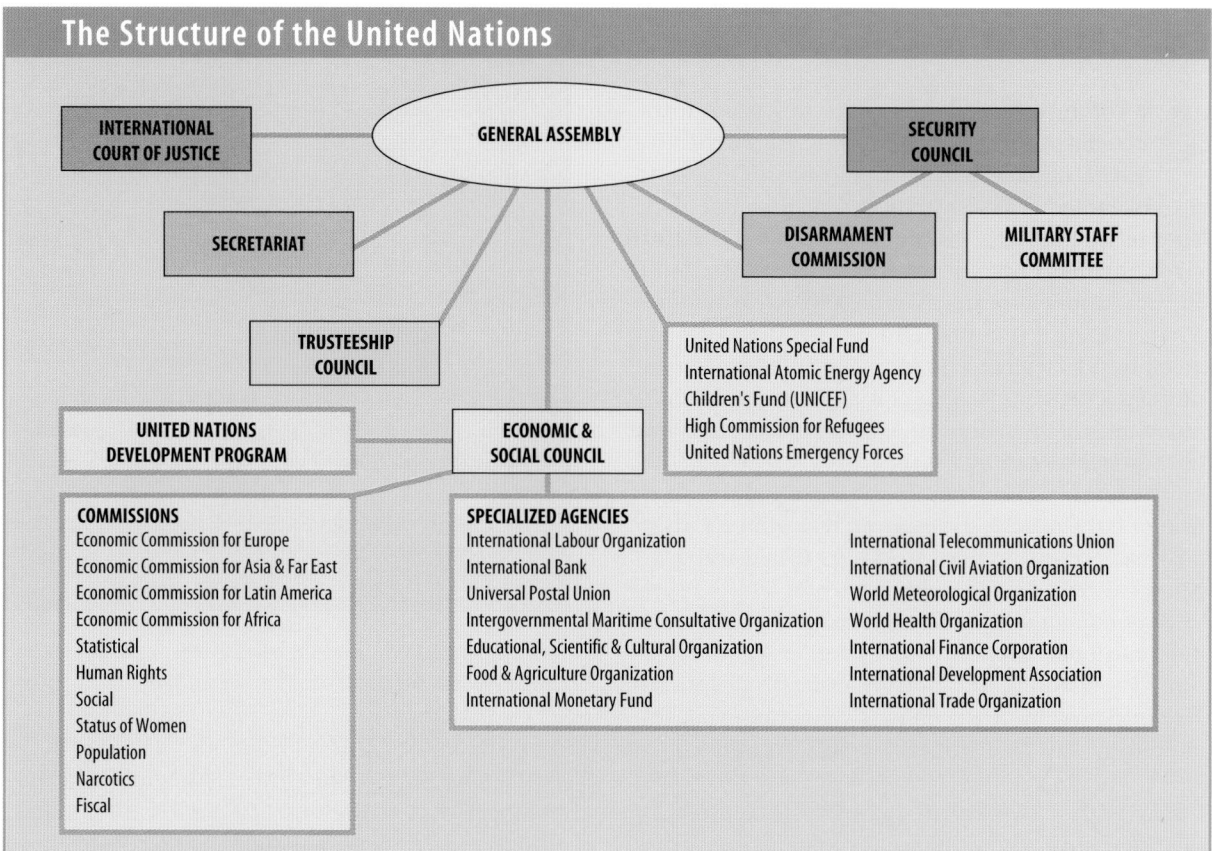

The Structure of the United Nations

INTERNATIONAL COURT OF JUSTICE

GENERAL ASSEMBLY

SECURITY COUNCIL

SECRETARIAT

DISARMAMENT COMMISSION

MILITARY STAFF COMMITTEE

TRUSTEESHIP COUNCIL

United Nations Special Fund
International Atomic Energy Agency
Children's Fund (UNICEF)
High Commission for Refugees
United Nations Emergency Forces

UNITED NATIONS DEVELOPMENT PROGRAM

ECONOMIC & SOCIAL COUNCIL

COMMISSIONS
Economic Commission for Europe
Economic Commission for Asia & Far East
Economic Commission for Latin America
Economic Commission for Africa
Statistical
Human Rights
Social
Status of Women
Population
Narcotics
Fiscal

SPECIALIZED AGENCIES
International Labour Organization
International Bank
Universal Postal Union
Intergovernmental Maritime Consultative Organization
Educational, Scientific & Cultural Organization
Food & Agriculture Organization
International Monetary Fund

International Telecommunications Union
International Civil Aviation Organization
World Meteorological Organization
World Health Organization
International Finance Corporation
International Development Association
International Trade Organization

The function of the United Nations has changed and expanded since its conception. This chart showing the structure of the UN illustrates how many international concerns are addressed.

The precarious financial situation of the United Nations has resulted primarily from the cost of its military peacekeeping operations. UN operations in Korea from 1950 to 1953 ($200 million), and in the Congo from 1960 to 1964 ($400 million), are examples of the economic strain imposed by military activities. These costs are over and above the salaries and equipment costs that were borne by those states whose soldiers were involved. The Soviet bloc, however, refused to pay its share for Korea, on the grounds that the action was a domestic matter outside the UN's mandate and was not a Council activity but one fostered by the Assembly, which did not have a mandate to allocate costs. The Latin Americans have suggested the costs of peacekeeping be borne exclusively by the permanent members of the Council, who have the responsibility to maintain world peace.

In 1962, the International Court of Justice ruled that peacekeeping costs are legitimate charges on all members of the organization and are to be paid.

Failure to pay assigned costs can result in expulsion. In 1964, both France and the Soviet Union were in danger of losing their seats in the Assembly for non-payment of arrears. Because of the threat of the Soviet Union to withdraw if pressed for payment, this session of the United Nations did its business by informal agreements, as no official votes were taken. The following year the matter was allowed to drop. Since then, members have been assessed their share of further United Nations operations costs, although in Cyprus, peacekeeping costs were borne by the governments involved.

Subsequent suggestions regarding a resolution of the United Nations' financial problems have ranged from a surcharge on all international mail, to a fee on the use of international waterways, a fee for all UN services, a resource tax on mining the ocean floors or Antarctica, a charge for ventures into outer space, and a tax on all international travel.

In the 1990s, the magnitude and proliferation of the UN peacekeeping forces around the globe has resulted in skyrocketing costs at a time when member nations are in default of payments. The resolution of its financial problems is critical to the United Nations if it is to be a credible security force in the global community.

THE SECRETARIAT

An administrative cadre of thousands of international civil servants comprises the Secretariat, which manages the day-to-day business of the United Nations. At the head of the Secretariat is the secretary general, who is nominated by the Security Council and appointed by the General Assembly. As chief administrator of the United Nations, the secretary general has the power to set agendas and call meetings, as well as to give advice and attempt to solve problems. The Secretariat is responsible for carrying out the wishes of the Security Council and the General Assembly, as well as for gathering data, disseminating information, and monitoring the work of the specialized agencies and commissions. An additional burden on the Secretariat has been the support and planning of an increasing number of United Nations sponsored conferences on matters of global importance—the use of outer space, the law of the sea, human habitat, the planetary environment, and technical development.

THE ECONOMIC AND SOCIAL COUNCIL

The Economic and Social Council is devoted to improving the standard of living of all the people of the world. The council has 27 member nations. Each year the General Assembly elects 9 members to serve for a three-year period. Each member has one vote, and decisions are made by majority. Although emphasis has been on global economic matters related to better health and cultural and educational opportunities, the question of social equality has become a major thrust with the adoption of the UN Universal Declaration of Human Rights. The Economic and Social Council gathers data, disseminates information, and administers commissions and agency programs. In addition, it cooperates with other global organizations, such as the Red Cross and labour unions, in the promotion of human welfare. The council planned and sponsored the First and Second Development Decades, aimed at improving conditions in the developing nations.

THE INTERNATIONAL COURT OF JUSTICE

Located in The Hague, the International Court of Justice is the principal judicial arm of the United Nations. Unlike its predecessor, the Permanent Court of International Justice, the International Court of Justice is an integral part of the UN Charter. Thus, it has the status of being a part of the multilateral treaty that is the "constitution" of the United Nations. The Court is composed of 15 judges elected by the Council and Assembly to nine-year terms. No 2 judges can be of the same nation. Judges are to represent the major legal systems of the world, and decisions are reached by a majority vote. In special cases, additional judges can be appointed by a nation whose legal codes are not represented. These judges have full voting rights for the case in question. Only nation-states can bring cases to the International Court of Justice. Distrust of the Court and of the United Nations defeated attempts to make compulsory the arbitration of disputes between nations. Appearance at the Court is voluntary, and its decisions are not binding unless a mutual agreement is reached. No serious clash has been referred to the Court: nations prefer other means of settling their disputes. The Court has the power to give advice on matters of international law and can rule on interpretations of the UN Charter.

THE TRUSTEESHIP COUNCIL

The Trusteeship Council was designed to administer territories that were not self-governing at the end of the Second World War. Some of these territories were former mandates of the League of Nations, and some were colonies of Japan and Italy. In addition, some territories voluntarily placed themselves in trust. Trust powers were to ensure the political, social, economic, and educational well-being of the inhabitants of these non-self-governing peoples. In 1950, there were still 11 trust territories, all but Somaliland being former mandates. The Trust Territory of the Pacific Islands was declared a strategic region under American administration. The mandate of South West Africa was not placed in trust, but was held by the Union of South Africa with the intent of annexation. In 1990, South West Africa obtained its independence and is now called Namibia.

BIOGRAPHY

BOUTROS BOUTROS-GHALI
(1922–)

The following is taken from the June 1992 report entitled *An Agenda For Peace* by Boutros Boutros-Ghali of Egypt, secretary general of the United Nations from 1991 to 1996. He was succeeded by Kofi Annan of Ghana.

The nations and peoples of the United Nations are fortunate in a way that those of the League of Nations were not. We have been given a second chance to create the world of our Charter that they were denied. With the cold war ended we have drawn back from the brink of a confrontation that threatened the world and, too often, paralyzed our Organization.

Even as we celebrate our restored possibilities, there is a need to ensure that the lessons of the past four decades are learned and that the errors, or variations of them, are not repeated. For there may not be a third opportunity for our planet which, now for different reasons, remains endangered . . .

Peace at home and the urgency of rebuilding and strengthening our individual societies necessitates peace abroad and cooperation among nations. . . Democracy within nations requires respect for human rights and fundamental freedoms, as set forth in the Charter. It requires as well a deeper understanding and respect for the rights of minorities and respect for the needs of more vulnerable groups of society, especially women and children. This is not only a political matter. The social stability needed for productive growth is nurtured by conditions in which people can readily express their will. For this, strong domestic institutions of participation are essential. Promoting such institutions means promoting the empowerment of the unorganized, the poor, the marginalized . . .

Reform is a continuing process, and improvement can have no limit . . . We must be guided not by precedents alone, however wise these may be, but by the needs of the future and by the shape and content that we wish to give it.

I am committed to a broad dialogue between the Member States and the Secretary-General. And I am committed to fostering a full and open interplay between all institutions and elements of the Organization so that the Charter's objectives may not only be served better, but that this Organization may emerge as greater than the sum of its parts. The United Nations was created with a great and courageous vision. Now is the time, for its nations and peoples, and the men and women who serve it, to seize the moment for the sake of the future. ●

When Palau, the last remaining trust territory, became an independent state in October 1994, the work of the Trusteeship Council was completed. As a result, the Trusteeship Council as originally conceived ceased to exist. Consideration is being given, however, to transferring its mandate to responsibility for the environment or to provide assistance to those states that have ceased to function effectively because of serious civil disputes.

PEACEKEEPING OPERATIONS

One of the major objectives of the United Nations is to maintain world peace through collective security. The Security Council has the responsibility of debating breaches of the peace and deciding what action should be taken against the aggressors. How to get agreement on the identification of the aggressor, and convince some 185 nations of an appropriate response, is another matter. Although the United Nations has had success when dealing with the less powerful nations, there is little it can do when conflict involving the major powers erupts. The United Nations is not a world government with sovereign powers and cannot easily enforce its resolutions. The ideological division between the major powers left the Security Council powerless to deal with Soviet aggression in Eastern Europe after the Second World War, with the Arab-Israeli dispute between 1967 and 1970, or with major-power involvement in Vietnam or Afghanistan. However, in 1990, the UN Security Council resolution protested Iraq's invasion of Kuwait and authorized the use of force when economic sanctions and diplomacy appeared to have failed.

KOREA: 1950–1953

The United Nations had barely recovered from the hectic events leading to the establishment of the state of Israel in 1948, when it was confronted with aggression in Korea. The Korean War (1950-1953) was to test the willingness of the organization to deal effectively with armed aggression. Unlike the League, which avoided the use of military force, the United Nations was determined to take action. In the absence of the Soviet delegate, the Security Council approved collective security

The United Nations peacekeeping forces are deployed whenever the international community deems situations between two or more countries to be escalating into a threat to universal collective security. The Swedish soldier in this picture was a member of the peacekeeping force in Cyprus in 1980.

INTERNATIONAL LAW

As the world becomes more complex and interdependent, a mutually acceptable approach to solving legal problems between states is increasingly necessary. Select a recent dispute between two or more states. Choose a major player and defend its position. Be sure to use legal arguments.

The UN Charter forms the basis for the development of international law, which emphasizes the resolution of disputes by peaceful means rather than by the use of force. The General Assembly has primary responsibility for the development of international law and for declarations of specific principles. For example, in 1961 the General Assembly declared South Africa's policy of apartheid to be a violation of UN principles.

To establish international rules to meet the demands of a rapidly changing world, nation-states must reconcile national aspirations with international goals. The United Nations has recognized the economic and environmental interdependence of the nation-states of the world.

Two examples of international law formulated by United Nations mandates are the Law of the Sea and the Treaty Governing the Exploration and Use of Outer Space.

In 1958, the first Law of the Sea conference convened. Ever since, the Law of the Sea has challenged international lawmakers. Despite a series of conventions, the international community has not been able to agree on ocean access and ownership of sea resources. In 1982, a vote in the General Assembly supported a resolution to establish a 320 km "exclusive economic zone" for coastal nations, in addition to sovereignty over oceanic resources for a distance of 560 km. Landlocked nations would have access to the ocean and a share of surplus ocean resources. The control and prevention of pollution was also addressed in the agreement.

Another contentious issue has been deep-sea mining. The United States strongly opposes the establishment of an international authority to regulate deep-sea mining. The international authority, proposed by a UN resolution, would be empowered to direct surplus resources to the development of Third World countries. Despite a negative vote by the United States, and abstention by the Soviet Union, the UN resolution was passed by an overwhelming majority (130 countries in favour, 4 against, 17 abstentions). This is an example of the power of developing countries in the General Assembly.

In 1967 the Treaty of Principles Governing the Activities of States in the Exploration and Use of Outer Space was made law. The installation of nuclear weapons in space was prohibited as was any military activity on the moon or any other planets. This treaty, in combination with others controlling nuclear weaponry, was deemed essential to the security of nations and the preservation of humankind.

1. What is the International Court of Justice at The Hague, Netherlands? What is its purpose?

2. Research the positions of the USA, Russia, Japan, or Canada regarding the creation of an international Law of the Sea convention.

3. Coordinate a convention on the use of the Antarctic. Assign the roles of the major players to individuals, pairs, or groups. Try to reach an agreement that everyone will sign.

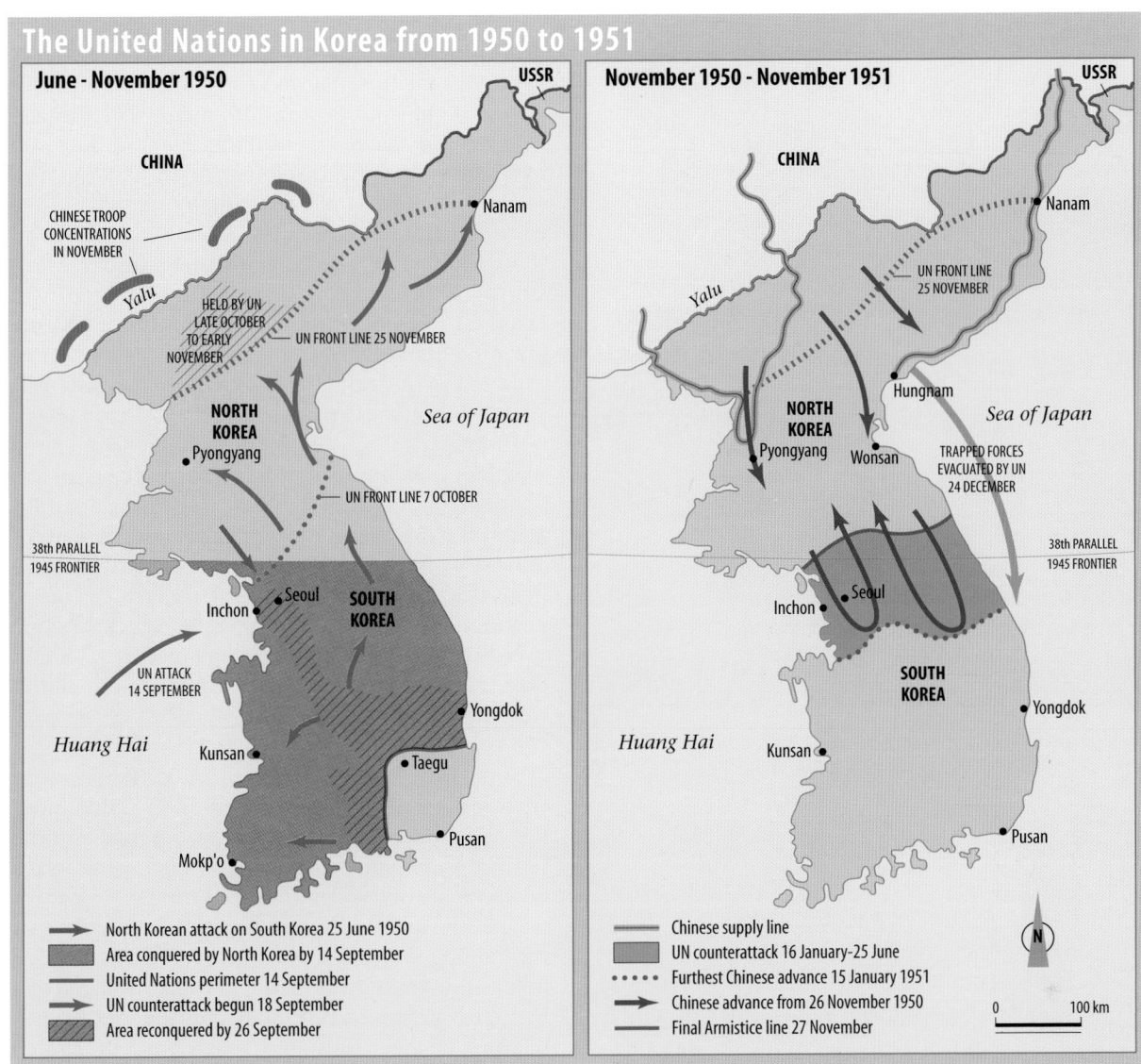

June - November 1950

CHINA

CHINESE TROOP
CONCENTRATIONS
IN NOVEMBER

Yalu

Nanam

USSR

HELD BY UN
LATE OCTOBER
TO EARLY
NOVEMBER — UN FRONT LINE 25 NOVEMBER

Sea of Japan

NORTH
KOREA
Pyongyang

UN FRONT LINE 7 OCTOBER

38th PARALLEL
1945 FRONTIER

Inchon • Seoul SOUTH
KOREA

UN ATTACK
14 SEPTEMBER

Huang Hai

Kunsan •

• Yongdok

• Taegu

Mokp'o •

• Pusan

→ North Korean attack on South Korea 25 June 1950
▨ Area conquered by North Korea by 14 September
— United Nations perimeter 14 September
→ UN counterattack begun 18 September
▨ Area reconquered by 26 September

November 1950 - November 1951

CHINA

Yalu

Nanam

USSR

UN FRONT LINE
25 NOVEMBER

NORTH
KOREA
Pyongyang   Wonsan

Hungnam

Sea of Japan

TRAPPED FORCES
EVACUATED BY UN
24 DECEMBER

38th PARALLEL
1945 FRONTIER

Inchon • Seoul

SOUTH
KOREA

• Yongdok

Huang Hai

Kunsan •

• Pusan

N

— Chinese supply line
▨ UN counterattack 16 January–25 June
• • • • Furthest Chinese advance 15 January 1951
→ Chinese advance from 26 November 1950
— Final Armistice line 27 November

0   100 km

measures and approved the formation of a multinational army to end the fighting in Korea.

The Korean peninsula was divided at the 38th parallel in 1945 as a result of an agreement between the United States and the Soviet Union. The USSR was to occupy the territory north of the 38th parallel, and the United States was to occupy the territory south of that line after the Japanese surrender. Once provisions for establishing a permanent government for the entire country were worked out, the occupying forces would withdraw. When negotiations for uniting the country reached an impasse in 1947, the United States referred the matter to the United Nations. The General Assembly passed a resolution providing for elections for a national assembly, to be conducted under United Nations supervision. When the United Nations was refused permission to enter North Korea, elections were carried out in the south,

The United Nations officially sanctioned military intervention when North Korea invaded South Korea. However, for all practical purposes, the United States was in command of the operations.

and the Soviets installed a rival government in the north. By 1949, the superpowers had withdrawn their forces and left in place two governments which both claimed sovereignty over one country.

On 25 June 1950 North Korea mounted a full-scale invasion of South Korea, capturing the capital of Seoul in the first days of the war. The Security Council declared the attack a breach of the peace and called for a halt to hostilities. It then asked member states to assist the Republic of South Korea in repelling the attack, and authorized a United Nations command under American leadership to enter the battle zone. The Security Council thus

Canada was one of the United Nations members to participate in the Korean conflict. In this photograph, a member of the Canadian Provost Corps examines a Korean child who was injured in napalm attacks.

gave legitimacy to the massive United States involvement that was to follow.

The United Nations force that fought in Korea was hardly a model of collective security. The Americans supplied most of the soldiers and equipment. Only 15 other states furnished military forces of any size, although 40 states contributed medical and economic aid. The United Nations provided moral and psychological support to the American effort to assist South Korea in repelling the invasion by North Korea. However, before the United Nations resolutions were passed, President Truman had already authorized American military intervention in Korea.

During the next 12 months, virtually all of Korea became a battleground. United Nations forces halted the initial invasion and pushed the North Koreans back across the 38th parallel. At that point, the UN approved the forcible reunification of the peninsula. The objective was no longer to repel the invader, but to conquer North Korea. Under General MacArthur's command, the United Nations forces advanced toward the Yalu River, which separates Korea from China.

Early in October 1950, first contact was made with Chinese volunteer forces. The war had assumed new dimensions. The newly created People's Republic of China viewed the American presence only 200 km from Beijing with alarm. The Chinese believed the Americans would move from Korea to overthrow the government of Mao Zedong, and reinstate the USA's old ally Chiang Kai-shek. They were determined to keep the Americans as far from their borders as possible. Chinese forces drove United Nations forces southward, and Seoul was taken for the second time in six months. It was not until the new year that sufficient strength could be gathered to push the Chinese back to the 38th parallel and stabilize the front.

In January 1951, the People's Republic of China rejected UN proposals for a cease-fire, and was branded an aggressor. In May, the United Nations asked all states to place an embargo on shipments of arms, war *matériel*, petroleum, and transportation items being sent to China or North Korea. Armistice negotiations began in July 1951, but quickly stalled over the repatriation of prisoners of war. A demilitarized zone separating the two parts of the peninsula was finally agreed to in July 1953. In February 1954, the foreign ministers of France, the Soviet Union, Great Britain, and the United States met in Geneva to settle the Korean and Indo-China questions. No agreement on Korea was reached and the status quo remains to this day, with hostile forces on each side of the demilitarized zone.

The Korean War demonstrated the difficulties of conducting collective-security operations. Lack of unanimity among the major powers hindered the United Nations force. Small contingents from a handful of member states gave a United Nations facade to an operation that was, in effect, carried out by the United States and South Korea. Member states were left free to decide what, if any, support they would give the operation. Sanctions were voluntary rather than mandatory. The cost of the operation came close to bankrupting the organization, and the Soviet bloc refused to pay its share of the costs on the grounds that the Korean foray was an Assembly decision and therefore not binding. They saw the North Korean invasion of South Korea as a breach of the peace and not as open aggression.

The United Nations action in Korea did not end in a unification of the Koreas, but it did result in pushing North Korea back behind the 38th parallel once more. A precedent had been set when the Assembly took over from a deadlocked Security Council and, what is more important, the United Nations demonstrated its willingness to take action.

SUEZ: 1956–1967

The qualified success of military intervention in Korea had taught the United Nations a lesson. In future, the organization would try to avoid active military ventures, pursuing instead a peacekeeping role. United Nations forces would be placed between the combatants to police a cease-fire and move the dispute to the negotiating table. In contrast with the Korean action, the major powers would not be invited to take part in peacekeeping operations. In this manner, disputes would be localized and the possibility of major power conflict would be lessened.

The first opportunity for the UN to exercise a peacekeeping role occurred in 1956 when Israeli, French, and British forces invaded the Suez Canal Zone. Egypt had just nationalized the canal and was in the difficult process of working out new arrangements over ownership and canal management when Israel invaded. Claiming that the canal itself was endangered, the French and British intervened to protect the crucial waterway. The Egyptians began to sink ships in the canal to deny its use to the invaders. Attempts by the Security Council to resolve the dispute were met by French and British vetoes, and the General Assembly was forced to take the matter in hand. On 2 November, the Assembly called for a halt to hostilities and a withdrawal of forces from the area. The British and French agreed, provided that a United Nations force be stationed in the disputed area to see to the re-opening of the canal. On 4 November, Lester Pearson of Canada introduced a resolution calling for the establishment of an emergency force (UNEF), and by mid-November the first contingents arrived on Egyptian soil. Israel steadfastly refused permission for United Nations forces to enter Israeli territory. A peacekeeping force of 6000 soldiers drawn from member states was posted to the area, and continued to patrol the borders between Israel and Egypt for the next 10 years.

The UN presence kept incidents to a minimum and protected the operation of the canal. The situation deteriorated, however, in May 1967, after an armed clash between Syrian and Israeli troops on the Golan Heights. On 18 May, the Egyptians asked the United Nations forces to withdraw. Placed in an untenable position, Secretary General U Thant reluctantly gave his approval for withdrawal. On 5 June, a full-scale war began between Israel and its neighbours. Nine United Nations soldiers were killed by Israeli gunfire during an artillery attack.

The United Nations has been active in the Middle East, with varying degrees of success, since the creation of Israel. In 1973, hostilities between Israel and Egypt escalated. The United Nations helped negotiate and implement a disengagement agreement between the two countries.

They were members of one of the last contingents to be withdrawn. On 6 June, the Security Council adopted a cease-fire resolution that attached no blame for the war, nor any specific conditions for peace. A resolution of the Middle East situation was far beyond the ability of the United Nations. A second UN force entered the region in 1973, after hostilities had erupted once more. Although the United Nations force was not able to prevent the eruption of hostilities in the Middle East at that time, it was successful in preventing superpower involvement and in promoting the success of peacekeeping ventures in other regions.

THE CONGO: 1960–1964

Of all the UN peacekeeping operations, the one in the Congo was the largest and one of the most controversial. The size of the UN force approached 20 000, mostly drawn from neighbouring African states. At one point the force was involved in aggressive action, even governance of the war torn Congo. Thirty-four countries, including some of the major powers, contributed to the campaign. The non-interventionist policy of peacekeeping was sorely tested by hostile governments, and by multinational corporations intent on securing

REFUGEES

Millions of people around the world have fled their homes because of civil unrest. Should stable industrialized nations be required to provide refuge for these people? Choose a current large-scale refugee situation. Research the causes and suggest both short and long-term solutions.

Today millions of people live and die far away from their homes, having been driven to seek refuge in strange places by wars, famine, poverty, and political upheavals. The most satisfactory solution to their plight would be repatriation, but most leave their homelands with little hope of being able to return. Their growing numbers have brought into question whether the world can care for them all. Since 1945, it is estimated that as many as 60 million people have been forced to seek haven in other lands. Small numbers are readily assimilated; but today's numbers are so large they affect the population and cultural patterns of host nations, alter domestic policies, and, in the case of the Palestinian situation, affect foreign policies. The refugee problem has become one of the most serious issues facing the world.

Refugees are recognized as displaced persons only after they have crossed an international boundary. Given this definition, there are millions of people around the world who are not considered refugees but "internal migrants." In the absence of domestic political and economic reform which would allow them to return safely to their homes, they are forced to remain for long periods of time in refugee camps.

The United Nations Relief and Rehabilitation Administration was created in 1943 to bring aid to areas stricken by war. Through its services, some 6 million people were rehabilitated by 1947. In that year, the International Refugee Organization took over the responsibility of the remaining 1.6 million European refugees. This organization was replaced in 1951 by the United Nations High Commissioner for Refugees (UNHCR), charged with assisting those people who seek asylum, fearing persecution and death at home. Since then, the UNHCR's mandate has been expanded to include aid to those fleeing external aggression, foreign occupation, foreign domination, and political turmoil. Originally established to deal with a purely European problem after the Second World War, the system now has global dimensions. The notion that the refugee problem is transient in nature and will disappear has proved unrealistic: new reasons for migration continue to arise.

Since 1990, millions of people have been forced to leave their homes to seek safety elsewhere as a result of political terror and armed conflict. Refugee populations in excess of 10 000 can now be identified in 70 of the world's states. No part of the world is untouched by the mass migrations. The UNHCR places the number at over 30 million, not counting the estimated more than 5 million displaced within their own nation. The latter are not formally recognized as refugees, because they have not crossed an international border.

Recent crises indicate that some of the population displacements have been a matter of planned policy on the part of warring parties within the nation. Half the population of Liberia has been uprooted by civil war, and some 500 000 were displaced by the warring clans in Somalia. In the first part of 1994, half a million people were massacred in Rwanda while, in the space of only a week, two million more fled to neighbouring Tanzania and Zaïre. Upon its breakup, 900 000 people left the former Yugoslavia, and millions remain homeless in this war-shattered region. Two hundred thousand or more people were displaced by the Russian actions in Chechnya, and it is estimated that displaced populations number 890 000 in Azerbaijan, 380 000 in Armenia, and 280 000 in Georgia. Other examples include the flight of a million Nepalese, the struggle of the Kurdish peoples in the four nations in which they live, and the outward movement of Latin Americans seeking a better standard of living in North America. Increasingly, larger numbers of the world's people are searching for safe havens and a better standard of living.

Many refugees are seeking a better life but are not at risk. If they are unable to obtain permission to emigrate, they sometimes enter countries illegally, hoping that they will evade discovery and enjoy a better lifestyle.

The changing nature of the world's refugee problem has led to new initiatives designed to manage large-scale human migration, provide humanitarian aid for those in genuine need, at the same time as

protect the interests of the host countries. In the early 1990s, the industrialized countries took action to reduce the flow of refugees into their nations. Entrance requirements were tightened; refugee boat people were intercepted at sea with the intention of sending them back to their country of origin; and work permits were withdrawn.

New initiatives include the provision of safe havens within the refugees' own countries where aid and security can be provided and monitored by international agencies. The safe havens in northern Iraq for the minority Kurds, or those established in the former Yugoslavia during its civil war, are examples of this initiative. Another is the action taken in 1994 when tens of thousands of Haitians and Cubans set out by boat to reach Florida. They were intercepted and conducted to a safe haven outside the USA, in Guantanamo Naval Base in Cuba. Here their claims of asylum were processed. The funding of special economic zones in impoverished nations is now viewed as the most practical solution to a very complex problem. This funding would create employment and entice those seeking a better life to stay where they are. Some $60 billion have been transferred to some states in the form of migrant remittances. This figure does not include the

The Universal Declaration of Human Rights proclaims the right of freedom of movement, the right to leave any country, and the right to seek and receive asylum from persecution. Many people are not given the opportunity to exercise these rights.

economic benefits that accrue from increased trade, investment, and other forms of aid designed to improve conditions at home.

1. What are the responsibilities of host nations toward refugees?

2. What are the responsibilities of refugees to host nations?

3. Should there be limits to the number of refugees a nation accepts? If so, what are they?

4. Devise plans for looking after 1 000 000 refugees to be settled in your country in the next months. What UN agencies and other volunteer organizations would you call upon for assistance?

the mineral wealth of the break-away province of Katanga.

The Belgian Congo (Zaïre) was granted its independence on 1 July 1960. No provision had been made to prepare the 14 million Congolese for political freedom. Only 30 Congolese were university graduates. Five days after independence, the Congolese army mutinied and Belgian troops intervened to restore order in the cities. On 11 July President Tshombe of Katanga announced the secession of his province from the Congo. On 14 July, the Security Council called upon Belgium to withdraw its forces and authorized a United Nations force to assist in restoring order. Within a month, 14 000 troops had arrived. They were to use force only in self-defence, and they were not to interfere in the internal operations of the Congo. Their role was to restore law and order, protect lives and property, and transform the Congolese army into a reliable instrument.

The restoration of stability in the Congo would take a chaotic four years. Between September 1960 and August 1961, no single government existed in the region. The Congolese army took over Léopoldville and was recognized by most United Nations members as the legitimate government. Gizenga controlled the city of Stanleyville and Orientale Province with the support of the Soviet bloc. Tshombe claimed the right to Katangan independence, and was supported by mercenaries in the interests of Belgium and the multinational corporations. Albert Kalonji sought autonomy for Kasi province.

Fighting broke out between Tshombe's mercenaries and the United Nations force in 1961. The world was shocked when the secretary general of the UN, Dag Hammarskjöld, was killed in a plane crash while on his way to meet Tshombe. In November, after a series of incidents, the Security Council gave the acting secretary general, U Thant, permission to use military force to resolve the chaotic situation. Limited military actions were authorized to capture and expel all mercenaries from the region.

The United Nations force was withdrawn in June 1964, but United Nations assistance in the form of technical aid and training programs continued. Although internal disorders and political upheavals did not stop, the United Nations can be credited with a major contribution to stability in the area. The $400 million price tag, however, created a financial crisis for the international organization.

INTERNATIONAL ECONOMIC COOPERATION

Global independence has resulted in the growth of international economic organizations outside of the UN. After the First World War, the Triple Alliance was crippled economically and not allowed to participate in international trade until reparations were paid. Protective tariffs and worldwide depression compounded their economic difficulties. The collapse of the international economic order dislocated governments and brought to power demagogues like Hitler and Mussolini, who promoted war to gain what peace had denied their people. Economic plans for reconstruction after the Second World War were aimed at preventing the reoccurrence of such events, by swiftly reconstructing the world's economic and financial systems.

Recognition of world interdependence, particularly in the area of economics, has led to the development of a number of agencies designed to foster trade and development, as well as to stabilize currency relationships. In 1944, the International Monetary Fund (IMF) was established by a meeting of 44 allied nations at Bretton Woods in New Hampshire, to provide stability among the world's currencies. The purpose of the IMF was to re-stabilize exchange rates that had been disrupted when nations left the gold standard in the 1930s. A modified system of fixed exchange rates was established, with the US dollar as the world's principal reserve currency. Dollars could be freely converted into gold at a fixed price. Exchange rates would be calculated according to the par values of currency in effect at the opening of the Bretton Woods conference. Any adjustment of a member country's currency required approval by the governing board of the IMF. The IMF consisted of a pool of currencies that member nations could draw upon to remedy balance-of-payments difficulties, without having to devalue their currencies or impose exchange controls. The fund proved successful in stabilizing international exchange, and allowing for the extension of international trade with little concern for currency exchange. The exclusion of the Soviet bloc from the IMF over the years increased the USSR's economic isolation.

The Bretton Woods meeting resulted in a second financial plan, the creation of the International Bank for Reconstruction and Development—commonly called the World Bank. The World Bank was to make a pool of credit available to countries which might not have sound credit ratings at the moment, but whose futures were promising. If a loan was made by a private institution, the World Bank would guarantee repayment. The purpose of the bank was to encourage reconstruction and development of member nations, and to enhance the development of international trade. Since the United States contributed one third of the seed money to the bank, it held one third of its decision making power. As well as America's dominance in the World Bank, the headquarters of both the IMF and the World Bank were in Washington so that many bureaucratic positions were most likely to be filled by Americans. Both institutions have been dominated by American policies and personalities.

Since 1945, world trade has grown more rapidly than world production, and a complex network of global exchange has developed. After the Second World War, it was recognized that a multilateral organization to promote and regulate trade was essential. National representatives were unable to reach agreement on the formation of an international trade organization, but they did reach agreement on a treaty on tariffs that was later to take shape as a permanent international organization. The **General Agreement on Tariffs and Trade (GATT)**, signed in 1947, was a legally binding code of conduct, agreed to by its members, to increase trade between nations. Since its inception, several multinational conferences were held to promote the concept of tariff reduction as a means to increase productivity and wealth. Opposed to domestic subsidies as providing an unfair advantage, GATT agreements had in some areas accomplished a major reduction in tariffs, from 60 per cent to less than 5 per cent. GATT constantly monitored trading practices and disciplined nations found guilty of protectionist practices.

Changes in international trading patterns provide new challenges in global economic management. In the 1960s, the European Common Market and Japan provided competition for American goods and dislocated America's predominance in world markets. New blocs have been particularly sensitive to protecting their textiles and farm produce through subsidies. For example, members of the European community agreed to buy farm produce from inside the bloc, despite high costs, before buying outside the bloc. Such a policy protects inefficient European producers from competition and leads to overproduction. Massive subsidies given to European steel producers in order to maintain employment and plants have invited American

Members of the United Nations have turned their attention to the world's economic problems. The World Bank was set up to provide affordable aid to all countries. However, many developing countries now have debt-loads which their economies cannot support.

retaliation in the form of quotas and the banning of some imports.

After 1971, the dramatic increase in energy costs, as a result of action taken by OPEC (the Organization of Petroleum Exporting Countries) led to a frenzied demand for a return to protective tariffs. The 1986 GATT negotiations in Uruguay sought a solution to the stagnation of trade brought about by increased tariffs and domestic subsidies. These had risen in

163

response to a stagnation in world markets brought about by a tremendous increase in productive capacity. "Dumping" of surplus goods in non-industrial nations became common practice, and resulted in the raising of protective tariffs by non-industrial nations to save their own economies. The free trade system devised at the end of the Second World War was no longer working, as global industrial production now outstripped market demands.

The impetus toward free trade was reversed. One example of this was the decision by members of the European Union (EU) not to buy from foreign producers until all similar products within the EU had been purchased. Canadian agricultural products could not be sold to Europe until those from Spain, France, and Poland had been consumed. Most industrial nations opened up branch plants within the EU, hoping to get their products in the back door. The North American Free Trade (NAFTA) region, including Canada, the USA, and Mexico, was formed in response to the EU. Foreign interests established branch plants in North America, too, under licence to the parent firm. They created employment in exchange for getting around tariff barriers. Many Asian car manufacturers, for example, have their automobiles assembled in Canada. The increasingly global nature of large corporations and industrial enterprise render economic nationalism obsolete.

In addition to international trade, economic interdependence involves the exchange of national currencies. The international money market remained relatively stable until the reconstruction of Germany and Japan was complete in the 1960s. During that decade, American imports and defence costs resulted in the first US balance-of-payments deficit. By 1971, continued and growing deficits caused grave concern for the American government. The Americans, who had borne a major part of the costs of the reconstruction and defence of Europe, as well as most of the costs of reconstruction in Japan, now demanded that the franc, mark, and yen be revalued upward in order to reduce the imbalance. The revaluation would cause imported goods from France, West Germany, and Japan to be relatively more expensive for American consumers, creating a lessening in demand for these goods and a lower balance-of-payments deficit.

French attempts to redeem hoarded American dollars in gold caused a political crisis. French president Charles de Gaulle made a bid to cripple the USA financially through redemption of American dollars in gold, which, fortunately for the USA, was not an example followed by other countries. The danger of having the value of the US dollar pegged to gold, however, was apparent, as it forced the American government to redeem dollars for a fixed amount of gold. President Richard Nixon took the United States off the gold standard and devalued the American currency. By 1980, the US dollar had shrunk to 45 per cent of its 1973 value. Nations holding American currency suffered heavy financial losses. Since then, exchange rates have been allowed to fluctuate according to the political and domestic needs of individual nations.

In 1995, the World Trade Organization (WTO) succeeded GATT. With a larger membership than GATT (120 by 1996), the WTO also has a broader scope. Whereas GATT applied only to trade in goods, the WTO includes services and intellectual property. The WTO is a legal and institutional body dealing with the multilateral trading system. It determines how governments deal with domestic trade legislation and regulations as well as provides collective debate, negotiation, and adjudication for international trade relations.

THE UNITED NATIONS IN THE 1990s

In the face of signs of increased cooperation between the Soviet Union, before it collapsed, and the USA, hope increased that the United Nations might begin to play a larger role on the international scene than it had in the past.

Through a series of UN resolutions put forward by the United States and supported by the USSR in 1990-1991, the UN authorized first sanctions, then armed intervention, against the Iraqi forces which had occupied Kuwait. Once formal hostilities had ceased, the UN established a peacekeeping force along the Iraq-Kuwait border, in keeping with the international organization's previous actions in Cyprus, Sinai, and Lebanon.

Less traditionally, members of the UN forces (particularly the USA, France, Britain, and the Netherlands) took subsequent steps to secure a large area in northern Iraq, adjacent to Turkey, to protect Kurds who had been persecuted by the forces of Iraqi leader Saddam Hussein. This action was an interesting precedent for the UN.

The United Nations Charter established the provision that the international community would

RWANDA

Secretary General Boutros Boutros-Ghali once commented that his inability to get the UN to act in Rwanda was one of his darkest failures. The seventeen nations that had promised to provide for a UN force to stop the killings in that region did not fulfil their promises.

When Rwanda gained its independence in 1962, the minority Tutsi began seeking refuge in neighbouring states in reaction to the violent seizure of power by the majority Hutu. By the 1990s, about half the Tutsi (480 000) had sought asylum in Burundi, Uganda, Zaïre, and Tanzania. They conducted border raids from these countries into their homeland in an attempt to destabilize the Hutu government.

In October 1990, the Rwandan Patriotic Front in Uganda mounted an attack on northeast Rwanda, hoping to force a solution to the refugee problem. Initial success saw the collapse of the Hutu government, and in 1993 the right of the Tutsi refugees to return home was negotiated. The repatriation agreement was barely signed when radicals on both sides started a civil war which displaced about one million people.

On 6 April 1994, presidents Juvenal Habyarimana of Rwanda and Cyprien Ntaryamira of Burundi, returning from a peace conference, were killed in a plane crash. While the cause of the crash remains undetermined, it touched off an orgy of killing, unsurpassed in recent years. Plans had been laid for the massacre of the Tutsi and moderate Hutus. An estimated 500 000 people were killed, although many analysts place the figures much higher.

As a result of the massacre, 250 000 refugees fled into Tanzania. They were followed by an additional 800 000, mainly moderate Hutus, fleeing to Zaïre. The latter was a calculated exodus designed to leave the advancing Hutu forces to conquer a desolate and depopulated countryside.

Relief agencies in Tanzania and Zaïre were unequal to the task of providing for the sudden influx. The UN was able to send monitors into the refugee camps; a force of 1500 soldiers from Zaïre was sent to police them. The process of repatriating the exiles ran into many roadblocks, not the least of which is the continued violence against the remaining Tutsi by the Hutus. Peace is unlikely to come in the near future, as sporadic fighting continues along the borders, pitting refugee organizations against government troops.

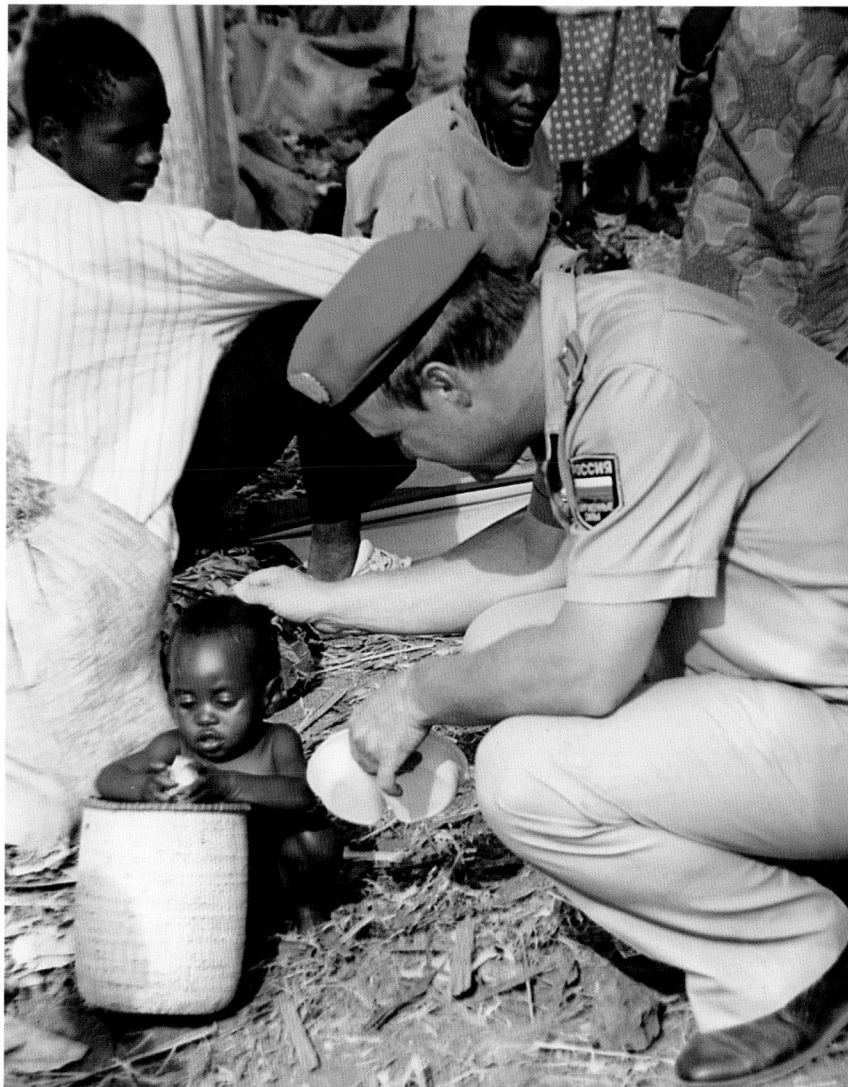

UN soldiers like this one were sent to Somalia in 1991 to feed and care for starving civilians. A year later, American troops came into Somalia to protect the UN workers. The situation, however, became increasingly volatile and the Americans had to withdraw after two years.

SOMALIA

In January 1991, rebel forces captured Mogadishu, the capital of Somalia. Civil war had raged for eighteen months and had resulted in over one million deaths in a nation of some six million. The UN sent in aid teams to feed and care for the starving civilians. In September 1992, after UN aid personnel had been killed, the Americans acted to protect the UN workers. On 21 December, 28 000 American troops went ashore to stabilize the situation. At first they were greeted as liberators; later they were drawn into the clan rivalries and perceived as having taken sides. When American troops were ambushed and many of them killed, the USA decided to leave Somalia. The American withdrawal was completed on 12 April 1994.

On 22 October 1995, 190 heads of state and other officials posed for this photograph to celebrate the United Nations' fiftieth anniversary. The dignitaries included US president Bill Clinton, UN secretary-general Boutros Boutros-Ghali, Cuban president Fidel Castro, Czech president Vaclav Havel, Israeli president Yitzhak Rabin, and PLO leader Yassir Arafat.

intervene in the interests of collective security when conflict between nation-states threatened the peace and security of the world. The intervention in Iraq, however, was undertaken in order to provide humanitarian aid to victims of human rights violations by their own government. Subsequent interventions to protect human rights were undertaken by UN forces in Somalia and Bosnia in 1992, and Rwanda in 1994. (You will learn more about the war in Bosnia in Chapter 17.) By 1996 the majority of UN actions were to support human rights within nations embroiled in civil wars.

The United Nations currently faces a complex challenge. On 24 October 1995, the organization celebrated its fiftieth anniversary. Those fifty years have been fraught with both success and failure.

With the end of the Cold War, a new role seemed to be forged for this international body. Perhaps it would now be able to work more effectively to maintain collective security if the United States and Russia were able to cooperate in the Security Council. Between 1989 and 1992 there were 89 armed conflicts. All but three of these conflicts were civil disputes resulting from ethnic hatreds, ambitious politicians, or economic disparity. In 1994 to 1995, the United Nations responded to international conflict by sending 18 peacekeeping missions, a record in any one year to date. Can the United Nations respond effectively to such a magnitude of threats to the security of the world in the face of financial crisis and serious questions regarding its peacekeeping operations? The immediate future may determine whether the major powers will allow the UN to play the role of "world police force" or whether regional organizations such as the North Atlantic Treaty Organization (NATO) will take over.

SUMMARY

The United Nations was structured as an instrument for collective security by the Allied nations of the Second World War. Determined to rehabilitate war-torn areas as well as maintain peace and security, this international organization was structured to include agencies that would encourage rehabilitation as well as development of ex-colonial areas. Membership was extended to all the major powers, and over the years, all of the world's nation-states have been encouraged to join. With headquarters in New York, the United Nations consists of six major bodies: the Security Council, the General Assembly, the Secretariat, the Economic and Social Council, and the Trusteeship Council. The International Court of Justice, which is the judicial arm of the United Nations, is located in The Hague.

United Nations peacekeeping operations have been instituted in a number of areas in an attempt to promote world peace. In 1950, a UN force was sent to Korea to support the South Koreans who had been invaded by North Korea. By the mid-1990s, most UN peacekeeping operations were taking place in nations embroiled in civil war.

International economic cooperation was a goal of a meeting of the four major allied nations at Bretton Woods, New Hampshire. Out of this meeting, the International Monetary Fund and the World Bank emerged. Recognition that world trade is dependent on international tariff agreement resulted in GATT, later replaced by the WTO. By 1990, major political change on the international scene heralded the possibility of changes in trading patterns and tariff structures.

QUESTIONS

1. Explain the philosophy of collective security as applied by the United Nations.

2. How does the United Nations differ from the League of Nations?

3. How does the United Nations enforce its decisions?

4. Name and briefly explain the duties of each of the six principal organs of the United Nations.

5. How has the composition and the role of the General Assembly changed since 1945?

6. Why is the United Nations suffering financial difficulty?

7. Why did the United Nations launch a peacekeeping mission in Korea in 1950?

8. Explain the results of the United Nations action in Korea, for Korea and for the UN.

9. Evaluate the success of the UN peacekeeping force in either the Suez or the Congo.

10. What is the International Monetary Fund? How does it affect international trade?

11. Explain the purpose of the World Bank.

12. What is GATT and the World Trade Organization? What actions by industries affect tariff regulations?

13. Explain how nations of the world are made interdependent through trade and currency exchange. What problems have occurred in this global network of interdependence?

14. Explain briefly the factors that could affect international trading patterns in the near future.

CRITICAL ANALYSIS

1. Explain why the principles of collective security and spheres of influence are irreconcilable.

2. Describe power as it is manifested in the post-war world.

3. Should every nation-state be given an equal voice in the decisions of the United Nations? Explain.

4. Study the concept of a supranational world government with global sovereignty. Can this concept be implemented?

5. What factors are necessary to the effectiveness of the United Nations?

RESEARCH PROJECTS

1. Write a report on one of the UN agencies. Evaluate its contribution to the improvement of living conditions in the world.

2. Research Canada's contribution to UN peacekeeping operations. Describe the Canadian involvement in any two "trouble spots" since 1950.

3. Research the work done by Lester Pearson, the former Canadian prime minister, that led to his winning the Nobel Peace Prize.

4. Research the work of the World Bank. Describe two projects it has funded recently and evaluate the effectiveness of these investments in furthering the development of the countries involved.

ACTIVITIES

1 Diary

Keep a record of the items you eat, wear, and use for a period of one week. Categorize them according to their country of origin. If they are manufactured goods, attempt to determine the source of their raw materials. Are they obtained in the country that houses the manufacturer? Compare Canada's attitude to imported goods with that of Japan. How do these attitudes affect the average consumer?

2 United Nations Assembly

Formulate a resolution on any current world issue for discussion by your UN Assembly. Students must each represent a member nation. Be sure to include all permanent members of the Security Council. Students must then research the countries they will represent, and be prepared to give a valid presentation of the position their countries would most likely take.

3 Immigration Hearing

Establish a group of students to sit as the Immigration Board which will then hear the appeals of a number of immigrants. Select students to play the following immigrant roles, all of whom are appealing to the board to allow them into Canada:

a) Kurdish refugee
b) Hong Kong businessperson
c) Rwandan refugee
d) Vietnamese refugee

HISTORICAL ANALYSIS

OPPOSING VIEWS OF THE UNITED NATIONS

The effectiveness of the United Nations as a body of collective security is dependent on the willingness of its members to operate within the mandate of the Charter of the United Nations in a cooperative manner. Consider the following views on the United Nations and evaluate the possibility for successful international action on global problems. Identify factors which point to support for the United Nations as well as those which indicate dissension among members.

1 The United States:

Convinced during the Second World War of the need for a global organization dedicated to maintaining world peace, the United States became a sponsoring member of the United Nations. In the absence of post-war cooperation with the Soviet Union, the United States determined to make the United Nations an instrument of American foreign policy.

Before 1957, the United States could count on majority support for its position on virtually any issue. After 1957, the Third World countries achieved a majority position and have turned the organization's focus from the superpower relationship to that of the non-industrialized world. In the Americans' view, this Third World bloc seems intent on availing themselves of American wealth through the auspices of the United Nations.

The trend to anti-Americanism which has developed in the United Nations has soured the American view of the United Nations. Apart from the Carter government, which supported issues of human rights which dominated United Nations business during its term in office, American administrations have treated the organization with disdain. As a principal financial contributor, the threat of American withdrawal from UN agencies such as UNESCO would prove disastrous for program development.

2 China:

Since joining the United Nations in 1971, China has blamed the organization for its recognition of Taiwan as representing one-fifth of the world's population. The UN activities in Korea are remembered as a pro-American strategy which promoted the isolation of China from the world forum and extended China's humiliation.

China would not take part in any UN committees which were reminiscent of Taiwan. The People's Republic of China (PRC) vetoed the acceptance of Bangladesh into the UN after Pakistan's civil war in which China sided with Pakistan and the Soviets aligned themselves with India. China condemned American use of defoliants in the Vietnam War and has criticized Soviet intervention in the Third World. Although committed to Third World programs of development, China does not agree with the Third World desire to abolish the veto in the Security Council.

3 The Third World:

The predominance of Third World countries in the UN has moved the preoccupation of the General Assembly from East-West concerns to North-South development concerns. The system of voting in the General Assembly gives small, underdeveloped countries the same voting power as the large industrialized superpowers. These underdeveloped nations have found a forum for the publication of their needs and through this body have received technical assistance, development loans, and national prestige. Their gratitude for development monies does not extend to any willingness to bear the cost of ecological concerns. They view ecological matters as low priority in their desire for rapid industrial growth to meet the needs of burgeoning populations. Environmental protection is a luxury which they feel they cannot afford.

4 Russia:

After the collapse of the Soviet Union, a number of new nations arose from the ashes of the former empire. Their membership in the United Nations has added a new direction to the UN debate. Russia still exists as the largest part of the old Soviet Union. Surprisingly, the political leadership of Russia see in the UN a forum which can be useful to them. Equally as surprising, the USA has participated in discussions with Russia within the United Nations. An example of this is American and Russian cooperation during the Gulf War of 1991. Allied intervention would not have been possible had Russia not agreed that the invasion of Iraq was acceptable. Such cooperation heralds a new era for UN activities.

USA/USSR THE COLD WAR

RIVALRY FOR GLOBAL SUPREMACY: 1945–1962

Two thousand years ago the proudest boast in the world was **Civis Romanus sum.** *Today, in the world of freedom, the proudest boast is* **Ich bin ein Berliner.**

There are many people in the world who do not understand what is the great issue between the free world and Communism. Let them come to Berlin. And there are some who say in Europe and elsewhere that we can work with the Communists. Let them come to Berlin.

American president John F. Kennedy, addressing a crowd from the balcony of the (West) Berlin Town Hall, 26 June 1963.

FOCUS ON THE COLD WAR

The emergence of two nuclear superpowers after the Second World War led to what became known as the Cold War. Some argue that a rough balance of Soviet and American atomic arsenals prevented global war during this period. What is your opinion?

OVERVIEW

The end of the war in Europe revealed signs of growing mistrust between the USA and the USSR. Issues such as the Polish question, confrontation in Iran, containment, the Marshall Plan, the Czechoslovakian Crisis, the Berlin Blockade, NATO, Cominform, Tito in Yugoslavia, the Korean War, Khrushchev's reforms, the Hungarian Revolution, the Berlin Wall, and Cuba are all developed in the context of the Cold War.

BACKGROUND OF THE COLD WAR
During the Second World War, differences in strategy for the defeat of Hitler, a lack of agreement on the settlement of Central Europe, and fear and mistrust of each other led to the creation of intense rivalry between the United States and the Soviet Union.

THE POLISH QUESTION
Poland's strategic location made it the first major source of disagreement between Western leaders and Stalin.

CONFRONTATION
In 1946 confrontation in Iran and Turkey was followed by the British withdrawal from Greece. A power struggle ensued. Why did the United States and the Soviet Union feel a need to stake out their territory at this time?

THE MARSHALL PLAN
The USA's determination to shore up Western Europe against the possible spread of communism led to the provision of funds for reconstruction.

CZECHOSLOVAKIAN CRISIS
How did the Communist coup d'état in Czechoslovakia alarm the American public? The Communist party in Czechoslovakia promoted a commitment to support a foreign policy of containment of communism.

BERLIN BLOCKADE
In 1948, the Soviets attempted to force the West out of Berlin. The Americans and the British airlifted supplies to the city for 11 months.

NATO
In 1949, twelve Western nations banded together in an alliance structure committed to resist Soviet expansionism.

COMINFORM
The Soviet Union turned to the consolidation of communism in Eastern Europe and established the Cominform as a bulwark against American imperialism.

TITO IN YUGOSLAVIA
In 1948, Yugoslavian leader Tito was expelled from the Cominform for refusing to adhere to Soviet dictates.

THE KOREAN WAR
The Korean War illustrated the extension of Cold War rivalry into Asia. When North Korean troops invaded South Korea, the United States sent aid immediately.

THE KHRUSHCHEV ERA
Khrushchev consolidated his power in 1956 and brought an air of reform to the Soviet Union.

POLISH AND HUNGARIAN UNREST
Khrushchev's suggestion that there are "many roads to socialism" led to attempts by both Poland and Hungary to free themselves of Soviet political and economic domination in 1956.

BERLIN: TENSION BUILDS
The changes in East and West Germany increased tension in Berlin until finally the Berlin Wall was constructed in 1961.

THE CUBAN MISSILE CRISIS
Cold War tension came to a head in October of 1962 when the Soviet Union attempted to place missiles in Cuba.

BACKGROUND OF THE COLD WAR

The seeds of the Cold War were sown during the Second World War. Because they faced a common enemy in Hitler, the Grand Alliance became a marriage of necessity forged by the United States, Great Britain, and the Soviet Union. From the beginning, disagreements over wartime strategy foreshadowed post-war conflict, especially between the Soviets on the one hand and the British and Americans on the other. Stalin's suspicions of Great Britain and the United States were heightened when, at the liberation of Italy in 1944, the Soviet Union was excluded from the Allied Control Council. Recognizing a precedent—that the army that liberated a country would determine that country's future government—Stalin did not strenuously object. He expected to apply this precedent in Central Europe, where the Red Army was already in a position to be the army of occupation. Then, in an October meeting with Churchill in Moscow, Stalin achieved full agreement on spheres of influence in Central Europe, and won the USSR a commanding position in the region.

At Teheran in 1943, then at Yalta and at Potsdam in 1945, the Allies worked out the broad outline for a settlement once Germany was defeated. Three issues defied resolution: the boundaries of Poland; the types of governments in Eastern Europe; and the future of Germany. Between the Yalta and the Potsdam conferences, fears about the European balance of power were heightened. The determination of each of the major powers to act unilaterally prevented the resolution of these major issues at Potsdam. The dispute over the boundaries of Poland festered throughout 1945, and fostered dissension between the Americans and the Soviets. Eastern Europe, it was agreed, fell clearly within the Soviet sphere of influence, but would be allowed to determine its own political future through free elections. Stalin's promise was an empty one: free elections failed to materialize in areas dominated by the Red Army. The most contentious area of all was Germany, where the United States and the Soviet Union faced each other squarely in their respective occupation zones.

An Allied Control Council was established to manage post-war Germany. Designed to facilitate reunification, it was hamstrung by the rule of unanimity. As no common goal for Germany existed, problems surfaced immediately in the operation of the council. The British and the Americans wanted a politically unified and industrially self-sufficient country; the French and the Soviets wanted a politically weak Germany. The issue of reparations illustrated these conflicting goals. In 1946, the West ceased the collection of any reparations in their zones, intending instead to foster German economic recovery. The Soviet Union, on the other hand, renewed its demands for $10 billion in reparations payments and continued to strip its zone bare of resources and industrial goods for the reconstruction of the Soviet Union. The Western occupation zone in Berlin was particularly contentious, as it gave the West a firm presence inside the general Soviet sphere of influence. The foundation of a bipolar power structure had been laid. For the next two decades, international power would be wielded through competing blocs, dominated by the United States and the Soviet Union.

THE POLISH QUESTION

The issue causing most dissension initially was the Polish question, which became a contest of wills. The problem was twofold. Who would govern Poland, and where would Poland's borders lie? At the beginning of the war, a group of government officials dominated by Polish army officers, landowners, and Roman Catholic Church officials had sought asylum in Great Britain and declared themselves the Polish government in exile. The British supported this group as the legitimate Polish government. However, the Soviets created a Polish government in Lublin, which was officially recognized by Stalin in January 1945, and operated as a puppet of the Soviet Union. At Yalta, both Churchill and Roosevelt insisted that Stalin allow free elections and encourage a Polish regime composed of members of both the London government in exile and the Lublin government. Instead, Stalin increased his support for the Lublin government and suppressed freedom of speech, the press, and religion. He believed the West's pronouncements on free elections were posturings for the benefit of domestic electorates.

Not having an electorate of his own to deal with, and Poland being within his sphere, Stalin ignored opposition to his policy of repression. Poland was placed firmly under Soviet army control. In the matter of borders, Stalin insisted on establishing the western border of Poland at the Oder-Neisse line, which would force the relocation of 6 to 9 million Germans from East Prussia, Silesia, and East Pomerania. Setting the line this far west was to compensate Poland for the loss of 21 336 sq km of territory taken by the Soviet Union in its westward expansion. Although Western powers objected, they were not willing to confront Stalin so soon after the war.

CONFRONTATION

The first serious confrontation between the Soviets and the Americans occurred not in Germany, but in Iran. Strategically located in the Middle East, and possessing vast reserves of oil, Iran had been occupied by Soviet and British troops during the Second World War, to ensure that Allied supply lines were kept open. The agreement between the British, Soviet, and Iranian governments provided for withdrawal of foreign troops six months after the end of the war. The Soviet troops, however, did not withdraw; in fact, they supported a communist revolt in the northern province of Azerbaijan. Continued occupation of northern Iran, along with the formation of a Soviet-Iranian stock company to develop oil resources, led to British and American fears that the Soviet Union would obtain control of the entire country. Intense diplomatic pressure from both the British and the Americans resulted in Soviet withdrawal from the area, and by mid-1946 the Iranian government had been persuaded to purchase American military equipment. The groundwork was laid for the Washington-Teheran link, an arrangement that was to last until the shah was deposed in the Iranian Revolution in 1979.

Another problem area in the period 1945-1946 was Turkey. Turkey had remained neutral during the war. Because of Turkey's strategic location in regards to shipping routes between the Black Sea and the Mediterranean, the Soviet Union made an overture to the capital city of Turkey, Ankara, to secure access to the straits, and thus control the waterways linking it to the mineral resources of North Africa and the Middle East. When Ankara rejected the Soviet proposal, Stalin responded by sending 25 Soviet divisions into Turkey. This action was viewed by the Truman administration as a direct attempt to interfere in the eastern Mediterranean, which had long been regarded as a Western sphere of influence. An American naval task force was dispatched to the area and the Soviets were reminded of the American monopoly of nuclear weaponry. In the face of this show of force, the Soviets backed down and Western domination of the eastern Mediterranean prevailed.

At the same time as the Iranian and Turkish crises, trouble loomed in Greece. When German troops were evacuated from Greece in November 1944, communists hoped to take over. Traditionally, however, Greece had been considered part of the Western sphere of influence, and the British were expected to fulfil the role of protector. The British had confirmed this arrangement in 1944, when Stalin sought a free hand in Romania.

In Greece, the British backed the royalist government, which was threatened by communist insurgents in the north of Greece. By 1946-1947, however, Britain's economy was no longer able to support a British presence in Greece. The Greek government, threatened by the possibility of communist takeover, appealed to the United States for assistance. The Truman administration for the moment maintained an isolationist stance, and refused to become involved. The United Nations could not intervene because the Soviet Union exercised its veto power in

After the conferences at Teheran and Yalta, Great Britain and the United States were forced to recognize the Soviet sphere of influence in Eastern Europe. Joseph Stalin was the leader of the Soviet Union at the time.

the Security Council. Finally, in 1947, Churchill informed Truman that Great Britain would be forced to terminate all financial assistance to Greece and withdraw 40 000 troops by 31 March 1947.

Truman now feared that the Soviet Union would step in if the United States failed to act. Therefore, on 12 March 1947 President Truman in an address to Congress declared both economic and military support to Greece and Turkey, and appealed for authorization of an expenditure of $250 million in Greece and $150 million in Turkey. This historic declaration, which became known as the **Truman Doctrine**, stated that the United States must adopt

DENAZIFICATION

After the defeat of Germany the destruction of Nazism began. The Soviets and the Americans did not agree on the manner in which Nazism should be eradicated. Analyse the differences between the two approaches. Which approach seems more just?

General Eisenhower's first proclamation to the German people promised that in the area under his command, Nazism and German militarism would be abolished. Nazi rule would be overthrown, the Nazi party would be dissolved, and Nazis would be cast out of civilized society. What remained of the Third Reich was divided into four occupation zones, each of whose military commanders implemented the proclamation in different ways.

The Soviets approached **denazification** as merely another episode in the long struggle between capitalism and communism. Within the Eastern zone, populated by 17 million East Germans, the occupation forces eliminated the top layer of society. Landowners, politicians, industrialists, bankers, and business people were arrested and executed, or deported to the Soviet Union for forced labour. The remainder, provided they had no private property and thus no vested interest in capitalism, could avoid punishment for past actions by joining any one of a number of communist organizations. Joining the East German Communist party (SED) before 31 March 1946 erased all traces of past actions. The East German government established a blanket waiver of punishment for all ex-Nazis and former German army officers—if they had not committed war crimes. Such people were restored to full citizenship, as were scientists who agreed to continue their research under Soviet direction.

The French zone included the Saar region of coal mines and steel mills. To maintain, as reparations, continuous production for shipment back to France, the French found it necessary to overlook past Nazi leanings, especially with mine managers and industrialists. The German *Direktoren* went back to their desks. General Perrin-Pelletier, the French deputy governor of the military, expressed a belief that virtually all Germans were ex-Nazis, and "if one didn't want to kill them all, then one had to work with them." Denazification was not going to take place under his command. The French argued that the total defeat of Germany, with its cities destroyed and millions dead or wounded, had likely denazified it in the best possible way.

The British took a legal rather than a moral stance. They sought out Nazis guilty of war crimes for punishment. Tribunals were presided over by judges, not political or military appointees. The British zone held the largest population: 22.7 million Germans, compared with 18 million in the American zone, 17 million in the Soviet zone, and 3.8 million in the French zone. Within their own zone the British conducted 22 969 trials of former SS and Nazi leaders. The Americans held 169 000 trials, and the French and Soviets, approximately 18 000 each.

The Americans were confident they too could eradicate Nazism. All Germans in the American zone were to provide detailed information about their past and their activities during the Hitler years. The plan was to force confessions regarding the extent of service to the Third Reich. The Americans were aided in their efforts by the discovery of the Nazi party master membership lists in Munich, which included the names of 8 million full members and 4 million associated members. On the basis of a questionnaire, 3.5 million Nazis were identified and indicted for war crimes. The Americans had neither the staff nor the desire to spend a decade processing so many cases. The case-load was reduced to under 1 million by granting amnesty to the young, the old, the disabled, and associate members who had paid dues but were not active within the party itself. The remainder were placed in the hands of German authorities.

Things began to go badly after that. Germans who had so recently endorsed Hitler's policies were not going to have a change of heart overnight and condemn their compatriots. Ex-Nazis were denied all but menial jobs. Thousands of bureaucrats were out of work at a time of already high unemployment. Without their services, the economy began to collapse.

1. Compare the treatment of Nazis in each of the occupation zones.

2. Explain why the European and American views on war crimes differed.

a policy "to support free peoples who are resisting subjugation by armed minorities or by outside pressures." The doctrine was outward-looking and interventionist in nature. Truman was determined to reverse the isolationist tendencies of the USA. From this time forward, American foreign policy would be shaped by a desire to maintain a buffer zone of friendly governments on the Soviet periphery in order to contain communism within Soviet borders.

A foreign policy dedicated to containing communism was supported by Department of State official George Kennan, who had spent considerable time in the USSR. In an 8000-word document anonymously submitted to the journal *Foreign Affairs,* Kennan asserted that the Soviet Union could be expected to extend its power into those areas on its borders too weak to resist domination. The best way to prevent Soviet expansion was to strengthen governments politically, economically, and socially. Kennan thus provided justification for American intervention in the affairs of Greece and Turkey and laid the foundation for the American policy of containment that was to shape American external affairs for many years.

THE MARSHALL PLAN

Soviet expansion in Western Europe was even more alarming to Americans than the possibility of Soviet expansion in Greece and Turkey. The United States recognized that an economically devastated Western Europe was ill-equipped to resist Soviet forces. On 5 June 1947 Secretary of State George Marshall addressed the problem of Western Europe's vulnerability. Speaking at Harvard University, Marshall suggested that the impoverishment of Western European nations invited action by communist-controlled labour organizations, and eventual political domination by the Soviet Union. The best defence against Soviet expansion into Western Europe, he said, was to strengthen the economies of Western European nations, including Germany's. The **Marshall Plan,** as his proposal came to be called, provided funds for the reconstruction of 16 European nations outside the Soviet sphere of influence. Initially, the United States also offered aid to the Soviet Union and its satellites; but the USSR refused aid for itself and those nations in its sphere of influence because the Americans insisted on the monitoring of funds, and would have discovered the full weakness of the Soviet economy. After the war, 25 million Soviet people were homeless and most of

Under the Marshall Plan, the United States provided financial aid to devastated European countries, including parts of Germany. The German girls in this picture rebuilt their school with the help of American funding.

their lands were totally devastated. People subsisted on cabbage and potatoes, keeping warm in winter in felt boots and tattered coats. The Soviet economy did not recover to 1940 levels of production until 1952.

While the Soviet Union was suffering grave consumer deprivation, the United States entered one of the greatest consumer booms of its history. The assistance provided to Western Europe further stimulated the American economy. The program extended $13.2 billion in aid from 1948 to 1952. The economic expansion and redevelopment of European economies allowed them to re-establish trade with the United States. The gap between the standard of living in Western Europe and the United States was beginning to close, even as that between Western and Eastern Europe widened.

CASE STUDY

SWEET CAPORALS

The economic instability in Germany which followed the Second World War led to rampant inflation and the switch to a barter economy based on American cigarettes. Compare the German economy of 1947 to that of Germany in 1922.

The Second World War was a punishing defeat for Germany. Its cities were transformed into piles of rubble, and its military and industrial base was devastated. Survivors eked out the essentials of life. Food, shelter, and employment were hard to come by. Some 45 million West Germans were joined by 10 million German refugees from the East; the latter aggravated savage competition for shrinking resources.

Hitler had vowed to take the German people down with him. To the effects of Allied bombing were added the effects of a scorched earth policy. The Germans themselves destroyed industrial, transportation, and communication facilities. Nothing of value would be left for the occupiers.

In the Ruhr, the industrial heartland of the Reich, not a factory building was left standing. For the first time in years, survivors in the Ruhr could see clear blue sky, untainted by the pall of industrial pollution. Later, when the rubble had been cleared away by hand and piled in hills in the centre of the cities, it was discovered that a good deal of the machinery was still usable.

Of greater immediate concern was the shortage of food and fuel. Diets dropped to 600 calories a day during the bitter winter of 1946-1947. Hamburg reported 10 000 cases of hunger edema. In the British zone, 250 000 cases of tuberculosis were reported and the death rate among those afflicted topped the 50 per cent mark. Malnutrition stalked the land, saddling the young with rickets and other diseases. The food shortage became critical when the Soviets cut off supplies of potatoes and grain in retaliation for nonpayment of reparations from the Western zone.

People reverted to barter, exchanging possessions for the necessities of life. No one would produce or sell valuable goods for paper Reichsmarks, and instead, a cigarette economy sprang up. Every day there was an exodus from the cities to outlying farms to obtain food for personal and household goods. China, jewellery, cloths, rugs, and tools were bartered for food. Farmers, at least, began to prosper.

The Soviets began to pay their forces, for the full period of the war, in occupation marks. The Americans had, as a gesture of good will, sent the Soviets a set of plates which they now used to crank out hundreds of millions of marks. The marks were not redeemable in rubles but were worth 10 cents each in the Western zone. Soviet soldiers flooded into the British and American zones to buy anything they could take home. A wristwatch bought at the PX (the American army base store) for $15 could be sold to a Soviet for 5000 marks, and then the marks could be redeemed for $500 American. A $1 carton of cigarettes could fetch 1500 marks— $150 American. There was no limit to the number of marks an individual could redeem. The British and American sectors were subsidizing the Soviet forces of occupation, not to mention their own entrepreneurs. By the time Soviet marks were declared invalid, some $800 000 000 had been lost under the redemption program.

The cigarette now took the place of the old occupation mark, and became the basic unit of value in the German economy. There was never a shortage of cigarettes among the Western victors, and even more began arriving in packages from relatives at home. A carton of cigarettes worth $1 in the USA was valued at 1000 marks in Germany. An average weekly wage was 80 marks. Tobacco was literally worth its weight in gold, and goods and services were priced in cigarettes. A contractor bid 155 cartons of cigarettes to rebuild the *New York Herald Tribune* building in Frankfurt. The national bank counted its assets in cartons of cigarettes. The volume of cigarette traffic eventually paralyzed the postal service. Cigarettes were finally banned from the mails, at which point American soldiers switched to other commodities, like soap, coffee, and nylons.

If you can't beat 'em, join 'em. The American army decided to get into the black market business by opening its own barter marts in Berlin and Frankfurt. Cartons of cigarettes were exchanged for sets of Meissen china and sterling silver. The army would now regulate the trade. The barter marts attracted Germans from all over Germany. Extra trains had to be added to the schedule to accommodate happy shoppers. It was not unusual for the marts to have an 85 per cent turnover in goods each day. The trade became even more profitable when the USA permitted spouses and dependents of service members to accompany them abroad. Life became an adventure in shopping—all the more attractive for free shipment of goods back to the United States. A grand piano could be purchased for 50 cartons of cigarettes, and a mink coat for only 200.

All this came to an end in June 1948. Convoys of US army trucks protected by heavy machine guns fanned out all over Germany, carrying 500 tonnes of new Deutschmarks. In the period immediately before the currency change there was mass panic buying, to get rid of the old marks. The fever hit an all-time high when a carton of cigarettes rose to 23 000 marks ($2300 American). The revaluation of the mark meant wiping out the country's savings, securities, bonds, and indebtedness at one fell swoop. Germans were permitted to exchange 400 old marks for new ones at par and, two months later, another 200 old marks. Then the exchange stopped. The Americans substituted a mere 10 billion new marks for hundreds of billions of old marks. Now the German economy could begin its recovery with new currency based on real purchasing power.

1. Describe the Soviet Reichsmark gambit.

2. What effect did the barter economy established after the war have on Germany's real wealth?

3. Who suffered most in the revaluation of the German currency in 1948, and why?

CZECHOSLOVAKIAN CRISIS

The polarization of Europe was dramatically furthered by events in Czechoslovakia in 1948. When elections were held in May 1946, the Czech Communists won 38 per cent of the vote. Although Prime Minister Gottwald was closely associated with Moscow, neither President Eduard Beneš nor Foreign Minister Jan Masaryk were Communist. Czechoslovakia had wanted Marshall Plan assistance, but had been pulled out of discussions on Stalin's orders. The nation seemed willing to follow Moscow's lead while trying to retain a measure of independence. On 25 February 1948 the Communists pushed Beneš aside and seized complete control. Masaryk's mysterious death two weeks later was officially described as suicide, but there is little doubt that he was murdered. Suicide pictures printed in Western newspapers shocked the American public, who began to demand American intervention in European affairs. The Communist *coup* in Czechoslovakia left no doubt the Soviet Union intended to clamp tight control on the satellites within its sphere. On 11 March 1948 the American Senate voted 69 to 17 to extend Marshall Plan aid to Europe in the hope of preventing communist success elsewhere.

BERLIN BLOCKADE

The most serious crisis between the Soviet and American spheres occurred in 1948, in Berlin. The four-power agreement on Berlin had guaranteed the Allies the security of three air corridors into West Berlin from West Germany, but had not guaranteed access by land or rail. By the spring of 1948, Stalin viewed the Western occupation of Berlin as a festering sore deep in the Soviet zone. He was disappointed the Allies had not left Berlin as they had hinted they might when the war ended. He was convinced they would not fight to save what had formerly been the enemy's capital.

Marshall Plan investment had stimulated the West German economy, but the East German economy had been pillaged by the Soviets in an attempt to rebuild their own domestic economy. When the Western powers extended currency reforms to West Berlin, the Soviets—fearing a strong united Western sector of Germany, and desiring to push the West out of Berlin—imposed a blockade on all road and rail traffic into the former national capital. It was

The 1948 Soviet blockade of all road and rail traffic into Berlin helped usher in the era of the Cold War. Supplies, like the ones being unloaded above, were airlifted in by Britain and the United States. Half of Berlin remained under the Western sphere of influence.

now obvious that German reunification was an illusion. Why, therefore, should the old capital continue under four-power occupation?

When the blockade began on 24 June 1948, Berliners feared they would be abandoned by the West. Indeed, some politicians thought this the wisest course. Why risk a third world war to protect former Nazis? However, the view of the Americans, voiced by General Clay, who was in command of West Berlin, was that if the West allowed the takeover of Berlin, the Soviets would be encouraged to continue into West Germany. The Americans and the British decided to remain in occupation and to supply West Berlin by airlifting in all supplies necessary to maintain life in the city.

It was an ambitious task. The city consumed 12 000 tonnes of goods a day in peacetime. At least 5500 tonnes of goods would be needed to maintain a subsistence level of food, light, and warmth during the winter blockade. Average caloric consumption dropped to 1600 per person per day. Berliners existed on dehydrated vegetables and powdered milk, with biscuits instead of bread. Vitamin supplements were flown in. Canned meats and dried eggs provided protein.

Some 1500 tonnes of food were required daily to meet minimal standards, but the problem of supplying energy was even more challenging. A minimum of 2500 tonnes of coal was required every day. The challenges of transporting this huge amount finally prompted the cutting of timber within the city to supplement the coal supply.

Bad weather, Soviet harassment of cargo planes, radar foul-ups, and stacking of aircraft to provide maximum numbers of flights, all contributed to hazardous and extremely stressful flying conditions. Planes landed continuously, sometimes every three minutes. In order to discourage the Soviets from shooting down cargo planes, the Americans announced that they had stationed B-29 bombers in Britain. The Americans brandished their nuclear monopoly once again.

Stalin's decision to end the blockade, however, was made on the basis of its ineffectiveness. The Soviet Union did not gain the control it had hoped for, and the blockade was proving prohibitively expensive. It lifted the blockade on 12 May 1949. The following day, oranges, lemons, cucumbers, and fresh fish arrived in Berlin by rail. On 23 May 1949, West Germany was declared to be the Federal Republic of Germany, formalizing the division of Germany. The Soviets had suffered a major post-war defeat. They had not driven the West from Berlin, nor had they prevented the formation of a new state in the west.

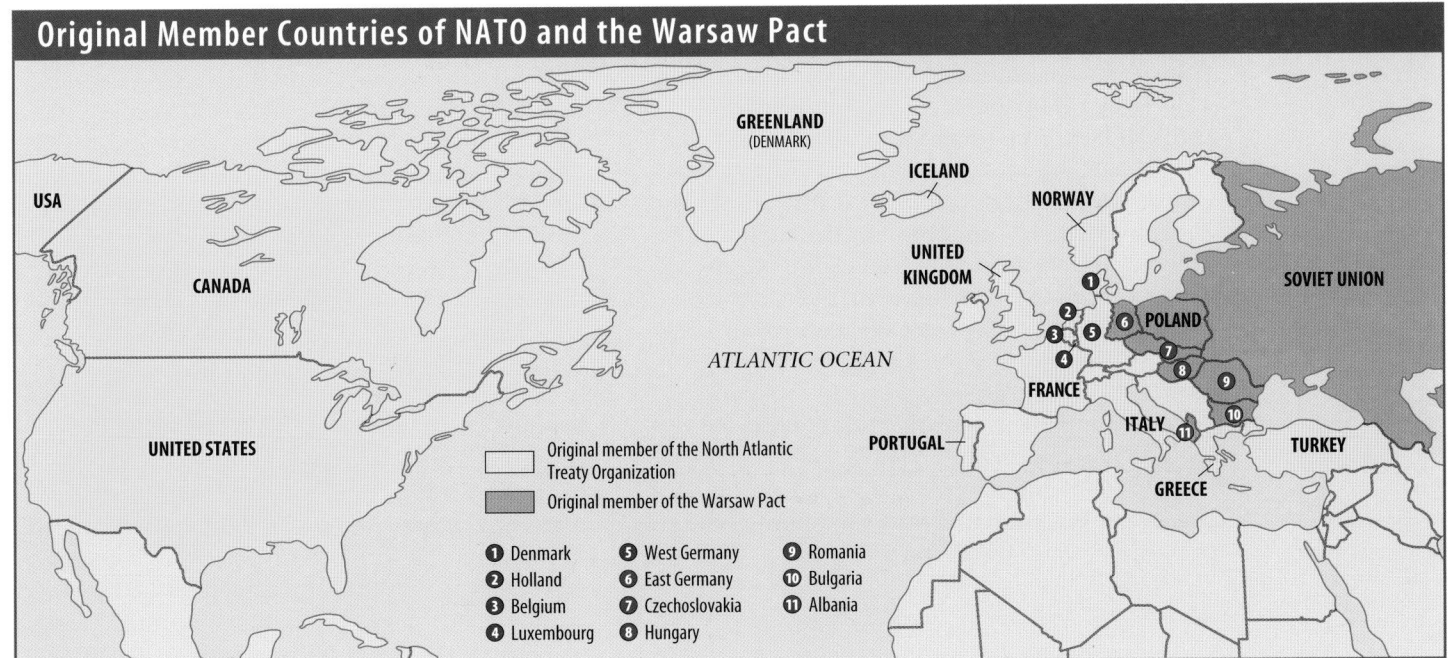

Original Member Countries of NATO and the Warsaw Pact

GREENLAND
(DENMARK)

ICELAND

NORWAY

UNITED KINGDOM

USA

CANADA

ATLANTIC OCEAN

SOVIET UNION

POLAND

FRANCE

ITALY

PORTUGAL

TURKEY

GREECE

UNITED STATES

☐ Original member of the North Atlantic Treaty Organization

■ Original member of the Warsaw Pact

❶ Denmark ❺ West Germany ❾ Romania
❷ Holland ❻ East Germany ❿ Bulgaria
❸ Belgium ❼ Czechoslovakia ⓫ Albania
❹ Luxembourg ❽ Hungary

NATO

The North Atlantic Treaty Organization was formed in 1949 and the Warsaw Pact was finalized in 1955. This map shows the countries involved in both agreements.

The Czechoslovakian *coup* and the Berlin Blockade gave impetus to the formation of a Western European military alliance supported by the United States. Since 1947, the relationship between the Soviet Union and the Western powers had become increasingly tense. The United States feared that without a strong military defensive system, Western Europe was threatened by Soviet expansionism. Thus on 17 March 1948 five European nations—Belgium, France, Luxembourg, the Netherlands, and Great Britain—signed the Treaty of Brussels, which called for a pooling of their military resources to face potential Soviet aggression. Just as the United States had engineered the economic reconstruction of Western Europe with the Marshall Plan, it would now lay the foundation of its defensive military realignment. On 11 June 1948 the American Senate passed a resolution that paved the way for American support of a European security system. The Vandenberg Resolution (named for Senator Arthur Vandenberg, who instigated it) called for the United States to align itself with other regional alliances designed to promote national and regional security. The United States could now join those countries already linked by the Brussels pact, and form a military union between the United States and Western Europe.

In moving toward a regional defence alliance with the nations of Western Europe, the United States openly acknowledged its security was closely linked to that of Western Europe. The Berlin Blockade, designed as it was to drive the West out of Berlin, had clearly been a direct threat to the security of Western Europe and, ultimately, the United States. On 4 April 1949, therefore, the five Brussels pact signatories—plus Denmark, Iceland, Italy, Norway, Portugal, Canada, and the United States—signed the North Atlantic Treaty. The agreement stipulated that an act of aggression against any one of the signatories would be interpreted as an attack against all. It was a defensive military alliance, binding its members to assist each other in the event of attack by an aggressor nation. The North Atlantic Treaty Organization (NATO) was specifically designed to warn the USSR that the West was committed to stand united in the face of any Soviet expansion. It was also hoped, initially, that NATO would present a psychological barrier: Western nations stood united against a collection of Eastern European countries not yet formally aligned. Although there was no significant commitment to military buildup at this time, it was hoped the American monopoly of the atomic bomb would prove to be a deterrent to the Soviet Union. The Berlin Blockade had signaled a serious turn of events in the Cold War, indicating to the West that it must secure a military balance with the USSR in Europe. NATO also, of course, strengthened the American position in Europe.

The partition of Europe into rival spheres of influence had been fostered by the West: diplomatically by the Truman Doctrine; economically by the Marshall Plan; and, finally, militarily by the formation of NATO. Reaction on the part of the Soviet Union was evident diplomatically in Andrei Zhdanov's speech to the founding conference of the Communist Information Bureau (Cominform); economically in the formation of the Council for Mutual Economic Assistance (Comecon); and militarily in the organization of the Warsaw Pact in 1955.

Discussions about the role of NATO after the dissolution of the Warsaw Pact (1991) were ongoing in the late 1990s. Should NATO disband, or should it open its membership to former Communist nations and act as a world police force?

WARSAW PACT

On 14 May 1955 Albania, Bulgaria, Czechoslovakia, the German Democratic Republic (East Germany), Hungary, Poland, Romania, and the Soviet Union signed the Warsaw Pact, a defensive military treaty obligating the signatories to come to the aid of any member that fell victim to attack by an aggressor nation. Throughout the period of the Cold War, the Warsaw Pact aligned Soviet bloc countries against the Western alliance of NATO. However, the disintegration of Soviet control over Eastern Europe in 1989 led to the withdrawal of Soviet forces from the region and the formal dissolution of the Warsaw Pact on 31 March 1991.

COMINFORM

The Cominform replaced the old Comintern, or Communist International. It had as its goal the consolidation of communism in Eastern Europe under the leadership of the Soviet Union, not the promotion of international communism. The USSR had been somewhat unsuccessful in promoting international communism: its leadership had been rejected in China, Vietnam, the Philippines, and Greece. None of those countries had turned to the Soviet Union for liberation; each had determined to attempt a revolution of its own. By consolidating Eastern Europe, Stalin hoped to revitalize the role of the Soviet Union in a global revolutionary communist movement. When Zhdanov spoke to the Cominform, he identified the United States as an expansionist power that was determined to exert economic, ideological, and military control over all of Europe. He called upon communist parties in Western Europe to oppose the Marshall Plan, and was successful in instigating strikes in both France and Italy. The Cominform crystallized opposition to the West and marked the end of any possibility of cooperation between the nations of Eastern Europe and the West. It facilitated the consolidation of Soviet power in Eastern Europe, which the Czechoslovakian *coup* served to highlight.

TITO IN YUGOSLAVIA

Soviet success in Czechoslovakia was in striking contrast to failure in Yugoslavia. The leader of Yugoslavia was Josip Broz, more commonly called Tito. During the Second World War, Tito had led a group of communist partisans that had managed, with British support, to liberate Yugoslavia from Nazi forces. The Red Army arrived in February 1944, but it proved more a hindrance than a help. The Red Army committed so many serious assaults on Yugoslavian citizens in the course of their operations that tension developed between Yugoslavia and the USSR.

The real problems between the Soviet Union and Yugoslavia arose, however, over the issues of political and economic control. Stalin would not accept Tito as an equal. He insisted upon the same unrivaled control he had established in Poland, Czechoslovakia, and East Germany. Tito had broad-based support in Yugoslavia, where he enjoyed a hard-won victory over the Germans. Yugoslavia was the only Eastern European country to have expelled the Nazis with only minimal help from the Allies. It was also the only Eastern European country to have established a communist dictatorship without the assistance of the Red Army.

Tito ruled with an audacity that angered Stalin. Tito acted independently in his attempts to control Trieste and its surrounding region. Determined to consolidate and firmly entrench his rule, Tito approached Bulgaria about the creation of a Balkan federation that would include all Eastern European countries in a customs union. The Soviet Union was not mentioned as part of this union. Enraged, Stalin summoned the Bulgarian and Yugoslavian leadership to Moscow. Tito refused to attend, instead sending a delegation of minor officials. But the Bulgarian leader, Georgi Dimitrov, bowed to Stalin's demands. Stalin now proposed a union of Bulgaria, Yugoslavia, and Albania as an alternative to Tito's Balkan federation. Tito saw this proposal as little more than an opportunity for Red Army troops to occupy Bulgaria and threaten Yugoslavia. He was not willing to consider the proposal.

Since gaining power, Tito had taken charge not only of domestic affairs but foreign policy as well. Stalin strongly disapproved of Tito's foreign policy. Its grave implications for Soviet control of the communist world were clear. Throughout the spring of 1948, an exchange of correspondence between Moscow and Belgrade revealed a widening and irreconcilable split. Finally, on 28 June 1948, Yugoslavia was expelled from the Cominform. Economic sanctions against Yugoslavia followed. As Yugoslavia received 26 per cent of its imports from, and sent 24 per cent of its exports to, the Soviet Union, the blockade would have serious repercussions. Food shortages and rising prices threatened the country's already shaky economy. Tito had not totally severed ties with the West, however, and American economic aid was extended without any strings attached.

During the period 1947-1948, it became apparent that Stalin objected not only to Tito's independence but also to his support of the communist rebellion in Greece. Stalin demanded that Tito withdraw his support since Greece was in the Western sphere of influence. Tito was not only supplying *matériel*, but also allowing Greek insurgents to reorganize on Yugoslavian soil. Stalin was bent on consolidating his own sphere of influence in Eastern Europe at this time and could hardly approve of Tito's tampering in a country falling within Britain's sphere.

COMECON

In 1949 the Council for Mutual Economic Assistance (Comecon) was established under Moscow's leadership. Designed to coordinate the economic and social development of the Soviet Union's satellite states in Eastern Europe, this organization established trading patterns and industrial plans for the region. Economic integration was encouraged with the creation of the International Bank for Economic Cooperation (IBEC) and an International Investment Bank.

The move to market economies and the establishment of international trade in hard currencies in January 1991 resulted in the dissolution of Comecon. The Soviet Union, Bulgaria, Czechoslovakia, Hungary, Mongolia, Poland, Romania, Cuba, and Vietnam joined together in the Organization for International Economic Cooperation in order to establish trade with the West.

Yugoslavia was geographically isolated from the Soviet Union and thus very difficult to restrain. After Yugoslavia's expulsion from the Cominform, the Soviet Union launched a campaign of political, military, diplomatic, and economic pressure to bring Yugoslavia back into the Soviet fold. The failure of this campaign had grave implications for the future. Tito's Yugoslavia blended communism with nationalism, and represented a direct challenge to the Soviet model.

The lessons of Yugoslavia helped Stalin deal more effectively with the Communists in China, when Mao surprised the Soviets by his victory over Chiang Kai-shek's Nationalist army. Since 1927, Soviet control of the Communist party in China had been limited. Stalin was not convinced that Mao and his followers were true communists; and he was concerned about his own ability to maintain concessions in Manchuria once Mao consolidated power. Both sides recognized, however, that a Sino-Soviet agreement was necessary, both for the maintenance of the trade concessions in Manchuria, and

BIOGRAPHY

JOSIP BROZ—TITO (1892–1980)

Josip Broz, popularly known as Tito, was the Communist Yugoslavian leader who organized partisan forces to harry Axis conquerors of his country during the Second World War. Because his troops rendered ineffectual about 30 enemy divisions, a price of 100 000 gold marks was placed on Tito's head. Also during this time, Tito managed to turn the Anglo-American support from his rival partisan leader, Mikhailovich, to himself. British prime minister Churchill explained this change in the following terms: "The reason why we have ceased to supply Mikhailovich with arms and support is a simple one. He has not been fighting the enemy and moreover some of his subordinates have been making accommodations with the enemy." Mikhailovich reported that his forces, in fear of a communist take-over of Yugoslavia, found it expedient to collaborate with Axis powers. This flew in the face of Tito's strong instinctive national pride and single-minded dedication to turning back Axis gains. However, Mikhailovich's fear was realized when, during the war, Tito announced and partially implemented basic communist policies in Yugoslavia.

From 1945 to 1953, Tito acted as prime minister and minister of defense for Yugoslavia. The form of dictatorship implemented by Tito was, at times, extreme and ruthless. His intent was to build into Yugoslavia a system of government based on the Soviet system. He alone was able to hold the separate ethnic groups of his country together.

Tito was different from other Communist leaders of his time, insofar as he let situations—rather than communist theory—dictate his actions. Edvard Kardelj, one of the active Yugoslavian Communist party members Tito surrounded himself with in the 1930s, had the following to say about Tito:

> We found him very direct of speech and manner. He was nothing like the old Party leaders. When you asked him a question, he didn't always come back at you with a quotation from Marx, Engels, or Lenin. Instead he spoke in practical, common-sense terms. "This," he would say, "is the problem we are facing. This is what I think ought to be done. Do any of you think differently?"

That Tito was different from other Communist leaders became a point of contention when he refused to join the East European Communist bloc, thus defying Stalin's desire to make Yugoslavia a Soviet satellite. Yugoslavia was expelled from the Cominform, and Tito embarked on his own brand of communism—a more tolerant and democratic brand. Needless to say, Stalin viewed Yugoslavia's decentralized profit-sharing workers' councils and the decentralization of economic and social control as dangerously "revisionist."

In January 1953, Tito was named the first president of Yugoslavia and president of the Federal Executive Council. With the 1963 constitution he became president for life. Of the many legacies he left behind with his death in 1980 was his common-sense—an ability to deal in reality rather than only in theory—and his ability to unite the disparate factions within his country. The country began to unravel after his death. ●

for the presentation of a united communist front to the world.

These events in China occurred at a time when the Truman administration was focusing on the threat of communist expansion in Europe. NATO stood as a symbol of Western power, but without German rearmament and large numbers of American forces in Europe, its effectiveness was questionable. The rearmament of Germany was still politically unacceptable, and the Americans were unwilling to commit the forces necessary to strengthen the NATO presence in Europe. To make things worse, Truman announced on 22 September 1949 that the Soviets had just exploded an atomic bomb. The American monopoly on nuclear power had ended. There was now a growing feeling in the United States that the Cold War was being lost. On 9 February 1950 Senator Joseph McCarthy charged in a speech at Wheeling, West Virginia that 57 members of the Department of State were communists. The resulting hysteria was to last for the next three years. In combination with events in both Europe and Asia, the "Red Scare" reinforced the American conviction, called **McCarthyism**, that communism must be stopped before it enveloped the United States itself.

On 12 April 1950 the National Security Council issued a policy paper, *NSC 68*, that was the most comprehensive statement yet of a US strategy in the Cold War. A practical extension of the Truman Doctrine, *NSC 68* allocated funds to support a massive military buildup in order to counter communist expansion around the world. In essence, it designated the United States as the global police officer for the maintenance and preservation of democracy against forces of change perceived as communist-inspired, and thus a threat to the free world. Department of State officials estimated that the cost of implementing this program would be about $35 billion US or 13 per cent of the gross national product. To raise this amount of money (a doubling or trebling of then-current defence spending), taxes would be increased, and a variety of domestic economic controls would be imposed. It was obvious that this program was virtually impossible to sell to the American public, without help from crises like the ones in Greece in 1947, or in Czechoslovakia in 1948.

THE KOREAN WAR

The needed crisis was not long in coming. On 25 June 1950 North Korean troops crossed the 38th parallel and invaded South Korea. Korea was strategically located—a peninsula jutting out from the Communist mainland of China just next to Japan. After the Second World War, Korea had been divided at the 38th parallel. The Red Army had occupied the country in a move on Japan late in the war, despite American insistence that Soviet help was no longer necessary. On 15 August 1945 the United States proposed joint occupation of Korea, to which proposal Stalin agreed. He hoped to establish a similar Soviet zone of occupation in Japan. Stalin assumed that when the Soviet and American occupation troops left Korea, Moscow-trained communists would gain control. However, it soon became obvious that both North and South Korea wished to dominate the entire peninsula, and no compromise seemed possible. All hope of reconciliation faded when North Korean troops invaded the south.

Within hours of the invasion, Truman ordered assistance to South Korea, as well as to counter-revolutionary forces in the Philippines and Indo-China. Also, he dispatched the US Seventh Fleet to the Formosa Straits to ward off any attempted invasion of the Nationalist-held island of Formosa. Truman's motive was to prevent the spread of communism in the Pacific. The gesture was contrary to the general understanding that the American sphere of influence ran from the Philippines through the Ryukyu Archipelago, before bending back to Japan, then along the Aleutian island chain to Alaska. Since leaving Korea in 1948-1949, the United States had failed to appreciate either the strategic significance of Korea or the moral responsibility it had incurred by stationing occupation forces in the south for three years following the war.

The invasion of South Korea brought Americans to the realization that failure to support South Korea would be an act of betrayal. Truman had promised the world that the United States would assist in the defence of any nation threatened by communist forces. How could he now ignore South Korea? Within hours of the invasion, the United States pushed a resolution through the United Nations Security Council branding the North Koreans as aggressors, and requesting UN assistance in dealing with the crisis.

The Korean War escalated the Cold War and also turned the world's attention away from Europe. Alliances on both sides were solidified by the conflict.

The Soviet Union also recognized the strategic importance of Korea, with its well-positioned warm-water ports. The memoirs of Nikita Khrushchev suggest that the North Korean leader, Kim Il-Sung, convinced Stalin that once North Korean forces entered the south, they would be able to end the civil war quickly by encouraging South Koreans to join them. The United States would not support South Korea because it lay outside the Americans' proclaimed defence perimeter.

At the time of the invasion, the USSR had walked out of the United Nations Security Council, and was thus unable to exercise its veto on the resolution to assist South Korea. Stalin had counted on the apparent lack of American interest in Korea to ensure the success of the North Korean incursion. He had not counted on any sudden shift in policy.

The Korean War was a turning point in the foreign policies of both the Soviet Union and the United States. From 1945 to 1950, the USSR had worked to consolidate its power in, and control over, Eastern Europe, and had discouraged the establishment of communist regimes that might rival Moscow's. Recognizing the failure of threats and intimidation in Yugoslavia, Stalin determined to keep China's Communist leadership in place by economic and military measures. When Mao trav-

eled to Moscow early in 1950, seeking assistance to rebuild a China ravaged by two decades of civil war, Stalin extended $300 million in long-term credits in exchange for Soviet bases in Dalian and Lüshun, joint stock companies to develop the mineral resources in Manchuria and Xinjiang (Sinkiang), and Soviet dominance in Mongolia. Stalin thus found ways to support a communist colleague, while maintaining Moscow's pre-eminence.

Support for the North Korean invasion seemed to Stalin to provide the opportunity to consolidate communism in Asia, and block any reconciliation between China and the United States. This decision led in turn to increased military assistance to China itself. The Korean War turned Soviet foreign policy outward, and provided the foundation for Khrushchev's later thrust into the Third World.

The United States made even greater changes in its foreign policy as a result of the Korean War. Although its main focus was still Europe, the USA made a commitment to a stronger presence in Asia. On 30 August 1951 an American military agreement with the Philippines (which had been granted independence in 1946) reaffirmed American rights to air and naval bases there. On 1 September 1951 the ANZUS Pact with Australia and New Zealand established the United States rather than Great Britain as protector of those Pacific states. In 1954, the **Southeast Asia Treaty Organization (SEATO)** brought together European and Asian nations, as the United States, Britain, France, Australia, New Zealand, Pakistan, the Republic of the Philippines, and Thailand agreed to mutual defence.

Of even greater significance were changes in the American relationship with Japan. Recognized now as a counterweight to the communist presence in Asia, the United States began a program of capital investment in, and technology transfer to, Japan, which would spark a spectacular economic recovery. Japan was also encouraged to rearm to a certain extent, in order to provide for its own defence. These measures would restore Japan's political sovereignty and place it securely in the American sphere of influence. As with West Germany, Japan's economic reconstruction and military self-sufficiency were seen as essential to the Western alliance in its attempt to limit Soviet expansion.

The Korean War was also the catalyst for the rearmament of Western Europe. The United States committed four divisions to NATO forces already in Europe. Its annual defence budget rose from $11.5 billion to $45 billion between 1950 and 1952. West Germany was still perceived as the key to the security of the West. France objected strongly to the rearmament of Germany, but Great Britain mediated, suggesting that German troops be subject to the control of the United States and Great Britain. This suggestion allayed France's fears and allowed the integration of German troops into the NATO alliance. By 1955, the Western **Military Defensive Alliance's** maze of interlocking treaties was consolidated, and stood as a bulwark against Soviet expansion in Asia as well as Europe.

THE KHRUSHCHEV ERA

Stalin died on 6 March 1953 and left no clearly identified successor. A number of subordinates were determined to replace him. Georgi Malenkov became the Soviet prime minister and Nikita Khrushchev the head of the Communist party. For the next three years, party officials jockeyed for power, but by 1956, it appeared Khrushchev had enough support to take control of the government.

In 1955, Khrushchev had been instrumental in a conciliatory gesture to the West: the signing of the Austrian State Treaty. This agreement, signed on 15 May 1955, provided for the withdrawal of all Allied occupation forces—including Soviet forces—from Austria and the restoration of political sovereignty there. In exchange, Austria agreed to a policy of strict neutrality and isolation from any political or economic associations with other Western European states. This was the first time the Soviet Union had voluntarily withdrawn forces from any area in Europe, and was an indication of a change in Soviet policy. From now on, the Soviet focus would be on Eastern Europe, as well as the situation at home. The **de-Stalinization** of the Soviet Union had begun.

De-Stalinization was one of Khrushchev's primary goals. Stalinist policy was a major issue in the leadership struggle. Most leadership contenders were themselves involved in the Stalinist terror, as were the rest of the Politburo members. Most party members, however, wished simply to forget Stalin and go forward. The anti-Stalin campaign was necessary to purge the Soviet Union of the horror that Stalin's regime had represented for most Soviet citizens. Khrushchev was determined to denounce Stalin and propose a new direction for the USSR. In February 1956, he addressed the 1500 delegates to the Twentieth Party Congress in a secret speech that would establish a new direction for the Soviet Union in international affairs, even as it indirectly encouraged challenges to Soviet control in Eastern Europe.

Khrushchev's denunciation was a clever combination of praise for Stalin's collectivist and industrial policies from 1929 to 1933 (which had laid the economic foundation of the new Soviet state), and condemnation of Stalin's autocratic rule (which had terrorized party members and caused military disasters in the Second World War). Khrushchev was attempting to appease some members of the Politburo who wanted to establish a new direction, without alienating Stalinists, who maintained a hard-line conservatism and feared criminal charges as accomplices of Stalin. Khrushchev's message was essentially reformist, and he promised personal safety to Stalinists by identifying only a small group of the dictator's accomplices, who had already been exposed and punished.

A second theme of Khrushchev's speech was Lenin's contention that "there are many roads to socialism." This was the position Tito had taken when he refused to bow to Stalin's demands for control over Yugoslavian affairs. Khrushchev hoped to bring Tito back into the Soviet fold by approving diversity within the Soviet bloc. By this means, Khrushchev also hoped to establish stronger ties with socialist parties in Western Europe.

A third theme in Khrushchev's speech was Soviet recognition of the growing importance of the Third World. Decolonization movements had begun around the world after the Second World War. As new nationalist governments struggled to establish themselves, it became obvious to both the United States and the Soviet Union that sheer numbers of new states could drastically alter the international order. The United States had begun an outward thrust into Asia as a result of the Korean War. Khrushchev now suggested an ideological rationale for Soviet support to newly emerging nations. With Soviet aid, he argued, Third World countries could escape capitalist imperialism and launch programs of industrialization. The Soviet Union had already indicated its commitment to this philosophy by financing a giant steel mill at Bhilai, in India. India had refused to participate in SEATO, and hence was identified as strategically desirable in the ongoing struggle between the USSR and the West. The underlying tenet here was peaceful coexistence. Khrushchev recognized the existence of two different social systems, but advocated the victory of socialism through non-violent transition, not by the war or violent revolution his predecessors had promoted.

Khrushchev's speech proved to be a Pandora's box. The denunciation of Stalin created an expectation that Khrushchev could remedy the ills of the Stalinist regime. Over the next eight years he attempted to fulfil these expectations by changes in both domestic and foreign policy.

Since the collectivization process of the first Five Year Plan (1928-1932), when the Soviet agricultural system was reorganized, the USSR had been unable to produce enough food to feed its population. Agricultural reform was one of Khrushchev's top priorities. Maize was to be the primary crop, and Khrushchev set a goal for its production to match those for meat, butter, and milk. All were to equal output in the United States by 1962.

It was an unrealistic program, doomed to failure from the beginning. Bureaucratic red tape and the lack of investment capital made progress impossible. Instead of instituting change, the Soviet bureaucracy, from Khrushchev down to minor party officials, looked for scapegoats. Instead of seeing an increase in production, Soviet agriculture suffered an enormous setback. Of 22 million privately owned cows in 1958, only 10 million remained by 1962. No reserves of grain were accumulated, and when the harvest failed in 1963, bread shortages occurred across the country.

Unlike Stalin, who simply allowed the peasants to die of hunger, Khrushchev bought almost 12 million tonnes of grain abroad. In an attempt to reform agriculture, Khrushchev launched a program of chemicalization in order to increase production. This program, too, was a dismal failure. The Soviet economy simply could not produce enough chemical fertilizer to supply agricultural units, and did not have the funds to buy abroad. These failures in agricultural reform contributed substantially to the political demise of Khrushchev in 1964.

Khrushchev's policy also altered the Soviet Union's relationship with China. The change in foreign policy disturbed the Chinese, who detected in the new Soviet thrust into the Third World a weakening of the Sino-Soviet alliance. The USSR now appeared unlikely to promote the Chinese Communist government's desire for international recognition, or assist any attempt to overthrow the Nationalist regime in Taiwan.

The most significant effect of Khrushchev's new policy, however, was its impact on Eastern Europe. People in Poland and Hungary, particularly, harboured old and deep anti-Soviet sentiments, and wanted to institute governments more in tune with their own nationalist sentiments. The anti-Stalinist reaction in the Soviet Union spread quickly to all countries in the Eastern bloc, encouraging resistance to Soviet control in general.

POLISH AND HUNGARIAN UNREST

In June 1956, labour unrest in Poznan in Poland grew into riots protesting Soviet economic and political domination. Recognizing the gravity of the situation, Moscow agreed to allow Poland greater control of its own affairs and permitted the Polish Communist party to expel pro-Moscow Communists from the Central Committee of the Polish United Workers' party. By October, Moscow had agreed to the elevation of Wladyslaw Gomulka to the post of party secretary. Khrushchev flew to Warsaw to persuade Polish Communists to maintain a pro-Soviet position, but Gomulka had announced a national communism in Poland and refused. Soviet tanks were ready to roll on Warsaw, but Khrushchev recognized war was ill-advised and decided to compromise instead. Soviet military control was curtailed, many restrictions on individual liberties were removed, and a *de facto* alliance between the Polish state and the Catholic Church was formulated. Gomulka, for his part, recognized the strategic nature of Poland's geographical position between the Soviet Union and Germany, and affirmed Poland's allegiance to Soviet foreign policy. Poland had achieved some measure of independence without incurring the wrath of the Red Army.

Events in Poland raised liberalization hopes in Hungary. The Hungarians demanded independence from Soviet control, economic decentralization, and improvements in the standard of living. Many Hungarians were not only anti-Soviet but also anti-communist.

After the brief rule by Béla Kun's Communist government in 1919, the Hungarian government fell into the hands of right-wing reactionaries, who sided with the Nazis in the Second World War. Hungary was liberated by the Red Army in 1945, and Matyas Rakosi became first the Hungarian Communist party's general secretary and then, in 1952, prime minister. A hard-line Stalinist, Rakosi established an atmosphere of terror and persecution. The Hungarian standard of living—which had not been luxurious, but had been superior to that of most of Eastern Europe before the war—fell dramatically. After Khrushchev's speech, both workers and intellectuals openly demanded liberalization of the economy, and improvements in the supply of consumer goods.

On 6 October 1956 some 200 000 residents of Budapest demonstrated against the abuses of Rakosi's regime. The city's largest factories were the backbone of the revolt, and workers were joined by intellectuals and large numbers of Hungary's youth. It was a grass-roots movement which began to look very much like a popular revolution. The Soviet leadership reacted almost immediately. They removed Rakosi from power and installed Imre Nagy as prime minister on 23 October. By this time, Budapest was filled with workers' councils, all presenting social and political demands. Thousands of people took to the streets. Skirmishes resulted as Soviet troops attempted to maintain a semblance of order. Hungarians on the march wished to withdraw from the Warsaw Pact, declare neutrality, and become a sovereign nation.

The government of Imre Nagy already included non-Communists, and Nagy now proclaimed that free elections would be held in the near future. On 30 October Moscow promised in negotiations to support the Hungarian national government and eventually withdraw Soviet troops from Hungarian soil. It seemed that the Hungarian Revolution would achieve its goal of independence.

However, as Soviet troops left Budapest, on 1 November 1956 Nagy declared a Hungarian withdrawal from the Warsaw Pact. This announcement aborted the revolution. The Soviet Union could not allow Hungary to establish a precedent that could bring about the disintegration of the Soviet bloc. On 4 November 1956, 5000 Soviet tanks and an army of 250 000 soldiers entered Budapest. The Hungarians fought valiantly, but in three days the struggle was over. Armed resistance in the countryside continued until 14 November, also without success.

The destruction in Budapest was enormous. Many buildings bear the marks of the Red Army assault to this day. As many as 20 000 people were killed and another 20 000 imprisoned. Some 200 000 Hungarians fled abroad, many to Canada or the United States. The Communist Janos Kadar was installed as the new prime minister. Imre Nagy was taken to Romania, where he was tried and executed in 1958. Twenty years after his death, he was, as he had predicted, exonerated by a reformed Hungarian government.

The brutal suppression of the Hungarian Revolution was instructive in a number of ways. Nationalism remained a vital force in Eastern Europe even among communists and bolstered an

This picture shows citizens of Budapest watching Soviet tanks roll through their city a month after the brief and violent struggle of the Hungarian Revolution. Soviet military presence in Hungary continued for over 20 years.

HUNGARY IN THE SOVIET SPHERE

The Hungarian Revolution coincided with the Suez Crisis and US presidential elections. These events, along with the recognition that Hungary was clearly in the Soviet sphere of influence, precluded any supportive action for Hungary from the West.

anti-Soviet stance in some areas. Military force, not ideology, bound the Soviet bloc. It was evident that Soviet control could be preserved only by the Red Army. It seemed, though, that the Soviet Union might be forced to allow a measure of economic, political, and cultural autonomy if a nation were willing to continue adherence to the Soviet-dominated Warsaw Pact.

This crisis reminded the West of the importance of Eastern Europe to the Soviet Union. Eastern Europe was the key to the military defence of the Soviet Union. The Soviet Union was prepared to use military force to preserve its hegemony in the region. Hungary's appeal to the United States for assistance went unanswered because the United States recognized that Hungary was in the Soviet sphere of influence. Entry into the conflict would have been an open confrontation with the Soviet Union.

During the early months of 1960 it seemed as if the Cold War was beginning to thaw. However, after May, relations between the Soviet Union and the United States became even more strained. This picture shows Khrushchev addressing the United Nations in September of that year.

BERLIN: TENSION BUILDS

In November 1958, tension between East and West once again centred on Berlin. The situation in Germany had changed dramatically in the decade since the Berlin Blockade. West Germany, governed by Konrad Adenauer, who made no secret of his anti-communist stance, now contributed a strong military contingent to NATO. The West German economy was thriving and provided a high standard of living for its citizens. East Germany, in contrast, was economically depressed and politically repressed. Over 2 million East Germans had fled to the West by 1958. Many of them were skilled workers or highly trained professionals, and their exodus jeopardized the economic recovery of their homeland. The long border between East and West Germany had been sealed to prevent any further "brain drain," but Berlin itself remained an escape hatch.

Khrushchev, alarmed at the growing military and economic strength of West Germany, as well as by the loss of valuable labour, demanded that the Western powers occupying Berlin evacuate within six months. Unless they did so, the Soviets would turn over administration of their sector to the Pankow regime of East Germany, with whom the West had no diplomatic ties nor agreement for access to Berlin. The ultimatum was designed to remove the Western showplace of West Berlin from the Soviet sphere of influence, to weaken ties between the United States and West Germany, and provoke disunity among NATO allies. However, the Western alliance stood firmly united in refusing to budge, and by March 1959, Khrushchev had to back down. He proposed a summit meeting to settle the issue and met with President Dwight Eisenhower at Camp David in September 1959. The meeting proved cordial and **détente** seemed likely as a moratorium was declared on the Berlin question. A summit conference was planned for the following May in Paris to work out a comprehensive settlement of Cold War issues. Many people had great hopes that the Cold War would be resolved through **summitry**.

The Paris summit of 16 May 1960 was not to be. On 5 May 1960 the Soviets announced that they had shot down a high-altitude American reconnaissance plane, a U-2, piloted by Gary Powers. The U-2 was obviously on an intelligence-gathering mission over Soviet territory. Khrushchev demanded Eisenhower apologize for the violation of Soviet air space, punish those responsible, and promise to discontinue the flights. Eisenhower had no choice but to refuse all of Khrushchev's demands. Khrushchev in turn refused to meet with Eisenhower in Paris. An opportunity to settle the most pressing issues of the Cold War was lost.

Why would Khrushchev have changed the position he had held at the Camp David meeting so dramatically? Two reasons seem likely. Khrushchev had been severely criticized by the hard-line faction in the Politburo over conciliatory moves made in Berlin in particular, and in European issues in general. As well, his attempts at rapprochement with the West had antagonized the Chinese. The Chinese were openly critical of Khrushchev's foreign policy of peaceful co-existence and resentful that Moscow had not supported China in border disputes with India, in attempts to regain Formosa, and in attempts to develop nuclear weapons. The U-2 incident left Khrushchev vulnerable. His plans to negotiate a settlement on Berlin and obtain concessions from the West on both Berlin and Germany were now aborted. Khrushchev declared he would not negotiate with the Americans so long as Eisenhower was in office.

The election of John F. Kennedy was greeted favourably by the Soviet Union. Determined to resolve the situation in Berlin, Khrushchev used the summit meeting in Vienna in 1961 to present the new American president with an ultimatum

The Berlin Wall became the symbol of the Cold War which separated Eastern and Western Europe. East German police are shown here repairing the Berlin Wall while West Berlin police and others gather on the other side. This section of the wall was damaged in 1963 when a mechanic rammed an armoured car into the structure during his escape to West Berlin.

demanding a peace treaty with Germany, the evacuation of occupation troops from Berlin, and the creation of a free city. He followed up his ultimatum with an announcement of a 33 per cent increase in the Soviet military budget to establish a position of strength in Berlin. Kennedy responded by announcing a $3 billion increase in the American defence budget and a doubling of draft calls. Tension mounted, and no resolution of the Berlin issue seemed likely.

Some 103 000 East Germans poured into the West via West Berlin in the first six months of 1961. As Khrushchev continued to press publicly for an agreement with the West, he determined secretly to close off the escape route to the West. On 13 August 1961 the border between East and West Berlin was permanently closed, with a few heavily guarded checkpoints. The Berlin Wall was initially barbed wire, but over the years it became concrete slabs. All buildings on the east side of the wall were removed, and a mined buffer zone was developed.

The Berlin Wall stabilized the situation in Berlin but it did not resolve the issue. Khrushchev faced tough opposition from the hard-line faction in the Politburo. During the Twenty-second Congress of the Communist party of the Soviet Union in late October, fellow Politburo member Kozlov and his supporters seemed to challenge Khrushchev for leadership and chastised him for backing down on his ultimatum to the Americans. Khrushchev, however, showed toughness when he allowed Soviet tanks in Berlin to come nose to nose with American tanks at Checkpoint Charlie from 25 to 27 October. This demonstration of force did not escalate, but it was a sure indication that the situation in Germany remained unresolved. Khrushchev would have to find another means of dislodging the West from Berlin.

THE CUBAN MISSILE CRISIS

In 1962, Cold War tension shifted from Europe to the Caribbean. Khrushchev's memoirs suggest that while visiting Bulgaria in May 1962, he had the idea of installing missiles in Cuba to gain an advantage in the East-West balance of power, and a position of strength in negotiations over Berlin. If he could install the missiles before they were discovered by the United States, he would occupy a strong position in the American sphere of influence and be able to negotiate more effectively the removal of Western powers from the Soviet sphere of influence in Berlin.

The relationship between Cuba and the Soviet Union began after the dictatorship of Fulgencio Batista was overthrown by Fidel Castro in 1959. Cuba and the Soviet Union had, in 1960, signed a $100 million trade agreement—the beginning of massive Soviet involvement in the Cuban economy. Soviet arms and equipment were sent to Cuba to help defend the island. Cuban émigrés, supported by the American Central Intelligence Agency (CIA), conducted a number of isolated raids on Cuba in an attempt to upset the Castro regime—culminating in 1961 with the notorious Bay of Pigs disaster. On 17 April 1961 Cuban émigrés, backed by the CIA, landed at the Bay of Pigs hoping to gain control of the whole island. The venture was a complete fiasco, a deep embarrassment for the new administration of John Kennedy.

During 1962, the Soviet Union stepped up its supply of arms to Cuba while at the same time assuring the Kennedy administration it intended no threat to the United States. However, on 14 October 1962 an American U-2 overflying Cuba photographed an area around San Cristobál that showed evidence of medium-range ballistic missile sites. The next 13 days brought the Soviet Union and the United States to the brink of nuclear war.

Once they had discovered the sites, the United States had to decide what to do about them. Opinion in the US Department of State was divided. The "hawks" favoured direct action—either an air strike or an invasion. The "doves" wanted to solve the crisis by diplomacy alone, perhaps by removing American Jupiter missiles in Turkey in return for the Soviets removing their missiles in Cuba. The "owls" preferred a mild use of military force, perhaps to close Cuba to Soviet ships.

The "owlish" or middle-of-the-road position prevailed, primarily because the Executive Committee (ExComm) had a very real fear of nuclear war. On 22 October 1962, President Kennedy went on national television to inform the American public that offensive missile sites had been established in Cuba by the Soviet Union, and that in response he was imposing an air and naval quarantine of Cuba to prevent any further deliveries. Although Cuba requested a UN Security Council meeting to resolve the crisis, direct negotiation between the United States and the Soviet Union was ultimately the method used to bring about resolution of the crisis. The UN secretary general U Thant, meanwhile, appealed to Khrushchev to suspend arms shipments to Cuba, and he asked Kennedy to suspend the quarantine. Khrushchev accepted the appeal, but Kennedy rejected it.

Meetings between Robert Kennedy (US attorney general and John F. Kennedy's brother) and the Soviet ambassador to the United States, Anatoly Dobrynin, secretly established the compromise publicly agreed to by Khrushchev and John Kennedy. On 27 October 1962 Khrushchev proposed the trade of Soviet missiles in Cuba for Jupiter missiles in Turkey. That same morning Major Rudolf Anderson, the pilot who originally spotted the missile sites, was killed when his U-2 plane was shot down over Cuba. The Americans protested this action and demanded the Soviets agree to the immediate dismantling of the missiles; the Americans refused any public trade of missiles, even though the Jupiters were obsolete anyway and scheduled to be removed. The Americans did not wish to imply to any of their allies that they would abandon their commitment to them. However, the Americans did agree to remove quarantine measures and promised not to invade Cuba.

By this time Khrushchev realized he had badly misjudged the Americans and decided to accept the compromise Kennedy held out to him. The crisis was over.

The Soviet missiles were removed from Cuba under UN supervision in the six months following the crisis. The next year, the United States quietly dismantled the Jupiter missiles in Turkey. Throughout 13 days of crisis, the two sides had negotiated in a conciliatory fashion. One of the lessons of the Cuban Missile Crisis, in fact, was the value of diplomacy. By allowing an opponent to save face, one could avert disaster. Although the Soviets had installed the missile sites with the hope of bargaining in Berlin, they took no further action against the West in Berlin. The West learned, however, that the American commitment to NATO must be strengthened, as must the West's position in Berlin.

The Cuban Missile Crisis made both the Soviet Union and the United States aware of the vulnerability of a world dominated by nuclear weaponry. On 20 June 1963 these two superpowers demonstrated their determination to avoid accidental nuclear war by the establishment of a hot-line between Moscow and Washington. As well, talks were begun on the issue of nuclear proliferation and testing. As a result of these talks, the Partial Test Ban Treaty was signed on 5 August 1963 by the Soviet Union, the United States, and Great Britain. The treaty banned nuclear tests in the atmosphere, under water, and in space. It was later signed by more than one hundred nations—though China condemned the treaty as a bargain between imperialists. China's reaction indicated a split with the Soviet Union, but 1963 began a détente between the Soviet Union and the United States.

SUMMARY

The Cold War was a period of intense rivalry between the United States and the Soviet Union as they sought to stake out their spheres of influence and maintain hegemony within these spheres. Although it is difficult to determine the precise time frame of the Cold War, the period between 1945 and 1963 was the most tense. During this time, the critical issue of the Cold War was Eastern Europe. Neither the Soviet Union nor the United States wanted strong independent governments in this region.

After the First World War, Woodrow Wilson had attempted to support democratic governments in the new countries created from the old Austro-Hungarian Empire in order to prevent expansion by the new Soviet regime. The end of the Second World War once again raised the question of Eastern Europe's political fate. The Red Army's liberation of this area gave the Soviet Union a strong claim to dominate it. The United States was unwilling to allow this domination, however, fearing that Western Europe was threatened as well. The period from 1945 to 1950 was characterized by the struggle of the United States and the Soviet Union to secure their positions in Europe.

In 1950, the Cold War moved to Asia, with the outbreak of the Korean War. From this time forward, superpower hostility was global in nature. However, Europe would remain the focal point, with Germany the crucial issue. The United States wanted a strong West Germany to counter the threat of Soviet expansion, and the Soviet Union wanted the West out of Berlin. Hence, from 1958 to

1961, the Berlin issue dominated East-West relations. In 1962, the issue came to a head with the Cuban Missile Crisis, which brought the world to the brink of nuclear disaster. Diplomatic resolution of this crisis and subsequent easing of tension between the United States and the Soviet Union paved the way for a new era of détente.

QUESTIONS

1. Name two results of the Second World War that led to the Cold War.

2. Name the three issues that defied resolution at Potsdam in 1945. Compare the positions of the USA and the USSR on these issues.

3. Explain the disagreement that erupted over Germany.

4. What was the "Polish question"?

5. What caused the Soviet-American confrontation in Iran? How was the issue resolved?

6. Why was Turkey considered of strategic importance to the Soviet Union?

7. What was the Truman Doctrine? What was its significance for American foreign policy?

8. Explain George Kennan's role in shaping American foreign policy.

9. What was the Marshall Plan? Explain why the United States implemented the Marshall Plan.

10. What were the results of the Marshall Plan for Western Europe? What were the results for the United States?

11. What was the significance of the Communist *coup* in Czechoslovakia in 1948?

12. What were the causes and results of the Berlin Blockade?

13. Describe the NATO agreement. How is it significant in international power politics?

14. What was the Cominform? What was its significance?

15. Explain how Tito was able to remove Yugoslavia from Stalin's grip without suffering the fate of Czechoslovakia.

16. Explain the significance of *NSC 68* to American foreign policy.

17. How did the Korean War affect the foreign policy of the USA? How did it affect the USSR? How did the war affect the situation in Europe in the 1950s?

18. Explain the role played by China in Cold War politics from 1949 to 1960.

19. Identify the three primary features of Khrushchev's speech to the Twentieth Party Congress.

20. What did Khrushchev mean by peaceful co-existence?

21. Name and explain three consequences of Khrushchev's speech to the Twentieth Party Congress.

22. How did the Soviet Union and Poland resolve the unrest that occurred in Poland in June 1956?

23. Explain how events in Hungary in October 1956 differed from those in Poland in June 1956.

24. How did the Soviet Union deal with the Hungarians in the 1956 uprising?

25. Explain what the resolution of the Hungarian Revolution revealed about the Soviet Union's relationship to Eastern Europe.

26. Why did the United Nations fail to help Hungary in 1956? Why did the United States not help?

27. Explain why tension developed once again in Berlin from 1958 to 1961. How was it resolved?

28. What was the significance of the shooting down of Gary Powers' U-2 spy plane?

29. Why did Khrushchev order the installation of missiles in Cuba?

30. What options did the United States consider when trying to resolve the Cuban Missile Crisis?

31. Explain how the Cuban Missile Crisis was resolved.

32. What lessons did the United States learn from the Cuban Missile Crisis? What did the Soviet Union learn?

33. What were two results of the Cuban Missile Crisis?

CRITICAL ANALYSIS

1. How did the Second World War alter the balance of power?

2. How did the development of nuclear forces alter defence strategies in the USA and the USSR?

3. Evaluate containment (political, military, economic, cultural) as an international-relations strategy.

4. What role do the media play in arousing public support for containment? Explain and give an example.

5. Why did the USA refrain from using nuclear weapons during the Cold War?

6. Should every nation have nuclear capabilities? Explain and justify your position. Will having nuclear weapons help smaller nations gain major-power status?

RESEARCH PROJECTS

1. Research the causes, course of events, and the results of one of the following Cold War confrontations: (a) the Berlin Blockade; (b) the Korean War; (c) the Hungarian Revolution; (d) the Cuban Missile Crisis. Evaluate the impact of the event chosen on the superpower relationship.

2. The Marshall Plan invested large sums of money in Europe between 1948 and 1952. Research this investment and show how reconstruction occurred in Western Europe. Evaluate the effectiveness of the plan and comment on current suggestions that a similar plan be instituted for Eastern Europe today. Is a Marshall Plan of the 1990s likely to be effective in reconstructing Eastern Europe? Explain.

3. Compare and contrast the political and economic system of Yugoslavia with that of Poland, Czechoslovakia, or Hungary. Evaluate the success of the Yugoslavian model by studying current conditions in Yugoslavia.

4. Compare and contrast life in West Berlin with that of East Berlin in the 1960s. Comment on the presence of the Berlin Wall.

ACTIVITIES

1 Guest Speaker

Invite an individual who has lived in Eastern Europe or the Soviet Union to talk about life under a communist regime.

2 Debate

Be it resolved that the United States policy of containment furthered the peace and security of Western Europe in the post-war world.

3 Panel Discussion

Establish students to play the roles of Nikita Khrushchev, John Kennedy, Fidel Castro, Lester Pearson, and any two European leaders in power in 1962. In these roles, discuss the rationale for the Cuban missile construction and the point of view of each country represented. Students should discuss the global implications of the crisis and their reactions to the way in which the crisis was resolved.

HISTORICAL ANALYSIS

THE COLD WAR

After the Second World War the United States and the Soviet Union staked out rival spheres of influence and developed foreign policies designed to maintain hegemony in their respective territories. Possessing incompatible political and economic systems, the two superpowers maintained rivalry and diplomatic confrontation which came to be known as the Cold War.

Analyse the following excerpts from speeches by Churchill and Khrushchev to determine the rationale for the Cold War. Consider the audience for which each speech was prepared. Determine what each side perceives as aggression and what action each recommends in response.

1. When speaking at Fulton, Missouri on 5 March 1946, Churchill warned that a shadow had fallen over Europe and Asia, a shadow cast by Soviet hostility and aggression. He urged military strength and unity of purpose to stop the communist advance in Western Europe.

We understand the Russians need to be secure on their western frontiers from all renewal of German aggression.

From Stettin in the Baltic to Trieste in the Adriatic, an iron curtain has descended across the continent. Behind that line all the capitals of the ancient states of central and eastern Europe ... and the populations around them lie in the Soviet sphere and are all subject ... to an increasing measure of control from Moscow ... The Communist parties which were very small have been raised to pre-eminence and ... are seeking everywhere to obtain totalitarian control. Police governments are prevailing ... this is not the liberated Europe we fought to build. Nor is it one which contains the essentials of permanent peace ...

2. In the Soviet view, the Cold War represented a desperate attempt to preserve capitalism in the face of socialist expansion. Khrushchev made these comments in a speech to the Twentieth Party Congress in February 1956.

Soon after the Second World War ended, the influence of ... militarist groups began to be increasingly evident in the policy of the United States of America, Britain, and France. Their desire to enforce their will on other countries by economic and political pressure, threats, and military provocation prevailed. This became known as the position of strength policy. It reflects the aspirations ... of present-day imperialism to win world supremacy, to suppress the working class and the democratic and national liberation movements.

The inspirers of the Cold War began to establish military blocs and many countries found themselves ... in restricted aggressive alliances—the North Atlantic bloc, Western European Union, SEATO and the Baghdad Pact ... The organizers of military blocs allege they have united for defence ... [but] this is a smokescreen to cover up the claims of one power for world domination.

SUPER POWER DÉTENTE

FOCUS ON SELF-DETERMINATION

We and you ought not now to pull on the ends of a rope in which you have tied the knot of war, because the more we pull, the tighter the knot will be tied. And a moment may come when the knot will be tied so tight that even he who tied it will not have the strength to untie it; and then it will be necessary to cut the knot ... and thereby doom the world to the catastrophe of thermonuclear war.

The chairperson of the Soviet Council of Ministers, addressing the Kennedy administration during the Cuban Missile Crisis, October 1962.

At the same time as the superpowers began attempts to settle some of their most outstanding differences, a desire for complete self-determination among nations and regions within their respective spheres of influence arose. Select an example of this (Nicaragua, Afghanistan, the Middle East, etc.) and examine it in the context of ongoing superpower détente. Has détente helped or hindered the struggle for self-determination in the nation or region you have selected?

OVERVIEW

Brezhnev, the Prague Spring, unrest in Poland and China, and Vietnam's effect on the USA are dealt with in the context of détente in this chapter. The arms race from 1945 to the present and then arms control from 1963 to the present are developed.

THE SOVIET BLOC: 1962–1975

After the Cuban Missile Crisis, Khrushchev was deposed and in 1964 the Soviet Union entered a new era of repression under Leonid Brezhnev.

PRAGUE SPRING

Liberal changes introduced in Czechoslovakia by Alexander Dubček in March 1968 were brought to an end in August 1968 when Soviet forces supported by Warsaw Pact troops entered Czechoslovakia.

POLAND

During the 1970s Poland experienced serious social and economic difficulties but maintained a peaceful relationship with Moscow.

CHINA

The United States recognized the Sino-Soviet split as an opportunity to secure a foothold in China. In 1972, Nixon visited China in an effort to re-establish diplomatic ties.

AMERICAN INVOLVEMENT IN VIETNAM

Implementing the policy of containment in Vietnam led to American involvement in a war which was highly controversial.

THE NUCLEAR ARMS RACE AND ARMS CONTROL

The development of nuclear weaponry introduced new challenges in the area of arms control. Both superpowers embarked on programs to develop nuclear technology which threatened to destroy the world.

SALT I AND SALT II

In 1972 progress was finally made in the limitation of strategic weaponry as the United States and the Soviet Union signed SALT I and began immediately to discuss its extension to SALT II.

REAGAN AND GORBACHEV

Gorbachev's rise to power introduced a new era of détente between the superpowers and from 1985 to 1988 the leaders held five summit meetings.

THE SOVIET BLOC: 1962–1975

During the Khrushchev era, the Soviet Union concentrated on military control of the Eastern bloc while allowing some economic and cultural diversity. As long as satellite countries remained loyal to the Warsaw Pact and committed to communism, some domestic autonomy was allowed. Hungary, Bulgaria, and East Germany maintained stability; but Romania, Czechoslovakia, and Poland challenged Soviet control and signaled a change in the relationship between the Soviet Union and its satellites.

In October 1964, Nikita Khrushchev was deposed. Leonid Brezhnev became general secretary of the Communist party, and Alexei Kosygin gained the post of prime minister. The new Soviet leadership was faced with the challenge of improving relations with the West while at the same time asserting control over the Soviet bloc in Eastern Europe. The first challenge to Soviet control of Eastern Europe came from Romania. Even before Nicolae Ceaușescu gained power in Romania in 1965, Romanians had asserted their independence by refusing to participate in the Comecon plan to create a division of labour within the Soviet bloc. The Comecon plan had called for Romania to develop agriculture at the expense of industry. However, the Romanians made overtures to Western governments in order to establish access to technology and promote industrial development. Because there was no question of Romania's loyalty to communist doctrine, and because Romania made no move to leave the Warsaw Pact, the Soviets allowed its independence to go unchecked. Romania soon developed into one of the most Stalinist or closed societies in Eastern Europe, with Ceaușescu skilfully balancing autonomy with deference to Moscow.

PRAGUE SPRING

Events in Czechoslovakia, however, could not be ignored by the Soviet Union. In January 1968, Alexander Dubček replaced Antonín Novotný as party secretary in Czechoslovakia. Although Dubček was not initially viewed as a threat by the Soviet Union, liberal changes began almost immediately. On 4 March, censorship of the press, radio, and television was abolished. Even more alarming to the USSR was the tolerance of non-communist organizations with the potential of developing into

BIOGRAPHY

NICOLAE CEAUŞESCU (1918–1989)
ELENA CEAUŞESCU (1919–1989)

Nicolae Ceauşescu was the third of ten children born to Andruta and Alexandra Ceauşescu in the village of Scornicesti, in the low rolling hills of Olt County, Romania. Nicolae's parents were peasants, and at the age of 11 he went to Bucharest to find work. Because detailed information on Nicolae's early life is limited to that which is found in government-commissioned biographies, the facts of his early life can only be guessed at, intertwined as they are with propaganda and myth. Although Nicolae's impoverished and harsh start in life is true, it became part of the myth, carrying with it the message that any Romanian could rise from obscurity and poverty to become president. One must just persevere, work hard, and be devoted to the Romanian Communist Party (RCP).

As a teenager, Nicolae joined the RCP and was imprisoned twice for anti-fascist activities. When the Soviets entered Romania in 1944, Nicolae was released from prison and shortly after became the secretary of the Bucharest branch of the Communist Party. Thus began his steady rise within the RCP ranks. In 1946, Elena and Nicolae married: two years later, Valentin, their eldest son was born, followed by daughter Zoia in 1950, and son Nicu, their favourite, in 1951. Nicolae was promoted to Committee secretary and candidate member of the Political Bureau in 1954, and in 1965 to secretary-general of the RCP and president of the State Council, thereby attaining the leading position in both party and state. He was elected president of Romania in 1974, and was re-elected in 1980 and 1985.

During his years of presidency, Nicolae emphasized Romanian nationalism and rapid industrialization. In response to the economic problems of the 1980s, he tightened central control and further entrenched his own cult of power and personality into the Romanian psyche. Any reform measure that was undertaken had to ensure the continued rapid accumulation of goods and the strict adherence to socialist principles. Ceauşescu was even more inflexible than Lenin, whose New Economic Policy of the 1920s tolerated some private agriculture and enterprise. Biographer Mary Ellen Fischer has compared Ceauşescu to East German Walter Ulbricht, of whom it was said: "His terrifyingly simple world had no room for the individualist, the flabby-muscled, the hedonist, the Christian, the doubter, the bourgeois, the dreamer, or the artist." Every effort was to serve the state and to contribute to the socialist development of Romania.

Although not a bloody dictatorship, the Ceauşescu-era provided the impetus for the relentless wearing down of the economic, spiritual, and psychological well-being of a whole country's population. This was an era during which people spied on their own family and friends in return for pathetic rewards—small improvements in living standards and personal conveniences.

During the Ceauşescu years, the Romanian press constantly praised Elena for her "prodigious political activity and decisive role in the assertion of Romanian science, education and culture." After Elena's death, a retired schoolteacher produced a report she had kept hidden for over half a century. It uncovered that 14-year-old Elena had failed every subject except singing, gymnastics, and needlework. On the report the schoolteacher had scrawled "Must stay in the same form a second year." Instead, Elena quit school, worked in the fields for several seasons, then moved to Bucharest. According to former diplomat, Mircea Codranu, had Elena lived, she would have been tried "for genocide not of people but of culture and education."

The Ceauşescus remained in power until 1989, when both Nicolae and Elena were tried and executed after attempting to flee Romania during a revolutionary *coup*. At Nicolae and Elena's December 1989 trial, many laws were broken in order to proceed rapidly with their execution. To the questions and charges piled up against them, they were silent and refused to respond, saying "I shall only answer to the Grand National Assembly and to representatives of the working class."

The struggles of the Romanian people have continued long past the December 1989 executions. The National Salvation Front under Ion Iliescu—which came to power immediately following the Ceauşescus—was based largely on tactics and power-mongering similar to that of its predecessors. Ana Blandiana, who had been part of the National Salvation Front for a short time, and who is also one of Romania's best-known poets and rare genuine dissidents, said the following: "In light of what has happened since 25 December 1989, and the way the power holders have behaved since that date, I wonder whether we were right to judge Ceauşescu so harshly." Ceauşescu biographer, Edward Behr, while in a queue for gasoline near Piesti, heard a motorist shout: "Under Ceauşescu we had electricity but no gasoline. Now we have neither."

The fact of post-Ceauşescu Romania was that the civil service, police, and courts remained largely intact, except for in those cases where a person was hopelessly compromised by their loyalty to Ceauşescu. Former Securitate expert Liviu Turcu felt that most Romanians had been tainted by and implicated in the corruption of the Ceauşescu system—if only through blackmail, to help them to get a divorce quickly, to get a passport, or to take a trip. "If you are talking about moral recovery [for Romania]," says Turcu, "I believe it will take at least one or two generations to start putting things right, and this is perhaps Romania's biggest tragedy." ●

political organizations. Club 231 was organized on 31 March to monitor the treatment of political prisoners. On 5 April, rights to travel abroad, to freedom of speech, and to a free press were guaranteed. The party announced that the *nomenklatura*, the system of appointing bureaucrats only from party ranks, should be abolished. All of these reforms were to be formalized at the Fourteenth Party Congress scheduled for 9 September 1968.

Although Dubček continued to support the Warsaw Pact, his attempts to promote "socialism with a human face" were viewed with alarm in Moscow. Strategically located in Central Europe, Czechoslovakia was essential to the security of the Soviet bloc. Recent Warsaw Pact manoeuvres on Czechoslovakian soil had revealed vulnerability on the western border. Thus, a combination of strategic, ideological, and domestic considerations led to the Soviet decision to invade Czechoslovakia. If the Prague Spring—which had introduced political, cultural, and social freedoms—was allowed to continue, would other members of the Soviet bloc attempt similar reforms? If, for example, nationalism was allowed to flourish in Czechoslovakia, would the Ukrainians also agitate for national autonomy?

On 20 August 1968, at 11 PM, a four-pronged Soviet invasion began. Tanks and armoured carriers rolled in from Ukraine, Poland, East Germany, and Hungary in support of the Soviets. The Czech forces were overwhelmed by 250 000 combat troops in 29 divisions, 1000 aircraft, and 7500 tanks. An additional 250 000 support troops ensured the success of the invasion. The Czechoslovakians met the invasion with passive resistance: only 80 civilians were killed. The lesson of Hungary in 1956 had not been forgotten.

On 17 April 1969, Gustav Husák replaced Alexander Dubček as party secretary in Czechoslovakia. Moscow announced the **Brezhnev Doctrine**, which proclaimed the right of the Soviet Union to determine when intervention might be necessary in order to preserve socialism and protect against counter-revolution within the Eastern bloc. Units of the Red Army were permanently stationed in Czechoslovakia, and the Czechs were subjected to one of the most repressive regimes in Eastern Europe. Ironically, the country that in 1968 seemed the birthplace of reform would two decades later refuse to allow the sale of *Pravda*, because it contained articles outlining Mikhail Gorbachev's new policies of *glasnost* and *perestroika*.

Relations between China and the West improved in the late 1960s. China was admitted to the United Nations in 1971, and in 1972 US president Richard Nixon made a highly publicized visit to China.

POLAND

Events in Poland from 1968 to 1970 were affected by the events in Czechoslovakia. Wladyslaw Gomulka, Poland's leader, recognized that economic reform was essential, but he was not willing to allow any political reform. When student demonstrations broke out in Warsaw against Soviet domination, Gomulka was able to rally working-class support for the police in putting down the protests. University students were considered a privileged group and much class resentment could be rallied against them. Also, Gomulka stirred up anti-Semitic feelings and made the Jews scapegoats for the economic problems facing Poland. Most of Poland's remaining 30 000 Jews were forced to leave during this period. Gomulka had decided that promoting class divisions and racism in his own country was safer than allowing hostility to be directed at the Soviets. In December 1970, as the

economy worsened, price increases on food items had to be imposed. Strikes beginning in the Gdansk shipyards spread rapidly throughout the country, and violence became widespread. Gomulka was replaced by Edward Gierek, but no Soviet intervention occurred. The Polish Communist party maintained control of the population. The working class was subdued for the time being, but economic problems were to persist throughout the 1970s.

CHINA

The other problem area for the Soviets was China. During the 1960s, the Sino-Soviet dispute developed into a power struggle as a result of the inability of the two countries to resolve a number of key issues. Ideological leadership for the communist world still emanated from Moscow, and any deviation from Soviet strategy or challenge to Soviet leadership was not permitted. China wished to initiate its own militant policies in Third World countries and resented Soviet overtures to India in particular. The Chinese were also resentful of their military dependence on Moscow, which resulted from Soviet unwillingness to assist them in the development of nuclear technology. As well, longstanding border grievances existed between the Soviet Union and China. On 2 March 1969, Soviet troops were ambushed by the Chinese near Damansky Island. The Soviets took steps to reinforce their border, and by 1972, the 7242 km border with China was guarded by 44 Soviet divisions, and one quarter of the Soviet air force was moved from west to east. The Soviets now had a greater concentration of forces along the Chinese border than they did in Eastern Europe, where only 31 divisions were deployed.

The United States viewed the Sino-Soviet split as an opportunity to step in between the two communist powers and mend its own relationship with China. In 1969, trade and travel restrictions that had been in place since the Korean War were relaxed. The Chinese responded in 1971 with an invitation to an American table-tennis team to compete in China. This "ping-pong diplomacy" was followed by the startling American announcement that President Nixon would travel to China to re-establish diplomatic relations with China. Gestures of good will preceded the visit. The Americans refrained from exercising pressure on the United Nations when Nationalist China was replaced in the

Security Council by Communist China in October 1971. In December, the Americans took the side of Pakistan against India, China's enemy, in a war which resulted in the creation of the new state of Bangladesh (formerly East Pakistan). In February 1972, Richard Nixon became the first American president to set foot on Chinese soil. The most notable agreement reached during this visit was a statement of joint opposition to attempts by outside nations at establishing hegemony in East Asia—a clear warning to the Soviet Union. Cultural and commercial contacts were also to be cultivated.

AMERICAN INVOLVEMENT IN VIETNAM

The United States had re-established its relationship with China at a time when American armed forces were hopelessly mired in the Vietnam War. The American intervention in Vietnam had begun in the 1950s, with military assistance to the French. By 1954, the Americans were paying for 80 per cent of the French war effort in Indo-China. In 1957, Eisenhower applied the domino theory to Indo-China. Vietnam lay on the West's defensive perimeter and was therefore of strategic significance in the American sphere of influence. According to Eisenhower, if the United States did not take a stand against communism in Vietnam, all of Southeast Asia could fall under communist control. Thus began one of the most controversial wars in the USA's history. From 1959 to 1975, some 55 000 Americans were killed, 303 000 were wounded, and $150 billion was spent in a war that ended with American withdrawal and a communist takeover. Even today there is no agreement on the validity of American involvement in Vietnam. There is agreement, however, that the war had dramatic effects on American society.

Escalating American involvement in the Vietnam War began in 1965, with the American bombing of North Vietnam and a significant increase in the number of troops committed. Between 1965 and 1968 there were more than 500 000 American military personnel stationed in Vietnam. By the end of 1967, more bombs had been dropped on Vietnam than on Europe throughout the Second World War. This commitment to war came at a time when President Lyndon Johnson was implementing his war on poverty in an effort

In 1970, four students were killed and numerous others were wounded when the National Guard opened fire on a group of anti-war protesters in the USA. This caused even more unrest among Americans. This photograph was taken as students ran from the bullets and tear gas at Kent State University.

VIETNAM'S LEGACY

The Vietnam War continued to divide the American people even after its conclusion. Returning war veterans were denied the heroes' welcome accorded to veterans of former wars; instead, they faced either contempt or indifference. Even the building of the Vietnam Veterans Memorial proved to be contentious. Dedicated in 1982, this black granite wall is imbedded deep in the soil, much as the war is buried in the American psyche. Listed in chronological order of their deaths, all the names of the American casualties of Vietnam appear. This monument is now one of the three most visited sites in Washington, D.C.

to produce the Great Society. The American economy was expected to fund two kinds of war without substantial increases in taxation. By 1971, although the defence budget remained at 4 to 5 per cent of the GNP, the welfare budget had risen to absorb 12 per cent of the GNP. At the same time, the United States' share of the world's gold reserves had shrunk from 68 per cent in 1950 to 27 per cent in 1973. The American economy appeared to be floundering. The dollar was taken off the gold standard and allowed to float against other currencies. Signs of recession and economic decay appeared.

The Vietnam War occurred at a time when American society was undergoing fundamental change. The civil rights movement, the women's movement, the environmental movement, and anti-establishment groups that manifested themselves in communes of flower children all challenged the traditional bases of American society. Civil disobedience, draft-dodging, and widespread anti-war demonstrations indicated a decline in the number of those who supported the war. The growing divisiveness was promoted by the mass media: for the first time in history a war was fought in the living rooms of the USA. Though the Tet Offensive of 1968—the attack by the Viet Cong on all American bases in Vietnam—was a military failure for North Vietnam, it proved to be the undoing of the American war effort. Faced by a now-monumental resistance of the American public to involvement in Vietnam, the American government appeared to lose resolve. If an escalation of American commitment prior to 1968 had not deterred so widespread an attack as the Tet Offensive, then surely the whole war was a hopeless venture. The election of Richard Nixon as president came largely as a result of his promise to extricate the United States from Vietnam.

THE NUCLEAR ARMS RACE AND ARMS CONTROL

In 1945, the United States had a monopoly of nuclear weaponry unchallenged until the Soviets tested their first atomic device four years later. Initially, the United States hoped to use nuclear superiority as a deterrent to Soviet aggression; most military analysts estimated conventional Soviet forces at twice those of the United States. In fact, some figures suggested upwards of 4 million Soviet

soldiers under arms against about 1.4 million Americans. More conservative estimates placed Soviet conventional forces at slightly less than double those of the Americans. Whatever the case, the difference was significant and to the USA's disadvantage. For almost two decades, the superpowers waged an arms race, each attempting to achieve superiority in numbers and types of weapons. Until the late 1960s or early 1970s, the United States retained nuclear superiority, but the Soviet Union maintained conventional superiority. During this time, agreement was reached on testing and nonproliferation, but it was not until the 1970s that any agreement on the limitation of numbers of armaments was reached.

Once the United States and the Soviet Union mastered the production of thermonuclear power, they became preoccupied with developing delivery systems, to convey these nuclear weapons to their targets. Both relied heavily on personnel, documents, and materials captured at German laboratories, factories, and missile sites. The 1950s and the 1960s were characterized by technological innovations that resulted in a vast array of new weapons, none of which could be used without the risk of an all-out nuclear holocaust. The arms race developed out of a desire on each side to possess enough new and technologically superior weaponry to prevent the opposition from striking first.

In August 1957, the Soviet Union successfully tested an intercontinental ballistic missile. On 4 October 1957, the Soviets launched *Sputnik I,* the first earth satellite to achieve space orbit successfully. The following month, they launched a satellite containing a test animal. Khrushchev, emboldened by these successes, determined to bluff regarding the true size and quality of the aircraft and missile force of the Soviet Union. Using supposed superiority of Soviet technology as leverage, Khrushchev attempted in 1958 to wrest control of West Berlin from the West. The United States had, however, developed the U-2 spy plane, capable of flying surveillance missions without being detected by radar. In May 1960, the U-2 plane piloted by Gary Powers was shot down on a routine flight over Siberia. It was now obvious to the world that the United States had been monitoring missile sites in Siberia and had been able to ascertain Soviet strategic inferiority. Khrushchev's bluff had been called.

The United States conducted its first satellite launch in February 1958, but the Soviets continued to be in the forefront of space technology. In 1960, they sent two dogs into space and then successfully

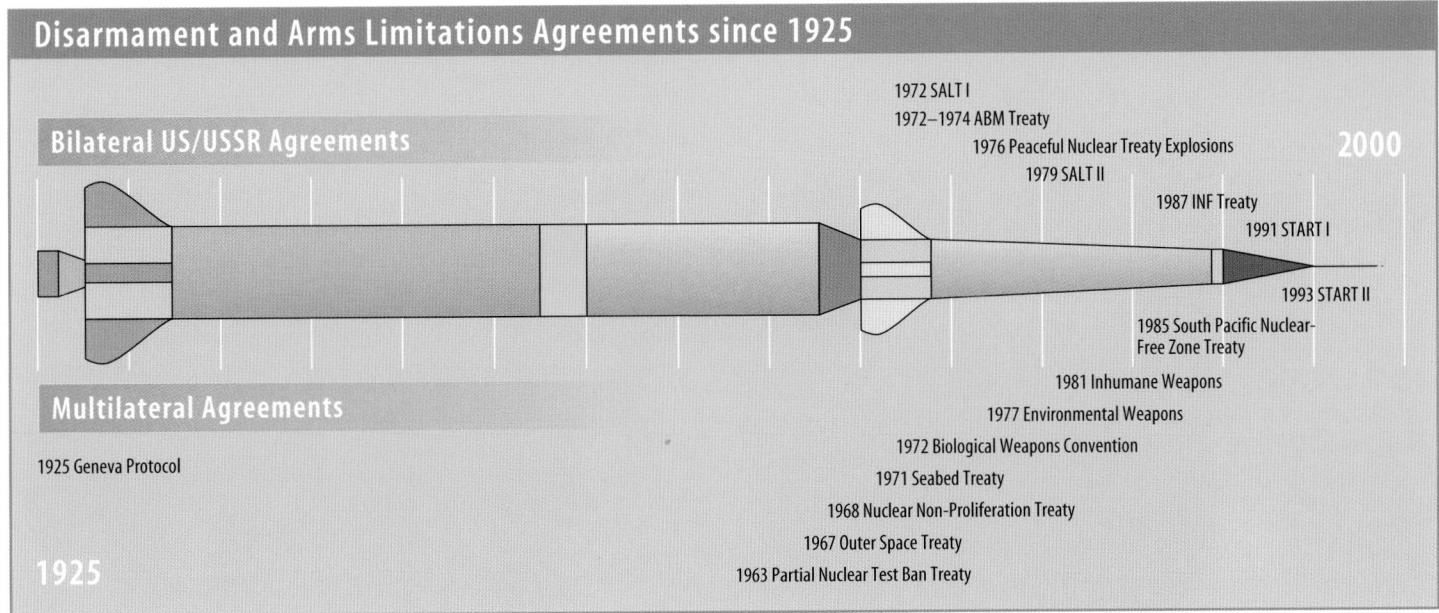

Disarmament and Arms Limitations Agreements since 1925

Bilateral US/USSR Agreements

1972 SALT I
1972–1974 ABM Treaty
1976 Peaceful Nuclear Treaty Explosions
1979 SALT II
1987 INF Treaty
1991 START I
1993 START II

2000

Multilateral Agreements

1925 Geneva Protocol

1985 South Pacific Nuclear-Free Zone Treaty
1981 Inhumane Weapons
1977 Environmental Weapons
1972 Biological Weapons Convention
1971 Seabed Treaty
1968 Nuclear Non-Proliferation Treaty
1967 Outer Space Treaty
1963 Partial Nuclear Test Ban Treaty

1925

retrieved them from orbit. On 12 April 1961, Yuri Gagarin was the first human being to travel in space. On 14 April, this Soviet cosmonaut returned triumphant to parade through Moscow with Khrushchev. Despite these achievements, the Soviets lagged behind the United States in the arms race. The U-2 flights had revealed that significantly fewer missiles were in place than the Soviets suggested, and that the Americans had the lead in long-range strategic weapons. The development of the Polaris missile, with a range of 1700 and later 2500 nautical miles, gave the United States strategic superiority, for no point on earth lay outside that range. By 1964, the United States possessed 1880 strategic delivery units to the Soviet Union's 472. The Cuban Missile Crisis was in part precipitated by the Soviet attempt to overcome inferiority in missile deployment by strategic missile placement within the American sphere of influence.

Following the Cuban Missile Crisis in 1962, the Soviet Union and the United States agreed on the Partial Test Ban Treaty, which limited nuclear testing in the atmosphere, under water, and in outer space. Despite the realization that nuclear war would wreak devastation on the whole earth, the superpowers continued throughout the 1960s to stockpile nuclear arsenal. The superpowers still were engaged in brinkmanship. By 1969, the Soviet Union had tripled its stock of intercontinental ballistic missiles (ICBMs) and increased significantly its supply of submarine-launched ballistic missiles (SLBMs). The USA's superiority was at an end, and the new American goal became sufficiency. Thus, in the early 1970s, rather than build increasing numbers of the

After the Second World War, the world community attempted to establish total nuclear disarmament. Later, the focus shifted to arms limitations agreements when it became apparent that world powers would never agree to total disarmament.

STRIVING FOR PEACE

After the destruction of Hiroshima and Nagasaki, efforts were made to secure total disarmament. This proved impossible and by the 1960s arms limitation had become the objective. Negotiations have had only a limited effect and the superpowers have built up arsenals of lethal weapons including many with nuclear capability. In 1987 the INF Treaty between the USA and the USSR was signed. The agreement was the first to eliminate medium range nuclear weapons, and some progress was made on cutting back on other nuclear arms.

same type of weapons, the Americans embarked on a program designed to develop innovation in nuclear technology. A new anti-ballistic missile program was created. In addition, the Multiple Independently Targeted Re-entry Vehicle (MIRV), which would give the ICBM three to ten separately targeted nuclear warheads, was developed.

To check this dangerous and expensive arms race, the United States and the Soviet Union began in the late 1960s to discuss the possibility of limiting the

201

The Soviet Union and the United States engaged in a heated arms race throughout the 1970s. Both conventional and nuclear weapons were developed. These Soviet troops are just a minuscule part of the USSR's firepower.

numbers of strategic weapons. In 1968, the United States, the Soviet Union, and Great Britain signed the Nuclear Non-Proliferation Treaty. By the time it came into force in March 1970, 97 countries had agreed to limit the nuclear fraternity to those countries currently in possession of nuclear technology. The exceptions to the agreement were China and France.

SALT I AND SALT II

Throughout these discussions, no limits had ever been placed on the numbers of nuclear weapons possessed by the nuclear powers. This changed on 26 May 1972 when the United States and the Soviet Union signed the **Strategic Arms Limitation Talks agreement (SALT I)**. The agreement limited both sides to two ABM (anti-ballistic missile) sites and 200 interceptors each. The ABM was designed to intercept and destroy incoming missiles before they reached their targets. Equality in ABMs would presumably preserve strategic balance and limit the possibility of either side gambling on a first strike.

Limits were also placed on offensive weapons. American ICBMs were frozen at 1054 while the Soviet Union was allowed to expand its arsenal from 1530 to 1618. The Americans could deploy 44 submarines with 710 launchers and 1000 land-based missiles, while the Soviets could deploy 62 submarines with 950 launchers and 1410 land-based missiles. Although the Soviet Union retained superiority in total numbers of weaponry, the United States enjoyed superiority in those weapons systems not covered by treaty limitations, notably long-range bombers and MIRVs. SALT I was a historic accord in the limitation of strategic weaponry. Because many types of weapons were left unregulated, however, it did not stop the arms race. The Soviets were anxious to develop the MIRV and the United States was working on the Trident submarine, the MX, and cruise missiles.

The SALT I agreement had a five-year life span. Soon after signing it, the Soviets and the Americans began talks on SALT II, which would control weapons technology. By 1974, Presidents Ford and Brezhnev had agreed in principle to limit strategic missiles. The United States and the Soviet Union would each be allowed 2400 strategic missiles, of which 1320 could be equipped with MIRVs. The United States would be allowed 525 strategic bombers to the Soviet Union's 160. Instead of placing a freeze on the development of nuclear weapons, the agreement placed limits on the numbers of weapons both sides could actually build.

SALT II was sharply criticized in the American Senate and this, along with the Soviet invasion of Afghanistan, prevented ratification of the treaty. In spite of this failure to ratify, however, both sides maintained the spirit of the agreement until 1985.

Arms-control agreements in the 1970s failed to prevent the development of a world with two superpowers determined to maintain first-strike capability and an arsenal of weaponry designed to intimidate opponents. A situation of **Mutually Assured Destruction (MAD)** was maintained as both sides raced to develop new and technologically superior nuclear and conventional weapons. With the Soviet invasion of Afghanistan in December 1979, NATO decided to ask the United States to deploy 572 cruise and Pershing II missiles in Western Europe to counter the perceived threat from Soviet SS-20s. From 1980 to 1985, the American defence budget rose from $ 197 billion to $ 296 billion, an increase of 51 per cent. Over 25 per cent of this increase went to strategic weapons systems like the B-1 bomber, the MX missile, and the Trident submarine. The remainder of the budget was spent on conventional forces, including amphibious and airlift forces used in Third World operations. Claiming that the Soviets had achieved military superiority rather than equality, President Ronald Reagan put all arms-control negotiations on hold for the first year and a half of his presidency, and concentrated on a nuclear defensive strategy.

The most dramatic of Reagan's proposals was the **Strategic Defense Initiative (SDI)**—the Star Wars project—a defensive shield which would hit and destroy incoming enemy missiles. Proposed as early as 1983, SDI was not given much attention until 1984 and 1985, when it came to the forefront of the nuclear debate. The concept was touted as scientifically based, but was in fact vague and ambiguous. The total defensive shield or astrodome proposed by Reagan would protect all of the United States' territory from attack by Soviet missiles. The cost and impracticability of this proposal encouraged the concept of a selective shield, one that would protect American missiles needed for a counter-strike. A third proposal was an offensive laser system based in outer space, designed to attack Soviet cities directly and incinerate them within a matter of hours. The fantasy of SDI was contrary to the terms of the ABM treaty (a part of SALT I) and seemed destined to unleash a new arms race. It may have been a bargaining chip designed for use in arms negotiations with the Soviets, or a means of achieving nuclear superiority over the USSR. Whatever the

intention, SDI did alarm the Soviet Union and became a point of contention in any attempts to hold arms negotiations.

In 1977, the Soviet Union led the United States three to two in megatonnage—the explosive yield of bombs measured in tonnes of TNT. However, it lagged significantly in missile accuracy. From 1971 to 1984, defence spending in the Soviet Union grew by 5 per cent per annum. Because of the nature of a planned economy like that of the Soviet Union, it is difficult to compare defence spending with any assurance of accuracy, but estimates suggest that while the United States devoted 5.5 per cent of GNP to defence, the Soviet Union spent between 13 and 17 per cent. In the late 1970s, Soviet warhead accuracy improved, and technology imported from Japan allowed their submarines to move more quietly. In the 1980s, the quality, sophistication, and capability of Soviet aircraft, submarines, warships, and missiles improved significantly. But by 1985, the large commitment of monies to the defence sector of the economy was causing serious problems in the domestic economy. Soviet citizens were no longer willing to forego consumer goods in order to maintain a large military establishment.

From 1979 to 1985, the superpowers could not agree about arms control, and the arms race continued to escalate. They could not agree on arms control because they could not agree on matters such as the Soviet invasion of Afghanistan and NATO's nuclear policy. Ronald Reagan portrayed the Soviet Union as the evil empire and the ageing leadership of the Soviet Union—Leonid Brezhnev, Yuri Andropov, and then Konstantin Chernenko—as rigid in its approach to arms negotiations. In 1981, Reagan proposed the zero option, according to which the Americans would not deploy missiles in Europe if the Soviets dismantled their SS-20s there. The Soviets refused after intensive bargaining, fearing that French and British missiles would remain to give NATO an advantage. In November 1981, Reagan proposed the Strategic Arms Reduction Talks (START) in place of the Strategic Arms Limitation Talks (SALT) in an effort to reduce the number of ballistic missiles as well as nuclear warheads. The agreement would require the Soviets to destroy two-thirds of their missiles and the United States to destroy half of its own. No limits were placed on cruise missiles or bombers, however, in both of which areas the United States maintained superiority. No progress was made in any area of arms control until Gorbachev came to power in the Soviet Union in 1985.

On 8 December 1987 Mikhail Gorbachev and Ronald Reagan signed the intermediate-range nuclear forces (INF) treaty in Washington, D.C.

REAGAN AND GORBACHEV

A number of factors converged in the period 1985 to 1989 to usher in a new era of détente. Reagan, in his last four-year term of office, was concerned with his historical legacy and was anxious to erase the unpopular anti-communist stance he had developed in his first term in office. The new Soviet leader, Mikhail Gorbachev, inherited a backward economy that spent disproportionate amounts of money on the military at the expense of consumer goods. The two leaders held summit meetings on five separate occasions from 1985 to 1988.

The first meeting between Reagan and Gorbachev occurred in November 1985, in Geneva. At this time, Gorbachev announced his intention to modernize the Soviet economy, and the two leaders agreed that a nuclear war could never be won and must not be risked. The meeting established a friendly relationship that laid the groundwork for future negotiations.

In Reykjavik, Iceland, in late 1986, Gorbachev presented Reagan with sweeping proposals for arms reductions that would eliminate 50 per cent of the strategic missiles held by both sides and limit the testing of Reagan's Strategic Defense Initiative (SDI) to the laboratory. Unwilling to kill SDI, Reagan rejected the proposal. The tables had now been turned; the United States had to this point taken the initiative in arms-reduction proposals. The Soviet leader was now directing the negotiations. Gorbachev began to concentrate on the zero option proposal Reagan had made in 1981.

The Washington summit of December 1987 proved to be an important occasion in the struggle for arms control: Reagan and Gorbachev signed the first Soviet-American disarmament treaty ever. The intermediate-range nuclear force (INF) treaty called for the destruction of 1600 Soviet missiles and 400 American missiles, and established a system for on-site verification that made cheating impossible. The unequal ratio reflected the vast superiority of Soviet conventional forces in Europe. Although the missile reduction touched only 4 per cent of the total arsenal, the INF treaty was viewed as an auspicious beginning to a new era of friendliness between the Soviet Union and the United States.

When Reagan traveled to Moscow in May 1988, the primary topic of discussion was human rights. Freedom of speech, religion, and emigration were promoted by Reagan as he met with prominent Soviet dissidents. A little progress was made on arms control as well. The United States Senate ratified the INF treaty on the eve of the Moscow summit, and Reagan retracted his statement that the Soviet Union was an evil empire. Although no concrete agreement on START was reached, both sides agreed that progress had been made.

In December 1988, Gorbachev paid a farewell visit to Reagan in New York. Speaking before the United Nations, Gorbachev pledged a reduction in total Soviet armed forces of 10 per cent, withdrawal of 50 000 troops from Eastern Europe, and a reduction by 50 per cent of Soviet tanks in East Germany, Czechoslovakia, and Hungary. He reiterated his commitment to restructure the Soviet economy in an atmosphere of openness, or *glasnost,* thus directing the Soviet Union on a new path. In three short years, Gorbachev had announced revolutionary change in the Soviet Union and provided the framework for constructive negotiation with the United States. A new era had indeed been born.

CASE STUDY

STAR WARS DEFENCE

The highly controversial Strategic Defense Initiative was a futuristic proposal promising to defend the United States by the establishment of a missile shield. Is a superpower justified in spending the enormous amount of money essential for such a project when so much of the world's population is denied the basic necessities of life? Debate this question with your classmates.

On 23 March 1983, President Reagan announced his Strategic Defense Initiative (SDI) to build and deploy a space umbrella that would make North America immune to intercontinental missile attacks from outer space. No enemy would fire its missiles at the USA if it knew none of them would reach their targets. And without their own antiballistic missile (ABM) defence, their cities and military installations would be vulnerable to an American retaliatory strike. Thus, the construction of the shield would change forever the shape of military strategy and foreign policy. It would ensure American predominance among the world's powers, and negate the Soviet Union's missile forces. Not only would it make North America safe from missile attack, it could bring about peaceful co-existence among the world's nuclear powers and bring an end to the possibility of nuclear warfare.

SDI was the latest in a long line of strategies designed to protect North America from nuclear attack. Before the development of intercontinental-range missiles, defences were established against the manned bomber attack expected over the North Pole. Bomb shelters were built and plans were developed to evacuate cities in the four to six hours available before the bombers arrived. The development of missiles cut the warning time to under 15 minutes and strategies were changed to ensure a retaliatory strike could get off the ground before being destroyed. Thousands of missiles were built to ensure that even if North America suffered major damage, enough missiles would survive to hit back. Mutually Assured Destruction (MAD) meant that war would be avoided if both sides realized that the damage they would sustain, even in victory, would be unacceptably high.

Anti-missile defences were then designed that would shoot down the incoming missiles before they got to their target. The American system (Spartan-Sprint) consisted of two missiles. The first was designed to explode a nuclear device in space to melt the incoming missiles, although the flash would likely set fire to the surface below. A second, and faster, missile was designed to engage missiles that the initial firing had missed. It was agreed that the two superpowers could deploy two of these systems—one around a military target and the other around a centre of population. Despite the best efforts of designers and technicians, it was found that 90 per cent of the missiles would always get through, doing unacceptable damage.

The Americans and the Soviets agreed to give up on all but token missile defences in the ABM treaty of 1972. The systems simply did not work and they could not guarantee security from attack. The key to missile defence is totality. If only one missile gets through, is its damage unacceptably high? In the 1970s, there was doubt as to how many missiles, if any, could be stopped. In the 1980s, SDI held out the promise that no missile would get through the defence screens.

The American High Frontier plan, in part a response to the experimentation of the Soviets with a laser-shield defence called Red Shield, called for a three-layered defence. The first layer would consist of 432 satellites armed with chemical lasers that would intercept enemy missiles after their launch. A second layer would protect American missile bases against missiles that did get through. A third layer of particle-beam weapons would be constructed in space in subsequent years. The development of particle-beam weapons depended on the ability of scientists to control and direct the laser against thousands of individual missiles during the milliseconds of a hydrogen-bomb explosion. At the time, Defense Secretary Weinberger doubted if the idea of particle-beam defence was based on anything but hope. Many believed that even if the system could be made, it would be too vulnerable to Soviet attack to be a credible deterrent.

There are three phases in a missile's flight when the missile is vulnerable to attack. The first is the booster phase, when the missile is being carried through the atmosphere into space. During this

Nations with Nuclear Weapons (1996)

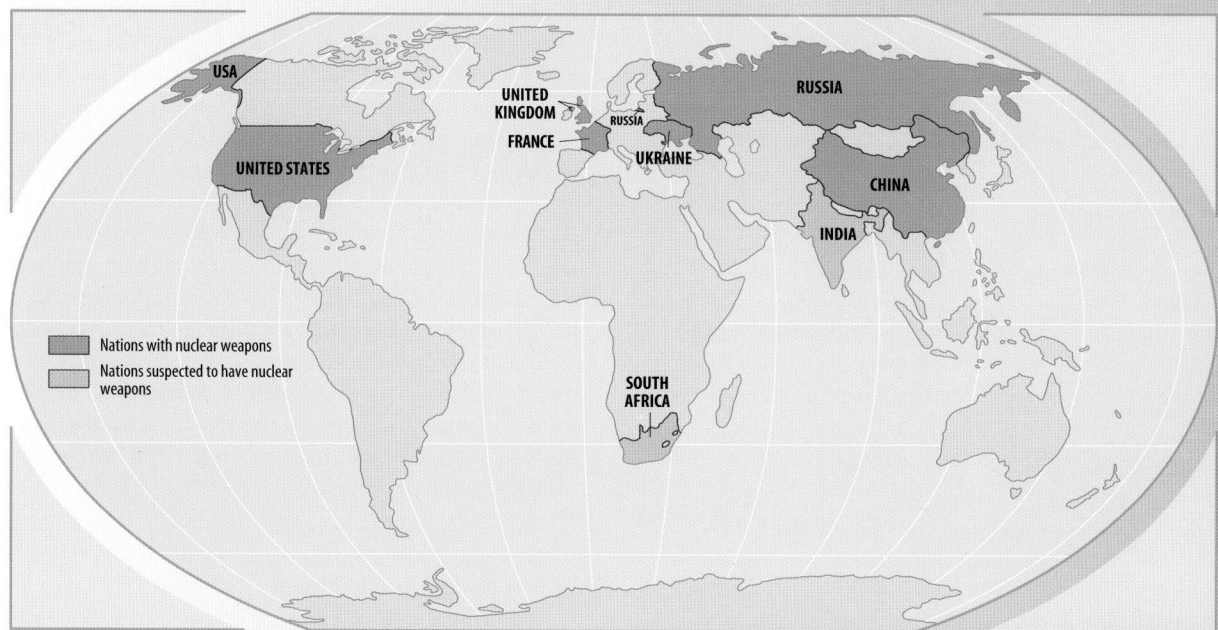

Nations with nuclear weapons

Nations suspected to have nuclear weapons

The United States and Russia are no longer the only countries with nuclear weapons.

phase, the missile's multiple, independently targeted warheads are still attached. Attack during the booster phase has the advantage of destroying all the warheads before they separate from the main missile. Also, only during the booster phase does the burning of the rocket engines emit infra-red signals that facilitate detection.

Defences have to be situated close to the enemy to be able to attack the thousands of missiles within five minutes of their firing from silos or submarines. Only lasers and particle beams are capable of this task. To get particle-beam weapons close enough to the launch sites would require their positioning on space platforms overlooking Soviet missile bases. These platforms would be obvious targets for Soviet attack.

An alternative would be to construct Earth-based lasers whose concentrated beams would bounce off relay mirrors orbiting 45 000 km above the atmosphere. These would direct energy beams at the rising missiles. The mirrors would have to be kept perfectly synchronized for this system to work. Another proposal would be to use X-ray lasers powered by nuclear explosion and carried aloft by their own interceptor missiles.

The second phase during which missiles are vulnerable is when they reach outer space. At this point their warheads have separated and begun the descent toward individual targets. As many as 10

warheads could be deployed from each missile. One way to destroy missiles in this phase would be to blanket their path with nuclear explosions that would melt them. The fields of intense radiation would, builders hoped, be drawn out into space. Attempts to track individual targets would be difficult because of hundreds of decoys, clouds of aluminum chaff, and infra-red-emitting aerosol sprays. A firing of 10 000 missiles would register as hundreds of thousands of potential targets and overload defence computer systems. Unable to identify the targets, computers would not give the command to fire, so all the warheads would get through.

The third-phase defence depends on getting at the missiles when they are well within the atmosphere and close to their targets. However, missiles can be primed to explode upon sensing interception, as well as when they are within a few kilometres of targets. Exploding as much as 20 km above the target would effectively incinerate whatever lay below.

The task of designing any SDI system is challenging to scientists and technicians. Can every enemy missile on land, and sea, or in the air be identified, targeted, and destroyed within minutes of its firing? Is there the technology to construct and control the laser and particle-beam devices required for a guaranteed defence? Is it really possible to establish platforms in deep space that are immune from attack? Even if the SDI system becomes functional, it would not defend against cruise missiles and nuclear bombers designed to fly under land-based radar screens.

The announcement of SDI placed tremendous strain on Soviet resources. Convinced that, given enough incentives, American industry would no doubt at some future date create an anti-missile umbrella, the Soviets started to develop their own SDI system and, in addition, to develop plans to destroy American SDI facilities.

History has shown that new weapons systems have only a brief period of predominance. Any SDI system would only trigger a new system to overwhelm it. And if obviously outdistanced, would a superpower be tempted to carry out a pre-emptive strike, if they had nothing to lose by it?

The American Defense Department announced that as early as 1987 it would begin tracking and targeting enemy missile sites from space shuttles. The development of the Aegis class of cruisers, using computer-controlled firing systems, has indicated that the SDI concept is possible on a small scale. But will SDI turn outer space into a battlefield? Can we risk placing continental defence into the circuits of pre-programmed computers? Would war of such magnitude place the survival of humankind at risk? SDI has raised more questions than it answers.

With the vast changes within the Soviet bloc in the late 1980s and early 1990s, however, Reagan's successor, George Bush, was less enthused about SDI. In his 1991 budget, Bush downplayed the importance of SDI. Still, the USA has now been able to intercept dummy warheads in outer space with success. President Bill Clinton, Bush's successor, has continued the policy of downsizing the American nuclear arsenal.

1. Devise a scenario to achieve SDI. What resources and technology would be needed?

2. How would SDI change North American military planning?

3. Although radiation from the initial intercepts would be sucked into the vacuum of space, what danger would high altitude nuclear explosions present to the globe?

4. Devise strategies to overload or get through the SDI shield.

5. Relate what the SDI shield does not protect against.

6. How do breakthroughs in the technology of other countries affect a nation's defence program?

SUMMARY

After the Cuban Missile Crisis in 1962, the superpowers entered an era of détente. This period was characterized by a relaxation of international tension as both sides worked to avoid the nuclear confrontation that had threatened to erupt over Cuba. The Soviet Union was determined to establish peaceful co-existence with the West, an atmosphere in which they could focus on achieving nuclear equality with the United States. Ironically, though the missile crisis had revealed the potential horrors of nuclear confrontation, the superpowers now engaged in an arms race of unprecedented proportions.

Although the world was still dominated by the threat of superpower hostility, there were signs of change in the international power structure—in particular the Sino-Soviet split and the subsequent establishment of diplomatic ties between the United States and China.

The tension in Western Europe eased as the question of Germany and Berlin was resolved. The growth of the West German economy as well as that of Japan introduced two new economic powers. While the superpowers still dominated world affairs, it was evident that a multipolar power structure was evolving.

Over this period, arms control became the subject of superpower negotiation. The SALT I agreement lent substance to the claim that détente did in fact exist between the United States and the Soviet Union. While superpower conflict was not direct, difficulties existed in a number of other areas. The Soviet Union faced unrest in Czechoslovakia and Poland while the United States was embroiled in Vietnam.

QUESTIONS

1. What was Brezhnev's twofold challenge when he came to power in 1964?

2. What reforms did Czechoslovakia formulate in 1968?

3. Why did Moscow refuse to allow the Czechoslovakian reforms to be formalized?

4. How did the Soviet Union resolve the Prague Spring?

5. What were the key issues in the conflict between the Soviet Union and China?

6. Why did the United States re-establish a relationship with China?

7. Why did the Americans become involved in the affairs of Vietnam?

8. Describe American society at the time of the Vietnam War. How did the American people react to the war?

9. Briefly compare and contrast the USA's nuclear arsenal to that of the USSR before 1970.

10. How did weapons production in the United States and the Soviet Union change after 1970?

11. Explain the terms and the significance of SALT I and SALT II.

12. Explain the Strategic Defense Initiative.

13. Compare defence spending in the United States with that of the Soviet Union. How does level of defence spending affect the domestic economy of each country?

14. What is START?

15. Between 1985 and 1989 Gorbachev and Reagan met five times. Make a chart identifying the location, year, and results of each meeting.

CRITICAL ANALYSIS

1. Explain how war might be effectively deterred.

2. Which has the greater degree of stability, an arms race or co-existence? Explain.

3. Why did nuclear war not break out between the USA and the USSR?

4. Study the possibility of establishing SDI. Given time, would the USA be able to put SDI in place? How might this change the balance of power?

5. Explain the danger a superpower faces in being first to disarm.

RESEARCH PROJECTS

1. Compare and contrast the Prague Spring of 1968 with Prague in the autumn of 1989. Discuss the role of the Soviet Union in both cases.

2. Research the anti-war movement that emerged in the United States during the Vietnam War. Identify the reasons for this movement, as well as the actions taken against the war.

3. The Brezhnev years were difficult years for dissidents. Explain Soviet policy on dissidence, and research means by which dissent was controlled. Illustrate by examining the life of a dissident like Alexander Solzhenitzyn.

4. Research the advances made in nuclear weapons technology during the period 1970 to 1985. Evaluate the effectiveness of the arms race during this period.

ACTIVITIES

1 Chart

Make a chart illustrating the arms race from 1963 to 1985. Identify the types and numbers of weapons possessed by the United States and the Soviet Union.

2 International Summit Meeting

Topic: Disarmament

Students will represent a variety of individuals to discuss the viability of world disarmament. Students must promote the viewpoint of the individual which they represent. Some participants might be Ronald Reagan, Mikhail Gorbachev, Alexander Solzhenitzyn, Pierre Trudeau, Margaret Thatcher, George McGovern, David Lewis, and Helmut Kohl.

3 Panel Discussion

Establish a panel to discuss the American involvement in the Vietnam War. Students might represent a Vietnam veteran, a draft dodger, a Canadian journalist, Lyndon Johnson, and a student of Kent State University.

HISTORICAL ANALYSIS

THE VIETNAM WAR

The intervention of the USA in the Vietnam War was highly controversial. Analyse the following quotations in order to determine the rationale for foreign involvement in what was perceived by some people as a civil war. Should any of the major powers have been involved in the Vietnam conflict? Explain.

> 1. ... we shall pay any price, bear any burden, meet any hardship, support any friend, oppose any foe in order to ensure the survival and success of liberty.
>
> —John Fitzgerald Kennedy

> 2. Kennedy and Johnson both had good information. They escalated the war because politically they could not accept defeat in war ...
>
> —Leslie Gelb, the *Pentagon Papers*

> 3. Were not the communists getting around containment and penetrating the American defence perimeter through wars of national liberation? The United States is committed by treaty and pledge to the defence of Vietnam. What would our other allies think of our will to arrest the spread of communism should we fail?
>
> —Dean Rusk

> 4. The United States had made excessive commitment to an area that was not essential to the global balance of power. It was a guerrilla war supported by the people and could only be won by killing everyone in sight.
>
> —George Kennan

> 5. Hanoi saw the war as one of liberation from imperialism. The people would defend the nation against invasion in a people's war of freedom.
>
> —Melvin Gurtov

THE MIDDLE EAST:
TURBULENCE & INSTABILITY

FOCUS ON CONFLICT AND STABILITY

Today Egypt is entirely free. Not a single foreign flag flies over Egyptian soil. For the first time in centuries, we are completely free to fight for our destiny ... [We must strengthen our forces, in order] to liberate all Arabs so that the lands of the Arabs may belong to them, and so that the Palestine tragedy may not be repeated and we may be able to restore to the people of Palestine their right to freedom and existence.

Egyptian president Gamal Abdel Nasser, in an address to a mass rally in Cairo's Republic Square, 19 June 1956.

It is with a feeling of deep reverence and consecration that I open the Constituent Assembly of the State of Israel— the first Knesseth Israel *of our time—in this eternal city of Jerusalem. This is a great moment in our history. Let us give thanks and praise to the God of Israel, who in His mercy has granted us the privilege of witnessing this redemption of our people after centuries of affliction and suffering.*

Dr. Chaim Weizmann, provisional president of the new state of Israel, on the opening of its first parliamentary session in Jerusalem, 14 February 1949.

The creation of Israel in 1948 brought a new set of

political circumstances to the Middle East. Examine the

results of the creation of Israel and the implications for

future stability in the region, from the perspective of one

of the following: Israel; surrounding Arab countries; the

Palestine Liberation Organization (PLO); the United States.

Be prepared to defend your position.

OVERVIEW

In this chapter, the creation of Israel, the Suez Crisis, the Six-Day War, the Iran-Iraq War, Lebanon, the PLO, and the Gulf War are all discussed. In addition, the importance of the Middle East as an oil-producing region is examined in the context of its international relationships with the USA and the former USSR.

A JEWISH HOMELAND

In 1948 the state of Israel was carved out of Palestine in order to provide a homeland for Jews fleeing Europe.

ARAB–ISRAELI WAR: 1948

The first conflict between the Arabs and the Jews occurred as soon as the new state of Israel was created.

THE SUEZ CRISIS

In 1956, Nasser of Egypt emerged as a leader in the Arab world. When he closed the Suez Canal to British and French shipping, the Israelis attacked in a bid to reduce the threat of Egyptian hegemony in the Middle East.

THE SIX–DAY WAR: 1967

In 1967, the Israelis significantly increased their territory in a lightning war against Egypt, Syria, and Jordan.

THE YOM KIPPUR WAR: 1973

Egypt and Syria retaliated against Israel in a surprise attack on the holy day of Yom Kippur in 1973.

IRAN–IRAQ WAR

From 1980 to 1988, Iran and Iraq fought a devastating war over control of resources, the Shatt-al-Arab waterway, and hegemony in the Middle East.

THE GULF WAR

In 1990, Iraq's occupation of Kuwait threatened stability in the Middle East and instigated the UN actions to restore peace to the area.

ENVIRONMENTAL WARFARE

In 1991, during the Gulf War, it is estimated that 1.1 billion litres of oil spilled into the Persian Gulf, and hundreds of oil wells were set on fire. These tragedies have serious environmental implications.

Jerusalem, a holy place for Muslims, Jews, and Christians, has often been a focal point of conflict in the Middle East. This street in old Jerusalem is shown during a peaceful moment.

SUPERPOWER INVOLVEMENT IN THE MIDDLE EAST

Although both the United States and the former Soviet Union have been involved in the Middle East, neither superpower has been able to attain any significant amount of control in the region.

Even before Palestine was partitioned by the United Nations, Jewish refugees were flooding in. Britain refused to allow these 4700 illegal Jewish immigrants on this ship to stay in Palestine in 1947.

A JEWISH HOMELAND

The area commonly referred to as the Middle East covers the expanse of territory from Morocco to Turkey, as well as countries bordering the Red Sea, the Gulf of Aqaba, and the Persian Gulf. The strategic location of the Middle East and its enormous oil resources have made the area attractive to industrial powers throughout the twentieth century. Britain and France maintained a foothold in the region prior to the Second World War as a result of the mandate system developed under the League of Nations after the First World War and the collapse of the Ottoman Empire. The Soviet Union and the United States attempted to impose their presence in the region after the Second World War with a view to influencing events in this strategic area.

Hostility between Jews and Arabs has helped fuel the tensions in the region in the twentieth century, a confrontation that seems to defy resolution. Both the United States and the Soviet Union have acted as arms suppliers and negotiators in the area. Although no direct confrontation has occurred between them in the Middle East, there have been a number of close calls, especially during the Yom Kippur War in 1973.

The creation of the new Jewish state of Israel out of the British mandate of Palestine in 1948, and the subsequent displacement of Palestinian Arabs in the region, created the pivotal Middle East problem as it exists today. Both Arabs and Jews claim the right to Palestine, and each side maintains that its very survival depends on its control of this tract of land.

Members of the Zionist movement, which began in Europe in the mid-nineteenth century, hoped to create a Jewish state in Palestine to provide a homeland for European Jews. In 1917, Britain, anxious to enlist the support of Jewish people in the war effort, issued the Balfour Declaration, which promised British support for the establishment of a Jewish homeland in Palestine. The declaration also claimed that no action would be taken to infringe on the rights of non-Jewish Palestinians. These promises were contradictory: the rights of Muslim inhabitants were bound to be infringed upon by a large influx of Jewish immigrants.

Although the United States never formally endorsed Zionism, President Wilson had privately indicated his reluctant approval of the Balfour Declaration. Throughout the 1930s and 1940s, the Palestinian Jewish communities received substantial support from American Jews. The Second World War and the ensuing holocaust created a crisis in Palestine. As the world closed its doors to Jews desperately trying to get out of Europe to escape Hitler's concentration camps, many groups pressured the British to raise the quotas imposed on immigration to Palestine. Zionist forces began to attack both the British and the Arabs. Tensions rose as refugees were smuggled into Palestine. When illegal immigrants were caught by the British, they were interned in camps on the island of Cyprus. Finally, the United Nations stepped in and, with the support of the Soviets, who wished to see the British leave Palestine, agreed to partition the region into separate Arab and Jewish states. Thus, on 14 May 1948, the new Jewish state of Israel was created and granted membership in the United Nations. Hostilities erupted immediately, and war between Arab and Jew quickly ensued.

ARAB–ISRAELI WAR: 1948

When the state of Israel came into being in 1948, it was threatened on all sides by Arab states that had denounced the partitioning of the region of Palestine. Although the Arabs vastly outnumbered the Israelis, they were ill-trained in the art of war and unable to unite behind their field commanders. The *Haganah,* Israel's fighting force, initially had limited numbers of weapons. Czechoslovakian communists, fronting for the Soviet Union, provided the Zionist forces with arms. These weapons, along with a tremendous increase in their numbers, allowed Zionists not only to defend themselves but to expel, largely through terrorist acts, the Arabs from a number of surrounding territories. By the time this first round of fighting was over, the new state of Israel had significantly increased the size of its territory from that assigned it by the UN.

Dr. Ralph Bunche, an American who was working with the United Nations, encouraged the Arabs and Israelis to disengage in 1949. The Arabs blamed the USA for the imposition of this Jewish state in the heart of Arab territory, even though it was the Soviet Union that had supplied weapons to Israel. From this time onward, the United States found itself inevitably drawn into the Israeli camp, while the Soviet Union took an increasingly pro-Arab stance.

This first Arab-Israeli War increased rather than diminished the animosity between the two peoples. The Arabs were furious over the additional loss of territory, but resented even more the rising tide of Arab refugees out of Palestine. Many Arab soldiers left the battlefield expecting to be permitted to return home when the fighting was over. This was not to be. As many as 900 000 Palestinian Arabs became refugees—many of whom would occupy refugee camps administered by the United Nations in the West Bank, Gaza Strip, or other nearby areas. These refugee camps became hotbeds of discontent and further inflamed the already hostile atmosphere in the Middle East. Groups like the **Palestine Liberation Organization (PLO)**, which was founded in the early 1960s, recruited many fervent new members from the refugee camps.

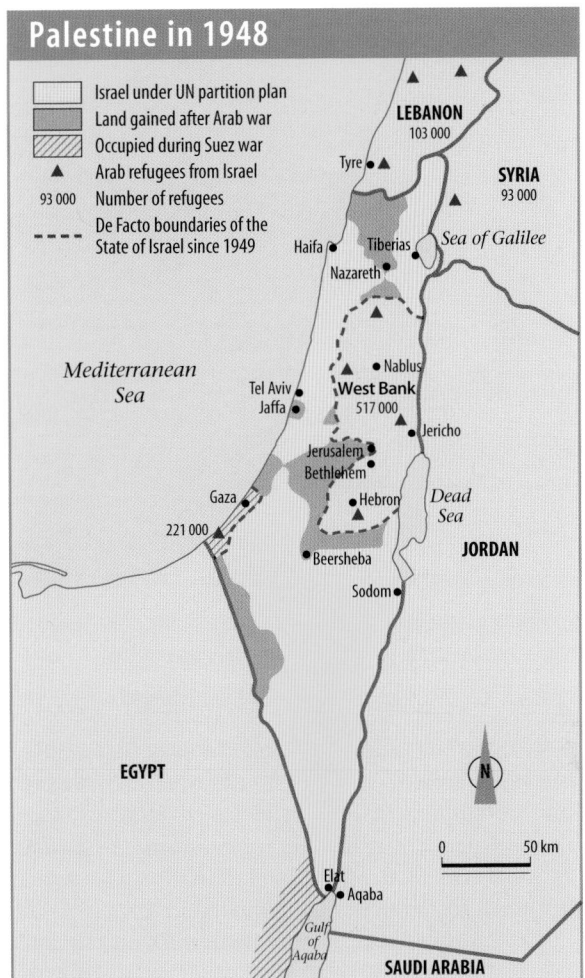

Palestine in 1948

Israel under UN partition plan
Land gained after Arab war
Occupied during Suez war
▲ Arab refugees from Israel
93 000 Number of refugees
- - - De Facto boundaries of the State of Israel since 1949

The partitioning of the region of Palestine led to the first of many wars between Israel and its neighbours. During these wars, Israel increased its territory.

THE SUEZ CRISIS

The second confrontation between Arabs and Israelis occurred in Egypt in 1956. On 23 July 1952, Colonel Gamal Abdel Nasser deposed King Farouk of Egypt and emerged as the leading Arab nationalist in the Middle East. Nasser was determined to modernize the Egyptian economy and build up the armed forces, in order to maintain the struggle against Israel. He was also influenced by the movement against colonialism that had emerged from the Bandung Conference in 1955, and did not wish either American or Soviet influence to dominate his country. Nasser requested American aid for the construction of the Aswan Dam on the Nile River, which was expected to provide vast amounts of electric power and irrigate

213

Peace keeping forces from the United Nations helped negotiate a cease-fire in the Suez Crisis. These Yugoslavian troops were on patrol duty in the Sinai Peninsula in 1957.

large tracts of land. American aid was at first granted but later refused, when it was discovered that Egypt had obtained arms from the Soviet Union. Nasser then turned to the Soviets for economic assistance as well, and established a relationship that would last until the Soviets were expelled in 1972.

On 26 July 1956, Nasser **nationalized** the Suez Canal, taking control of the canal away from the British. Although British troops had withdrawn from the region, Egypt planned to keep the canal open to European shipping. The canal was a critical trade link with the Far East. To reassert international control of the canal, the British and the French devised a plan, together with the Israelis, to go to war with the Egyptians. Keeping the plan secret from the Americans, the Israelis would launch a pre-emptive strike on Egypt, and the British and the French would intervene under the guise of restoring order. The purpose of the attack was to regain control of the canal, and to destroy Egypt's ability to threaten Israel. On 29 October 1956, the Israelis invaded the Sinai Peninsula. The next day, the British and French bombed military targets in Egypt and then followed through, on 5 November, with paratroopers and an amphibious force. The British and French were unsuccessful in their bid to regain the canal, and the heavy damage the canal suffered closed it to navigation for some time.

The Americans, for a number of reasons, took the issue to the United Nations. They did not want the British or the French to re-establish their influence in the area. The Americans wanted to strike a balance between Arab and Jew that would enable the USA at the same time to protect Israel and maintain access to Arab oil. The United Nations called for a cease-fire and the withdrawal of all foreign forces from the area. The UN also sent a peacekeeping force to maintain an international presence in the area.

The Suez Crisis resulted in the eclipse of British and French influence in the Middle East. Although the Israelis had scored a dramatic military victory, they were forced to withdraw from Egyptian territory by the threat of American economic sanctions. Nasser emerged a hero to the Arab world. The Soviet Union, which at the time of the crisis was involved in the Hungarian Revolution, suffered some recrimination for not supporting the Arab cause. However, it was obvious that the United States was not sympathetic to Nasser's goals, and the Soviet Union became the source of economic and military aid to much of the Arab world. Perhaps the most devastating outcome of the war was the negation of any possible peace talks between the Arabs and the Israelis, and the likelihood of future hostility in the area. The withdrawal of the Israeli forces and the presence of the United Nations emergency force did provide 10 years of relative stability in the area, but more fighting was to come.

THE SIX–DAY WAR

In May 1967, President Nasser of Egypt requested the withdrawal of the UN emergency force that had patrolled the Egyptian side of the truce line since the Arab-Israeli War in 1956. Nasser mobilized Egyptian forces, blocked the Straits of Tiran to Israeli shipping, and announced that he intended to promote the full restoration of an Arab Palestine. Syria, Jordan, and Iraq joined Egypt in the mobilization, and Arab oil-producing countries threatened to cut off supplies to any country that supported Israel. Nasser believed he could force the Israelis to give in without fighting. However, the Israelis determined that they had a possibility of success in a war if they stopped the Egyptians at the border. On 5 June 1967, the Israeli air force launched a pre-emptive strike against Egypt, Syria, and Jordan. The Egyptian air force was destroyed and Syrian and Jordanian troops were decimated. Within six days, the Israelis occupied the Sinai Peninsula, the West Bank of the Jordan River, and the Golan Heights in Syria. Israel now occupied three times as much territory as it had before, and in the process had significantly improved its defensive and strategic position.

The Six-Day War served to heighten tension between the Arabs and the Israelis. Guerrilla warfare was used more frequently, as the Palestine Liberation Organization and other political or paramilitary organizations carried out small-scale military operations against Israeli targets. Israel responded with massive retaliation on Arab villages and guerrilla bases. Attempts by the United Nations to negotiate a settlement between the Arabs and the Israelis were unsuccessful.

The overwhelming military victory of the Israelis led them to feel great confidence. In 1970, the United States increased the sale of arms to Israel, as Israeli forces continued to press their advantage in the area of the Suez. But an intense Palestinian nationalism had developed in the region. Because Israel now occupied such a significant portion of former Arab territory—including Jerusalem, sacred to Muslims as well as Jews and Christians—most Arab states aligned themselves solidly against Israel. The Arabs were determined to regain Arab territories and viewed the defeat in the Six-Day War as only a temporary setback.

Another significant consequence of this war was the Arab discovery of the diplomatic power of an oil embargo. European nations depended heavily on Middle East oil. Although the United States had provided an emergency supply during this crisis, it was obvious that increasing demand in all areas of the West would make a secure oil supply an important consideration in the future. Peace in the Middle East seemed an elusive dream, and the stalemate seemed indefinite.

THE YOM KIPPUR WAR: 1973

On 2 October 1973, while Jews were celebrating the holy day of Yom Kippur, Egyptian and Syrian forces launched a surprise attack on Israel. Egypt had previously attempted to negotiate the return of its territory lost to Israel, but Israel's military successes had made the Israelis unwilling to negotiate. So, by unexpectedly attacking Israel, Egypt hoped to win back territory, as well as pressure the United States into demanding settlement of the issue.

Crossing the Suez Canal, Egyptian forces breached the Bar Lev Line and opened the Sinai and

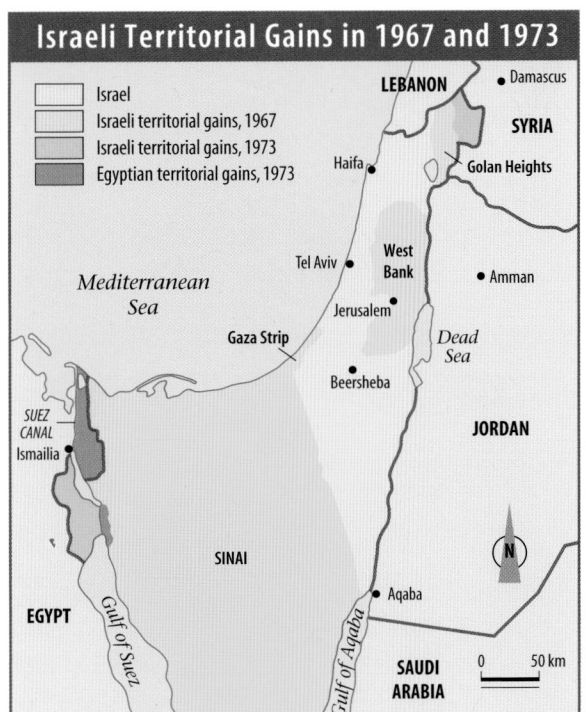

Israeli Territorial Gains in 1967 and 1973

□ Israel
□ Israeli territorial gains, 1967
■ Israeli territorial gains, 1973
■ Egyptian territorial gains, 1973

LEBANON
• Damascus
SYRIA
Haifa • ○ Golan Heights
Mediterranean Sea
Tel Aviv • West Bank
Jerusalem • • Amman
Gaza Strip *Dead Sea*
Beersheba •
SUEZ CANAL
Ismailia • JORDAN
SINAI N
EGYPT • Aqaba
Gulf of Suez *Gulf of Aqaba*
SAUDI ARABIA 0   50 km

Both in 1967 and 1973 war broke out again between Israel and its neighbours.

southern Israel to attack. Simultaneously, Syrian forces moved onto the Golan Heights with 800 tanks. It seemed a complete reversal of the events of 1967, with the Arabs in control and taking the initiative. Israeli defenders suffered heavy losses at first, but after two weeks of the bloodiest tank battles since the Second World War, the Israelis gained the upper hand. Rearmed by American military supplies which were airlifted to the region, the Israelis drove back the Syrians and for a time threatened the city of Damascus. They also launched a formidable counterattack against Egypt, and only diplomatic pressure from Washington prevented them from crossing the Suez Canal in force and occupying more Egyptian territory.

In late October, both sides finally accepted a UN-sponsored cease-fire agreement. The United States was instrumental in forging this cease-fire, and once fighting stopped in early 1974, the American secretary of state, Henry Kissinger, began the diplomatic search for a lasting peace in the region. Several obstacles blocked the path, however, and it was not until 1977 that the visit to Israel of the Egyptian president, Anwar Sadat, provided the breakthrough necessary to forge an uneasy peace. Israeli prime minister Menachem Begin responded by visiting Egypt soon afterward. These overtures culminated

OPEC

The Organization of Petroleum Exporting Countries is an oil cartel which controls the production and distribution of one of the world's most important energy resources. Select a member state of OPEC. Write a brief report outlining "your" nation's oil policies to the year 2010, within the context of OPEC.

On 10 September 1960, an intergovernmental group was established by Kuwait, Iran, Iraq, Saudi Arabia, and Venezuela to study the international pricing structure of oil. These were the original members of OPEC—the Organization of Petroleum Exporting Countries. During its first decade, OPEC was largely a public-relations group, with a small staff that made pronouncements according to the wishes of its members. The real power lay within the group of oil ministers representing the producing states. Jealously guarding their own production figures, the ministers never gave OPEC sufficiently accurate information to be of value, until 1971. In that year, the oil companies insisted that an umbrella organization negotiate all new oil contracts for the producing states. The increased demand for oil, coupled with the uncertainties of supply from Libya and the political difficulties of the Iranian shah, led the companies to demand negotiations be conducted as a single bloc. OPEC was chosen to represent the 13 sovereign producer-governments.

In 1971, OPEC helped negotiate the five-year Teheran agreements, which called for an increase of the posted price of oil to $2.18 a barrel over the next five years. The ink was hardly dry on the paper when oil prices spiraled up, as each government attempted to gobble up a larger share of the market. One by one, the governments nationalized the oil concessions in their countries, asserting control over all aspects of production. Attempts to build reserves by the world's industrial nations became even more urgent as a result of the threatened embargo during the Yom Kippur War of October 1973. Saudi Arabia and the other OPEC members began to charge what the market could bear. Oil stocks were put on auction as the producer nations ignored the OPEC agreements and raised their prices as high as possible.

Despite the threat of an oil embargo aimed at the United States and Western Europe, all the OPEC states actually increased production and exports at this time, except for Saudi Arabia, whose enormous but relatively steady volume of export was essential to global supplies.

The dramatic increase in oil prices directly affected a number of developing nations who had begun extensive industrialization programs based on low-cost energy. Having borrowed heavily at high interest rates in order to undertake these developments, they now found themselves heavily in debt and unable to complete their projects. In many Third World countries, development programs were set back decades, or were abandoned. Many were forced to default on their loans and declare bankruptcy. The gap between these countries and the industrial world widened considerably.

By 1982, world demand for oil had fallen. During the crisis decade, the oil-dependent nations had built up their reserves so that future embargoes would not be as effective. New technologies, such as more efficient automobile engines and more efficient use of supplies, had also eased demand, as had the bringing in of new oil fields outside of OPEC. North Sea discoveries in particular made the British Isles and Western Europe more self-sufficient in energy products. By 1990, OPEC's share of global oil markets had shrunk to under 70 per cent. Today, the proposal to bring the vast Siberian reserves on stream would continue the erosion of OPEC power.

The attempt by oil-producing states to form a global **cartel** to control the petroleum industry has so far failed. The goal of a cartel is to keep prices high by keeping consumer demand high. OPEC has not been successful as a cartel because its members have, in the past, flooded the market with oil, thereby lowering its price. This failure is the result of not having every oil-exporting nation within the organization; the inability of the 13 OPEC member governments to reach and maintain a common policy; and the swift way in which the industrial nations have built up their reserves and opened up new oil fields outside of OPEC control.

1. Explain how the global oil cartel affected global politics.

2. What are the strengths and weaknesses of cartels? Use OPEC as an example.

in the historic Camp David summit conference of September 1978.

The Camp David peace accords were orchestrated by the USA's Carter administration, which pledged economic support to both Israel and Egypt. Some $3 billion in military assistance would be sent to Israel and $1.5 billion to Egypt. In addition, $500 million worth of economic assistance would go to Egypt. The Camp David framework for peace was followed by a treaty of peace signed by Israel and Egypt on 26 March 1979. This treaty officially ended the state of war between the two countries, called for the withdrawal of Israeli forces from the Sinai and the return of Egyptian sovereignty in this area, established diplomatic relations between Egypt and Israel, and required that the two nations live in peace with each other.

The Camp David meeting was successful in that it allowed Egypt to concentrate more of its resources on pressing domestic needs, and increased Israel's national security. Other Arab states, however, denounced the treaty. Several key issues remained unresolved and the region remained one of the most volatile in the world. Factions of the Palestine Liberation Organization continued their guerrilla raids against Israel. As champions of the dispossessed, some Palestinian organizations today are a threat to Israeli security and a key element in the tensions of the region. The Arab refugee problem has grown since the 1947-1948 war. Some estimates suggest that as many as 3 million Palestinians have been displaced over the last four decades. Israel insists that there are also about 1 million Jewish refugees from Arab states. The refugee issue is a complex problem with no easy solution. Finally, there is the problem of the West Bank territories. These are Arab-inhabited lands under Israeli military occupation. The West Bank has become a critical issue in the future of Middle East settlement. The Arabs view this area as an important part of an Arab Palestinian nation, while the Israelis consider occupation of this territory central to Israeli security.

The Yom Kippur War had serious consequences for the United States and Western Europe as well, because the oil-producing nations of the Middle East cut off petroleum supplies and created an energy crisis. Although the embargo lasted only five months, the world economy was adversely affected by the increase in oil prices when trading resumed. Between 1973 and 1975, OPEC quadrupled the price of crude oil and produced one of the most serious economic crises of the world since the Great Depression of the 1930s.

In 1974, the General Assembly of the United Nations agreed to allow the participation of Yassir Arafat, leader of the PLO, in UN deliberations on the Palestinian question.

IRAN–IRAQ WAR

Although the Arab-Israeli conflict has monopolized international attention, the oil-rich area of the Persian Gulf has also fostered rivalry between Iran and Iraq, with both states seeking hegemony in the area. The first direct clash between the two countries came in 1969, after a decade of unrest, when Iran aided Kurdish guerrillas in Iraq, and Iraq supported Arab dissidents in the southern Iranian province of Khuzistan. The following decade saw skirmishes on either side, but only limited fighting. The two primary issues causing conflict were control of the Shatt-al-Arab—the waterway that carries the waters of the Euphrates and Tigris rivers to the Persian Gulf—and command of oil resources in the region.

Two major developments paved the way for the war between Iran and Iraq. In Iraq, Saddam Hussein emerged to seize control of his nation's administration. Determined to reassert Iraq's position in the

Ayatollah Khomeini returned to his homeland from Paris after the shah was deposed. While in power, his actions would have world-wide implications.

increased its production of oil, becoming the world's second largest exporter, with 98 per cent of its export revenue coming from the sale of oil. This revenue financed the army, technical training, industrial expansion, educational programs, and agricultural development.

In Iran, an Islamic revolution in 1979 deposed Shah Mohammed Reza Pahlevi and brought to power Ayatollah Ruhollah Khomeini. This change in leadership had profound implications for the United States, as well as for countries in the Persian Gulf area. The shah had maintained close ties with the USA. He had embarked on a Westernization process he hoped would transform his country. The reforms, called the White Revolution, were intended to provide sweeping improvements in education, health care, agriculture, and the emancipation of women. The shah's revolution was a failure. Any gains accrued only to the élite, and widened the gap between rich and poor. Although the shah claimed to be working toward democracy, his reign was dictatorial and repressive. SAVAK, the shah's secret police, suppressed any dissent through killing and brutal torture of Iranians who opposed the regime.

By the late 1970s, all segments of Iranian society objected to some aspect of the shah's rule and were ready to support his removal. In 1979, the shah's government was overthrown and Ayatollah Khomeini seized control. Khomeini intended to establish an Islamic republic, which would impose a new political order based on Islamic principles. He set out to rid Iran of Western and secular influence, believing both were responsible for the corruption of Iranian society.

In September 1980, Iraq launched an attack on Iran that resulted in massive destruction of Iran's oil facilities and Iraqi occupation of much of southwestern Iran. Two reasons for the attack appear to have been a desire to overthrow Khomeini, whom Hussein despised, and a desire to establish the Iraqi government as the dominant power in the Persian Gulf. Iraq clearly initiated the war, but many authorities concede that Iran had been guilty of persistent provocation, by trying to stir up trouble among Iraq's minority groups.

The weakness of Iran after the fall of the shah, and Iraqi uneasiness about the consequences of Khomeini's **Shi'a** fanaticism, were contributing factors as well. Also, the 1975 agreement that provided for shared ownership of the Shatt-al-Arab had been signed only reluctantly by Iraq. Iraq now wished to nullify the treaty and assume sole ownership of the critical waterway. Hussein expected an electrifying victory. He was certain that Iran, still suffering from

Persian Gulf, Hussein identified Iran and Saudi Arabia as his chief adversaries. Since both of these countries were supported by the United States, he turned to the Soviet Union for support. In 1972, before even becoming leader of Iraq, he had concluded a treaty with the Soviet Union for Soviet aid, particularly arms. Not wishing to tie himself exclusively to the Soviet Union, however, Hussein concluded an agreement with France for a nuclear reactor and research facility, and with Italy for naval and air force training. During this time, Iraq purges within its military leadership, low morale, and lack of *matériel* due to an American economic boycott, would be unable to mount an effective defence. He did not expect the determined resistance that materialized and quickly bogged the armies down in a stalemate.

In September 1981, Iran launched a successful counter-offensive in which troops fought to recapture the land initially occupied by Iraq. In 1984, Iran invaded Iraqi territory and, in February 1986, captured the Fao Peninsula that connects the Persian Gulf to the Shatt-al-Arab, effectively eliminating Iraq's access to the Gulf. At this point, it seemed that Iran was winning, but events in 1987 seemed to turn the war in favour of Iraq. Between February and April, Iran launched a concentrated assault on the southern port city of Basra, the second largest city in Iraq. Despite the deployment of 200 000 men along a 3 km-wide front, the Iranians were unable to seize the city. Concentrated Iraqi fire resulted in 50 000 to 70 000 Iranian casualties.

By 1988, it seemed clear that Iran was losing both the war and the battle to influence world opinion. The secretary general of the UN, Javier Pérez de Cuéllar, announced that a cease-fire in the Iran-Iraq War would begin on 20 August 1988, and that a 350-strong observer force would be sent to the area to monitor the truce.

The Iran-Iraq War devastated both countries and led to the largest United States naval buildup since the Second World War. Half a million lives were lost over an eight-year period. Iran seemed to have suffered the most serious devastation and was both physically and emotionally exhausted, its people's commitment and zeal drained by the Iraqi offensive in 1987. Much of Iran's industry and oil production were crippled by Iraqi air attacks. By 1988, Iran was earning only $6 billion per year from the export of oil though it needed $10 billion per year to buy arms, food, and other necessities. Iraq, for its part, owed $40 billion to Western Europe alone for arms, not counting money owed to rich Gulf creditors. It seemed that a long recovery period would be necessary to rebuild the war-torn area.

Two aspects of the Iran-Iraq War suggested a frightening legacy for the Gulf region. The use of chemical warfare and missiles as decisive weaponry on both sides gave a new dimension to conflict in the region. Saddam Hussein launched a program to develop nuclear weapons, hoping to make Iraq the first nuclear power among Islamic nations. Iraq's preoccupation with nuclear weaponry raised grave concern not only in nearby Israel, but around the world.

Iraqi leader Saddam Hussein attended an emergency Arab summit in 1987. The summit was called in hopes of reconciling Iran and Iraq. Even after it was over, the war between the two countries contributed to the instability in the Middle East throughout the late 1980s.

THE GULF WAR

Iraq emerged from the Iran-Iraq War as the dominant military power in the Persian Gulf region. In July of 1990, Saddam Hussein enhanced his power in the region by successfully charging Kuwait and the United Arab Emirates with exceeding the oil production quotas established by OPEC. Emboldened by his success at the OPEC conference and hoping to intimidate Kuwait into paying Iraq an indemnity to make up for the lower oil prices which had resulted from over-production, Hussein amassed his troops on Kuwait's border. Iraq was informed by the American ambassador in Baghdad that the United States had "no opinion" on the dispute between Iraq and Kuwait.

Hopes for stability in the Middle East were once again shattered with the Iraqi invasion of Kuwait on 2 August 1990. The United Nations Security Council immediately condemned the invasion and called for Iraq to withdraw. On 6 August 1990, a Security Council resolution imposed economic

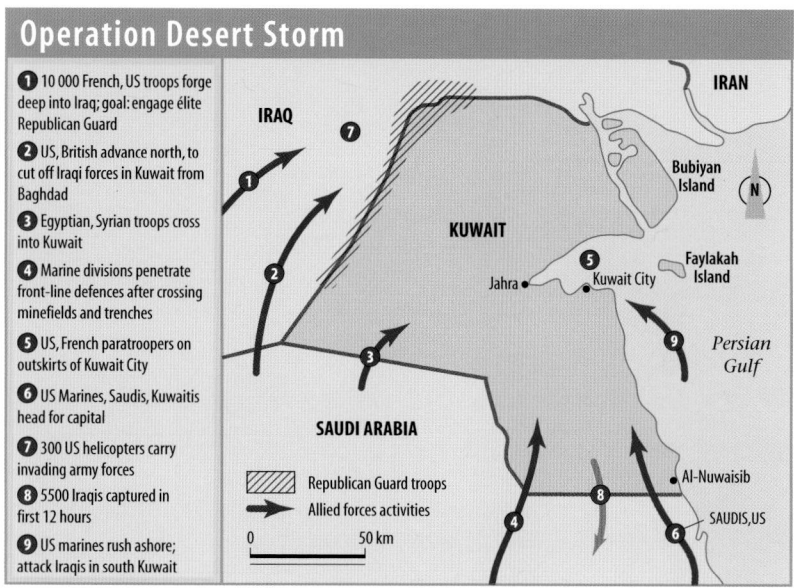

Operation Desert Storm

1. 10 000 French, US troops forge deep into Iraq; goal: engage élite Republican Guard

2. US, British advance north, to cut off Iraqi forces in Kuwait from Baghdad

3. Egyptian, Syrian troops cross into Kuwait

4. Marine divisions penetrate front-line defences after crossing minefields and trenches

5. US, French paratroopers on outskirts of Kuwait City

6. US Marines, Saudis, Kuwaitis head for capital

7. 300 US helicopters carry invading army forces

8. 5500 Iraqis captured in first 12 hours

9. US marines rush ashore; attack Iraqis in south Kuwait

In January of 1991, Operation Desert Storm went into action. The Middle East was once again torn apart by war. This map shows the coalition troops' movements on the first day of the ground war.

sanctions on Iraq with a vote of 13 to 0 (Cuba and Yemen abstained). On 25 August, the Security Council approved the enforcement of the embargo on goods shipped to Iraq, and warships were stationed in the Persian Gulf to enforce the edict and monitor traffic. Seemingly immune to international pressure, Iraq declared Kuwait to be its 19th province on 28 August 1990.

Diplomatic talks throughout September and October proved futile. The United States, then, assembled a coalition force of ground troops, ships, and aircraft from 25 countries. On 29 November 1990, the Security Council approved "all necessary means" to secure the freedom of Kuwait and established 15 January 1991 as the date by which Iraq must withdraw its forces from Kuwait. Thus, for the first time since the Korean War in 1950, the UN Security Council approved an action of collective security against an aggressor state. Negotiations continued throughout December and, although Hussein released foreign hostages, he refused to relinquish Kuwait.

In an apparent attempt to pressure the United States, Hussein suggested on 24 December that Israel would be attacked first in the event of war. On 13 January, Javier Pérez de Cuéllar, secretary general of the United Nations, met Saddam Hussein in Baghdad in a last-ditch attempt to resolve the issue diplomatically. The meeting failed to secure Iraq's withdrawal from Kuwait and, 19 hours after the 15 January deadline expired, the Gulf War began.

The coalition force launched a massive aerial assault on Iraq, with intense bombing of the city of Basra, of the Republican Guard assembled along the Kuwait border, and of targets in Kuwait.

Iraq retaliated with sporadic Scud missile attacks on Israel and Saudi Arabia. The missile attacks on Israel were seen as a ploy by Saddam Hussein to draw Israel into the war thereby breaking the allied coalition which contained Arab nations, including Saudi Arabia, Syria, Egypt, and Kuwait. Unopposed by the Iraqi air force, coalition planes devastated Iraq's military and communications infrastructure, and severely damaged the country's ability to fight on the ground.

When coalition ground forces launched a multi-pronged attack on Iraqi positions in Kuwait and southern Iraq, they met with surprisingly little resistance. In three days, the fighting was over. By 28 February, Saddam Hussein's government was forced to accept all 12 UN resolutions adopted since Iraq's invasion of Kuwait.

The Gulf War is illustrative of the economic, territorial, and political causes of war. In 1988, Iraq was $80 billion in debt as a result of its eight year war with Iran. About half of this sum was owed to Western nations, which had to be repaid in hard currency, while the remainder was owed to Gulf states, which Hussein expected to be forgiven. Instead of repaying any of the debt, Hussein persuaded his creditors to extend further credit.

Much of Iraq's financial difficulty stemmed from Hussein's lack of economic expertise. Forty per cent of Iraq's export earnings was spent on military and economic development directed at increasing Iraq's regional power rather than providing jobs for returning soldiers. Thus, reconstruction projects were not designed to assist in the demobilization of the army after the Iran-Iraq War. To compound the problems, inflation soared to 40 per cent and consumer goods were in short supply. Eighty per cent of Iraq's foodstuffs and consumer goods were imported.

Hussein hoped to solve Iraq's problems by selling more oil, but when the price of oil fell from $20 to $14 per barrel, Iraq faced a cash shortage. No longer considered credit worthy and unable to repay any of its debt, Iraq moved on its wealthy neighbour to the south. The Rumailah oil field extends from Iraq into Kuwait. Saddam Hussein demanded ownership of the entire oil field and presented Kuwait with a bill for $2 billion for oil which it claimed Kuwait had illegally sold during the Iran-Iraq War.

The boundary problems which erupted over the Rumailah oil field were compounded by Iraq's lack of access to the Persian Gulf. There is no Iraqi port on the Gulf's 40 km of shoreline, making Iraq dependent on the port of Basra on the Shatt-al-Arab waterway for traffic into the Persian Gulf. Iraq wanted the Kuwaiti island of Bubiyan in order to gain direct access to the Persian Gulf. Thus, both these territorial and financial difficulties could be solved by the annexation of Kuwait.

Politically, Saddam Hussein sought hegemony in the Middle East and intended to establish himself as the leader of the Arab world. He encouraged a liaison with the PLO and encouraged the Palestinian refugees on the West Bank and the Gaza Strip to look to him as their saviour. In diplomatic negotiations with the United States he maintained that the Gulf crisis could not be resolved unless the United States and Israel were willing to resolve the Palestinian issue.

In the end, defeat plunged Iraq into bitter internal feuding, with Shi'a forces in southern Iraq, and Kurdish groups in the north, challenging the government's authority. At the same time, Iraq's defeat seemingly opened the possibility of a US-brokered settlement of the Palestinian issue, one of the most vexing problems in the Middle East.

Egyptian troops are shown arriving in Saudi Arabia in September of 1990. Over 30 countries sent troops to the Middle East as part of the United Nations coalition forces. However, the United States sent the largest number of troops and equipment, and was the dominant force in the coalition.

ENVIRONMENTAL WARFARE

One of the most devastating battles waged in the Gulf War in 1991 was waged against the environment. As much as 1.1 billion litres of crude oil spilled into the Persian Gulf as a result of Saddam Hussein's sabotage of Kuwait's Sea Island oil terminal.

The oil slick threatened the water supply of neighbouring Gulf states and posed a deadly threat to the plant and animal life which inhabits the region. Environmentalists were frustrated in the clean-up strategy by their inability to begin until the war ended.

A second environmental disaster occurred in Kuwait as a result of the sabotage of hundreds of oil wells which were set on fire by Iraqi soldiers. As the wells burned out of control the skies darkened and poisonous gases filled the air. The total environmental cost was enormous. Although estimates of as long as two years were originally given for extinguishing the oil well fires, the job was completed faster than that by Canadian and American companies.

SUPERPOWER INVOLVEMENT IN THE MIDDLE EAST

The reasons for conflict in the Middle East are complex and the political reality is that all components leading to conflict are important. Although both the United States and the former Soviet Union have had a vested interest in the region, reasons for Middle East tensions cannot be reduced to a simple East-West equation. Neither superpower can claim overwhelming success in the region as regional disputes are characterized by shifting alliances and a lack of any long-term commitment to either superpower. It would appear, on balance, that the Soviet Union enjoyed even less success in maintaining its presence in the Middle East than has the United States.

The United States has maintained a special interest in the Middle East, and has had four specific goals in its relationship with the region: to contain Soviet influence, to retain access to the oil resources of the Gulf region, to limit Arab radicalism, and to maintain Israel's security and well-being. Unfortunately, the USA's commitment to Israel has come into conflict with its attempts to deal with the

BIOGRAPHY

YITZHAK RABIN (1922–1995)

After spending seven years at Bet Hinuch, and two years at another school, Givat Hashlosha, Rabin began studies at Kadoorie Agricultural High School for Boys. Kadoorie was repeatedly attacked by Arab gunfire, and because of the isolated position of the school, it was up to the students to protect themselves. Before the end of Rabin's first year, the school was closed due to these attacks. The experiences at Kadoorie were the beginning of Rabin's move away from the life of a farmer and toward the life of a soldier.

His education having been interrupted, Rabin accepted an offer to move to Ginossar and learn the use of revolvers, rifles, and hand grenades. Yigal Allon—who had extended this offer to Rabin, and who was the sergeant responsible for training the Kadoorie boys—remembered Rabin as having "a sort of analytical approach to problems. He would never say he understood something before he really did understand all that was involved. Once he said he understood, you knew he really did." Other character qualities attributed to Rabin in his early years include introversion, self-confidence, humility, and stubbornness. His wife-to-be, Leah Schlossberg, compared him to Israel's first king, King David: "chestnut hair and beautiful eyes."

Rabin fought in the Arab-Israeli War in 1948-49, which saw the birth of an independent Jewish state, the world-wide immigration of 2 000 000 Jews to Israel by 1962, and the large-scale relocation of Arabs from the same regions. Rabin also represented Israeli Defense Forces (IDF) at the armistice in Rhodes. In 1964, Rabin became chief-of-staff of the IDF and headed the armed forces during the successful Six-Day-War of 1967. Between 1968 and 1973, Rabin was the ambassador to the United States, after which time he became Labour Party leader and prime minister of Israel from 1974 to 1977. In 1984, he became Israel's defense minister. Then in 1992, Rabin and the Labour Party defeated Yitzhak Shamir and the Likud Party and Rabin again became Israel's prime minister. In a talk to the Labour Party Central Committee before the election, Rabin raised many of the themes that would come to dominate his government.

Yitzhak Rabin's mother, Rosa Cohen, was the parent who is said to have been the more influential in Yitzhak and his sister Rahel's lives. Significantly, Yitzhak once said of her: "She had her own position, her own principles, she was ready to fight for anything that seemed to her a worthy cause." In contrast to the hectic pace of Rosa's life, Nehemiah, Yitzhak's father, was quiet and easy-going. However, he too had a strong sense of civic duty and was actively involved in bettering the lot of those he worked with. Steadfast to the socialist ideal, Nehemiah refused promotions into managerial positions, remaining a worker for 30 years at the Palestine Electric Corporation.

Yitzhak was born in Jerusalem to Rosa and Nehemiah in 1922. In 1923, the family moved to Tel Aviv. At the age of six, Yitzhak started school at Bet Hinuch, a school established by the workers of Tel Aviv. The goal of the school was not to create intellectuals or business people but to create workers for the new Kibbutzim that were being established around the country. As Kibbutzniks—farmers who would settle the land and establish a Jewish presence— the former Bet Hinuch students would be living up to the Zionist and workers' mandate.

Whoever travels around the country and meets the various publics can perceive the beginning of change, the beginning of a new hope, the beginning of a popular understanding that it is necessary to replace the Likud in order to give the State of Israel a chance.

I believe that this change stems from two sources. The first is the realization that the Likud misses, is missing and will continue to miss the great opportunities which present themselves to the state, whether in the sphere of advancing peace while preserving security, or in the sphere of the national priorities. In the current erroneous and distorted order of priorities, political settlements in the territories precede everything else: immigration absorption, the future of the younger generation, the war against unemployment, and social and economic progress. There is widespread disappointment with the deficient functioning of this government in almost all spheres of life . . .

Should I form the next Israeli government I undertake to reach an agreement with the Palestinians in the territories over the establishment of an autonomy within six to nine months. After the agreement with the Palestinians, we shall reach an agreement with Jordan and then with Syria. The second thing which I undertake is to stop the political settlements, whose only purpose is to prevent any possibility of finding a political solution to the conflict.

If the construction were taking place in Greater Jerusalem, the Jordan Rift and the existing settlements on the Golan Heights, I would not complain. But the Likud is diverting thousands of millions of shekels to political settlements which have no value in security terms, and in addition to blocking any possibility for peace, prevent the channelling of resources into those spheres where they are really needed.

Several months later, Rabin told the *Jerusalem Post* that, "Once you solve the problem between us and the Palestinians in the territories, there is no problem with Jordan. Once you solve the problem between Israel and the Syrians, there is no problem with the Lebanese."

On 4 November 1995, Yitzhak Rabin was assassinated by a 27-year-old Israeli law student identified as Yigal Amir. Since the 1993 Oslo Accord, Rabin's government had been threatened by right-wing extremists who opposed the authority granted to the Palestine Liberation Organization. Following the assassination, Benjamin Netanyahu was elected prime minister of Israel. Although he took a right-wing stance, he publicly committed Israel to continue the peace process with the PLO. ●

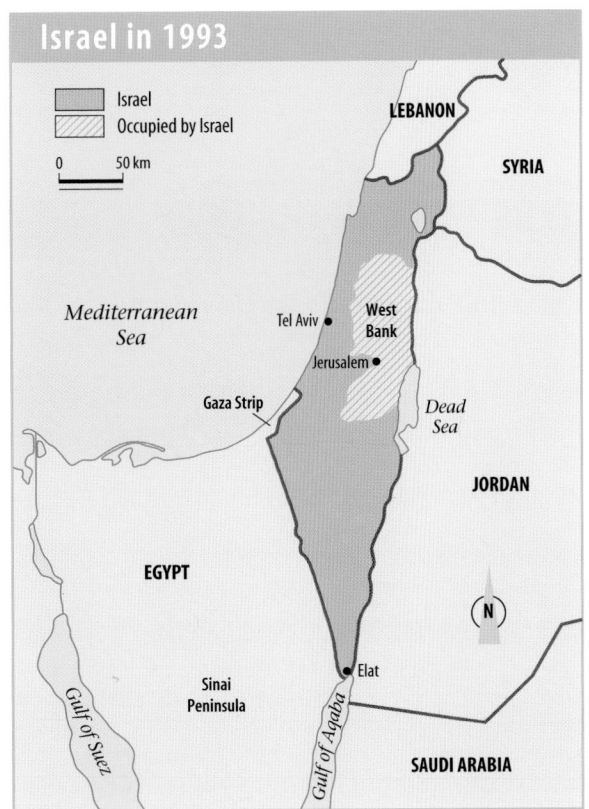

Israel in 1993

In 1993, Arafat and Rabin signed the Oslo Accord. Israel withdrew from the Gaza Strip and promised to extend gradual autonomy to the West Bank.

Soviets and the Arabs, creating a complex and frustrating situation for diplomats and residents of the region alike. When Ronald Reagan came to power, he based his Middle East policy on four main assumptions: the threat to the security of oil-producing countries of the Gulf was the central problem for the United States, the Arab-Israeli conflict was now less acute, the Gulf region and the Arab-Israeli conflict can be dealt with in isolation, and the Middle East must be defended against Soviet incursion.

Acting on the basis of these policy assumptions, the United States supported Israel's attack on Lebanon in May 1982. The attack was really designed to crush the PLO and eliminate the threat it posed to Israel. The purpose of the invasion of Lebanon was to destroy the PLO and weaken Palestinian nationalism, thereby facilitating the absorption of the West Bank into Greater Israel. American peacekeeping troops were deployed in Beirut, and a naval armada was stationed offshore.

The fighting in Lebanon, however, demonstrated that Israel's stability was questionable and its

TERRORISM IN THE SKY

One of the most frightening international developments for the ordinary citizen has been that of terrorism. Sabotage of aircraft, bombings, and hostage-taking are terrorist techniques which are both unpredictable and attention-getting. Can you imagine any political ends which might justify terrorist acts? Debate this question with your classmates.

Terrorism became a frightening political weapon in the 1970s, as groups such as Germany's Baader-Meinhof Gang and Italy's Red Brigades carried out bombings and murder at will. Armed and financed by foreign governments, these terrorists waged a type of war against the West, bent on destabilizing democratic political processes. The terrorists took hostages, stormed banks, and planted bombs in shopping centres, school buses, and railway and airport terminals. Special security forces trained to counter their attacks quickly discovered they were not dealing with ordinary criminals. The terrorists' purpose was to publicize their cause. Having achieved world-wide coverage in the media, they were prepared to die rather than surrender.

Terrorists believed that the dramatic act of killing innocent people would focus world attention on their cause. They tried to instill a sense of guilt among well-off Westerners over their past exploitation of the oppressed peoples of the Third World. In this they gained some support in universities, where some students took up the cause.

Out of dozens of terrorist organizations, two have consistently held territorial ambitions. These are the Irish Republican Army (IRA), bent on the return of Northern Ireland to the Republic of Ireland, and Palestinian groups determined to secure the return of Palestine to Arab control. The Palestinian groups are financed by Arab governments and oil-rich sheiks and supplied with Soviet weapons and training. Of these groups, the People's Front for the Liberation of Palestine (PFLP) has been one of the most active.

The PFLP gave new dimensions to air piracy. The PFLP gained immediate attention by hijacking, and threatening to destroy, jumbo jets full of passengers. At first, governments and airlines were at a loss as to how to deal with the situation. The terrorists did not respond to the usual offer of money for lives. More often than not, the airplanes had to be stormed by special commandos, who hoped to kill the terrorists before the terrorists could harm their hostages. Before the commandos went in, officials would try to wear down the skyjackers through prolonged negotiations. Initial response to the threat took the form of trying to identify dangerous individuals and deny them access to the aircraft before it left the ground. The screening of luggage and the use of dogs to sniff out explosives added another security dimension.

The first PFLP skyjacking took place on 23 July 1968, when an Israeli E1 A1 707 flying out of Rome was captured and forced to land in Algiers. The Israelis responded by placing armed guards on their aircraft. This was largely successful. Yet despite increased security at airports and the use of electronic scanners to detect weapons and bombs, skyjackings continued. Terrorists bypassed security by using ground crews and cleaners to smuggle weapons and bombs aboard aircraft while the planes were on the ground. Once in the air, the terrorists could recover the weapons and take control of the aircraft. They could then send out radio transmissions to a global audience.

In September 1970, Leila Khaled and Patrick Arguello were captured when their skyjacking of an E1 A1 flight ended in the Netherlands in failure. Khaled failed to remove the pin from her hand grenade and was taken alive. In efforts to force her release, other terrorists took an American TWA 707, a Swissair DC-8, and a British VC-10 to an airstrip outside Amman, Jordan where they demanded Khaled's return. At the same time, a TWA jumbo jet was taken to Cairo, where it was blown up after its passengers were released.

One unexpected reaction to the skyjackings was that of King Hussein of Jordan: he unleashed his Bedouin army against the PFLP camps in Jordan's border regions. This drove the PFLP and other Palestinian refugee groups into Syria and Lebanon, where they regrouped before carrying on their activities.

The rash of skyjackings brought on international cooperation in hunting down and destroying organized terrorism. Anti-terrorist commando squads like the British Special Air and Boat Services, the Dutch Marines, and the German GSG 9 became proficient in handling terrorist attacks. By the end of the decade, they had taken their toll of the PFLP, IRA, Red Brigades, and other terrorist organizations. The dramatic decrease in terrorist effectiveness resulted in Yassir Arafat directing his Palestine Liberation Organization towards peaceful efforts to create a Palestinian state.

Terrorism continued into the 1980s. This time, right-wing terrorist groups acted in support of neonazi movements. The Armed Revolutionary Nuclei of Italy set off a bomb in a crowded railway station in Bologna, and killed 85 people. Another 13 were killed in a bombing incident at the Munich Oktoberfest, and a bomb incident in Paris in the Rue Copernic claimed 4 victims outside a synagogue. In 1985, Americans were targets at the Rome and Vienna airports for Libyan and Syrian government-backed terrorist groups. In that year there were 2200 terrorist incidents, in which 198 Americans were killed or wounded. Americans in Madrid, Athens, Rome, Berlin, and Frankfurt were now at risk. As the number of American tourists in Europe dropped to less than half the normal amount, European economies began to feel the effect. The unified response was agreement to combat terrorism and punish those governments that supported terrorist activities.

In 1986, the taking at sea of the Italian liner *Achille Lauro*, and the murder of an American passenger, caused revulsion throughout the world and triggered an American military reaction. The Americans were certain that the Libyan government was behind the more recent violence. Libyan support of terrorists had already caused several international incidents. When Libyan missiles were fired at US warships in the Gulf of Sidra, the Americans struck at Libyan radar and port facilities. When Libya's leader Colonel Qaddafi ordered his People's Bureaus (embassies) to plan acts of terrorism against Americans, other governments, headed by the USA, began to react.

On 14 April 1986, the Americans carried out air strikes against the Libyan cities of Tripoli and Benghazi, bombing Qaddafi's compound and killing members of his family. The air strikes were meant as a deterrent to further terrorism. The raids were effective: Libyan-supported terrorism quickly came to an end. Some Arab states were mildly critical of the American attack, while others signaled tacit approval through their silence. European governments were slower to respond, but in the end approved the air strikes.

Also in April, European governments began imposing economic sanctions on Libya. The sale of arms, the transfer of technology, and construction contracts were canceled. More than 500 Libyan diplomats were expelled and sent home. The sanctions were extended to Syria after an incident at Heathrow Airport, where a bomb was intercepted before it could be taken aboard an E1 A1 flight with 350 passengers. The bomb was to have been carried on board by the unsuspecting fiancée of a Syrian terrorist. Her tragic plight turned public opinion against Syria. This incident was followed in June by the discovery of another bomb destined for an El Al flight out of Madrid, again linked to Syrian officials.

Many governments supported an agreement to bring terrorists to public trial and deal with them through normal legal procedures. The trials would help convince the public of the terrorists' ruthlessness, and turn public opinion against them. In further agreements, governments concurred not to ransom hostages or negotiate with terrorists, but instead to act firmly to kill or capture them. Hostages would have to face the risk of death in this no-barter policy.

The no-negotiation policy could not stand the test. When its own time came, Israel agreed to the release of 1200 Arab prisoners for the return of 3 Israeli soldiers. France got hostages back after reinstating loans to the Khomeini regime in Iran. And the United States government, which itself had forced the pace of anti-terrorist agreements, secretly made a deal to exchange arms for Americans held in Teheran.

Today, terrorism is still a fact of international relations. Although the number of incidents has dropped dramatically, they still occur—such as the destruction of a Pan American jumbo jet over Lockerbie, Scotland.

1. Why might negotiation with terrorists not be effective? Is terrorism effective?

2. By what means other than violence can terrorists attract public attention?

3. What rationale do terrorists give for killing innocent victims?

4. What responsibility does the media have regarding the relative effectiveness of terrorism?

5. Describe alternative measures to combat terrorism.

These Palestinian children may one day live in an autonomous Palestinian state.

by the character of regional political forces. Communism has been unsuccessful in eroding the national and religious forces which dominate the Middle East. As a result, the communist movement has been weak in most countries and severely repressed in others.

The Soviet Union made its entry into the Middle East in 1955 with the signing of an arms agreement with Egypt. The Egyptian tie was maintained until Egyptian president Anwar Sadat terminated the relationship in 1974. The Soviets backed the Arab states in both the 1967 and 1973 conflicts with Israel. Although the Soviet Union strongly opposed the Iraqi attack on Iran in 1980, it remained a major arms supplier and economic partner to Iraq. Iraq aside, the Soviet Union did not have a single reliable long term ally in the entire Middle Eastern region. Syria, Egypt, and Libya were all difficult partners, leaning to the West when advantage suited them.

In the overall pattern of global relationships since the Second World War, the Middle East has not been an area of intense superpower conflict. The reason for this is twofold: the area is dominated by regional disputes which transcend the East-West conflict, and the superpowers' priorities, although very different, are often compatible. Hence, the Americans agreed to refrain from installing missiles in the Gulf region, and the Soviets did not interfere unduly with American access to oil. The critical ongoing issue in the Middle East is the Palestinian problem. Until the problems of Palestinian autonomy and Israeli security are resolved, the possibility of a peace settlement remains elusive. Although the resolution of the Palestinian question would not solve the regional instability, it would ease tensions and facilitate negotiation of a comprehensive Middle Eastern peace initiative.

On 13 September 1993, Yassar Arafat and Yitzhak Rabin shook hands on the lawn in front of the American White House in a symbolic gesture confirming their acceptance of the Oslo Accord which hammered out agreement over the disputed territories in the Middle East. The accord called for the withdrawal of Israel from Gaza and the gradual extension of autonomy to the entire West Bank. The most contentious issues of refugees, borders, and Palestinian statehood were reserved for future settlement. The peace accord was recognized by the international community as a giant step toward the resolution of tension in the Middle East. Yitzhak Rabin and Yassar Arafat shared the 1993 Nobel Prize for Peace.

aggressive stance to its national security could make it a liability rather than an asset to the United States. Uncritical support of Israel had damaged American credibility in the eyes of the world, and dealt a serious blow to the USA's prestige in the Arab world. Whether directly or indirectly, by contributing to the destruction of Lebanon, the Americans contributed to the collapse of regional order.

Soviet policy in the Middle East met with more frustration than success. Although the area was of strategic concern to the USSR, the Soviets had less success in maintaining a presence in the Middle East than in any other region. The Soviet Union divided the Middle East into two areas when shaping policy: the Central East or the Northern tier which includes Turkey, Iran, Afghanistan, and sometimes even Pakistan, and the Near East which includes Israel and the Arab countries. Of utmost concern was rivalry with the American presence in the area and the vulnerability of the Soviet Union's southern border. The deployment of American missiles, for example in Turkey and Iran, would threaten Soviet security. Hence in the 1960s the Soviets' primary concern in their relationship with Turkey and Iran was that these areas remained free of American missiles. The Soviet impact on internal policies of Middle Eastern nations was tempered

SUMMARY

Since the demise of the Ottoman Empire, the Middle East has proven to be one of the world's most volatile areas. Ethnic, religious, political, and economic disagreements, pitting at various times Arabs against the West, Jews against Arabs, Arabs against Arabs, and Shi'a Muslims against Sunni Muslims, have often led to bloody confrontations and many a complex diplomatic impasse.

Conflict has dominated the region for decades. Fighting surrounding the formation of the state of Israel in 1948, the Suez Crisis of 1956, the Six-Day War of 1967, the Yom Kippur War of 1973, the ongoing struggle in Lebanon, the Palestinian issue, the Iran-Iraq War of 1980-1988, and the Gulf crisis of 1990-1991 all have tended to mask the underlying causes which have so often led to violence in the Middle East.

It remains to be seen whether superpower intervention into the affairs of the region will finally prove successful at the end of a century marked by frequent great-power failures, from the British and French at Suez, to the USSR in Egypt, and the USA in Lebanon. Failures and successes aside, the strategic and economic importance of the Middle East will ensure continued superpower interest well into the twenty-first century.

QUESTIONS

1. Describe the Zionist movement and explain how it affected the politics of the Middle East.

2. What was the Balfour Declaration?

3. What were the short term causes of the Arab-Israeli War of 1948?

4. What were Nasser's goals for Egypt after he seized power in 1952?

5. Why did Israel invade Egypt in 1956?

6. What was the American response to the Suez Crisis?

7. Why didn't the Soviet Union become involved in the Suez Crisis?

8. Explain how the Suez Crisis was resolved.

9. What were the consequences of the Six-Day War in 1967?

10. Describe the Yom Kippur War of 1973. What were the results?

11. How did the Camp David peace accords attempt to solve the problems in the Middle East?

12. Name and explain two issues of importance to the Middle East which were not resolved by the Camp David accords.

13. How did the Yom Kippur War affect the industrial nations of the world?

14. What two issues were central to the Iran-Iraq conflict?

15. What were the results of the Iran-Iraq War?

16. Name and explain three causes of the Gulf War.

17. Name four goals which the United States has in relationship to the Middle East.

18. What two issues concern the Soviet Union in the Middle East?

19. Evaluate the effectiveness of American and Soviet actions in the Middle East in relation to their goals.

CRITICAL ANALYSIS

1. Explain how the establishment of the state of Israel has destabilized the Middle East.

2. Evaluate the effectiveness of OPEC's oil cartel in influencing foreign policy.

3. Are global relationships becoming increasingly vulnerable to economic forces? Explain.

4. How can organized terrorism be eliminated? What protection does the individual have against terrorism?

5. Explain how direct confrontation between the superpowers was averted in the Middle East.

RESEARCH PROJECTS

1. Research the development of the PLO. Identify leadership, goals and objectives, techniques of operation, and its current status in the Middle East. Evaluate the PLO's effectiveness in furthering the Palestinian position in the Middle East today.

2. Research the causes, events, and results of the Iranian Revolution of 1979. Evaluate the impact of the revolution on the Iranian people as well as on the stability of the Middle East.

3. Trace the origins of Zionism and evaluate the impact of this movement on the conditions in the Middle East today.

4. Write a biographical account of one of the following individuals and evaluate the role he or she played in the political conditions of the Middle East: (a) David Ben Gurion; (b) Golda Meir; (c) Ayatollah Khomeini; (d) Anwar Sadat; (e) Saddam Hussein.

ACTIVITIES

1 Role Play

The possession of the West Bank remains one of the most contentious issues in the Middle East. Select three students to research the Israeli position, three students to research the Arab position, and a panel of five students to act as arbiters in the dispute. Establish a conference which will be structured to hear the viewpoints of the two opposing sides and make recommendations for settlement. The students presenting the opposing positions must play the role assigned them while the students selected as arbiters must be neutral and objective in their decision. Remaining students may play a role by questioning the participants.

2 International Linkage

Compile a global wall map showing the OPEC oil reserves and the destination of OPEC's oil exports.

3 Debate

Be it resolved that the United States should intervene to protect displaced people, like the Kurds in Iraq.

HISTORICAL ANALYSIS

THE MIDDLE EAST

The Middle East is a strategic area not only in terms of resources but also of trade routes which link East and West. Major powers have always attempted to establish spheres of influence in areas which serve as lifelines for their economic well-being. The United States has maintained a presence in the Persian Gulf region since the Second World War. Analyse the following statement by Carter, made in the 1970s, and evaluate its significance on American action in the Gulf War in 1991. Explain why the Soviet Union remained outside of the conflict. Should the United Nations have acted against Saddam Hussein?

> Any attempt by an outside force to gain control of the Persian Gulf Region will be regarded as an assault on the vital interests of the United States of America, and such an assault will be repelled by all means necessary including military force.
>
> —Carter Doctrine, 1979

Following this statement and during his term of office in 1979, President Carter acted to establish American bases in Kenya, Somalia, Oman, and Diego Garcia. He also created a rapid deployment force.

Research the current relationship between the United States and Iraq.

NATIONALISM IN ASIA

CHAPTER 13

TIME LINE

16 August	1945:	Japan surrendered
2 September	1945:	Ho Chi Minh proclaimed Vietnam's independence
1946 - 1954:		French returned to Vietnam
	1947:	USA referred Korea to UN
15 August	1947:	India gained independence from Britain—Pakistan created
30 January	1948:	Gandhi assassinated
25 June	1950:	North Korea invaded South Korea
September	1951:	Peace treaty signed between Japan and 48 nations
	1954:	Dien Bien Phu
	1955:	SEATO was formed
	1956:	Japan acknowledged Soviet territorial claims
	1964:	Gulf of Tonkin incident
1965 - 1975:		Americans entered Vietnam
	1968:	Tet Offensive
	1972:	US and China rapprochement—Nixon visited China
	1973:	Paris agreement on US withdrawal from Vietnam
	1975:	Vietnam united
	1976:	Peace declaration between Japan and China
	1978:	Vietnam invaded Cambodia (Kampuchea)
	1979:	China invaded Vietnam
	1989:	Vietnamese troops left Cambodia (Kampuchea)
	1994:	Americans ended the trade embargo against Vietnam

FOCUS ON NATIONALISM

I personally would wait, if need be, for ages, rather than seek to attain the freedom of my country through bloody means. I feel in the innermost recesses of my heart, after a political experience extending over an unbroken period of close upon 35 years, that the world is sick unto death of blood spilling. I have therefore no hesitation whatsoever in inviting all the great nations of the earth to give their hearty cooperation to India in her struggle.

Mohandis 'Mahatma' Gandhi, in a broadcast to North America, 13 September 1931.

Decolonization in Asia was paralleled by a growth in nationalism. This expressed itself in various forms, ranging from Gandhi's non-violent movement in India to Ho Chi Minh's war of national liberation in Vietnam. Choose an Asian nationalist leader during the period 1945-1975. Analyse this leader's successes or failures. Draw conclusions regarding the role of nationalism in reshaping the political map of Asia.

OVERVIEW

From 1945 to 1980, Japan developed into a major industrial power. This occurred gradually, through the defeat and reconstruction of Japan, and the industrial growth and expansion of Japanese defence forces. Also covered in this chapter are wars of national liberation, India, Pakistan, Korea, and the Vietnam War.

JAPAN: 1945–1980

Reconstruction of Japan after the Second World War resulted in an industrial nation whose economy rivals that of Western nations.

WARS OF NATIONAL LIBERATION

Independence movements flourished after the Second World War as Asian countries shook off their colonial masters.

INDIA AND PAKISTAN

India's independence was characterized by religious conflict which resulted in the partition of India and Pakistan to recognize Muslim and Hindu territory.

KOREA

In 1945, Korea was divided at the 38th parallel with the North occupied by Soviet Communist forces and the South occupied by American forces.

VIETNAM

The struggle for Vietnamese independence resulted in division at the 17th parallel with Communist support in the North and Western democratic support in the South. It was not until 1975 that Vietnam was reunited under a Communist government.

JAPAN: 1945–1980

At 11 AM on 16 August 1945, the Japanese people were summoned to their radios to hear an important message from Emperor Hirohito. They listened to a voice they had never heard before, speaking a special dialect that few understood, telling them that the war had not developed to their advantage. The enemy had used a new and cruel bomb with a power so great it could destroy all of civilization. In order to save humankind, he, the emperor, had taken the unprecedented step of intervening with the government to end the war. The military had already stopped fighting, and he urged them to remain calm and confident as they awaited the occupation forces. There was an immediate national outpouring of grief and shame intermingled with relief. Crowds milled about the streets not knowing how to behave and feeling confused about their nation's first defeat in 2000 years. Shattered both physically and psychologically, the Japanese prepared to bear defeat.

The realities of global strategy were to determine the nature of Japan's occupation. In the five years after the Second World War, the Americans, Soviets, and the Chinese sought to expand their spheres of influence in the region, even as Britain, France, and the Netherlands moved to regain their colonies. In the midst of a fluid political situation that at times came to the brink of war, Prime Minister Yoshida allied Japan closely with the United States. The future lay in the hands of the American occupation forces under General Douglas MacArthur who, as Supreme Allied Commander, assumed the powers of a shogun. American experience with the difficulties of four-power control in Germany resulted in a blunt refusal to repeat that failure in Japan. Demands by the USSR and other allies to participate in the occupation of Japan were denied. The Allied Council for Japan, located in Tokyo, and the 11-member Far East Commission, in Washington, had little influence over American policy. The British, French, and Dutch were not to reassert their claims in the Pacific until after the formality of surrender had taken place. The Pacific theatre was to become an American sphere in which the USA's allies were not welcome.

Tensions already building between the two superpowers in war-torn Europe now increased. Asia was drawn into the global bargaining that marked the delineation of the spheres of influence of the USA and the USSR. Soviet forces continued to advance into Manchuria and Korea for some days after the Japanese surrender. In response, American troops occupied the south half of Korea to the 38th parallel, and airlifted Chiang Kai-shek's Nationalist armies into the coastal cities and into the north of China. In the process, Japan became the major staging base for American forces in the Pacific.

As a result of its defeat, Japan was stripped of its empire and limited to the four main home islands. Japanese troops were withdrawn from all overseas regions. They were to turn their equipment and bases over to the nearest Allied commander. All airplanes were to be destroyed to stop any attempt to continue the kamikaze attacks mounted in the last months of the war. At the same time, the USSR regained its position of 1904—including the Kurile Islands and the southern half of Sakhalin—despite having been in the Pacific War for only a matter of days. The Soviets also took over railways, mines, and industrial facilities in Manchuria. In Japan itself, Emperor Hirohito lost his divinity, a democratic form of representative government was established (which included the right of women to vote), the military was denied any part in the government, and 200 000 military officers were banned from public life. The military staffs were abolished, and in Tokyo 28 war criminals were put on trial for making war. Seven were sentenced to death. Another 9000 Japanese were sent to trial for war crimes in various parts of Southeast Asia; over 900 were executed.

The immediate task was to rebuild Japan's agricultural sector. Food supplies were at a premium: Japan could not feed itself, let alone look after millions of service members returning from overseas. In the first weeks of the occupation, food and medicine were airlifted in, while tonnes more arrived in naval transports. New land development policies led to the breakup of large estates and land was distributed to some 2.5 million tenant farmers. This redistribution facilitated the modernization of farming practices and the re-equipment of farms; use of the latest in farm machinery resulted in sharply increased yields and effective food production.

The initial decision to break up Japan's large industrial firms was set aside. The demand for consumer goods was so great that their destruction would have caused serious disruption in supply. American strategists also began to take into account the potential of Japanese industry to supply American forces in the western Pacific. A rebuilt Japanese industry would be a considerable asset to the American military. As a result of the strategic needs of the USA, and with American technology and direction, Japan was producing enough food and goods by 1948 for its own needs and those of the occupation forces.

In the summer of 1947, anxious to reduce its costly military commitment in the Pacific, the USA moved to normalize relations with Japan. Events in China and Korea, and the growing hostility between the USA and the Soviet Union, resulted in efforts to strengthen Japan beyond what had been considered wise in 1946. To gain the agreement of other Asian nations to Japanese reconstruction, the USA would have had to guarantee their security against a rearmed Japan. A peace treaty was signed between Japan and 48 other nations in San Francisco in September 1951, but the Soviets and their allies

General Douglas MacArthur landed in the Philippines in 1944. After war in the Pacific ended, MacArthur directed the occupation of Japan. Later, he was the commander of the UN forces during the first part of the Korean War.

refused to sign it. It was not until after Stalin's death in 1953 that relations between Japan and the Soviet bloc eased. In 1956, Japan acknowledged the USSR's territorial claims in return for the Soviets removing their veto of Japan's membership in the UN. A declaration that the state of war existing between Japan and the USSR had ceased to exist was then signed. A similar agreement was signed by the USSR and the People's Republic of China in 1976.

Japan renounced its claim to Korea, Taiwan, the Kuriles, and the south half of Sakhalin island, gave up its mandates from the First World War, and agreed to American occupation of Okinawa and Bonin. At the same time, Japan signed a mutual defence treaty with the USA and gave the Americans continued use of 1400 military bases and the right to station 200 000 troops in Japan's home islands. The growing presence of Soviet military forces in

Japan's recovery after the Second World War was facilitated by aid and trading agreements with the United States. Modern Japan is a manufacturing giant in its own right. Most, if not all, of the buildings surrounding this park in Tokyo have been built since 1960.

the Pacific, and the potential threat from a resurgent China, made the Japanese anxious about the future. Japan's newly formed Self-Defence Force (JDF) began to receive heavy weapons and expanded to 300 000 members. However, Japan consistently refused to become partner to any formal military alliance, or to send troops to Korea or Vietnam. Although Japan considered acquiring nuclear weapons, it chose not to. Japan's future lay in collaboration with the USA, firmly within the American sphere.

Between 1982 and 1987 Premier Nakasone moved Japan's defence policy closer to that of the United States. At the same time, he greatly expanded the JDF. Reasoning that the centre of the global economy was shifting to the Pacific, Nakasone claimed a strategic role for Japan. During the 1980s, Japan acquired a high-technology anti-submarine, anti-invasion, and air defence network. The rapid growth of the Japanese forces in numbers and quality caused concern amongst its neighbours.

Today, Japan has the capability to protect its sea lanes and air lanes for at least 1000 km outside its boundaries. Its modern forces include F-15 and F-16 fighters, while the more modern destroyer-like patrol craft have missile capacity and will soon have the ship-based Aegis antimissile defence system.

Japan's first post-war aircraft carriers and nuclear-powered submarines are being considered for the 1990s. On land, Japan's forces have anti-tank helicopters and surface-to-surface missiles.

The amazing recovery of Japan's industrial strength was in part the result of the wars in Korea (1950-1953) and Vietnam (1965-1975), an economic bonanza. Japan's strategic location made it the supplier of American economic and military needs. Japan became the arsenal for these wars without being a participant. Everything the American forces needed by way of equipment and repairs could be supplied by Japan, and orders poured into Japanese industries. The large injection of American money advanced Japanese prosperity.

A shift in emphasis from light industry to heavy industry and high-technology production was accompanied by massive reforms in state-controlled education. Education became and still is a high priority. Massive funds were invested in universities and technical schools to produce the human resources necessary for industrial supremacy. By 1960, Japanese industry was seeking out markets among its former enemies and securing the raw materials required to fuel industrial growth. Having no resources of its own, Japan depends on ownership and control of offshore minerals and fuels. Profit from exports maintains a favourable balance of trade and a high living standard for the upper economic classes. Throughout the post-war period, Japan's largest trading partner has been the United States; about one third of Japan's exports go to the USA, with the European Union close behind.

In 1962, Japan concluded a five-year commercial arrangement with China on a barter basis. The vast potential of China as a commercial partner has yet to be felt, and the gains to this date have been small. Japan was also inhibited in its China trade by American hostility to Beijing, until the United States normalized relations with the People's Republic of China in order to take full advantage of the widening rift between the Soviet Union and China. By the 1970s, Japan had become an economic giant, but this move caused a profound reassessment of economic policies.

The benefits of friendlier relations between the USA and China, which has one quarter of the world's population, was not lost on the American public, but Japan felt betrayed and resentful of a move that could result in a major shift of trade patterns. At this time, Japan also had to face the first of American trade restrictions on access to the American market. American textile interests had forced their government to impose a ban on some Japanese imports and a 10 per cent surcharge on other Japanese goods. This halved Japanese economic growth from an expected 10 per cent and fostered anti-American feelings in the nation. Relations were not improved even with the return of Okinawa, which had been captured by the Americans during the Second World War, for the USA maintained its nuclear presence on the island. American attitudes eased somewhat in 1972, when President Nixon and Prime Minister Sato met in Honolulu, and Japan agreed to a massive purchase of American goods to redress the USA's imbalance of payments.

In the 1970s, Japan became an insatiable consumer of materials and goods from outside its boundaries. Oil from the Middle East was critical to its economic growth. Over 90 per cent of Japan's energy supplies came from this region. OPEC price increases hit Japan hard. The tripling of energy costs led to a rapid diversification of oil suppliers as well as investment in oil exploration in Southeast Asia—both of which have reduced Japan's dependence on OPEC to about 60 per cent of the country's needs. Also, all of Japan's power corporations have developed nuclear power plants. But future energy supplies are a matter of continuing concern.

By 1980, Japan was using one tenth of the world's raw materials and more than one tenth of the world's oil production. The entire industrial base was vulnerable, and a decision was made to embark on a policy of **economic imperialism**. Japan would make world-wide investments in property, businesses, industrial plants, and mines in order to secure future supplies. By 1986, Japan stood ahead of West Germany and behind only the USA in industrial strength. Japan's annual exports to the USA, its largest market, were close to $90 billion, almost one third of its total export trade. Its imports from the USA were over $30 billion. The growing trade imbalance has led to American demands for greater access to the Japanese market or protective tariffs to halt the flow of Japanese goods.

Half a century after its defeat in the Second World War, Japan is in the first rank of industrial nations. Once a nation in ruins, its cities destroyed, its people dazed and unable to feed themselves, Japan has emerged as a major economic power. This remarkable transition was brought about by Japan's ability to adapt to change and the willingness of its people to try new ways.

In 1949, the Chinese Communists under Mao established the People's Republic of China, defying the imperial powers and Chiang Kai-shek's Nationalists. This photograph shows the People's Liberation Army triumphantly entering central China.

WARS OF NATIONAL LIBERATION

At the end of the Second World War, China, the Soviet Union, Great Britain, and the United States prepared to redraw the map of Asia in their own interests. Each sought to expand its sphere of influence in the Pacific. They were opposed by nationalist forces led by people such as Jawaharlal Nehru, Sukarno, Ho Chi Minh, and Mao Zedong, whose unalterable anti-imperial stance gained them overwhelming national support. The Japanese war was over, but the Asia for the Asians movement was far from dead.

Agreements reached by the major powers at Yalta and Potsdam made it clear that the imperialist powers intended to reassert their authority over their colonies in Asia once Japan was defeated. They planned to administer their former colonies as they had for the better part of a century. As victors in command of finely tuned war machines, they thought there was little the peoples of Asia could do but submit.

Although the Americans were opposed to the re-establishment of the colonial system, favouring instead democratic self-government, they did not oppose their European allies. The need for a combined effort to contain what they saw as the global

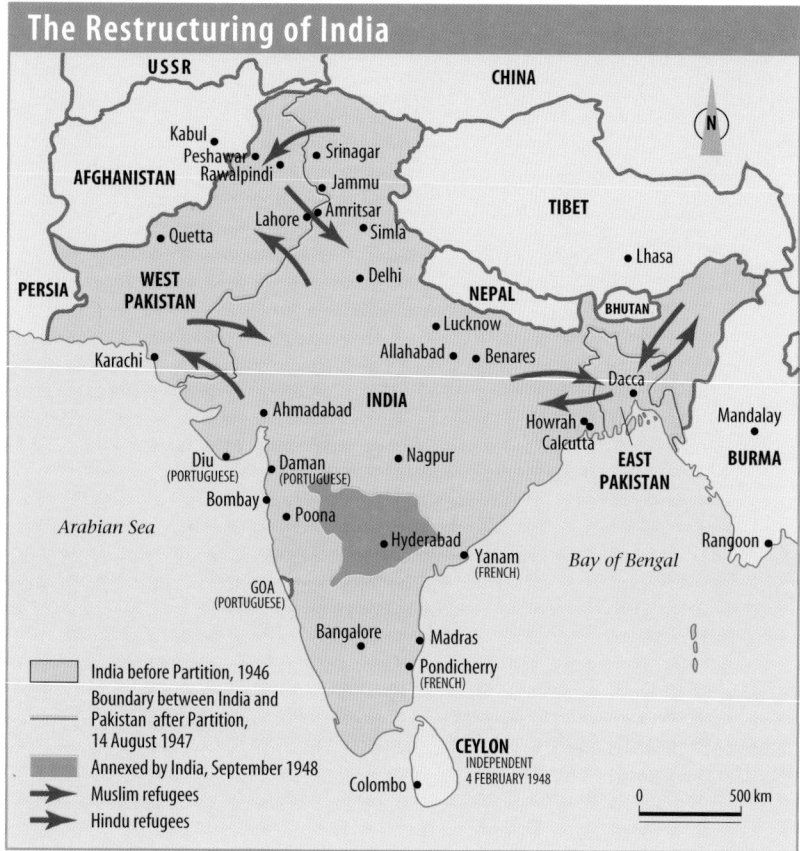

The Restructuring of India

USSR
CHINA
Kabul
Peshawar
Srinagar
Rawalpindi
AFGHANISTAN
Jammu
TIBET
Lahore
Amritsar
Quetta
Simla
N
Lhasa
PERSIA
WEST
PAKISTAN
Delhi
NEPAL
BHUTAN
Lucknow
Karachi
Allahabad
Benares
Dacca
Ahmadabad
INDIA
Mandalay
Howrah
Calcutta
EAST
BURMA
Diu
(PORTUGUESE)
Daman
(PORTUGUESE)
Nagpur
PAKISTAN
Bombay
Poona
Rangoon
Arabian Sea
Hyderabad
Yanam
(FRENCH)
Bay of Bengal
GOA
(PORTUGUESE)
Bangalore
Madras
India before Partition, 1946
Pondicherry
(FRENCH)
Boundary between India and
Pakistan after Partition,
14 August 1947
CEYLON
INDEPENDENT
4 FEBRUARY 1948
Annexed by India, September 1948
Colombo
0   500 km
Muslim refugees
Hindu refugees

By 1947, British India had been divided into two independent nations, India and Pakistan. East Pakistan later broke away and became Bangladesh. (Today, Ceylon is known as Sri Lanka.)

spread of communism ruled out any breach between them. But the grandiose plans of empire were swept away by the **wars of national liberation** that characterized the decade following 1945.

Japanese conquests had quickened the pace of nationalism throughout Asia. Experience gained in administration through collaboration with the Japanese, or through guerrilla organizations opposed to the occupation, brought forward popular leaders with massive national followings. The sudden surrender of the Japanese in the summer of 1945 created an unstable situation for several weeks before the imperial nations could get their troops into the Pacific. In the meantime, provisional governments dedicated to the exclusion of foreigners sprang up in China and the former colonies. Nationalism, running rampant amongst Asian peoples, was too strong to be controlled. More often than not this deep-seated feeling was ignored by all except Britain. The British experience in India brought about a decision not to contest independence, but to assist nationalist movements in as

friendly a manner as possible. Force of arms could not maintain an empire—as they had discovered in North America in 1776. India and Pakistan were given independence in 1947, Burma in 1948, and Malaya in 1957. France and the Netherlands attempted to retain their colonies by force and failed.

INDIA AND PAKISTAN

In 1945, Britain began the transfer of sovereignty to Indian leaders. It had promised independence to Indian leaders before and during the Second World War in return for their support of Britain's war efforts. With the war over, the question became one of timing and form. Britain suggested a three-level government: an All-India Congress, which would manage foreign affairs, defence, and communications; a middle level of three large regional groupings (of provinces and princely estates); and a lower level of local officials. Religious leader Mohandis 'Mahatma' Gandhi and future prime minister Nehru rejected the plan since it would permit provinces to choose which regional grouping they wished to belong to. They also opposed Britain's proposal to hold plebiscites in Muslim-dominated regions, fearing that a plebiscite would result in Muslim demands for a sovereign government.

During the war, the Muslim League made great strides in gaining support for a separate Muslim nation to be formed by **partitioning** the subcontinent. Muslims in the six northern provinces favoured partition and the creation of a separate state. They were convinced that in the long run there was no future for them within a Hindu-controlled union.

Despite objections from the Congress party, the British agreed to partition along religious lines, but found it difficult to determine and establish what in effect was a religious border. This was to be most difficult in Bengal and the Punjab, where Muslim and Hindu populations were mixed and more or less equal in numbers.

The Muslim League began demonstrations in favour of separation from India. Spurred by vitriolic propaganda, atrocities against the minorities began to take place throughout India. Rioting began in Calcutta, where some 4000 people were killed, but soon spread across the north. Muslims and Hindus fled their homes to the safety of friends in neighbouring regions. Reprisals led to increased strife that verged on civil war: tens of thousands were butchered in savage exchanges. There were not enough troops loyal to the central government to put down the fighting. It was also feared they might join in the massacres that raged well into the autumn.

As all authority except for that of the religious leaders seemed to have vanished, the British dispatched Lord Mountbatten to India as governor general to hurry forward the date of independence to 15 August 1947. The Mountbatten Plan proposed an exchange of populations between Hindu and Muslim regions. The 6 million Sikhs were not accorded a separate state because they did not form a majority in any of the regions they were in. A new Muslim state of Pakistan would be formed, a state further separated into two parts. East Pakistan later broke away to form Bangladesh. As the date of partition approached, 12 million people jammed the dusty highways seeking sanctuary in new homelands. For weeks on end, bewildered throngs threaded their way across a countryside filled with danger and violence. Estimates of the total loss of life during the partition were in excess of 250 000. Ironically, non-violence advocate Mahatma Gandhi was assassinated on 30 January 1948.

Since partition, India and Pakistan have resolved most of their differences. Each nation has developed in its own way and has maintained some economic ties with Great Britain.

KOREA

The surrender of Japan in 1945 led to political chaos throughout Asia. The readiness with which nationalist leaders were able to exploit the situation led to major conflicts in China (1945-1949), Korea (1950-1953), and Vietnam (1945-1975). The reaction of the superpowers to nationalist movements was to establish alliances that would expand their spheres of influence. This practice led to global expansion of the Cold War. One of the oddities was the series of attempts by both the USA and the USSR to contain the imperialistic policies of China—the Soviets through normalizing relations with Japan and signing mutual assistance treaties with India and Afghanistan; the United States by establishing the MacArthur line of island military bases stretching from Japan to the Philippines.

Jawaharlal Nehru and Mahatma Gandhi are pictured above in 1946, immediately after Nehru was elected president of the Indian National Congress Party. Although the two men worked closely to achieve India's independence, both had different ideas of how India should develop after that independence was achieved.

In August 1945, Japanese forces were ordered to stockpile their weapons in the centres of towns and await the Allied advance. In many instances, they had no one to surrender to, since Allied forces were far away and, in some cases, it was days before the formalities could be arranged. During the period before order was restored, the Soviets raced into Manchuria and Korea, and American forces advanced northward up the Korean peninsula until they met the Soviets at about the 38th parallel. The **military demarcation line**, which was to become the political boundary between North and South Korea, was made by two junior field officers.

Since then, all attempts to establish a single government for Korea have failed. In 1947, the United States took the Korean issue to the United Nations, which adopted a resolution calling for national elections under UN supervision throughout the entire peninsula. After the elections, both occupying powers were to withdraw. Elections were held in the south in May 1948, but the UN commission was denied access to the north. A government was established in the south under Syngman Rhee and it claimed to be the government of all of Korea,

NUCLEAR THREAT

North Korea is suspected of having developed

nuclear bombs in an effort to gain military strength.

When this became clear, the USA took swift action.

President Clinton demanded UN inspection of the

North Korean nuclear power plants in return for

safe fuel and light-water cores for the reactors. Two

issues are raised by the North Korean nuclear threat.

Should all nations have access to nuclear weapons?

And should disarmament be linked to economic

benefits?

The Korean peninsula was divided along the 38th parallel at the end of the Second World War. The North Korean economy, controlled by the Communist government of Kim Il Sung, had been geared to military defence and provided few consumer goods to the people. During that same period, South Korea developed a thriving industrial economy and even the USSR engaged in billions of dollars in trade with the republic in the South.

Kim was succeeded in power by his son Kim Jong Il who has continued his father's policies of isolationism. He holds power with the support of the armed forces and sees it as his duty to forcibly reunite the two Koreas. To this end, it is suspected that North Korea has developed the ability to produce nuclear bombs. In fact, many believe North Korea may have as many as five bombs already assembled.

The Americans reacted swiftly to the possibility of North Korea becoming a nuclear power. President Clinton promised the American people that he would not tolerate nuclear weapons in North Korea. He demanded that North Korea open up its nuclear power plants to UN inspection teams. Previous attempts at inspection had proven frustrating. Inspectors were certain that at least two of the nuclear plants were erected outside their view along with technical processing equipment that could transform waste products into weapon-grade plutonium.

Now, on Clinton's urging, the inspectors would be permitted to count the number of waste rods to ensure that none of the plutonium had been transferred to weapons production. One billion dollars in currency, earned by Koreans working in Japan and in the process of being sent home, was frozen until the inspection was completed. This move affected North Korea's economy as did the threat to blockade the import of oil that made up 75 per cent of North Korea's energy needs.

The North Korean stance was somewhat modified when the USA offered to supply $4 billion in safe fuel for North Korea's nuclear plants. Included in the deal were 500 000 tonnes of fuel oil and the promise to provide light-water cores for the reactors. The provision of light-water cores would render them unable to process weapon-grade plutonium.

Kim Jong Il jumped at the offer of aid. His people were desperately short of food, and there were no consumer goods on North Korean shelves. Reopening trade with the West was to his advantage. Also to his advantage was the timing of opening his nuclear program for inspection. The 8000 spent fuel rods do not have to be removed from the peninsula for another eight years. Unlimited inspections of the nuclear plants will not begin for another five years. Yet, Kim has learned that outsiders will not permit North Korea to have nuclear weapons, and that he will have to come to terms with the outside world if his economy is to improve.

1. What incentives were offered North Korea to halt its nuclear arms program?

2. Why did Kim Jong Il agree to the demands of the international community to allow nuclear inspections?

though its mandate ran only to the 38th parallel. A rival communist-backed government was established in the north. In 1949, the Americans and the Soviets both withdrew their forces according to previous agreements and left opposing hostile governments behind. On 25 June 1950, northern troops crossed the border and captured the southern capital of Seoul the next day.

The United States referred the invasion to the UN's Security Council and in the absence of the Soviet delegate, the Council passed a resolution requiring cessation of hostilities and withdrawal of the northern forces. When this resolution was ignored on 27 June, the Security Council called on all members of the UN to help South Korea repel the attack and restore peace. The return of the Soviet delegate (and Soviet veto) to the Security Council in August put an end to any chance of cooperation and collective action. The Soviet Union and China then protested against UN involvement, claiming that the invasion was not a threat to the international order and, being a domestic civil war, was outside the boundaries of UN activity. Since the Council had come to a deadlock over Korea, the USA referred the matter to the General Assembly.

The UN resolutions gave legitimacy to American military operations on the mainland. Only a handful of nations supported the UN intervention. On 8 July, General MacArthur was given command of a UN force. Over 50 per cent of the army, 85 per cent of the naval forces, and 90 per cent of the air force were American. South Korea and 15 other nations contributed sizable forces. Canada was one such nation, which sent naval and army contingents.

UN forces were able to push the North Koreans back beyond the 38th parallel. The question then became whether the task was merely to repel the aggressor or to unify the peninsula forcefully. On 7 October, the General Assembly voted for unification; and by the end of the month the UN forces were approaching the Yalu River, the boundary with Manchuria. The approach of the UN forces to the Chinese border caused panic in Beijing. Chinese Communist leaders were convinced the UN operation was a smoke screen to cover an American invasion of China to reinstate Chiang Kai-shek and the Kuomintang. There was enough warmongering in the American press to warrant such an assumption. When Premier Zhou Enlai, speaking at the UN, warned the Americans to stay away from China's boundaries and was ignored, significant numbers of Chinese troops entered Korea on 16 October, and drove the UN armies south. Chinese alarm over a

A member of the Canadian battalion in Korea is shown helping a wounded rifleman to an aid station. This picture was taken in 1951, the year negotiations for a cease-fire began. However, these soldiers would be on the battle field for two more years before a formal cease-fire could be established.

war just 700 km from Beijing was surely as genuine as American alarm at a war 8500 km away. All together, about 700 000 Chinese volunteers took part in the war. Seoul was captured by the Chinese, then retaken by the UN army. The Chinese and North Koreans were pushed back to the 38th parallel where the front stabilized until armistice negotiations began in July 1951. These talks dragged on for two more years before a formal cease-fire was agreed upon in 1953.

The People's Republic of China entered the war out of fear that the Americans intended to invade

French Indo-China from 1859 to 1954

CHINA
TONKIN
BURMA
Dien Bien Phu
Hanoi
Haiphong
Mekong
Luang Prabang
Gulf of Tonkin
Hainan Island
Vientiane
1954 PARTITION LINE
LAOS
SIAM (THAILAND)
Hué
Tourane
FRENCH SPHERE OF INFLUENCE 1904-1940
ANNAM
FRENCH 1884-1954
Bangkok
CAMBODIA
Trat
Phnom Penh
Mekong
Dalat
Gulf of Siam
Saigon
FRENCH 1867-1954
COCHIN-CHINA

French Indo-China
Annexed by Siam, 1940–1947
★ French defeat, 1954
Controlled by Ho Chi Minh:
1946–1950
1952–1954

0   200 km

This map shows the rise and fall of the French sphere of influence in Indo-China over almost 100 years.

China through Korea and reinstate Chiang Kai-shek. There had been considerable debate in the United States on the advantages to be gained by allowing the Chinese Nationalist forces in Formosa (Taiwan) to attack the Communist regime. Toward the end of the fighting, the war became more and more a Sino-American conflict. General MacArthur made no effort to conceal his desire to wage full-scale war against China if it meant using atomic bombs on China's centres of population. General MacArthur's views did not carry weight in Washington, and he was dismissed for pursuing a policy not approved by his government. The United States deliberately chose not to use nuclear weapons to achieve a military victory.

The Korean question was taken up at the Geneva conference in 1954, but the conference failed to produce an agreement on the Koreas. The status quo remains in effect, even though all parties agree that unification is desirable.

VIETNAM

The French established themselves in Asia in the later part of the nineteenth century, when they took under their control the protectorates of Annam, Tonkin, and Cochin-China, called the Three Kys, and the protected kingdoms of Laos and Cambodia. Together these made up French Indo-China, which the French held unopposed until 1940. The Japanese occupied Indo-China from 1940 to 1945. During the occupation, the Three Kys became the autonomous state of Vietnam. While other nationalist groups fled to China or collaborated with the French or Japanese, the Communist party led by Ho Chi Minh resisted the invaders and gained popular nationalist support in a united front called the Viet Minh (Independence League). The Japanese set up a new government in Vietnam under Bao Dai to safeguard their position, but upon Japan's surrender, the Communists took power in Vietnam under a provisional government.

At the end of the war the British liberated the southern part of Vietnam, to the 17th parallel, and the Chinese Nationalist forces liberated the northern part. Both the Chinese and the British withdrew in 1946 in favour of the returning French, but not before Chiang Kai-shek had officially recognized Ho Chi Minh's provisional government in North Vietnam. At one point, Ho Chi Minh tried to get the Americans involved in hastening Chinese Nationalist withdrawal from his country, but to no avail. Indo-China was not a priority for the USA at the time, nor were the Americans about to create a rift with France, whose support they needed in Europe.

The French refused to recognize Ho Chi Minh's government and re-established their own control over the region from Saigon in South Vietnam. They offered Ho Chi Minh's provisional government an associate-state status within the French Empire, but this was not the full independence Ho Chi Minh desired. In November 1946, the French bombed Haiphong, and the Viet Minh responded the following month with raids against the French in Hanoi, killing 40 and abducting 200 people. The resulting war was to last 7.5 years, ending in the French defeat at Dien Bien Phu in 1954. In the next few years, the French attempted to win other nationalist parties to their side, with only modest success.

The war taking place simultaneously in Korea transformed the fight in Vietnam into an anti-communist crusade. This brought a massive influx of

American aid, which by 1954 had risen to $1.1 billion—78 per cent of the French war effort. It was not enough for South Vietnam to win the war. In 1952, for example, the Viet Minh guerrilla forces took control of the countryside. French losses of soldiers and *matériel* from ambush and sabotage escalated, while the kingdoms of Laos and Cambodia gained their independence. In November 1953, hoping to bring the guerrillas out in the open to do battle, the French established a small garrison camp in the north-west at Dien Bien Phu. The camp was well sited to interdict supplies coming from the North down the Ho Chi Minh Trail. The trail was a network of paths that formed a highway for goods sent by Ho Chi Minh to support the Viet Minh in the South. At Dien Bien Phu, the French general Navarre hoped to draw the bulk of the Viet Minh forces into the open to destroy them. Instead he found himself surrounded by the Viet Minh, who overran his defences after a six-month siege. This defeat convinced the French to leave Indo-China.

On 26 April 1954, a nine-power conference on Vietnam and Korea met at Geneva. The USSR and Britain, the co-chairs, pushed the pace of negotiation, fearful lest the war escalate to the international level and the Americans use their nuclear bomb in support of a NATO ally. Both hoped to arrange a graceful withdrawal for the French and a smooth transfer of power to a nationalist government. When neither objective could be attained, they made provision for the division of Vietnam along the 17th parallel, an exchange of populations, and withdrawal of forces to be supervised by Canada, Poland, and India. The new boundaries were to be guaranteed by China, Britain, France, and the USSR. Elections were to be held throughout the two zones within two years to choose a government. Had these elections been held, the larger population in the North would have guaranteed a communist government. The USA was not party to the agreements and not bound by their terms, although the superpower promised not to upset the situation if stability was restored. Certain of American support, the South also disassociated itself from the Geneva agreements.

The Americans acted to support a southern regime under Bao Dai and later Ngo Dinh Diem, and by 1955 long-range American-led patrols were active in the North around Hanoi. The USA further moved to reinforce its position through the formation of SEATO, an alliance of three Asian and five non-Asian nations (Pakistan, Thailand, and the Philippines, the USA, Australia, New Zealand,

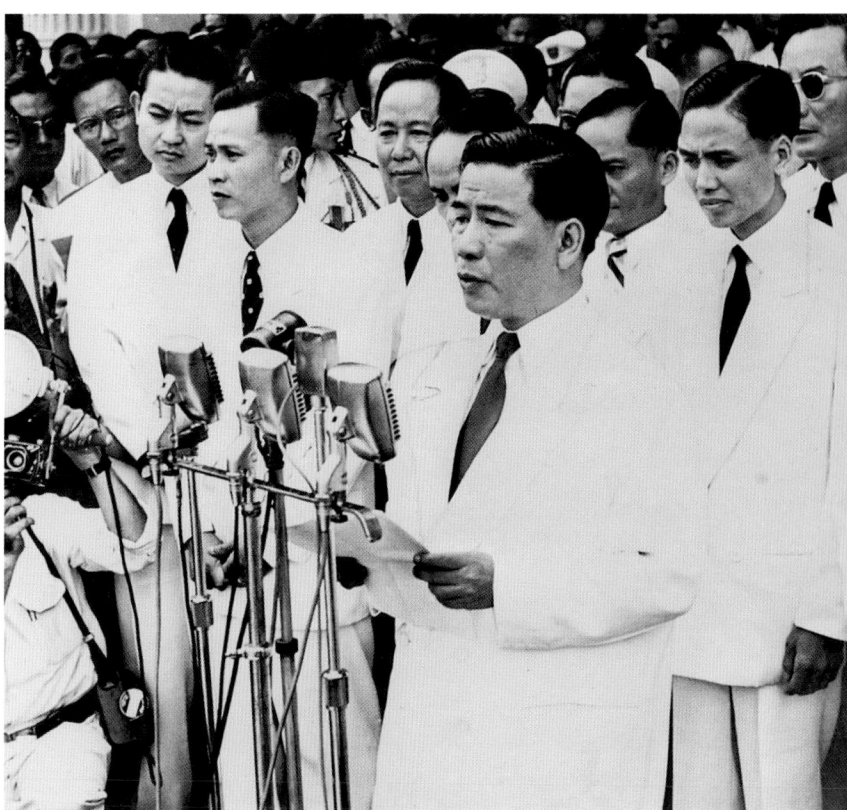

Ngo Dinh Diem took the oath of office as the first president of the Republic of Vietnam in 1955. Although originally supported by the United States, Diem was murdered in a 1963 military *coup* which was reportedly backed by the United States.

Britain, and France). SEATO was to provide joint action in the case of a renewal of war in Vietnam. The alliance never got off the ground and did not help to save Vietnam from communist dominance. SEATO was dissolved in 1975.

In the North, Ho Chi Minh began a program of agrarian reform modeled on the Chinese collective. The program ended in a bloody peasant uprising during which 50 000 people were killed. Essential foodstuffs had to be imported from the South and attempts to industrialize required support from the USSR and Czechoslovakia.

Meanwhile, the Americans moved to support the South. The great fear was that if South Vietnam fell to the communists, all the other states in Asia would follow suit—the **domino theory**. By June 1955, the number of American advisors to South Vietnam surpassed the limits established at Geneva.

After the war, the South was reasonably prosperous; but one million refugees from the North, mostly Catholic, were a burden. The new prime minister, Ngo Dinh Diem, was one of these refugees, and in 1955 declared himself president of the

BIOGRAPHY

HO CHI MINH (1890–1969)

With the start of the first Chinese revolution, it was decided, in consultation with his father, that the fiercely patriotic Ho should expose himself to Western ways and sciences before embarking on a revolutionary career. Because Ho had little money, his ticket to the West was a job as a messboy aboard a French liner. From 1912, Ho visited London and the USA, settling in Paris in 1918. While in Paris, Ho worked as a photo-retoucher, cook, and gardener while writing for the anti-colonial newspapers *Paria* and *Viet Nam.* In his second publication, Ho stated his Eight-Point Programme which he tried to submit to US President Wilson at the Versailles Peace Conference. Ho's demands on behalf of Vietnamese colonials included: "the right of self-determination; constitutional government; democratic freedom; equality of the law for Vietnamese and French; amnesty for political prisoners; freedom of the press; freedom to organize and assemble; abolition of forced labour, the salt tax and forced consumption of alcohol." This Eight-Point Programme, however, never made it onto the Versailles agenda.

With this last show of western indifference towards Vietnam's plight, Ho wholeheartedly turned toward the Soviet Union—bastion for the oppressed—for understanding and support. A further push in this direction came when the French Socialist party, of which Ho was a member, refused to take seriously Lenin's program which called for the immediate freedom of colonized peoples. Out of this difference within the French Socialist party, the French Communist party was formed, with Ho as one of its founding members. From 1922 on, Ho was often in Moscow. Tran Ngoc Danh, compatriot with Ho, made the following observation about Ho's communism:

How many times in my life have I been asked: you who know Ho Chi Minh so well, can you say whether he is a nationalist or a communist? The answer is simple: Ho Chi Minh is both. For him, nationalism and communism, the end and the means, complement one another; or rather they merge inextricably.

After having been away from Vietnam for many years, Ho returned in February of 1941 and successfully brought all those factions that resisted the French under his control. Paul Mus, the French expert on Vietnam during those years, was struck by the fact that Ho's long absence from his

Ho Chi Minh, whose birth-name was Nguyen That Thanh, was born into a household of scholar-revolutionaries in the village of Kim Lien, in the province of Nghe An, in central Vietnam on 19 May 1890. In the preceding years, family members and relations had been dismissed from government service for anti-French activity. When Ho was 9 years old, he and his mother fled to Hue, after having been charged with stealing weapons from the French to pass on to the anti-French rebels. His mother died in Hue a year later, and Ho returned to Kim Lien to finish his schooling. At 17 he journeyed to the south and became an elementary school teacher for a brief time.

homeland had not made him lose touch with it at all. On the contrary, as Ho biographer David Halberstam noted, Ho had kept his thumb on the earth, thereby realizing the simple Chinese proverb that a thumb-square of planting rice is more precious than a thumb-square of gold. Ho was deeply connected with the millions of peasants in the rice fields, who at the sight of him would be willing to give their life blood to realize their independence as a nation.

At this time Ho founded an independence league known as Viet Minh, whose mandate it was to coordinate all nationalist activities in the struggle for independence. At the end of the Second World War, the Viet Minh took over Vietnam, and Ho proclaimed Vietnam's independence on 2 September 1945. However, the French would not be turned away that easily, and war broke out against the French in 1946, lasting until a humiliating French defeat in 1954 at Dien Bien Phu. The peace agreement that was reached at the time partitioned Vietnam along the 17th parallel and promised that country-wide elections would take place within two years to reunify Vietnam. Because it was not in the interests of any Western countries to uphold this agreement, it was never carried out.

In 1954-55, Ho became prime minister and president of North Vietnam, and the Viet Minh resumed terrorist attacks in the South. Representing Ho in the South was the Viet Cong, also supported by China. The USA responded to the terrorism by increasing their assistance to the South, sending combat troops into Vietnam and later beginning the systematic bombing of the North. American involvement in Vietman continued until 1975. With hardly a respite, Americans had replaced the French as the foreign invaders of Vietnam, and like the French they began sinking into the quagmire of Vietnamese desperation and fierce patriotism.

During the Vietnam War, United Nations secretary general U Thant tried in vain to mediate between Washington and Ho. Furthermore, Thant put out a statement which concluded that it was not the communist threat which had devastated Vietnam, but foreign intervention. This was in keeping with Ho's conviction and bottom-line of reaching a peace with the United States, namely that all foreign troops leave Vietnam, and that the Vietnamese people in the North and South be allowed to settle their own affairs.

US president Lyndon Johnson kept insisting that Ho did not want peace, when in fact what Ho did not want was peace on American terms. An American peace would have undermined Ho's government and kept Vietnam a divided people with the South under a puppet regime. In the years between 1967 and 1969, Ho had little need to defend his position: Western journalists did the job for him. Most journalists returning from a first-hand look at Vietnam guiltily questioned or openly railed against American involvement.

This far-away war in defense of people they hardly know, even today, has created deep chasms among adults and helped to trigger a rebellion among the young. It has destroyed many well-established assumptions. It has led to the abdication of the American president and the electoral defeat of his party, and has cruelly scarred the US reputation around the world. The war has undermined America's confidence in the judgment of their leaders, in their institutions, their military establishments, and their foreign policy. It has enflamed the young to the extent that they have begun to resist military service as perhaps never before in American history.
—Henry Brandon. *Anatomy of Error.* (1970)

Ho died of a heart attack on 3 September 1969, without having realized his lifelong dream of uniting all of Vietnam under communism. At his death, *Time* magazine featured his face on their front cover for the fourth time. The following tribute was written:

Ho Chi Minh's life was dedicated to the creation of a united Vietnam, free from foreign control, and the 19 million people of his tortured land suffered mightily from his total devotion to that vision. Even so, they affectionately knew him as "Bac Ho" (Uncle Ho). So did many in the South. No national leader alive today has stood so stubbornly or so long before enemy guns. ●

republic. To the USA he was an anti-communist ally. But Diem treated the South as a family business, to be administered not by democracy but by secret societies antagonizing the dominant Buddhist sect. His administration was particularly corrupt and, what is more important, without public support. In 1960, when Diem cut off food supplies to the North to force the North to beg for unification on his terms, Ho Chi Minh decided to send aid to the anti-Diem forces around Saigon. From then on, an active communist opposition grew in the South under the name Viet Cong. The Viet Cong had broad support in the countryside, stemming in part from the brutal exactions the Diem government inflicted on its peasant population.

American policy at this time was to support what to them was an anti-communist regime and potential ally on the American defence perimeter. With a heightened sense of public mission, the Americans were intent on protecting the peoples of Asia from communist aggression.

The role of the Viet Cong in what happened next is open to debate. One version is that the revolution in the South began as a spontaneous protest against a repressive Catholic regime, and that the communists belatedly became part of the movement. The other version is that the uprisings in the 1960s were orchestrated by Hanoi in North Vietnam with Soviet help. In hindsight, the former seems more plausible. In any case, in 1963 Buddhist hostility to the Catholic regime reached a climax: Buddhist monks publicly burned themselves to death to protest government corruption. They were the spearhead of mass demonstrations against the Diem regime in the South. The authorities responded by sacking Buddhist monasteries and torturing monks. At this, the Americans cut off aid to the Diem government and began to plot Diem's removal. After Diem's overthrow, government followed government, *coup* followed *coup*, until some semblance of stability was reached under Generals Nguyen Ky and Nguyen Van Thieu, in 1965.

During the early 1960s, the Viet Cong extended their operations to drive the Americans out of the countryside and into the cities, but an increase in the number of American forces blunted the Viet Cong offensive. At this point, North Vietnam decided to send regular divisions into the South to rescue their allies. The American response was to send special forces (the Green Berets) into the countryside to win the people to their side. Under the "protected hamlet plan," peasants were to be gathered in defensible strong points to deny food and

shelter to the guerrillas. The system had worked in Malaya, where the Malayan peasants did not support the Chinese guerrillas, but in Vietnam, the peasants and guerrillas were of the same ethnic background. The peasants continued to support their people. Some 12 000 villages were relocated and placed under government protection. The system caused even more opposition to the Diem regime. Most of the villagers resisted resettlement. They were content to stay in their homes and deal directly with the Viet Cong, whom they did not see as their enemy.

The war was extended to the North in 1964, when an American destroyer was allegedly attacked by Vietnamese gunboats in the Gulf of Tonkin. American president Lyndon Johnson used the incident to get Congressional approval to fight back. In 1965, bombing reprisals were begun against Haiphong harbour; and by the end of 1968, the Americans had 500 000 soldiers in the field.

By 1967, it was becoming clear the Americans could not win the war without destroying the very people and country they had come to protect. The massive aerial bombardment of enemy strongholds was marginally more effective than the bombing raids in the Second World War, but it could not defeat the enemy. A military solution was impossible; only a political solution could end the fighting. President Johnson offered to negotiate an end to the war, provided that South Vietnam could remain an independent state, that it be supported by American economic aid, and that the USA supplied a further $16 billion in aid to Southeast Asia, including North Vietnam. The proposal hinged on a division of the country and Ho Chi Minh rejected it. Premier Pham Van Dong of the Communist party countered the American bid with another calling for the evacuation of all foreign troops from the Vietnams and for the Vietnamese to decide their future internally. The two positions were irreconcilable.

In 1968, the Viet Cong made a spectacular but militarily ineffective attack, called the Tet Offensive, on all the American bases during Tet holiday celebrations. The Viet Cong attacked the cities with a strength of 84 000. They had smuggled in stockpiles of weapons and ammunition in the previous weeks and hoped to rouse the citizens against the government. Yet some 35 000 Viet Cong were killed, and the Viet Cong effectively lost their ability to wage conventional warfare. Seeing the enemy reeling, General Westmoreland asked for a dramatic increase in American military forces to finish the job. When this request was leaked to the press, the American public reacted with some of the largest anti-war demonstrations ever staged.

The Viet Cong besieged the southern city of Saigon and took and held Hue, the ancient capital, for a few weeks, but the hoped-for insurrection in Saigon had not occurred. At the same time, however, television reporting brought events into American homes and strengthened domestic criticism of the war. The use of napalm and defoliants caused particular revulsion. So great was the public backlash against the war that President Johnson decided not to run for reelection and, in November, Richard Nixon became president of the United States.

President Nixon was faced with the dilemma of how to get the Americans out of an unpopular war. Intensive bombardment had not worked. The dropping of 7.8 million tonnes of bombs on an area a bit larger than France—in the most intensive strategic bombing campaign in history—had not brought North Vietnam's surrender. Industrial, transportation, and oil and gas facilities were repeatedly hit, but this did not weaken the North Vietnamese resolve to persevere. Nor could the bombing curtail the shipment of soldiers and arms to the South in support of the Viet Cong. After particularly heavy raids in 1972, virtually all industrial and communications facilities were destroyed.

In May 1968, talks opened between the USA and North Vietnam in Paris. They were joined by the Viet Cong and representatives from South Vietnam. The talks were to drag out over the next four years. The delay brought renewed American attempts to cut the Ho Chi Minh Trail by invasion of Laos and Cambodia. These invasions of what the anti-war movement termed neutral countries caused further furor, though the Viet Cong controlled such border regions and built up supplies there. Nixon also began to turn more of the fighting over to the South Vietnamese Army. Lavishly equipped with weapons and supplies, the South Vietnamese Army were to take over the defence of their own country as the Americans withdrew. Beginning in 1969, the Americans began to cut their own forces in Asia by half, creating doubt among other Asian allies about American commitment to hemispheric defence.

The Paris agreements of January 1973 called for a cease-fire in Vietnam, removal of all foreign troops from Vietnam, Laos, and Kampuchea (known as Cambodia before 1976 and after 1989), and recognition of the sovereignty of both Vietnams. Prisoners of war were to be released within 60 days, the time allotted to American evacuation. After the

In the weeks immediately before the 1975 fall of Saigon, the United States scrambled to evacuate American citizens and certain Vietnamese citizens. However, many Vietnamese citizens who had wanted to flee the country were prevented by a lack of ready transportation.

American withdrawal, the war heated up again and the North forcefully unified the nation. When the fighting came to an end in 1975, some 2 million Vietnamese had been killed and the country laid waste. The Americans had spent over $ 100 billion and suffered 55 000 dead. Saigon was renamed Ho Chi Minh City.

After the communist victory, hundreds of thousands of Vietnamese sought to flee the new government by crowding into small boats and heading out to sea in hope of rescue. The exodus was a spontaneous movement, but it was encouraged by the government. It is thought that as many as 70 per cent of the boat people were killed by pirates, storms, drowning, or starvation; only 400 000 made it to relative safety. After world attention was drawn to the plight of the boat people, a solution was found for the almost 840 000 Vietnamese refugees. Seven hundred fifty thousand were resettled in countries like Canada, the USA, Australia, France, Great Britain, and Germany. Others were placed in camps in Hong Kong, Singapore, Thailand, and the Philippines. They are now being forcibly repatriated to Vietnam with promises that the Vietnamese government will not conduct reprisals on them.

The unification of the Vietnams did not stop the fighting in the region. In efforts to dominate the region, the Vietnamese invaded Cambodia (Kampuchea) in 1978 and repulsed a Chinese invasion in 1979. In both instances Vietnam received support from the USSR. Vietnam had become an important factor in the USSR's attempt to contain China. The Soviets vetoed the condemnation of Vietnam by the Security Council and stationed guided-missile equipped squadrons in Vietnam waters from time to time. In the later part of the 1980s, the United States attempted once more to gain some influence in the region. On 11 July 1995, President Bill Clinton announced his intention to normalize relations with the Vietnam government. This initiative resulted from a recognition that Vietnam has adopted a free market economy and a more open society. An improved relationship between the USA and Vietnam will allow a substantial increase in American investment in the region as well as a resurgence of tourism. Steps were taken in this direction in 1994 when the American trade embargo on Vietnam was lifted. However, lingering American concerns regarding those soldiers still identified as "missing in action" or "prisoners of war" continue to plague relationships between the two countries.

MISSING SOLDIERS

As of July 1995, there were 2198 Americans still unaccounted for as a result of the Vietnam War. The USA spends upwards of $100 million US annually in attempts to locate those soldiers identified as MIA (missing in action) or POW (prisoner of war). Vietnamese MIAs number 300 000. Citizens of Vietnam are openly concerned about their government's reluctance to invest in the search for these individuals.

SUMMARY

The American occupation of Japan in 1945 was the beginning of Japan's transformation into a modern industrial power. Adapting to the ways of the conqueror, Japanese society was in a position to benefit from American involvement in wars on the Asian mainland. Japan became the staging base for the Korean and Vietnam wars and anchored the American island defence line that limited Chinese expansion. Allied to the United States, the Japanese experienced rapid economic growth in the last half-century and became one of the world's great economic powers.

The sudden surrender of Japanese forces in August 1945 caught the Allies off guard. In the interval between the surrender and the arrival of Allied forces, a number of nationalist leaders established their own governments in the former colonies. They wanted recognition of national sovereignty and an end to imperialism in Asia. Local heroes then led the movement for independence against attempts by the colonial powers to reassert their control. Britain moved quickly to grant the Indian subcontinent its independence in 1947 and, soon afterward, to give independence to other British colonies. The Dutch and French attempted to maintain their colonies by force, and failed. The nationalist movement got caught up in Cold War rivalry between the USA and the USSR when the Korean War (1950-1953) drew the attention of the superpowers to the Pacific. Attempts by nationalists to seize power were seen as communist expansion and were challenged by American military action in both Korea and Vietnam.

The French attempted to regain control over Vietnam between 1945 and 1954. Unable to persevere against Ho Chi Minh's forces, they withdrew in 1954. Their place was taken by the Americans, who gave increasing military support to the South Vietnamese government after 1962. The Vietnam War ended in bitter defeat for the South in 1973, with the withdrawal of US forces. The Vietnams were forcibly reunited in subsequent military action by North Vietnam. More recently, Vietnam has been engaged in action in Laos and Cambodia (Kampuchea).

QUESTIONS

1. Explain the nature of the United States' occupation of Japan after the Second World War.

2. Why did the United States support the reconstruction of Japan?

3. How did Nixon's rapprochement with China in 1972 affect Japan?

4. Evaluate the economic power of Japan and comment on its place in the international marketplace.

5. What was the major issue in the achievement of India's independence from Britain? How was this issue resolved?

6. Explain the significance of Korea in post-war Asia.

7. What role did the United Nations play in the Korean War? Why?

8. Explain why China became involved in the Korean War. Evaluate Mao's policy on the Yalu border. Was it reasonable?

9. Why was General MacArthur dismissed by Truman? Why was the war in Korea limited?

10. Explain the French position in Indo-China.

11. How did the Korean War affect the Vietnam War?

12. What occurred in 1954 at Dien Bien Phu? Explain its significance for the French and the Americans.

13. What was the aim of Ho Chi Minh and his followers? Why did the USA not recognize Ho Chi Minh's government?

14. Evaluate the Gulf of Tonkin incident in 1964 in relation to subsequent events. How was it important?

15. What were the terms of the Paris agreements in 1973?

16. What was achieved by the fighting in Vietnam for the Vietnamese, the Americans, and the Soviets?

CRITICAL ANALYSIS

1. Describe how decolonization altered the world's power structure.

2. Explain the differences between conventional and guerrilla warfare.

3. What role did civil disturbances in the USA have on military strategy in Vietnam?

4. Is consistency or flexibility more realistic in conducting a nation's foreign affairs?

5. Should a nation's foreign and military policies be open to public scrutiny?

6. Why could the superpowers not defeat national liberation movements?

RESEARCH PROJECTS

1. Research the reconstruction of Japan after the Second World War. Evaluate the role played by the United States and comment on the current economic power of Japan in relation to that of the United States. Predict how this power distribution might change by the year 2010.

2. Research the role of the Viet Cong in the Vietnam War.

   Describe the tactics they used in fighting the war.

3. Research one of the following battles: (a) Dien Bien Phu; (b) Gulf of Tonkin; (c) Tet Offensive. Describe the course of events, immediate results, and long-term impact on the course of the war.

4. Research MacArthur's role in the Korean War. Evaluate his impact on the war.

ACTIVITIES

1 Debate

Be it resolved that the Korean War was, in fact, an American military venture in support of the US policy of containment, rather than a United Nations operation.

2 Collage

Make a collage of goods exported by Japan.
or
Make a collage of goods imported by Japan. Indicate the cost of these imported goods and note the average Japanese wage at the bottom of your collage.

3 Panel Discussion

Structure a panel to discuss Japanese investment in western Canada. Should Canadians be concerned about foreign ownership? What sort of liaisons should be established with the Japanese in the promotion of cultural and business exchange? Are there some mutual benefits to consider?

HISTORICAL ANALYSIS

ASIA TODAY

The decolonization of Asia established a variety of regimes ranging from the totalitarian government of the People's Republic of China to the democracy of Taiwan, but the feature common to the entire area was a powerful surge of nationalism. Wars of national liberation and proxy wars, resulting from the Cold War conflict, were essentially over by 1990. As we approach the twenty-first century, the dynamics of the region are shifting. No longer dominated by western colonial powers, Asian nations are carving out their place in Asia, as well as in the global network. In doing so, they risk political and military conflict over territory strategic to their security and those territories containing natural resources such as oil. The potential for conflict is compounded by the threat of nuclear weapons' development in North Korea and the threat of nuclear development in Japan. China has been a nuclear power since 1968.

Select one of the following countries for research: China, Taiwan, Vietnam, the Koreas (consider the possibility of reunification), Thailand, Malaysia, or Indonesia.

Analyse the way in which the political and economic systems are changing to propel these countries into a more influential role in international relationships. What factors suggest that the country can change its position in the international community? What political system prevails? What economic development is occurring? How is this country's relationship with others in the region likely to develop? Are there any territorial disputes currently at issue? What is the country's relationship with North America and Europe?

Suggested resources:

Bih-jaw Lin and James T. Myers (ed). *Contemporary China in the Post-Cold War Era.* Columbia: University of South Carolina Press, 1986.

Copper, John F. *Taiwan: Nation-state or Province?* 2nd edition. Boulder: Westview, 1996.

Schwarz, Adam. *A Nation in Waiting: Indonesia in the 1990s.* Australia: Allen & Unwin, 1994.

THE PEOPLE'S REPUBLIC: CHINA AFTER 1945

CHAPTER 14

TIME LINE

1 October	1949:	Mao Zedong proclaimed the People's Republic of China
	1950:	Mutual defence treaty re-negotiated between China and the USSR
1953 - 1957:		China's first Five Year Plan
2 May	1956:	Mao's one hundred schools of thought speech
	1956:	Great Leap Forward
1966 - 1976:		Cultural Revolution
	1971:	China allowed into the United Nations
	1972:	American president Nixon visited China
	1976:	Mao Zedong died
	1978:	Deng Xiaoping became leader
	1980:	China's One Child Policy was introduced
	1987:	Student demonstrations
June	1989:	Tiananmen Square demonstration
February	1997:	Deng Xiaoping died
1 July	1997:	Hong Kong reverted from British to Chinese Control

FOCUS ON NATIONAL DEVELOPMENT

One year is but a flash in the endless flow of history. Nevertheless in this fleeting year, the Party Central Committee headed by Chairman Hu has led us from victory to victory in grasping the key link of class struggle and running the country well. From their own experience the people of China have come to understand more and more deeply that socialist revolution and socialist construction in China have truly entered a new period of development, and that the Party Central Committee headed by Chairman Hu deserves to be called the vigorous fighting command of the proletariat which holds aloft the great banner of Chairman Mao. The whole Party, the whole army, and the people of all nationalities throughout the country are delighted to have such a wise leader and supreme commander as Chairman Hu. When drinking water think of its source. Therefore we all the more cherish the memory of our great leader and teacher Chairman Mao who showed great foresight in choosing such an excellent successor for us. And it is invincible Mao Zedong Thought that has guided us to advance from victory to victory.

A joint editorial issued by Beijing's leading daily newspapers on 1 January 1978, translated and republished in *Peking Review*, 6 January 1978.

"When drinking water, think of its source." The student demonstrations in Beijing's Tiananmen Square in 1989 shocked a world which believed that the People's Republic of China had begun to forcefully and conclusively move away from its Maoist/Communist past. Is China actually changing? If so, what does the future hold for the world's most populous country? Using the historical data in this chapter and popular media sources, prepare a "briefing paper," outlining and defending your predictions for China to the year 2010.

OVERVIEW

China's unusual history includes civil war, superpower involvement, social revolution, agricultural and industrial reform, the Great Leap Forward, the Cultural Revolution, and Deng's economic reforms.

INTERNATIONAL INTEREST IN CHINA

Both the former Soviet Union and the United States viewed with interest the struggle between the Nationalist Chinese and the Communist Chinese. In 1949, Mao's Communist forces were successful in driving the Nationalists into exile in Taiwan.

THE PEOPLE'S REPUBLIC OF CHINA

The new Communist government in China moved immediately to consolidate its political control and attempt to achieve recognition internationally.

AGRARIAN AND INDUSTRIAL REORGANIZATION

The collectivization of agriculture and state planning of industry resulted in widespread economic reform.

FOREIGN POLICY

Conflict with the Soviet Union and the USA, and competition with Taiwan, hampered China's attempts to achieve international recognition, and entry into the United Nations was not granted until 1971.

THE CULTURAL REVOLUTION

In 1967, Mao directed the youth in a campaign against the intellectuals and urged destruction of tradition.

DENG XIAOPING

In 1978, Deng Xiaoping attained control of China and embarked on a radical new economic program which injected some market characteristics into China's command economy.

CHINA: TIANANMEN SQUARE 1987-1990

Economic reforms in China brought hopes for political reforms as well. These hopes were effectively dashed in June 1989 when the government forcefully put down student demonstrations in Tiananmen Square and imposed martial law.

INTERNATIONAL INTEREST IN CHINA

In the summer of 1945, Chiang Kai-shek's Nationalist armies streamed out of the interior into the cities of central China and beyond to eastern seaports that had been under Japanese control since 1937. It was a race against time: civil war was about to break out between the Kuomintang and Mao Zedong's Communist forces in the North. Chiang also wanted to get hold of the huge stores of materials the Japanese had left behind in Manchuria, close to Mao's centre of power. The Americans assisted the Nationalist forces by providing air and sea transportation as well as by moving 100 000 men onto the mainland to occupy Beijing and South Korea.

In order to avert a civil war, the Americans urged Chiang to broaden the base of the Kuomintang to take in other parties, including Mao's Communists. A united front could bring peace and prosperity to the world's most populous nation. President Truman wanted some kind of accommodation between the Nationalists and the Communists, and American threats to withhold supplies brought an uneasy truce between contending factions throughout most of 1946. Discussions were held between a number of political groups on proposed land reform, free elections, the merging of rival armies under a national command, civil liberties, and an end to the rampant corruption amongst Chinese bureaucrats. All these initiatives were still-born. Chiang reopened his war against the Communists. Misled by his armies' swift advance on China's cities, he believed he was strong enough to rid China of his enemies with or without American support.

Stalin too was concerned about the future of China. Sharing a 7500 km border with the republic, the Soviets saw themselves in a position to influence China's post-war direction. They decided to support Chiang instead of Mao, for Mao wanted all foreigners to leave China, and this included Soviets. The Soviets also felt that Mao's communist movement was too weak to be of permanent value to them. It was made up of an illiterate peasantry without a concentrated proletariat unlike the Soviet model. Chiang was of more use to them than Mao. The Soviets genuinely believed that the Chinese communist revolution would have to wait until China was industrialized. The Soviets accordingly urged Mao to negotiate with the Kuomintang.

Mao complied in the short term. But he had already decided against using the Soviet model. He would create a **China model** and use the peasantry as his soldiers in social revolution. China's peasantry was formidable in numbers if not expertise—95 per cent of a population of 500 million. A protracted guerrilla war in the countryside could deny the cities food and other materials and it would cut communications and bottle up the Nationalist armies in their fortresses. Peasant soldiers would not assault the cities defended by the Kuomintang but would isolate garrisons in smaller towns and villages. In the final stage, guerrilla bands would link up as armies to administer the final blow. This model has since been adopted by movements in many Third World countries, who have found themselves without an urban proletariat.

The Soviets concluded a treaty with Chiang in which they promised to withdraw their forces from Manchuria and limit Mao's operations in the North. In return, they would regain their boundaries of 1904, get access to Lüshun as a warm-water port, use Dalian as a Pacific base, and take ownership of the mines and industrial plants in Manchuria, as well as control the Chinese Eastern and Southern Manchurian railways. A plebiscite was to be held in Outer Mongolia to see which sphere that country would belong to.

The Soviets proposed even more aid if China would rid itself of American influence. The very fact that Chiang was prepared to consider this proposal made the Americans furious. Such a proposal was unthinkable after all the aid the USA had given Chiang over the years. Unaware that the Americans had already decided to not get involved in any fighting on the mainland, Chiang believed that no matter what he did, his American allies would never let him lose.

In 1946, the Soviets abruptly abandoned Manchuria and allowed the Chinese Communists access to the resources they had left behind. Nationalist troops rushed into the North to counter the Communist threat, and bitter fighting broke out. The war resulted in a military victory for the Communists in 1949 and the flight of Nationalist leaders and forces to the island of Taiwan (Formosa), where they came under the protection of the American Seventh Fleet. There, with American support and to the detriment of the native population, Chiang reorganized his government in hope of returning to the mainland. In Beijing, amid the victorious and jubilant Communist forces, Mao

In Shanghai, the municipal police, with the support of the Nationalist armies, executed Communists in the streets. Soon after this photograph was taken, the Red Army took Shanghai.

proclaimed the People's Republic of China on 1 October 1949.

Mao had risen to popular support on an anti-Japanese crusade. Now he called upon the masses to rise against the Kuomintang and the landowners, and to rid China of all foreign influence. He demanded an end to government corruption that dehumanized the people. The Kuomintang had been unable to make any headway toward economic reforms. In many instances, urban and rural people had been better off under the Japanese; at least they had had enough to eat. Corruption was so rampant that Kuomintang officials sold off factories and land and pocketed the cash, misused millions of dollars allocated for defence, squeezed the poor for all of their savings, and squandered not just large-scale American aid but also a $500 million United Nations loan. The hearts and minds of the people began to shift to the Communists, to Mao's promise of land reform and honest government.

Mao had wanted to carry out the first social revolution in China in 2000 years. Few realized how simple it was going to be. China was a land of peasant farmers, and 70 per cent of them (350 million farmers) were landless. Without land ownership, the peasant had no social status. Mao promised

249

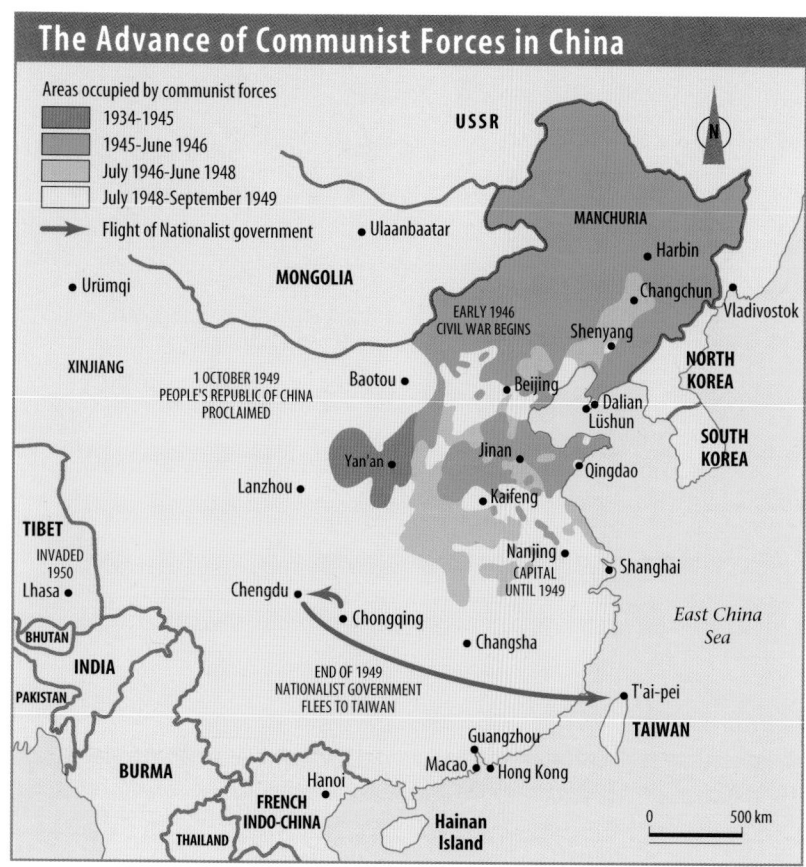

The Advance of Communist Forces in China

Areas occupied by communist forces
- 1934–1945
- 1945–June 1946
- July 1946–June 1948
- July 1948–September 1949
→ Flight of Nationalist government

USSR

MONGOLIA

MANCHURIA

Ulaanbaatar

Urümqi

Harbin

Changchun

Vladivostok

Shenyang

EARLY 1946
CIVIL WAR BEGINS

XINJIANG

1 OCTOBER 1949
PEOPLE'S REPUBLIC OF CHINA
PROCLAIMED

Baotou

Beijing

NORTH
KOREA

Dalian
Lüshun

SOUTH
KOREA

Yan'an

Jinan

Qingdao

Lanzhou

Kaifeng

TIBET
INVADED
1950

Lhasa

BHUTAN

Nanjing
CAPITAL
UNTIL 1949

Shanghai

Chengdu

Chongqing

East China
Sea

INDIA

PAKISTAN

Changsha

END OF 1949
NATIONALIST GOVERNMENT
FLEES TO TAIWAN

T'ai-pei

TAIWAN

BURMA

Guangzhou

Macao
Hong Kong

Hanoi

FRENCH
INDO-CHINA

THAILAND

Hainan
Island

0   500 km

Mao's forces steadily gained support throughout China after the Japanese withdrew. This map shows the areas occupied by the Communist forces from the 1930s to 1949.

them land ownership. Of the peasants who were landowners, very few had large estates. The country gentry who had controlled the countryside had vanished during the Japanese occupation. Their collaboration in Japanese plundering of farms destroyed what loyalty they once commanded; many of them fled with Chiang to sanctuary in Taiwan in 1949. In the cities, financiers and bureaucrats took what they could—and when the time came, they too fled to Taiwan or elsewhere.

THE PEOPLE'S REPUBLIC OF CHINA

The People's Republic of China (PRC) now had to gain diplomatic recognition from other nations. It was more difficult than the new government had imagined. Only the Soviets extended immediate recognition. Britain and a few other nations followed suit shortly. The Americans could give recognition only if they were prepared to give up Taiwan—which was out of the question. Many withheld recognition because of Mao's eagerness to export revolution far beyond his own borders. In an address in Beijing to the Australasian Trades Union Congress in 1949, Mao threw China's support behind all wars of national liberation. It appeared China was indeed embarking on its own brand of imperialism. Mao's policy of promoting instability among his neighbours caused other Asian nations to join together to contain China within its own borders.

The Americans were actually moving to recognize Mao's government when the Korean War broke out in 1950. This war changed everything. Chiang's forces on Taiwan were now deemed necessary to the American defence perimeter, an important factor in the containment of communism. Someday, they could even be transported back to the mainland to fight as America's ally. Recognition of the People's Republic of China was shelved indefinitely.

The Soviets moved swiftly to make the PRC an ally. The USSR and China signed a mutual defence treaty in 1950, one aimed against the USA and its ally, Japan. The Soviets gave up their claim to Lüshun and their interests in Manchurian industry and railways. They approved a $300 million loan to China and agreed to erect and operate a number of model factories. They would also supply technical information, send 12 000 scientists and technicians to help reconstruct China's industry, and accept 6000 Chinese students in Soviet universities. Stalin thus hoped to dominate Mao, whom he suspected of being more nationalist and imperialist than communist.

Mao's immediate problems, however, were political and economic. The China he conquered was one of the most backward nations in the world. The devastation of the previous quarter century had destroyed political unity and economic progress. Primitive technology could not keep pace with population increase. The Chinese now faced famine. The first task was to establish a strong central authority in Beijing. The nation was divided into six military regions, and by 1952 outlying regions, including Tibet, had been brought into the fold. Until 1954, China was effectively under military rule, as Mao used the army and secret police against counter-revolutionaries. Under the control of the Public Security Forces, the nation was divided into urban and rural residence committees that comprised an average of 100 households. Centralization of power proceeded rapidly since there was no one to oppose the PRC. The old bureaucracy had vanished, and Communists quickly took power. Needing some kind of direction and leadership, hundreds of thousands of villages and towns quickly fell into line. Their chief concern was to get on with the harvest, not to think about politics. Besides, the Communists were a symbol of nationalism and were greeted by the peasantry as their own.

The only immediate threat to the new regime was Taiwan, where Chiang's armies prepared for a return to the mainland. The American intervention in Korea in 1950 seemed to be the first step in a counter-revolution to unseat the PRC. American success in Korea hardened the Chinese landowner class in its resistance to land redistribution. Their resistance was put down with severity by the Public Security Forces, and even the mildest criticism of the regime could result in arrest. Over 2 million counter-revolutionaries were executed at this time, and millions more were sent to concentration camps by people's courts. For two and a half years, Chinese and Americans faced each other in Korea, not far from Beijing. The Chinese losses in soldiers were staggering, but they held American forces at bay and generated intense national pride throughout the country.

For Mao, gaining control of Chinese cities was almost as easy as gaining control of the countryside. Many public officials and bureaucrats had already fled, leaving extreme desolation and deprivation behind. Few if any municipal services were working, and food was extremely scarce. There was massive unemployment, and 60 million urban dwellers contributed their share to daily riots and lootings. Not even China's disciplined secret societies could stave off anarchy. Factories and workshops dosed for want of materials, and small shopkeepers closed their shops in the crime-ridden streets. The Communists turned the municipal services over to young **cadres** who learned on the job, but got the services going again. The general public had always been apathetic in their attitude to the Kuomintang, so the Communist takeover was relatively unop-

The Nationalists declared Taiwan the seat of the Republic of China, claiming the right to rule over all of China. This photograph shows Chiang Kai-shek reviewing troops in 1954. He died in 1975 without having regained control of the mainland.

LAND REFORM

Although Mao implemented land reform, he did so only gradually. The critical economic situation demanded an ideologically mixed approach to land redistribution. The primary aim was to increase yields, not to socialize the farming sector.

posed. Industrial production revived fitfully but surely. The first priority was to get factories back into production, not nationalize them. State controls came later. In 1951, the cadres began conducting mass public meetings, followed by smaller struggle sessions to hear the public confessions and self-criticism of those with capitalist leanings. Intellectuals and teachers were especially singled out for re-education. The remaining assets of the middle classes were seized. The remnants of the old authority were cleansed from the system by 1952.

The Korean War brought new problems and new opportunities for the PRC in the midst of its efforts to stabilize control of the cities. The security forces were given a free hand to root out counter-revolutionaries. The army and security forces organized the population into urban committees and then proceeded to gather up all weapons, but the cost of the war in human and other resources further drained an already overburdened minority. Both the Soviets and the Americans took action to limit China's influence in Asia. The USSR normalized relations with Japan, and Khrushchev visited India and Afghanistan, offering aid to Third World nations. The USA began giving aid to the French in Indo-China and established an island containment perimeter from Japan through to the Philippines and Australia. By 1955, the spheres in Asia had hardened into defensible political boundaries. In response, the PRC modified its policy of supporting revolutions in Africa and Latin America. China's new, more acceptable foreign policy was based on five principles: a policy of co-existence; respect for each other's boundaries; a promise not to subvert national governments; equal treatment of other states; and renouncement of expansionism.

AGRARIAN AND INDUSTRIAL REORGANIZATION

The land reform of the period 1950-1952 effectively eliminated what remained of the agrarian élite. The overall aim was to abolish private ownership and redistribute the land on an equitable small-plot basis. Later, the plots would be merged into collectives and, finally, communes, to take advantage of economies of scale, but mergers were to be gradual and voluntary. Landowners were not treated totally like non-citizens. They were given equal shares and, after proper penance and re-education, had the stigma of "owner" removed from their records. Any farming operation that was in support of industry was to remain untouched— nothing was to stand in the way of industrial revival. Cadres were sent into the villages to create enthusiasm for the reforms and identify the 20 million landowners to be re-educated in class struggle. Village associations, under the security forces, were to administer the reforms. The public humiliation of the landowners gave vent to violence and revenge that grew in intensity as the Korean War threatened counter-revolution.

Redistribution proceeded quickly through the cadres. By 1952, the initial reorganization of the farming sector was complete. Redistribution did not solve the problem of inadequate yields or rural poverty, though grain production did increase at the rate of about 13 per cent a year. The state tax of 30 per cent of the harvest was more honestly and fairly collected under the PRC, but it was still an onerous levy. The new incentive brought harvests almost sufficient to keep pace with the growth in population. Economies of scale and mechanization were necessary. Labour intensive irrigation and transportation projects were already under way in preparation for merging the household plots into larger collectives. All in all, the lot of the peasant was marginally better.

Agricultural surpluses were needed to pay for the nation's industrialization. The government hoped to revitalize industry by implementing Soviet-style five year plans. The first plan was to produce energy and hydroelectric power, and Soviet technicians were to assist the Chinese in its development. But Soviet assistance was meagre and far from adequate. Little was heard about the plan except that progress had been made. Even today, China has a relatively small industrial base for a nation its size.

A state planning commission modeled on the Soviet Gosplan was established to provide central control over all production processes. More and more industries and businesses were nationalized at this time. Industrial growth was designed for the interior of the country. The 427 new factories were to help bind the region to the rest of the country. The new factories would also remove industrial complexes from vulnerable coastlines and bring them closer to raw materials and markets. By 1957, output in farm machinery, trucks, tractors, and jet planes had doubled.

Growth in industry came at the expense of the peasantry. The growth of industry revitalized the cities and attracted tens of millions of people to them. Urban population leaped from 60 to over 100 million and caused major problems. Cities simply could not handle this rapid growth. Growth of the cities led in turn to increased bureaucratization, and political cadres began to see themselves as a new urban élite. Technicians, engineers, and scientists began to rival the cadres in bidding for power.

Industrialization had a profound effect on the Communist hierarchy. Some party leaders grew comfortable in urban centres and abandoned their rural roots. The party began to split into a group of right-wing conservatives (who favoured industrial and economic growth) and a group of left-wing radicals (who savoured their ties to the egalitarianism of the farm)—a split that disturbs the party to this day. The question was which path to take to the socialist utopia—urban or rural? Should power be decentralized to the village or centralized in the Communist party? The new urban political élite fought to retain control of the direction of the revolution.

The neglect of the farming sector during the first Five Year Plan could not be ignored. Something had to be done to increase yields to keep pace with population growth and pay for industrial development. Peasant individualism had created a new class of farm owners who would resist collectivization. Yet collectives and even larger communes were what the state needed to achieve industrial growth. The conservative wing of the party advised a gradual approach, but Mao wanted the pace of collectivization increased before Chinese kulaks settled into a comfortable anti-revolutionary social class. Mao overrode the party and appealed to the masses to revitalize the revolutionary spirit of social change. Amazingly enough, hundreds of millions of peasants followed his lead, and by 1960 almost all farms had been organized on a village-collective basis. The event still astounds observers. Mao's populist appeal generated a self-sustaining momentum, as hundreds of thousands of villages rushed headlong into reorganization. Within a few months, 100 000 000 households had merged into 485 000 collectives.

By 1956, seven years after the establishment of the People's Republic, Mao reasoned that socialism had come and been accepted by all of the people. Most control over farms and industry was in the hands of the state. A primary concern was the bureaucratization of the Communist party—its forgetfulness of its egalitarian beginnings. As well, new political and economic élites had risen to challenge the authority of the party itself. More thinkers and planners were needed to guide economic growth, but they would only augment the rival power groups already within the state. On 2 May 1956, Mao gave a speech in which he called for one hundred schools of thought and gave free reign to scientists to debate theories that had no political connotations. He also talked of "flowers" blooming together: writers and artists were thus encouraged to comment on society without criticizing the socialist system.

There was no doubt Mao was using his position to rid the party of its conservative elements. The situation quickly got out of hand as a long-pent-up spate of criticism was directed at the party and at socialism as a system. Mao soon termed these criticisms the poisonous weeds that would have to be rooted out. In the autumn Mao ordered repressive measures against the intellectuals who had dared to speak out. The state retained its monopoly of power, but Mao and the party hierarchy had learned the hard way that the people were not united behind the socialist system.

Six months later, Mao launched his **Great Leap Forward** to release the latent energies of the masses, to foster both industrial and agrarian growth at the same time. He felt growing urban unemployment could be solved by sending millions in the cities back to the countryside where they could be the vanguard of local industries. Peasants could participate in industrial growth by establishing their own backyard businesses in the off-seasons. They could manufacture the fertilizers, tools, and other equipment they required for farming. Decentralization of control would lead to an increase in consumer goods and a general rise in the standard of living. There was no prospect of foreign investment and, with China's split from the Soviet Union, no foreign technological aid. The modernization of the nation had to come from within.

Mao's proposal required a shift of investment to light industry. Light industry, he reasoned, would provide the consumer goods that would spur peasants to greater productivity. Higher yields would then sustain growth in heavy industry. There would be simultaneous development on three fronts: agriculture, light industry, and heavy industry. One of the most highly publicized programs was the making of backyard iron and steel. Large amounts of metal and metal products resulted, but all of it was shoddy and of only marginal use; still, the villages did begin to make and repair their own implements.

Conservatives in the party thought the Great Leap Forward was irrational and doomed to failure. They believed that China did not have the resources to make progress in all areas at the same time. The worst-case scenario was that with extra responsibility for light industry, the peasants would become exhausted. Most questioned whether the illiterate masses could in fact handle the technology essential for change. The idea that each village could look to itself for its own resources was good in theory but there was no allowance in the plan for differences in size or resources. Cadres of youths flooded out into the countryside bringing the new message from Mao that few dared openly to oppose. The resulting chaos and disruption, along with drought and flood, put an end to the program in 1960.

Mao also hastened the merging of village collectives into regional communes. Economies of scale were the aim, as always. Agricultural bureaucrats

In 1971, the People's Republic of China was admitted to the United Nations. Kurt Waldheim, the UN secretary general at that time, visited China in 1972. This photograph shows him being greeted by Premier Zhou Enlai.

of forced reorganization had taken their toll on the farms. The party moved to end the communization movement and reassert its central authority. Private ownership was reintroduced to stimulate production, and by 1960 most of the communes had been abandoned. At this point, Mao stepped aside from the party for a number of months, his only support being the People's Army. Though a father figure to the masses, he was ignored within the party hierarchy. In 1960, typhoons and drought affected 60 per cent of the arable land, and only massive wheat purchases from Canada and Australia saved the situation. The Great Leap ended in tremendous human suffering.

FOREIGN POLICY

The late 1950s was also a time of international difficulties for China. The death of Stalin in 1953 led to a bitter rift between China and the Soviets. Mao felt he was in line for the leadership of the world's communist movement. Ignored by Stalin's successors, who had no intention of letting international leadership slip from their hands, Mao began soliciting support from other communist nations and promoted a division in the socialist world. Mao intervened on behalf of Gomulka in Poland, but approved of the crushing of the Hungarian Revolution because the dissidents criticized the socialist system. He was angered at not being forewarned of or consulted about Khrushchev's de-Stalinization speech to the Twentieth Congress. Criticism of Stalin, leader of a personality cult, could be extended to Mao himself. Mao also disagreed with Khrushchev's policy of peaceful co-existence. If the USSR had the military power it claimed, why did it not use that power to destroy NATO as Mao would have done in the same position?

were sent down to the communes to gain first-hand experience and guide the program to a successful conclusion. They were also to reacquaint themselves with the people they were governing. Over two years (1958-1960) the communization movement affected the lives of 500 million peasants. Again, millions of frenetic cadres flooded the countryside encouraging the masses to action. By the end of 1960, 750 000 collectives had merged into 24 000 communes of around 5000 households (30 000 people) apiece. Mao hoped communization would be the first step in the withering away of the state, for self-sufficient communes would have little need for party apparatus. The movement also drew women into the work force as men went off to work on construction brigades. There was an associated growth in the number of state nurseries. A whole new welfare support system, including doctors, clinics, and schools, developed for rural people.

Unrealistic work assignments and harvest quotas killed the program. Out of exuberance and fear, the local cadres reported amazing growth in crop yields and industrial output that simply did not exist. Shortfalls in food production were evident in 1958. Lack of harvesters in the countryside and the chaos

Although the Soviets had provided moderate aid to China, they were not about to make China a rival global power. The Soviets in effect adopted the American policy of containment toward China. The Soviet Union did not support China in its border war with India in 1959, and even appeared to threaten China in its normalization talks with Japan and Camp David meetings with Eisenhower. Khrushchev openly criticized Mao's opposition to co-existence, ridiculed the Chinese attempts at agrarian revolution, and in December 1960 ordered all Soviet technicians and scientists in China to return home, bringing all plans and blueprints with them.

Mao became even more nervous about the Soviet Union's Asian policies after Brezhnev replaced Khrushchev in 1964. The Brezhnev Doctrine of 1968 stated that the Soviet Union had a responsibility to intervene in other socialist countries in the interest of communist solidarity. The USSR's invasion of Czechoslovakia was a prime example of the doctrine in operation. Would China be next? In 1969, sporadic fighting broke out between Soviet and Chinese border patrols on the Ussuri River. There was talk in Moscow of the need for a pre-emptive nuclear strike against China, before the Chinese developed their own nuclear arsenal. As one million Soviet troops took up positions along its northern borders, China began to seek a rapprochement with the United States.

Negotiations with the United States in 1972 resulted in President Nixon's historic visit to Beijing. Nixon was quick to exploit the rift between China and the Soviet Union, seeing future political and economic advantages in so doing. A year earlier, in 1971, the People's Republic of China had displaced Taiwan in the UN, and took its seat on the powerful Security Council. The USA declared China's relationship with Taiwan to be a domestic matter, though it pledged to support Taiwan as it had in the past.

The 1970s witnessed a retreat from socialism in China to a position of modified private enterprise. Firm lines of central control were imposed upon the people as the party rose above the masses and reasserted its authority. New cadres were sent into the countryside, along with the People's Army, to regain political control from the villages. Small and inefficient backyard industries were shut down, and priority was given to improvement of transportation and distribution systems in the country. In the cities the work force was cut by half, and the newly idle were sent by the millions into the country to work on brigades. Above all, central planning was re-imposed on both industry and agriculture.

During these five years of recovery, Mao plotted to counter the reassertion of party supremacy. He blamed the party, not the masses, for China's continuing backwardness. The masses supervise the party, and not the other way around. The party was corrupt and bourgeois, and the masses must cleanse it of privilege and élitism. The People's Army introduced Mao's thoughts in political indoctrination sessions in 1964. The *Red Book* of Mao's quotations was to play a predominant part in the cultural revolution that began in 1966.

Students from the Transport School in Kirin Province are shown marching to Beijing in January of 1967.

THE CULTURAL REVOLUTION

Mao called for a million successors to carry forward revolutionary ideals after his death. The energy of the masses was to be generated in permanent revolution: youth must be co-opted into his crusade. The **Cultural Revolution** of 1966-1976 was to be Mao's last revolutionary act. A decade of internal chaos and tragedy began that at times resembled a civil war. The movement was anti-intellectual in nature. The educated were its earliest victims, although every sector of the economy was affected in varying degrees.

Mao's strategy was to use youth to raise the mass consciousness to the dangers of privilege and modified capitalism. The revolution began in universities and spread to the schools. Student activists donned red arm bands and mounted a growing campaign of criticism against authority

255

CHINA'S ONE CHILD POLICY

In 1980 the Chinese government ruled that each family must limit itself to one child in order to reduce population growth. Since the policy was implemented, China's population has surpassed one billion and the country is faced with the challenge of feeding and housing enormous numbers of people. Should governments implement population control programs? Debate reasons for the success or failure of the Chinese program.

China is one of the largest political units on Earth. Its 9.6 million sq km make it slightly larger than the United States, but over half of that area is composed of mountains and steep hills unsuitable for human habitation. Less that 15 per cent of the total land area is fit for cultivation, though it must support just under a quarter of the world's population. The Chinese people are concentrated in the south and east where 90 per cent of the population lives along major rivers and the Pacific coastline. China's population density is one of the highest in the world. On 7 per cent of the land area, there are 828 people per sq km (compared to just over 62 per sq km in the USA). At its most extreme, in Shanghai, the density reaches 4952 per sq km. However, most Chinese live in rural villages and maintain a traditional village culture.

On 25 September 1980 an open letter to the Chinese people from the Central Committee sounded the alarm. China's population was growing faster than agricultural or industrial development could warrant. Since 1949, there had been a net increase of over 430 million people. China would soon double its population of 1949, adding an additional 100 million people every six years. It could not withstand a second doubling in the next 30 years. The urban, industrial working class showed the largest gain, growing from only 3 million in 1949 to 120 million in 1985. The increase in population alone would use up half of the nation's fixed assets.

The rapid 30-year growth was terrifying. The nation could not possibly feed, house, transport, educate, or provide welfare and health services to such a number. Another disturbing feature was that over 65 per cent of the population were under 35 years of age, and more than half were under 20. If the current birth rate continued, China might have an additional 192 million people by the turn of the century. The Central Committee created a strategy to limit population growth, hoping to achieve a zero population growth rate by the year 2000.

The goal of the Central Committee was to stabilize population at about 1.2 billion by the 1990s. A one-child-per family policy had to be implemented. With life expectancy up and the mortality rate dropping (as a result of improved diet and health care), the population was growing too quickly. It was already beyond the capacity of the state to maintain, let alone its capacity to improve, people's standard of living. Physical resources ran critically low. Farm plots were halved under an equal share policy. The national goal was to rear four generations a century instead of five. With a 2.2 birth rate per year (many women would not bear any children at all), the total population could stabilize by the mid-twenty-first century.

The central government decided to coerce its people into accepting such a policy. The cadres were schooled in mass persuasion and they were ordered to "sell" the strategy to their 20-30 households. Their position and wages were made in part dependent on how well they managed to reduce the birth rates in their districts. Women were urged to sign a pledge to have only one child, to marry later (the minimum age of marriage for men is 22 and for women 20), to take advantage of free abortions, to accept sterilization, to use birth-control devices, and to practise a variety of voluntary restraints. True to form, the cadres embarked on their mission to make family planning a priority.

Generous funding was made available to the 30 million families that had only one child. Social status and educational advancement in day-care and pre-school facilities were only part of the reward. Local councils were to provide cash incentives from communal funds. Under the taxation laws, farmers were given incomes, from which they paid taxes, since few were willing to increase taxes to pay for the one child policy. The necessary weekly work points were reduced, additional grain allocations were made available, promises of land were given, promises of equal pay in the work force were made, and other incentives were given to those who produced only one child.

The policy was accepted to a greater extent in urban rather than in rural areas. Family planning seminars in the cities had a dramatic effect in reducing the birth rate, along with a growing welfare system that included care for the elderly. Voluntary restraints reduced the anticipated number of births by over 10 million.

But 90 per cent of China's infants are born in the countryside. Attempts to persuade rural inhabitants to limit families to only one child failed. Where the policy was implemented, mothers resorted to infanticide if the child was a girl. In the traditional Chinese culture, men have a sort of feudal indifference toward women. Farming families want sons who can manage heavy farm work and look after their parents in their old age, as according to traditional Chinese culture. The armed forces wanted males and openly encouraged the murder of baby girls. Global outrage over this infanticide led the Central Committee to modify its strategy in 1984.

Before this, the strategy had already run into difficulties. Local cadres often neglected to enforce the central government's will. Many farmers were willing and able to pay the fines levied on a second child. Farm women earned enough extra money from their private plots to bribe local officials into letting them try for a boy and a girl. By 1984, so many exceptions had been approved that a two child policy had come into effect. The state itself recognized that more children meant more productivity and wealth. Reasons given for a second child ranged from a need to guarantee care for the elderly to a need to have a brother to play with.

In the early 1990s, China faced a minor baby boom as the 25 million women who had so far voluntarily put off having a child until they were over 25 had reached child-bearing age.

1. Why was the one child policy put into effect? With what results?

2. Is it advisable for a state to achieve zero population growth? How can this be done?

3. Look at the chart below. What age group did most of China's population belong to in 1990? What significance does this have for China's population growth?

4. Calculate the resources needed to feed and shelter an additional 100 million people. What does this increase do to development budgets?

5. Devise solutions to China's population difficulty.

6. Research another country with a rapidly growing population. What has this country's government done to control population growth? Compare this situation to China's.

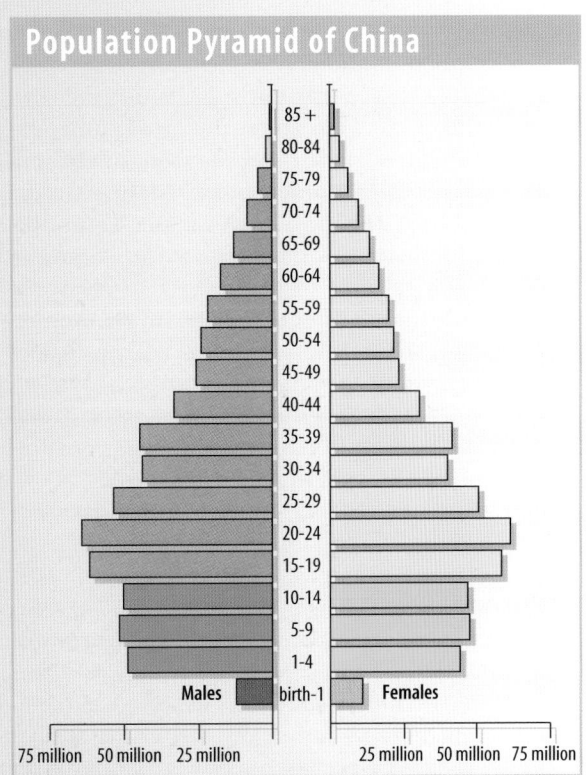

The population pyramid shows the age distribution within the total population of China. The figures are from 1990. Age demographics are important to China.

This photograph shows members of Mao's Red Guard mourning his death at the Mass Memorial Service.

and corruption. Millions of students left their studies to root out revisionists across the country. Called Red Guards, they were given free provisions and transport while on Chairman Mao's business, and the People's Army was ordered to assist them. In the summer of 1966, the movement caught fire. Youths from every town and village traveled to Beijing to receive Mao's personal blessing. On 18 August, the first of the major rallies was held in Tiananmen Square. One million Red Guards greeted their leader with mass hysteria. That summer, over 12 million student activists paraded before Mao prior to the start of their revolutionary mission. The government was powerless to intervene.

The students became uncontrollable in their quest to destroy all symbols of the past. Public buildings were ransacked and government files destroyed. Empowered by the army, the students brought anarchy to the land. Factory workers joined them that winter, and industrial production was paralyzed. The Red Guards established local councils that refused to recognize any authority but their own. Rival groups battled for power in the larger centres, and for a time the government completely lost control of the cities. On 5 January 1967 the workers in Shanghai, the nation's largest industrial centre, carried out their own revolution and established their own dictatorship of the proletariat. The resulting commune of students, workers, and the army defied the central government for weeks.

Similar organizations sprang up in other strike-ridden cities. By the following summer, all semblance of central authority had been replaced by a chaos of local councils. Production had come to a halt, and the economic progress to date had been destroyed. The nation appeared to be headed for civil war when, in September, Premier Zhou Enlai ordered the People's Army to restore order by force. Conservative estimates are that 400 000 died in the resulting army action, and millions more were sent to correctional camps for re-education. Some 17 million people were sent out to work brigades in the country, to labour in a Spartan life and learn proper ethics and morals. The government backlash hit students and intellectuals hardest. Wandering China, unable to return to their studies, now bereft of any assistance from Mao, they flooded back into the cities as a lost generation. It would take China more than a decade to recover what had been lost.

Mao died in 1976. He had guided the revolution from its early days, through the long civil war with the Nationalists, and the Japanese invasion, to political victory. Under his leadership China became a united nation for the first time since 1911. He had rid the country of imperialists and set its course towards modernization. His ability to involve hundreds of millions of peasants in mass movements remains unexplained. Mao carried out the aims of Sun Yat-sen in returning the sod to its tillers. He was unmatched as a populist leader, but he was unable to create a popular mass government. Toward the end, his idea of an agrarian socialist utopia (in which the state had withered away) was directly at odds with his idea of a modern industrial power. The tragic conflict between these two ideals has yet to be resolved in China.

DENG XIAOPING

Mao's death in 1976 set off a bitter power struggle within the Communist party that was to last until 1978. The forces of radicalism and egalitarianism were arrayed against those who favoured a pragmatic approach to economic development that included rapprochement with the West. Deng Xiaoping favoured the latter approach and urged foreign trade regardless of the dangers of foreign influence. China's resources would have to be traded for equipment and technology if China were to become an industrial power. After the fight for succession, the new government under Deng was to be judged on how well it met economic needs and managed industrial growth, not on the basis of political ideology.

The liberalization in economics did not extend to politics. Students and intellectuals had taken advantage of the period after Mao's death to demonstrate and establish political forums denouncing authority and demanding a full range of democratic freedoms. The ban on criticism of the socialist system and government authority was reasserted. Anarchists were denounced and unofficial political meetings were once again suppressed.

Deng's administration was wedded to modernization in agriculture, industry, defence, and science. A modest return was made to a form of private enterprise, in which the market system operated and profits could be made, to improve the standard of living. Though only 16 per cent (400 000) of the businesses and factories were permitted a measure of autonomy in wages and hiring, the effect was far-reaching. As consumer goods entered the marketplace, inflation soared and unemployment rose to 20 per cent. Only a 1 per cent growth in GNP resulted, so the government returned many resources to central control. Stable and significant economic growth was not achieved until 1984.

In a major break with the immediate past, Deng reinstated an Open Door trading policy with the rest of the world. **Special economic zones** were established to conduct foreign trade. From an initial four zones in 1980, the program expanded to eighteen in 1984. Foreign investors received preferential status in China's market. Within the zones, price and profit mechanisms were used to guide transactions. In an effort to attract more foreign currency, the government more recently proposed turning the entire seaboard into a customs-free zone. This policy would make available 160 million workers to

By the early 1980s, Chinese citizens began to have access to a variety of goods. Only a few years before, consumers like those pictured above would have been denounced as greedy capitalists.

assemble finished products less expensively than can be done in Taiwan, Haiti, or South Korea.

Opening up parts of China for trade created a demand for Western consumer goods. For the first time, China had to face the reality of a trade deficit with the outside world. This deficit reached $40 billion in 1987, climbing rapidly as China sought to modernize its industrial base with Western equipment. China accordingly expanded its export trade in weapons and soon won fourth place in world armament sales. New initiatives in 1987 saw the beginnings of normalized relations with the USSR. But in all this China still had little that other countries wanted—save a vast consumer market.

Politically and socially, Deng brought a Western flavour to China in his efforts to develop a more balanced approach to modernization. This change in policy direction did not admit criticism of the system itself. Student demonstrations for an increased voice in decision-making were not acceptable, nor was the liberalization of government structure permitted. Student demonstrations in Tiananmen Square in 1987 were crushed and their organizers sent to correctional camps outside the major cities.

BIOGRAPHY
DENG XIAOPING
(1904–1997)

To build socialism it is necessary to develop the productive forces. Poverty is not socialism.

—Deng Xiaoping in 1987
to the premier of Czechoslovakia

Deng was born in 1904 in Sichuan province as the oldest son of a landowner. After attending middle school, Deng took part in a preparatory course for candidates with potential for studies and work in France. He succeeded in the course, and while studying in Paris (1920s)—likely at the University of Lyon—Deng joined the China Communist Party (CCP), adopting the name Xiaoping `Little Peace' in 1925. In 1926, he went to Moscow to study for several months. During the Long March (1934-36), Deng probably served as director of the Political Department of the 1st Front Army. After this, he served as a commissar to the People's Liberation Army in the years of the civil war (1937-49). In 1955, Deng entered the Politburo of the CCP and headed the secretariat during the early 1960s.

In his daughter's biography, Deng is depicted as a good-hearted man of few words—a lover of food and football. Deng, the introvert, was philosophical when questioned about his personal fate, and optimistic in the face of adversity. Mao described Deng as a "needle wrapped in cotton," and in recognition of Deng's determination and proactive stance, Mao commented that "Deng's mind is round and actions are square"—attributes of significance in a career that included three forced military marches, and three purges from power.

The Cultural Revolution of the 1960s attacked the CCP and undermined its authority. This flew in the face of Deng's profound respect for and belief in the importance of the CCP. Deng was convinced that only the solid political base of an efficiently functioning CCP could ensure the economic reform and growth that China so needed. During the Cultural Revolution, Deng was dismissed as a 'capitalist roader' and sent to a tractor factory in Nanchang for re-education. The charges against Deng, as listed by the Red Guard in their publication *Red Flag Struggle* and *The East is Red,* included the following:

1. Unauthorized actions as secretary general of the Party.

2. Condemnation of the personality cult with resulting damage to the position of Mao Zedong.

3. Insult to Mao Zedong Thought at Party conference in 1961.

4. Advocacy of a system of academic degrees and titles (1963).

5. Rejection of criticism in the field of culture.

6. Suppression of revolutionary students at Beijing University.

7. Rejection of Mao Zedong's educational theory combining studies with manual labour.

An important element in Deng's political down-fall during the Cultural Revolution included his low opinion of Jiang Qing's—Madame Mao's—efforts to revolutionize the Beijing Opera. From 1965 on, Deng conscientiously did not attend theatre performances, whereas all his Politburo colleagues did.

Deng's patron, Zhou Enlai, helped in Deng's rehabilitation in 1973, and Deng returned to politics to serve as acting prime minister after Zhou's heart attack in 1974. With Zhou's death in 1976, Deng was forced into hiding, but came back again in July 1977 as vice premier. By December 1978, although nominally a CCP vice chair, state vice premier, and Chief of Staff to the PLA, Deng was the controlling force in China. Working with his protégés Hu Yaobang and Zhao Ziyang, Deng introduced a pragmatic new economic modernization program. In 1987, Deng retired from the Politburo. Despite old age, Deng remained China's paramount leader into the late 1990s.

Some would say that Deng's political system and beliefs were created by what he considered to be the elements which went into the making of the Communist utopia of the 1940s or 1956. Deng's political message and mandate were formulated in response to conditions in China resulting from losses in the Sino-Japanese War (1898). His political mandate included economic construction and production, democratic centralism and minority rights within the CCP, the separation of party and government, and the emphasis on attaining the widest possible popular support using a variety of methods. Although economic modernization was a priority for Deng, party rule was an even greater priority. In 1958, he made the statement to the Young Communist League that "there is only one party. If you hold firm on this point, then whatever mistakes you make you will remain basically correct." Deng's policies, although sometimes misinterpreted as a drift toward capitalism, were actually socialism with Chinese characteristics.

Deng died in February 1997, after a lengthy hospitalization. He was 92 years old. The transition in leadership from Deng to Jiang Zemin had already begun five years before. In 1997, many people considered Jiang to be a transitional figure between China's revolutionary giants and a new generation that has yet to come into its own. ●

Sino-Soviet relations thawed enough for Mikhail Gorbachev to make a state visit to China in May of 1989. This photo shows Deng Xiaoping greeting the Soviet leader at the Great Hall of the People.

CHINA: TIANANMEN SQUARE 1987–1990

China's economy boomed during the 1980s and became one of the "hottest" in the world. But by 1987 it was overheating, and by 1988 it was raging out of control. While productivity often grew by 20 per cent per year the critical infrastructure of support to industry—energy and transportation facilities, for example—lagged far behind. In efforts to create greater amounts of goods the government allowed prices to fluctuate in a free market. This seemingly reasonable policy resulted in rampant inflation and caused deep discontent among the third of China's population that existed on fixed salaries. The 30 per cent increase in the cost of living early in 1988 seemed mild when, in the latter part of the year, prices occasionally jumped 80 per cent above the previous year's levels. The bureaucracy could not approve wage increases fast enough to compensate for an economy seemingly out of control, and inflation erased the savings of the middle class. Deng ordered a return to centralized price controls and imposed quotas on industries. Monopoly control was returned to the state in order to bring stability and re-establish economic order.

261

HONG KONG

In 1997 Hong Kong was removed from British administration and reverted to control by China. Apprehension over this event caused the emigration of many residents of Hong Kong to North America. Using current media sources, investigate who stayed behind, and why. Make a presentation based on your findings.

Between the city of Victoria on Hong Kong Island and the New Territories on the mainland lies one of the world's best deep-water passageways. Through trade, Hong Kong has become the world's largest financial centre after New York and London. Situated at the mouth of the Pearl River, and just downstream from Guangzhou (Canton), Hong Kong is the West's most important gateway to China. In the 1990s, Hong Kong merchants and bankers established important trading ties with the People's Republic of China. Billions of dollars are traded annually. Hong Kong's 950 sq km house well over 6 million inhabitants, of whom only some 150 000 are non-Chinese. Its population density of 5000 per sq km makes the city the most densely populated region on Earth.

The British administered Hong Kong from 1841 to 1997 as a strategic naval base and centre for Asian trade. In 1839, Imperial Chinese Commissioner Lin attempted to do away with the opium trade in Guangzhou. He forced British traders to turn over their opium stocks, which he then publicly destroyed. The British community withdrew down river to Hong Kong on the coast. In the ensuing war, Britain occupied Shanghai and forced China to cede Hong Kong and five other ports. After the Sino-Japanese War of 1898 Britain agreed to lease the territory from China for 99 years. This lease expired in June 1997. In 1982, China announced its intention to integrate Hong Kong upon expiration of the lease. The announcement of forced reunification with China raised many important issues, one of which is the principle of self-determination.

The 1982 declaration caused panic. Capital was transferred from Hong Kong to Singapore and other major cities around the world. Lineups for visas from foreign legations to leave the colony mushroomed. American dollars were flown in to stem the run on the banks and stabilize the skidding market. By 1984, Britain was forced to agree to the turnover, but it did seek to get the best deal possible for the people of Hong Kong.

The advantages to China of the repatriation of Hong Kong are many. Hong Kong is permitted to retain its capitalist status and prosperity as a special economic zone within the PRC. The existing social and economic lifestyles will not be changed for at least 50 years after unification. Property rights and personal freedoms of the capitalist world will be permitted to continue unopposed. The territory's custom of negotiating treaties with other countries will not be touched, although there is no precedent for such a degree of autonomy within China. All agreements in force at the time of unification will remain so. Hong Kong will continue to have its own currency, financial market, and customs union. A comprehensive list of distinctive administrative and social practices, ranging from taxation policy to health care, will remain in place. It appears China is determined to fund the high standard of living enjoyed by the colony, whatever the cost to itself.

The British have demanded continued guarantees of freedom of the press, freedom to travel, free trade, private property rights, full economic capitalism, and retention of the legal and educational systems. The property and personal safety of colonial administrators, the 6000-strong police force and intelligence services, and property owners along with their wages, pensions, and jobs are to remain unmodified until 2047. All contracts in effect are to be honoured, there is to be no increase in farm taxation, and China must allow a quasi-elected government to function.

The Chinese government, however, is making its mark on Hong Kong. The press has limited freedom. Appointed advisory councils have replaced the British parliamentary system. Beijing's administrative machinery has not been forced onto the colony, but there is no negotiation on the right of the

People's Army to be there. As well, no public official who had ties with Taiwan will be tolerated. China naturally claims Taiwan as part of its *irredenta*.

Before 1997, the lack of confidence in Deng's promises exploded in Hong Kong after the massacre in Tiananmen Square in 1989. If Beijing was prepared to use the army against its own students and the people of its capital, what might it do once in control of Hong Kong? Fear that Deng would not live up to his promises prompted an outcry in Britain against turning the colony over to China. Could Britain in all conscience hand over to China 7 million people who did not want to be handed over? What other choices were there?

Although the British had considered absorbing the total population of the colony through assisted immigration to England and (they hoped) Canada, Australia, and the USA, they had to shelve this plan as unmanageable. Instead, they proposed to provide a limited number of British passports to those who agreed to remain in their posts until the turnover date—at which time they were to train others to do their work before leaving. In 1990, Britain agreed to accept 50 000 Hong Kong families, or about 250 000 people. Britain also warned its partners in the European Union and Commonwealth that by 1997, there could be a massive emigration from the territory. In 1990 alone some 50 000 top professionals and financiers emigrated to the USA, Canada, and Australia. China saw this exodus of highly skilled people as a breach of the 1984 agreement and was totally opposed to it.

The government of Hong Kong has acted to ease tensions in the colony in another matter: Vietnamese boat people. Some 47 000 Vietnamese are to be sent back to Vietnam. The first groups have already been sent to Hanoi. Gathered in camps along the Chinese border, the refugees are indoctrinated with the need to go back. So far, Hanoi has given them reasonable treatment upon their return. Hanoi has hinted that it might permit upward of 500 000 former American sympathizers and officials in Vietnam to emigrate to the USA.

Both China and Britain forecast continued prosperity for Hong Kong after the transfer of power. The Chinese government hopes China's own economic reforms will close the gap between the two economic systems. They are also wary lest Hong Kong become an open door to Western culture, especially since a growing number of sons and daughters of Beijing's bureaucracy who have already taken up residence in the colony bring back Western ideas on regular visits. China is prepared to abide by the one country, two systems policy as long as there is no danger to Beijing. But the executions and other penalties after the Tiananmen demonstrations throw some doubt on the government's guarantees.

The Chinese government has turned their attention to Taiwan. Disputes with the Americans over that island's status had soured relations with the USA since 1949. In the 1990s, Taiwan's agreement to purchase eight frigates from France increased tensions in the region. China hopes that a successful repatriation of Hong Kong might eventually lead to a similar reunification with Taiwan.

1. Why did the British agree to turn Hong Kong over to China in 1997? Were there alternatives?

2. How have the businesses of Hong Kong reacted to the reunification with China?

3. Why will China permit Hong Kong to keep its capitalist system for at least 50 years?

4. Why did China insist on stationing its troops in Hong Kong? What message does this give the people?

5. What is the relationship of Hong Kong to Taiwan in the eyes of the Chinese government?

6. What might happen should the people of Hong Kong proclaim independence under the doctrine of self-determination?

7. Research the effects that immigration of Hong Kong residents has had on either Canada, the United States, Australia, or Britain.

CASE STUDY

TAIWAN

A comparison of the situation in Hong Kong, taken over by China in 1997, and that of Taiwan would be interesting. When Haiti was the only nation prepared to recognize Taiwan as a sovereign state, China used its veto power in the Security Council to stall a UN force designated for Haiti until the recognition was dropped. In view of this, what should the UN position be on Taiwan's claim to independence?

On 23 March 1996, in the first presidential election held in over 4000 years of Chinese history, the people of Taiwan elected Lee Teng-hui as president. This followed the dramatic precedent of parliamentary elections held in 1992. Up until that time, Taiwan had been governed by a single-party, authoritarian political system complete with tight censorship and ruthless martial law.

The presidential election was not without its dangers. China chose the election issue to send a clear message to the Taiwanese that it would not tolerate the election of anyone who advocated independence for the island. China's president, chosen by the Communist Party, repeatedly stated China's position that Taiwan is considered part of its *irredenta*. At some future date, Taiwan is to be merged with the mainland government. The example of an elected president in Taiwan is seen as a lethal thrust at China's own dictatorial regime. Should the democratic practice of popular elections be transmitted to the mainland, it would spell the end of the Chinese Communist Party's dominance of power.

In order to put pressure on the elections, and to warn Taiwan against any rash move toward independence, the Chinese armed forces staged war-games in the Straits of Formosa in the South China Sea that separates Taiwan from the mainland. As election day drew nearer, the war-games picked up in intensity. The Chinese naval manoeuvres threatened to blockade Taiwan ports. As Taiwan is heavily dependent on trade, this would have been a serious matter if carried too far. It was psychological warfare aimed at ensuring that the Taiwanese were clear about their future role as part of China.

Some feared that China might even be tempted to invade Taiwan to force the island back under its control. One response to the military threat was a counter-threat created by the arrival in waters off Taiwan of American carrier combat groups creating a local balance of naval power. This military escalation raised the possibility of an accidental war.

China's efforts to influence the election were checkmated by the American presence. Some doubted that China's large but obsolete forces would have been able to capture Taiwan had the occasion arisen. This may be true at the moment, but experts predict that with a population of 1.2 billion and increased expenditures to modernize the army through the purchase of high-tech weapons from Ukraine and Russia, China could be a bona fide superpower within ten years.

The future of China's relationship with Taiwan depends upon Deng's successor and how he views the Taiwanese situation, as well as how much support the USA is prepared to give Taiwan to ensure its independence.

1. What event sparked the crisis between China and Taiwan in 1996?

2. Why is China threatened by events in Taiwan?

3. What circumstances point to the possibility of China becoming a superpower?

The inflation of 1988 caused a conservative reaction. Deng had to admit that the right-wingers in his government had been correct, and that reform had caused undue hardship for the people. There was now a renewed emphasis on ideology and intolerance. Marches and demonstrations were made illegal, and all forms of dissent were discouraged because the government feared these would lead to civil war.

Some members of the government, however, continued to make demands for political reforms. Zhao Ziyang and his followers in the Politburo argued for more reform instead of cutting economic spending. They favoured private ownership that would remove political interference in the market place. Prime Minister Li Peng opposed Zhao and argued that concentrated authority would guarantee individual freedoms. Li feared a return to the days of the Cultural Revolution that had ravaged China's economy for more than a decade. The debate was brought to a head with the death of former party secretary Hu Yaobang in April 1989.

Hu had been party secretary and a liberal within the Politburo who proposed solving problems by other means than Marxist ideology. He was deposed in 1987 after student demonstrations in Tiananmen Square. After Hu's downfall, students demonstrated for educational reforms that would have seen an end to party control. They demanded freedom of the press, freedom of assembly, an end to corruption, and more spending on education.

The fortieth anniversary of the founding of the Chinese Republic was used by Zhao to push for new political reforms. The occasion was the Qinming festival in April 1989, honouring the dead. Initial student demonstrations began as a demand to attend the funeral of Hu, who had died on 8 April. Then, up to 10 000 students marched on Tiananmen Square to demand political reforms and intellectual freedom. Hard-liners remembered what had occurred when Mao had encouraged student activists to mount the Cultural Revolution. That mistake was not going to be repeated. Deng and his government were deeply afraid of what could happen if political reforms were authorized.

The power of the students increased as their numbers increased. By late April, some 100 000 had gathered in the square to demand political change. The government rejected their petitions and brought in police to clear the square. The crowds then put up wall posters that claimed China would have been better off with Chiang Kai-shek.

During late May 1989, Chinese student activists built a statue of the "Goddess of Democracy," modeled on the Statue of Liberty. Within days of this scene, the world watched in horror as the Chinese government's decision to send troops into Beijing resulted in thousands of deaths.

An open split developed in the Politburo near the time of Mikhail Gorbachev's mid-May visit. By then, a thousand students had started a hunger strike that was receiving much publicity. Soon student demonstrations spread to other cities, where they were joined by workers' organizations. On 4 May, the students demanded an independent student council. Zhao championed their cause. By 18 May, more than one million people had joined the demonstrations. On 19 May martial law was proclaimed.

The imposition of martial law deepened the crisis. The people of Beijing responded by coming into the streets and taking control of the city. Protest had become insurrection. Deng called in the army. All processions were banned and foreigners and journalists expelled, and on the evening of 3 June troops moved into the city.

The troops entered the central districts of Beijing firing indiscriminately at students and civilians. At Muxidia, a housing enclave for senior government bureaucrats, élite troops fired at will, killing a number of onlookers and cowing party liberals by destroying their homes. By midnight, some 50 000 troops had blasted open the barricades that held them out of the square. During the next few days an estimated 4500 or more civilians and 1000 soldiers died. Deng appeared publicly on 9 June 1989 and claimed victory for the government over those who wanted to make China a bourgeois republic. Some 2000 people had already been arrested, and hangings began on 17 June. The army was to be the key factor in China's future.

Police occupied Tiananmen Square before the period of the Qinming festival in 1990 to ensure there would not be a repetition of the disorder. The traditional black and white flowers of mourning for the festival were forbidden, and soldiers guarded the streets of the capital. Over 30 000 arrests had been made in the previous year and top police officers had been replaced by army generals. Censorship of the press had been reimposed and foreigners were made subject to police surveillance. Some 564 000 graduating students were assigned jobs at the grassroots level in the countryside, where they could be re-educated. In 1990, 600 000 first-year students were forbidden to mix with more senior classes, and had already received intensive ideological and military training. One of the top groups of intellectuals in China had been, in effect, destroyed to re-establish government authority throughout the land.

SUMMARY

In 1945, with American aid, Chiang Kai-shek attempted to reassert Kuomintang authority over China. This attempt failed in 1949 when the Kuomintang lost the civil war with Mao Zedong. Chiang was forced to flee to Taiwan, where he established a new government with American support and protection. The PRC claims Taiwan as an integral part of China, to be reincorporated into the PRC at a future date.

Upon gaining military control in 1950, Mao set out to consolidate his political hold, reorganize the farming sector, and modernize the industrial base. Sweeping land reforms gave hundreds of millions of peasants title to the land they worked. Those of the landowner class who remained on the mainland increased their opposition to reforms at the time of American intervention in the Korean War. Many landowners hoped the Americans would re-establish the Kuomintang. This was not to be, and their resistance to change resulted in their abolishment as an economic class. Crop yields improved, but not fast enough to keep pace with a demographic explosion. In the late 1950s and in the 1960s Mao undertook to reorganize small farms into large collectives where economies of scale could prevail. In the 1980s Deng Xiaoping moved to abolish collectives in favour of modified private enterprise. Throughout all these changes the farming sector has continually lagged behind the rising needs of the nation.

Industrial modernization has had a difficult history since China does not have the resources to develop more than one critical sector at a time. Industrial development was to be financed through sale of surplus farm production. Emphasis on heavy industry led to the degradation of the farming sector; it also created a strong centralized bureaucracy and competing power élites in major cities. Mao attempted to maintain the revolutionary fervour of the peasantry by undermining the Communist party's central control. With the support of students and the People's Army, he twice confronted the party with populist movements dedicated to eliminating bourgeois tendencies in the government. These mass movements brought economic dislocation and ruin to the nation. Since Mao's death in 1976, the government has attempted to make good the losses through a form of modified private enterprise. Special economic zones have been established to attract and manage economic ties with the outside world. In the late 1980s Deng proposed turning the entire eastern seaboard into a duty-free zone to make available 160 million people who could rival the workers of Taiwan, South Korea, or Haiti in inexpensive assembly of consumer goods.

Deng's attempts to liberalize the economy have not been carried over into the political sphere. The Communist party still maintains a monopoly on power. Repeated demonstrations in favour of free speech and democracy have been crushed, and many of those involved were sentenced to service in the army or rural work brigades as a form of "re-education."

QUESTIONS

1. How did the Japanese occupation of China affect the fortunes of the Kuomintang?

2. Why was the Kuomintang unable to maintain support in the countryside? What was Mao's revolutionary goal for China?

3. Briefly describe the Chinese civil war. What was its result?

4. Explain why the United States continued to support Chiang Kai-shek.

5. Explain the Soviet position on China in the 1940s, which resulted in a mutual defense treaty in 1950.

6. Explain how Mao reorganized agriculture. Compare this reorganization to Stalin's collectivization of agriculture.

7. What was the Great Leap Forward? Evaluate its effectiveness.

8. Explain how the Soviets readjusted their relationship with China after the Communist Revolution of 1949. What caused the split between China and the USSR?

9. On what was China's new foreign policy based?

10. What was the purpose of the Cultural Revolution of 1966-1976? Evaluate its effects on China.

11. Describe the impact of industrialization on Chinese society. Explain the Soviet influence on China's industrialization policy.

12. Evaluate Mao's leadership of China from 1949 to 1976.

13. Describe how Deng Xiaoping revolutionized China's economy.

14. Why were the student demonstrations in 1987 and 1989 put down?

CRITICAL ANALYSIS

1. What place does individual freedom have in a nation such as China, which contains a quarter of the world's population?

2. Which is most effective, central control or decentralized control?

3. Can states exist without a central government?

4. How will China get the resources to improve the standard of living of its people?

5. Is zero population growth a realistic target? Why or why not?

6. Should the industrialized world help China industrialize?

7. Debate the following:
Be it resolved that China failed to develop into the socialist utopia envisioned by Mao Zedong.

RESEARCH PROJECTS

1. Compare and contrast the Chinese Revolution of 1949 with the Russian Revolution of 1917. Consider leadership, goals, and course of events.

2. Research the Gang of Four. Identify who they were, what role they played in China's development, and the impact they had on the country's social and political conditions.

3. Research the Cultural Revolution. Evaluate its impact on China's economic and social structures.

4. Compare and contrast the Soviet approach to agriculture with the Chinese one. Evaluate the success of each.

ACTIVITIES

1 Debate

Be it resolved that China's one child policy must be enforced in order to ensure China's economic success.

2 Newspaper

As a class, create a newspaper designed to inform Canadians about current conditions in China. You must agree upon an editor and support staff. Include all types of articles usually found in a daily newspaper, and structure your articles to reflect the political, economic, and social conditions of China today. Pictures, cartoons, and advertisements should be included.

3 Interview

Interview a number of people on the issue of Hong Kong citizens immigrating to Canada. Select long-time Canadian residents from three or four ethnic groups and recent immigrants from Europe, Africa, Asia, or the Caribbean. Structure your questions in a manner which allows you to understand each individual's reasons for the position which they hold on this issue. Write a short summary of your findings or present them orally to the class.

HISTORICAL ANALYSIS

MAO'S CHINA

By defeating the Nationalist Chinese in 1949, Mao Zedong and his Communist followers established the People's Republic of China and set out to revolutionize all aspects of life. Land reform and industrial development were followed by the Cultural Revolution of 1966-1976. Mao succeeded in drawing the Chinese people together and driving out foreign influence, but at his death in 1976, China was still a backward nation struggling to modernize its industry.

Analyse the reforms of the 1950s and the events of the Cultural Revolution in an attempt to determine the impact of Mao's policies on China. How did "land reform" affect agriculture in China? What were the consequences of the Great Leap Forward? How did the Cultural Revolution affect the Chinese people? Evaluate Mao's contribution to modern China. To what extent were his policies supportive of China's attempts to industrialize and achieve a higher standard of living for its people?

Suggested resources:

Byron, John & Robert Pack. *The Claws of the Dragon: Kang Sheng, The Evil Genius Behind Mao and His Legacy of Terror in People's China.* New York: Simon & Schuster, 1992.

Karnow, Stanley. *Mao and China: A Legacy of Turmoil.* New York: Viking Penguin, 1990.

CHAPTER 15

REVOLUTION IN THE GLOBAL POWER STRUCTURE:
1975–1990

The sovereignty of a people is not up for discussion—it is to be defended with arms in hand.

Nicaraguan folk hero Augusto César Sandino, 1929.

"Do you think you are going to win?"

"Yes, yes of course."

"What makes you think so? What makes you think you are going to win?"

"I believe we are going to win. It's evident!"

Afghan guerrilla commander Ahmad Shah Massoud in an interview from the French documentary *Valley against an Empire,* summer 1981.

FOCUS ON GLOBAL INTERACTION

The global power structure has shifted considerably since 1975. Assume the role of a senior United Nations official. Write a report or give a speech, outlining the major changes which have taken place since 1975, and predicting the shape of global political systems in the early twenty-first century.

OVERVIEW

In the 1970s it became apparent that the bipolar world was changing to a multipolar structure which included the economic powers of Japan and Western Europe.

THE HELSINKI ACCORD

In 1975, thirty-five nations met in Helsinki to discuss the security of frontiers in Central Europe and issues of human rights.

THE SOVIET UNION: 1975–1985

Political and economic challenges characterized the Soviet Union in the stagnant years termed the "Brezhnev Era."

AFGHANISTAN

In 1979, the Soviet Union began its involvement in Afghanistan, in a war comparable to the Vietnam War.

POLAND

Poland's labour unrest resulted in the formation of a labour union called Solidarity led by Lech Walesa. Threatened by civil unrest and the popularity of Solidarity, the Polish government imposed martial law in 1981.

THE SOVIET UNION

Productivity in the Soviet Union deteriorated during the Brezhnev years, resulting in a serious chronic shortage of consumer goods.

THE UNITED STATES: 1975–1985

The era of détente between the Soviet Union and the United States ended in 1979, with the Soviet invasion of Afghanistan. This change signaled a new arms race which proved immensely costly to both sides.

CENTRAL AMERICA

Central America has always been closely tied politically and economically to the United States. Why is this area an important sphere of influence for the USA?

EL SALVADOR

American involvement in El Salvador has consisted of military aid to assist the government in repelling Communist rebels, but the atrocities committed by both sides has made American involvement very controversial.

NICARAGUA

American support for the Contra resistance to the Sandinista government resulted in the Iran-Contra arms scandal. The defeat of the Sandinista government in 1990 raised hopes that stability might return to Nicaragua.

BY 1975, THE BIPOLAR WORLD of the United States and the Soviet Union had begun to change. Both superpowers experienced domestic challenges that threatened their international status. Military, economic, and political power and influence must be considered in defining a global superpower. The Soviet Union achieved its superpower status because of military strength and an apparent willingness to use its strength. After crushing the Prague Spring of 1968, Moscow introduced the Brezhnev Doctrine, which justified the use of force in eliminating either external or internal forces "hostile to communism" in Soviet bloc countries. Clearly, the Soviet Union would not tolerate any challenge to Moscow's control of Eastern Europe. Political control, however, was achieved only by military coercion. During the 1970s, it became apparent the Soviet economy was struggling to continue the disproportionate defence spending essential to the maintenance of power. How long would Soviet citizens sacrifice personal needs and desires to the interests of the state?

On the other side of the globe, the Americans, suffering from the military defeat in Vietnam and the disillusionment of the Watergate scandals, struggled through the indecisiveness of the Carter years. Economically powerful, but to some extent morally bankrupt, the United States tended toward introspection in an attempt to determine what had gone awry with its society. The Vietnam issue had pitted American against American, and the forced unification of the Vietnams under Communist rule in 1975 illustrated that the USA's costly involvement had been futile. The Watergate scandals, which revealed evidence of widespread political espionage among members of the Nixon administration, eroded Americans' faith in the office of the president and held the country up to international ridicule.

Signs of the gradual disintegration of the two Cold War superpower blocs had appeared during the 1960s. The unswerving allegiance of nations shielded by the Warsaw Pact or NATO alliance systems had disappeared, and the international system took on new characteristics. Three factors seem most important in this change: the large number of newly independent and non-aligned countries resulting from the decolonization process; the reluctance of Western European nations to act as pawns in the Cold War, and their subsequent overtures to Eastern Europe on the issue of nuclear armaments in Europe; and the emergence of China as an independent power after its split with the Soviet Union in 1962. In combination with the growing economic power of Japan and Western Europe, these factors paved the way for a new **multipolar** system of international relations. Although the world was still dominated in large measure by decisions made in the Soviet Union and the United States, China, Japan, and Western Europe were now forces to be reckoned with.

THE HELSINKI ACCORD

During the period of détente, negotiations between the United States and the Soviet Union focused primarily on arms control. However, issues of human rights and security of frontiers were also in the forefront of discussion. The United States hoped to encourage a greater emphasis on human rights in Eastern Europe and the Soviet Union, to make life more bearable in those regions. The Soviet Union wanted a guarantee of the borders established in Eastern Europe after the Second World War. In Helsinki, on 1 August 1975, 33 European nations and the United States and Canada signed the Final Act of the Conference on Security and Cooperation in Europe. The only European power to abstain was Albania, long a Stalinist "hermit nation." The **Helsinki Accord** represented 10 years of diplomatic negotiation between the Soviet Union and its Warsaw Pact allies, and the United States and its Western European associates. Bargaining focused on the recognition of post-war Central European borders and was finally structured in a three-part agenda.

The first part, "Questions Relating to Security in Europe," gave the Soviet Union and its allies what they had been seeking on border issues in Europe. The frontiers of Eastern Europe were stated to be inviolable, but provision was made for their alteration in accordance with international law, by peaceful means and by agreement. Seemingly in

This photo shows a Swedish member of a United Nations peace keeping force in Cyprus. This picture could be said to symbolize the intent of the Helsinki Accord in 1975.

conflict with the Brezhnev Doctrine was the stipulation of nonintervention in the internal affairs of other nations. The first section ended with a note on security and disarmament that required 21 days' notice for military manoeuvres which involved more than 25 000 soldiers and came within 250 kilometres of national borders—as well as an exchange of observers at such manoeuvres.

The second section, "Cooperation in the Fields of Economics, of Science and Technology, and of the Environment," was politically insignificant by comparison with the other two sections, but it did at least herald a new awareness of the necessity of international cooperation in these areas.

The third section, "Cooperation in Humanitarian and Other Fields," bound the signatories to respect human rights and was specifically directed at the Soviet Union, whose record in this area was abysmal. This part of the agreement aimed to facilitate freer movement and allow for freedom of choice in both private and professional associations. The Helsinki Accord thus held out hope for the oppressed people of Eastern Europe and the Soviet Union, especially dissidents and Jews wishing to leave the Soviet Union, known as refuseniks. However, because the accords were not entrenched in international law, their value was primarily symbolic.

Following the signing of the Helsinki agreement, the Soviet Union and the United States became embroiled in affairs within their own spheres of influence. By 1980, détente seemed to have deteriorated to Cold War again. The Soviet invasion of Afghanistan in 1979 brought an American boycott of the Moscow Olympics and the USA's refusal to ratify SALT II. Economic problems in Poland led to the formation of **Solidarity**, a labour-union-based association of groups that challenged the Communist party's hold on the country. Within the Soviet Union an ageing leadership, a stagnant economy, and the struggle to control dissidents and refuseniks all signaled cracks in the Communist system.

The election of Ronald Reagan to the presidency of the United States in 1980 heralded a new era of right-wing militancy that directed American nationalism against the "evil empire" of the Soviet Union. The invasion of Grenada, interference in El Salvador, and aid to the Contra rebels in Nicaragua were all aimed at restraining Communist insurgency in Central America. Reagan embarked on a massive buildup of arms to ensure military superiority over the Soviets. Increased defence spending and a determination to reduce taxation resulted in a huge budgetary deficit that drove interest rates higher and made American manufactured goods less competitive on the international market. It was not until 1985, when Mikhail Gorbachev came to power in the Soviet Union, and when Ronald Reagan won a second term in office, that relations between the superpowers warmed once again.

THE SOVIET UNION: 1975–1985

The Nixon-Ford-Carter policy of détente enabled the Soviet Union and its Eastern bloc satellites to import vast amounts of Western technology and machinery, paying for them with money borrowed from Western banks. This activity fostered an illusion that the Soviet Union was making economic gains by comparison with the United States. Though most of this money was poured into the military sector, some of it reached the consumer sector. The invasion of Afghanistan, however, ruptured the relationship between the Soviet Union and the West. The Soviet bloc, owing about $80 billion to Western banks, now suffered a serious economic downturn. Poland, which accounted for about $27 billion of the Soviet bloc debt, faced its own economic crisis in 1980, and the Soviet Union itself was forced to sell off much of its gold reserves. Severe economic pressures, agitation by political dissidents, and Western support for Jewish people who wished to emigrate challenged the ageing leadership of Brezhnev, Andropov, and Chernenko and proved to be problems beyond their ability to solve.

AFGHANISTAN

Since 1945, Afghanistan had been firmly in the Soviet sphere of influence, though both Washington and Moscow had aided a succession of Afghan governments. Because of its geographical proximity, however, the Soviet Union had a vested interest in the security of its southern neighbour and committed more economic and military aid to the area.

Afghanistan is a dry, mountainous country populated by diverse ethnic and linguistic groups. It has not developed economically and socially despite efforts by a succession of rulers to stimulate development. In 1973, the monarchy was overthrown by the king's cousin, Mohammad Daoud Khan. Daoud was supported by a faction of the People's Democratic Party of Afghanistan (PDPA)—the Parcham, led by Babrak Karmal. The Parcham believed collaboration with other political forces was necessary to instigate change and promote democratic reforms that might possibly, but not inevitably, lead to socialism. Most of the members of the Parcham came from the urban establishment. The other faction of the PDPA was the Khalq, led by Hafizullah Amin. The Khalq was composed of social classes lower than those of the Parcham. Amin opposed collaboration with other political groupings and was determined to effect social change. He began to recruit support from the army.

Daoud established a dictatorship and began a program of economic development. Determined to secure his power, he repressed all opposition, including the leftists that had supported his bid for power. Daoud attacked Islamic fundamentalists and moved his country closer to the pro-American shah of Iran. This rapprochement suggested that Daoud was now less dependent on the Soviet Union. Alarmed by Daoud's concentration of power in his own person, members of the two factions of the PDPA attempted a reconciliation. By the spring of 1978, Daoud had begun to arrest members of the PDPA. Mir Akbar Khyber, member of the PDPA central committee and editor of the Parcham newspaper, was assassinated. Anti-government demonstrations followed and Daoud reacted by arresting PDPA leaders on 26 April. Amin, leader of the Khalq faction, was able to alert his army supporters before his arrest, and on 27-28 April, a *coup d'état* forced Daoud from office. The Parcham and Khalq factions of the PDPA formed the government, and Daoud, his family, and his top government officials were executed. In December 1978, the Soviet government signed a treaty of friendship with the new Afghan government, thus signaling its support of the PDPA.

The new regime began a program of radical reform aimed at dismantling Afghanistan's still-feudal society. However, the PDPA itself was unable to present a united front on either social or economic issues, and internal squabbling hampered its efforts to institute reforms—ranging from the cancellation of peasant debts to reforms of traditional social customs like arranged marriages and dowries. The chief stumbling block proved to be land reform: the urban roots of the PDPA made it ill-equipped to deal with rural issues.

The PDPA determined that peasant holdings would be limited to 6 hectares of irrigated land and 60 hectares of unirrigated land. The problem was that Afghanistan had a shortage of irrigated land, and even limiting such plots to 6 hectares could not assure irrigated land for the entire population. Water was in short supply almost everywhere. The land issue, and problems associated with debt cancellation (many smallholders were creditors as well as debtors), created a crisis in the countryside.

A resistance movement began within a month of the *coup.* The movement was backed by most of the country's 320 000 mullahs, or Muslim religious

Thousands of Soviet lives were lost during the war in Afghanistan. These Soviet soldiers are shown checking a road for mines.

AMBASSADOR KIDNAPPED

In February 1979, the American ambassador, "Spike" Dubs, was

kidnapped by four Afghans and held hostage in the Kabul Hotel in

an effort to force the release of the Afghans' friends from prison.

Afghan police, backed by Soviet snipers, burst into the room, killing

the kidnappers as well as Ambassador Dubs.

This photograph shows the first troops crossing the Soviet-Afghan border after the Soviet Union pulled out of the war.

leaders learned in sacred law. As if the disorders related to land reform were not enough, the government suffered from factional competition. The Khalq now triumphed over the Parcham. But the Khalq found itself beset by rivalry between Amin and Nur Mohammad Taraki for leadership of the regime. Taraki collaborated with the Soviets but was arrested and executed by Amin when his duplicity was discovered. Taraki's death meant the death of the regime. The Soviets distrusted Amin and feared the continuation of civil turmoil and the loss of their potential satellite.

On Christmas Eve, 1979, Soviet paratroopers of the 195th Airborne Division descended on Kabul. By 27 December, some 5000 Red Army soldiers were in control of the Afghan capital. The Soviet invasion was underway. A revolutionary tribunal sentenced Amin to death, and on 1 January 1980, Babrak Karmal was installed as leader of a Soviet puppet government. By the end of January, the invasion had been supported by 1850 tanks and squadrons of MiG-21s, MiG-22s, and SU-17 fighter bombers. However, 90 per cent of the countryside was in the hands of rebel troops, the *mujaheddin*. Just as the Americans had failed to annihilate the Viet Cong in 1965, the Soviets now failed to subdue the *mujaheddin* in their initial strike.

The countryside and the people of Afghanistan proved indomitable. A country of 400 000 sq km, roughly two-thirds the size of Alberta, Afghanistan is a wild, inhospitable region covered with deep valleys, mountain escarpments, and the Baluchi desert in the south. Landlocked, and with few natural resources other than natural gas, it depends on cash crops of wool and hashish. In 1979, the largely Muslim population numbered 15.2 million, 90 per cent of whom were illiterate. Many of the Afghan people are tribal, resourceful, and given to feuding among themselves. Soviet divisions, trained to fight conventional warfare, were no match for guerrilla forces used to the different terrain. The Soviets soon realized they now had their own Vietnam, a war they could not win, but a war they could not easily abandon.

By 1985, Soviet troop strength had risen to 120 000, but the *mujaheddin* refused to surrender. In a bid to win support by seeming more Afghan than Communist, Karmal outlined 10 theses for extending the Afghan revolution. This ploy did not result in increased popularity, and in May 1986 Karmal was replaced by Major General Mohammed Najibullah, director of the secret police, who was in league with the Soviet secret police (the KGB). Early in 1987, Najibullah announced a unilateral cease-fire, a gesture rejected by resistance leaders. Najibullah's leadership did, however, begin Soviet troop reduction and provide hope for the end of a protracted war.

On 14 April 1988, the Geneva Accords on the war in Afghanistan were signed by Pakistan and Afghanistan, and an additional declaration guaranteeing the agreement was signed by the United States and the Soviet Union. The accords, which came into force on 15 May 1988, provided a timetable for Soviet troop withdrawal in 1989 and an end to the war in Afghanistan. They also called for the voluntary return of 3.5 million Afghan refugees who fled to Pakistan during the war. On 15 February 1989, the last Soviet soldier crossed the Afghan border on his way home.

Some 15 000 Soviet soldiers lost their lives in the Afghan war. Although the Soviets have not disclosed how much the war cost them, it is estimated they had to spend $12 million per day. The cost to the Afghans is incalculable. Soviet weaponry transformed the country into a barren wasteland. Of 22 000 villages, an estimated 15 000 were destroyed and 5000 made uninhabitable. Millions of farm animals were slaughtered, homes were reduced to rubble, irrigation systems were destroyed, and agricultural areas were riddled with hundreds of thousands of land-mines. The United Nations budgeted $1 billion for reconstruction and resettlement in the first year. This money was channeled through the regime in Kabul, and not only supported the regime, but gave it the leverage in rural areas it had sought for the last 10 years. Humanitarian agencies feared a repetition of the Ethiopian situation, where rebels had to accept government control or face starvation.

POLAND

From 1970 to 1976, three factors allowed Poland's government to contain labour unrest and maintain some measure of economic stability: the Soviet Union extended economic aid; Western banks offered easy credit to fund industrial expansion and the import of new technology; and world demand for traditional Polish exports, especially coal, remained strong. Productivity could thus be increased without sacrifices by the working class. Wages were allowed to rise by 40 per cent during the period of 1970-1975, and food consumption increased. But, since agriculture was heavily subsidized, increased food consumption severely strained the nation's budget and forced importation of both food and animal fodder. At the same time, Western economies suffered recession and the demand for Polish exports weakened. As Poland's debt to Western banks increased, the Polish government found it increasingly difficult to meet interest payments. By 1976, the government was forced to announce price increases. Meat alone was to cost 60 per cent more than before. This and other price increases raised the cost of living by 16 per cent. Strikes broke out immediately, and the government withdrew its price increases the next day. In order to prevent reprisals against striking workers, a number of dissident intellectuals organized to defend the workers and assume a major role in Polish society.

The workers had the support of the Roman Catholic Church, which was one of the few institutions in Poland whose authority did not come from the Communist state. The reorganization of Poland's borders after the Second World War made it the most homogeneous state in Europe: 95 per cent were ethnic Poles, and virtually all were Roman Catholics. The Roman Catholic Church naturally

Thousands of Solidarity members demonstrated on May Day of 1981. By the end of the year, the Polish government imposed martial law, and protests like the one above became illegal.

provided the focus for resistance to the Communist regime after 1945. Proportionately more citizens attended mass and participated in the ceremonies of the Catholic Church in Poland than anywhere else in the world.

As Poland was the most intense centre of Catholicism, it was appropriate that Karol Wojtyla, cardinal-archbishop of Cracow, be elected pope on 16 October 1978. Pope John Paul II was the first non-Italian to be chosen as pope since 1522, and the youngest pope since 1846. No bishop from Slavic East Europe had ever before achieved such honour. Pope John Paul II reflected the conservative and authoritarian nature of traditional Catholicism, but he combined this with a humanitarianism gained in wide-ranging travel. His largest audience was in his homeland where 3.5 million people attended the service he conducted at Czestochowa.

By July 1980, the Polish government was forced to impose substantial price increases. Export markets had not recovered, and service charges on the foreign debt now consumed the country's hard currency. Meat prices rose by 100 per cent. Strikes swept the country, with the Gdansk shipyards leading the way. The government then granted pay increases of 10-15 per cent. However, the crises in 1970 and 1976 had given the labour force a sense of political power, and there was now a sit-down strike at the Lenin Shipyards in Gdansk on 14 August 1980. Although substantial pay increases were offered to break the strike, the workers refused them, demanding recognition as a trade union. On 17 August, they received symbolic support from the Catholic Church when a mass was conducted just outside the shipyard gates. The leader of the Lenin Shipyard strikers was an electrician named Lech Walesa. Supported by an inter-factory strike committee, Walesa achieved the Gdansk Accord on 31 August 1980. This agreement granted the workers' right to establish independent unions, the right to strike, better working conditions, Saturdays free of work, radio broadcasts of mass, relaxed censorship, and an easing of political control. By mid-September the government conceded these terms could be extended to unions throughout the country. In order to establish greater bargaining power in their dealings with the government, unions throughout Poland united. *Solidarnosc,* or Solidarity, was born on 22 September 1980.

At the first sign of trouble in Poland the Soviets had begun Warsaw Pact military manoeuvres in East Germany and the Baltic region, hoping to intimidate the recalcitrant Poles. However, the Soviets understood the wisdom of allowing the Polish Communist party to resolve the crisis itself—a tactic that had worked in 1956 and 1970. Polish nationalism ran deep, and any Soviet intervention would be met with fierce resistance. Besides, the Soviets were now mired in Afghanistan. When Poland's rural areas demanded a Rural Solidarity, however, the Soviets began a new round of Warsaw Pact manoeuvres and seemed poised for intervention. Walesa struck a conciliatory pose, however, and while some members of Solidarity objected to his cancellation of a general strike, his prudence was rewarded when the Polish supreme court accepted Rural Solidarity as a legal organization.

By the autumn of 1981 Solidarity's membership had grown to comprise 8 million or more of a population of 35 million. The government wanted workers to make sacrifices in the interests of resolving the economic crisis, and Solidarity wanted a say in the management of the country's affairs in return. While negotiations were underway, a new round of food and tobacco price increases was imposed. In October, General Jaruzelski, prime minister and defence minister, took over as Communist party chief. By the end of November it was obvious that Jaruzelski was not going to allow Solidarity any real power; talks between government and Solidarity reached an impasse. Sporadic strikes staged around the country throughout the autumn now escalated, and in December, Rural Solidarity

suggested that it merge with both Solidarity and the student organizations.

On 12 December 1981 the national leaders of Solidarity abandoned the middle ground maintained by Walesa, and proposed that 17 December be designated a national day of protest—to be followed in the New Year with a national vote on Communist leadership, free elections, and the military relationship of Poland and the Soviet Union. This was a direct challenge to the authority of the Communist state, and Jaruzelski proclaimed martial law on 13 December 1981, establishing a Military Council of National Salvation. Telephone and telex communications were cut, transport of goods was halted, factories were occupied, strikes were outlawed, and the arrest of Solidarity leaders began.

The American response to the imposition of martial law was to apply economic sanctions in an attempt to force the government to liberalize its regime. In August 1984, the Polish armed forces released large numbers of political prisoners, and the Americans lifted many of the sanctions they had applied. However, Poland continued to suffer economic difficulties. Its foreign debt had grown to $30 billion by 1986, contributing to the already great difficulties the Poles had in obtaining the necessities of daily life.

THE SOVIET UNION

From 1964 to 1982, during the Brezhnev years, the Soviet Union continued to pour vast amounts of money into armaments and in the 1970s achieved parity with the United States in some types of weaponry. The commitment to an enormous nuclear arsenal was made at the expense of the manufacture and distribution of consumer goods, which remained relatively scarce and of poor quality. Although comparisons are difficult to make because the GNP of a centrally planned economy is difficult to assess, it is estimated that during the 1970s the average Soviet citizen had a standard of living comparable to that of the average North American worker in the 1920s. This comparison must be qualified, however. The urban Soviet had three further disadvantages. Housing had not kept pace with immigration from rural areas. It was very difficult to find accommodation, and per-capita floor space was only 6.7 square metres (compared to 111 square metres in North America). Only 1 in 46 Soviet citizens owned a

During the 1970s and early 1980s, the average Soviet citizen had little or no access to consumer goods that Western tourists to the USSR had.

car—and ownership came only after a waiting period of about 10 to 15 years, and was very expensive. Finally, as agriculture continued to deteriorate under Brezhnev, food shortages persisted and citizens had to endure long line-ups daily to obtain the necessary items. Meat and fresh produce were in short supply and often simply unavailable at state stores.

The Soviet Union's difficulties with food supply persisted despite annual investment of about $78 billion and annual subsidies of about $50 billion to keep retail prices down. Socialization of agriculture had led to a lack of incentive and a denial of responsibility among workers on state farms. Chronic inefficiencies and enormous wastage due to poor storage, ramshackle distribution networks, and lack of efficient transportation created a dependency on imported grain. Private plots, which comprised only 4 per cent of Soviet arable land, contributed 25 per cent of food output; but any conversion of the collective farms to smallholdings would pose a threat to bureaucratic control that Brezhnev was not willing to risk. His successors, Andropov and Chernenko, both ill and aged, simply continued to oversee a stagnant economy. It was not until the accession of Mikhail Gorbachev that any significant changes occurred in the Soviet Union's organization of agriculture.

THE UNITED STATES: 1975–1985

By the mid-1970s, the United States was faced with a multitude of challenges, both domestic and international. The American people still demanded that their government take a leading role in policing the world while at the same time providing high-quality consumer goods at reasonable prices. American industry was no longer able to compete in world markets for automotive, steel, or textile products. Competition from Asia—particularly from Japan, Korea, and Taiwan—pressured American industrialists to become more innovative. The automotive industry was particularly under siege: the energy crisis of 1973 made fuel economy imperative, and Japanese cars were far superior in fuel efficiency. The combination of skyrocketing energy prices and trade imbalances led to a recession in the United States by the end of the decade.

The years President Jimmy Carter was in office were characterized on the international scene by the end of détente but also the development of the notion that use of nuclear weapons need not destroy humanity. The USA's national security advisor Zbigniew Brzezinski saw the world in bipolar terms and clearly viewed the Soviets as a global threat to be met militarily. Secretary of State Cyrus Vance, by contrast, believed that peace could be achieved by negotiation and economic ties with the Soviets. Faced with two competing positions, Carter had to make foreign policy decisions without either a settled framework or a personal background in such matters. As a result, Carter adopted a humanitarian approach and focused on the human rights issue in the Soviet Union. Carter's open encouragement of Soviet dissidents infuriated Brezhnev and lessened any opportunities for meaningful negotiations between the superpowers.

The most serious rupture in American-Soviet relations at the end of the 1970s occurred when Brzezinski played his "China Card," hoping to "trump" Soviet policies in the Third World and in arms control. On 1 January 1979, Carter and Deng Xiaoping had exchanged diplomatic representations and ended 30 years of American non-recognition of China. Brzezinski capitalized on this opportunity, and American exports to China nearly doubled in 1979. This increased trade was viewed as a real *coup* by the Americans, who now faced worldwide trade competition from Japan. The Chinese used the relationship to imply American complicity in the Chinese invasion of Vietnam, and thus disrupted the Soviet-American relations while SALT II agreements were still unratified. When the Soviets invaded Afghanistan, détente effectively ended; the Americans boycotted the 1980 Moscow Olympics and refused to ratify SALT II.

In 1980, Ronald Reagan won a landslide victory over Jimmy Carter in the presidential race. Reagan seemed to symbolize all the pent-up frustration and aggressive nationalism of the American public, and he focused attention on the "evil empire" of the Soviet Union—promising to take a hard-line stand in foreign policy. The Soviet Union, Reagan argued, had continued to produce arms at a time when the United States had directed its attention to domestic issues. It was now time to redress the imbalance and equip the United States to fight a protracted war with conventional as well as nuclear weaponry. The belief that a nuclear war could be fought and won had been popularized already; and despite evidence to the contrary, the Reagan administration operated on such a premise.

Believing that the American economy could afford a massive military buildup, the administration ignored the budgetary deficit it was running, and subsequent dramatic increases in interest rates. The result for the American economy was devastating: factories became less competitive and workers faced increased prices and fewer jobs. Committed to "taking the government off the backs of the people," Reagan refused to raise taxes. The government's share of GNP accordingly rose to 25.2 per cent, its highest degree of involvement since the Second World War.

The Reagan administration was supported largely by a militant right wing anxious to protect the world from communism. Central America was an area too close to the United States for it to allow communist success there. The Reagan government thus attempted, in both El Salvador and Nicaragua, to secure friendly governments and prevent infiltration by either Soviet or Cuban communists.

CENTRAL AMERICA

Throughout the twentieth century, Central America has been more tightly integrated into the American economic and security system than any other region of the world. As early as 1823, when President James Monroe issued the Monroe Doctrine that warned European nations to refrain from further meddling in the western hemisphere, the Americans had declared their hegemony in the region. By the 1900s, the United States challenged Great Britain in the area by investing heavily in banana and coffee plantations, railroads, gold and silver mines, and finally, in utilities and government securities. By 1914, Central America's economic survival had come to depend on its trade with the United States.

As American economic leverage grew, so did its political influence. The construction of the Panama Canal, which opened in 1914, accelerated the growth of American power in Central America as British power receded. Determined to maintain stability in the region, the Americans have since supported autocratic and reactionary governments threatened by popular revolution. Lately encouraged by Cuba, these revolutionary movements have, especially in Nicaragua, attempted to oust governments that favour small, wealthy élites. Their goal is to break monopolies held by a combination of foreign investors and local élites that turn countries into producers of one or two primary export crops at the expense of healthy economic diversification. Land is monopolized by crops exported to industrial nations and is therefore unavailable for the production of foodstuffs required domestically. The result is malnutrition and even starvation among the peasantry and excessive wealth among the élite.

EL SALVADOR

El Salvador is a prime example of some of the difficulties facing the small nations of Central America. Some 2 per cent of the population was made up of the Fourteen Families that controlled nearly all the fertile soil and 60 per cent of the total land area. The ordinary people of El Salvador rank among the five most poorly fed populations in the world. At 3.5 per cent per year, El Salvador has one of the world's highest population growth rates, and demands on the land have resulted in the

Villagers in Colombia cast their ballots for local leaders. In many cases, the United States has used its influence to establish democratic governments in Central and South America. Often these governments are democratic in name only.

wholesale destruction of both plant and animal life. El Salvador had for some time been in the grip of a civil war whose roots can be traced to the 1972 presidential elections that saw José Napoléon Duarte deprived of victory when the army declared its own candidate the winner. A *coup* attempt by Duarte and other opposition forces ended in failure, and Duarte was exiled to Guatemala. Guerrilla groups organized in the countryside. The Roman Catholic Church also helped to mobilize the population. Oscar Romero, who was archbishop in 1977, became outspoken in condemning government and vigilante terrorism. With the election of Pope John Paul II in 1978, the Church advised Latin American Catholic leaders to commit to community, but not partisan causes. Archbishop Romero continued his criticism of government supported vigilante groups and condemned the military for committing atrocities on the civilian population.

Government repression increased, and most church leaders withdrew from political involvement as Pope John Paul II voiced disapproval of political activism. Romero was silenced by a right-wing

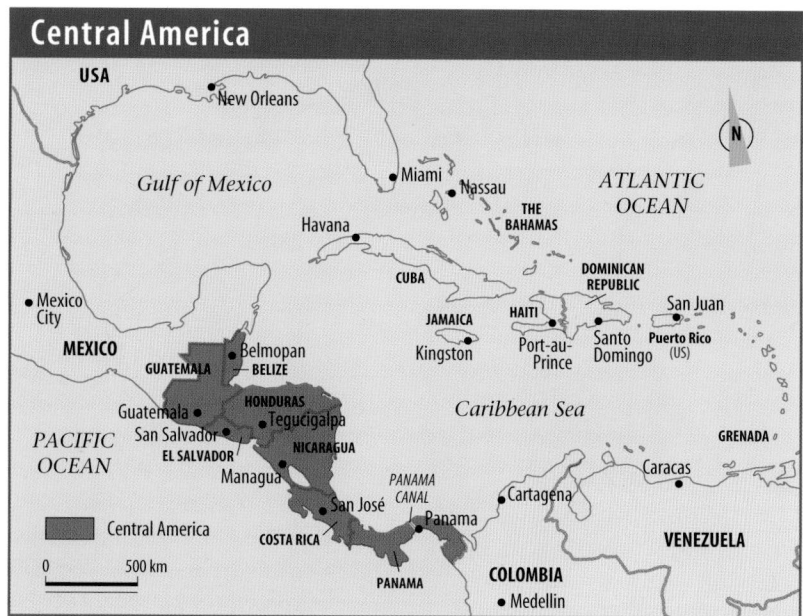

Central America

The United States has been involved in Central American politics throughout the twentieth century.

SANDINO, HERO OF THE SANDINISTAS

The charismatic Augusto César Sandino was born in Nicaragua's wealthy élite but developed a mission to rid Nicaragua of its American presence and distribute land to disadvantaged peasants. In 1927 Sandino engaged in a war with US troops. For five years he eluded detection by US Marines, staging guerrilla raids from his camps in the hills. When the marines finally left, in January 1933, Sandino agreed to negotiate with the government—and gave General Somoza of the National Guard the opportunity to arrest and execute him. Claiming to have the approval of the American minister to Nicaragua, Arthur Lane, Somoza implicated the United States in the execution of Sandino—a man who was even then a folk hero.

political group, who murdered him in the capital city of San Salvador while he was celebrating mass. The military dictatorship lost much of what little support it had when the bodies of three nuns and a Catholic layperson, all American citizens, were found in a shallow grave. Support of revolutions that sought to overcome poverty and disease put the Church on the firing line in Central America and aided attempts to unseat ruling dictatorships.

The American protest against Salvadoran government atrocities was short-lived. The military aid that Carter suspended to protest the slaying of US churchwomen was resumed under the Reagan administration. By 1984, annual US military aid to the Salvadoran government amounted to $196.6 million, in response to the support Salvadoran rebel groups received from Cuba through Nicaragua. The United States was committed to the government in power to prevent a leftist revolution. In 1984, Duarte won the presidential election, but the army remained the dominant force in the country. Guerrilla forces and pro-government death squads terrorized the countryside. A vicious cycle of repression and rebellion left at least 45 000 civilians dead and made 750 000 Salvadorans refugees.

NICARAGUA

Nicaragua has long been a key state to American dominance in Central America. From 1911 to 1933, the United States was in military occupation of Nicaragua to control the natural system of waterways and the site of a contemplated transisthmian canal much like that in Panama. During this period, Nicaragua was essentially an American protectorate as the United States sought to prevent German and Japanese interests from constructing a canal through the region to rival its own. From 1936 to 1979, the Somoza family dynasty ruled Nicaragua with American support. Willing instruments of American foreign policy, the Somozas were unhindered in their manipulation of the Nicaraguan economy. They controlled the Nicaraguan state airline and shipping line, and over half the country's arable land.

The earthquake that struck the capital, Managua, in 1972 was the beginning of the Somoza family's downfall. Relief supplies totaling $600 million were stolen by the National Guard, who resold the goods on the black market. Anastasio Somoza Debayle personally profited from the disaster by demanding that Managua be rebuilt on land he owned, even though studies showed the area liable to future earthquakes. The Somoza family fortune now reached about $1 billion as they profited from reconstruction contracts and further crowded out the already small economic élite outside their ranks. It was this small group, now dispossessed of its wealth, that formed the first effective opposition to the Somozas. In December 1974, this group of moderates, led by Joaquin Chamorro, editor of *La Prensa*, formed the Union Democratica Liberacion (UDEL). The UDEL was soon obscured by the Frente Sandinista de Liberacion Nacional (FSLN), a radical group founded in 1962 and named after the guerrilla leader, Sandino. The **Sandinistas** were initially unsuccessful in their attempts to organize a resistance movement against the Somoza regime, but in 1977 they staged a series of guerrilla raids that identified them once more as a significant threat to the government. The assassination of Joaquin Chamorro on 10 January 1978 provoked rioting and a general strike. The moderates, though wary of the Sandinistas, joined them in a coalition to mobilize the masses and unseat Somoza. The Sandinistas acted unilaterally in August, however, when they seized 1500 hostages from a legislative session and demanded the release of political prisoners. Sandinista support emerged in the countryside; and sporadic uprisings resulted in the death of about 3000 people in a three-week period as the National Guard attempted to retain control. Despite American attempts to get Somoza and the Sandinistas to negotiate, the Sandinistas gained control of most of the country the following year.

On 17 July 1979, Somoza fled the country and was assassinated in Paraguay on 17 September 1980. The Sandinistas emerged victorious during the formation of a provisional government, which included representatives of both the left-wing and the moderate groups. Violeta Barrios de Chamorro, widow of the assassinated Joaquin Chamorro, was one of the country's most important moderates and a representative of the business community. The Sandinistas, represented by Daniel Ortega Saavedra, were now the dominant faction and encouraged a land-reform program that created both state farms and state cooperatives as well as granting private holdings. By 1981, moderate members of the provisional government feared the continued dominance of radical Sandinistas and attempted to initiate elections. The Sandinistas recognized a growing resistance to their dominance and refused to allow elections. As a result, a counter-revolutionary movement led by former members of Somoza's National Guard launched guerrilla raids into Nicaragua from bases in Honduras.

These guerrilla groups, known as the Contras, received $10 million in covert American aid in 1981, and another $19 million in 1982. The Reagan administration, of course, hoped to undermine the Sandinista government. In 1983, it gave $24 million

This photograph, taken in 1984, shows new recruits for the Sandinistan army brandishing Soviet-made rifles. Their foes, the Contras, were supplied similarly by the United States.

MISKITO UPRISING

Nicaragua's Miskito Indians, in an attempt to gain recognition of their right to sovereignty in their own Atlantic Coast region, staged an uprising in 1981 that resulted in the wholesale resettlement of as many as 10 000 people. Some Miskitos fled to Honduras, and many joined the **Contras**. The resistance the Miskito offered the Sandinistas only enhanced the latter's determination to centralize power in Managua. Finally, in 1985, the Sandinistas drafted a plan to allow autonomy in the Miskito region in matters other than defence, and small numbers of Miskito refugees were repatriated.

BIOGRAPHY

VIOLETA BARRIOS DE CHAMORRO

(1929–   )

Violeta Chamorro was the president of Nicaragua from 1990 to October 1996. Her election, as head of the National Opposition Union (U.N.O.) in 1990, saw the defeat of Sandinista Daniel Ortega. After years of civil war in the 1980s between the American-backed Contra rebels and the Soviet-backed Sandinistas, Nicaraguans hoped that Chamorro's rise to power would be followed by great economic improvements. Although Chamorro was the candidate supported by the USA, within several years of her leadership the USA had drastically reduced aid to Nicaragua. This came in response to Chamorro's policies, which did not make a clean break with the Sandinistas. Neither did her policies call for the conviction or punishment of key Sandinistas responsible in part for the conflict that had preceded Chamorro's presidency.

Some have called Chamorro elegant, while at the same time denouncing her as ineffective. Others have seen her as the one who ruled, while her son-in-law, Minister of the Presidency, Antonio Lacayo, reigned. Although many Nicaraguans respected and liked Chamorro during her years as president, there were those who looked back longingly to the ruthless dictatorship of Somoza, which lasted from 1946-1979. (Chamorro's deceased husband, Pedro Joaquin Chamorro Cardena, was owner/editor of the newspaper *La Prensa* during the Somoza years and was a leading critic of the Somoza regime. Violeta took over *La Prensa* in 1978 when Pedro was assassinated.) A small business owner in Managua said: "There was much repression [under Somoza] but the economy was very solid." Nicaragua's annual per capita income is $540 Cdn, less than it was in 1960. The United Nations estimates that some 70 per cent of Nicaraguans live in extreme poverty, and 60 per cent are unemployed. The infant mortality rate is 81 deaths in 1000, ten times higher than in Canada. Ecological destruction in Nicaragua has been proceeding at an alarming rate. Nearly 200 000 hectares are being lost each year. The soil is being depleted by cotton crops and poisoned by pesticides. Breast milk contains up to 400 times the DDT once allowed in the USA.

Sixty per cent of voters in Nicaragua do not associate closely with any political party. They are unable to believe that any politician can solve their deep-seated economic and political problems. Rather than helping Nicaragua to realize its vast potential in terms of human and natural resources, Chamorro's efforts focused on the country's $14.7 billion foreign debt and its runaway inflation. These priorities were set in response to pressure from the International Monetary Fund and the World Bank. What followed were drastic spending cuts, the privatization of hundreds of government operations, and tighter control of credit for agricultural and business enterprises. Economist and former Sandinista Alejandro Martinez Cuenca compared these measures to "dropping a bomb without even looking where the bomb is going."

Among Chamorro's four children are Sandinistas and bitter anti-Sandinistas, but presiding over a divided family is a far less-ominous task than presiding over a country with Nicaragua's problems. Luis Carrion, one of nine top Sandinista leaders, said that Nicaraguans have little experience in the art of compromise: "Nicaraguan politics are anti—anti-Zelayista, anti-Chamorrista, anti-Somocista, anti-imperialist, anti-Sandinista." He went on to say that where there is no history of "positive, constructive policies, distrust is profound."

Several of Chamorro's presidential victories included bringing an end to run-away inflation and slashing the size of the Sandinista People's Army from 96 000 members to less than one sixth of that. Besides cooperating with the Sandinistas, Chamorro also preached reconciliation between rival factions. On 21 July 1993, after 150 renegade ex-soldiers swept into the northern city of Esteli, leaving 45 dead and 98 wounded, Chamorro called on the some 1300 former combatants still roaming the mountains to enter nine security zones and await the proposed amnesty. "I ask all of you to stop this practice of war and the use of violence. Let's embrace the cause of peace, understanding and brotherhood."

While some of Chamorro's adversaries belittled her knowledge of politics and the feeble authority she held, a Latin ambassador in Managua cautioned that Chamorro was in control of the situation and that her failing may have amounted to the irreconcilable nature of her stated commitment to unity and what many perceived as her visceral hatred of the Sandinistas. ●

to the Contras, whom Reagan now termed "freedom fighters;" but by 1984 fears of a new Vietnam caused Congress to prohibit any further aid. In 1985, however, Congress approved nonmilitary aid. While the CIA had been funding the Contra resistance, the Cubans had been providing military aid to the Sandinistas, to whom the Soviet Union had given a $300 million subsidy.

In 1984, the Sandinistas finally allowed elections and Daniel Ortega gained the presidency. As commander-in-chief of the Sandinista army, Ortega had proven himself in the 1979 expulsion of union organizers who had attempted to ruin the Nicaraguan branches of American companies like Coca-Cola and Standard Fruit. This episode seemed to indicate Sandinista willingness to cooperate with American interests; but soon after their accession to unrivaled power, the Sandinistas began to pull away again from American influence. By the time Ortega became president, he was in open opposition to the United States and traveled to the Soviet Union in 1985 to enlist its support.

As the war in Nicaragua continued, not only the Americans, but also the Latin American neighbours sought its resolution. In August 1987, the president of Costa Rica, Oscar Arias, put forward a peace initiative based on three principles: cessation of aggression among Latin American countries, cessation of foreign aid to insurgencies, and respect for political freedoms. In March 1988, a cease-fire was negotiated between the Sandinistas and the Contras. Although both sides were guilty of atrocities, they now maintained the cease-fire with only minimal sporadic violence. Then, in 1989, the Sandinistas, worn down by the protracted war and faced with an inflation of 1700 per cent per year in a devastated economy, agreed to let the Nicaraguan people choose their government in an election to be held on 25 February 1990.

The Sandinistas agreed to the electoral process, believing they would win; instead they were the victims of a stunning upset. Violeta Chamorro won 55 per cent of the vote to Ortega's 41 per cent. Chamorro faced a considerable challenge in her new post: she headed a 14-party coalition of groups ranging from conservative to communist—the common thread being a hatred of the Sandinistas. On 25 April, Chamorro was inaugurated as Nicaraguan president, and Contra rebels began the

Colonel Oliver North's testimony at the Iran-Contra hearings stunned the citizens of the United States. However, Oliver North emerged from the scandal as something of a hero to many Americans.

IRAN–CONTRA AFFAIR

In November 1986, the American public learned that profits from the sale of arms to Iran had been diverted to the Contra rebels in Nicaragua. Colonel Oliver North revealed that, in addition to the arms money, $14 million in private donations had been raised to aid resistance to the Sandinista government.

This revelation created a furor among Americans since Congress had determined to halt military funding to the Contras in 1984.

centralization of both agriculture and industry under the Sandinistas was reversed. Chamorro's advisors suggested that the private sector should once again operate the sugar, coffee, and cotton sectors of the economy. Ortega was vocal in his opposition to any move to return banking to the private sector and warned against confiscation of land given to peasants in the agrarian reform. Chamorro promised to allow peasants to keep the land they received, but also to compensate owners who were victims of nationalization programs.

The World Bank estimates that Nicaragua will need $1.3 billion per year for the next 10 years to cope with population pressures and begin reconstruction. Chamorro's government requested $2 billion in aid from the United States, which was already beleaguered by requests from Eastern European countries for Marshall Plan-style assistance. American president Bush responded by first stopping the trade embargo on Nicaragua and then promising to resume diplomatic relations.

The defeat of the Sandinista regime removed one of the most destabilizing factors in Central America. Nicaragua had played host to the Cuban regime's attempt to export communism throughout Latin America. The strategic nature of Nicaragua's location in the American sphere of influence outweighed the Soviet Union's wish to limit its own involvement in the area lest it provoke the USA. Determined to ensure that communism did not gain a foothold on its doorstep, the United States had committed itself to a program of support for forces opposing the Sandinistas. A return to democratic government and the reconstruction of the economy depend partly on continued support by the American government.

In October 1996 a poorly organized but fair election took place. According to election rules, Chamorro was not allowed to run for re-election. Right-winged candidate, Arnoldo Aleman, popular ex-mayor of Managua and head of the Liberal Constitutional Party (PLC), won the election over Sandinista Daniel Ortega. There were 30 political parties in the running. Although the PLC is the legacy of the dictator Anastasio Somoza, a return to the terror and dictatorship of the Somoza years is unlikely. Aleman, a politician "who gets things done," recognizes—as did Chamorro—that there is still a large support base within Nicaragua for the Sandinistas. Likely his rule will be by constitutional means and responsive to the overwhelming majority of Nicaraguans who are committed to democracy.

surrender of weapons to international observers. The disarmament process was complete by 10 June 1990, at which time the Contras were demobilized.

Chamorro inherited a country devastated by 10 years of Sandinista rule. A civil war lasting 19 years had taken 50 000 lives and destroyed more than $500 million in property. A top priority of the new government was to revitalize the economy. The

SUMMARY

The bipolar world of the United States and the Soviet Union, which had emerged after 1945, began by 1975 to give way to a multipolar international system that included Japan, China, and Western Europe. In 1975, the Helsinki Accord was signed by 33 European countries, as well as the United States and Canada. This agreement was symbolic evidence of an attempt by these nations to guarantee European borders and ensure human rights.

Both of the superpowers faced challenges within their spheres of influence in the 1970s and 1980s. The Soviet Union became involved in a long and costly war in Afghanistan. The Soviet invasion of Afghanistan in 1979 resulted in renewed tension with the United States and the failure of the USA to ratify SALT II. Economic problems in Poland resulted in the formation of Solidarity and demands by labour unions for political and economic change. The Soviet Union, beset by economic problems, refrained from direct intervention but supported the Polish Communist government's imposition of martial law.

The United States faced serious economic recession in the late 1970s and thus welcomed Ronald Reagan's promises to allow free market forces to rejuvenate the economy. Increased government spending without increased taxes led to budget deficits as the United States embarked on an arms buildup to resist the "evil empire" of the Soviet Union. Central America proved to be one of the United States' major challenges as fighting continued in El Salvador and Nicaragua. American aid to the Contras in Nicaragua was discontinued by Congress, but a covert operation to divert money to the Contras from the secret sale of arms to Iran blew up in the Iran-Contra Affair. The period ending in 1985 saw both the United States and the Soviet Union more willing to negotiate since each recognized that cooperation on the international scene was essential to providing conditions necessary for their own domestic renewals.

QUESTIONS

1. Give three factors that contributed to the change in superpower status after 1960.

2. Explain the three sections of the Helsinki Accord.

3. Evaluate the significance of the Helsinki Accord to the USA, and to the USSR.

4. Why did the Soviet Union invade Afghanistan in 1979?

5. Explain how the Afghan landscape and its people affected the Soviet attempt to control the region.

6. What were the results of the war in Afghanistan?

7. Describe Poland's economic difficulties of 1980.

8. What is Solidarity? Explain its role in the attempted reform of 1980.

9. How did the Polish government respond to Solidarity's demands for change in 1980-1981?

10. Describe Soviet economic conditions during the Brezhnev years.

11. Describe the foreign policy put forward by President Carter.

12. Explain the term "China Card." How did this new alignment of the United States and China affect American-Soviet relations?

13. Describe the foreign policy initiated by Ronald Reagan upon his taking office in 1980.

14. Why is Central America of such concern to the United States?

15. Who was responsible for Archbishop Romero's death in El Salvador? Why was he assassinated?

16. Why did the United States support the Somozan dynasty in Nicaragua?

17. How did the Sandinistas gain control of Nicaragua?

18. Who were the Contras in Nicaragua? Why did they receive American aid?

19. Explain how the Nicaraguan situation was resolved in 1990.

20. What were the results of the war in Nicaragua?

CRITICAL ANALYSIS

1. Describe the costs—political, social, and economic—of suppressing nationalist movements within a sphere of influence.

2. Are boycotts, like the Western withdrawal from the 1980 Moscow Olympic Games, effective? What are the costs of boycotts to both sides? Who benefits? Give specific examples in supporting your answers.

3. Evaluate the Soviet Union's success in Afghanistan.

4. Who should the USA support in Latin America? Make a list of conditions that should be met before support is given.

5. How effective is American intervention in Latin America? How effective is it in Canada? Does the United States have the right to intervene in either Latin America or Canada? Why or why not?

RESEARCH PROJECTS

1. Compare and contrast Soviet involvement in the war in Afghanistan with American involvement in the war in Vietnam.

2. Trace the development of the Solidarity movement in Poland and evaluate its role in changing Poland's political and economic system.

3. Research the role of multinational corporations in Central America and evaluate their impact on social and economic conditions.

4. Write a biographical account of one of the following individuals and evaluate his or her impact on the social, political, and economic conditions of his or her country:
(a) Lech Walesa; (b) Daniel Ortega;
(c) José Napoléon Duarte; (d) Somoza;
(e) Arnoldo Aleman.

ACTIVITIES

1 Debate
Be it resolved that, in an interdependent world, cooperation in international trade must supplant economic imperialism and protectionism.

2 World Bank Meeting
Stage a meeting of World Bank members to discuss how the economic problems of either Nicaragua or Poland might be solved. Structure a plan that takes into account the current infrastructure in the country, resources available, skill and education of the people, and government support for programs that might be established.

3 Debate
Be it resolved that American involvement in Central America was essential to the preservation of American security.

HISTORICAL ANALYSIS

SOLIDARITY

In September 1980, a labour movement under the leadership of an electrician named Lech Walesa emerged in Poland. Since the Soviet Union's control of central Europe after the Second World War, the Polish government had managed to establish an uneasy peace with Moscow. However, this new development was too aggressive for Moscow to ignore, and ultimately the Communist government in Poland was encouraged to bring the group under control. As a result, martial law was imposed in Poland in December 1981.

Analyse the significance of the Solidarity movement in implementing change in Poland in the 1980s. What role did Lech Walesa play? Was he a key figure who established policy direction, or was he a figurehead? How was Poland's political and economic system affected by this large labour organization? What sort of foundation was laid for the change which came as a result of the revolutions in 1989 when the "iron curtain" was raised? How did the changes under Solidarity affect the move toward democracy and capitalism at the end of the 1980s?

THE GORBACHEV REVOLUTION

Expressing the will of the nation, the Congress demands that the policy of perestroika steadily continue. At the same time, the Congress notes that the process of perestroika is running into many difficulties and controversies and the situation in the country remains difficult and tense. The country has not yet come out of the crisis. The renewal of social life is being impeded by the persistence of old structures and practices and a stereotyped mentality. On the one hand, there is a need to overcome resistance by the conservative forces; on the other, radical elements are coming to the fore who are ignoring objective conditions and demanding that all problems be solved overnight.

From the resolution of the Congress of People's Deputies of the Union of Soviet Socialist Republics, on major directions of the USSR's domestic and foreign policy, 9 June 1989.

FOCUS ON

CHANGE IN THE USSR

The political, social, and economic systems of the former USSR have undergone significant change. Based on your studies, media reports, and your own opinions, attempt to describe the future of this vast collectivity of peoples and regions.

OVERVIEW

Gorbachev's policies of *glasnost* and *perestroika* made an impact not only on the Soviet Union but also on Central Europe. In what ways? This chapter discusses the nationalities question in the former Soviet Union, and the revolutionary changes in 1989 in Poland, Hungary, Czechoslovakia, East Germany, and Romania.

GORBACHEV'S REFORM PROGRAM

In 1986, Gorbachev introduced policies of *glasnost* and *perestroika* in an attempt to reform both the political and economic systems of the Soviet Union.

1989 REVOLUTION

In 1989, the Iron Curtain separating Eastern and Western Europe was removed as Poland, Hungary, East Germany, Bulgaria, Czechoslovakia, and Romania swept aside their Communist governments.

THE AFTERMATH OF REVOLUTION: 1990 EASTERN EUROPE

The euphoria of revolution in 1989 was replaced in 1990 with the reality that both economic and nationalist problems must be addressed.

THE SOVIET UNION

Gorbachev's political and economic reform was unsuccessful in solving the Soviet Union's problems. Gorbachev's leadership was challenged, and he was unable to stem nationalist and labour unrest.

On 11 MARCH 1985, the Politburo of the Soviet Union approved Mikhail Gorbachev as general secretary. A member of the generation profoundly affected by Khrushchev's speech to the Twentieth Party Congress, Gorbachev brought to office an attitude signifying change. Gorbachev first attracted the attention of party officials by successfully dealing with agricultural problems in Stavropol. In 1978, he was moved to Moscow, where he was given responsibility for all Soviet agriculture by the Central Committee of the Communist party.

In 1982, in an attempt to reduce wastage between the field and the processing plant, Gorbachev created the Regional Agricultural Industrial Organization, or RAPO. RAPO consisted of agribusiness units modeled on successful American companies like Cargill or Ralston Purina. It was hoped this large-scale industrialization of agriculture would solve the problem of food shortages, but in fact by 1987 production of vegetables fell below that of the previous year. Consumers were faced with even greater shortages of meat and vegetables on store shelves. It appeared RAPO had actually eroded agricultural production. Although Gorbachev's initiatives in the agricultural sector of the whole country did not meet with the same degree of success as his efforts in Stavropol, he exuded confidence and won the support of enough Politburo members to attain the leadership.

GORBACHEV'S REFORM PROGRAM

When Gorbachev came to power in 1985, he discovered the severity of the problems inherent in the Soviet economy. His initial policy was one of moderate reform, emphasizing modernization of the machine-tool industry, limited reorganization of the economy, and encouragement of innovation in science and technology. During his first year as general secretary, Gorbachev moved quickly to revitalize the Politburo by replacing ageing and unimaginative members with younger people who possessed technical expertise. He soon fashioned a Politburo largely supportive of his policies, but one that would not guarantee his role as leader would go unchallenged. In fact, as Gorbachev unveiled his program of political and economic reform for the Soviet Union, he suffered attack from both the radical left and the conservative right of the party.

The cornerstones of Gorbachev's reform program were ***glasnost*** (openness) and ***perestroika*** (restructuring). These were to be enhanced by *uskorenie* (acceleration) and *demokratizatsiya* (democratization). Of these concepts, *perestroika* emerged as the most significant as it involved the restructuring of both the political and the economic systems. In order for *perestroika* to revitalize the Soviet system, however, it had to be supported by policies of democratization and openness to counteract the bureaucratic inertia that had resulted in economic stagnation. Acceleration meant simply that the country had to get moving again and set production targets that encouraged an increase in the quality of manufactured goods. Production had to be monitored, and factories that did not operate efficiently would be closed down.

Applying *perestroika* to the economy was both challenging and disappointing. Gorbachev was criticized for not decollectivizing agriculture as the Chinese did. The Chinese system allowed peasant farmers to deliver specified quantities of grain to the collective farm and to keep any produce in excess of this contract. The result was tremendous incentive to produce surplus goods to sell on the open market, and Chinese city-dwellers benefited by the greater availability of foodstuffs.

RAPO, however, discouraged any move to break out of collective farming. Worse, when the six ministries concerned with agriculture were consolidated into *Gosagroprom,* this monolith was unable to delegate responsibility or direct agricultural production effectively. During the winter of 1989-1990 it was often impossible for Soviet citizens in Moscow to obtain butter, meat, or fresh fruit and vegetables. Quality foods were available only in the private markets, at prices which many average citizens could not afford.

One of the key elements of Gorbachev's economic reform was the encouragement and reward of private initiative. On 30 June 1987, the Enterprise Law established the independence of small business operations (enterprises) from the state ministries and Gosplan. These enterprises were expected to be economically self-sufficient and could no longer count on a subsidy from the state ministry if unprofitable. Contracts would be negotiated directly with customers, but the state could also order as much as 50 to 70 per cent of an enterprise's output. Unfortunately, ministries began to demand more and more of the enterprise's production and left little or nothing for private sale. As a result, certain ministries had neutralized one of the key elements of economic reform.

Cooperative ventures established on a similar premise also faced challenges. The small cottage industries that produced luxury goods, like perfumed soaps, fell victim to their own success. In the Russian Republic, particularly, there was a strong aversion to economic inequality and hostility to those who achieved higher incomes by their own efforts. The Ministry of Finance imposed a marginal tax on cooperatives that began at 30 per cent but quickly rose to 90 per cent, effectively stifling incentive. In an unprecedented move, however, the Supreme Soviet intervened and reduced the tax to a maximum of 50 per cent.

One of the primary problems of Gorbachev's attempt to adopt some characteristics of a market system is the absence in the former Soviet Union of

In 1989, a McDonald's restaurant was opened in Moscow in a flurry of publicity. Soviet citizens lined up for hours to sample the fare.

a history of private business. Moving almost directly from feudal serfdom to radical collectivization, the Soviet citizen had little or no experience with individual responsibility for his or her own economic well-being.

It became apparent that without far-reaching political changes, economic progress was impossible. Gorbachev's changes in personnel in his first year in office were not sufficient to pave the way for his reform movement. Structural change in the Soviet political system was essential; but once middle managers in the bureaucracy recognized the impact of reorganization on them, open resistance developed. The first serious challenge to Gorbachev's leadership came at the 1987 plenum of the Central Committee. The challenge came, surprisingly enough, from Boris Yeltsin, one of the most vocal supporters of radical reform.

Boris Yeltsin, the Moscow party chief, had been a staunch supporter of Gorbachev, but he had grown impatient with the pace of change and with the power he perceived conservatives still held. In his indictment, Yeltsin condemned both the party and Gorbachev. He suggested that the ruling Politburo was not only moving too slowly and promising too much, but was also divided on the manner in which reform should be instituted. Yeltsin was supported by large numbers of students and intellectuals in his home constituency who protested Yeltsin's dismissal by Gorbachev as being Stalinist. Gorbachev's criticism of Yeltsin came from a suspicion that

CHERNOBYL DISASTER

The social and environmental impact of the disaster at the Chernobyl factory has raised questions regarding the safety and feasibility of nuclear power as an alternate energy source. Should the international community impose tighter controls on the production of nuclear power? Debate this question, referring to both Chernobyl and the increasing global demand for cheap, efficient, non-polluting energy.

On 26 April 1986, a nuclear accident at the Chernobyl power plant resulted in the destruction of one of 4 RBMK-type reactors (a reactor cooled by water and moderated by graphite). Ironically, the accident occurred during a safety test. In conducting the test, power must be maintained at 30 per cent but the operator in charge erred and allowed the power to drop to 1 per cent. Instability was created in the reactor and the operator attempted to correct the problem by overriding the control rods.

In order to complete the test, the shutdown signals were disabled and thus no safety mechanism was in place when a sudden power surge occurred. The explosion destroyed the top of the reactor core and started a fire which threatened the other three reactors. Firefighters worked to extinguish the blaze but exposure to radiation made them Chernobyl's first casualties.

The radioactive cloud which emanated from the Chernobyl explosion spread across a large area including the western regions of Ukraine, Belorussia, Russia, Eastern Europe, and some parts of Scandinavia. The first report of the disaster came from Sweden which picked up excessive amounts of radioactivity in its monitoring of the air. Questions were immediately raised regarding the Soviet Union's failure to report a nuclear disaster to a world which would share in the fall-out. It appeared that *glasnost* was not yet fully operative.

Long after the accident, a shroud of secrecy surrounded Chernobyl, suggesting a cover-up masking the numbers of victims and the extent of environmental damage. Details regarding the accident as well as medical reports of those affected by radiation were top secret by order of the central government.

Although only about 100 000 people were evacuated from the Chernobyl area, an estimated 1.7 million people were exposed to dangerous levels of radiation. Of these 850 000 still live in contamimated areas, and another 280 000 should be relocated but have nowhere to go. Birth defects have risen by 20 per cent and doctors estimate that thousands of people will develop some form of cancer as a result of overexposure to radiation. The Soviet government announced the official death toll of 31 as a result of the Chernobyl accident. Western media reports estimated the total to be much higher. It is unlikely that any definitive total will ever be established.

The Chernobyl disaster clearly illustrated the perils of operating a nuclear power plant with insufficient safety mechanisms and ill-trained operators. Thousands of hectares of arable land have been laid to waste by contamination. Damage to the food chain in the first month was extensive but more frightening was the discovery that sheep in northern Scotland and reindeer herds in Scandinavia registered high levels of radioactivity.

1. Should nuclear power be promoted as an alternate energy source?

2. What appeared to be the cause of the Chernobyl disaster?

3. What were the results of the accident at Chernobyl?

4. Research the accident in 1979 at Three Mile Island in Pennsylvania. Compare and contrast this accident with that at Chernobyl.

Yeltsin wanted to revolutionize rather than restructure the system. Gorbachev stood firm in his belief that various stages of socialism must be ascended on the ladder to reform. Conservatives were encouraged by Yeltsin's dismissal and became even more vocal in their resistance to reform.

In March 1988, conservative criticism of Gorbachev culminated in the publication of a letter supposedly written by a Leningrad chemistry teacher, Nina Andreeva, but was actually written by propagandists for the Central Committee. Highly critical of Gorbachev's reforms, the letter suggested that with his de-Stalinization program and liberalization, Gorbachev had destabilized society. Central Committee secretary Yegor Ligachev praised the letter publicly and promoted it as illustrative of the true party line. Ligachev hoped to discourage reform and promote the election of anti-reform delegates to the upcoming Nineteenth Party Congress. His was a direct challenge to Gorbachev's leadership.

In early April, Gorbachev mounted a counteroffensive that began with a special Politburo meeting designed to confront Ligachev and his supporters and demand an explanation for their attack on *perestroika*. On 5 April, *Pravda* published an article that repudiated Ligachev's attack and promoted the party line as enunciated by Gorbachev. *Pravda* suggested that the letter of 13 March, in attacking *perestroika*, actually provided a defence of Stalin and encouraged a return back to the socialism of the past. *Pravda* went on to suggest that it was not possible to turn back now and that no matter how difficult *perestroika* was, restructuring was essential for the renewal of Soviet society. The Ligachev incident was resolved in Gorbachev's favour, but the reactions of Politburo members and the Soviet citizenry during this incident showed that independent action and freedom of expression were not yet fully developed nor tolerated in the Soviet Union.

Glasnost has been touted as one of Gorbachev's most innovative reforms because it promised an openness unknown in Soviet society since the 1917 revolution, and even before that. While greater freedom of expression and greater freedom of the press were allowed, there were limits, including state secrets, war propaganda, and medical records. Despite its limitations, *glasnost* allowed a glimpse into Soviet society impossible before Gorbachev's time. Crime, alcoholism, and prostitution, the existence of which were denied in earlier times, now became staples in the Soviet media. It was now possible to criticize medical care, government construction projects, and the government's involvement in Afghanistan. Books like Boris Pasternak's *Doctor Zhivago* and Rybakov's *Children of the Arbat* were finally available to Soviet citizens. Perhaps of even greater importance, Soviet historians were finally allowed to deal with topics that had been "revised" or ignored. The infamous Katyn Forest massacre of Polish officers by the Soviet army in the Second World War, previously blamed on Nazi forces, was officially acknowledged by the Soviet government, as was the murder or starvation of millions of people during Stalin's reign.

While *glasnost* provided a welcome openness in Soviet communications, it also promoted a discussion of ethnic concerns and historical disputes that led to instability in a number of areas, notably Armenia and Azerbaijan, Georgia, the Baltic states of Estonia, Latvia, and Lithuania, and the Soviet south-west (populated by Ukrainians, Belorussians, and Moldavians). The Soviet Union was initially structured as a federal state, accommodating its diverse ethnicities by allowing them autonomy in their regions. In 1923, Lenin organized a strong, centralized Communist party to maintain political control while non-Russian languages and cultures developed. Stalin reversed this policy of accommodation and promoted Russian culture and language to bind the diverse nation together. Local cadres who had promoted and sustained local ethnicity were purged. After Stalin's death the nationalities issue emerged as an undercurrent of destabilization: non-Russian nationalities were growing at substantially greater rates than the Russian nationality, and were making themselves heard. Non-Russian peoples viewed Russification as a grave threat and began to express grievances about language, religion, and immigration. After the Soviet Union signed the Helsinki Accord, national groups attempted to have their grievances heard. Gorbachev inherited this nationalistic dissatisfaction when he came to power in 1985.

On 28 June 1988, the Nineteenth Party Conference convened in Moscow. Gorbachev used the conference as a platform to promote his program of radical reform and to institutionalize the concepts of democratization and *glasnost*. Although *perestroika* had focused on economic matters, there was now a general realization that economic reform required political reform. It was the political system, then, that was the focus of the Nineteenth Party Conference. Gorbachev proposed a major restructuring of the Soviet political system. Party apparatus

BIOGRAPHY
ANDREI SAKHAROV (1921–1989)
YELENA BONNER (1923–   )

Andrei Sakharov will be remembered as the Soviet physicist who developed the Russian H-Bomb, and openly criticized Soviet repression. Sakharov was born in Moscow, the son of a scientist. He graduated from Moscow State University in 1942, where he did his doctoral work on cosmic rays. In the years following his graduation, Sakharov became primarily responsible for development of the hydrogen bomb. In 1953, he became the youngest-ever entrant to the Soviet Academy of Sciences. Sakharov's involvements in the 1960s—namely his campaigning for a nuclear test-ban treaty and for improved Soviet relations with the international community—strained his relations with Soviet authorities. He also spoke out against the civil rights abuses within the USSR, and was a founder of the Soviet Human Rights Committee. In 1975, Sakharov became the first Soviet citizen to receive the Nobel Peace Prize. Following his criticism of Soviet action in Afghanistan, and in the midst of a cold war crackdown against dissidents, Sakharov was arrested and exiled internally to the closed city of Gorky (1980). During his time in Gorky, Sakharov undertook a number of hunger strikes in an effort to secure permission for his wife, Yelena Bonner, to receive eye treatment from a specialist in Italy. Sakharov's protests had the desired effect, and Yelena received the treatments in 1981 and 1984.

Yelena Bonner, also a Soviet civil rights campaigner, was born in Moscow. In Stalin's 'great purge' of 1937, Bonner's parents were arrested, after which her father was executed and her mother imprisoned. Bonner became the ward of her grandmother in Leningrad. During the Second World War, Bonner served in the army and achieved the rank of lieutenant. It was also during this time that her eyes were seriously injured.

When the war ended, Bonner became a doctor. Upon separating from her first husband in 1965, she joined the Communist Party of the Soviet Union (CPSU). Eventually, however, Bonner became disillusioned with some of the policies and activities of the CPSU—particularly the Soviet invasion of Czechoslovakia in 1968—and she began to dissent. In 1971, she and Sakharov were married. A year later she resigned from the CPSU. For the next 14 years, Bonner and Sakharov led the Soviet dissident movement.

As part of Gorbachev's liberalization policy, the couple was released from Gorky in December 1986. They returned to Moscow and Sakharov resumed his position in the Soviet Academy of Sciences. In 1989, Sakharov was elected to the Congress of the USSR People's Deputies. Sakharov's published non-scientific works include *Progress, Co-existence and Intellectual Freedom* (1968) and *Alarm and Hope* (1978). ●

would be cut by as much as 50 per cent. This would entail a substantial reduction in personnel, an elimination of departments that duplicated government services, and the removal of party functionaries from local economic problems. In theory, it would eliminate some bureaucratic administration and it would free economic units to solve their problems without Gosplan. It would also allow the central bureaucracy to concentrate on economic problems that affect the entire country.

The changes which Mikhail Gorbachev hoped to institute in the Soviet Union promised to change radically both the political and economic structure of the country. However, by late 1988, spurred on by *glasnost* and democratization, national unrest threatened the stability of the Soviet Union. Along with the lack of improvement in access to consumer goods, this rising unrest signaled very serious dangers to Gorbachev's program of reform.

1989 REVOLUTION

During 1989 Gorbachev stood by and watched as the countries of Eastern Europe one by one cast off communist domination. The domino effect that the free world had feared after the Second World War appeared to be working in reverse. First Poland and Hungary, in well-planned moves, sought to hold free elections and eliminate the Communist monopoly on power. Then came spontaneous movements against communism in East Germany, Czechoslovakia, Bulgaria, and Romania. The world watched in shock and disbelief while the changes occurred with no interference from Moscow and little or no resistance from the Communist governments under attack. Except in Romania, communism collapsed in Central Europe without significant bloodshed.

It seemed fitting that the first country to secure release from the Communist party was Poland. It was the first country subjected to communist domination after the Second World War. On 5 April 1989, Solidarity leaders signed an accord with the Polish government that provided for the restoration of the legal status of Solidarity and free and open elections. The accords also reinstated the upper house of parliament which had been disbanded after the war. This upper house would have 100 freely elected members and would be able to veto legislation from the lower house. Of the 460 seats in the lower house, 35 per cent would be open to

Although the Polish reforms were relatively peaceful, there were some isolated incidents of violence. During the last Communist-controlled Congress, protesters battled with riot police outside of the Palace of Culture, in Warsaw.

Solidarity candidates. The election was held 4 June 1989 and proved to be a stunning defeat for the Communist party. Solidarity candidates swept 99 of the 100 seats in the upper house and all 161 seats that they were allowed to contest in the lower house. Many Communist candidates did not obtain the 50 per cent of votes required to give them a seat in the lower house: many voters simply said "No" to the official candidates listed. The election upset likely contributed to the resignation of President Wojciech Jaruzelski as leader of the Polish Communist party on 29 July 1989. On 19 August 1989, Jaruzelski, still president, designated the Solidarity official Tadeusz Mazowiecki as prime minister, the first non-Communist to hold this post in the post-war period. The primary problem for the new government would be to rejuvenate a stagnant economy.

In Hungary, following the announcement early in 1989 that non-conformist political parties would be tolerated, Communist control eroded steadily. In a symbolic move to open the Iron Curtain, Hungary began on 2 May 1989 to cut the barbed wire that

THE NATIONALITIES ISSUE

The Soviet Union was ethnically very diverse, but historically the Russians have been the dominant nationality. Reform policies in the Gorbachev years raised hopes for nationalist independence in many of the country's fifteen republics. Should nationalist aspirations have been allowed expression in the Soviet Union? In a small group, discuss to what extent other nations should, or have the right to, support the desire of a group or political unit within another country to establish its independence. You may use examples from anywhere in the world to support your position.

The former Soviet Union had a population of 290 million people of whom 145 million were classified as Great Russians. The remaining 145 million people represented an ethnic diversity which manifested itself in religious, social, and cultural differences. Article 76 of the Soviet constitution identified the former Soviet Union as a union of sovereign republics. While each of the fifteen republics maintained its own Communist party organization, flag, hymn, and capital city; political, cultural, and social control was exerted by Moscow. Thus, the USSR was, in fact, a symbolic federation of nations with power centralized in Moscow and Russian the dominant nationality. This structure created the potential for conflict between centralized and decentralized control of political and economic decision-making.

The Soviet Union's nationalities question stemmed from almost 300 years of continual Russian imperial expansion from the time of Peter the Great. Since the Bolshevik revolution of 1917, the Communist regime, building on tsarist nationality policies of the past, suppressed nationalist aspirations and attempted to imbue these diverse nationalities with Russian language and culture. The Gorbachev era was welcomed by national groups who hoped to achieve nationalist aspirations long held in check by Communist repression. Smouldering discontent was given a voice by the policy of *glasnost,* and from 1986 onward ethnic groups around the former Soviet Union formed popular fronts and demanded sovereignty.

Despite the Communist attempt to erase nationalism and focus on an international proletariat, the old ethnic loyalties remained and national aspirations lay smouldering. Potential conflict arose not only from the Russian domination of minority groups but also from the commingling of nationalities in regions such as Armenia and Azerbaijan. Russification programs in non-Russian republics like Ukraine provided advantages for those individuals who learned the Russian language and became familiar with Russian culture. This policy, in combination with the practice of filling bureaucratic posts with Russian administrators, fueled resentment in the non-Russian republics and led to civil uprising once a free press and freedom of assembly was made possible by *glasnost.*

Nationalist unrest was most volatile in the Caucasus region of Armenia, Azerbaijan, and Georgia. Each state maintained a brief period of independence after the Bolshevik revolution of 1917, before being absorbed by the new Soviet state. Borders drawn in 1923 left ethnic differences unresolved and seventy years of Soviet rule accentuated national frustrations.

On 23 February 1988, one million Armenians poured into the streets of their capital, Yerevan, demanding the return to Armenia of the Nagorno-Karabakh region of Azerbaijan. Largely populated by Armenians, this area has been a source of bitter ethnic conflict for decades.

Armenia and Azerbaijan

The summer of 1988 was fraught with tension which finally spilled over into armed conflict on 4 December 1988 when troops put down a demonstration in Baku, Azerbaijan killing 3 people and injuring many. Violence continued throughout 1989 with anti-Armenian pogroms in the Azerbaijani cities of Sumgait and Baku. Guerrilla warfare continued along the border of the Nagorno-Karabakh region until finally the Armenian National movement and the Azerbaijani Popular Front were invited to attend conciliatory talks in Riga, Latvia in January 1990. The problem remains unresolved and 500 000 Armenians and Azerbaijanis are homeless because of the strife.

Georgia

On 9 April 1989, Soviet troops attacked a peaceful demonstration in the Georgian capital of Tbilisi, killing 19 people and injuring dozens more. Brute force and poison gas were used on the crowd which knelt in prayer before the government buildings. The demonstration was led by intellectuals and factory workers who sought Georgian independence. The Georgian situation is complicated by demands of independence by the small republic of Abkhazia, which is under Georgian control.

The Baltic States

The Baltic states of Estonia, Latvia, and Lithuania experienced a brief period of sovereignty between the two world wars. In August 1989, two million people formed a human chain stretching through the three capital cities of Tallinn, Riga, and Vilnius in a symbolic protest of the Nazi-Soviet pact of 1939 which had denied them their freedom. Popular front movements gained momentum in the region, and in December 1989 Lithuania initiated a multi-party system of government.

On 11 March 1989, Lithuanian president Landsbergis declared Lithuania independent of the Soviet Union. Gorbachev responded with a show of force as tanks and troops rolled into Lithuania. Tensions remained high and the Soviet Union imposed an economic embargo accompanied by a blockade to prevent goods entering from Poland. Estonia and Latvia followed Lithuania's lead, declaring their absorption into the Soviet Union had been illegal. Finally, by mid-June, Gorbachev was forced to concede that negotiations must be carried out on the Baltic issue.

Ukraine

Sometimes termed the "jewel in the Russian crown," Ukraine was both geographically and economically critical to the former Soviet Union. Much of the Soviet Union's agricultural land fell within the borders of Ukraine, and its location on the Black Sea gave it access to trade routes. Its importance as a republic was also recognized by its possession of a seat in the United Nations along with the republics of Belorussia and Russia. The Ukrainian movement toward independence, which developed more seriously in 1990, was ominous for the Soviet Union because secession by such a large and important republic would possibly encourage similar action on the part of other dissatisfied national groups.

The nationalities issues in the former Soviet Union was fueled by the success of Eastern European freedom from Soviet control in the revolutions of 1989. During the initial attempts at *perestroika,* Gorbachev encouraged economic innovation without relinquishing political control. The enforcement of central control would possibly incite a greater degree of civil unrest. To allow republics to secede would, however, mean a fragmentation of the Soviet Union, and much political and economic uncertainty.

Ukraine's declaration of independence in 1991 prompted the exodus of the other republics and was followed by the dissolution of the Soviet Union. Independence has not, however, resulted in stability in the region. Instead the former Soviet republics remain embroiled in ethnic tension.

1. What has been the result of Gorbachev's liberalization policy toward ethnic minorities?

2. What rights should minorities have in any country?

3. Why has the policy of Russification failed?

In 1989, cellist Mstislav Rostropovich played in front of the Berlin Wall to commemorate those killed while trying to flee East Germany. Rostropovich fled the Soviet Union in the 1970s and now makes his home in the United States.

suggesting they, too, were liberal and open to change.

Bereft of public support, facing a growing liberal movement confident of success in the promised 1990 free elections, the Communist party of Hungary formally disbanded itself on 7 October 1989 and reconstituted itself as a socialist party, the Hungarian Socialist party. It promised to follow democratic procedures in determining leadership and to reform its program to meet the needs of a changing Hungary. Thus, while Solidarity in Poland worked alongside a Communist party that remained virtually unchanged, the Communist party in Hungary seemed determined to play a dynamic role in changes by undergoing change itself.

As the barbed wire between Hungary and Austria came down, numerous East Germans sought permission through the Hungarian embassy to make their way through Hungary to Austria and then on to West Germany. Over the summer of 1989, about 6000 East Germans arrived in Vienna via Budapest, turning vacation into emigration. By September, as the number of East Germans attempting to flee to West Germany via Hungary increased, the East German government tightened restrictions to cut off the flow of refugees. East Germans responded by going instead to the embassy in Prague, since Czechoslovakia was one of the few destinations East Germans could reach without East German travel documents.

By 1 October 1989, freedom trains were transporting young East Germans to Prague, where they hoped to gain sanctuary at the West German embassy before going to West Germany. As the numbers of refugees grew, so too did demands in East Germany for the lifting of travel restrictions and—more importantly—for democratic reform. Demonstrations in East Berlin, Leipzig, and Dresden vividly illustrated the growing strength of the movement. Pressure from both its own population and from the Hungarian government finally led East Germany to allow about 30 000 East Germans to emigrate. In an attempt to pacify its discontented population, the East German Communist party replaced ageing hard-liner Erich Honecker with Egon Krenz on 18 October. But the change of leadership and easing of travel restrictions did nothing to stem the flow. It was the largest outpouring of East Germans since the Berlin Wall was constructed in August 1961.

On 4 November 1989, 500 000 people demonstrated in East Berlin, jeering the Communist party

sealed off its border with Austria, determined to remove the entire 240 km of barbed wire by the end of the year. Then on 16 June 1989, Imre Nagy, the Hungarian leader who defied Soviet domination in 1956 and was later murdered for his role in the Hungarian Revolution, was honoured with a hero's burial following a public ceremony in Budapest's Hero Square. As a variety of independent liberal parties emerged, Communist popularity waned. Karoly Grosz, who had succeeded Janos Kadar as party leader, was stripped of most of his authority, and Communists discussed changing their name to one and demanding democratic reform. On 7 November, the entire East German cabinet resigned and the Politburo announced a reorganization. It was still not enough, and on 9 November 1989 the world was astonished to see the Berlin Wall opened at midnight by East German border guards. Since 13 August 1961, the Berlin Wall had stood as a symbol of the Cold War. It seemed unthinkable that, even with changes in Poland and Hungary, there could be any significant freedoms granted in East Germany. Yet throughout the weekend East Berliners celebrated with West Berliners, and for the first time since the Second World War, there was speculation about German reunification.

Events in Berlin overshadowed simultaneous changes in Bulgaria. Some 310 000 ethnic Turks had fled from Bulgaria to Turkey in 1988 to escape forced assimilation. Bulgarian dissidents began in 1989 to voice concern about environmental pollution, opening a door to other expressions of dissatisfaction with government. The country had suffered economic difficulties, like its neighbours in the Eastern bloc, but until the resignation of Todor Zhivkov on 10 November 1989, there was little awareness that the Communist leadership faced any serious challenge. The new Communist party leader, Petar Mladenov, was forced to promise free elections in the spring of 1990 and to relinquish absolute power—after the newly formed Union of Democratic Forces led a demonstration of 50 000 people in Sofia on December 10. As a final show of reform, the Communist party expelled former leader Zhivkov from its ranks.

Changes in East Germany, Bulgaria, Poland, and Hungary seemed to have little influence on the hard-line Communist government of Czechoslovakia. When, on 28 October 1989, 10 000 people staged a demonstration in Wenceslas Square to demand change, heavily armed police were dispatched to quell the crowd. Temporary order was imposed by party leader, Milos Jakes, but dissent seethed throughout the country. Vaclav Havel, who had been arrested in January and served time in jail until May, became a powerful symbol of opposition to the government. On 20 November, more than 200 000 people marched through the streets of Prague demanding free elections and calling for a general strike. By 25 November, the Communist party leadership had yielded and resigned their positions. Ironically, the crowd, which had now grown to over 350 000 people, was addressed by Alexander Dubček, the leader ousted by Soviet-led Warsaw Pact troops in 1968. He quoted the words of an old wise

Wenceslas Square in Prague became the centre of activity for young Czech protesters after the initial demonstrations in October 1989. This young demonstrator marched with his flag in November of the same year.

man who said, "if there once was light, why should there be darkness again? Let us act in such a way as to bring the light back." It seemed unlikely that any changes the Communist party proposed would be acceptable to the demonstrators, and on 27 November the entire Czechoslovakian work force walked off the job in a two-hour general strike.

As demonstrations continued, dissent crystallized in a group called Civic Forum, a mass movement determined to create political opposition to the ruling Communist party in Czechoslovakia. Finally, on 7 December, Ladislav Adamec resigned as prime minister and was replaced by Marian Calfa. Negotiations between the Communist party and Civic Forum resulted in the resignation of Gustav Husák from the presidency on 10 December 1989. In the election on 29 December Vaclav Havel became Czechoslovakia's new president. Havel demanded that free parliamentary elections be held in the new year, at which time the new parliament would select a president. The office of premier was

Poet and playwright Vaclav Havel became president of Czechoslovakia in 1989. In this photograph, Havel holds his nose as he observes the Chabarovice toxic waste dump in northern Czechoslovakia. This toxic waste dump is one of the largest and most dangerous in Europe.

VACLAV HAVEL

Vaclav Havel was born on 5 October 1936 in Prague to a middle class family. He became a poet and playwright, and was highly critical of the censorship imposed by the Communist state on artists. He was a founding member of Charter 77, a dissident group determined to foster independence and opposition to the totalitarian regime. He spent numerous years in jail, most recently for attempting to lay a wreath at the grave of Jan Palach, the student who set himself on fire in Wenceslas Square in 1968 when Warsaw Pact troops invaded Prague.

turned over to Alexander Dubček. The old regime's most vocal opponents now held two of the government's most influential positions.

Throughout the summer and autumn of 1989—while reform came to Poland, Hungary, East Germany, Bulgaria, and Czechoslovakia—Romania, led since 1965 by the Stalinist regime of Nicolae Ceauşescu, seemed immune to the revolutionary fervour. Then, on 17 December in the city of Timisoara, anti-government demonstrators took to the streets to protest the arrest of the Reverend Toekes, an ethnic Hungarian and spokesperson for Romania's 2 million Hungarians. Ceauşescu's troops met the demonstrators with tanks and gunned down thousands of unarmed men, women, and children. A mass grave, purportedly holding 4500 bodies, was later discovered after the incident. Tensions ran high and both sides told different stories. As the week wore on, it became evident that the Romanian people were no longer willing to be terrorized by Ceauşescu and his **Securitate**, a special police force that had been savage in its suppression of dissent. On 25 December 1989, Nicolae Ceauşescu and his wife, Elena, were seized in a *coup* and later executed by firing squad. Now the people of Romania must rebuild a society deprived for years not only of human rights but even of the basic necessities of life. It is an immense task for a country with no history of **political pluralism.**

Ion Iliescu became the new president of Romania after the election of 20 May 1990.

THE AFTERMATH OF REVOLUTION: 1990 EASTERN EUROPE

During 1989, Gorbachev abandoned the Brezhnev Doctrine which would have imposed both ideological and military control on the revolutionary elements in Eastern Europe. Instead, he encouraged reform and stood by while Communist parties throughout the Soviet bloc lost their monopoly on power and gave way to the concepts of political pluralism and market economics. The free elections promised by Stalin at Yalta finally materialized in 1989 and 1990 in Eastern Europe. Only Romania, Albania, and Bulgaria are now under Communist control. Initially, in Czechoslovakia and East Germany non-Communist governments gained power, and in Hungary and Poland non-Communists figured prominently in both government and the military. Subsequently, free elections in the reunified Germany resulted in the election of Helmut Kohl's conservative coalition, and in Poland, the Communists were defeated and Lech Walesa became the new president.

While journalists reiterated that the Cold War was over, the superpowers had to forge foreign policies which recognized the changing face of Europe. The dominant problem for both the Soviet Union and the United States was in restructuring foreign policies so that they were at once optimistic and realistic: policies that acknowledged the challenges which Eastern European nations would face in their struggle for change. The instability that could result from failure of reform in Eastern Europe concerned both superpowers.

The two factors which most seriously threatened Eastern European reform in the 1990s were economic and nationalistic. Economies in this region have suffered from the bureaucratic stagnation of central planning and require enormous injections of capital as well as patience and entrepreneurship on the part of the people in order to transform their economies into modern technological economies. As the transition to market economies occurs, people must endure rising unemployment and higher prices for consumer goods. In Poland, where bold steps were taken to reform the state economy, consumer goods filled store shelves for the first time in decades. While the average consumer is still unable to afford many of these goods, the private sector is growing. Optimism has resulted from the increased availability of goods, and the absence of queues which used to occupy at least two hours per day.

During 1990, the Council for Mutual Economic Assistance (Comecon), which regulated trade in the Soviet bloc, ceased to exist. Soviet subsidies of energy ceased, and demands that Central European countries pay for Soviet oil with hard currency were aggravated by the Gulf crisis of 1990-1991, which suggested that Iraq would default on its $4 billion debt to Eastern European countries. As the currencies of these states are still not convertible to Western currencies, trade barriers prevent entry into Western markets. Without substantial investment by Western business, it seems unlikely that Eastern Europe will develop the infrastructure and industry to compete effectively in international markets.

Fears of a united Germany emerged almost as soon as the Berlin Wall came down. If Germany reunited, how would it figure in European security? Demands that it be part of NATO were met with outright refusal by the Soviet Union. France reiter-

Romania was the only Eastern European country to suffer a violent revolution in 1989. Thousands of protesters lost their lives before the fall of the Ceauşescu government.

ated its age-old concerns about German strength. Throughout the spring of 1990, the German question remained in the foreground of European affairs. Helmut Kohl, chancellor of West Germany, met with Gorbachev in February and again in July to discuss German reunification. These negotiations resulted in the Soviet leader's acquiescence to German reunification as a sovereign state with membership in NATO. In return, Kohl pledged his government's financial support in the reconstruction of East Germany as well as an aid package to the Soviet Union.

On 1 July 1990, the economic union of East and West Germany became a reality. Stores in East

Tens of thousands of Berliners gathered at the Berlin Wall to celebrate the opening of the Brandenburg Gate.

Germany were filled with Western goods which East Germans could now buy with East German ostmarks exchanged at par with the West German Deutschmark. Elation over the availability of goods was, however, tempered by concern about potential inflation and the likelihood of unemployment as East German state factories, unable to compete with the technology of the West, faced closure.

On 2 October 1990, East and West Germany were reunited politically. Helmut Kohl won the leadership of the newly unified Germany on 2 December 1990 and plans were begun to reinstate Berlin as the capital. Germany's task then became the reconstruction of the eastern region where decades of central planning had resulted in a stagnant economy. Billions of Deutschmarks must be invested in industry in order to revitalize the region and provide the consumer goods expected by people now entering the market system. The transition from central planning to a market economy was not to be made without hardship. Unemployment rose dramatically in the eastern regions as industry attempted to become profitable. German citizens were challenged to exercise tolerance as the reunified nation struggled to provide some measure of equity in living standards throughout the country.

THE COLLAPSE OF THE SOVIET UNION

On 15 October 1990, Mikhail Gorbachev was awarded the Nobel Peace Prize in recognition of the rapprochement he had established with the USA since his ascension to power in the Soviet Union. His success on the international scene stood in marked contrast to the challenges facing him at home. Economic, nationalist, and political difficulties threatened throughout the winter of 1990 to 1991 to tear the Soviet Union apart.

Economic reforms attempted under *perestroika* failed to revive the troubled centrally planned system. In spite of a record crop, food shortages existed. Inefficiencies in harvest, transportation, and distribution systems prevailed. As a result, food rationing was instituted and an appeal was made to the West for food aid.

Gorbachev refused to allow private property or conversion to the free market system. A Five Hundred Day Plan, proposed by his reformist economic advisor Stanislav Shatalin to convert the economy to capitalism over a 500-day period, was rejected. Instead, a currency reform aimed at removing excess rubles from the system and reducing inflation was undertaken. Soviet citizens were given three days to exchange 50 and 100 ruble notes into lower denominations. Only 1000 rubles per person

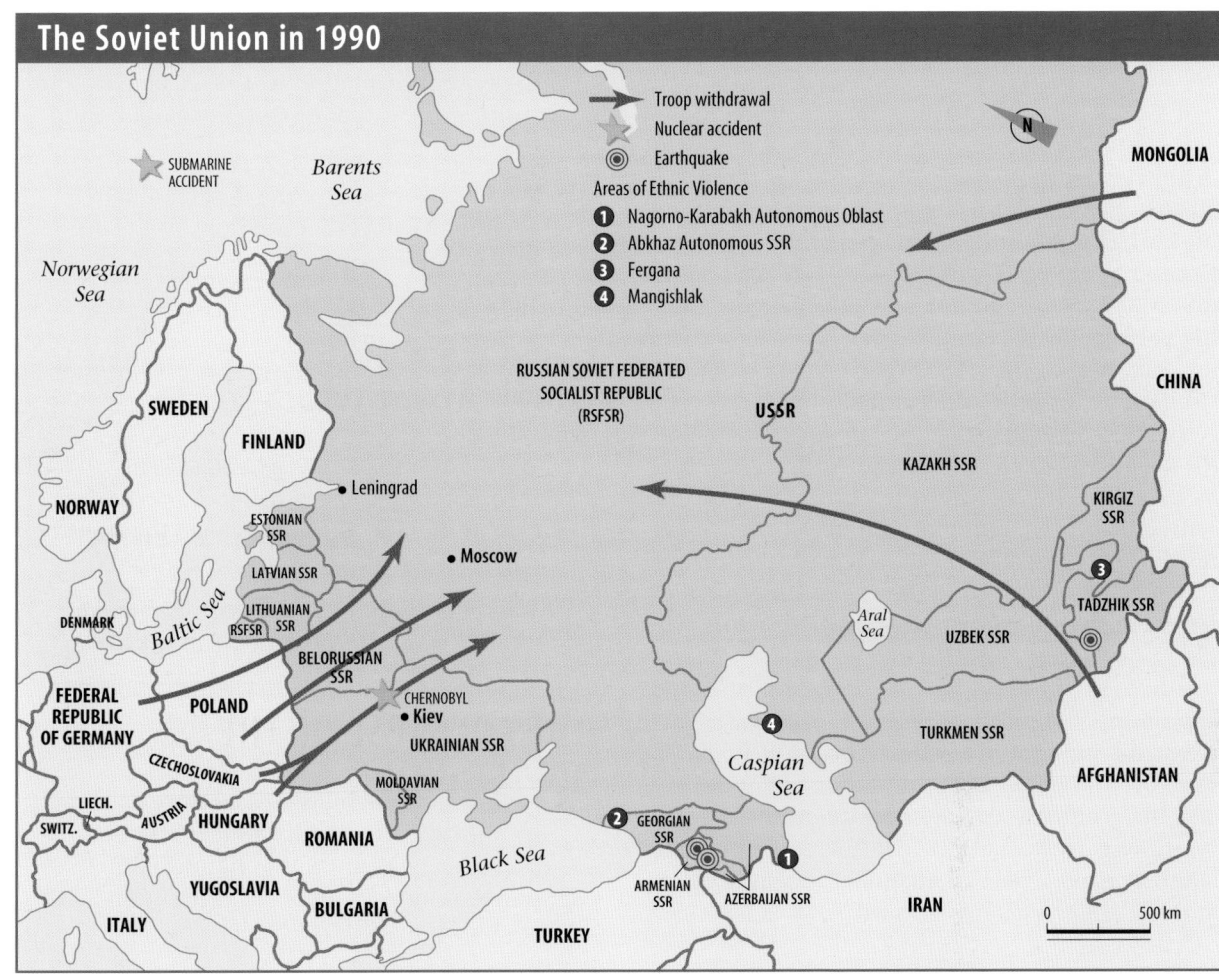

Troop withdrawal
Nuclear accident
Earthquake
Areas of Ethnic Violence
1 Nagorno-Karabakh Autonomous Oblast
2 Abkhaz Autonomous SSR
3 Fergana
4 Mangishlak

SUBMARINE ACCIDENT
Barents Sea
MONGOLIA
Norwegian Sea
CHINA
SWEDEN
FINLAND
RUSSIAN SOVIET FEDERATED SOCIALIST REPUBLIC (RSFSR)
USSR
KAZAKH SSR
Leningrad
NORWAY
ESTONIAN SSR
KIRGIZ SSR
LATVIAN SSR
Moscow
LITHUANIAN SSR
RSFSR
DENMARK
Baltic Sea
Aral Sea
TADZHIK SSR
BELORUSSIAN SSR
UZBEK SSR
FEDERAL REPUBLIC OF GERMANY
POLAND
CHERNOBYL
Kiev
UKRAINIAN SSR
TURKMEN SSR
CZECHOSLOVAKIA
MOLDAVIAN SSR
Caspian Sea
AFGHANISTAN
LIECH.
SWITZ.
AUSTRIA
HUNGARY
ROMANIA
GEORGIAN SSR
ROMANIA
Black Sea
YUGOSLAVIA
BULGARIA
ARMENIAN SSR
AZERBAIJAN SSR
IRAN
ITALY
TURKEY
0   500 km

could be exchanged. This measure further eroded confidence in the banking system and wreaked havoc with the private sector of business.

Separatist movements, resulting from nationalist forces, threatened the existence of the Soviet Union as all 15 republics declared their sovereignty. Despite such widespread dissent, Gorbachev remained determined to retain central control in Moscow. In a surprising move in the Baltic state of Lithuania in January 1991, Gorbachev backed his determination with the force of the Red Army. Thirteen people were killed as the army attacked Lithuanians supporting the independence movement. Gorbachev claimed no knowledge of the action, raising speculation about both his honesty and his control of the army. On 9 February 1991, Lithuanians voted 90 per cent in favour of establishing a sovereign independent state, despite intimidation from Moscow.

Political challenges faced Gorbachev as well. Initially viewed as a reformer, he consolidated his

By 1990, the Soviet Union had withdrawn its armed forces from Eastern European countries that had given up communism.

power during 1990 to give him more control than any other Soviet leader since Stalin. His old rival, Boris Yeltsin, leader of the Russian Republic, posed a serious challenge. Yeltsin advocated private property and conversion to free market forces. Other reformists, such as Nikolai Ryzhkov and Alexander Yakovlev, were driven out of power. Perhaps the most surprising move was the resignation of Eduard Schevardnadze, the Soviet foreign minister, who was credited with improved relations with the West. Schevardnadze warned that a dictatorship was on the horizon and he wanted no part of it.

SUMMARY

In 1985, Mikhail Gorbachev came to power in the Soviet Union, heralding a new era of reform. His policies of *glasnost* and *perestroika* promised greater openness in society as well as a restructuring of both the political and economic systems. Gorbachev's reforms were met with some scepticism from the Soviet people and outright challenge from his colleagues. Boris Yeltsin felt Gorbachev was moving too slowly, while Yegor Ligachev feared Gorbachev's reforms were too radical.

Glasnost allowed greater freedom of information for the Soviet people as well as their first clear view of their own history. However, acceptance of dissent encouraged national unrest in the Soviet republics of Georgia, Armenia, Azerbaijan, the Baltic states, and Ukraine. Gorbachev's encouragement of reform in Eastern Europe, along with his reluctance to impose control, resulted in a wave of revolution throughout the bloc in 1989. One by one, the Communist regimes of Poland, Hungary, East Germany, Bulgaria, Czechoslovakia, and Romania were overturned. By 1990, reforms were underway and the economic and political union of East and West Germany was a reality. The major powers were left to work out a new international system sensitive to the needs of a changing world.

QUESTIONS

1. Briefly describe Mikhail Gorbachev's background.

2. Name the four points of the reform program proposed by Gorbachev, and briefly explain each one.

3. Explain the Enterprise Law of 1987. Evaluate its success.

4. Compare and contrast the challenges to Gorbachev's leadership from Boris Yeltsin and Yegor Ligachev.

5. Explain how *glasnost* negatively affected the Soviet Union.

6. What political changes were announced at the Nineteenth Party Conference?

7. Choose three Eastern European countries that underwent revolution in 1989. Compare and contrast the causes of these revolutions and the outcomes.

8. What challenges face the international community now that the Cold War is over? Explain your answer.

CRITICAL ANALYSIS

1. What advantages did the USSR see in incorporating characteristics of the market system in its economy? Evaluate the country's potential for success in this endeavour.

2. What makes bureaucracies conservative in nature? What forces cause them to change?

3. Should the West enter freely into trade with the former USSR in all goods and technologies? Why? Why not?

4. Compare the stability of a country governed by a strong central government and the stability of a country that has distributed power among a number of regions. Apply this analysis to the former Soviet Union.

5. Examine the role of the media in events that lead to revolutionary change. Comment on the role the media played in the latter months of 1989 as change swept across Eastern Europe.

6. The former USSR, Eastern Europe, and China contain more than 25 per cent of the world's population. Western technology is needed to modernize the infrastructures and increase the standards of living of these people. Evaluate how enhancing the lifestyle of the people of China, the former Soviet Union, and Eastern Europe would affect your standard of living.

RESEARCH PROJECTS

1. Identify the problems facing the economy of the former Soviet republics and attempt to devise a workable solution.

2. Research the policy of *glasnost* and explain how this new openness affected political and social conditions in the former Soviet Union.

3. Select one of the following countries and research political and economic changes that have occurred there since 1989:
(a) Poland; (b) Czechoslovakia;
(c) East Germany; (d) Romania.

Evaluate the country's chance of successfully completing the political and economic changes now in progress. Consider factors necessary to this success, and problems that might prevent it.

4. Develop a strategy for ensuring the security of Europe. Evaluate the current status of NATO. What direction should European countries, the USA, and Russia take in establishing a defence strategy?

ACTIVITIES

1 Scrapbook

Choose one of the following topics and make a scrapbook that portrays the dynamics of the event: (a) the Berlin Wall; (b) the reunification of Germany; (c) Czechoslovakia: 1968-1989; (d) the Baltic republics; (e) the Russian economy entering into the 1990s—reform or stagnation?

Select pictures and articles from newspapers or magazines. Supplement them with drawings or articles of your own making. Include cartoons and maps to enhance interest.

2 Creative Analysis

In one of the following areas, analyse conditions in the Soviet Union before its collapse:
(a) Gorbachev's leadership;
(b) the Soviet economy;
(c) the Baltic republics;
(d) Soviet defence.
Then write a newspaper article, draw a cartoon, or write a poem or a short story describing conditions in that same area today.

3 Debate

Be it resolved that Gorbachev's policies of *glasnost* and *perestroika* were responsible for the problems faced by the Soviet Union in 1991.

HISTORICAL ANALYSIS

DISSIDENT LITERATURE

Vaclav Havel, who became Czechoslovakia's president after the fall of communism, was a writer and an active member of the dissident group, Charter 77. Andrei Sakharov, a physicist who helped the Soviet Union develop its nuclear technology, lived six years in internal exile for his active resistance to the Soviet government. Dissidents in Eastern Europe and the Soviet Union during the Cold War period, particularly in the 1970s and 1980s, were highly critical of totalitarianism and risked everything to promote individual freedom. Despite brutal repression these individuals created literary works which brought to life the society in which they lived. Most of these works were not readily available until after the fall of the Soviet Empire, although some of the more famous literary works were smuggled out to the West. Boris Pasternak's *Dr. Zhivago*, for example, won the Nobel Prize for literature, and Milan Kundera's novels were read widely in the West.

Select two pieces of literature written by dissidents. Analyse these works with a view to gaining an understanding of what life was like under the communist regime. Give specific detail regarding living conditions and opportunities which were available or denied the average citizen. How did the totalitarian government control life? How did people react to this control? What do you think people dreamed of or desired to do?

Suggested resources:

Kundera, Milan. *Immortality*. New York: Grove Press, 1991.

Rybakov, Anotoli. *Children of the Arbat*. New York: Dell Publishing, 1988.

Any other novel by Kundera and works by Vaclav Havel or other dissidents would also be appropriate.

THE LEGACY OF THE SOVIET COLLAPSE

FOCUS ON INTERNATIONAL STABILITY

Yeltsin, while less than the ideal democrat, represents the forces of beneficial change.

Headline from *Los Angeles Times,* about the results of the 1996 elections in Russia.

The breakup of the Soviet Union and Yugoslavia has challenged the international community with regard to both peacekeeping and economic development. Study the developments in both regions, particularly in Russia, by listening to media reports and by reading newspapers and magazines. What can the international community do to promote peace? What steps must be taken to build the infrastructure necessary and to develop a healthy economy in these areas? Does the West have a responsibility? If so, what is it?

OVERVIEW

Since the breakup of the Soviet Union, nationalist forces have threatened to destabilize the entire region. The war in the former Yugoslavia illustrates the severity of ethnic tensions and serves as a reminder that historic differences still influence the present. Events in the entire region, which comprised the Communist bloc, threaten the stability of Europe and have led to suggestions that the USA and other western industrialized nations must assist these areas to develop.

ATTEMPTED COUP: AUGUST 1991

From 19 to 22 August 1991, the world watched as eight party officials staged a *coup d'état* in Moscow. The *coup* failed but rang the death knell of the Soviet Union.

THE COMMONWEALTH OF INDEPENDENT STATES

Russia's Yeltsin, Ukraine's Kravchuk and Belarus' Shushkevich met on 8 December 1991 and agreed to the dissolution of the Soviet Union. The successor body was called the Commonwealth of Independent States and was a loose federation of sovereign states.

AFTERMATH OF THE SOVIET COLLAPSE

Representation in the UN, control of nuclear weapons, instability created by ethnic differences, and questions regarding political and economic systems are issues raised in the countries spawned by the collapse of the Soviet Union.

RUSSIA IN THE 1990s

It is important to the international community that the political and economic situation in Russia, the largest of the former Soviet republics, stabilizes.

RUSSIAN MILITARY

The Russian military has the potential to be a significant factor in the future development of the Russian state.

POLITICAL CHANGE IN RUSSIA

Is it realistic to expect western democracy to develop successfully in a society characterized by paternalism rather than individualism?

UKRAINE

The use of the Russian language in Ukraine, control of the Black Sea fleet, and control of the Crimea are three issues important in the relationship between Ukraine and Russia.

On 19 August 1991, Soviet tanks rolled into Moscow and took position outside the Kremlin, near St. Basil Cathedral.

THE BREAKUP OF YUGOSLAVIA

Croatia and Slovenia proclaimed their independence in 1991. When Bosnia-Herzegovina declared its independence, however, Serbia responded with military force. Despite UN intervention since 1992 and diplomatic efforts by western powers and Russia, Serbia remained a renegade state until the Dayton, Ohio meeting in the fall of 1995.

IN THE BEGINNING OF 1991, the Soviet economy was characterized by decreased production, soaring inflation, and a devalued ruble. The Soviet people suffered hardships comparable to the darkest days of Communist rule. Although goods were now readily available, most consumers could not afford more than the barest subsistence.

On 10 July 1991, Boris Yeltsin became the first democratically elected president of the Russian Republic. Mikhail Gorbachev, as President of the Soviet Union, maintained power in the Kremlin. A power struggle emerged between the two leaders. Gorbachev remained committed to the doctrine of communism which mandated central control. He refused, therefore, to allow private property or conversion to the free market system. Yeltsin, on the other hand, wanted to introduce free market reforms. He was popular not only around Moscow but threatened to overshadow Gorbachev in the Soviet Federation.

ATTEMPTED COUP: AUGUST 1991

The eight men who ousted Mikhail Gorbachev from power in August 1991 included (from left to right), Alexander Tiryakov, Vasily Starodubtsev, Boris Pugo, Gennady Yanayev, and Oleg Blakanov. They gave a press conference the same day that the *coup* began.

THE BALTIC STATES

The Baltic states of Latvia, Lithuania, and Estonia were the first to leave the Soviet Union, claiming their independence had been stolen from them by Stalin in 1940. They declared their independence in 1990. Soviet military force was used in Lithuania in 1991 but was unsuccessful in reigning in this renegade state. The loss of life which resulted from Soviet aggression served only to invite international censure against the Soviet Union.

Events in the Soviet Union came to a head in August 1991 when eight senior party officials staged a *coup d'état*. The tanks rolled into Moscow, and from 19 to 22 August the world watched the Soviet Union embroiled in revolution.

In hindsight, events in late July and throughout August 1991 suggested that political upheaval in Russia was imminent. Gorbachev and Yelstin squabbled over their roles when US president George Bush visited Moscow to sign a disarmament treaty. On the day of the meeting between Bush and Gorbachev, six Lithuanian customs agents were gunned down at their posts, presumably to send Lithuania a strong message regarding Moscow's view of its presumption of independence. Tanks were in evidence in Moscow, and after his meeting with Bush Gorbachev left Moscow for a vacation at his dacha at Foros in the Crimea. On 16 August, Yeltsin went to Kazakhstan, leaving Moscow without either president in residence. The eight *coup* plotters were all men whom Gorbachev had mistakenly trusted.

However, the *coup* was doomed to failure for a number of reasons. Communication lines were not cut, potential enemies of the revolution were not arrested, and troops were not strategically placed. The turning point occurred when Yelstin, who had returned to Moscow, climbed onto a tank and rallied the crowd in front of the Russian Parliament. Three Yeltsin supporters were killed in the crossfire, but it was an otherwise bloodless event. By 22 August order was restored, and Yeltsin and Gorbachev were poised to work out a power-sharing agreement. It was clear, however, that Yeltsin had emerged from the power struggle as the stronger candidate for leadership. He would be remembered atop the tank in the midst of the crisis while Gorbachev, on the other hand, was arrested at his dacha in the Crimea and returned to Moscow.

Within the week, the *coup* plotters were arrested and charged with treason. The crisis was over. Ultimately, the *coup* rang the death knell of the Soviet Union. No longer able to control the republics, the empire centred in the Kremlin began to fall apart. Ukraine declared its intention to become an independent nation, and on 1 December 1991 Ukrainians voted in a referendum to confirm their independence. Leonid Kravchuk continued as Ukrainian head of state.

THE COMMONWEALTH OF INDEPENDENT STATES

The Ukrainian decision to leave the Soviet Union sparked the exodus of other republics. Boris Yeltsin of Russia, Leonid Kravchuk of Ukraine, and Stanislav Shushkevich of Belarus (formerly called Belorussia) met on 8 December 1991 just outside of Minsk in Belarus and agreed to the dissolution of the Soviet Union. These three republics were the original signatories to the document which created the Union of Soviet Socialist Republics in 1922. The successor body was called the Commonwealth of Independent States. It would be a loose federation of sovereign states designed to empower these areas while at the same time link them economically.

Immediately following the meeting at Minsk, Nazarbayev of Kazakhstan began to lobby for the inclusion of Kazakhstan and the remaining republics in the union. A subsequent meeting was held on 21 December 1991 in Alma Ata, Kazakhstan. The Commonwealth of Independent States was declared to be the successor to the Soviet Union and now included eleven of the former Soviet republics. Only Georgia remained apart from this union. It joined in 1994. On 25 December 1991, Mikhail Gorbachev, who no longer had either a party or a political unit to lead, resigned as president of the Soviet Union.

After the 1991 *coup,* Yeltsin emerged as a leader more powerful than Gorbachev.

THE COMMUNIST PARTY

In November 1991, the Communist party was banned in the Soviet Union. It was allowed to reappear in 1993 and developed considerable support as the economic conditions in Russia deteriorated.

AFTERMATH OF THE SOVIET COLLAPSE

The breakup of the Soviet Union raised a number of issues. United Nations representation would fall to Russia, Ukraine, and Belarus as these three nations had occupied the seats granted the Soviet Union in the General Assembly. Russia, as the largest republic, would occupy the seat granted to the Soviet Union in the Security Council.

Of much graver concern was the control of nuclear weapons. Russia, Ukraine, Belarus, and Kazakhstan each had nuclear weapons. Negotiations to consolidate the stockpile of nuclear materials began, and by 1994 the START I (Strategic Arms Reduction Talks) treaty was ratified by the United States, Russia, Ukraine, Belarus, and Kazakhstan. By the end of 1994, one half of the 3300 strategic warheads were transferred from Ukraine, Belarus, and Kazakhstan to Russia. These states agreed that fissile material would be transferred to areas which would use the material at nuclear energy plants instead of for weapons production. Subsequently, some of the fissile material from Kazakhstan was transferred to nuclear energy plants in the United States.

Another concern relating to nuclear materials was the growth in theft and trafficking of these items which had occurred since the collapse of the Soviet Union. From 1992 to 1994, German authorities caught 58 smugglers in possession of nuclear substances and uncovered over 400 serious offers to deliver nuclear materials. In addition, there is real concern that nuclear scientists in the former Soviet republics will be attracted to wealthy but unstable Third World countries which would like to develop nuclear weapons. The expertise of these scientists, coupled with the illicit nuclear materials, would be a lethal combination.

Chechen fighters prepare for battle. Yeltsin sent Russian troops into Chechnya after Chechen president Dudayev declared the republic independent of the Soviet Union and Russia.

As the largest of the former Soviet republics, Russia is the acknowledged leader in the region. It is important therefore to the international community that the political and economic systems of Russia stabilize, because the entire area will be affected by whatever transpires here.

There are twenty-one republics in the great sprawling expanse of territory which defines Russia. One of the most pressing problems immediately following the collapse of the Soviet Union was the ethnic tension and apparent demand for sovereignty in far-flung corners of the country. The most contentious fighting broke out in the Caucasus.

Since the Russian conquest of the Caucasus in the nineteenth century, the Chechens resisted control. They staged a series of revolts between 1862 and 1942. In 1944, on the pretext of punishment for Nazi collaboration, Stalin deported both Chitin and Ingush peoples to labour camps in Kazakhstan and Siberia. Tremendous loss of life and serious damage to the Chechen culture resulted. When these people were rehabilitated by Khrushchev in 1957 and allowed to return home, they became embroiled in land disputes as they attempted to reclaim former holdings. Although Russian administrators continued to discriminate against Chitin and Ingush citizens, the area remained at peace from 1957 to the collapse of the Soviet Union.

On 1 November 1991, Chechnya's president Dudayev declared that the area of Chechnya-Ingushetia was independent of the Soviet Union. However, on 30 November 1991, the Ingush voted to remain with the Russian republic, leaving Chechnya on its own. Yeltsin declared a state of emergency in Chechnya and launched an invasion. The Chechens humiliated the Russians in this first round of fighting by capturing strategic facilities on the ground and seizing weapons which were flown in to the capital Grozny. Yeltsin responded to this defeat with an economic embargo on Chechnya. As a result, the Chechens turned to the promotion of their oil and gas reserves among terrorist groups in the Middle East and the Mafia in Russia to bolster their economy.

In late 1994, the Russians determined to resolve the Chechen intransigence by taking military action. Throughout January 1995, Grozny was bombarded. It was estimated that at the height of the bombing as many as 4000 shells an hour were dropped on the city. Many Chechens had already retreated to the mountains but an estimated 25 000 civilians, many of whom were ethnic Russians, died in the shelling.

A third issue was the instability created by ethnic differences in the now independent republics. Throughout the twentieth century, there has been a Russification of the entire region, and many republics contain large numbers of Russians. These people are now treated as foreigners, yet a return to Russia is not a viable option for most.

Significant differences in the development of the republics of the former Soviet Union continue to emerge, with the western region looking to Europe for economic and political ties, while the eastern region moves closer to Islam.

Finally, the political and economic systems of countries spawned by the collapse of the Soviet Union remain in question. The movement toward democracy has been tenuous at best. Reform efforts are challenged by both old guard communists and right-wing nationalists. Lacking any history of political freedom, people in this region seem unready for a democratic system modeled on Western principles. In addition, the attempt to make the transition from central planning to the market system has not yet been successful. As Russia is the largest of the successor states, a closer look at its political and economic progress is essential.

Atrocities spread to the countryside as well, and the slaughter of civilians was widespread.

As a result of the war, Chechen land and culture has been devastated. In addition, Russia sustained international censure, its military suffered embarrassment, and Yelstin suffered enormous political costs. The conflict has called into question the potential for Russian development in the direction of democracy.

RUSSIAN MILITARY

With the collapse of the Soviet Union, primary responsibility for defence in the region fell to Russia. Ukraine and Belarus inherited military personnel and equipment when the Soviet Union disintegrated, but much of the remaining military returned from the other republics to Russia. However, the Russian military now suffers from significant cutbacks in personnel, equipment, and overall funding. As military spending in Russia is just a fraction of that spent by the former Soviet Union, it has not been possible to maintain the prestigious force which the Soviet Union once displayed.

For example, in 1994 Russia spent about 4.6 per cent of its gross domestic product (GDP = GNP minus foreign investments) on defence, while in the past the Soviet Union typically spent 15 to 25 per cent of its GDP on the military. The armed forces in Russia are only about one-quarter the size of the armed force that was maintained by the Soviet Union. The Russian air force is less than one-half the size of the former Soviet air force. Defence cutbacks have resulted in a lack of spare parts for aircraft, lack of modernization as equipment wears out, and significant reduction in pilot flying time. These factors seriously threaten the credibility of the air force.

In addition, conventional armed forces suffer from a lack of conscripts and excessively high rates of desertion. Military life is viewed as a life of privation. There are no longer troops stationed anywhere in Eastern Europe, and returning soldiers have faced unemployment, lack of proper housing, and inadequate social programs in Russia.

However, the military remains an important factor in the development of Russia's political and economic future. To date, the military has refused to take political sides. Most analysts suggest that the 1991 *coup* would have succeeded if the military had been united and willing to support the *coup* plotters.

The 1991 *coup* ended three days after it began. On 21 August, the tanks and armoured cars left Moscow.

The Russian military has the potential to be a significant factor in the future development of the Russian state if one of the political leaders was able to marshal its support.

POLITICAL CHANGE IN RUSSIA

Russia has a long history of authoritarian government, first under the tsars and then under the Communist party. It is no surprise then that the democratic process is still relatively slow to develop in Russia. In fact, some analysts question whether it is realistic to expect western democracy to develop successfully in a society characterized by paternalism rather than individualism.

Gorbachev's reforms introduced an expectation of change which people believed would result in a much improved standard of living. In fact, when market reforms were introduced into the economy after the collapse of the command economy, there was a sudden influx of consumer goods. For the first time ordinary people in Russia had access to an array of goods. However, although store shelves were now well stocked, prices were so high that only the wealthy could purchase most items. Bacon, which had sold for 4 rubles per kilo, skyrocketed to 1200 rubles per kilo.

Prices had been freed from state control, but state monopolies still existed in many areas. This led to

On 2 October 1993, supporters of Alexander Rutskoi barricaded the Russian White House. The 12 days of fighting which ensued resulted in more violence than the 1991 *coup*. The man in the middle of the photograph is a pro-Communist waving a monarchist flag.

widespread speculation in which individuals bought goods from a state monopoly and sold them for a large profit on the open market. For example, an individual who bought gasoline from the state and sold it on the market could earn as many rubles in two days as a factory worker would earn in the entire month. This problem has continued and resulted in an environment where it is much more profitable to speculate than to produce. Young people are encouraged to reject jobs on farms or in factories by the promise of much higher earnings in speculative ventures.

By 1993, the failure of economic reforms was clearly evident in the widespread corruption, high prices of ordinary consumer goods, rising inflation, speculation in ordinary consumer goods, failure of privatization schemes, and the plummeting standard of living which resulted in severe economic hardship for the ordinary Russian. The newest joke circulating in Moscow was, "What has one year of capitalism achieved that 70 years of communism could not? It has made communism look good."

With economic conditions deteriorating daily in 1993, it is not surprising that there was a growing movement against Yeltsin, and the question of impeachment was raised repeatedly. Demonstrations were held in Red Square, and resistance against economic reforms grew. Parliamentarians who opposed Yelstin seized the opportunity to launch a power struggle in the Russian government.

Alexander Rutskoi and Ruslan Khasbulatov pitted themselves against Yeltsin and stirred the growing hostility of ordinary Russians against Yelstin into a revolt. On 2 October 1993, while Yeltsin was at his country dacha, Rutskoi, supported by Communists, neo-Nazis, and a motley crew of ruffians looking for a fight, barricaded the Russian White House and threatened to seize control of the government. Yelstin sent in the tanks, and over a 12-day period fighting occurred between the government and the rebels. While the 1991 *coup* attempt had resulted in only three deaths and little violence, this attempt was much more bloody and unsettling. More than 170 people were killed, about 900 wounded, and more than 1250 people were arrested as a result of the incident.

Although victorious, Yeltsin recognized the magnitude of the discontent and announced that he would rule by authoritarian decree until the elections were held in December 1993. Russia's political problems were partly the result of a government which had not made the transition from communism to democracy. Its parliament consisted of members who were elected while the Communist party was still in control, and its constitution dated back to 1978 when communism controlled the country. Although the December elections promised some democratic reform, the political organs needed restructuring and the average Russian voter had little or no knowledge of the election issues or the parties which promised to transform the country.

When elections were held in December 1993, Yelstin managed to hold on to power. Vladimir Zhirinovski, a right-wing nationalist who promised to restore the prestige of the old Russian Empire and to end the economic distress, received 18 per cent of the votes. For Westerners, the most unsettling aspect of Zhirinovski's platform was his anti-semitism and his goal to take territories lost by Russia during the twentieth century. His appeal to Russian voters seemed to stem primarily from his promise to restore stability and economic security by fighting the criminal elements in Russia and by controlling the economy.

In all, there has been a general trend in Russia since 1993 toward a more authoritarian form of government. The contenders in the June 1996 elections included Boris Yeltsin, Gennady Zyuganov, leader of the Communist party of the Russian Federation, Aleksandr Lebed, Vladimir Zhirinovski of the Liberal Democratic party of Russia, and Yegor Gaidar as leader of Russia's Democratic Choice party. Although Gorbachev declared his candidacy, he had no popular following in Russia and there was little chance

Vladimir Zhirinovski is a right-wing Russian nationalist who wanted to restore the prestige of the old Russian Empire. Western countries were concerned about Zhirinovski's imperialist and anti-semitist views.

that he would win many votes. The winner would have to garner 50 per cent of the total vote and, as predicted, the first ballot forced a runoff between Boris Yeltsin and Gennady Zyuganov. On 3 July 1996, Boris Yeltsin won 54 per cent of the vote despite his apparent unpopularity and ill health.

UKRAINE

On 1 December 1991, Leonid Kravchuk became Ukraine's first democratically elected president. He was a former Communist and was considered a moderate who would secure the newly independent Ukraine and ensure that its relationship with Russia remained amiable.

Three issues were of particular importance in the relationship between Ukraine and Russia. The first issue was that of the use of the Russian language in the Crimea and various parts of Ukraine. Ukrainians would like to abandon the use of Russian as a state language and use only Ukrainian. A second issue was the control of the Black Sea fleet. Recent agreements have allowed the Russians to maintain 75 per cent control, and they are determined to maintain their foothold on the Black Sea ports as well. Ukraine is not satisfied with these arrangements.

A third issue is the Crimea. In 1954, control of the Crimea was turned over to Ukraine. The Crimea is a prime vacation spot and is considered important also for its access to the Black Sea. In January 1994, it was requested that the Crimea become an autonomous area. This solution would solve the bickering between Ukraine and Russia for control of the region.

During his presidency, Kravchuk did not demonstrate the leadership skills necessary to solve the country's economic problems or to establish Ukraine's position in either Eastern Europe or the international community. Hyperinflation set in and the country seemed poised for economic collapse. On 10 July 1994, Kravchuk was replaced by his former prime minister Leonid Kuchma. Kuchma's strengths were his willingness to attack corruption in an effort to resolve the country's economic difficulties and his ability to act decisively.

Kuchma determined that Ukraine had no choice but to introduce radical economic reform. He advocated free prices, free trade, and a mass privatization program including land reform. The launching of such a radical reform program positioned Ukraine to gain support from the IMF (International Monetary Fund). Seven hundred fifty million dollars were committed by the IMF as an initial payment in 1994 with an additional $1.6 billion to follow. Kuchma's leadership of Ukraine has enhanced the status of Ukraine in the West. However, he has to continue his efforts to establish Ukraine's place in Western Europe and ensure a stable relationship with Russia.

BIOGRAPHY

LEONID KRAVCHUK (1934–   )

To many, Kravchuk is a study in contradictions: after three decades of working against the Ukrainian nationalists—during the 1980s as second secretary in the Ukrainian Communist party in charge of ideology— Kravchuk emerged in the early 1990s to be an ardent and influential defender of Ukrainian nationalism. Kravchuk said this conversion came about after reading government documents that he found in the National Archives in 1989.

> You cannot imagine what a strong influence documents have made on me. My attitude about the [Soviet] state and its policy and the Communist party change[d] overnight ... I have not come from being a Communist to being a nationalist, but to be more precise, from being a Communist to a democrat.

Many are skeptical of Kravchuk's conversion. The following is the sentiment of Ukrainian-Canadian Lubomyr Luciuk as it appeared in the *Ottawa Citizen* on 9 October 1992:

> We believed sincerely in Ukraine's struggle for an independent, united and democratic state. We got it all except democracy. This is not to say there are no democrats there ... But we must not fool ourselves, or try to hoodwink anyone else, into thinking that this "Absurdistan" is the Ukraine we had hoped for.

Like millions of Russians, Ukrainian Leonid Kravchuk enjoys a good game of chess. As he manoeuvres across the board, it is not hard to tell that here is a strategist who is an astute observer. Furthermore, Kravchuk claims to not need an umbrella during a downpour because he can walk between the drops. An optimist and an anomaly, Kravchuk became Ukraine's first democratically elected president in 1991 and the leader responsible for the movement towards Ukrainian independence. Both of these roles were a personal checkmate of sorts.

Leonid Kravchuk was born to Ukrainian Orthodox peasants in the village of Zhytyn in the Rivne Region of western Ukraine on 10 January 1934. He joined the Communist party in 1958. Kravchuk became well-educated, graduating from the Taras Shevenko State University in Kiev with a master's degree in political economics, and then from the Academy of Social Sciences in Moscow with a doctorate in economics. His wife, Antonina, is a professor of economics at Taras Shevenko State University.

After 1991, Kravchuk's leadership focused on building statehood and promoting inter-ethnic harmony. Several specific issues he tackled included sorting out Russian and Ukrainian claims to the Black Sea fleet, the fate of the Crimea, and disposing of the nuclear weapons stationed in Ukraine. Few would dare suggest that Kravchuk had an easy task ahead of him. The former Soviet republics are in the unique position of being relatively developed and of having evolved as component parts of an overarching Soviet political and economic system. For Ukraine and the other new states, the challenge is to extricate themselves from the devastating effects of past Communist policies at the same time as deal with a multitude of nasty economic, social, and environmental problems in their own countries. A tall order even for the most astute of strategists.

Unable to solve Ukraine's economic problems, Kravchuk lost his bid for re-election in July 1994. Leonid Kuchma took over the Ukrainian presidency with the goal of economic reform in mind.

●

RUSSIA AND BELARUS

On 23 March 1996, Russia and Belarus agreed to a political, economic, and cultural union. The agreement must be ratified by the parliaments of both countries and details regarding the proposal of a common budget have yet to be worked out.

This photograph of residents walking along a street in the Bosnian capital of Sarajevo was taken through a cracked window of a bus damaged by gunfire.

THE BREAKUP OF YUGOSLAVIA

Tensions in Yugoslavia had been building gradually since the death of Tito in 1980. Tito's brand of nationalistic communism held together a state composed of peoples influenced by their ethnic, religious, and historic diversity. Attempts to maintain the cohesion of Tito's leadership failed as separatist movements and economic difficulties pressured the Yugoslav government. In mid-1991, the region exploded.

The Yugoslavian crisis originated in the fourteenth century when the Ottoman Turks defeated Serbian forces in the Battle of Kosovo in 1389. For the next 500 years, this Slavic area was ruled by Muslim forces. It was not until Turkey's defeat at the hands of Russia in 1878 that Serbia regained its independence. Russia now became Serbia's patron because both areas were characterized by Eastern Orthodox Christianity and Slavic nationality.

Serbia began to agitate for a union of Slavs in the Balkan area. This union would include Serbs, Croats, Slovenes, and Bosnians, most of whom were under the control of the Austrian Hapsburgs. This nationalist agitation contributed to the outbreak of the First World War. The defeat of the Austrians, and subsequent breakdown of the Hapsburg Empire, made possible the creation of an independent Slavic state which in 1929 was called Yugoslavia. However, the creation of this state did not solve the ethnic and religious differences.

At the beginning of the Yugoslav crisis, the region was divided by ethnic and religious differences. The Serbs are Eastern Orthodox Christians, the Croats and Slovenians are Roman Catholic, and the Bosnians are a mixture of Serbs, Croats, and Slavic peoples who converted to Islam during the Ottoman rule. Although both the Serbs and the Croats have Slavic origins, the Serbs maintain ties to Russia and Eastern Europe while the Croats and the Slovenes wish to maintain closer ties to Western Europe. These ethnic and religious differences are compounded by bitterness over historic events such as the defeat of Kosovo in 1389 and the Croatian Fascist atrocities against the Serbs in the Second World War.

During the 1980s, Serbian leader Slobodan Milosevic rallied Serb forces throughout Yugoslavia to promote Serbian influence in the region. In 1991, Croatia and Slovenia proclaimed their independence in resistance to Serbian threats to envelop them in a Serbian-dominated state. They were admitted to the United Nations along with Bosnia and Herzegovina in 1992, and the international community hoped that this recognition would bring peace to the region. When Bosnia-Herzegovina declared its independence, however, Serbia responded with military force. The Serbian army moved against Croatia and Slovenia as well as Bosnia. The war against Croatia and Slovenia ended in a ceasefire. While Slovenia restored its political and economic systems to normalcy, Croatia remained embroiled in the conflict.

The bitter fighting persisted in Bosnia, where ethnic differences led to some of the worst atrocities of recent memory. The slaughter and systematic rape of civilian populations was termed "ethnic cleansing" and led an outraged international community to

313

Heavy smog sits on downtown Leipzig in former East Germany. Experts say that cleaning up this air pollution will cost billions of dollars.

INDUSTRIAL POLLUTION

Eastern Europe's industrial pollution presents an appalling picture. Acid rain, combined with industrial and domestic waste, has caused widespread environmental damage which has adversely affected the landscape and degraded the quality of life. The consequences of environmental pollution are alarming.

In many regions of Eastern Europe, entire populations have respiratory diseases, and life expectancies have been shortened by as much as five to ten years. The biggest culprit is the estimated 26 million tonnes of sulphur dioxide emissions which are added to the air as a by-product from burning soft lignite coal. In addition to this industrial pollution, the smoke from millions of coal-burning stoves in family homes filters out the rays of the sun, creating an eerie grey atmosphere. The smog over major cities, such as Budapest and Cracow, contains some of the highest concentrations of chemical emissions in the world. Visitors complain that they can taste the sulphur in the air. Conditions are so damaging in some industrial regions of Poland that children are routinely sent out of the area for a three-week respite from the pollution.

Initial estimates of cleaning up air pollution alone approach $200 billion. This is money that the impoverished nations do not have. Think of the problem of converting all the coal-burning energy sources to the cleaner natural gas. Even if it could be done quickly, where would the gas come from? Who would construct the necessary infrastructure of pipelines and refineries? What would be the effect of mass unemployment if the factories were to be closed down, as they should be?

An even greater danger is presented by the threat of a nuclear accident in one of the two dozen Soviet-built nuclear power plants that are scattered throughout the region. Safety devices often do not work, and personnel are not capable of maintaining plant integrity. One Chernobyl is enough, yet others threaten as economic necessity drives governments to continue to use outdated and unsafe nuclear power stations.

Eastern Europe's forests, rivers, and lakes have all been critically affected by industrial and domestic pollution. From Germany to its mouth in the Black Sea, the Danube River has been turned into an industrial sewer, receiving lethal doses of chemical waste along its path. Added to the chemical waste is an equally damaging influx of nitrogen run-off from agricultural fertilizers.

The solution to this problem is to halt industrial production in order to stop the pollution before the situation deteriorates beyond repair. However, the social and economic dislocation of such a measure would create problems of its own. In the euphoria of newly won political freedom, governments are loath to deal with a situation that could result in mass unemployment and lead to political turmoil. Industries that are inefficient and obsolete do not see the additional costs of cleaning up their wastes as a priority. Farmers chafe at the additional cost of pollution controls that would make their products uncompetitive in a competitive global market.

The region's initial decision to take concerted action toward the elimination of pollution has been stalled. Current priorities in every nation in Eastern Europe are for increased food production and increased availability of consumer goods rather than for pollution controls. Western European nations that are affected by the spread of air pollution have agreed to spend several billion dollars to pay for a partial cleaning of the air. This is in addition to attempts to clean up their own air and water pollution in order to create a clean environment for all.

How does one reform the production practices of the Eastern bloc? Who would cover the costs? Where does one begin? These questions all seem without answers at the present time.

1. What causes the pollution in Eastern Europe?

2. What social problems prevent the elimination of pollution in Eastern Europe? Why do farmers resist pollution controls?

3. What problems are evident in nuclear power plants in this region?

4. Propose a solution to the pollution problem, taking into account the economic realities in Eastern Europe.

heap condemnation on Serbia for its brutality. Despite United Nations intervention since 1992, and a variety of diplomatic efforts by both Western powers and Russia, Serbia remained a renegade state until the parties to the conflict finally agreed to meet at Dayton, Ohio in the fall of 1995. While the meeting produced an agreement that seemed to auger well for a protracted peace, the hostilities in the region seem to be deep-seated and resistant to permanent solution. The establishment of distinct areas for Serb and Croat civilians to re-establish their homes has proved difficult for police. However, 1996 has witnessed an end to the war and limited violations of the peace agreement.

NATO

NATO involvement in the Yugoslav crisis resulted in air strikes in response to the refusal of the Serbs and the Croats to maintain the ceasefire which was negotiated in 1994.

SUMMARY

The transfer from the authoritarian government of the Communist party to a more open democracy in Russia has been fraught with uncertainty. Gorbachev remained committed to the doctrine of communism while Yeltsin, who emerged as head of the Russian Republic, was open to market reforms. A power struggle between the two followed.

At this point, one republic after the other voted to leave the Soviet Union, and Gorbachev chose not to use military force to prevent this. The Soviet Union ceased to exist in 1991. The successor body was the Commonwealth of Independent States, a loose federation of sovereign states.

The largest and most powerful of these states was Russia, where Yeltsin assumed the leadership of what was left of the former USSR. He survived several *coups* and brought a degree of stability to the new Russian government. However, efforts at reuniting the old Russian Empire failed as republic after republic declared their independence. Ethnic differences within the republics caused instability. Significant differences emerged, with the western region looking to Europe for economic and political ties, and the eastern region moving closer to Islam.

Some issues created problems, such as the location of nuclear weapons in Ukraine and elsewhere. The USA and Western Europe acted to locate and disarm these weapons.

No less challenging was the desired change from a state-planned economy to a market-oriented model. A black market flourished as factories slowed to a halt and unemployment and starvation grew. Financial aid from the West helped ease the situation, but foreign aid cannot solve the problem of restructuring and modernizing the Russian economy.

Following the breakup of the Soviet Union, the member republics of the Yugoslav federation sought their independence. Unlike the Soviet Union, the central Serbian majority chose war to force Croatia and others to remain. When this failed, the Serbian government attempted to seize as much land as it could and to expel all non-Serbs. Efforts by the United Nations, and later NATO, created an uneasy truce in the ethnically mixed Balkan region.

Since the symbolic coming down of the Berlin Wall, the world has witnessed the breakup of two large federations, the Soviet Union and Yugoslavia.

QUESTIONS

1. What economic problems characterized the Soviet Union in 1991?

2. Compare and contrast the political roles played by Yeltsin and Gorbachev after Yeltsin's election as president of the Russian Republic.

3. Briefly describe the *coup* attempt of 1991.

4. What is the Commonwealth of Independent States?

5. Name and explain four issues which arose in the Russian Republic after the Soviet collapse.

6. Briefly describe the war in Chechnya. How has the war affected Chechnya? Russia?

7. What challenges does the military of the former Soviet Union face? What role does it play in the 1990s?

8. List the political and economic problems facing Russians in the 1990s.

9. Name and explain three issues which are important in the relationship between Ukraine and Russia.

10. Briefly describe the background to the conflict in the former Yugoslavia.

CRITICAL ANALYSIS

1. Does the communist philosophy contribute to the economic problems which plague the Russian Republic now that the Soviet Union has collapsed? Defend your answer.

2. Examine Russia's role in the international community in the 1990s. Why is stability in Russia important to the rest of the world?

3. Nationalism in the republics since the collapse of the Soviet Union threatens stability in the region. Identify and analyse the problems in Chechnya, Georgia, Azerbaijan, or any other area where nationalism is an issue.

4. Compare the conflict in the Yugoslav region to the conflict in Chechnya. Why is peace so difficult to establish in these regions?

RESEARCH PROJECTS

1. Research the process of Russification in the Soviet Union and explain how that phenomenon affected society.

2. Examine the new relationship which was forged between Belarus and Russia. Does this suggest the beginning of a new federation of former Soviet states? Analyse the potential for further unions to occur.

3. Research the role played by ethnic and religious differences in the Balkan War. How could these differences be overcome?

4. Analyse the results of the 1996 election in Russia. What do they suggest for the immediate future? How will this election affect Russia's international status?

ACTIVITIES

1 Role Play

Select students to role play Yeltsin, Zyuganov, Lebed, and Zhirinovski. (You could include any of the other candidates as well.) Hold a political forum with these candidates, outline their platforms, and reveal their plans to lead Russia to a more prosperous and stable future.

2 International Peacekeeping

You are a Canadian peacekeeper in Bosnia in 1994. Write an account of your experience as you move from village to village in the attempt to maintain the peace. What do you see, hear, and feel? Describe fully.

3 Debate

Be it resolved that the international community should intervene in civil wars such as that which occurred in the former Yugoslavia.

HISTORICAL ANALYSIS

NATIONALISM

Since the fall of the Berlin Wall in 1989, nationalist movements throughout the world have gained momentum. Czechoslovakia split peacefully into two separate countries, and some areas of the former Soviet Empire—such as Ukraine, Belarus, and Kazakhstan—have declared their independence without bloodshed. Other areas—such as Chechnya, Armenia, and Georgia—have not been able to establish national sovereignty peacefully. Yugoslavia's tragic dissolution exemplifies the irrationality of nationalism.

During the nineteenth and early twentieth centuries, some political leaders thought that borders should be drawn to allow ethnic homogeneity. Thus the defining feature of sovereignty would be nationalist: a common ethnic background, common language and traditions. As we approach the twenty-first century, we are becoming more aware of the global nature of our relationships and the interdependence which affects not only our economic but our political lives.

Research the concept of nationalism and assess how it affects current relationships. Can we expect to establish nations on the basis of ethnicity? What factors must be considered when borders are drawn? Is there any way to overcome the ethnic hatreds evident in an area like Bosnia? Should the international community be involved in establishing some guidelines for the settlement of civil disputes which originate from nationalist differences?

Suggested resources:

Drakulic, Slavenka. *The Balkan Express: Fragments from the Other Side of War.* New York: W.W. Norton, 1993.

Glenny, Misha. *The Fall of Yugoslavia: The Third Balkan War.* London: Penguin, 1992.

Kaplan, Robert D. *Balkan Ghosts.* New York: Vintage Books, 1993.

CONTEMPORARY GLOBAL INTERACTION

As WE APPROACH the end of the twentieth century, it is

clear that the world's political, economic, and social struc-

tures have changed enormously. It is equally clear that struc-

tural change is going to continue, at an accelerated pace,

into the next century.

What are the forces likely to be at the forefront of this change? While not a question easily or simply answered, it is a crucial one to consider. The most critical challenges facing the world today are the new world power structure, nationalist movements, population growth, refugees, trade blocs, environmental damage, and disparity in standards of living.

Most observers agree that non-governmental organizations or supranational actors will play an increasing role in international affairs in the future. This does not mean the death of the concept of the nation-state. It does, however, mean that there will be more players to take into account, and that many of them will represent collectivities which cross traditional political, economic, social, and ideological boundaries.

NEW WORLD POWER STRUCTURE

The collapse of the Soviet Union destroyed the bipolar power structure the world had seen since 1945. The USA has emerged as the only remaining superpower, a problem in itself. Other nations have subsequently begun to develop local spheres of influence through military power and economic dominance. China, Japan, North Korea, Israel, Iraq, Pakistan, and India have exerted influence over their neighbours, claiming to have arsenals of, or easy access to, weapons of mass destruction. Attempts by the USA and the UN to disarm these nations have led to confrontation in North Korea and Iraq. The bipolar world has given way to a multi-polar world, but is it less dangerous?

NATIONALIST MOVEMENTS

A destabilizing reaction to the end of the bipolar world has been the rise of nationalist movements. The break-up of Yugoslavia is a result of this, as is the demand of the Kurds for a nation to call their own. Nationalism has forced many countries to take a harder line on minorities and immigration. The expulsion of the Vietnamese boat people from Hong Kong, tribal warfare in Africa, and the closing of European borders to refugees are examples of this, and can be viewed as politically correct ethnic cleansing.

POPULATION GROWTH

Today, the world's population is about 5 billion. At the current growth rate, this could mean 10 billion by the year 2120 and 20 billion by the year 2150. Scientists tell us the Earth can sustain that number with due care and caution. However, what will happen in the next doubling? How can human growth be managed so as not to destroy the planet? Where will people find food, water, and housing? Western Canada is one likely prospect for increased immigration, as is Australia and Siberia. What would the Canadian West be like with 100 million people?

REFUGEES

In the world today, there are more than 37 million refugees who have been forced from their homes by civil unrest. They have fled to countries which are often unable to meet their need for sanctuary and a better life. This is especially true in Western Europe.

In 1990, France's president Mitterand commented that Western Europe had reached the threshold of tolerance toward refugees. Heavy influxes of displaced peoples had placed such demands on the infrastructure of the industrialized nations that it was increasingly difficult to provide food and shelter for the newcomers. Although the right to asylum would continue to be recognized, those who were in no danger would be repatriated.

France was not alone in its sentiment toward the deluge of those seeking to partake of Europe's wealth. In the summer of 1991, the Italians deported tens of thousands of Albanians who had ventured across the Adriatic. In England, Prime Minister Major pointed out that Western Europe could not be open to all those who preferred to live in London, Paris, or Rome instead of Bombay or Singapore.

The Germans regard forced repatriation with more sensitivity than the others, but even Chancellor Kohl was forced to stem the flow of immigrants. Germany has accepted more than half of the 3.5 million refugees who arrived in Europe between 1984 and 1994. Germany is also in the process of integrating 16 million East Germans into its economy and an estimated 1.5 million Germans returning from abroad. The $70 billion fund set aside to assist the integration of these peoples was quickly used up, and the total costs are now estimated at over one trillion dollars.

From Norway to Greece and Germany to Spain, European nations feel themselves to be under siege. Apart from immigration caused by opening boundaries with Eastern Europe, there has been an equally large increase in immigration from North Africa. An estimated 3.5 million Muslims of Arab origin are thought to be in Western Europe. Now, action is being taken in all nations to restrict granting asylum by refusing to accept refugees who come from what is considered a safe area. The result of these actions was an immediate 60 per cent decrease in refugees by 1994.

THE INTERNET

The exponential growth of the Internet has convinced many people that the world is quickly becoming a global village. Examine the potential effects of the Internet on developing countries.

The Internet has brought the world closer together by allowing people from different sides of the planet to find and communicate with each other in minutes. Through the inter-networked connection of high speed transmission lines and computers, a user can mail, join a discussion group, transfer digital files, or compute long-distance. One person can send a message across the world to another electronically, using a feature known as e-mail. USENET, or newsgroups, allow participation in ongoing discussions with people of similar interests—be it science fiction, medicine, horticulture, theology, etc., etc., etc. File transfer of any electronic digital information—documents, images, soundbites, video, 3-D animated graphics—is available to users with access to the many catalogues and libraries of information online. The ability to publish information, products and services has developed into new markets. Remote computing, Telnet, is available for long-range computing.

The Internet began as a think-tank research project in the early 1960s. The developers were faced with the strategic realities of the Cold War—technological vulnerability, national security, and the threat of nuclear holocaust. In 1969 the Pentagon's Advanced Research Projects Agency (ARPA) of the American Department of Defense decided to fund a command-and-control network that would continue to function in the event of nuclear war when traditional organizational structures collapsed. ARPANET linked military, university, and defense computing centres with high speed transmission lines to help scientists and researchers share information. E-mail and transfer capabilities were quickly added to ARPANET's potential tasks.

The founding principle of the Internet is no central authority. It is a great equalizer of sorts—there is no distinction between the user who is a Ph.D. and the user who is in grade four, if both are literate and have access to the Internet. Any node of the Internet can speak to any other node as a peer, as long as it conforms to the technical protocols. If one node fails, the message, or data packet, seeks an alternate route. The Internet has evolved out of its Cold War infancy to completely defy control. It thrives in an anarchical condition crossing traditional political, economic, social, and ideological boundaries. This emerging market, however, may yet become another arena for wealth and power as companies struggle for technological supremacy and financial gain.

The Internet's growth has been twofold—the accelerating number of online users and the increasing speed of electronic transmission. In 1969 there were four nodes to the network; in 1972, there were 37. By 1996 an estimated 57 million users were online with a growth rate of 20 per cent per month. Some of the submarine fibre-optic cables that now encircle the globe are capable of carrying 120 000 simultaneous phone conversations at speeds up to 10 gigabits per second. This increase in inter-connectivity means that people can communicate from just about anywhere. To be a part of this exploding growth of global communication all one needs is access to a computer with a modem. Students can log-on at a number of schools—universities were among the first to link up—and people who cannot afford their own system can go to an increasing number of online public libraries or one of the Internet cafés popping up in almost any city you can think of.

Some of the advantages of the Internet are less expensive communication, reduced time to find information, increased knowledge, increased user control, and an increased audience. Conversely, the gap between those who have Internet access and those who do not creates a new kind of border.

The developing countries are rushing to wire-up. Particularly in Southeast Asia—India, China, Malaysia, Singapore, and Taiwan—all expect high speed links. Their advantage may be that they can take the lead with state-of-the-art technology and are not restricted by existing infrastructures. Surfing the net, however, is still far from a possibility or priority for the majority of the world's people in developing countries who struggle to feed, clothe, and shelter themselves. They will not be sitting in Internet cafés, drinking coffee.

1. What was the original purpose of the Internet? What is its purpose today?

2. What possible advantages and disadvantages could the Internet have for developed and developing countries?

The European Union

Members of the European Union

0   500 km

Countries belonging to the European Union constitute a single economic market.

TRADE BLOCS

Global interdependence is a predominant characteristic of the modern world. Nations are coming together to form trade blocs that look out for their collective economic interests.

The European Union (EU) is the most powerful economic unit in the world today. Fifteen European countries—Austria, Belgium, Denmark, Finland, France, Germany, the United Kingdom, Greece, the Republic of Ireland, Italy, Luxembourg, the Netherlands, Portugal, Spain, and Sweden—form a single economic market, populated by over 300 million people and in command of resources comparable to those of the USA. Their combined GDP is in excess of $4 trillion.

The North American Free Trade Agreement (NAFTA), established in 1994, is another formidable trade bloc. The member countries of Canada, the United States, and Mexico have a combined market of 370 million people.

While some economic analysts fear that these trade blocs will result in protectionist economies in Europe and North America, others suggest that the need to invest capital and know-how abroad will ensure that these collectives pursue outward-looking economic and political strategies.

The European Union (EU)

The concept of a European economic bloc was first proposed after the Second World War by the French statesman Jean Monnet, who urged European union in the interests of preventing future wars. In 1951, Robert Schumann, France's foreign minister, proposed an amalgamation of French and German coal and steel resources. The Schumann Plan became the foundation of the European Coal and Steel Community (ECSC) which in 1951 united Belgium, France, Italy, Luxembourg, the Netherlands, and West Germany. These six member nations abolished trade barriers on coal, steel, iron ore, and scrap metal and allowed workers in these industries to move freely in the ECSC. In 1957, the six founding members of ECSC signed the Treaty of Rome which established the European Atomic Energy Community, or Euratom, and the European Economic Community. Euratom was directed at producing nuclear energy for peaceful purposes and has been instrumental in nuclear power production for European states. The European Community expanded its membership with the addition of Denmark, Ireland, and Great Britain in 1973, Greece in 1981 and later Spain and Portugal. In 1994, Austria, Finland, and Sweden joined what was by then called the European Union.

The union has experienced substantial economic growth as a result of the abolition of tariffs on goods traded within the community and the imposition of a common tariff on imported goods. The Single European Act of 1986, which laid the foundation for the European Union, proposed standardization in the areas ranging from the type of electrical plug to be adopted to pollution control devices. The elimination of border controls has raised security concerns, but some countries started early to categorize travelers as European Community or Other in recognition of anticipated changes.

Member states are working toward the creation of a common currency and, in fact, some multinational companies already key their domestic currencies to the European Currency Unit (ECU). No agreement has yet been reached on the creation of a central banking system. Once economic union is complete, the next logical step would appear to be European political union. While it must be recognized that fierce nationalism persists in these European states, there is also a belief that only by operating as a unit can they attain the living standards they desire.

ENVIRONMENTAL DAMAGE

Industrial and population growth in the world will continue to place unacceptable pressures on the environment. One of the greatest challenges humans face is in managing the Earth's resources. This is a global problem and concerns us all. The limited success in the industrial world in controlling pollution, resource exploitation, and in recycling resources is matched by minimal efforts in the non-industrial world. When priorities are to house and feed a hungry population, environmental concerns are easily ignored.

How much abuse can the life support systems of the Earth take before they break down? Air and water pollution and expanding deserts are warning signs. Humans require precise living conditions; their tolerance of impurities is not without limits.

STANDARDS OF LIVING

It has been calculated that there are not enough physical resources on Earth to provide each individual with a wealthy lifestyle. The growing disparity between peoples of the industrial world—where material standards of living are advanced—and those of the non-industrial world—where people often live close to the subsistence level—will create future instability. When there are not enough resources to go around, who gets the better lifestyle? Experiences of the twentieth century guide us in what to expect when desperate people decide to take action against what they consider to be oppressive living conditions.

QUESTION

It is impossible to predict the future partly because human nature does not conform to set scientific patterns. However, using the analytical skills you have developed, and your intuition, decide what you consider to be the major challenge facing humankind in the twenty-first century. Give evidence and reasons to support your answer.

ACTIVITY

Debate

Be it resolved that regional trade agreements, such as the EU and NAFTA, are good for the world's economy.

GLOSSARY

A

Appeasement. A strategy that involves giving in to an opponent in the hope that war will be averted. Chamberlain's attempt at appeasement of Germany over Czechoslovakia failed because Hitler was not prepared to be appeased. The publicity given the failure of the Munich Pact has since deterred other national leaders from acting in the same vein.

Attrition. A strategy in which the objective is not to win territory but to wear down the human and physical resources of the enemy slowly, thus negating its ability to wage war.

Autarky. The state of being self-sufficient, or independent of imports from other countries.

B

Balance of Power. A situation in which peace is ensured by an equilibrium of alliances between major powers that check any move toward hegemony.

Bipolar. A world in which there are two major powers or spheres of influence.

Blitzkrieg. Lightning war waged by Germany's mechanized combined forces, designed to force rapid surrender by breaking through enemy battle lines and savaging rear areas.

Brezhnev Doctrine. A thesis justifying the policy of Soviet intervention in communist bloc nations to ensure cohesiveness and adherence to the communist ideology as determined by Moscow.

Brinkmanship. The strategy of taking a nation to the brink of war in pursuit of foreign policy goals. It is a policy of threatening large scale or total war to force an opponent to back down in a confrontation.

C

Cadre. A nucleus of specially trained personnel.

Cartel. A grouping of businesses that works together in controlling sources of raw materials, markets, and prices.

China Lobby. A politically powerful American group that helped direct and maintain American support for the Kuomintang and Chiang Kai-shek, and discouraged support of Mao Zedong and communism.

China Model. A revolutionary system in which a peasantry is the motivating force, as opposed to the Soviet model, in which the proletariat are the agents of change.

Civis Romanus sum. I am a Roman.

Cold War. The name given to describe the tension and diplomatic confrontation between the superpowers, the USA and the USSR, after the Second World War.

Collective Security. A system in which the collective power of several industrial nations is used to maintain international peace and security.

Collectivization. A policy of merging small, individually owned farms into larger state-owned units to increase production through mechanization and economies of scale.

Communist International (Comintern). A global organization that was formed in an attempt to unite workers around the world into a unified movement directed from the USSR.

Containment. A policy to limit the expansion of rival spheres of interest by economic, political, and military means on a global scale.

Contras. Guerrilla groups in Nicaragua that opposed the Sandinista government.

Coup d'Etat, or Coup. This French word, which means "decapitation of the state," is used to describe an overthrow of government.

Cultural Revolution (1966-1976). Mao's final battle with the party and bureaucracy. He enlisted the aid of students to travel across the land and identify revisionists. He hoped to instill the decentralized ideal of a rural peasant revolution in young minds. The students were joined by workers who established their own rival soviet government in the cities. The movement created educational and economic chaos and was finally put down by the People's Liberation Army, who regained control for the central government.

D

Dawes Plan. A financial plan offered by the United States to Germany to assist in the restructuring of reparation payments after the First World War.

Decolonization. The process by which subject peoples gained their independence after the Second World War.

Demographic Reordering. National policies are designed to bring territorial and cultural boundaries in line with each other.

Denazification. The process of getting rid of former, active members and sympathizers of the Nazi party from defeated Germany. Denazification was undertaken by Britain, the United States, France, and the Soviet Union.

De-Stalinization. Khrushchev's policy to reveal the truth about Stalin's policies and moderate the effect those policies were having on the Soviet Union.

Détente. A lessening of tension; an attempt on the part of nations to work together toward peaceful co-existence.

Domino Theory. A belief that if one of America's allies fell to communism, the others would follow suit.

Duma. In Russian, this word means "a place of thinking." The Duma is the Russian equivalent of an elected, representative national assembly.

E

Economic Imperialism. The ownership of goods, services, physical resources, and industrial processes in another country. This relationship implies indirect control of political decisions.

Enabling Act. An act passed by the German Reichstag that allowed Hitler to legislate for four years without the Reichstag's approval.

Enterprise. A small business operation.

Extraterritoriality. A principle whereby a country is permitted to send to another nation diplomatic personnel who are permitted to live under the laws of their own culture, and are not bound by the laws of the host country.

F

Fascism. A right-wing doctrine that places the needs and security of the state ahead of the individual, and demands complete obedience by the individual to single party political leadership.

Four Policemen Concept. The superpowers would divide the globe into spheres of influence in which they would guarantee stability and peace through their political, economic, and military power.

G

The General Agreement on Tariffs and Trade (GATT). A series of binding agreements between signatories to reduce tariffs and move toward free trade.

Glasnost. A Russian word meaning openness in public affairs.

Gosplan. The state planning committee that directed the Soviet Union's economy.

Great Leap Forward. Mao's unsuccessful plan to forge ahead in industry and agriculture at the same time, in order to advance China's economy dramatically.

Greater East Asia Co-Prosperity Sphere. The Japanese proposal for a unified East Asia, with a common market. The scheme was designed to give Japan hegemony over the region as the only industrial power.

H

Heartland. The central or important area of a land mass or nation.

Hegemony. The political domination of one state over others.

Helsinki Accord. An agreement signed by 35 nations, including Canada, the USA, and the USSR, which guarantees to retain the status quo of European borders and to strengthen respect for human rights and freedoms.

Holocaust. The persecution, deportation, and elimination of six million Jews under the Nazi rule in Europe.

I

Ich bin ein Berliner. I am a Berliner.

Ideology. A closed system of political beliefs directed towards specified goals, with officially sanctioned principles that permit no deviation. The principal political ideologies of the twentieth century are democracy, fascism, socialism, and communism.

Iron Curtain. The ideological and political boundary separating the Soviet Union and its allies in Eastern Europe from the rest of the world.

Irredenta. Unrecovered territory containing ethnic minorities claimed by other nation-states.

L

Lebensraum. This word means "living space," and refers to the German policy of eastward expansion which would provide living space for the German people and sources of raw materials.

"Let all flowers bloom together, Let the hundred schools of thought contend." Mao's statement of China's national policy to revive free discussion and criticism of government policies among writers, journalists, students, and professionals (1956).

Little Entente. A regional grouping in Central Europe of Czechoslovakia, Yugoslavia, and Romania directed principally against expansionist Hungary and any attempt to revive the Austro-Hungarian Empire. The entente was encouraged by France. France saw in the Little Entente the potential to revitalize the threat of a two-front war against Germany in the interests of French security.

M

McCarthyism. A right-wing movement in the USA which involved mass investigations and blacklisting of people suspected of communist sympathies.

Marshall Plan. American economic aid offered after the Second World War for the reconstruction of those nations of Europe that had fought against Nazi Germany during the war.

Military Defensive Alliance. An alliance of nations based on the belief that security is best maintained by a balance of power. NATO and the Warsaw Pact are examples of military defensive alliances.

Military Demarcation Line. When negotiations over a political boundary are not successful, the boundary is often left where rival armies have met.

Multipolar. New economic as well as political and military power has created a new international structure in which the bipolar world of the USA and the former USSR has been transformed into a multipolar one.

Mutually Assured Destruction (MAD). The reality that losses in nuclear war would guarantee unacceptable destruction of victor and loser alike.

N

Nation-State. A human-made territorial political unit that holds sovereignty, the ability to make laws and impose punishment, including death, over its people.

Nationalism. A patriotic loyalty among the people within a state resulting from common bonds of language, culture, and tradition.

Nationalization. Government seizure of industry from foreign ownership. This can occur with or without compensation.

Nazi. A member of the National Socialist German Workers' Party, and a follower of Hitler.

New Deal. A legislative program of temporary government intervention in the American economy to counter the effects of the depression.

New Economic Policy (NEP). Lenin's reversion to modified capitalism to encourage greater production through profit incentives.

New Order. The demographic, economic, and political reorganization of Europe under German hegemony.

The Night of the Long Knives. On this night in 1934, Hitler purged his party of dissidents.

The North Atlantic Treaty Organization (NATO). A military defence group formed by Canada, the USA, and Western European countries to maintain peace and collective security among themselves.

O

Open Door Policy. An American proposal to permit every nation to trade freely with every other nation, with no nation creating a sphere of influence or claiming special privileges over any other state.

Organization of Petroleum Exporting Countries (OPEC). An organization that used a near global cartel to influence Western foreign policy into a pro-Arab stance.

P

Palestine Liberation Organization (PLO). A Palestinian organization determined to return Arab Palestinians to their homeland, including lands occupied by Israel.

Partition. A policy of separating a state into parts and exchanging populations in order to attain homogeneity within each new state.

Peaceful Co-existence. A situation in which divergent political systems exist together peacefully.

Peacekeeping. A policy of the UN to place multinational forces from "middle powers" between warring armies to halt fighting and force negotiation. It also was designed to keep major powers out of local disputes.

Perestroika. A Russian word meaning restructuring. Gorbachev applied this to both the political and the economic systems in the former USSR.

Political Pluralism. A conception in politics that if political power is spread among various groups, then government will serve the interests of all.

R

Resistance. Civilian underground organizations in World War II dedicated to carrying on warfare against German, Japanese, and Italian occupation forces after the formal surrender of their governments.

S

Sandinistas. A broadly based revolutionary group in Nicaragua—named after Nicaraguan folk hero Sandino—which obtained power in 1979.

Securitate. The Romanian secret police.

Self-Determination. A principle that people should have the right to determine their own system of law and government without intervention by outside forces.

Shi'a. One of two mainstream sects of Islam, the other being Sunni. Whereas the Shi'as appeal to the underprivileged, oppressed, and defeated, the Sunnis appeal to the more conservative and privileged classes.

Solidarity. A working class labour movement that gained national support in Poland after it demanded better working conditions and a freer form of government.

The **Southeast Asia Treaty Organization (SEATO).** A collective defence group formed by the USA, Britain, Australia, France, Pakistan, New Zealand, Thailand, and the Philippines to resist communist attacks in the area.

Soviet. An elected council.

Special Economic Zones. Areas in China in which an open door, free trade policy is established in efforts to acquire a share of world trade and technology.

Spheres of Influence. The extent to which a nation-state exerts its power beyond its borders.

Status Quo. Things as they are, or an existing state of affairs.

Stimson Doctrine. An American policy of not recognizing boundary changes made under duress or as the result of war.

Strategic Arms Limitation Talks (SALT I). These conferences were held between representatives of the United States and the Soviet Union to discuss the maintenance of acceptable levels of weaponry by limiting the possession of strategic weapons.

Strategic Defense Initiative (SDI). A strategy of creating an impenetrable missile defence shield of North America.

Successor States. Those nations that were created out of the collapse of the Russian, German, Austro-Hungarian, and Turkish empires after the First World War. Poland is often included in the list, despite its ancient statehood.

Summitry. The belief that international tension is created by entrenched bureaucracies and can be eliminated by face-to-face talks between leaders.

T

Terrorism. Selected acts of organized sabotage, kidnapping, and murder to attain funds and publicity for a specified cause.

Total War. The military deadlock on the Western Front in World War II resulted in the marshaling of all human and industrial resources of the combatants in a total effort to gain victory. Thus war was carried from the battle fronts to civilian populations. Women entered the work force to take the place of men gone to war. The rationing of food and resources became common, as did the conscription of additional levies of soldiers. Airships, airplanes, and submarines added a third dimension to the battlefronts and extended the conflict behind the lines to cities and under the oceans.

Truman Doctrine. The US policy of supporting governments against insurrection incited from outside their national boundaries. Intended for Greece and Turkey, it led to the formation of NATO and was later extended globally.

U

Unconditional Surrender. The Allied policy of accepting no negotiations to end a war. The enemy was to trust in the mercy of the victors and be given no prior guarantees.

United Front. A strategy of socialist and communist parties to unite under a common platform in order to gain political power.

Uniting for Peace. A UN resolution that called on the General Assembly to take action when the Security Council was deadlocked by veto.

W

War Communism. The state of martial law introduced in Russia by the Bolshevik government during the civil war (1917 to 1920).

War Crimes. Violations of international law or customs, as determined by the international community of nations.

Wars of National Liberation. Anti-imperial conflicts that erupted after the Second World War for the purpose of establishing national, independent governments.

Washington Treaties. The Nine Power Pact and the Four Power Pact guaranteed the signatories' spheres in Asia and recognized China's territorial integrity. The Japanese viewed the treaties as a barrier to their planned expansion on the mainland.

World Trade Organization (WTO). An organization which came into effect in January 1995 to coordinate the economic relationships of nations within the world trading system. GATT comes under the umbrella of this parent body.

Z

Zionism. The Jewish national movement for the purpose of re-establishing the Jewish nation in Palestine.

BIBLIOGRAPHY

Ambrose, Stephen E. *Rise to Globalism: American Foreign Policy Since 1938.* 5th ed. New York: Penguin, 1988.

Behr, Edward. *Kiss the Hand You Cannot Bite: The Rise and Fall of the Ceausescus.* New York: Villard Books, 1991.

Bell, P.M.H. *The Origins of the Second World War in Europe.* London: Longman, 1986.

Bennett, A. LeRoy. *International Organizations.* 3rd ed. New Jersey: Prentice Hall, 1984.

Biddiss, Michael D. *The Age of the Masses.* London: Penguin, 1977.

Boutros-Ghali, Boutros. *An Agenda for Peace: Preventative Diplomacy, Peacemaking and Peace-keeping.* Report of the Secretary General pursuant to statements adopted by the Summit Meeting of the Security Council on 31 January, 1992. New York: United Nations, 1992.

Brogan, Patrick. *The Captive Nations: Eastern Europe 1945-1990.* New York: Avon Books, 1990.

Brzezinski, Zbigniew. *The Grand Failure: The Birth and Death of Communism in the Twentieth Century.* New York: Scribner, 1989.

Bush, Ray, Gordon Johnston, and David Coates. *The World Order: Socialist Perspectives.* Polity Press, 1987.

Calvocressi, Peter. *World Politics Since 1945.* 4th ed. London: Longman, 1982.

Calvocressi, Peter and Buy Wint. *Total War.* London: Penguin, 1972.

Chubb, Edmond. *China and Russia.* New York: Columbia University Press, 1971.

Combs, Jerald A. *The History of American Foreign Policy Since 1900, Volume 2.* New York: Knopf, 1986.

Conquest, Robert. *Harvest of Sorrow.* Oxford: Oxford University Press, 1986.

Cook, Don. *Charles De Gaulle: A Biography.* New York: Putnam, 1983.

Crabb, Cecil V. Jr. *American Foreign Policy in the Nuclear Age.* 4th ed. New York: Harper & Row, 1983.

Davies, R.W. *Soviet History in the Gorbachev Revolution.* Bloomington: Indiana University Press, 1989.

Diuk, Nadia and Adrian Karatnycky. *The Hidden Nations: The People Challenge the Soviet Union.* New York: Morrow, 1990.

Divine, Robert A. *The Cuban Missile Crisis.* 2nd ed. Markus Wiener, 1988.

Echikson, William. *Lighting the Night: Revolution in Eastern Europe.* New York: Morrow, 1990.

Eksteins, Modris. *Rites of Spring: The Great War and the Birth of the Modern Age.* New York: Doubleday, 1989.

Fathers, Michael and Andrew Higgins. *Tiananmen: The Rape of Peking.* New York: Doubleday, 1989.

Fenn, Charles. *Ho Chi Minh: A Biographical Introduction.* London: Studio Vista, 1973.

Fischer, Mary Ellen. *Nicolae Ceausescu: A Study in Political Leadership.* Boulder: Lynne Rienner, 1989.

Fitzpatrick, Sheila. *The Russian Revolution: 1917-1932.* Oxford: Oxford University Press, 1982.

Gelb, Norman. *The Berlin Wall: Kennedy, Khrushchev, and a Showdown in the Heart of Europe.* New York: Simon & Schuster, 1986.

Georgescu, Vlad. *The Romanians: A History.* Edited by Matei Calinescu. Translated by Alexandra Bley-Vroman. Columbus: Ohio State University Press, 1991.

Goodman, David S.G. *Deng Xiaoping and the Chinese Revolution: A Political Biography.* New York: Routledge, 1994.

Gwertzman, Bernard and Michael T. Kaufman (eds.) *The Collapse of Communism.* New York: New York Times Company, 1990.

Halberstam, David. *Ho.* New York: Random House, 1971.

Halle, Louis J. *The Cold War as History.* New York: Harper Torch Books, 1991.

Halliday, Fred. *The Making of the Second Cold War.* 2nd ed. Routledge, Chapman & Hall, 1986.

Holloway, David. *The Soviet Union and the Arms Race.* 2nd ed. New Haven: Yale University Press, 1983.

Howard, Michael. *War in European History.* Oxford: Oxford University Press, 1976.

Hsu, Immanuel CY. *The Rise of Modern China.* 3rd ed. Oxford: Oxford University Press, 1983.

Ikle, Fred Charles. *Every War Must End.* New York: Columbia University Press, 1971.

Jones, Walter S. *The Logic of International Relations.* 5th ed. Boston: Little, Brown, 1985.

Kawahara, Toshiaki. *Hirohito and His Times: A Japanese Perspective.* New York: Kodansha International Ltd., 1990.

Kennan, George F. *Russia and the West under Lenin and Stalin.* Boston: Little, Brown, 1961.

Kennedy, Paul. *The Rise and Fall of the Great Powers.* London: Unwin Human, 1988.

Kennedy, Paul (ed.) *The War Plans of the Great Powers 1880-1914.* London: Allen & Unwin, 1979.

Keylor, William R. *The Twentieth-Century World.* Oxford: Oxford University Press, 1984.

Killen, Linda R. *The Soviet Union and the United States.* Macmillan, 1989.

Kopacsi, Sandor. *"In the Name of the Working Class": The Inside Story of the Hungarian Revolution.* Toronto: Lester & Orpen Dennys, 1986.

Krawchenko, Bohdan. *Social Change and National Consciousness in Twentieth-Century Ukraine.* Edmonton: University of Alberta; Canadian Institute of Ukrainian Studies, 1985.

Lafeber, Walter. *Inevitable Revolutions: The United States in Central America.* Norton, 1984.

Lloyd, Alan. *Franco: The Biography of an Enigma.* New York: Doubleday, 1969.

Maclean, Fitzroy. *Josip Broz / Tito: A Pictorial Biography.* Maidenhead: McGraw-Hill, 1980.

Marples, David. *The Social Impact of the Chernobyl Disaster.* Edmonton: University of Alberta Press, 1988.

Mayer, Arno J. *Why Did the Heavens Not Darken?* New York: Pantheon Books, 1988.

Meisner, Maurice. *Mao's China and After.* Free Press, 1986.

Prince Michael of Greece. *Nicholas and Alexandra: The Family Albums.* Conceived and compiled by Andrei Maylunas. Translated from the Russian by Catherine O'Keeffe. London: Tauris Parke Books, 1992.

Morrison, John. *Boris Yeltsin: From Bolshevik to Democrat.* Toronto: Dutton, 1991.

Moynahan, Brian. *The Claws of the Bear: A History of the Soviet Armed Forces from 1917 to the Present.* London: Hutchinson, 1989.

Nathan, James A. and James K. Oliver. *United States Foreign Policy Since World War II.* 4th ed. Scott, Foresman, 1989.

Novek, Alec. *Stalinism and After.* 2nd ed. London: Allen & Unwin, 1981.

Ohmae, Kenichi. *The Borderless World: Power and Strategy in the Interlinked Economy.* McKinsey, 1990.

Paterson, Thomas G. and Robert J. McMahon (eds.) *The Origins of the Cold War.* Heath, 1991.

Pearson, Frederic S. and J.M. Rochester. *International Relations: Global Conduct in the Late 20th Century.* 2nd ed. New York: Random House, 1988.

Perret, Geoffrey. *A Country Made by War.* New York: Random House, 1989.

Pollard, Robert A. *Economic Security and the Origins of the Cold War, 1945-1950.* New York: Columbia University Press, 1985.

Riasanovsky, Nicholas V. *A History of Russia.* Oxford: Oxford University Press, 1984.

Ritter, Gerhard. *The Schlieffen Plan: A Critique of a Myth.* London: W.I, Oswald Wolff, 1958.

Ross, Graham. *The Great Powers and the Decline of the European States System 1914-1945.* London: Longman, 1983.

Rubinstein, Alvin Z. *Soviet Foreign Policy Since World War II: Imperial and Global.* 2nd ed. Boston: Little, Brown, 1985.

Sheehy, Gail. *The Man Who Changed the World: The Lives of Mikhail S. Gorbachev.* New York: Harper-Collins, 1990.

Silva, Michael and Bertil Sjogren. *Europe 1992 and the New World Power Game.* New York: Wiley, 1990.

Slater, Robert. *Rabin of Israel: A Biography.* London: Robson Books, 1993.

Smith, Denis Mack. *Mussolini: A Biography.* New York: Knopf, 1982.

Smith, Hedrick. *The New Russians.* New York: Random House, 1990.

Spanier, John. *American Foreign Policy Since World War II.* Washington, DC: Congressional Quarterly, 1988.

Steinberg, Mark D. and Vladimir M. Khrustalëv. *The Fall of the Romanovs: Political Dreams and Personal Struggles in a Time of Revolution.* London: Yale University Press, 1995.

Stoessinger, John G. *Nations in Darkness: China, Russia and America.* 5th ed. New York: McGraw-Hill Ryerson, 1990.

Terrill, Ross. *The White-Boned Demon: A Biography of Madame Mao Zedong.* New York: Morrow, 1984.

Treadgold, Donald W. *Twentieth Century Russia.* 8th ed. New York: HarperCollins, 1995.

Tusa, Ann and John. *The Berlin Airlift.* New York: Atheneum, 1988.

Ulam, Adam B. *The Rivals: America and Russia Since WW II.* New York: Penguin, 1977.

Vadney, T.E. *The World Since 1945.* New York: Penguin Books, 1987.

Wegs, J. Robert. *Europe Since 1945.* 2nd ed. New York: St. Martin's Press, 1984.

Wright, Gordon and Arthur Mejia. *An Age of Controversy: Discussion Problems in the 20th Century European History.* New York: Harper & Rowe, 1963.

Yglesias, Jose. *The Franco Years: The Untold Human Story of Life Under Spanish Fascism.* New York: Bobbs-Merrill, 1977.

INDEX

CREDITS

Editorial:

Nancy Mackenzie, Peter Smith, Jane Spalding, Leah-Ann Lymer, Melanie Johnson, Carolyn Routledge, Marianne Lindvall, Janet Pinno

Typesetting & Design:

Leslieanna Blackner Au

Maps:

Wendy Johnson,
Johnson Cartographics

Index:

Carolyn Dearden

Photos:

Abbreviations
National Archives of Canada: NAC
Provincial Archives of Alberta: PAA
Department of National Defence: DND
United Nations: UN

Entries are by page number, codes as follows: T = Top B = Bottom
L = Left R = Right

3 UN Photo 36252
4 UN Photo 134095/Yutaka Nagata
5 Corbis-Bettmann SF17589
6 Athlete Information Bureau/Canadian Olympic Association C88-4766
9 PAA/B 58
12 NAC/PA 2373
14 Sophia Smith Collection, Smith College CPFo
15 Sophia Smith Collection, Smith College Y/Doty/SRWP
16 NAC/PA 169
17 Sophia Smith Collection, Smith College Y/Pond/WAD
19 NAC/PA 622
22 The Bettmann Archive F4999
23 UPI/Corbis-Bettmann U92499INP
24 Corbis-Bettmann PL6460
29 Snark/Art Resource, NY Loan of Liberation, 1918 poster by Abel Faure
31 UPI/Corbis-Bettmann U125518INP
37 UPI/Corbis-Bettmann U856268INP
39 UPI/Bettmann Newsphotos U1608265
42 UPI/Corbis-Bettmann U507632INP
45 Heinrich Hoffman/NAC/PA 164759
46 Corbis-Bettmann PL5810
53 UPI/Corbis-Bettmann U1904393
57 UPI/Bettmann U855431INP
58 NAC/PA 114781
59 UPI/Bettmann U868376INP
61 Corbis-Bettmann U3899UNI
63 UPI/Corbis-Bettmann U856923INP
70 Novosti Information Agency

71 The Bettmann Archive PG10544
74 Novosti Information Agency
76 Novosti Information Agency 79-3765
77 Novosti Information Agency
83 Ford News Department, Dearborn, Michigan
85 NAC/C 13236
86 UPI/Corbis-Bettmann U334606ACME
88 The National Archives of the United States/16-G-162-S21748C
95 The Bettmann Archive PL4934
96 The Bettmann Archive PG6678
98 Sophia Smith Collection, Smith College
99 UPI/Bettmann U604311INP
103 The Bettmann Archive F12141
111 PAA/BL 618/15
114 Corbis-Bettmann U1384003
117 Novosti Information Agency
119 Novosti Information Agency X173302
120 Sophia Smith Collection, Smith College Y/Woodsmall/WABo
121 Gilbert A. Milne/DND/NAC/PA 137014
125 Joanne Tuffs
128 The Bettmann Archive UKD-1515
129 Gilbert A. Milne/DND/NAC/PA 131506
130 K. Bell/DND/NAC/PA 137452
135 UPI/Bettmann U669473ACME
140 UPI/Bettmann U1028711INP
142 E.W. Stedman/NAC/PA 125415
143 Reuters/Corbis-Bettmann R86155092
144 DND/NAC/PA 145984
148 UN Photo 145618/John Isaac
149 UN Photo
151 UN Photo 183790/E. Kanalstein, 1993
154 UN Photo 178980
155 UN Photo 151321/John Isaac
158 Philip Plastow/DND/NAC/PA 170294
159 UN Photo 125151/Yutaka Nagata
161 UN Photo 141085/John Isaac
163 UN Photo 154784
165 UN Photo 186790
166 UN Photo 190891
173 Novosti Information Agency
175 UPI/Corbis-Bettmann U1025645INP
178 UPI/Bettmann Newsphotos U905667ACME
182 The Bettmann Archive W2450
184 UN Photo 34333
187 UPI/Bettmann Newsphotos U1331358INP
188 UN Photo 67223
189 UPI/Bettmann U1376263
196 UPI/Corbis-Bettmann U1929860
198 UPI/Corbis-Bettmann U1731372
199 UPI/Corbis-Bettmann U1668174
202 Novosti Information Agency
204 Reuters/Bettmann News Photos R87350003B
211 UN Photo 137431/John Isaac
212 UPI/Bettmann U1068735INP
214 UN Photo 53061
217 UN Photo 126844/T. Chen
218 UPI/Corbis-Bettmann U1954365
219 Reuters/Bettmann R87322007
221 Reuters/Bettmann R90309078
222 Corbis-Bettmann A95318531
226 UN Photo 156230/John Isaac
231 UPI/Corbis-Bettmann U741691ACME
232 The Ministry of Foreign Affairs, Japan/Tokan Color Express, Tokyo Courtesy The Consulate-General of Japan, Edmonton, AB

233 The Bettmann Archive W450
235 UPI/Bettmann U804890
237 UN Photo 33585/Army Photo
239 UPI/Bettmann Newsphotos U1297042INP
240 Corbis-Bettmann U1515860
243 UPI/Bettmann U1833445
249 UPI/Bettmann U903898
251 UPI/Bettmann Newsphotos U1267389
254 UN Photo 119619
255 UPI/Corbis-Bettmann U1542496
258 UPI/Bettmann UHK091902
259 Reuters/Corbis-Bettmann R93164543
260 The Bettmann Archive U1954084
261 Reuters/Corbis-Bettmann R89152065
265 Reuters/Corbis-Bettmann R89200001A
271 UN Photo 151312/John Isaac
273 A. Solomonov/Novosti Information Service
274 TASS/Novosti Information Service
275 Reuters/Corbis-Bettmann RGDA1200790B
277 V. Arutyunov/Novosti Information Service
279 UN Photo 096097/Yutaka Nagata
281 UPI/Corbis-Bettmann U2146624
282 UPI/Corbis-Bettmann U90093052
284 UPI/Corbis-Bettmann U87237065
289 Novosti Information Service
292 Reuters/Corbis-Bettmann R86078101
293 Reuters/Corbis-Bettmann R90062031
296 DaD/AP Courtesy The Consulate General of the Federal Republic of Germany, Edmonton, AB 12579/1C
297 Reuters/Corbis-Bettmann R90002090
298 Reuters/Bettmann RPRA03080191
299 Reuters/Corbis-Bettmann RBUC10C241989
300 DaD/dpa Courtesy The Consulate General of the Federal Republic of Germany, Edmonton, AB 12638/1
305 Reuters/Bettmann RMOW08192091
306 Reuters/Bettmann R91289068CI
307 Reuters/Corbis-Bettmann R91281064
308 Corbis-Bettmann A96072059
309 Reuters/Bettmann R91273001
310 Reuters/Corbis-Bettmann R93277154
311 AFP/Bettmann A95345501
312 Reuters/Bettmann U91305162
313 The Bettmann Archive A95191514
314 Reuters/Bettmann R90150018

We have made every effort to correctly identify and credit the sources of all photographs, illustrations, and information used in this textbook.

Reidmore Books appreciates any further information or corrections; acknowledgment will be given in subsequent editions.